SOMETIMES I LIE AWAKE AT NIGHT, AND I ASK, "WHAT IS THE MEANING OF LIFE?"

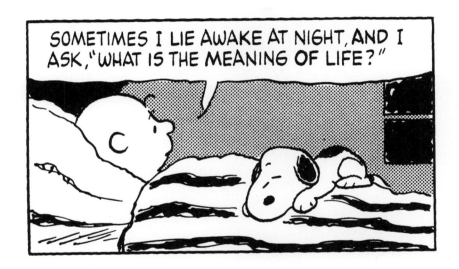

THE COMPLETE PEANUTS
by Charles M. Schulz

Fantagraphics Books, Inc.

Editor: Gary Groth

Designer: Kayla E.

Production, assembly, and restoration: Paul Baresh

Archival and production assistance: Marcie Lee, Elaine Lin, and Lucy Kiester

Associate Publisher: Eric Reynolds

Publisher: Gary Groth

Special thanks to Jean Schulz, without whom this project would not have come to fruition.

Thanks to Timothy Chow, and to Charles M. Schulz Creative Associates, especially Paige Braddock and Kim Towner.

PEANUTS and all related titles, logos and characters are trademarks of Peanuts Worldwide LLC © 2021 Peanuts Worldwide LLC.

The Complete Peanuts 1991–1992 (Volume Twenty-one) is copyright © 2024 Peanuts Worldwide, LLC. The introduction is copyright © 2024 Tom Tomorrow.

"Charles M. Schulz: 1922–2000" is copyright © 2021 Gary Groth. All rights reserved. Permission to duplicate materials from Peanuts comic strips must be obtained from Peanuts Worldwide. Permission to quote or reproduce for reviews and notices must be obtained from the publisher.

Fantagraphics Books, Inc.
7563 Lake City Way NE,
Seattle, WA 98115, USA

www.peanuts.com

www.fantagraphics.com

ISBN: 978-1-68396-936-5

Library of Congress Control Number: 2023944901

First softcover printing: 2024

Printed in China

PEANUTS

The COMPLETE PEANUTS by CHARLES M. SCHULZ 1991–1992

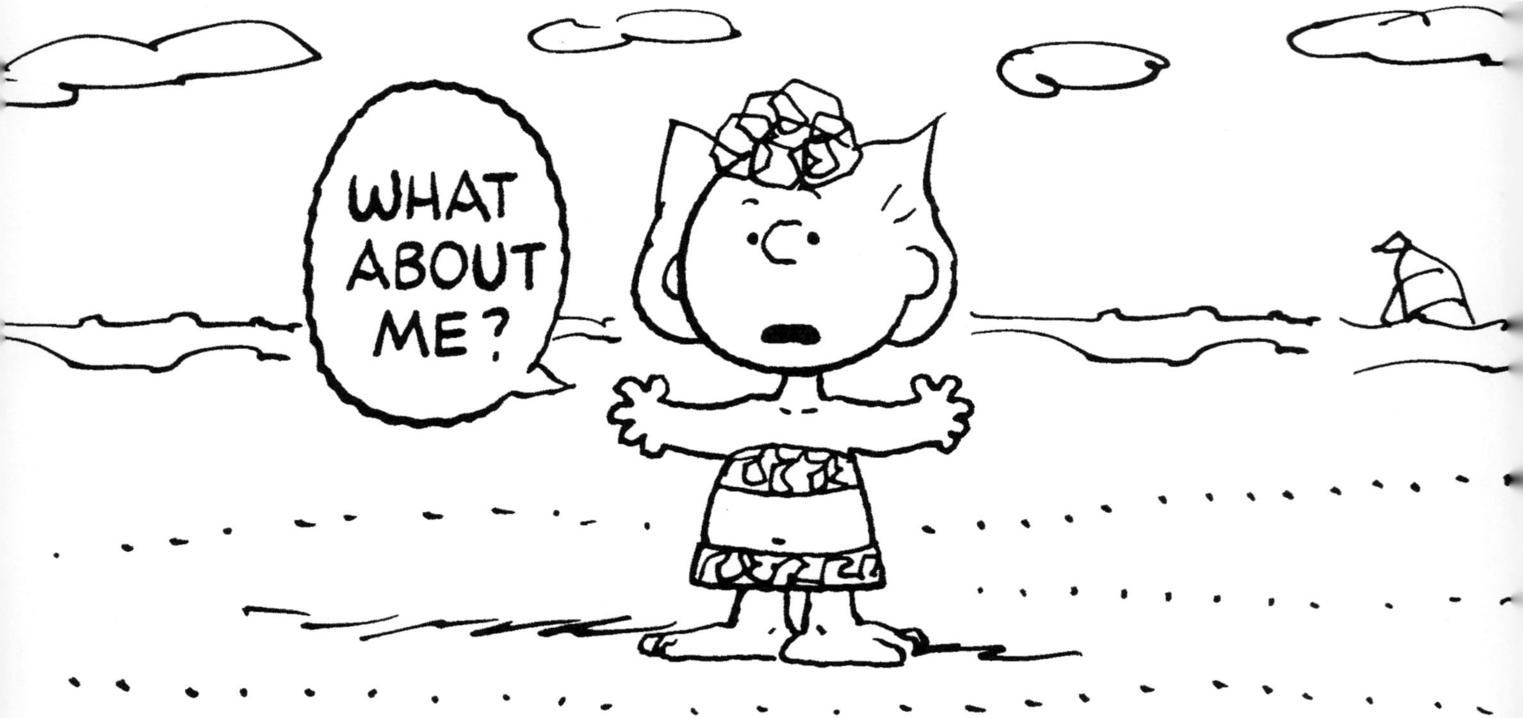
WHAT ABOUT ME?

Introduction by
TOM TOMORROW

WHEN FANTAGRAPHICS PUBLISHES THE LAST OF these volumes, the book series will contain 17,897 *Peanuts* comic strips drawn over the course of a 50-year career. It's an extraordinary body of work, and I'm grateful to have spent so much of my life watching it unfold. When people ask me about my own influences as a cartoonist, I can reel off a list ranging from *Mad* magazine to Garry Trudeau to Matt Groening — but there's absolutely no question that my earliest and most important inspiration was Charles M. Schulz.

As a kid in the 1960s, I think I hit the perfect sweet spot with *Peanuts* — old enough to understand the humor, young enough to truly appreciate the whimsy. Yes, the strip was often rooted in sadness and failure — with Charlie Brown as Sisyphus, eternally trying to kick the football — but it was also magical! And *that* was the part that delighted me the most as a young reader. It may have been a comic strip about a group of wise-beyond-their-years children who inhabited a (mostly) recognizable reality of school and summer camp and baseball games — but it also featured a dog who spoke to us in thought balloons, slept on top of his doghouse, and imagined himself to be a World War I Flying Ace or a world-famous author or an officer in the French Foreign Legion.

And that doghouse! Like Doctor Who's Tardis, it was apparently bigger on the inside. We were told that it had carpeting, and a pool table, and even a Van Gogh, though the latter was eventually destroyed in a fire and replaced with a Wyeth — a storyline inspired when Schulz's studio in Sebastapol, California, burned down in 1966. And that was *Peanuts* for you: a strip that spun heartbreak into wry humor, a cartoon about childhood anxiety that

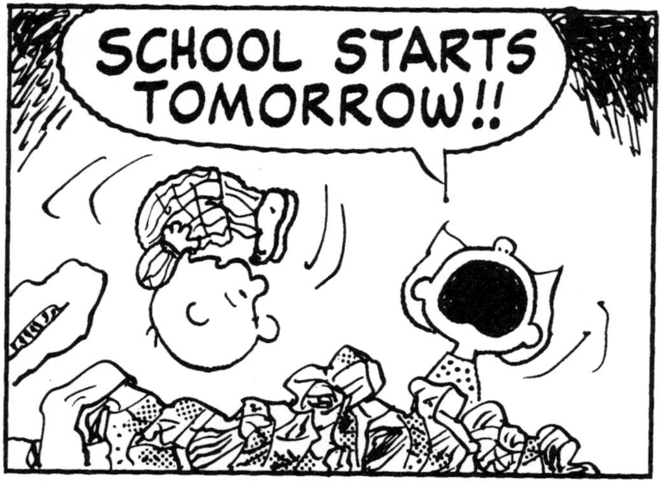
SCHOOL STARTS TOMORROW!!

veered frequently into the realm of magical realism. It was a balancing act that seemed entirely effortless, and as any artist or writer will tell you, things that seem effortless rarely are.

Schulz taught me to love this art form. I read each new strip in the morning paper, devoured the paperback collections of older work, treasured my copy of the Treasury. And, of course, *Peanuts* was more than a comic strip — it was ubiquitous in the culture as I grew up. The *Charlie Brown Christmas* special was a yearly holiday ritual in my home. My mother timed the purchase of our first color television set one December so that I'd finally be able to watch it in color: subsequent memories of technological transition pale in comparison.

The year that Charlie Brown and Snoopy became the unofficial mascots of the Apollo 10 mission (and some of Schulz's original art orbited the moon), I remember lying on a couch, sick with the flu and watching the Macy's Thanksgiving Day Parade on TV, mostly hoping to see the Snoopy balloon. And because I was so miserable, my mom had given me an early Christmas present — a Snoopy doll dressed up as an astronaut, with a red scarf and a big bubble helmet.

I still have one of those dolls, sitting on a shelf in my studio as I write these words.

In 1992, when I was a young adult and the cartoons in this book were new, I wrote Charles Schulz a fan letter, and he responded by inviting me up to Santa Rosa for lunch. It was crazy — I mean, I was just some goofball alt-weekly cartoonist, and he was *Charles Schulz* — but as it turned out, when it came to younger cartoonists, he was improbably generous with his time. We ate at the café adjacent to the skating rink he'd built, at the table that was always reserved for him (and on which you will still find a "reserved" sign to this day). And because we were both cartoonists, he was willing to spend the better part of an afternoon answering my questions and discussing our shared profession. Years later, after he passed away, I published the only obituary cartoon I've ever written, and quoted something he said that sums up the humility of a man who was already acknowledged to have created one of the great, lasting comic strips: "If I were a better artist, I'd be a painter, and if I were a better writer, I'd write books — but I'm not, so I draw cartoons."

After lunch he took me over to his studio, a large, comfortable room of wood and leather. As I imagine most people buying these volumes already know, he worked alone in that room, penciling and inking every strip himself. As he grew older, the lines grew a little shakier, but they were always authentically his.

After drawing the daily strip in a strict four-panel format his entire career, he had recently begun to experiment with different panel sizes and configurations. He told me it was something that he had always wanted to do, though when he finally proposed the change, there was some question in his mind as to whether the syndicate was going to allow it. Again I think this speaks to his fundamental humility and decency — the fact is, at that point in his career, he probably could have demanded a solid-gold drawing table and a full complement of chorus girls to entertain him while he worked, and the syndicate would have happily complied.

Schulz even gave me an original *Peanuts* strip, which has hung on the wall of every place I've lived since 1992 — so I mean it quite literally when I say that a day rarely passes that I don't think of the man and his work. In a happy coincidence, that strip is actually included in this volume — it's the middle cartoon on page 71, in which Linus says, "I'd really appreciate it if you'd take your stupid head off my blanket," and Snoopy complies, thinking, "It's nice to be able to do something for someone once in a while that's appreciated."

You were — and remain — appreciated, Mr. Schulz.

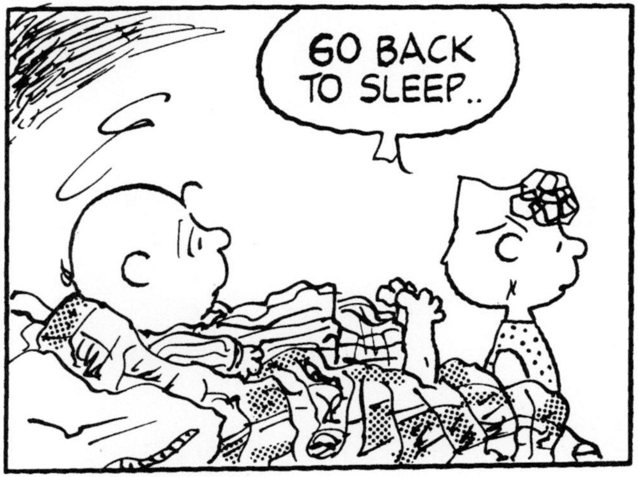
GO BACK TO SLEEP..

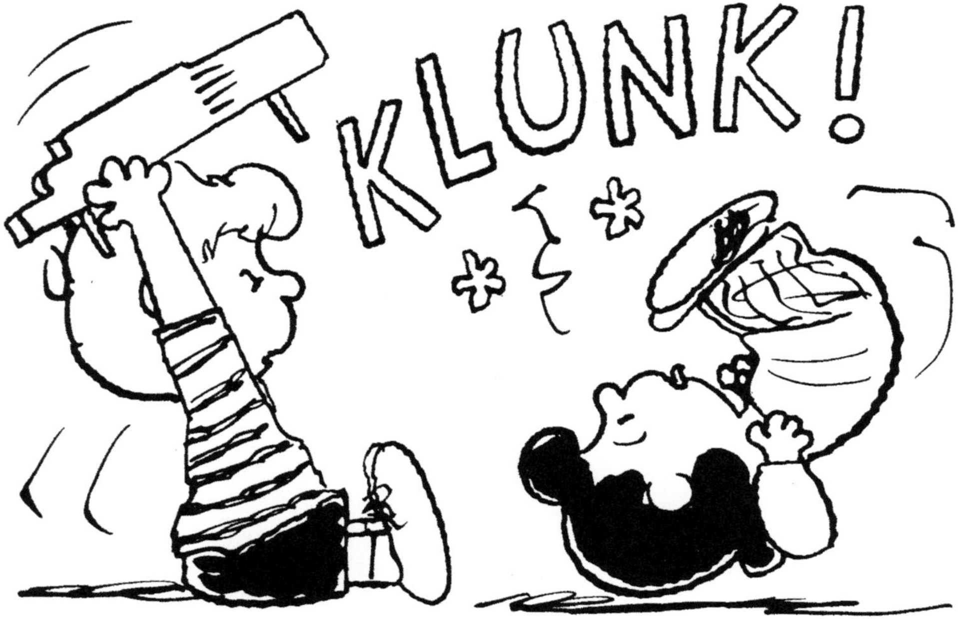
KLUNK!

I THOUGHT I WAS THE LIFE OF THE PARTY WHEN I PUT THE LAMP SHADE ON MY HEAD..
BUT THEN EVERYBODY HAD TO GET INTO THE ACT..
1-1-91
SCHULZ

SEE? I DIDN'T TAKE THE LAST COOKIE.. I SAVED IT FOR YOU..
1-2-91
I KNEW YOU WERE WORRIED ABOUT IT
COOKIES
THAT'S TRUE..
BUT NOW I CAN GET ON WITH THE REST OF MY LIFE..
SCHULZ

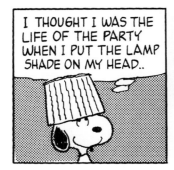

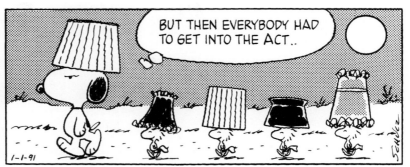

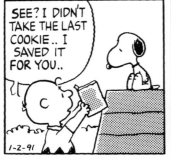

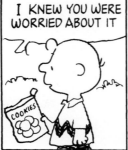

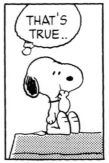

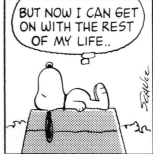

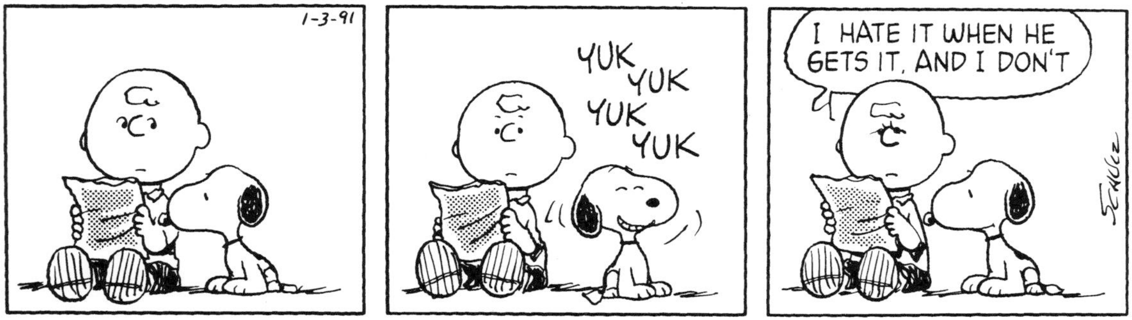
1-3-91
YUK YUK YUK YUK
I HATE IT WHEN HE GETS IT, AND I DON'T
SCHULZ

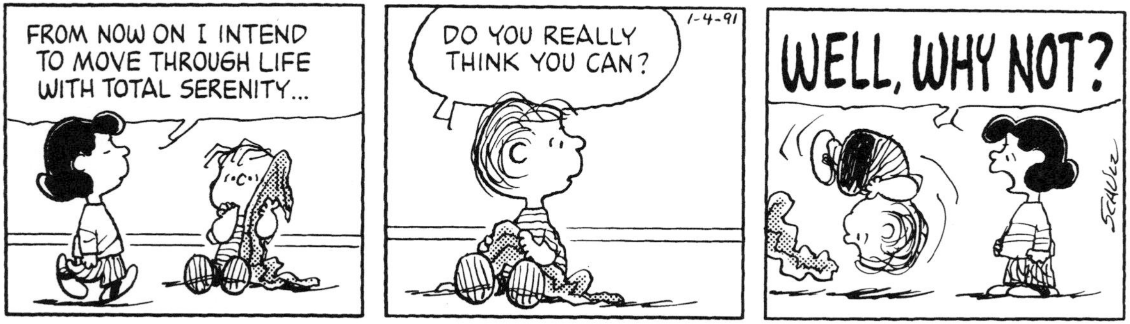
FROM NOW ON I INTEND TO MOVE THROUGH LIFE WITH TOTAL SERENITY...
1-4-91
DO YOU REALLY THINK YOU CAN?
WELL, WHY NOT?
SCHULZ

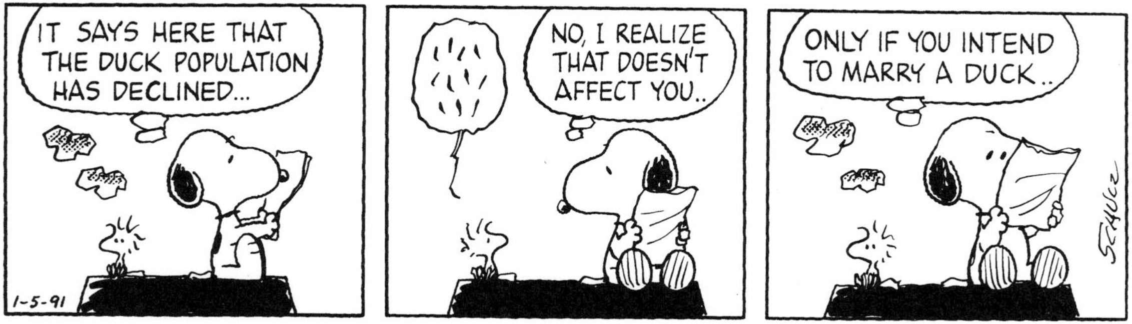
IT SAYS HERE THAT THE DUCK POPULATION HAS DECLINED...
1-5-91
NO, I REALIZE THAT DOESN'T AFFECT YOU..
ONLY IF YOU INTEND TO MARRY A DUCK..
SCHULZ

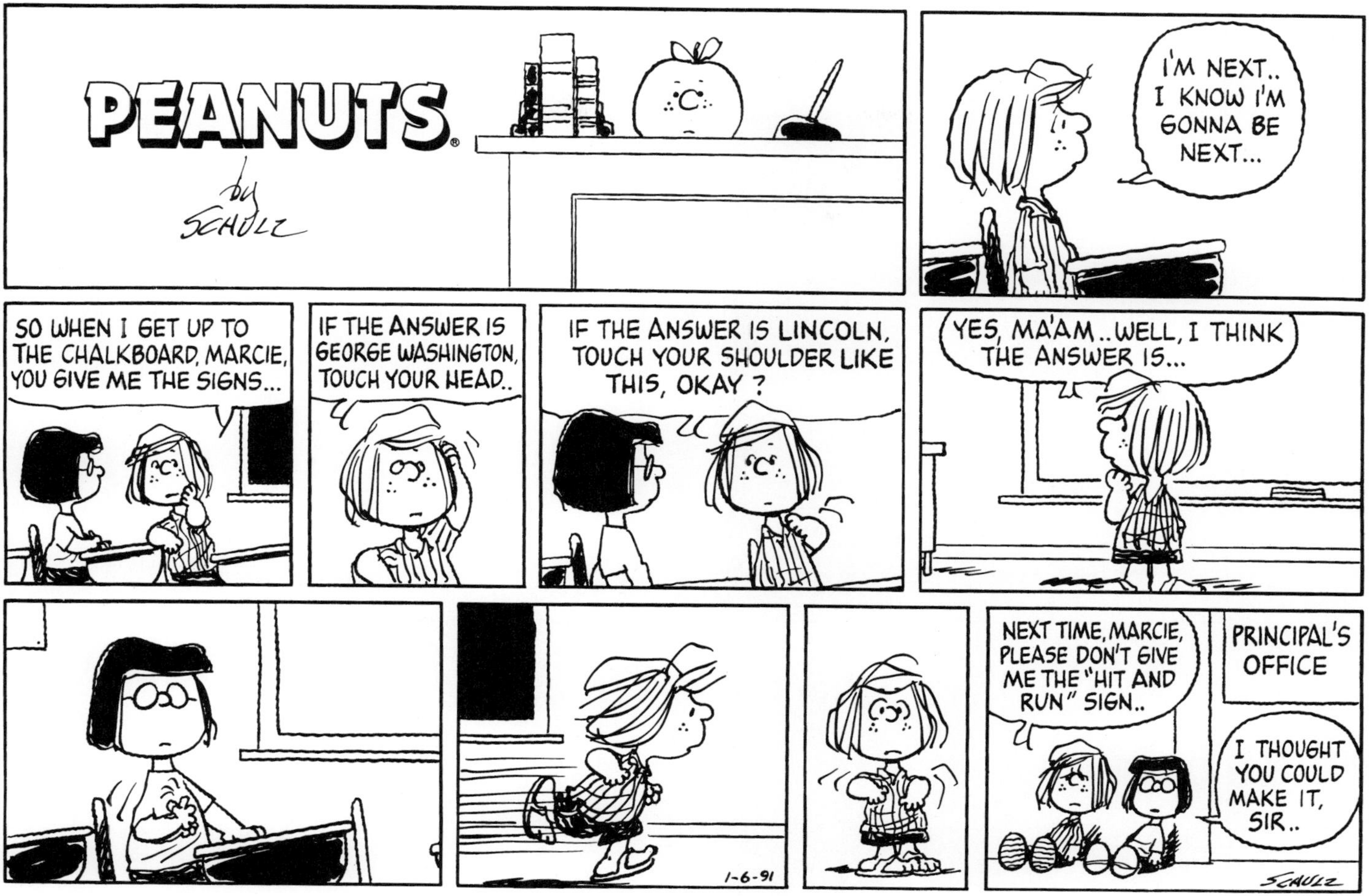
PEANUTS
by SCHULZ
I'M NEXT.. I KNOW I'M GONNA BE NEXT...
SO WHEN I GET UP TO THE CHALKBOARD, MARCIE, YOU GIVE ME THE SIGNS...
IF THE ANSWER IS GEORGE WASHINGTON, TOUCH YOUR HEAD..
IF THE ANSWER IS LINCOLN, TOUCH YOUR SHOULDER LIKE THIS, OKAY ?
YES, MA'AM..WELL, I THINK THE ANSWER IS...
1-6-91
NEXT TIME, MARCIE, PLEASE DON'T GIVE ME THE "HIT AND RUN" SIGN..
PRINCIPAL'S OFFICE
I THOUGHT YOU COULD MAKE IT, SIR..
SCHULZ

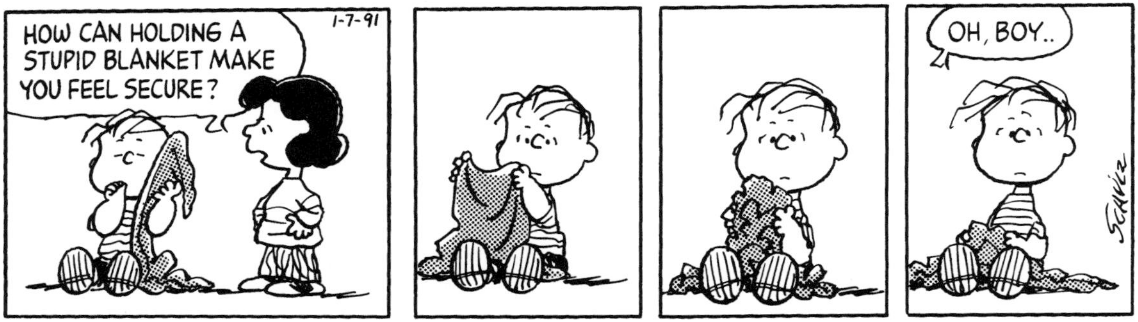
HOW CAN HOLDING A STUPID BLANKET MAKE YOU FEEL SECURE?
1-7-91
OH, BOY..
SCHULZ

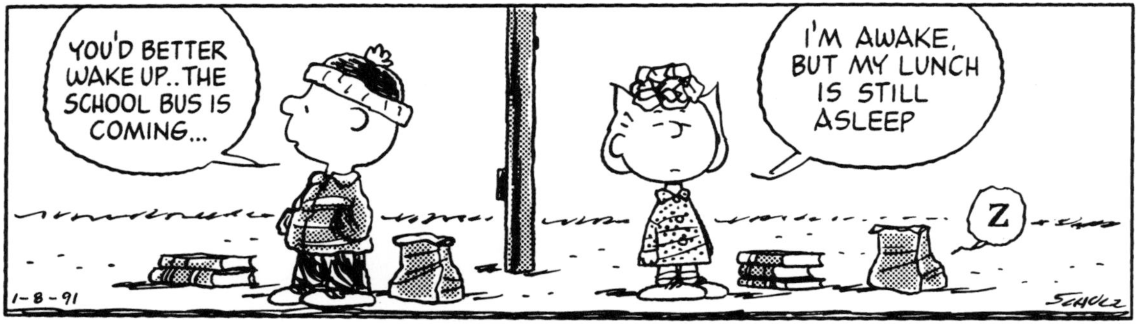
YOU'D BETTER WAKE UP.. THE SCHOOL BUS IS COMING...
I'M AWAKE, BUT MY LUNCH IS STILL ASLEEP
Z
1-8-91
SCHULZ

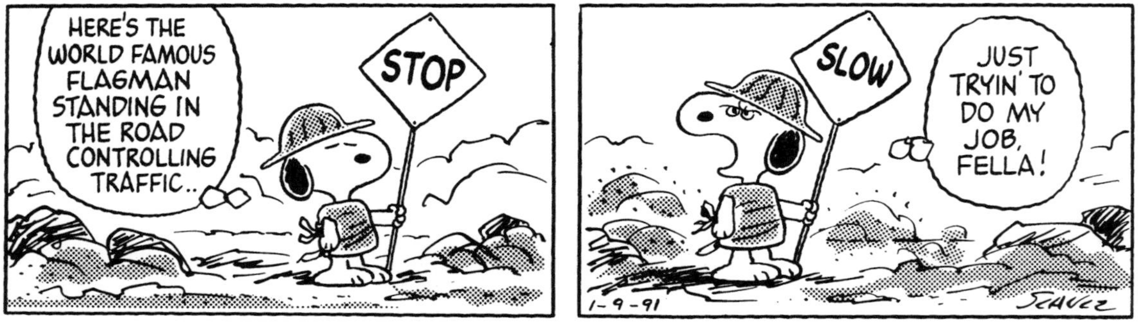
HERE'S THE WORLD FAMOUS FLAGMAN STANDING IN THE ROAD CONTROLLING TRAFFIC..
STOP
SLOW
JUST TRYIN' TO DO MY JOB, FELLA!
1-9-91
SCHULZ

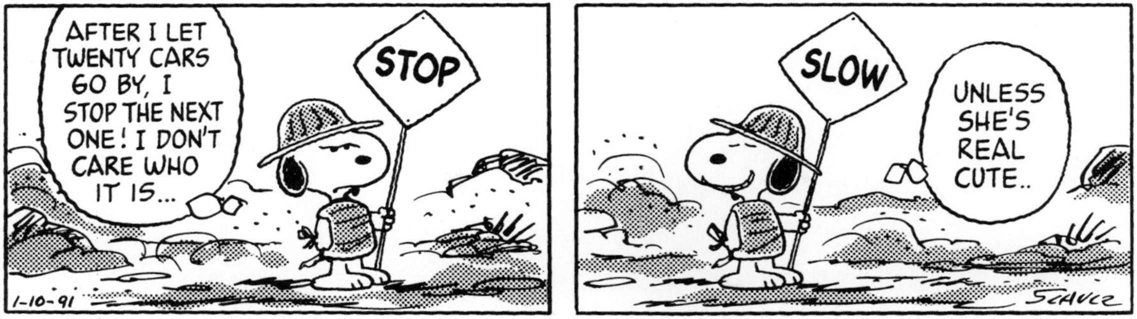
AFTER I LET TWENTY CARS GO BY, I STOP THE NEXT ONE! I DON'T CARE WHO IT IS...
STOP
1-10-91
SLOW
UNLESS SHE'S REAL CUTE..

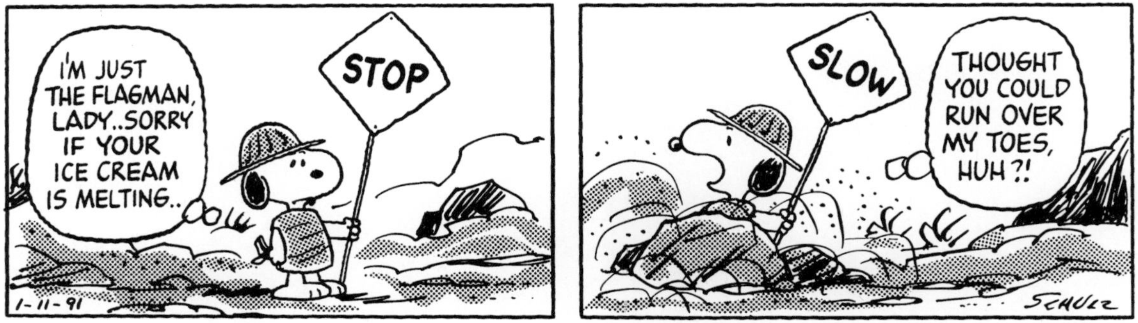
I'M JUST THE FLAGMAN, LADY..SORRY IF YOUR ICE CREAM IS MELTING..
STOP
1-11-91
SLOW
THOUGHT YOU COULD RUN OVER MY TOES, HUH?!

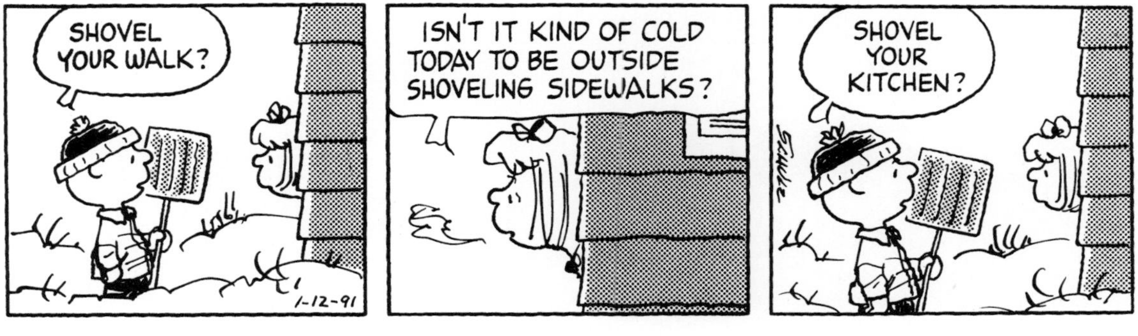
SHOVEL YOUR WALK?
1-12-91
ISN'T IT KIND OF COLD TODAY TO BE OUTSIDE SHOVELING SIDEWALKS?
SHOVEL YOUR KITCHEN?

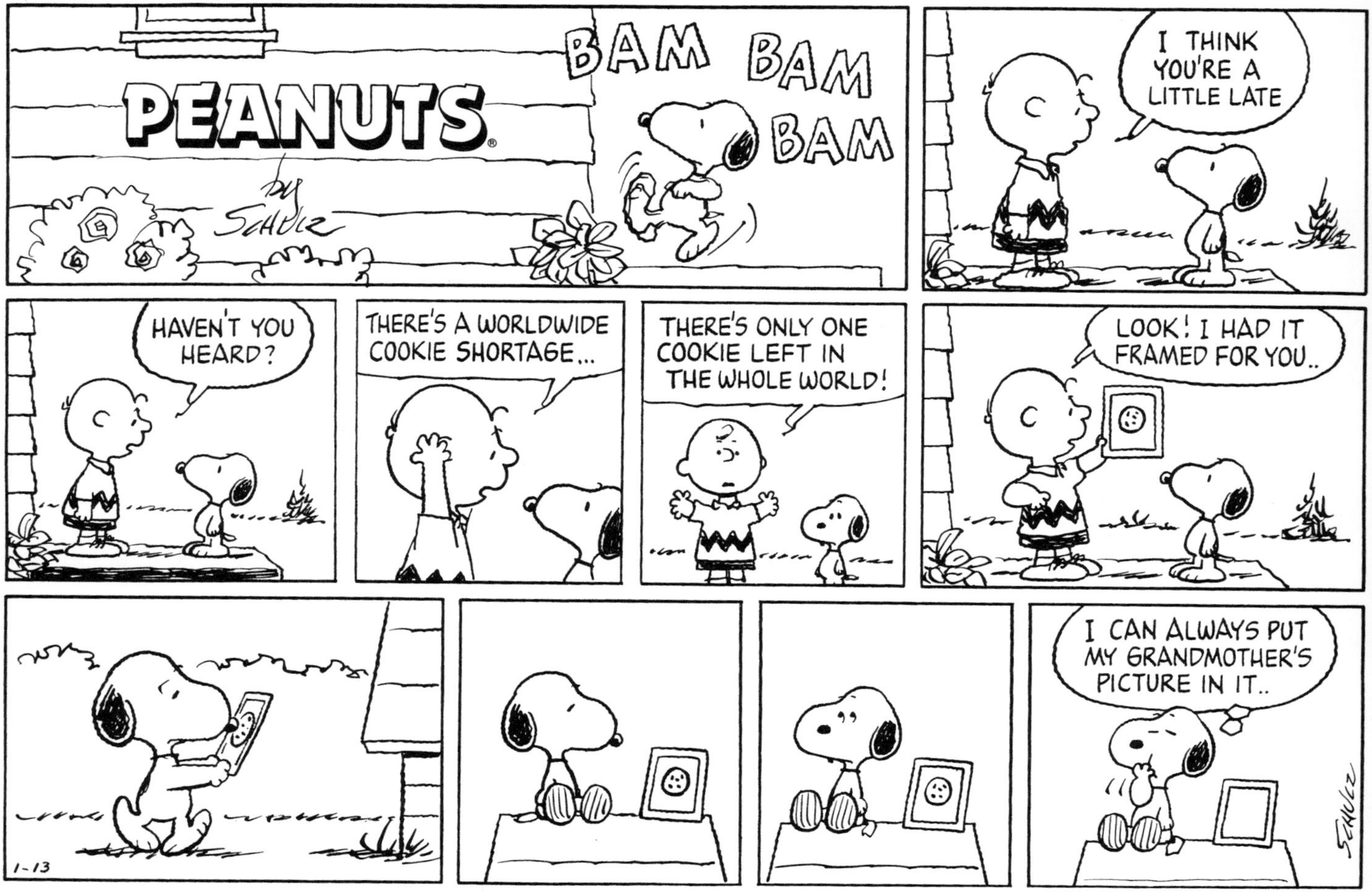
PEANUTS®
by Schulz
BAM BAM BAM
I THINK YOU'RE A LITTLE LATE
HAVEN'T YOU HEARD?
THERE'S A WORLDWIDE COOKIE SHORTAGE...
THERE'S ONLY ONE COOKIE LEFT IN THE WHOLE WORLD!
LOOK! I HAD IT FRAMED FOR YOU..
1-13
I CAN ALWAYS PUT MY GRANDMOTHER'S PICTURE IN IT..
Schulz

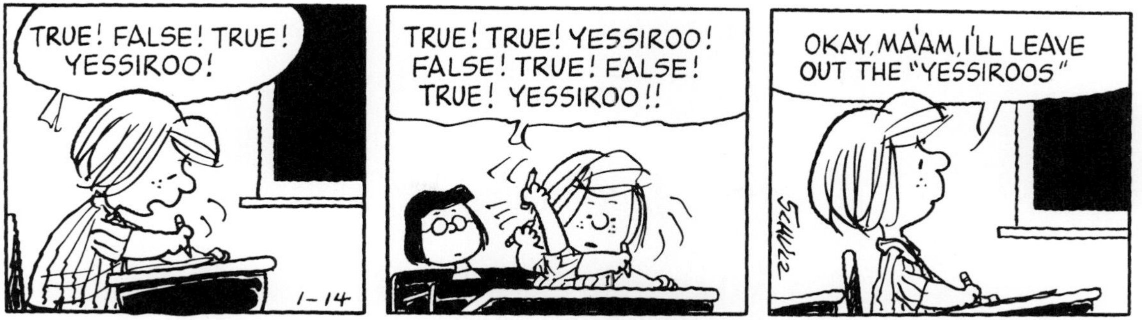
TRUE! FALSE! TRUE! YESSIROO!
TRUE! TRUE! YESSIROO! FALSE! TRUE! FALSE! TRUE! YESSIROO!!
OKAY, MA'AM, I'LL LEAVE OUT THE "YESSIROOS"
1-14

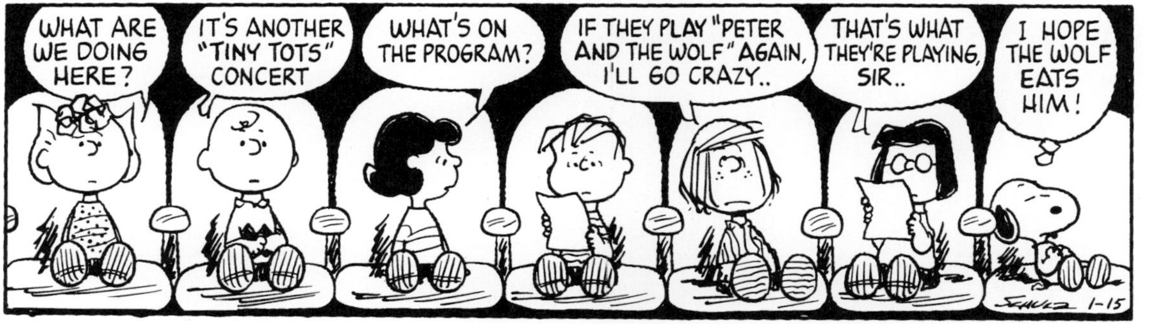
WHAT ARE WE DOING HERE?
IT'S ANOTHER "TINY TOTS" CONCERT
WHAT'S ON THE PROGRAM?
IF THEY PLAY "PETER AND THE WOLF" AGAIN, I'LL GO CRAZY..
THAT'S WHAT THEY'RE PLAYING, SIR..
I HOPE THE WOLF EATS HIM!
1-15

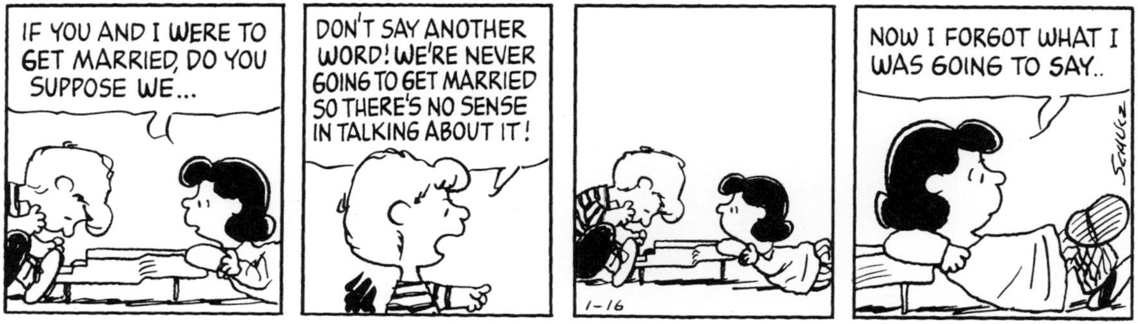
IF YOU AND I WERE TO GET MARRIED, DO YOU SUPPOSE WE...
DON'T SAY ANOTHER WORD! WE'RE NEVER GOING TO GET MARRIED SO THERE'S NO SENSE IN TALKING ABOUT IT!
1-16
NOW I FORGOT WHAT I WAS GOING TO SAY..

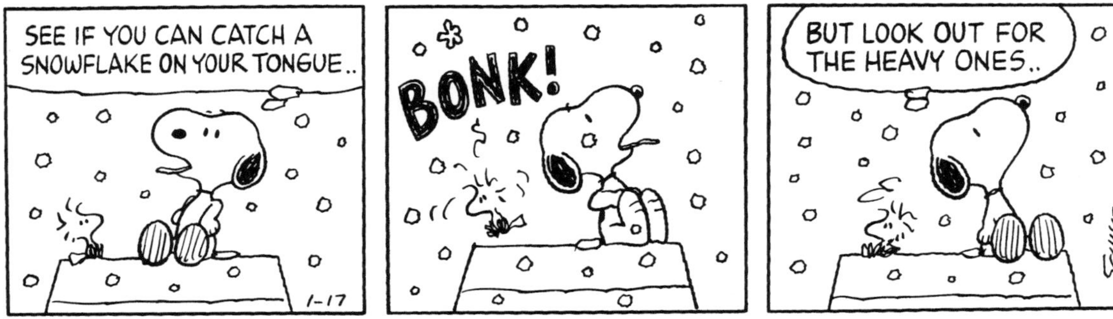
SEE IF YOU CAN CATCH A SNOWFLAKE ON YOUR TONGUE..
BONK!
BUT LOOK OUT FOR THE HEAVY ONES..
1-17
SCHULZ

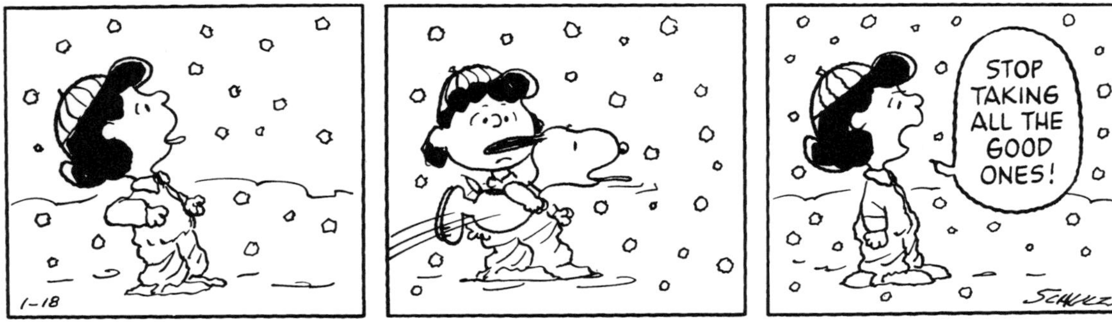
STOP TAKING ALL THE GOOD ONES!
1-18
SCHULZ

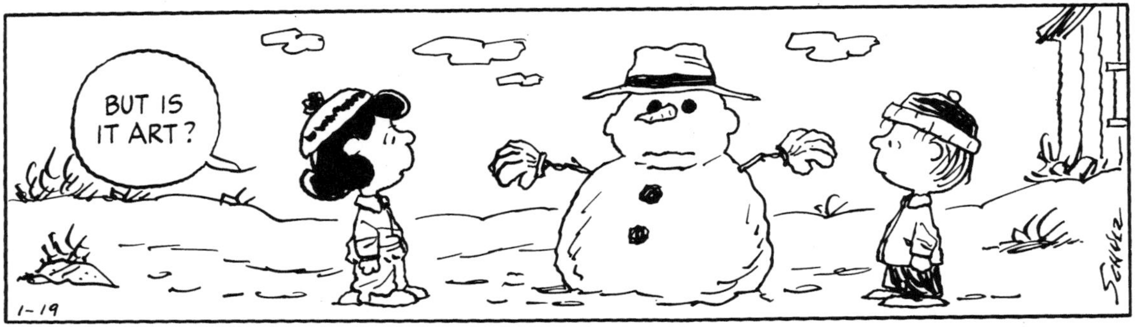
BUT IS IT ART?
1-19
SCHULZ

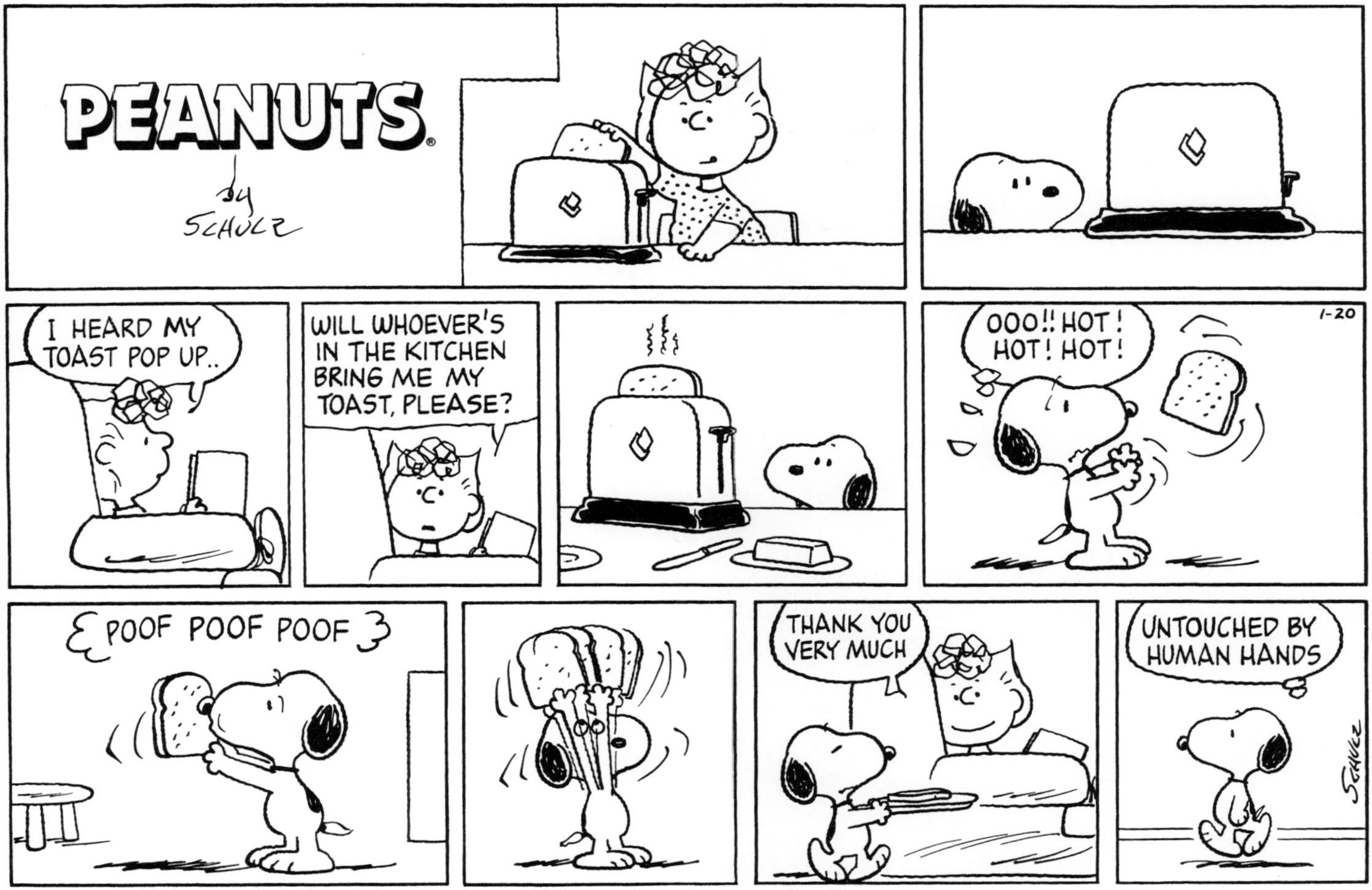
PEANUTS
by SCHULZ
I HEARD MY TOAST POP UP..
WILL WHOEVER'S IN THE KITCHEN BRING ME MY TOAST, PLEASE?
1-20
OOO!! HOT! HOT! HOT!
POOF POOF POOF
THANK YOU VERY MUCH
UNTOUCHED BY HUMAN HANDS
SCHULZ

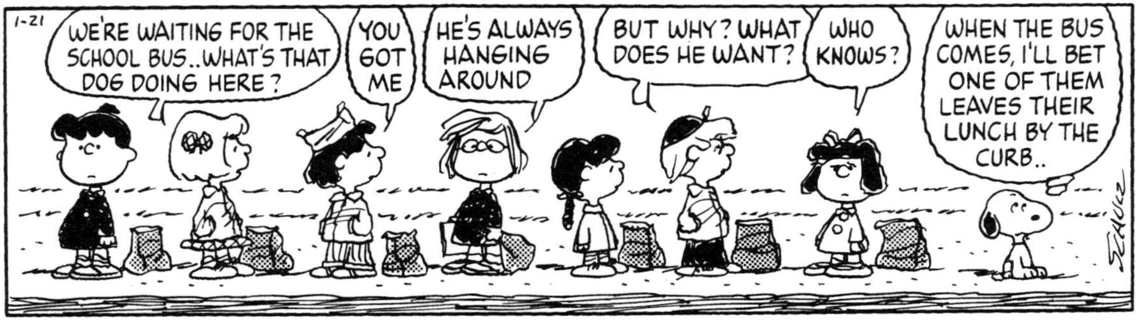
1-21
WE'RE WAITING FOR THE SCHOOL BUS..WHAT'S THAT DOG DOING HERE?
YOU GOT ME
HE'S ALWAYS HANGING AROUND
BUT WHY? WHAT DOES HE WANT?
WHO KNOWS?
WHEN THE BUS COMES, I'LL BET ONE OF THEM LEAVES THEIR LUNCH BY THE CURB..

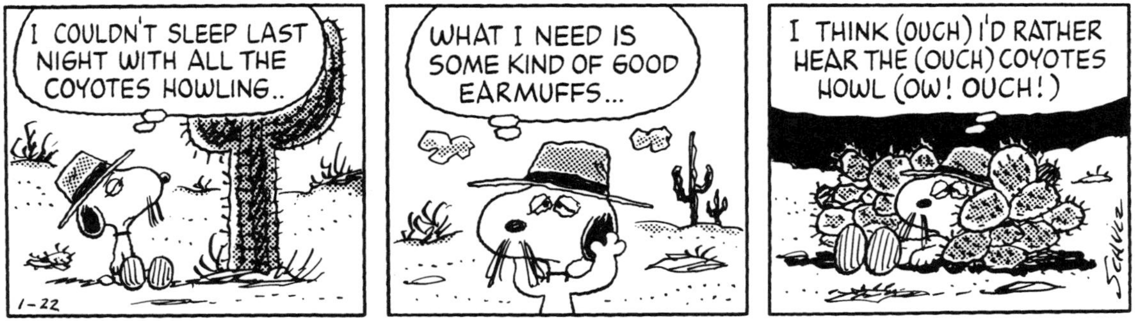
I COULDN'T SLEEP LAST NIGHT WITH ALL THE COYOTES HOWLING..
1-22
WHAT I NEED IS SOME KIND OF GOOD EARMUFFS...
I THINK (OUCH) I'D RATHER HEAR THE (OUCH) COYOTES HOWL (OW! OUCH!)

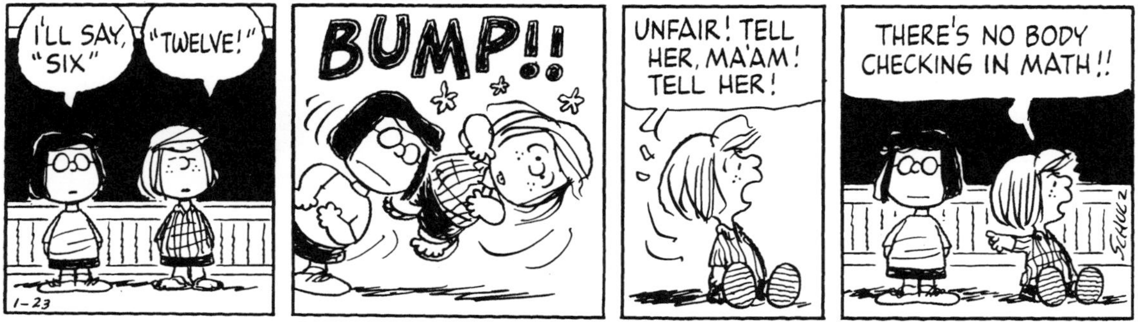
I'LL SAY, "SIX"
"TWELVE!"
1-23
BUMP!!
UNFAIR! TELL HER, MA'AM! TELL HER!
THERE'S NO BODY CHECKING IN MATH!!

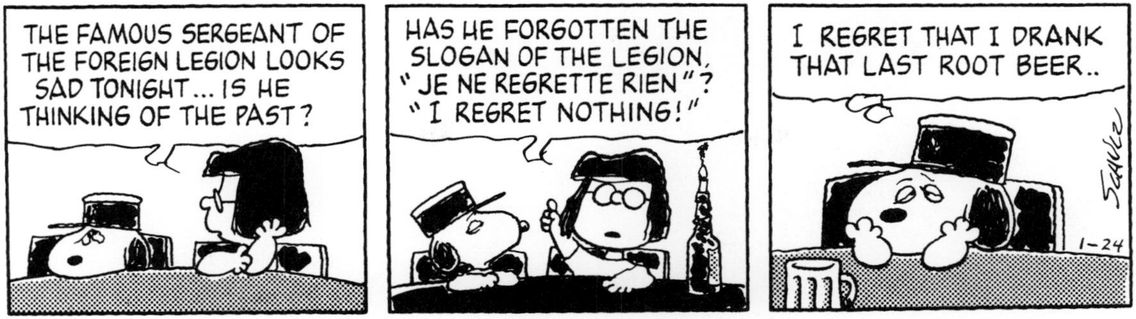
THE FAMOUS SERGEANT OF THE FOREIGN LEGION LOOKS SAD TONIGHT... IS HE THINKING OF THE PAST?
HAS HE FORGOTTEN THE SLOGAN OF THE LEGION, "JE NE REGRETTE RIEN"? "I REGRET NOTHING!"
I REGRET THAT I DRANK THAT LAST ROOT BEER..
SCHULZ
1-24

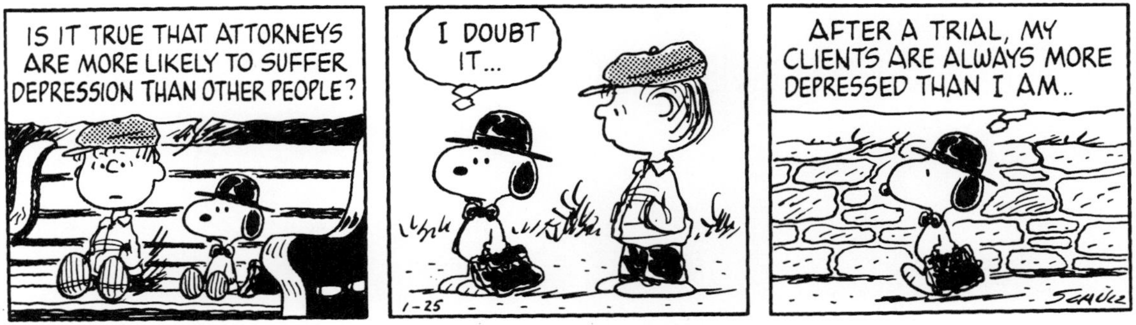
IS IT TRUE THAT ATTORNEYS ARE MORE LIKELY TO SUFFER DEPRESSION THAN OTHER PEOPLE?
I DOUBT IT...
1-25
AFTER A TRIAL, MY CLIENTS ARE ALWAYS MORE DEPRESSED THAN I AM..
SCHULZ

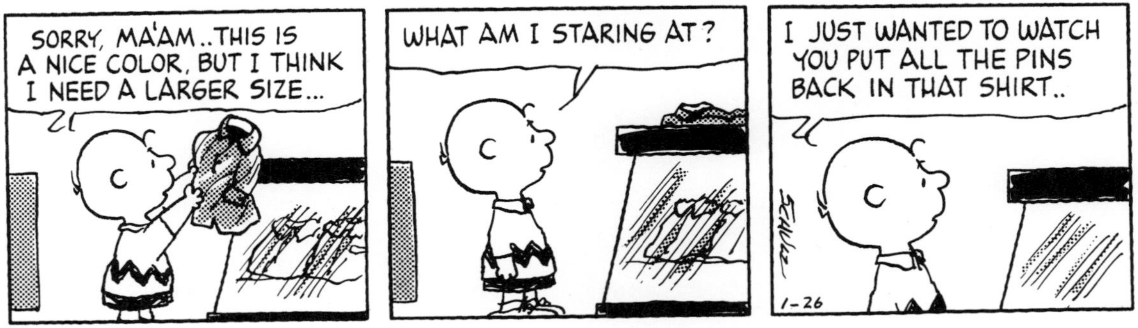
SORRY, MA'AM..THIS IS A NICE COLOR, BUT I THINK I NEED A LARGER SIZE...
WHAT AM I STARING AT?
I JUST WANTED TO WATCH YOU PUT ALL THE PINS BACK IN THAT SHIRT..
SCHULZ
1-26

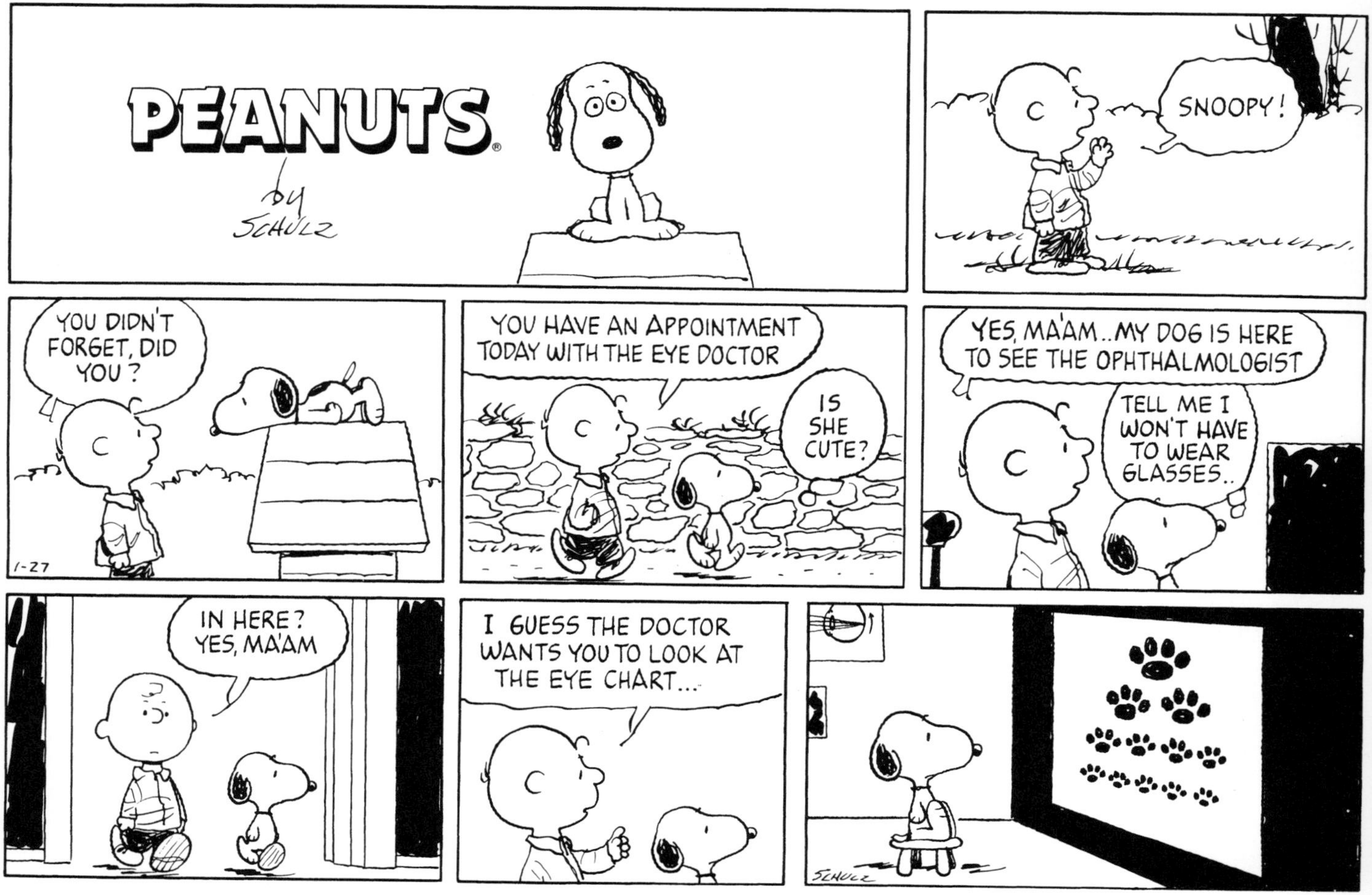
PEANUTS
by SCHULZ
SNOOPY!
YOU DIDN'T FORGET, DID YOU?
1-27
YOU HAVE AN APPOINTMENT TODAY WITH THE EYE DOCTOR
IS SHE CUTE?
YES, MA'AM..MY DOG IS HERE TO SEE THE OPHTHALMOLOGIST
TELL ME I WON'T HAVE TO WEAR GLASSES..
IN HERE? YES, MA'AM
I GUESS THE DOCTOR WANTS YOU TO LOOK AT THE EYE CHART...
SCHULZ

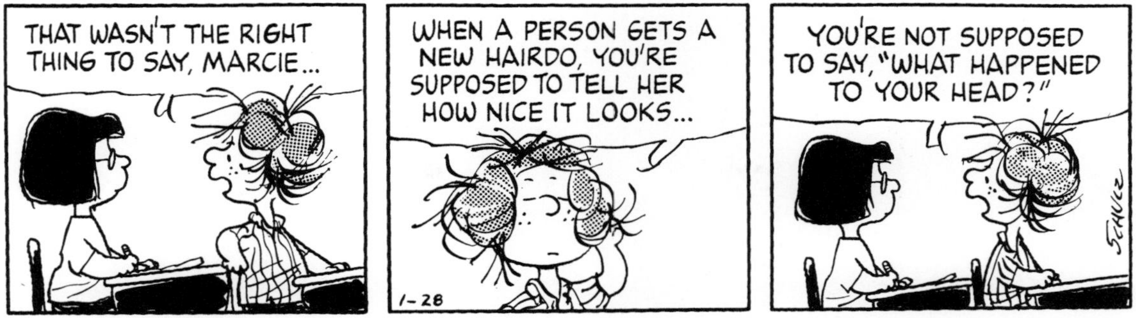
THAT WASN'T THE RIGHT THING TO SAY, MARCIE...
WHEN A PERSON GETS A NEW HAIRDO, YOU'RE SUPPOSED TO TELL HER HOW NICE IT LOOKS...
1-28
YOU'RE NOT SUPPOSED TO SAY, "WHAT HAPPENED TO YOUR HEAD?"
SCHULZ

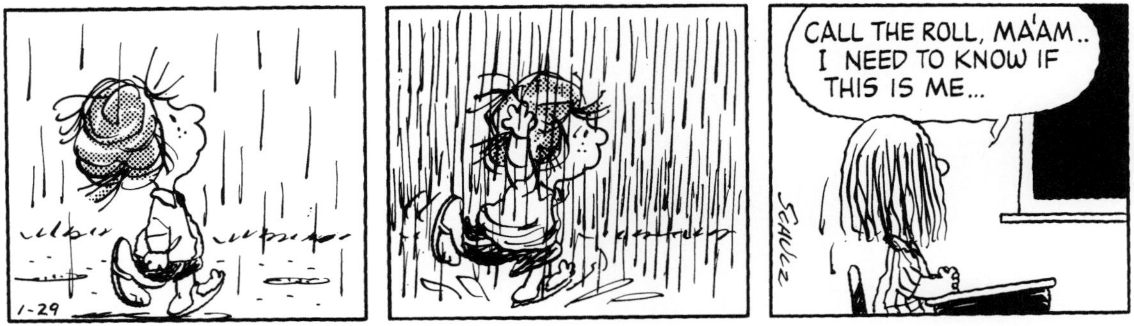
1-29
SCHULZ
CALL THE ROLL, MA'AM.. I NEED TO KNOW IF THIS IS ME...

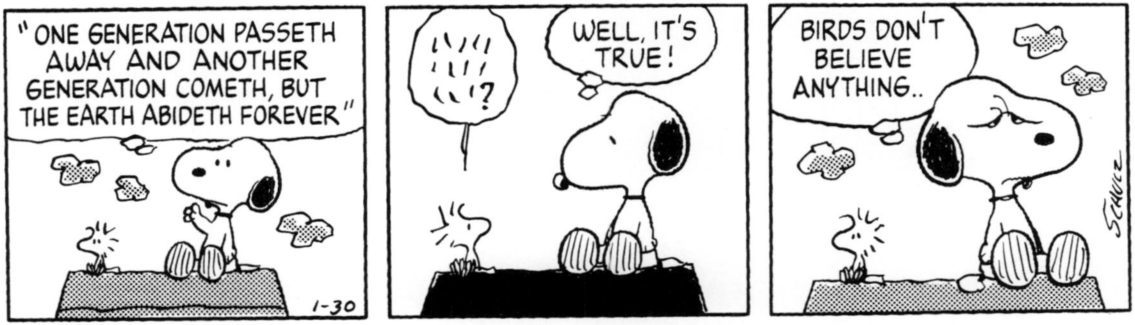
"ONE GENERATION PASSETH AWAY AND ANOTHER GENERATION COMETH, BUT THE EARTH ABIDETH FOREVER"
1-30
?
WELL, IT'S TRUE!
BIRDS DON'T BELIEVE ANYTHING..
SCHULZ

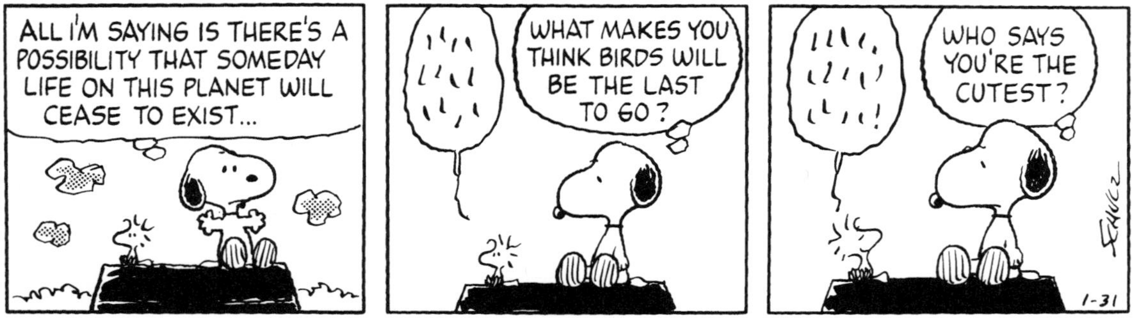
ALL I'M SAYING IS THERE'S A POSSIBILITY THAT SOMEDAY LIFE ON THIS PLANET WILL CEASE TO EXIST...
WHAT MAKES YOU THINK BIRDS WILL BE THE LAST TO GO?
WHO SAYS YOU'RE THE CUTEST?
SCHULZ
1-31

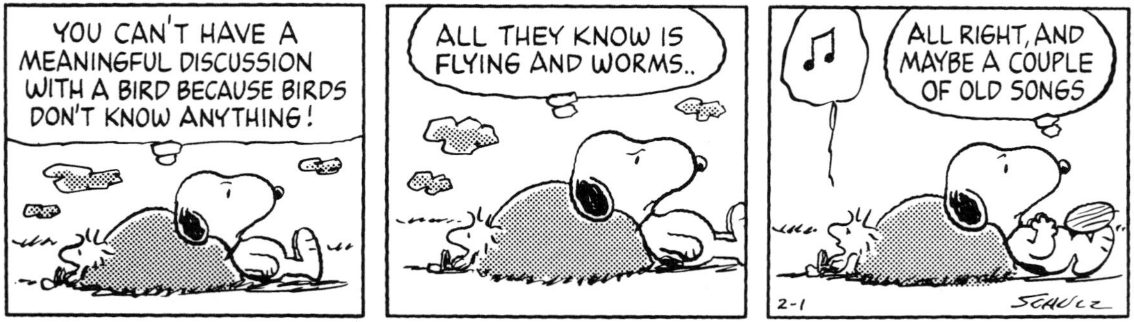
YOU CAN'T HAVE A MEANINGFUL DISCUSSION WITH A BIRD BECAUSE BIRDS DON'T KNOW ANYTHING!
ALL THEY KNOW IS FLYING AND WORMS..
ALL RIGHT, AND MAYBE A COUPLE OF OLD SONGS
2-1
SCHULZ

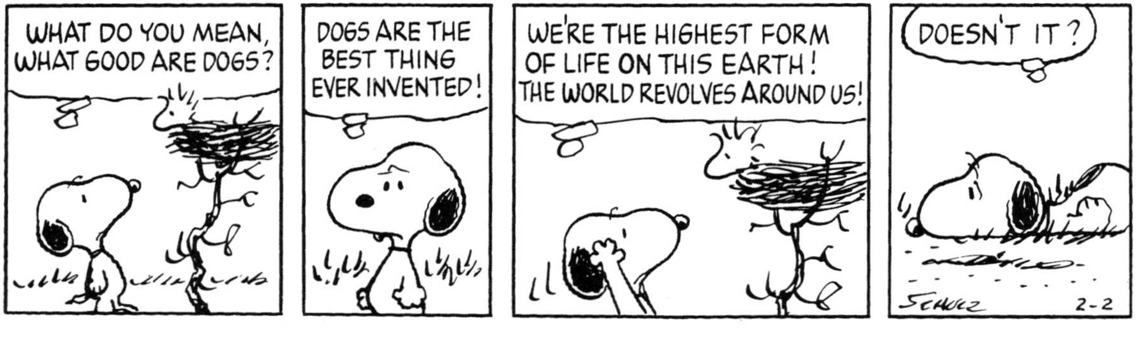
WHAT DO YOU MEAN, WHAT GOOD ARE DOGS?
DOGS ARE THE BEST THING EVER INVENTED!
WE'RE THE HIGHEST FORM OF LIFE ON THIS EARTH! THE WORLD REVOLVES AROUND US!
DOESN'T IT?
SCHULZ
2-2

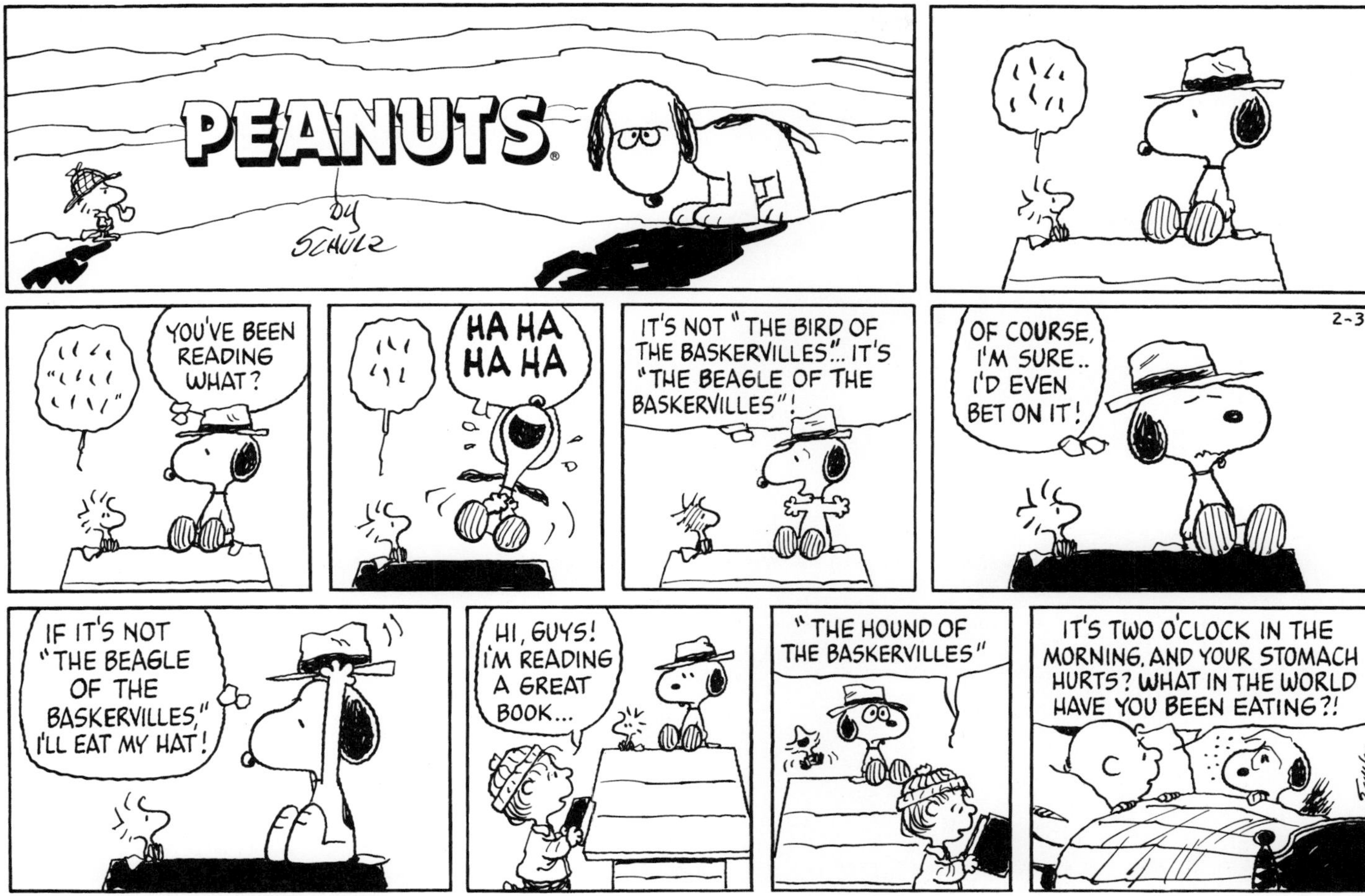
PEANUTS®
by SCHULZ
YOU'VE BEEN READING WHAT?
HA HA HA HA
IT'S NOT "THE BIRD OF THE BASKERVILLES"... IT'S "THE BEAGLE OF THE BASKERVILLES"!
2-3
OF COURSE, I'M SURE.. I'D EVEN BET ON IT!
IF IT'S NOT "THE BEAGLE OF THE BASKERVILLES," I'LL EAT MY HAT!
HI, GUYS! I'M READING A GREAT BOOK...
"THE HOUND OF THE BASKERVILLES"
IT'S TWO O'CLOCK IN THE MORNING, AND YOUR STOMACH HURTS? WHAT IN THE WORLD HAVE YOU BEEN EATING?!
SCHULZ

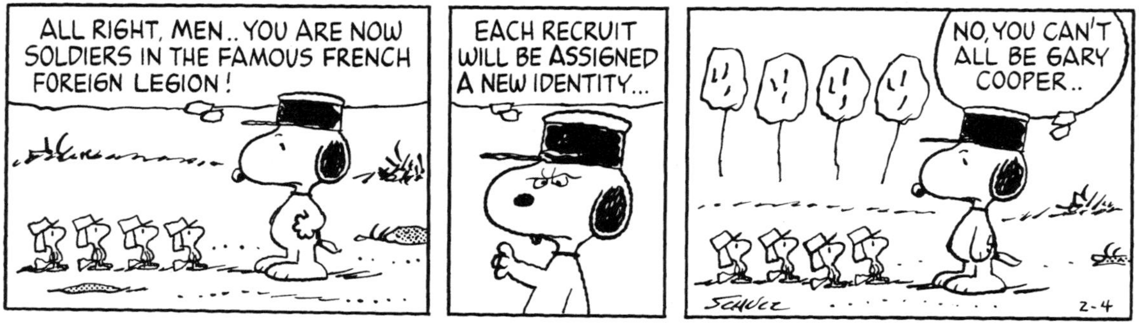
ALL RIGHT, MEN.. YOU ARE NOW SOLDIERS IN THE FAMOUS FRENCH FOREIGN LEGION!
EACH RECRUIT WILL BE ASSIGNED A NEW IDENTITY...
NO, YOU CAN'T ALL BE GARY COOPER..
2-4

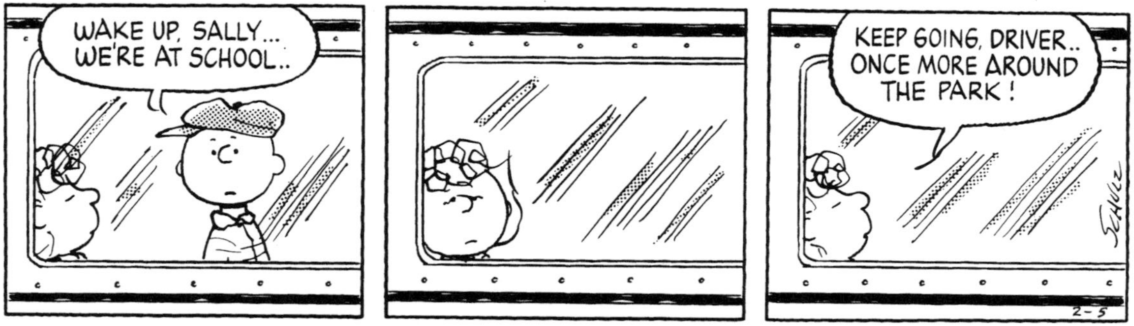
WAKE UP, SALLY... WE'RE AT SCHOOL..
KEEP GOING, DRIVER.. ONCE MORE AROUND THE PARK!
2-5

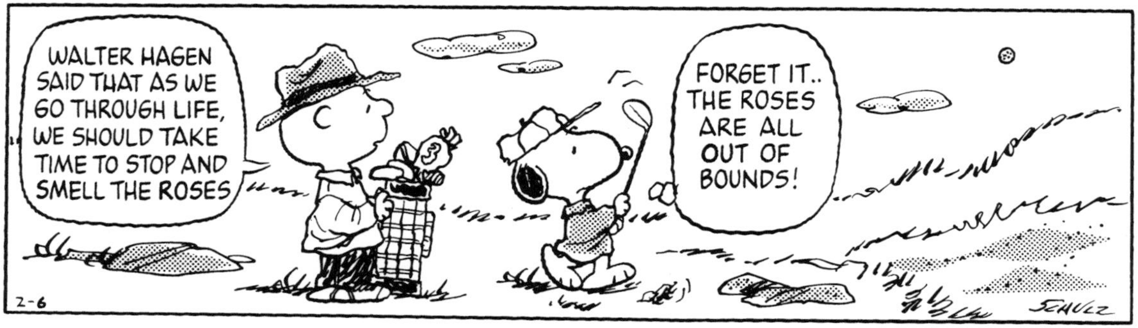
WALTER HAGEN SAID THAT AS WE GO THROUGH LIFE, WE SHOULD TAKE TIME TO STOP AND SMELL THE ROSES
FORGET IT.. THE ROSES ARE ALL OUT OF BOUNDS!
2-6

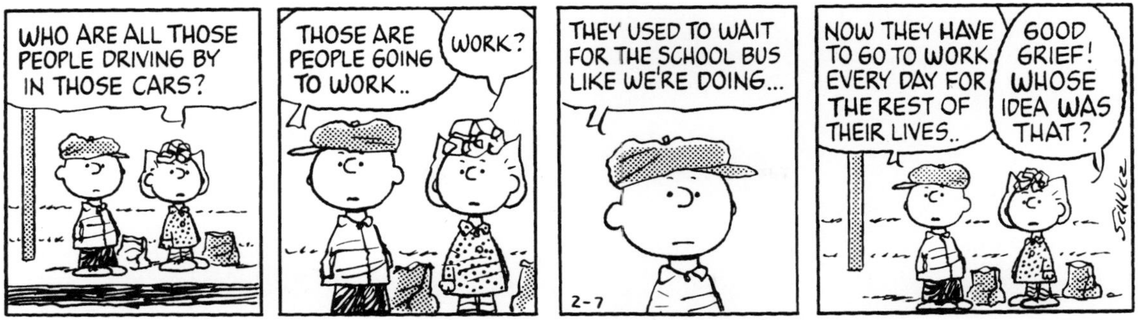
WHO ARE ALL THOSE PEOPLE DRIVING BY IN THOSE CARS?
THOSE ARE PEOPLE GOING TO WORK..
WORK?
THEY USED TO WAIT FOR THE SCHOOL BUS LIKE WE'RE DOING...
NOW THEY HAVE TO GO TO WORK EVERY DAY FOR THE REST OF THEIR LIVES..
GOOD GRIEF! WHOSE IDEA WAS THAT?
2-7
SCHULZ

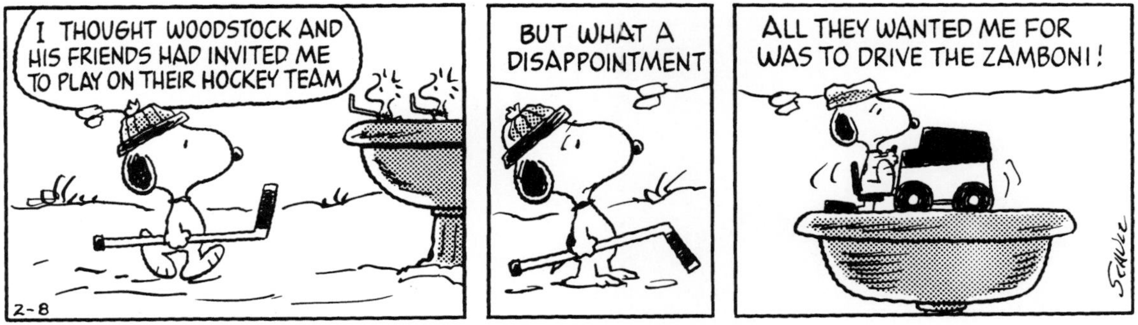
I THOUGHT WOODSTOCK AND HIS FRIENDS HAD INVITED ME TO PLAY ON THEIR HOCKEY TEAM
BUT WHAT A DISAPPOINTMENT
ALL THEY WANTED ME FOR WAS TO DRIVE THE ZAMBONI!
2-8
SCHULZ

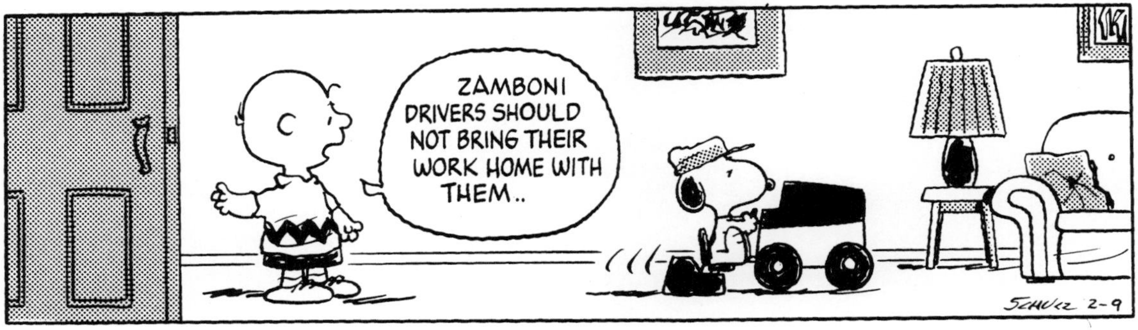
ZAMBONI DRIVERS SHOULD NOT BRING THEIR WORK HOME WITH THEM..
SCHULZ 2-9

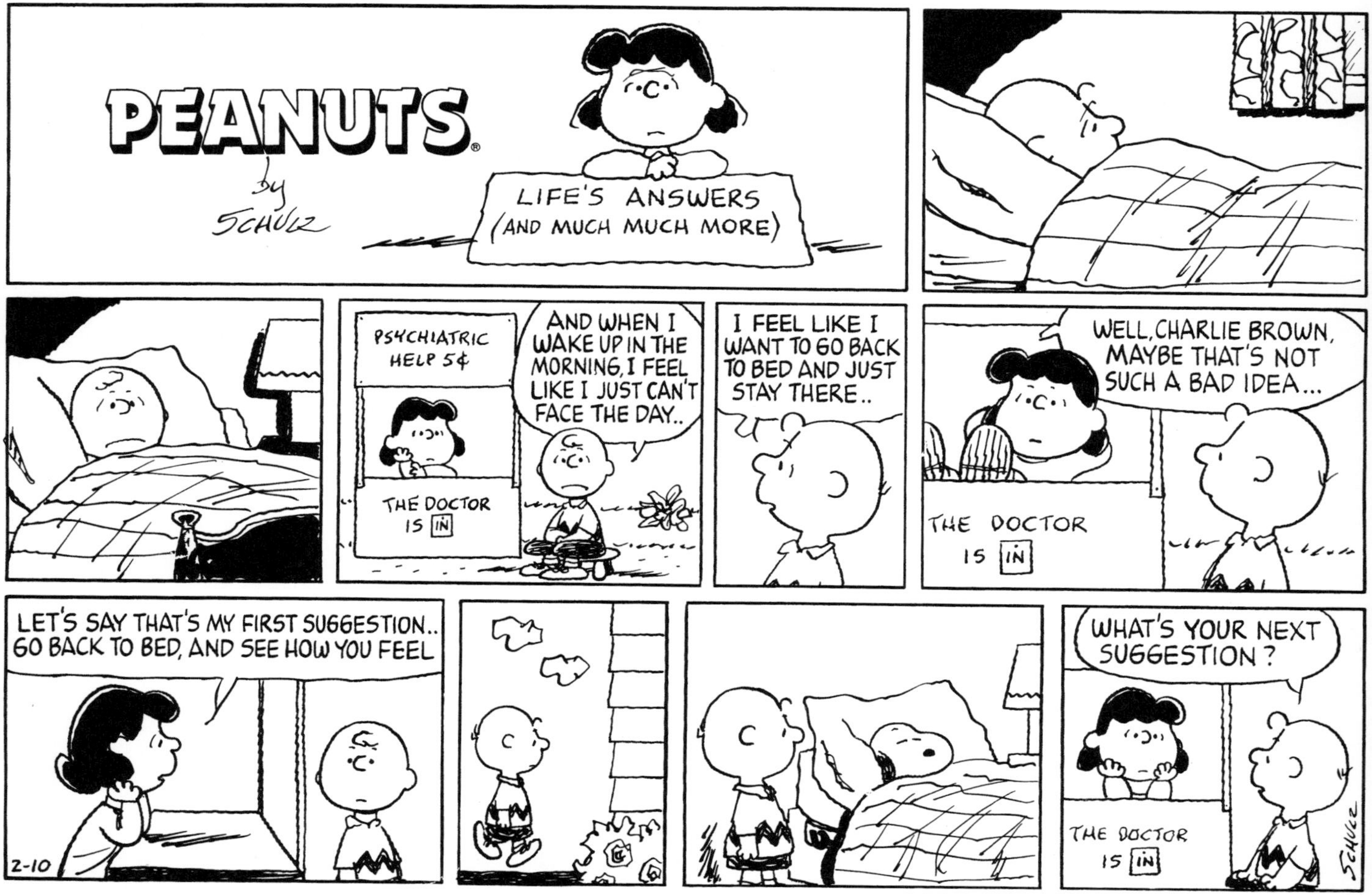
PEANUTS®
by SCHULZ
LIFE'S ANSWERS (AND MUCH MUCH MORE)
PSYCHIATRIC HELP 5¢
THE DOCTOR IS IN
AND WHEN I WAKE UP IN THE MORNING, I FEEL LIKE I JUST CAN'T FACE THE DAY..
I FEEL LIKE I WANT TO GO BACK TO BED AND JUST STAY THERE..
WELL, CHARLIE BROWN, MAYBE THAT'S NOT SUCH A BAD IDEA...
THE DOCTOR IS IN
LET'S SAY THAT'S MY FIRST SUGGESTION.. GO BACK TO BED, AND SEE HOW YOU FEEL
2-10
WHAT'S YOUR NEXT SUGGESTION?
THE DOCTOR IS IN
SCHULZ

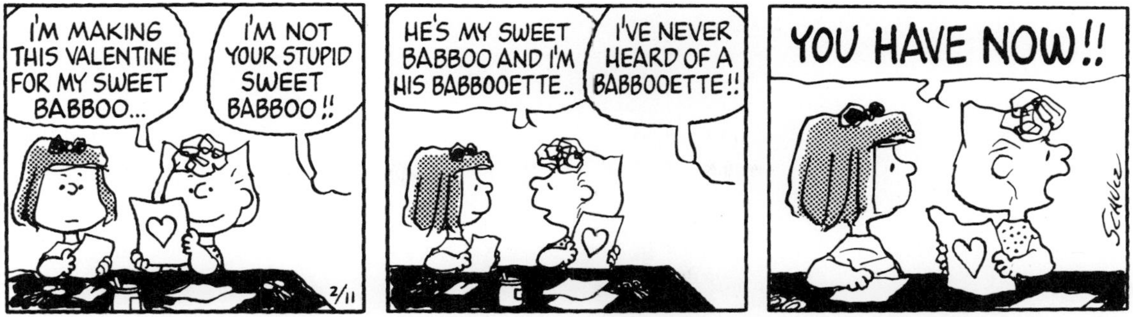
I'M MAKING THIS VALENTINE FOR MY SWEET BABBOO...
I'M NOT YOUR STUPID SWEET BABBOO!!
HE'S MY SWEET BABBOO AND I'M HIS BABBOOETTE..
I'VE NEVER HEARD OF A BABBOOETTE!!
YOU HAVE NOW!!

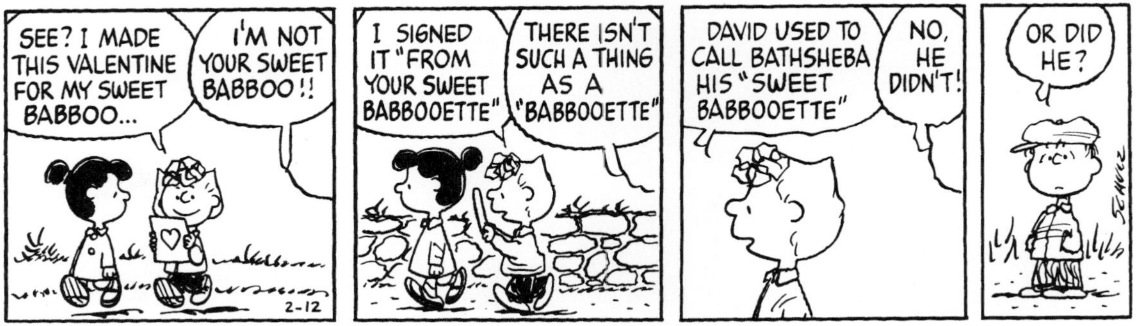
SEE? I MADE THIS VALENTINE FOR MY SWEET BABBOO...
I'M NOT YOUR SWEET BABBOO!!
I SIGNED IT "FROM YOUR SWEET BABBOOETTE"
THERE ISN'T SUCH A THING AS A "BABBOOETTE"
DAVID USED TO CALL BATHSHEBA HIS "SWEET BABBOOETTE"
NO, HE DIDN'T!
OR DID HE?

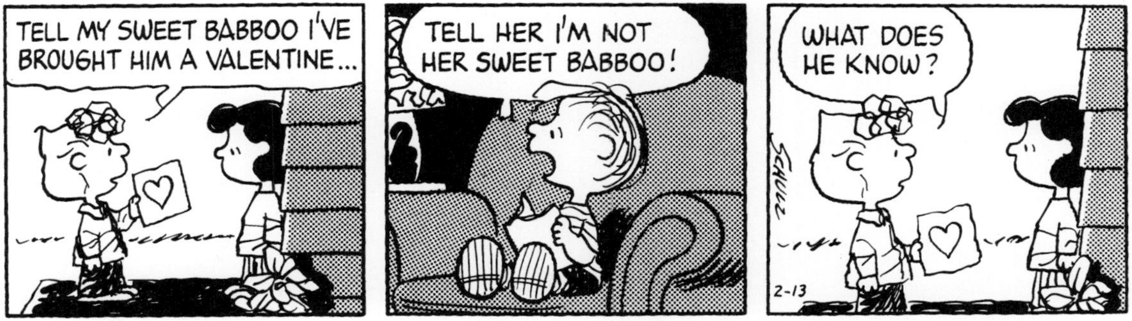
TELL MY SWEET BABBOO I'VE BROUGHT HIM A VALENTINE...
TELL HER I'M NOT HER SWEET BABBOO!
WHAT DOES HE KNOW?

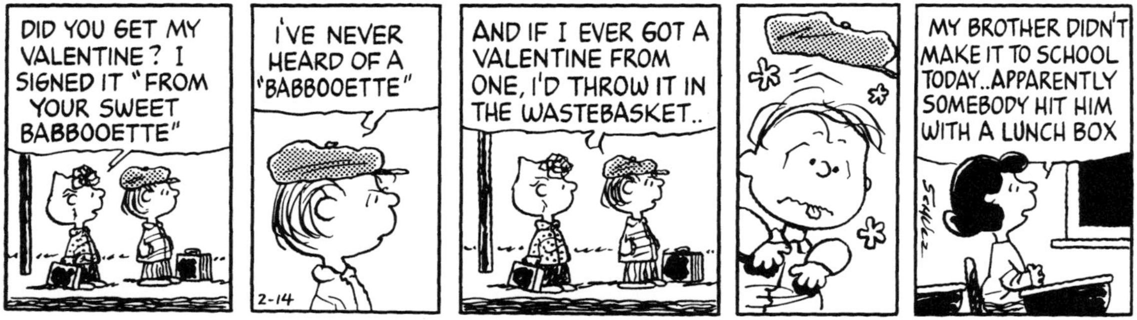
DID YOU GET MY VALENTINE? I SIGNED IT "FROM YOUR SWEET BABBOOETTE"
I'VE NEVER HEARD OF A "BABBOOETTE"
2-14
AND IF I EVER GOT A VALENTINE FROM ONE, I'D THROW IT IN THE WASTEBASKET..
MY BROTHER DIDN'T MAKE IT TO SCHOOL TODAY..APPARENTLY SOMEBODY HIT HIM WITH A LUNCH BOX
SCHULZ

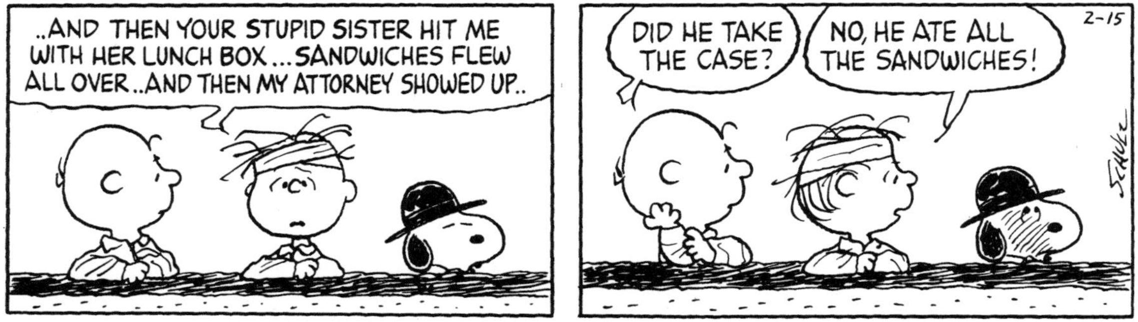
..AND THEN YOUR STUPID SISTER HIT ME WITH HER LUNCH BOX...SANDWICHES FLEW ALL OVER..AND THEN MY ATTORNEY SHOWED UP..
2-15
DID HE TAKE THE CASE?
NO, HE ATE ALL THE SANDWICHES!
SCHULZ

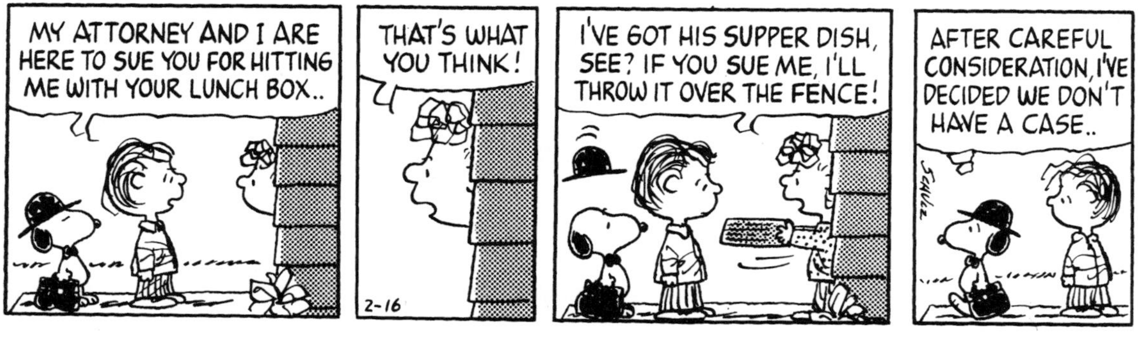
MY ATTORNEY AND I ARE HERE TO SUE YOU FOR HITTING ME WITH YOUR LUNCH BOX..
THAT'S WHAT YOU THINK!
2-16
I'VE GOT HIS SUPPER DISH, SEE? IF YOU SUE ME, I'LL THROW IT OVER THE FENCE!
AFTER CAREFUL CONSIDERATION, I'VE DECIDED WE DON'T HAVE A CASE..
SCHULZ

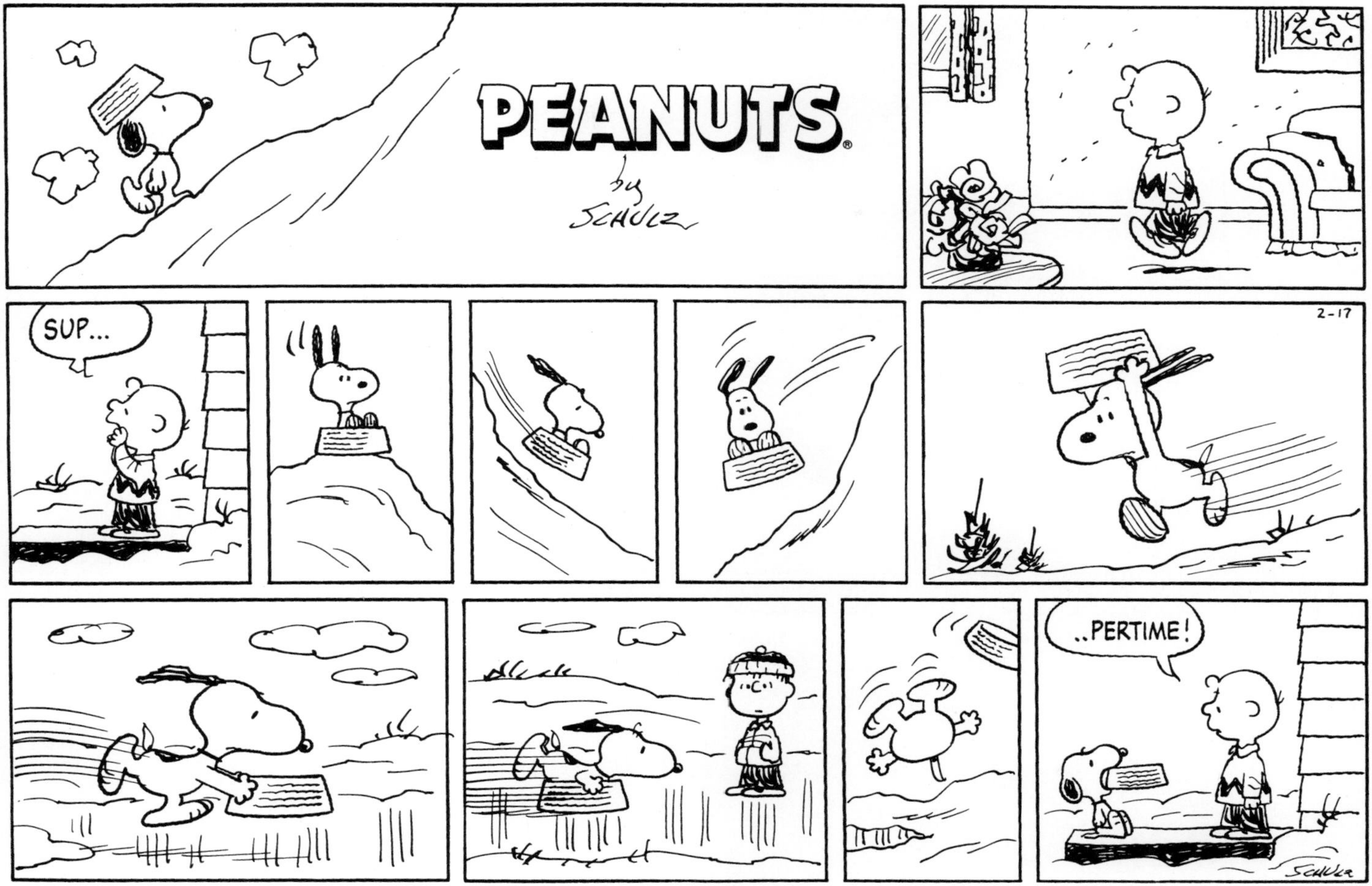
PEANUTS®
by SCHULZ
SUP...
2-17
..PERTIME!
SCHULZ

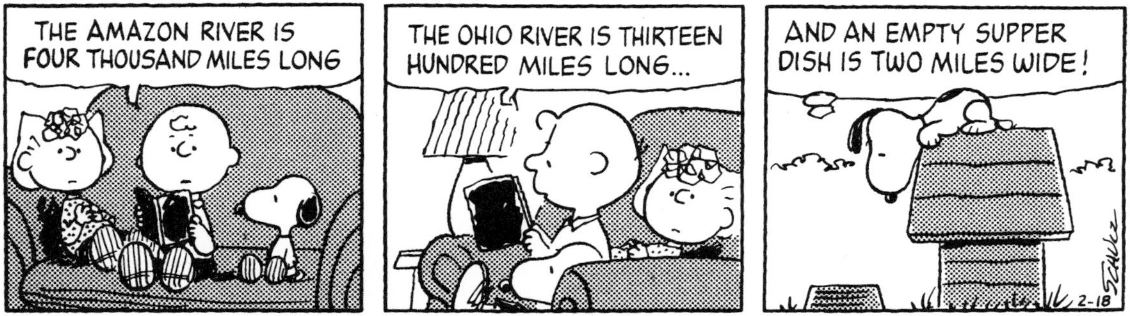
THE AMAZON RIVER IS FOUR THOUSAND MILES LONG
THE OHIO RIVER IS THIRTEEN HUNDRED MILES LONG...
AND AN EMPTY SUPPER DISH IS TWO MILES WIDE!
SCHULZ
2-18

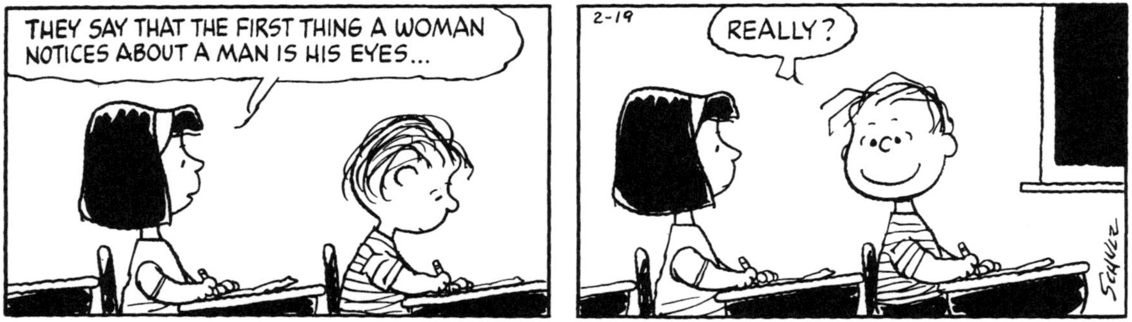
THEY SAY THAT THE FIRST THING A WOMAN NOTICES ABOUT A MAN IS HIS EYES...
2-19
REALLY?
SCHULZ

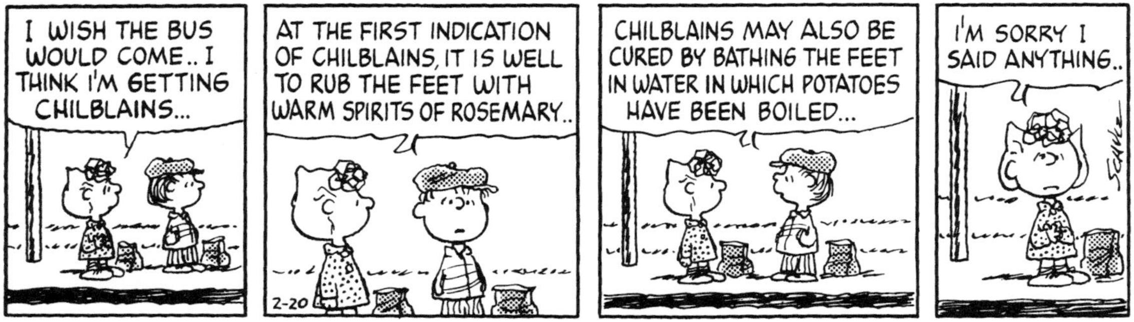
I WISH THE BUS WOULD COME.. I THINK I'M GETTING CHILBLAINS...
AT THE FIRST INDICATION OF CHILBLAINS, IT IS WELL TO RUB THE FEET WITH WARM SPIRITS OF ROSEMARY..
2-20
CHILBLAINS MAY ALSO BE CURED BY BATHING THE FEET IN WATER IN WHICH POTATOES HAVE BEEN BOILED...
I'M SORRY I SAID ANYTHING..
SCHULZ

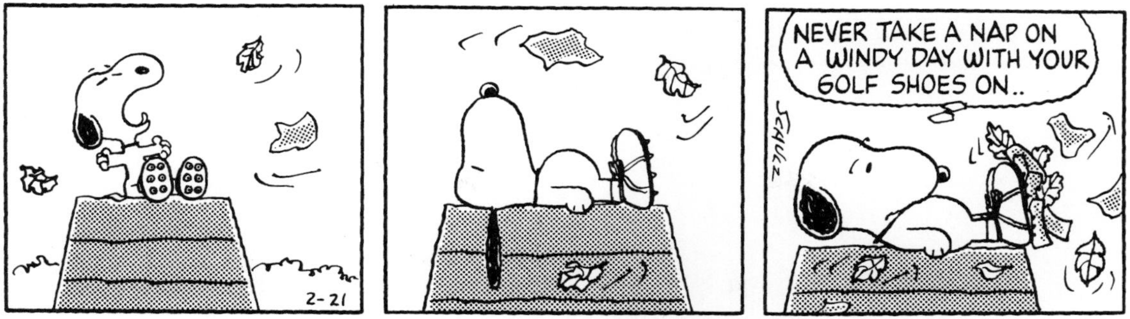
NEVER TAKE A NAP ON A WINDY DAY WITH YOUR GOLF SHOES ON..

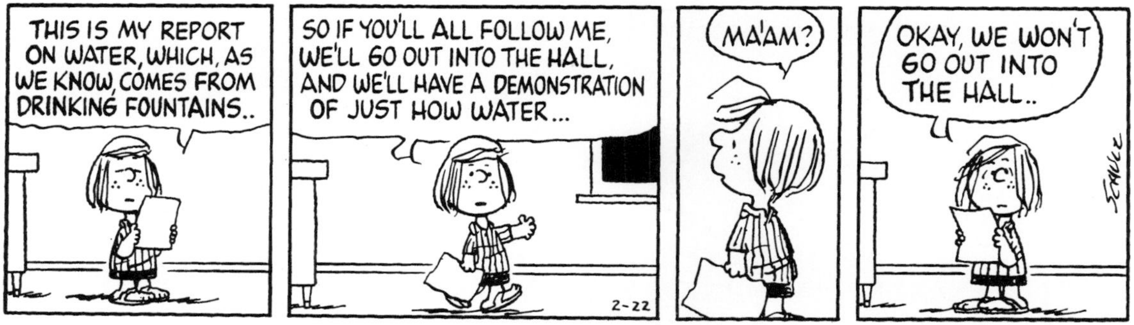
THIS IS MY REPORT ON WATER, WHICH, AS WE KNOW, COMES FROM DRINKING FOUNTAINS..
SO IF YOU'LL ALL FOLLOW ME, WE'LL GO OUT INTO THE HALL, AND WE'LL HAVE A DEMONSTRATION OF JUST HOW WATER...
MA'AM?
OKAY, WE WON'T GO OUT INTO THE HALL..

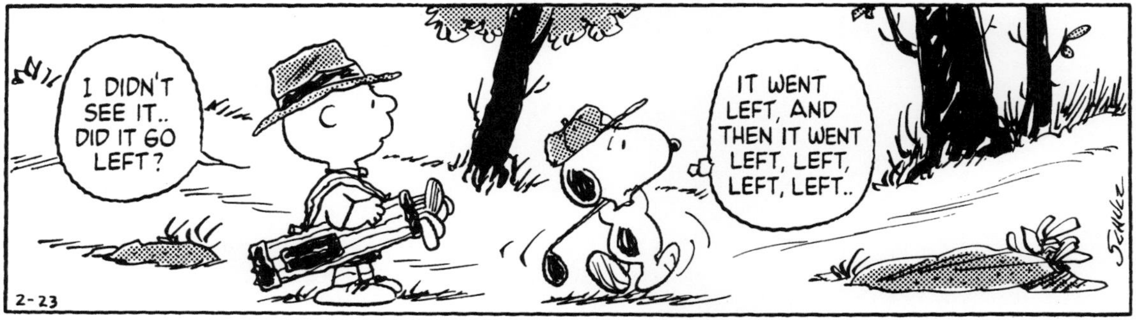
I DIDN'T SEE IT.. DID IT GO LEFT?
IT WENT LEFT, AND THEN IT WENT LEFT, LEFT, LEFT, LEFT..

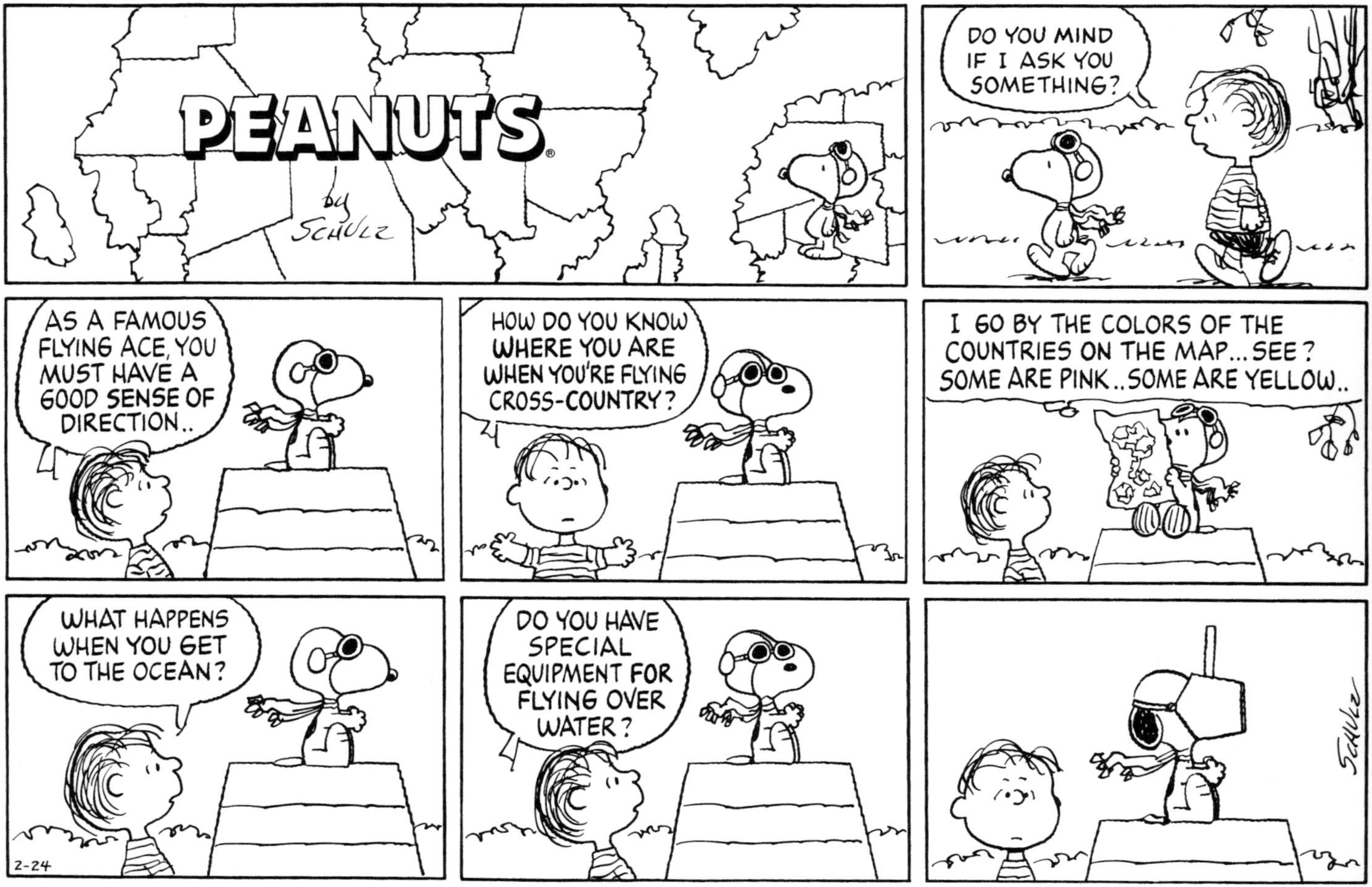
PEANUTS
by SCHULZ
DO YOU MIND IF I ASK YOU SOMETHING?
AS A FAMOUS FLYING ACE, YOU MUST HAVE A GOOD SENSE OF DIRECTION..
HOW DO YOU KNOW WHERE YOU ARE WHEN YOU'RE FLYING CROSS-COUNTRY?
I GO BY THE COLORS OF THE COUNTRIES ON THE MAP... SEE? SOME ARE PINK.. SOME ARE YELLOW..
WHAT HAPPENS WHEN YOU GET TO THE OCEAN?
2-24
DO YOU HAVE SPECIAL EQUIPMENT FOR FLYING OVER WATER?
SCHULZ

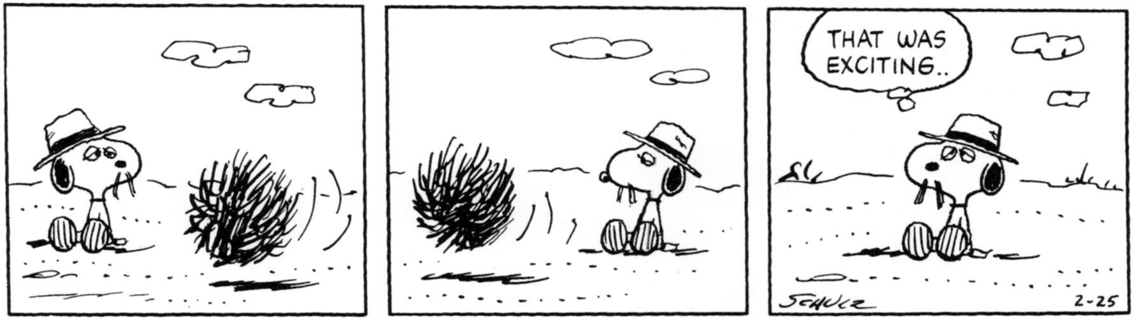
THAT WAS EXCITING..
SCHULZ
2-25

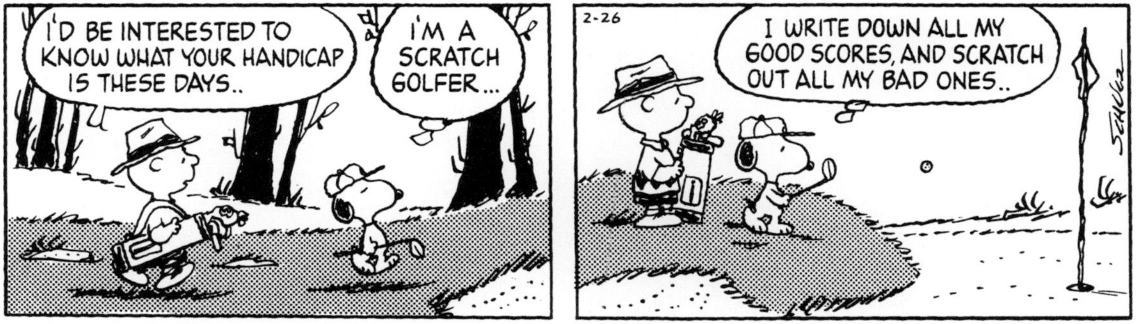
I'D BE INTERESTED TO KNOW WHAT YOUR HANDICAP IS THESE DAYS..
I'M A SCRATCH GOLFER...
2-26
I WRITE DOWN ALL MY GOOD SCORES, AND SCRATCH OUT ALL MY BAD ONES..
SCHULZ

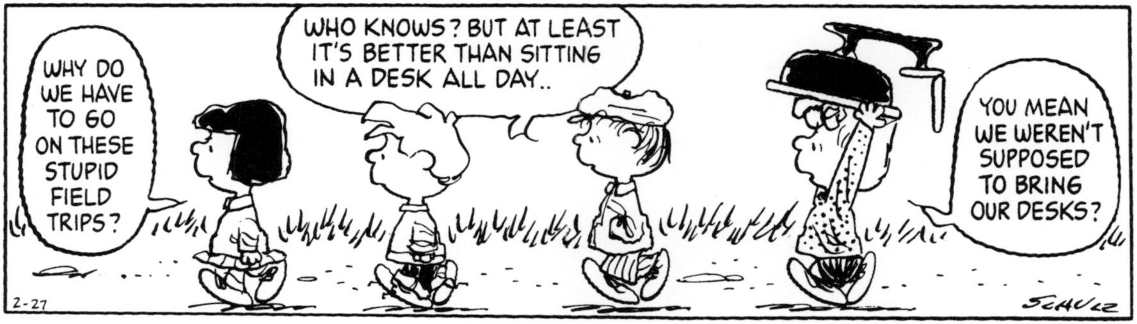
WHY DO WE HAVE TO GO ON THESE STUPID FIELD TRIPS?
WHO KNOWS? BUT AT LEAST IT'S BETTER THAN SITTING IN A DESK ALL DAY..
YOU MEAN WE WEREN'T SUPPOSED TO BRING OUR DESKS?
2-27
SCHULZ

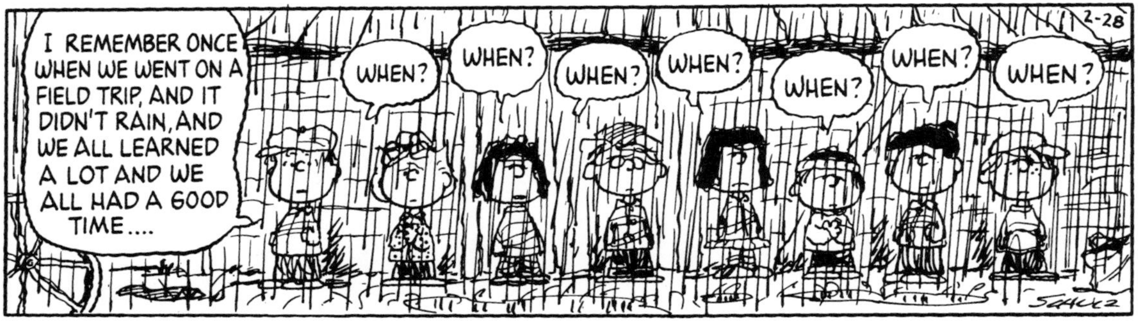
2-28
I REMEMBER ONCE WHEN WE WENT ON A FIELD TRIP, AND IT DIDN'T RAIN, AND WE ALL LEARNED A LOT AND WE ALL HAD A GOOD TIME....
WHEN?
WHEN?
WHEN?
WHEN?
WHEN?
WHEN?
WHEN?

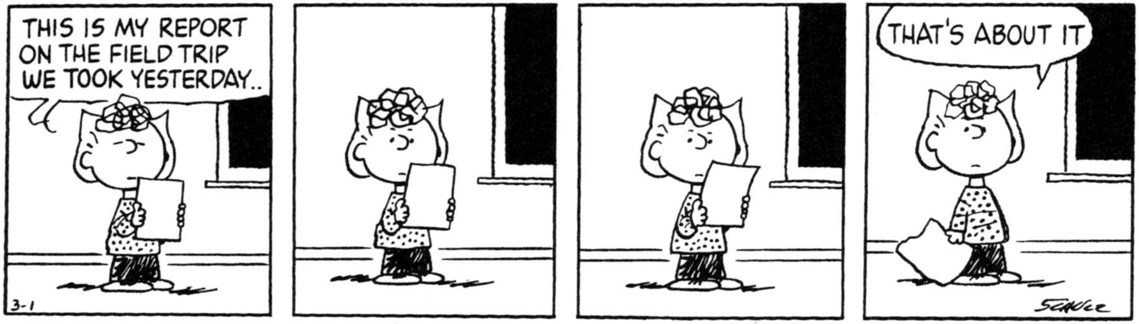
THIS IS MY REPORT ON THE FIELD TRIP WE TOOK YESTERDAY..
3-1
THAT'S ABOUT IT

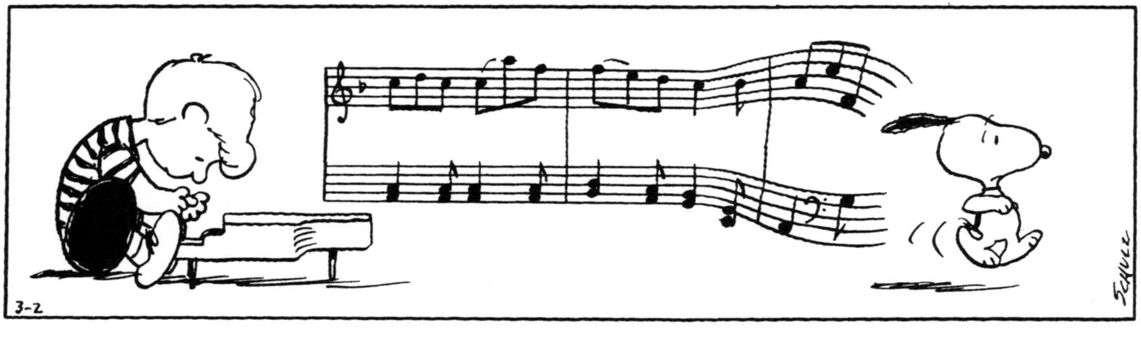
3-2

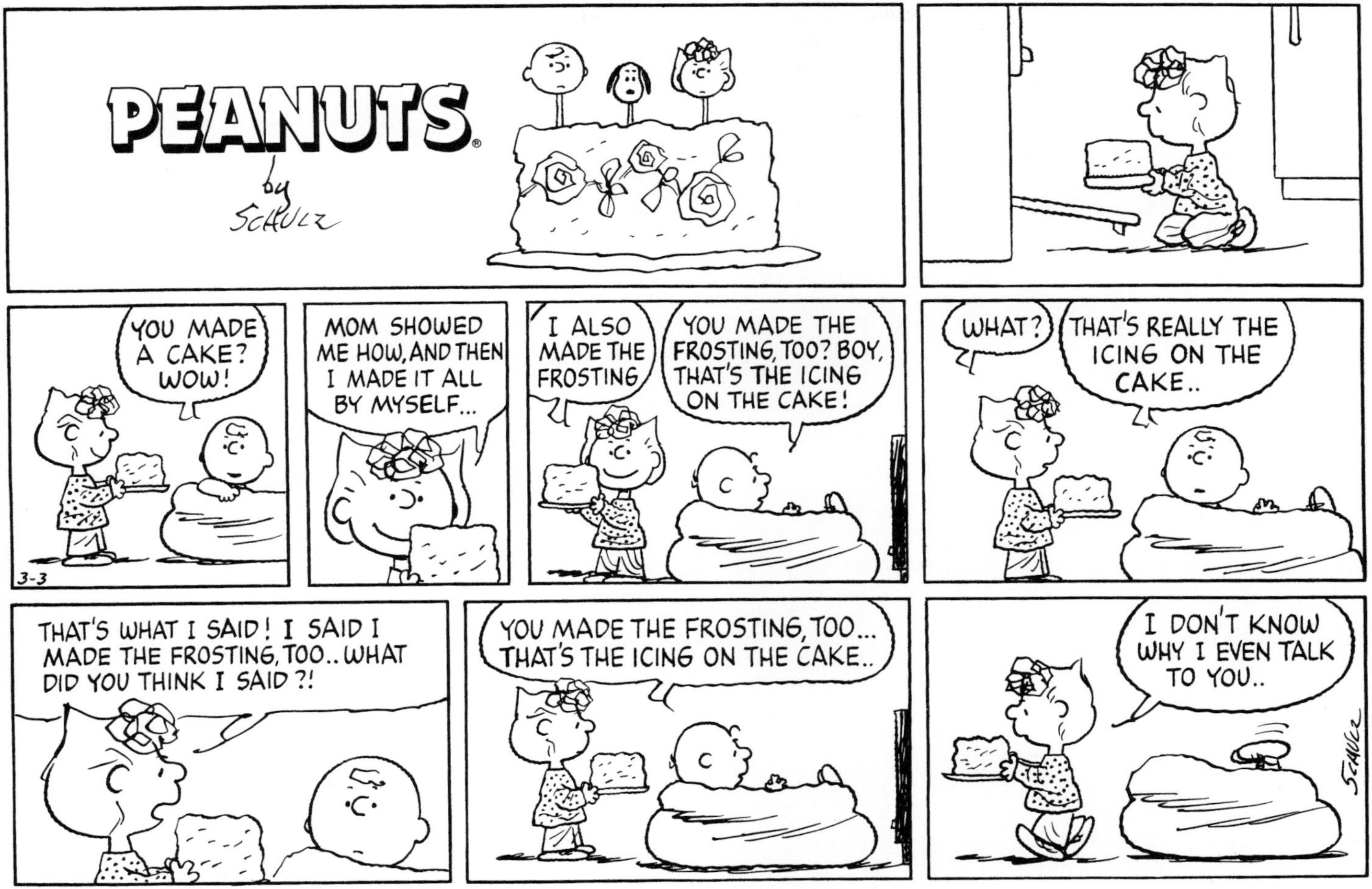
PEANUTS®
by SCHULZ
YOU MADE A CAKE? WOW!
3-3
MOM SHOWED ME HOW, AND THEN I MADE IT ALL BY MYSELF...
I ALSO MADE THE FROSTING
YOU MADE THE FROSTING, TOO? BOY, THAT'S THE ICING ON THE CAKE!
WHAT?
THAT'S REALLY THE ICING ON THE CAKE..
THAT'S WHAT I SAID! I SAID I MADE THE FROSTING, TOO.. WHAT DID YOU THINK I SAID?!
YOU MADE THE FROSTING, TOO... THAT'S THE ICING ON THE CAKE..
I DON'T KNOW WHY I EVEN TALK TO YOU..
SCHULZ

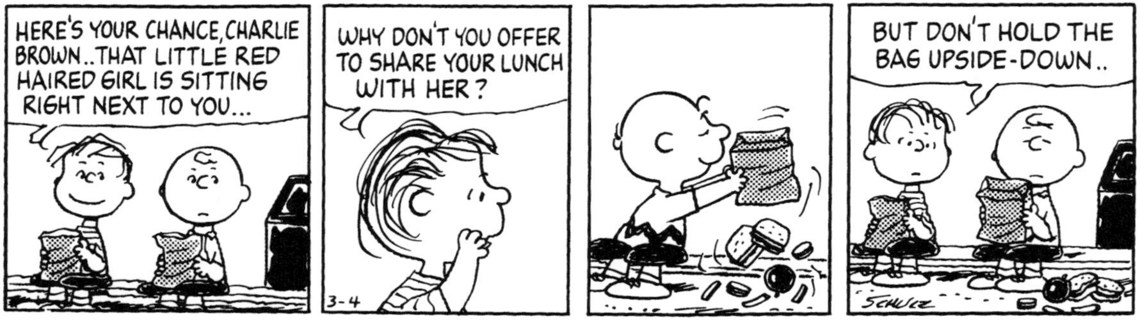
HERE'S YOUR CHANCE, CHARLIE BROWN..THAT LITTLE RED HAIRED GIRL IS SITTING RIGHT NEXT TO YOU...
WHY DON'T YOU OFFER TO SHARE YOUR LUNCH WITH HER?
3-4
BUT DON'T HOLD THE BAG UPSIDE-DOWN..
SCHULZ

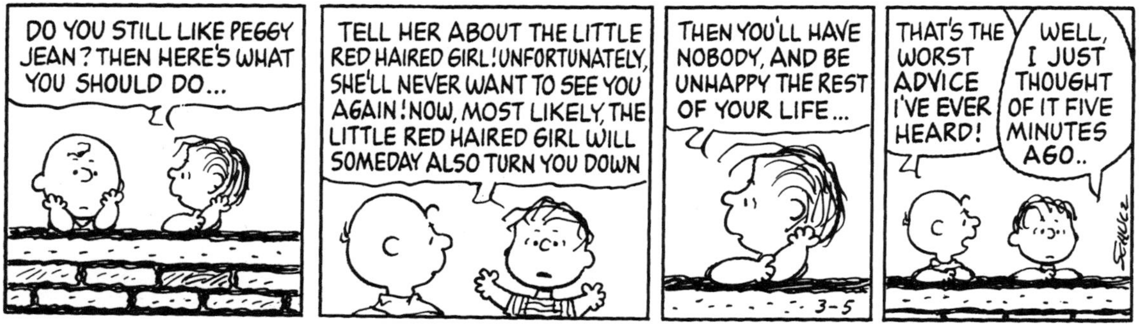
DO YOU STILL LIKE PEGGY JEAN? THEN HERE'S WHAT YOU SHOULD DO...
TELL HER ABOUT THE LITTLE RED HAIRED GIRL! UNFORTUNATELY, SHE'LL NEVER WANT TO SEE YOU AGAIN! NOW, MOST LIKELY, THE LITTLE RED HAIRED GIRL WILL SOMEDAY ALSO TURN YOU DOWN
THEN YOU'LL HAVE NOBODY, AND BE UNHAPPY THE REST OF YOUR LIFE...
3-5
THAT'S THE WORST ADVICE I'VE EVER HEARD!
WELL, I JUST THOUGHT OF IT FIVE MINUTES AGO..
SCHULZ

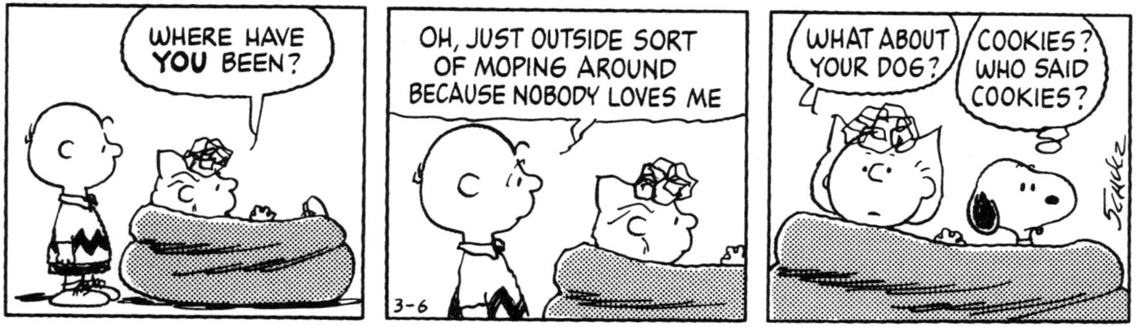
WHERE HAVE YOU BEEN?
OH, JUST OUTSIDE SORT OF MOPING AROUND BECAUSE NOBODY LOVES ME
3-6
WHAT ABOUT YOUR DOG?
COOKIES? WHO SAID COOKIES?
SCHULZ

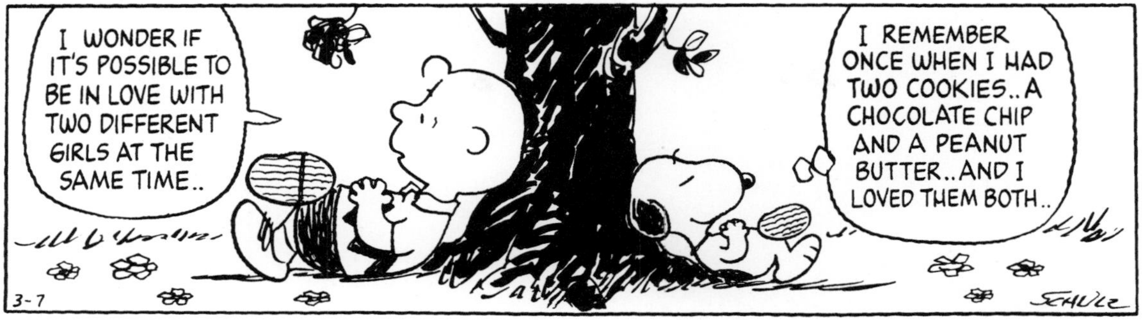
I WONDER IF IT'S POSSIBLE TO BE IN LOVE WITH TWO DIFFERENT GIRLS AT THE SAME TIME..
I REMEMBER ONCE WHEN I HAD TWO COOKIES..A CHOCOLATE CHIP AND A PEANUT BUTTER..AND I LOVED THEM BOTH..

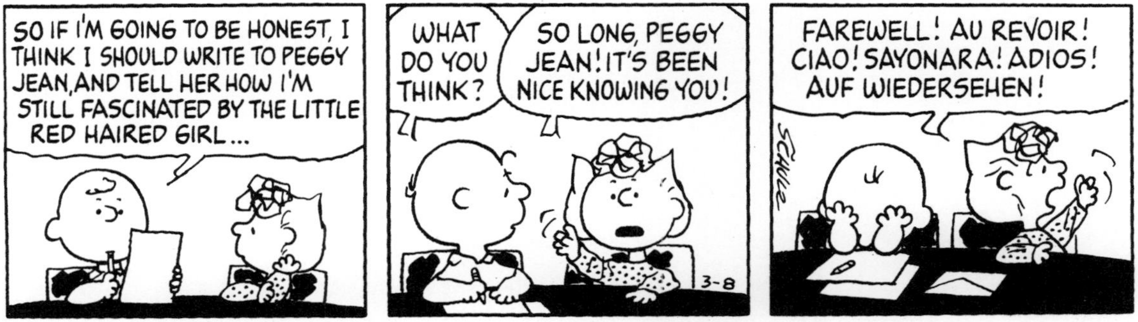
SO IF I'M GOING TO BE HONEST, I THINK I SHOULD WRITE TO PEGGY JEAN, AND TELL HER HOW I'M STILL FASCINATED BY THE LITTLE RED HAIRED GIRL...
WHAT DO YOU THINK?
SO LONG, PEGGY JEAN! IT'S BEEN NICE KNOWING YOU!
FAREWELL! AU REVOIR! CIAO! SAYONARA! ADIOS! AUF WIEDERSEHEN!

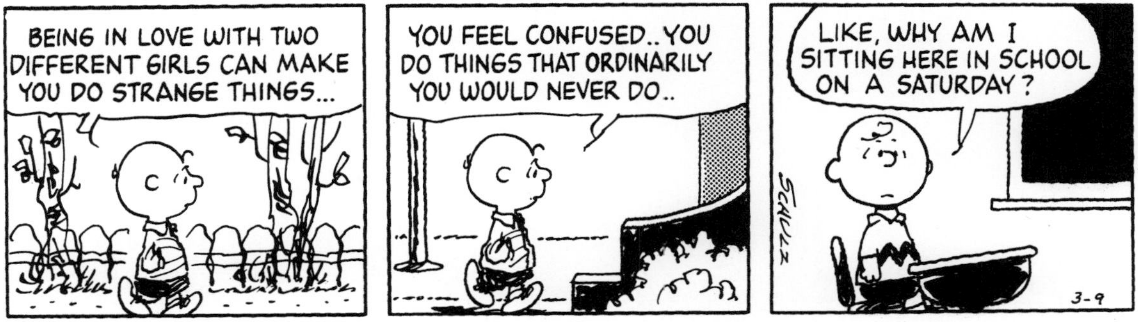
BEING IN LOVE WITH TWO DIFFERENT GIRLS CAN MAKE YOU DO STRANGE THINGS...
YOU FEEL CONFUSED..YOU DO THINGS THAT ORDINARILY YOU WOULD NEVER DO..
LIKE, WHY AM I SITTING HERE IN SCHOOL ON A SATURDAY?

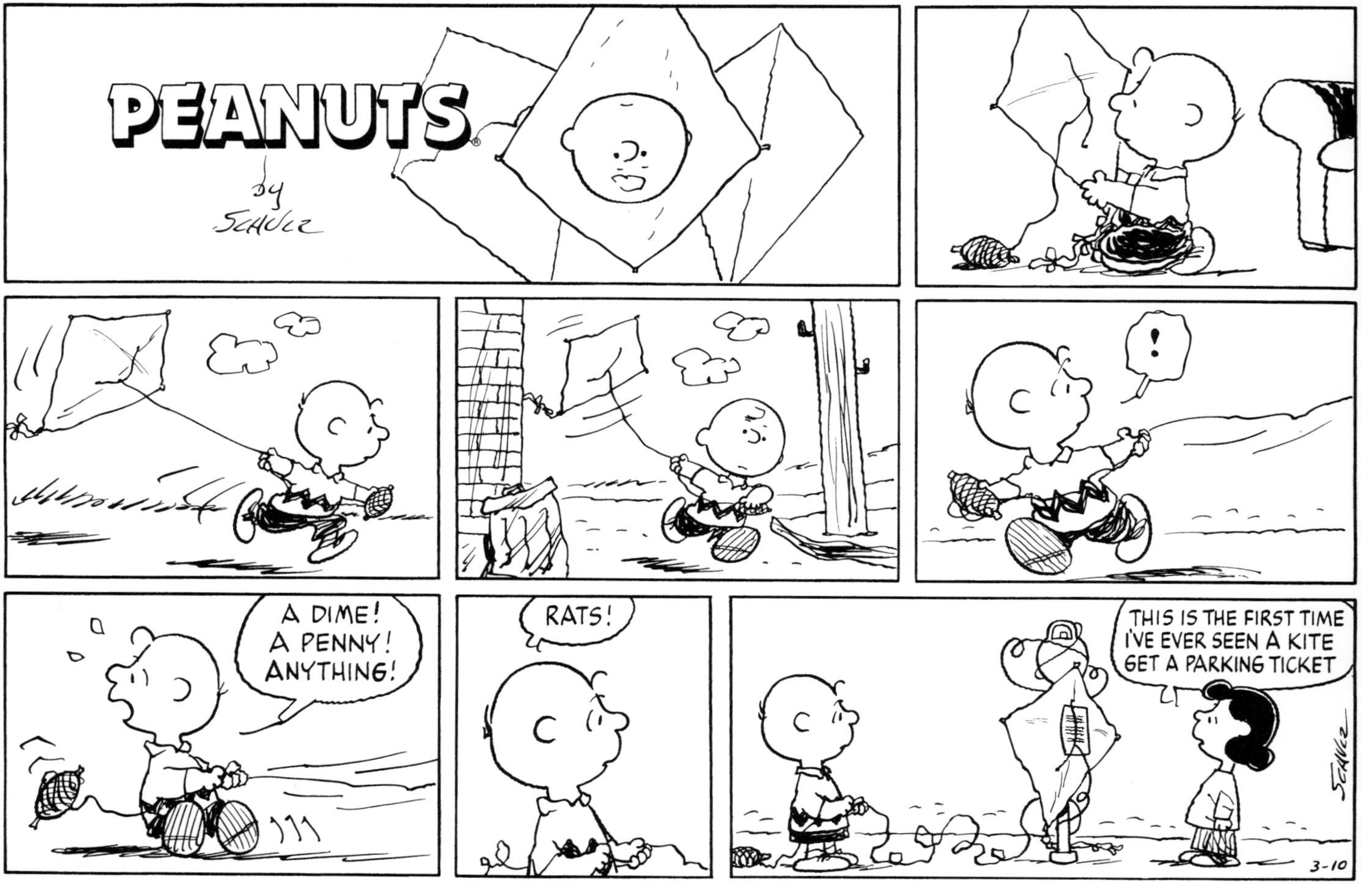
PEANUTS
by SCHULZ
!
A DIME! A PENNY! ANYTHING!
RATS!
THIS IS THE FIRST TIME I'VE EVER SEEN A KITE GET A PARKING TICKET
SCHULZ
3-10

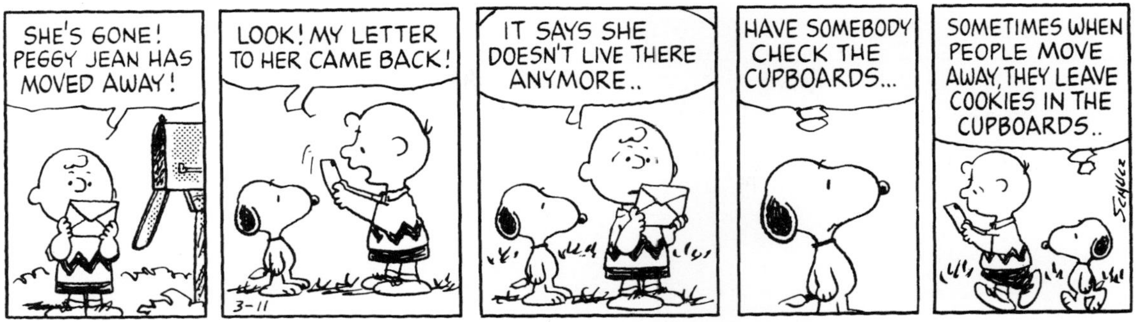
SHE'S GONE! PEGGY JEAN HAS MOVED AWAY!
LOOK! MY LETTER TO HER CAME BACK!
IT SAYS SHE DOESN'T LIVE THERE ANYMORE..
HAVE SOMEBODY CHECK THE CUPBOARDS...
SOMETIMES WHEN PEOPLE MOVE AWAY, THEY LEAVE COOKIES IN THE CUPBOARDS..

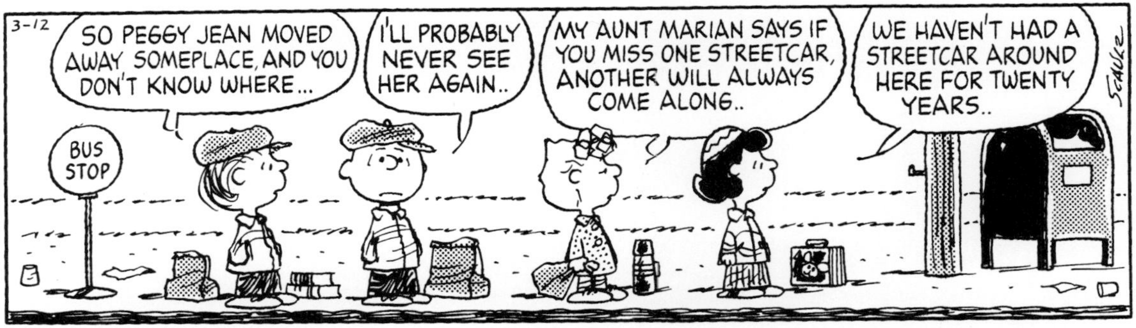
SO PEGGY JEAN MOVED AWAY SOMEPLACE, AND YOU DON'T KNOW WHERE...
I'LL PROBABLY NEVER SEE HER AGAIN..
MY AUNT MARIAN SAYS IF YOU MISS ONE STREETCAR, ANOTHER WILL ALWAYS COME ALONG..
WE HAVEN'T HAD A STREETCAR AROUND HERE FOR TWENTY YEARS..
BUS STOP

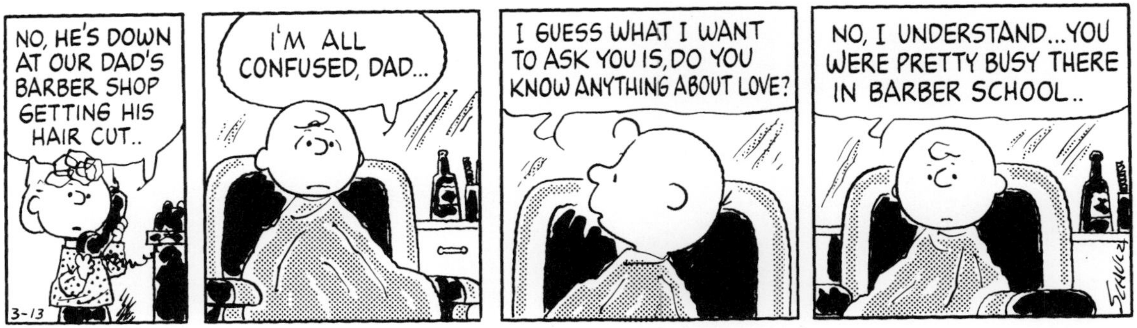
NO, HE'S DOWN AT OUR DAD'S BARBER SHOP GETTING HIS HAIR CUT..
I'M ALL CONFUSED, DAD...
I GUESS WHAT I WANT TO ASK YOU IS, DO YOU KNOW ANYTHING ABOUT LOVE?
NO, I UNDERSTAND...YOU WERE PRETTY BUSY THERE IN BARBER SCHOOL..

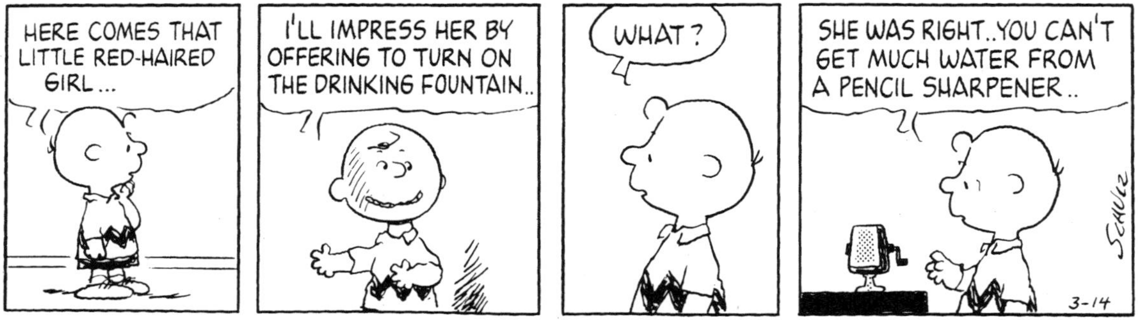
HERE COMES THAT LITTLE RED-HAIRED GIRL...
I'LL IMPRESS HER BY OFFERING TO TURN ON THE DRINKING FOUNTAIN..
WHAT?
SHE WAS RIGHT..YOU CAN'T GET MUCH WATER FROM A PENCIL SHARPENER..
SCHULZ
3-14

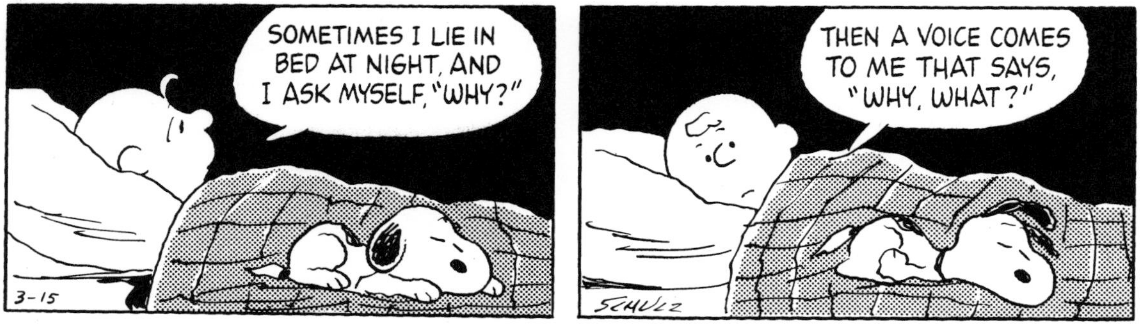
SOMETIMES I LIE IN BED AT NIGHT, AND I ASK MYSELF, "WHY?"
3-15
THEN A VOICE COMES TO ME THAT SAYS, "WHY, WHAT?"
SCHULZ

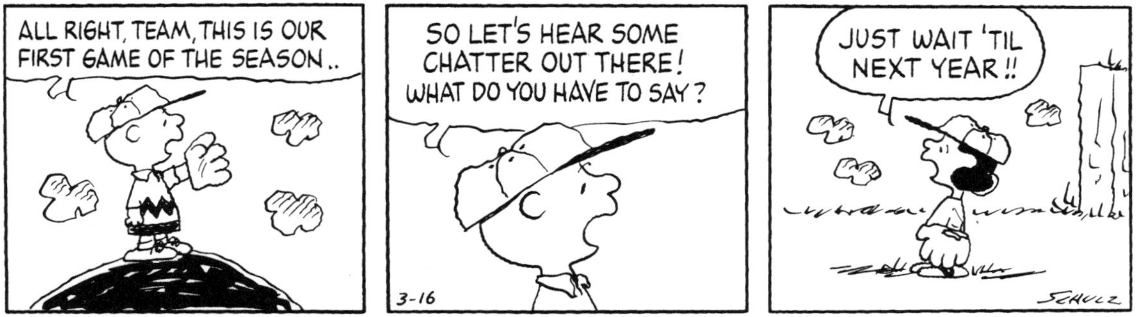
ALL RIGHT, TEAM, THIS IS OUR FIRST GAME OF THE SEASON..
SO LET'S HEAR SOME CHATTER OUT THERE! WHAT DO YOU HAVE TO SAY?
3-16
JUST WAIT 'TIL NEXT YEAR!!
SCHULZ

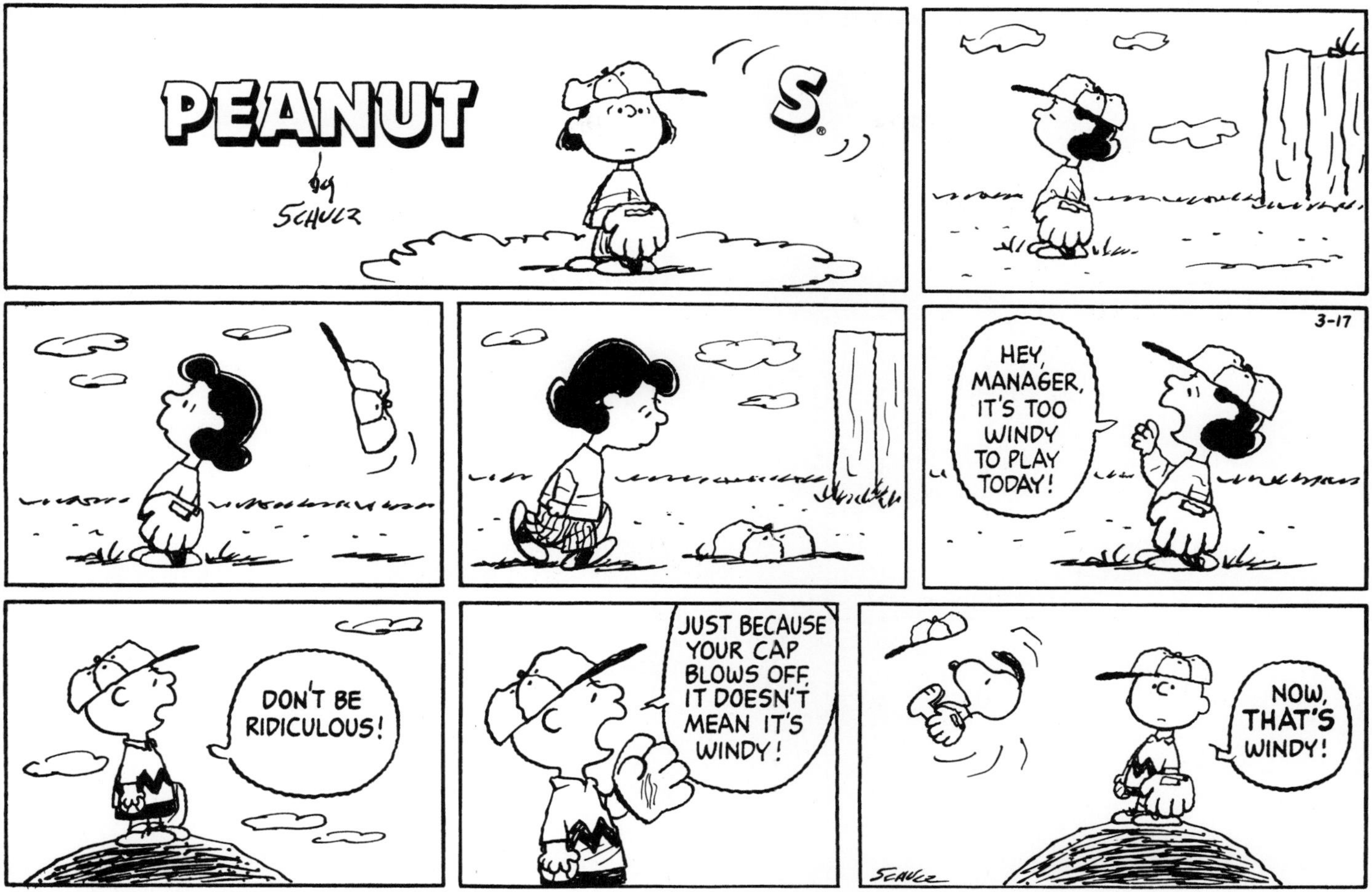
PEANUTS
by SCHULZ
3-17
HEY, MANAGER, IT'S TOO WINDY TO PLAY TODAY!
DON'T BE RIDICULOUS!
JUST BECAUSE YOUR CAP BLOWS OFF, IT DOESN'T MEAN IT'S WINDY!
NOW, THAT'S WINDY!
SCHULZ

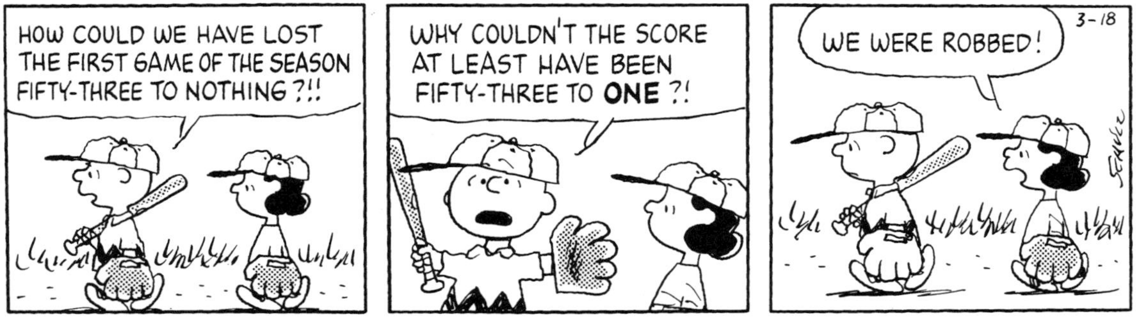
HOW COULD WE HAVE LOST THE FIRST GAME OF THE SEASON FIFTY-THREE TO NOTHING ?!!
WHY COULDN'T THE SCORE AT LEAST HAVE BEEN FIFTY-THREE TO **ONE** ?!
3-18
WE WERE ROBBED!
SCHULZ

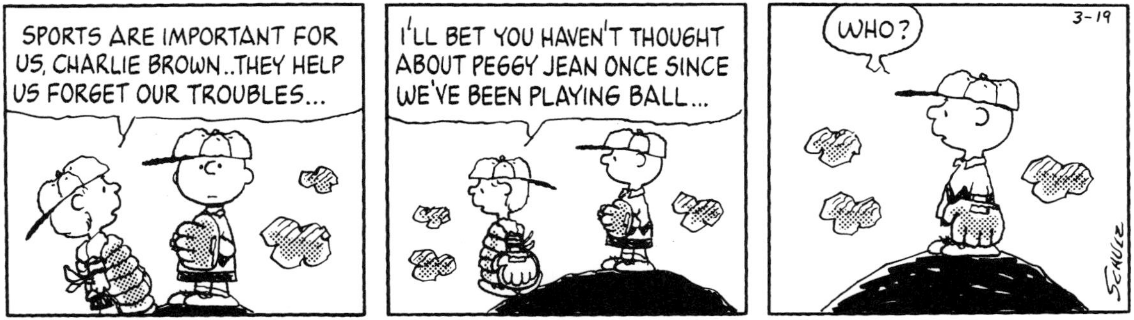
SPORTS ARE IMPORTANT FOR US, CHARLIE BROWN..THEY HELP US FORGET OUR TROUBLES...
I'LL BET YOU HAVEN'T THOUGHT ABOUT PEGGY JEAN ONCE SINCE WE'VE BEEN PLAYING BALL...
3-19
WHO?
SCHULZ

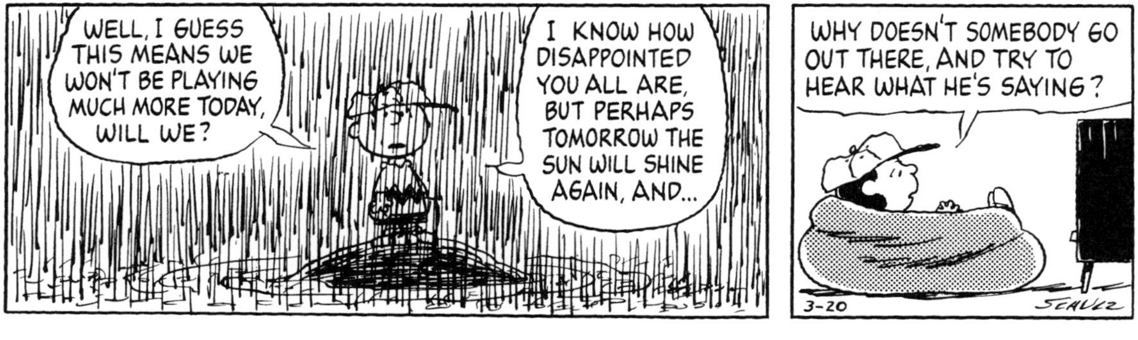
WELL, I GUESS THIS MEANS WE WON'T BE PLAYING MUCH MORE TODAY, WILL WE?
I KNOW HOW DISAPPOINTED YOU ALL ARE, BUT PERHAPS TOMORROW THE SUN WILL SHINE AGAIN, AND...
WHY DOESN'T SOMEBODY GO OUT THERE, AND TRY TO HEAR WHAT HE'S SAYING?
3-20
SCHULZ

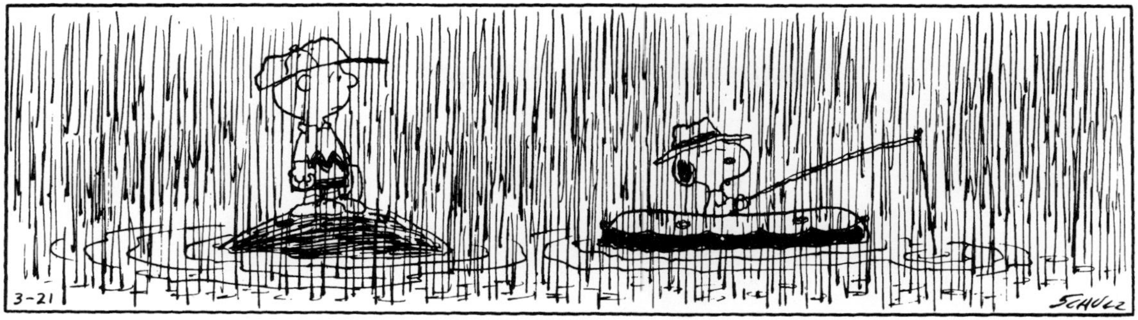
3-21
SCHULZ

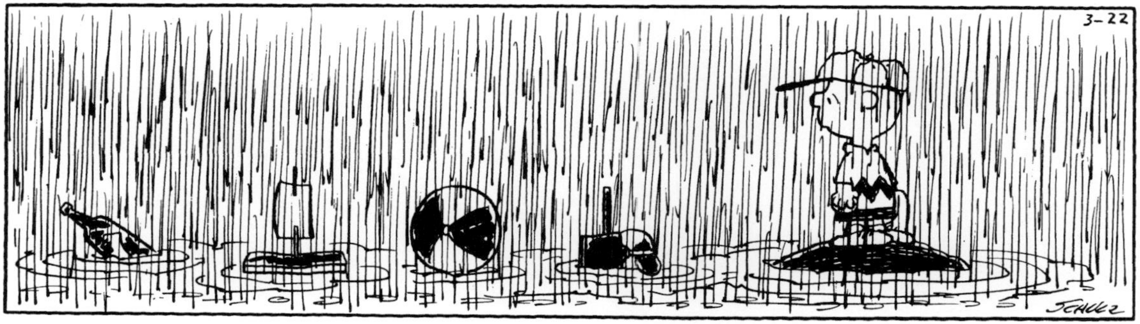
3-22
SCHULZ

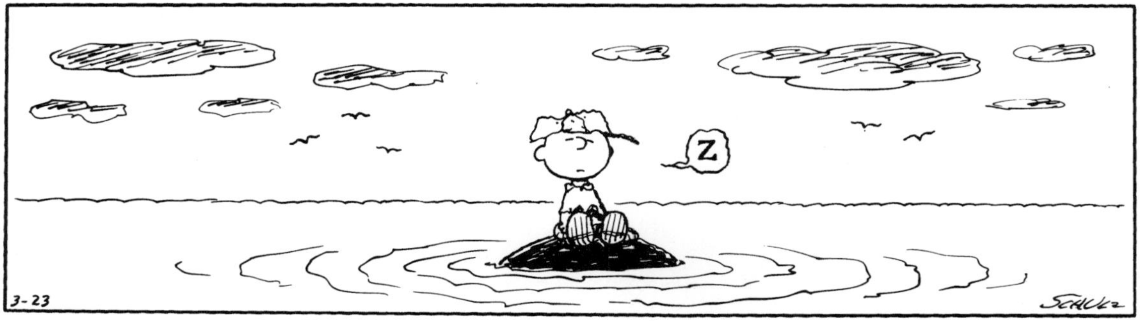
Z
3-23
SCHULZ

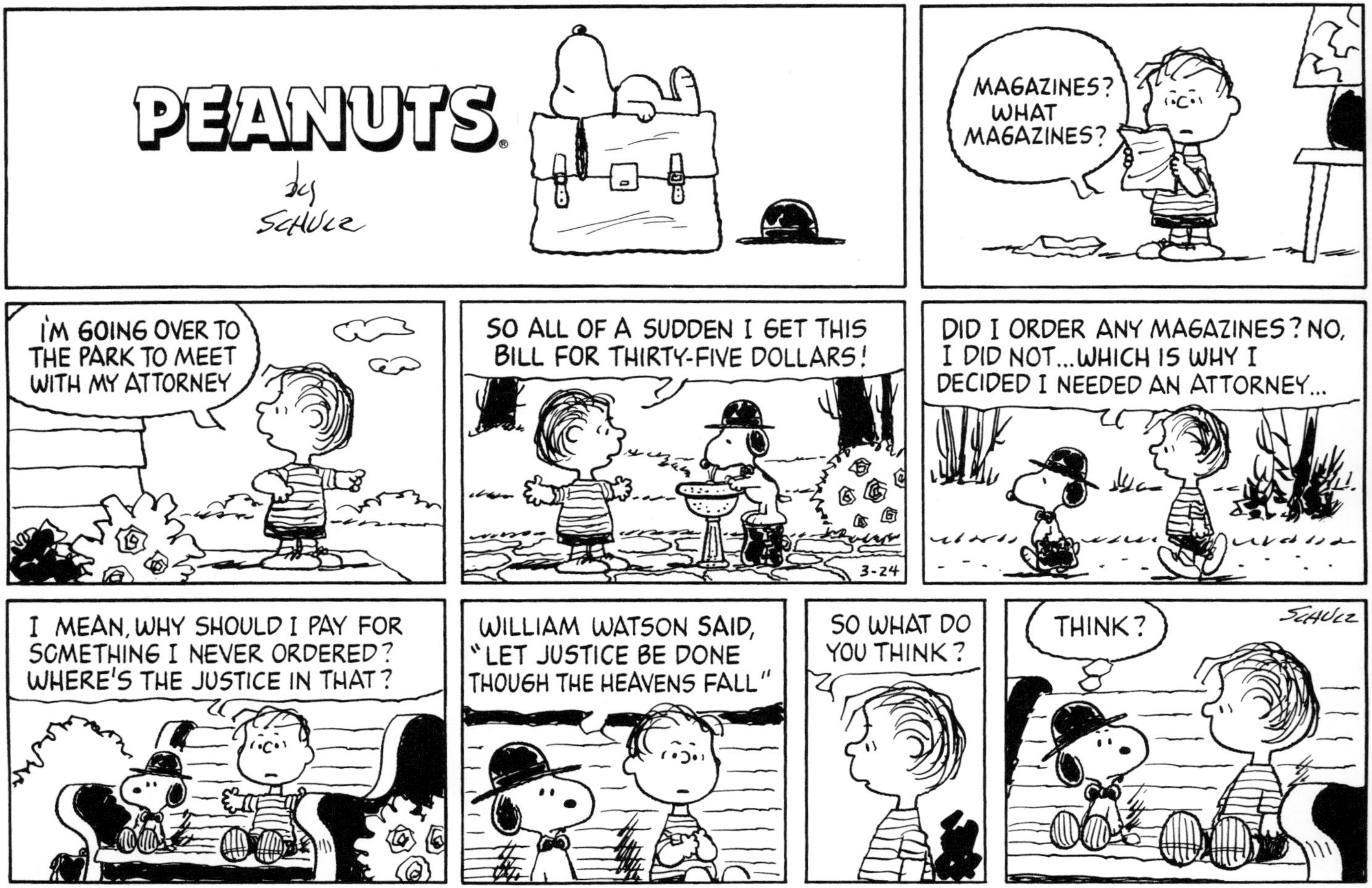
PEANUTS
by SCHULZ
MAGAZINES? WHAT MAGAZINES?
I'M GOING OVER TO THE PARK TO MEET WITH MY ATTORNEY
SO ALL OF A SUDDEN I GET THIS BILL FOR THIRTY-FIVE DOLLARS!
3-24
DID I ORDER ANY MAGAZINES? NO, I DID NOT...WHICH IS WHY I DECIDED I NEEDED AN ATTORNEY...
I MEAN, WHY SHOULD I PAY FOR SOMETHING I NEVER ORDERED? WHERE'S THE JUSTICE IN THAT?
WILLIAM WATSON SAID, "LET JUSTICE BE DONE THOUGH THE HEAVENS FALL"
SO WHAT DO YOU THINK?
THINK?
SCHULZ

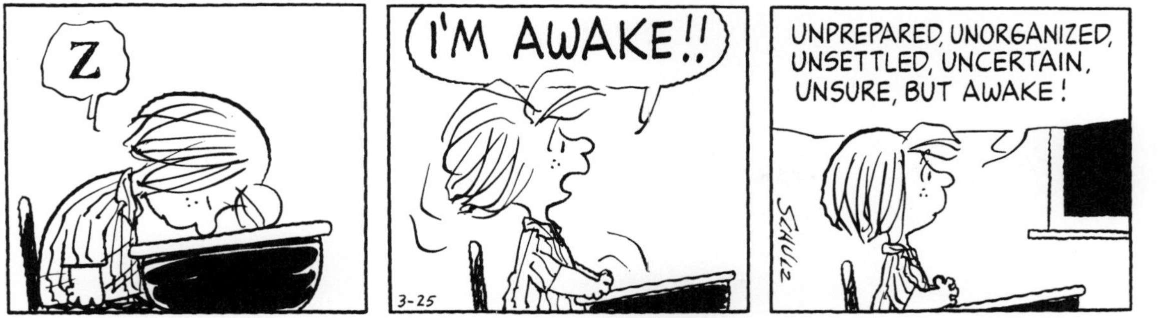
Z
I'M AWAKE!!
UNPREPARED, UNORGANIZED, UNSETTLED, UNCERTAIN, UNSURE, BUT AWAKE!

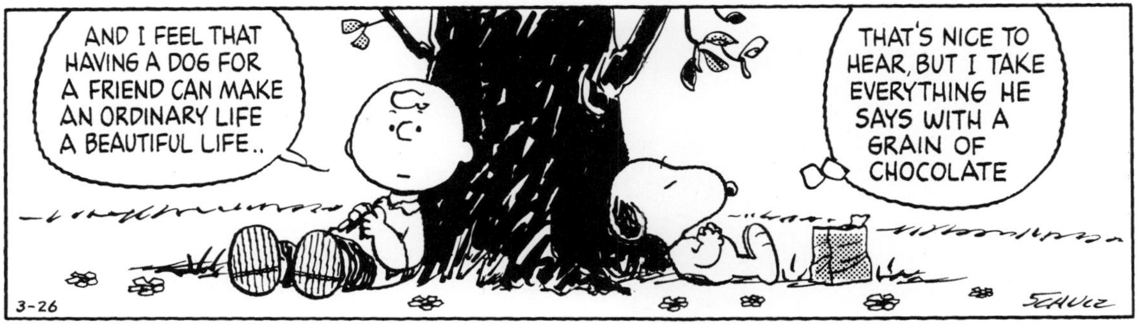
AND I FEEL THAT HAVING A DOG FOR A FRIEND CAN MAKE AN ORDINARY LIFE A BEAUTIFUL LIFE..
THAT'S NICE TO HEAR, BUT I TAKE EVERYTHING HE SAYS WITH A GRAIN OF CHOCOLATE

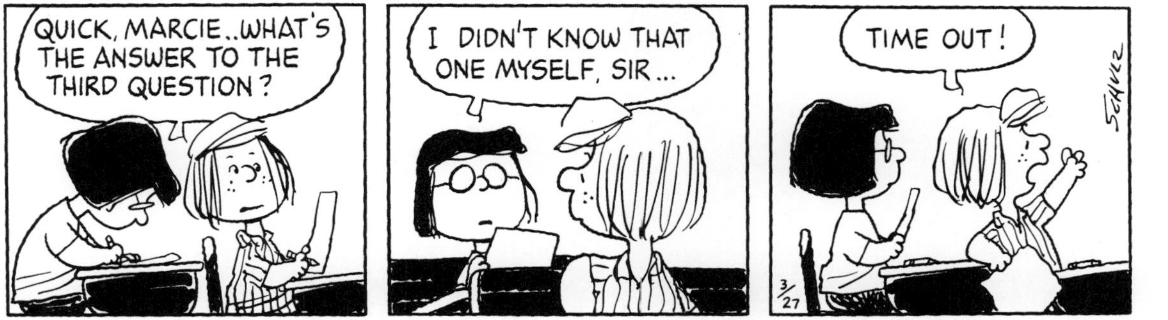
QUICK, MARCIE..WHAT'S THE ANSWER TO THE THIRD QUESTION?
I DIDN'T KNOW THAT ONE MYSELF, SIR...
TIME OUT!

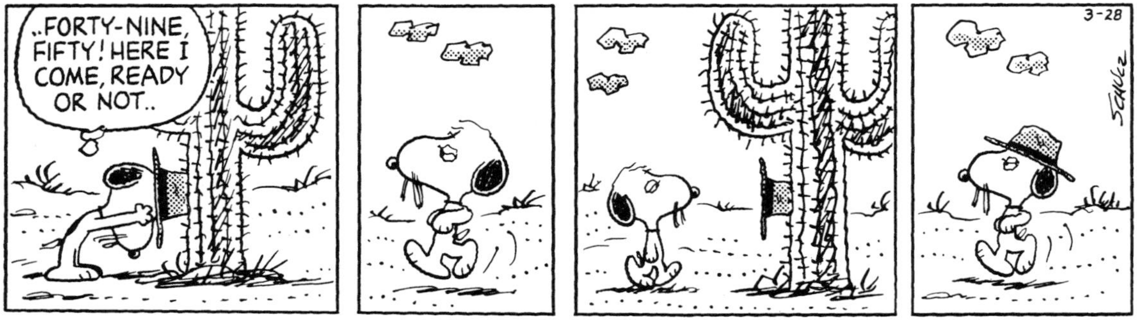
..FORTY-NINE, FIFTY! HERE I COME, READY OR NOT..
3-28

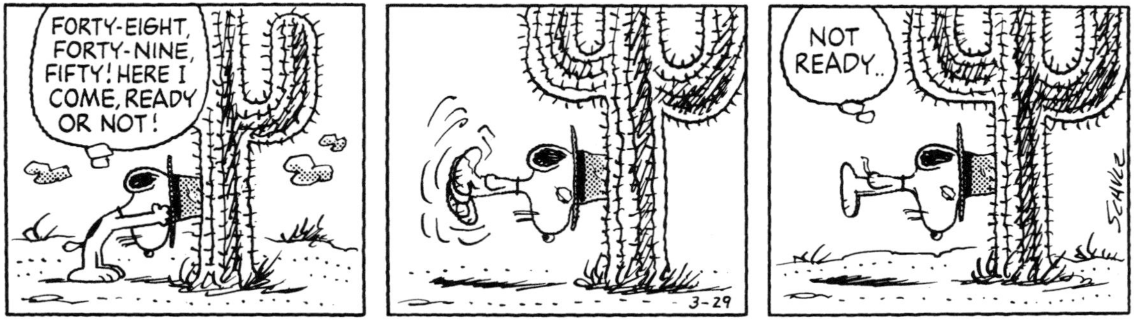
FORTY-EIGHT, FORTY-NINE, FIFTY! HERE I COME, READY OR NOT!
3-29
NOT READY..

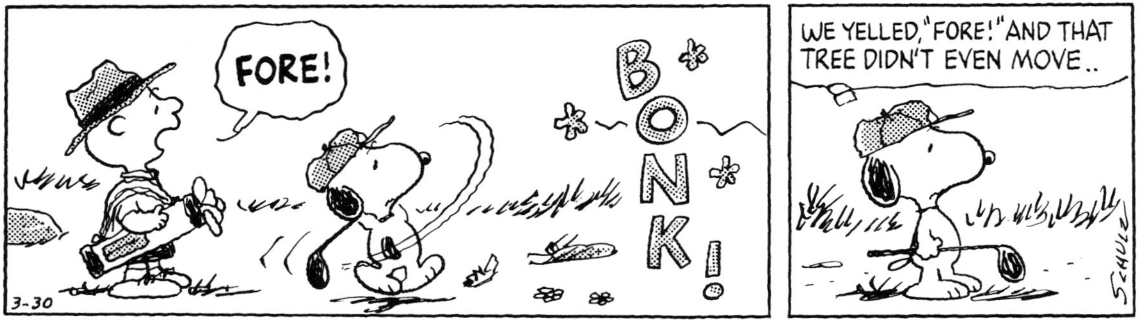
FORE!
BONK!
3-30
WE YELLED, "FORE!" AND THAT TREE DIDN'T EVEN MOVE..

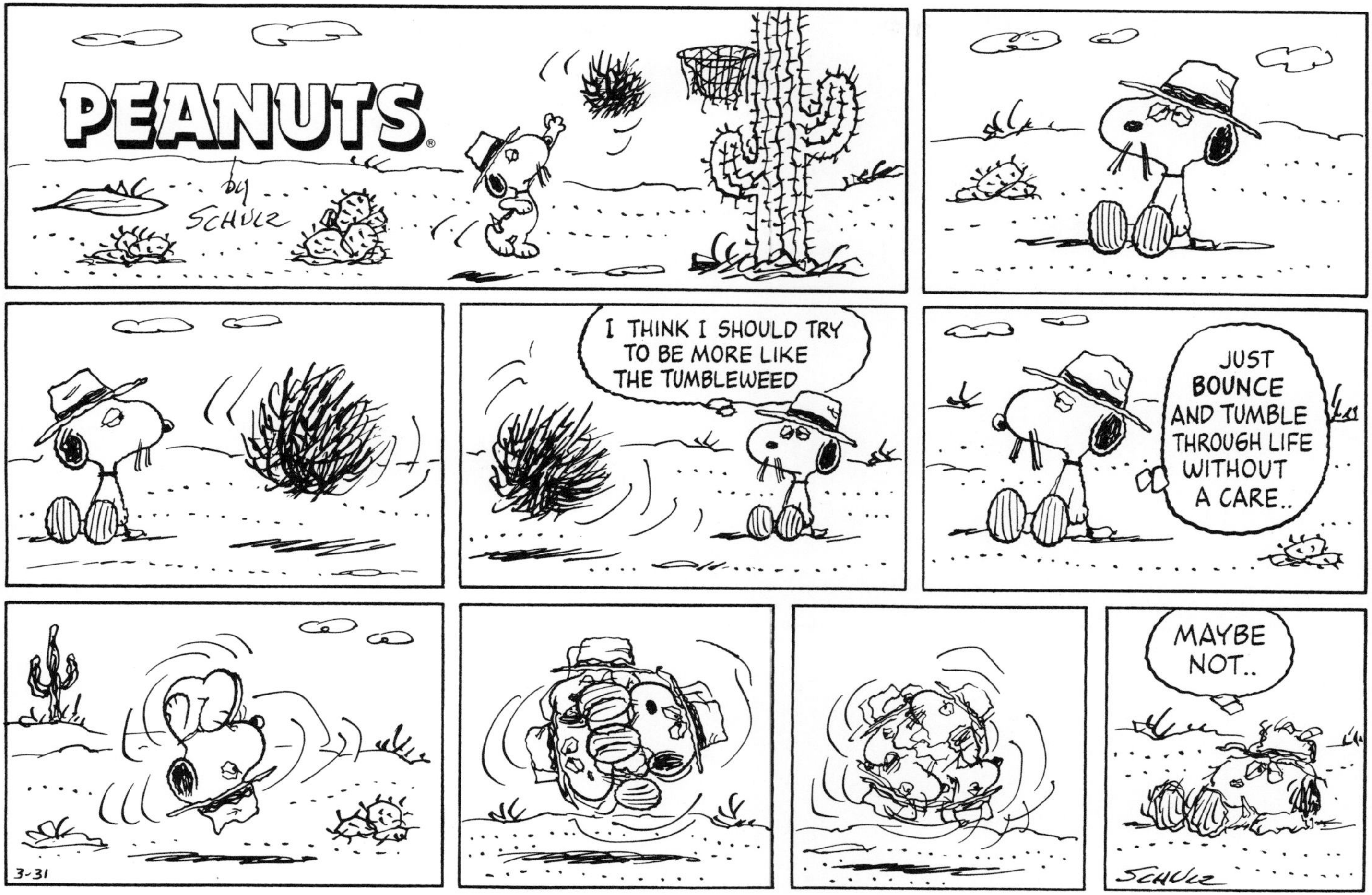
PEANUTS
by SCHULZ
I THINK I SHOULD TRY TO BE MORE LIKE THE TUMBLEWEED
JUST BOUNCE AND TUMBLE THROUGH LIFE WITHOUT A CARE..
MAYBE NOT..
3-31
SCHULZ

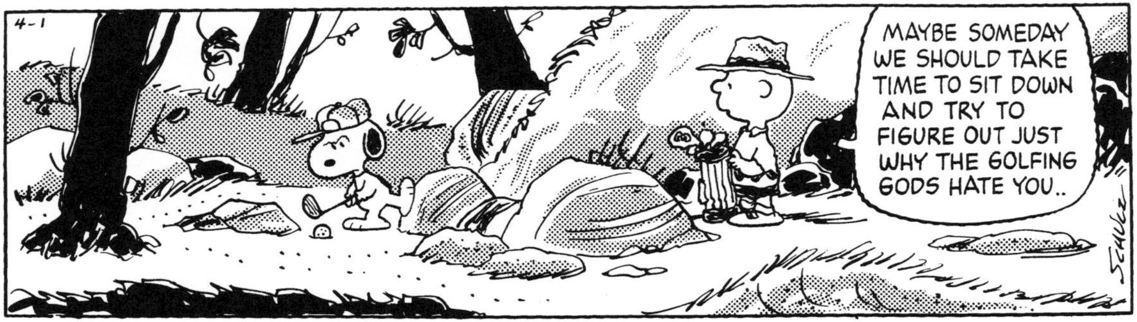
4-1
MAYBE SOMEDAY WE SHOULD TAKE TIME TO SIT DOWN AND TRY TO FIGURE OUT JUST WHY THE GOLFING GODS HATE YOU..
SCHULZ

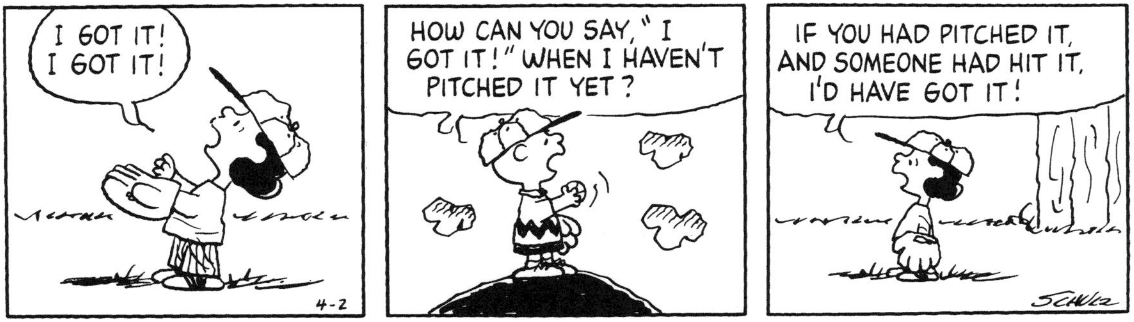
I GOT IT! I GOT IT!
4-2
HOW CAN YOU SAY, "I GOT IT!" WHEN I HAVEN'T PITCHED IT YET?
IF YOU HAD PITCHED IT, AND SOMEONE HAD HIT IT, I'D HAVE GOT IT!
SCHULZ

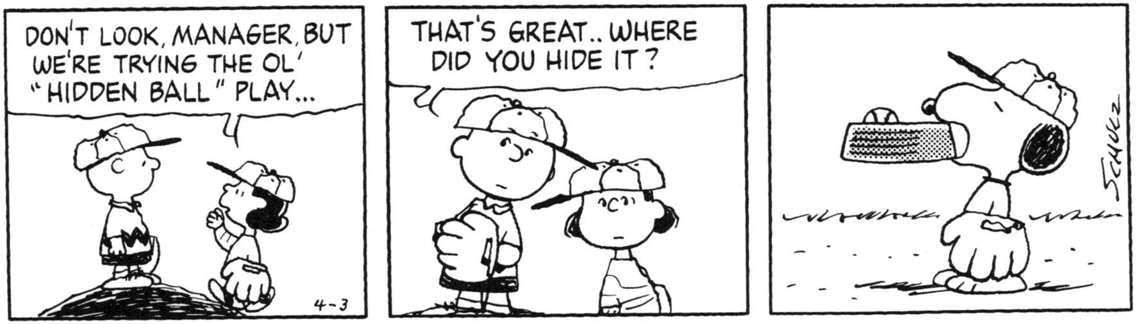
DON'T LOOK, MANAGER, BUT WE'RE TRYING THE OL' "HIDDEN BALL" PLAY...
4-3
THAT'S GREAT.. WHERE DID YOU HIDE IT?
SCHULZ

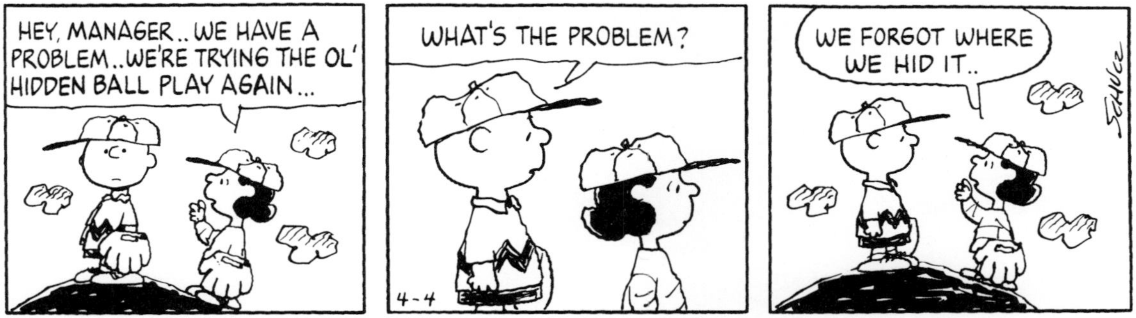
HEY, MANAGER.. WE HAVE A PROBLEM..WE'RE TRYING THE OL' HIDDEN BALL PLAY AGAIN...
WHAT'S THE PROBLEM?
4-4
WE FORGOT WHERE WE HID IT..

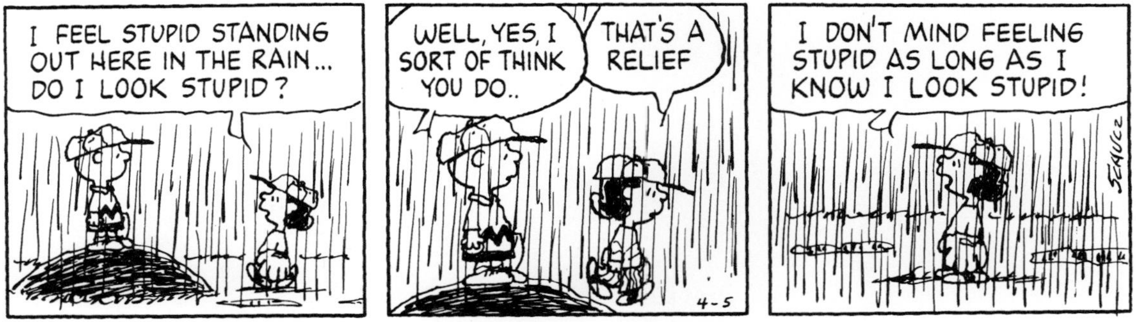
I FEEL STUPID STANDING OUT HERE IN THE RAIN... DO I LOOK STUPID?
WELL, YES, I SORT OF THINK YOU DO..
THAT'S A RELIEF
4-5
I DON'T MIND FEELING STUPID AS LONG AS I KNOW I LOOK STUPID!

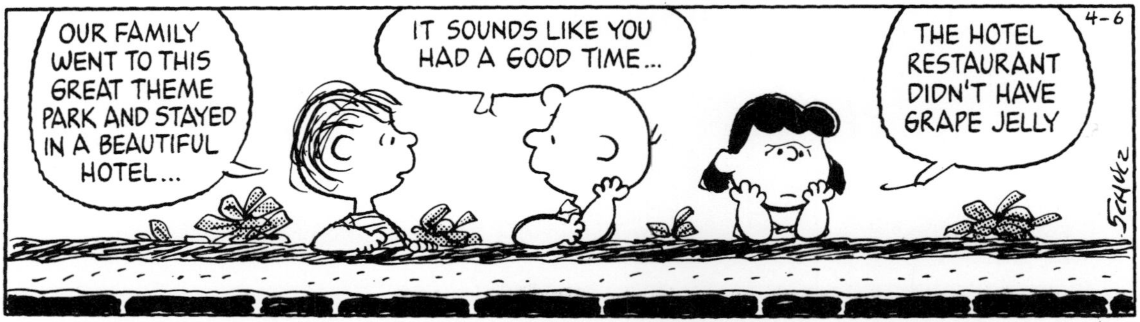
4-6
OUR FAMILY WENT TO THIS GREAT THEME PARK AND STAYED IN A BEAUTIFUL HOTEL...
IT SOUNDS LIKE YOU HAD A GOOD TIME...
THE HOTEL RESTAURANT DIDN'T HAVE GRAPE JELLY

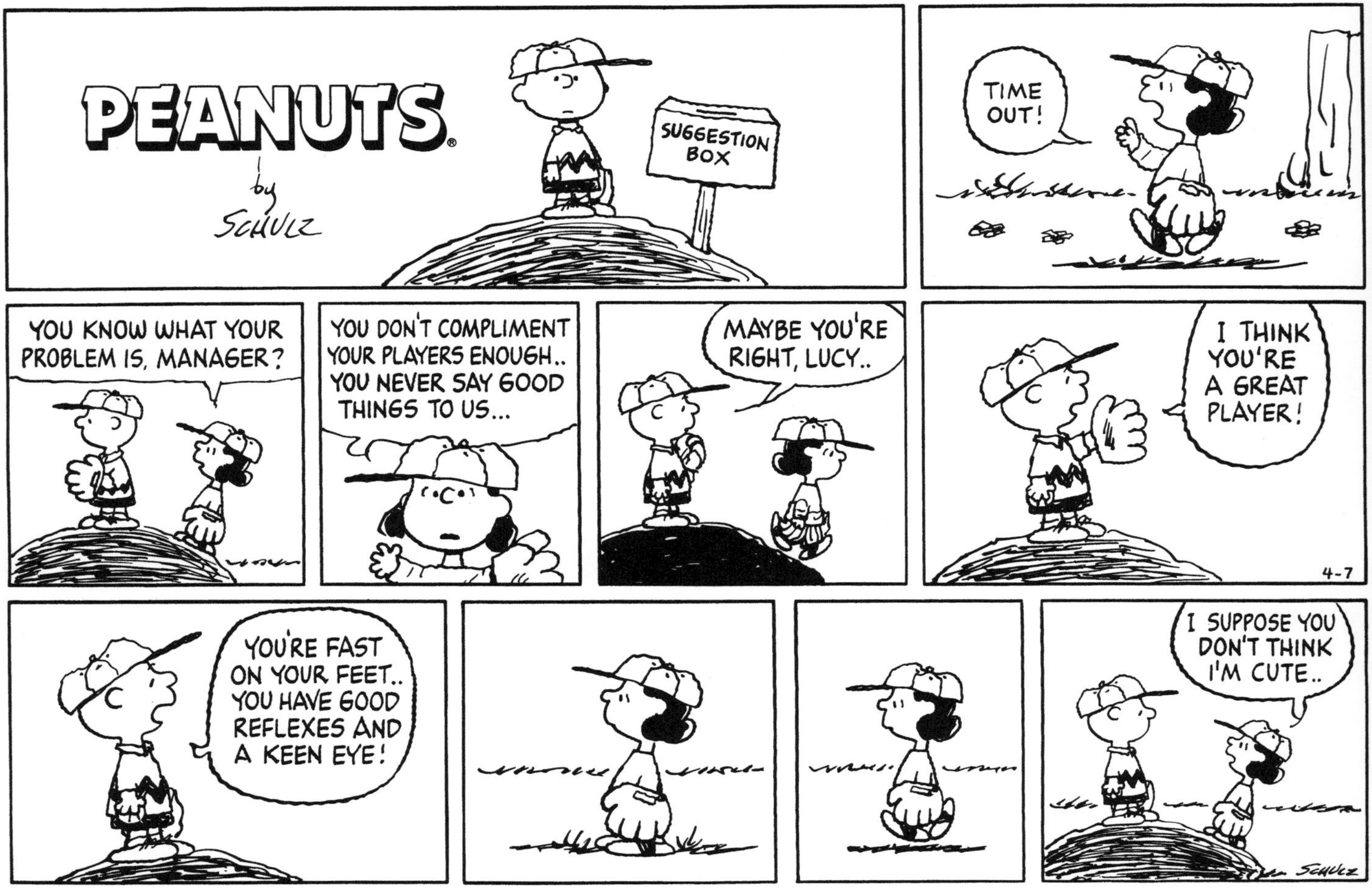
PEANUTS
by SCHULZ
SUGGESTION BOX
TIME OUT!
YOU KNOW WHAT YOUR PROBLEM IS, MANAGER?
YOU DON'T COMPLIMENT YOUR PLAYERS ENOUGH.. YOU NEVER SAY GOOD THINGS TO US...
MAYBE YOU'RE RIGHT, LUCY..
I THINK YOU'RE A GREAT PLAYER!
4-7
YOU'RE FAST ON YOUR FEET.. YOU HAVE GOOD REFLEXES AND A KEEN EYE!
I SUPPOSE YOU DON'T THINK I'M CUTE..
SCHULZ

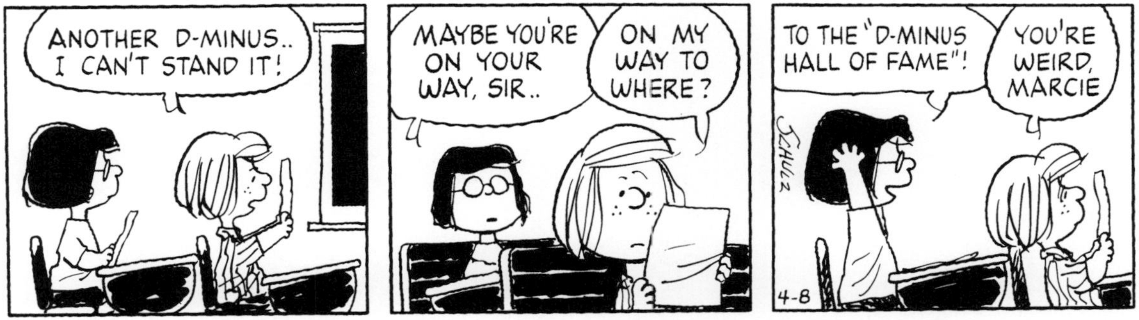
ANOTHER D-MINUS.. I CAN'T STAND IT!
MAYBE YOU'RE ON YOUR WAY, SIR..
ON MY WAY TO WHERE?
TO THE "D-MINUS HALL OF FAME"!
YOU'RE WEIRD, MARCIE
SCHULZ
4-8

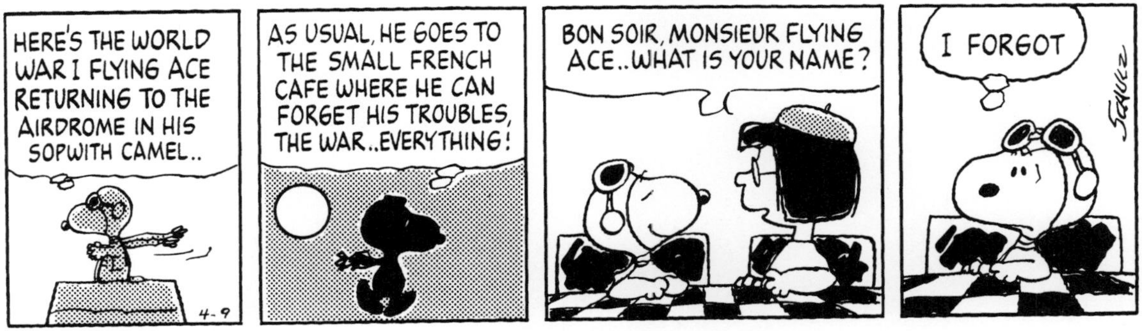
HERE'S THE WORLD WAR I FLYING ACE RETURNING TO THE AIRDROME IN HIS SOPWITH CAMEL..
4-9
AS USUAL, HE GOES TO THE SMALL FRENCH CAFE WHERE HE CAN FORGET HIS TROUBLES, THE WAR..EVERYTHING!
BON SOIR, MONSIEUR FLYING ACE..WHAT IS YOUR NAME?
I FORGOT
SCHULZ

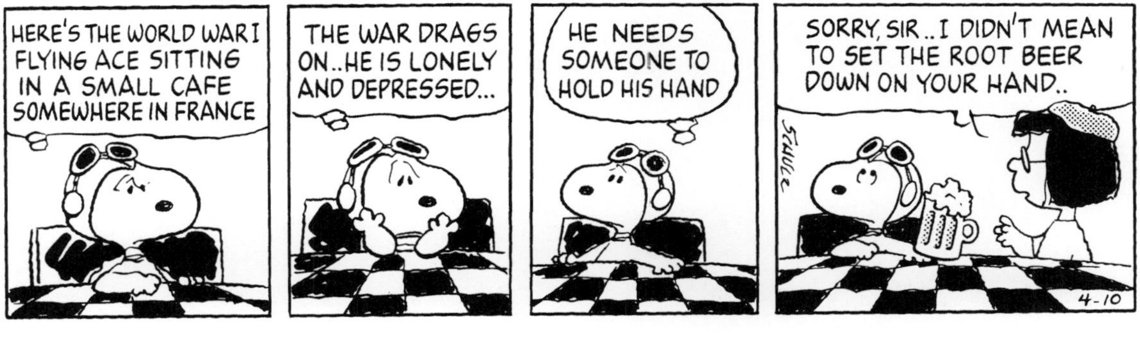
HERE'S THE WORLD WAR I FLYING ACE SITTING IN A SMALL CAFE SOMEWHERE IN FRANCE
THE WAR DRAGS ON..HE IS LONELY AND DEPRESSED...
HE NEEDS SOMEONE TO HOLD HIS HAND
SCHULZ
SORRY, SIR..I DIDN'T MEAN TO SET THE ROOT BEER DOWN ON YOUR HAND..
4-10

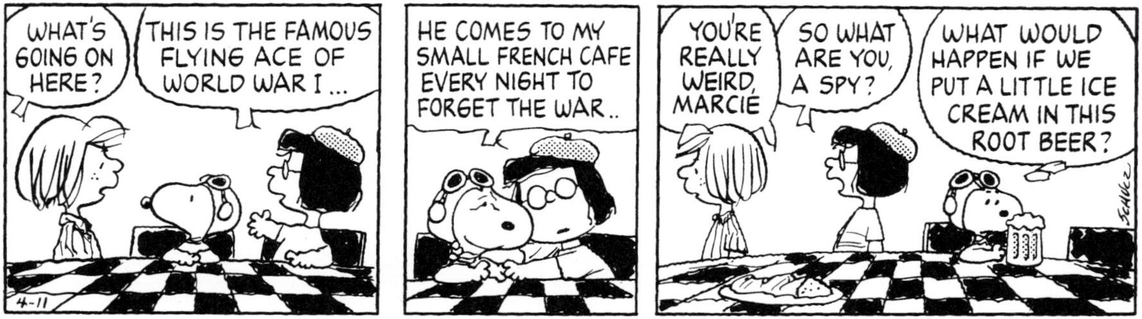
WHAT'S GOING ON HERE?
THIS IS THE FAMOUS FLYING ACE OF WORLD WAR I ...
4-11
HE COMES TO MY SMALL FRENCH CAFE EVERY NIGHT TO FORGET THE WAR..
YOU'RE REALLY WEIRD, MARCIE
SO WHAT ARE YOU, A SPY?
WHAT WOULD HAPPEN IF WE PUT A LITTLE ICE CREAM IN THIS ROOT BEER?
SCHULZ

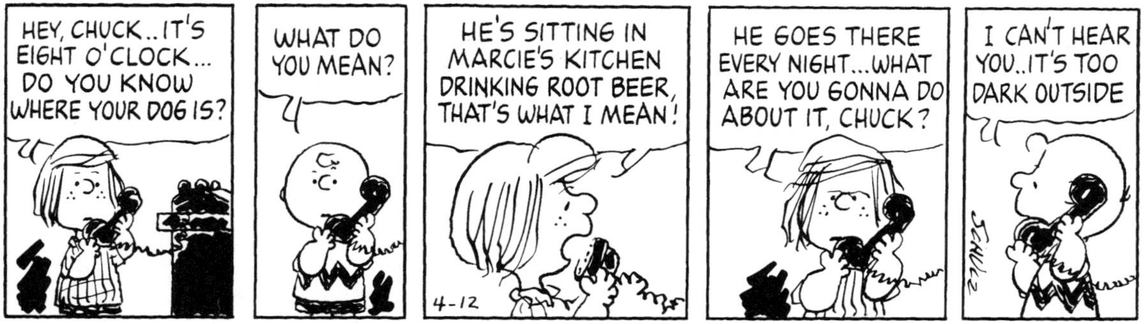
HEY, CHUCK..IT'S EIGHT O'CLOCK... DO YOU KNOW WHERE YOUR DOG IS?
WHAT DO YOU MEAN?
HE'S SITTING IN MARCIE'S KITCHEN DRINKING ROOT BEER, THAT'S WHAT I MEAN!
4-12
HE GOES THERE EVERY NIGHT...WHAT ARE YOU GONNA DO ABOUT IT, CHUCK?
I CAN'T HEAR YOU..IT'S TOO DARK OUTSIDE
SCHULZ

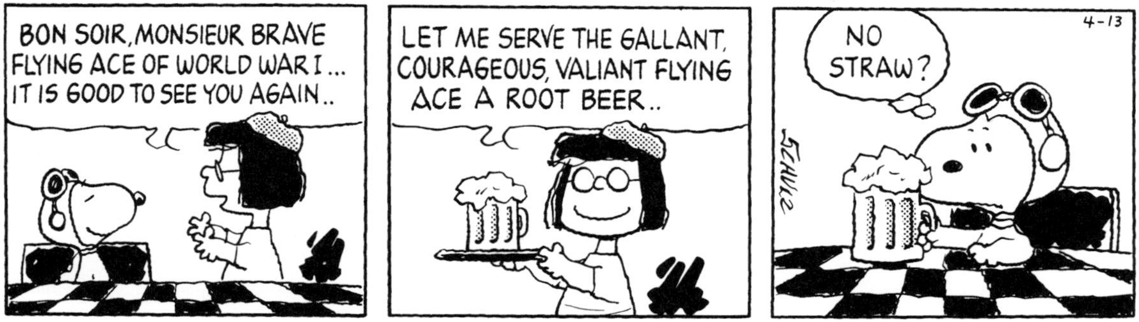
BON SOIR, MONSIEUR BRAVE FLYING ACE OF WORLD WAR I ... IT IS GOOD TO SEE YOU AGAIN..
LET ME SERVE THE GALLANT, COURAGEOUS, VALIANT FLYING ACE A ROOT BEER..
4-13
NO STRAW?
SCHULZ

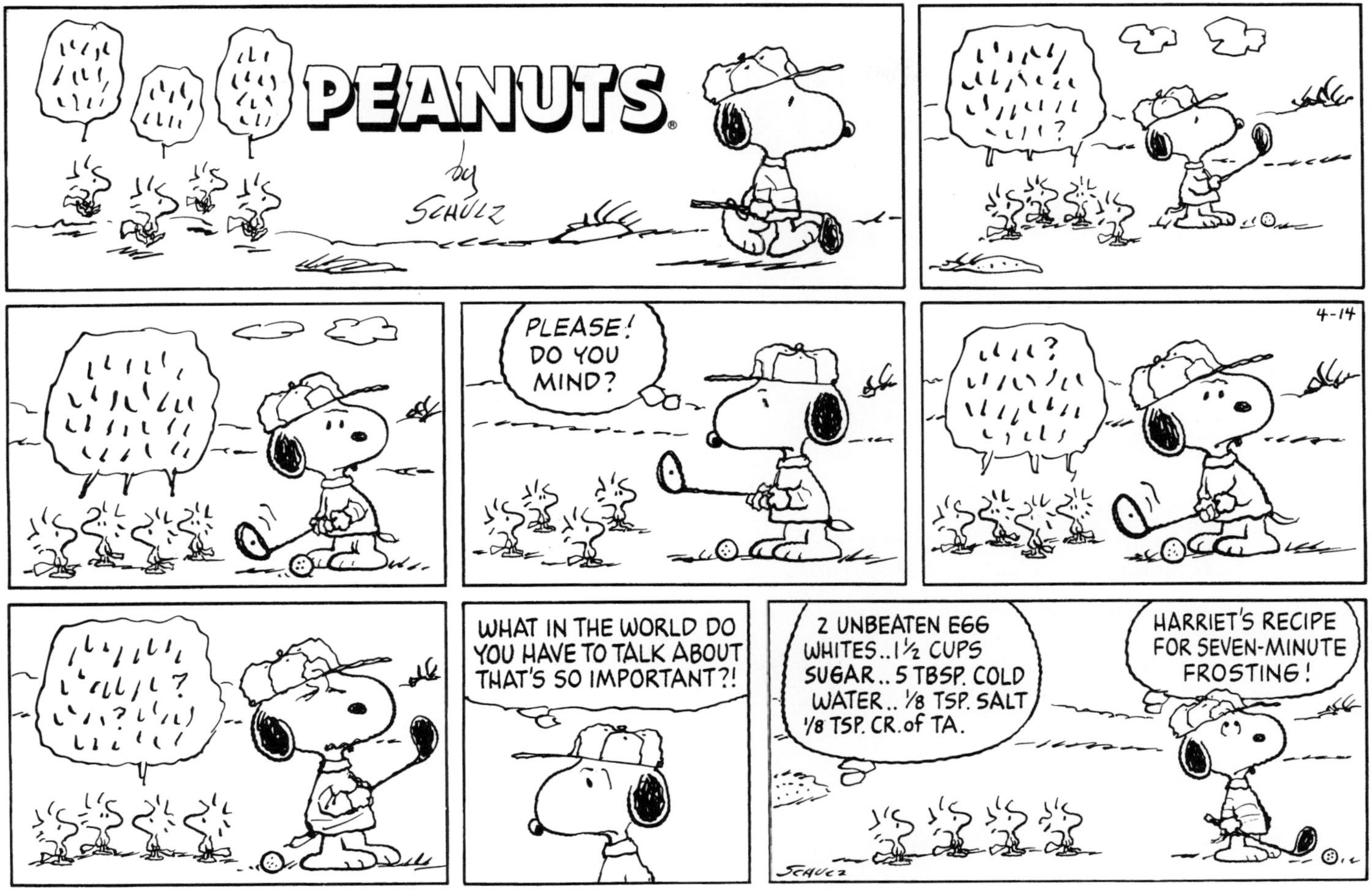
PEANUTS
by SCHULZ
PLEASE! DO YOU MIND?
4-14
WHAT IN THE WORLD DO YOU HAVE TO TALK ABOUT THAT'S SO IMPORTANT?!
2 UNBEATEN EGG WHITES..1½ CUPS SUGAR..5 TBSP. COLD WATER..1/8 TSP. SALT 1/8 TSP. CR. of TA.
HARRIET'S RECIPE FOR SEVEN-MINUTE FROSTING!
SCHULZ

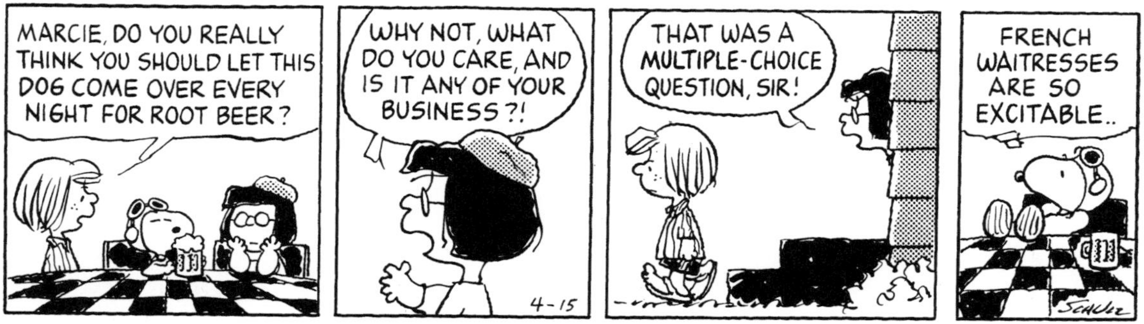
MARCIE, DO YOU REALLY THINK YOU SHOULD LET THIS DOG COME OVER EVERY NIGHT FOR ROOT BEER?
WHY NOT, WHAT DO YOU CARE, AND IS IT ANY OF YOUR BUSINESS?!
THAT WAS A MULTIPLE-CHOICE QUESTION, SIR!
FRENCH WAITRESSES ARE SO EXCITABLE..

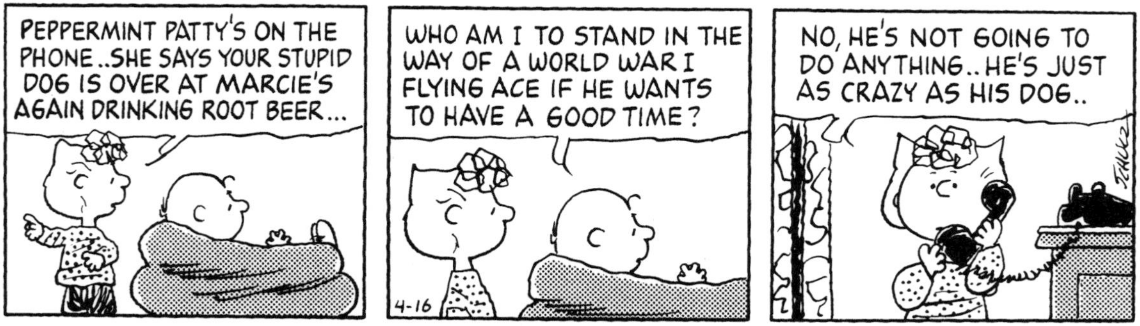
PEPPERMINT PATTY'S ON THE PHONE..SHE SAYS YOUR STUPID DOG IS OVER AT MARCIE'S AGAIN DRINKING ROOT BEER...
WHO AM I TO STAND IN THE WAY OF A WORLD WAR I FLYING ACE IF HE WANTS TO HAVE A GOOD TIME?
NO, HE'S NOT GOING TO DO ANYTHING..HE'S JUST AS CRAZY AS HIS DOG..

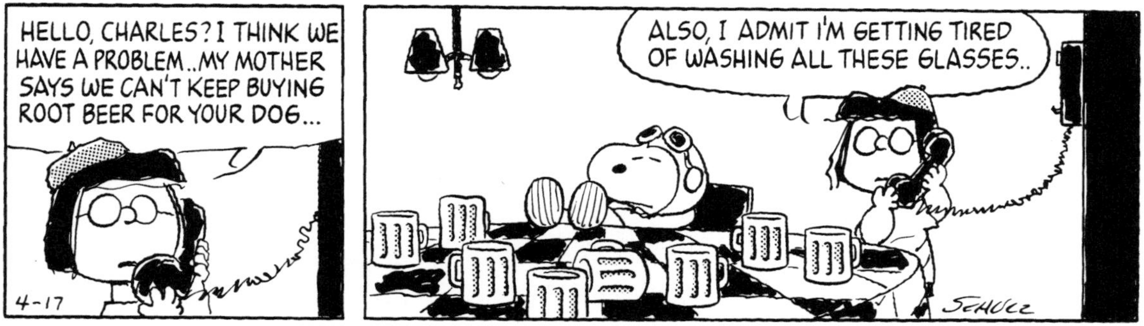
HELLO, CHARLES? I THINK WE HAVE A PROBLEM..MY MOTHER SAYS WE CAN'T KEEP BUYING ROOT BEER FOR YOUR DOG...
ALSO, I ADMIT I'M GETTING TIRED OF WASHING ALL THESE GLASSES..

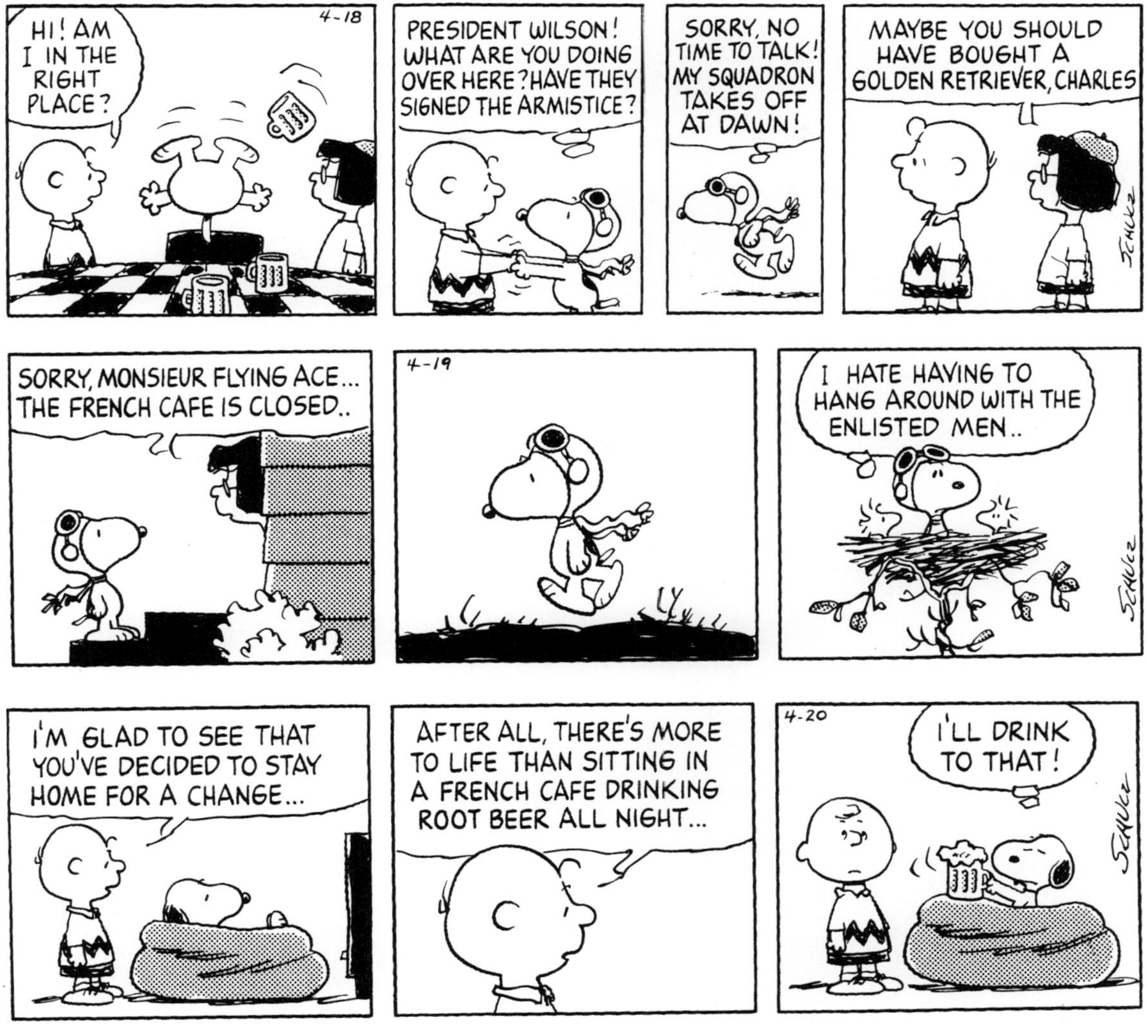
4-18
HI! AM I IN THE RIGHT PLACE?
PRESIDENT WILSON! WHAT ARE YOU DOING OVER HERE? HAVE THEY SIGNED THE ARMISTICE?
SORRY, NO TIME TO TALK! MY SQUADRON TAKES OFF AT DAWN!
MAYBE YOU SHOULD HAVE BOUGHT A GOLDEN RETRIEVER, CHARLES
SCHULZ
SORRY, MONSIEUR FLYING ACE... THE FRENCH CAFE IS CLOSED..
4-19
I HATE HAVING TO HANG AROUND WITH THE ENLISTED MEN..
SCHULZ
I'M GLAD TO SEE THAT YOU'VE DECIDED TO STAY HOME FOR A CHANGE...
AFTER ALL, THERE'S MORE TO LIFE THAN SITTING IN A FRENCH CAFE DRINKING ROOT BEER ALL NIGHT...
4-20
I'LL DRINK TO THAT!
SCHULZ

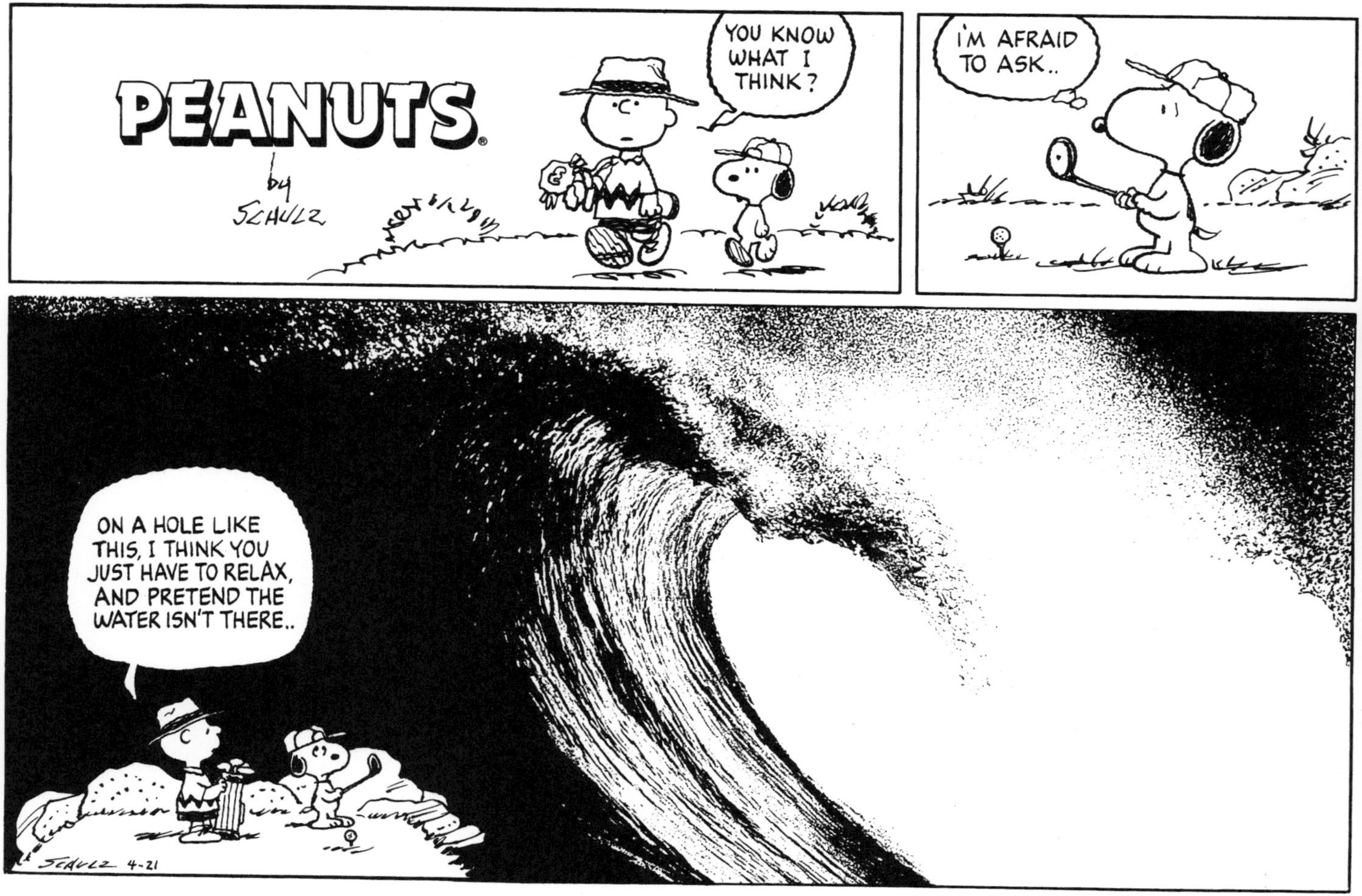
PEANUTS
by SCHULZ
YOU KNOW WHAT I THINK?
I'M AFRAID TO ASK..
ON A HOLE LIKE THIS, I THINK YOU JUST HAVE TO RELAX, AND PRETEND THE WATER ISN'T THERE..
SCHULZ 4-21

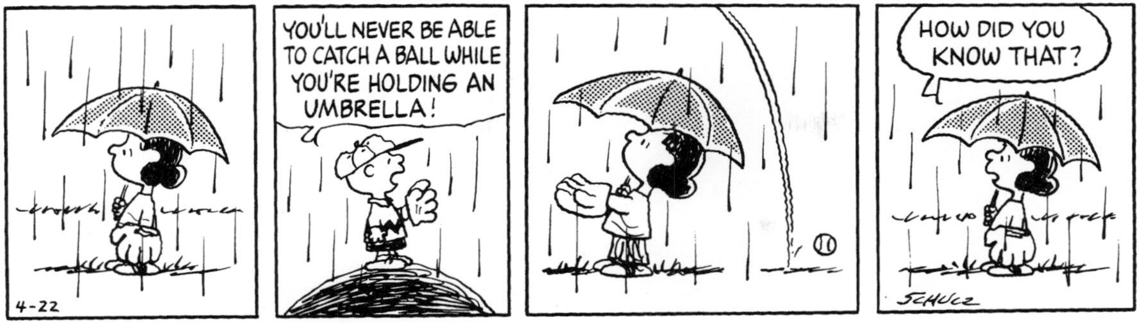
4-22
YOU'LL NEVER BE ABLE TO CATCH A BALL WHILE YOU'RE HOLDING AN UMBRELLA!
HOW DID YOU KNOW THAT?
SCHULZ

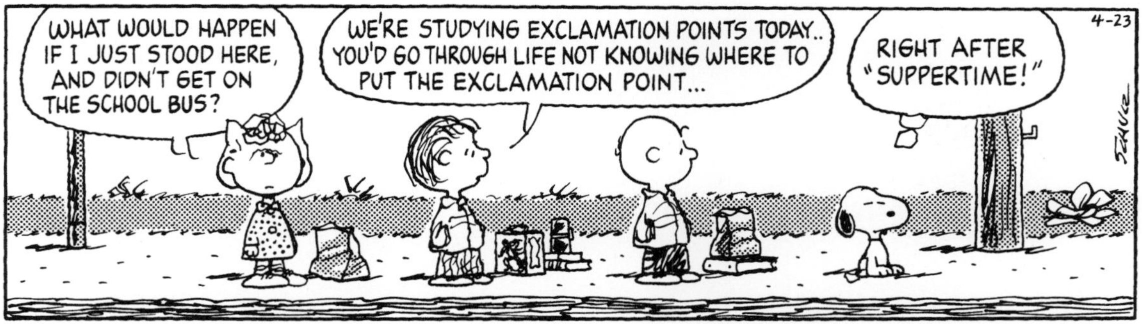
4-23
WHAT WOULD HAPPEN IF I JUST STOOD HERE, AND DIDN'T GET ON THE SCHOOL BUS?
WE'RE STUDYING EXCLAMATION POINTS TODAY.. YOU'D GO THROUGH LIFE NOT KNOWING WHERE TO PUT THE EXCLAMATION POINT...
RIGHT AFTER "SUPPERTIME!"
SCHULZ

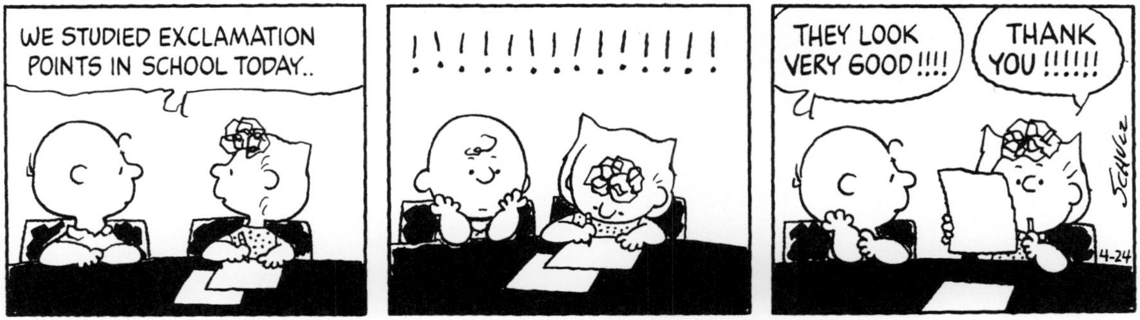
WE STUDIED EXCLAMATION POINTS IN SCHOOL TODAY..
!!!!!!!!!!!!!!!
THEY LOOK VERY GOOD!!!!
THANK YOU!!!!!!
SCHULZ
4-24

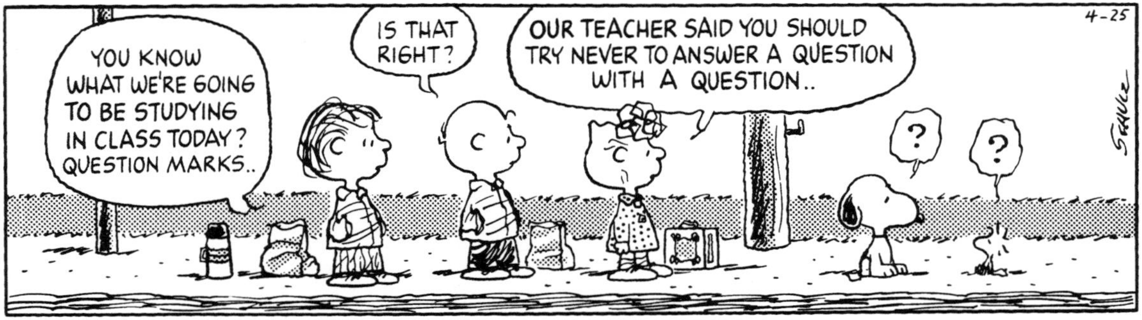
4-25
YOU KNOW WHAT WE'RE GOING TO BE STUDYING IN CLASS TODAY? QUESTION MARKS..
IS THAT RIGHT?
OUR TEACHER SAID YOU SHOULD TRY NEVER TO ANSWER A QUESTION WITH A QUESTION..
?
?

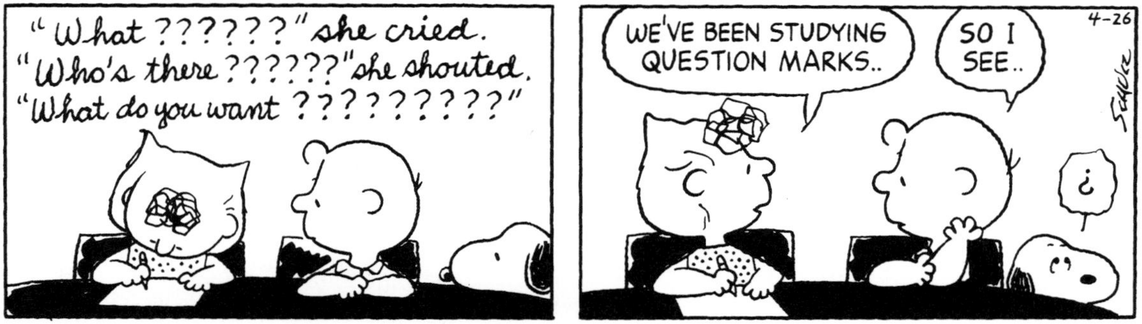
"What ??????" she cried.
"Who's there ??????" she shouted.
"What do you want ?????????"
4-26
WE'VE BEEN STUDYING QUESTION MARKS..
SO I SEE..
¿

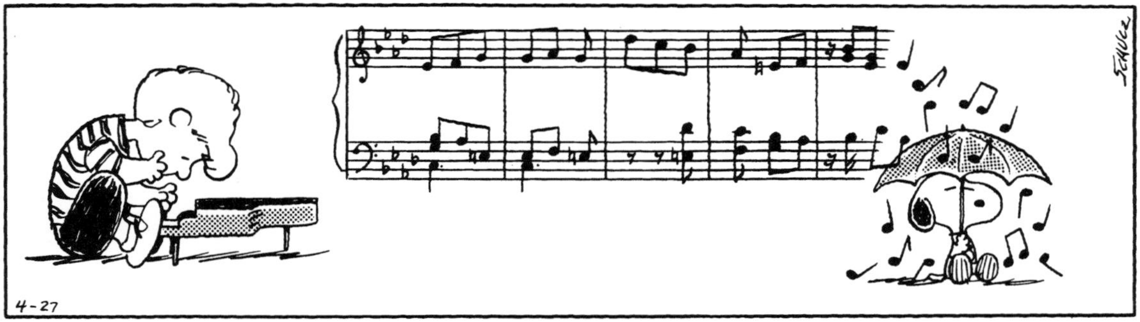
4-27

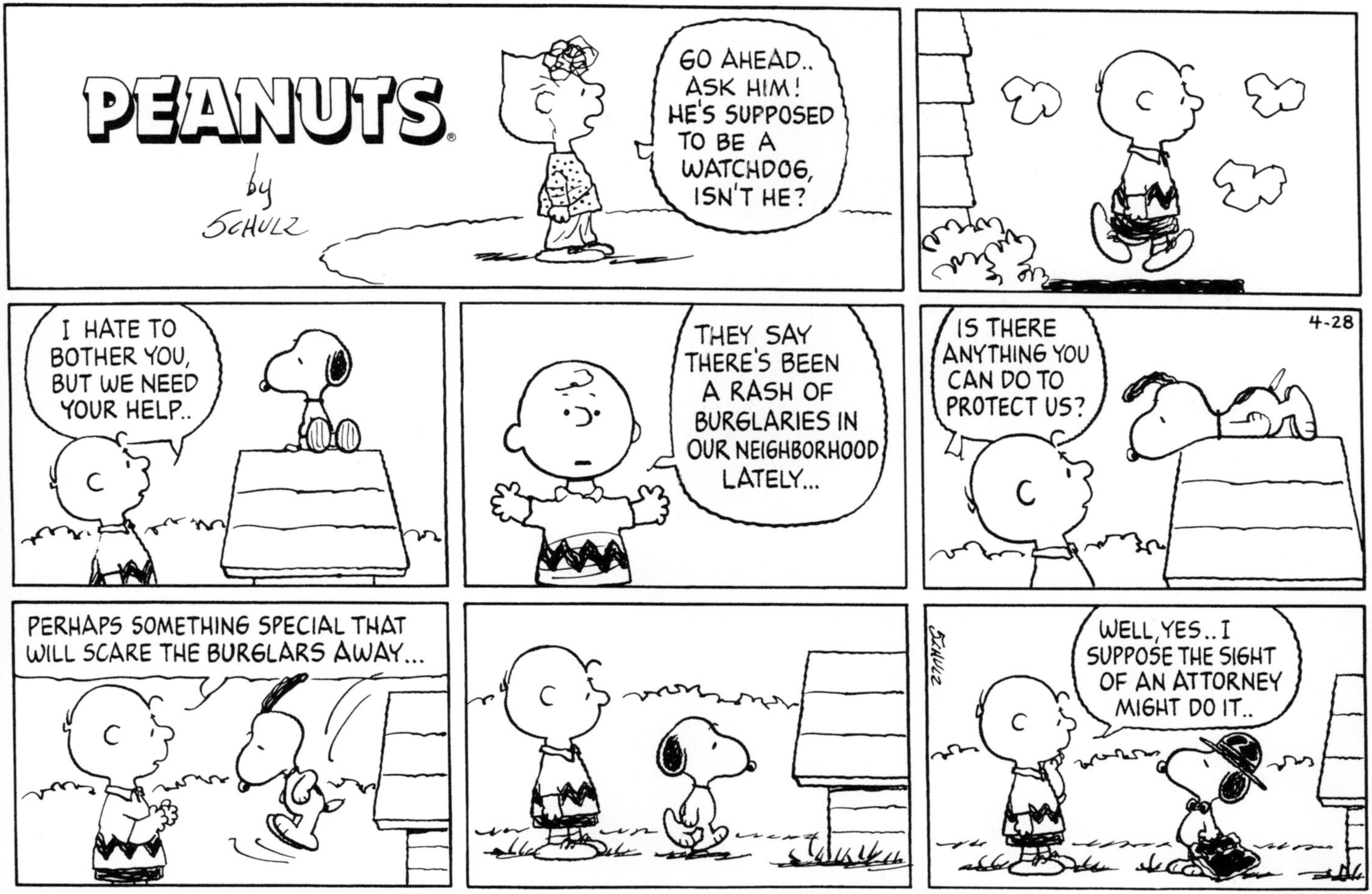
PEANUTS
by SCHULZ
GO AHEAD.. ASK HIM! HE'S SUPPOSED TO BE A WATCHDOG, ISN'T HE?
I HATE TO BOTHER YOU, BUT WE NEED YOUR HELP..
THEY SAY THERE'S BEEN A RASH OF BURGLARIES IN OUR NEIGHBORHOOD LATELY...
IS THERE ANYTHING YOU CAN DO TO PROTECT US?
4-28
PERHAPS SOMETHING SPECIAL THAT WILL SCARE THE BURGLARS AWAY...
SCHULZ
WELL, YES.. I SUPPOSE THE SIGHT OF AN ATTORNEY MIGHT DO IT..

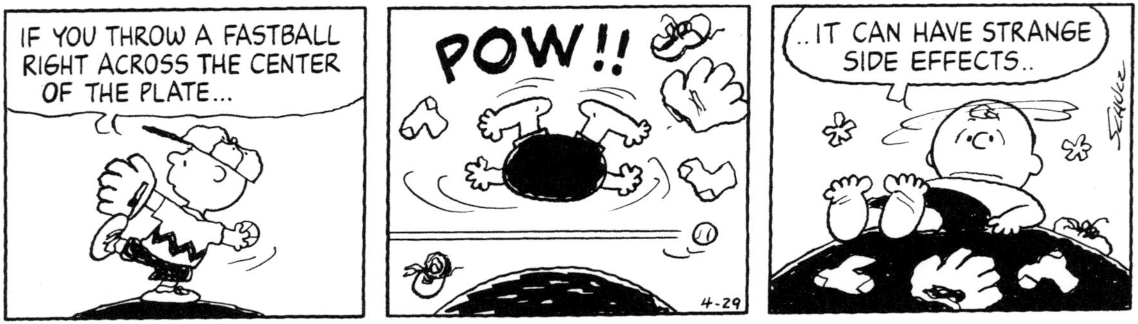
IF YOU THROW A FASTBALL RIGHT ACROSS THE CENTER OF THE PLATE...
POW!!
4-29
..IT CAN HAVE STRANGE SIDE EFFECTS..
SCHULZ

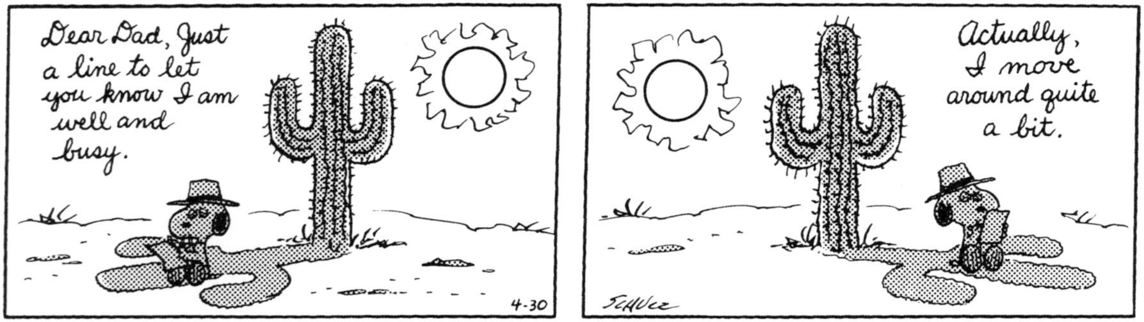
Dear Dad, Just a line to let you know I am well and busy.
4-30
Actually, I move around quite a bit.
SCHULZ

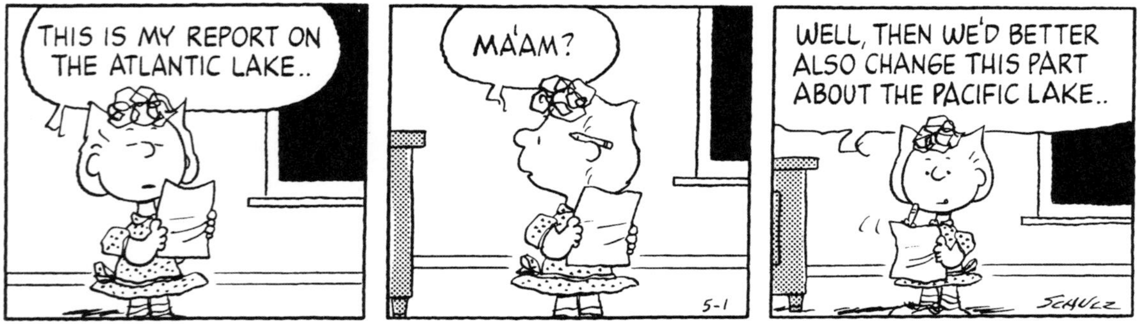
THIS IS MY REPORT ON THE ATLANTIC LAKE..
MA'AM?
5-1
WELL, THEN WE'D BETTER ALSO CHANGE THIS PART ABOUT THE PACIFIC LAKE..
SCHULZ

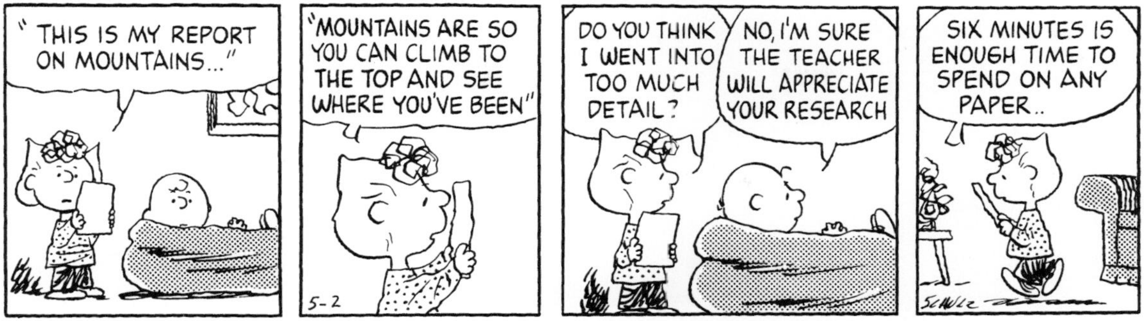
"THIS IS MY REPORT ON MOUNTAINS..."
"MOUNTAINS ARE SO YOU CAN CLIMB TO THE TOP AND SEE WHERE YOU'VE BEEN"
DO YOU THINK I WENT INTO TOO MUCH DETAIL?
NO, I'M SURE THE TEACHER WILL APPRECIATE YOUR RESEARCH
SIX MINUTES IS ENOUGH TIME TO SPEND ON ANY PAPER..

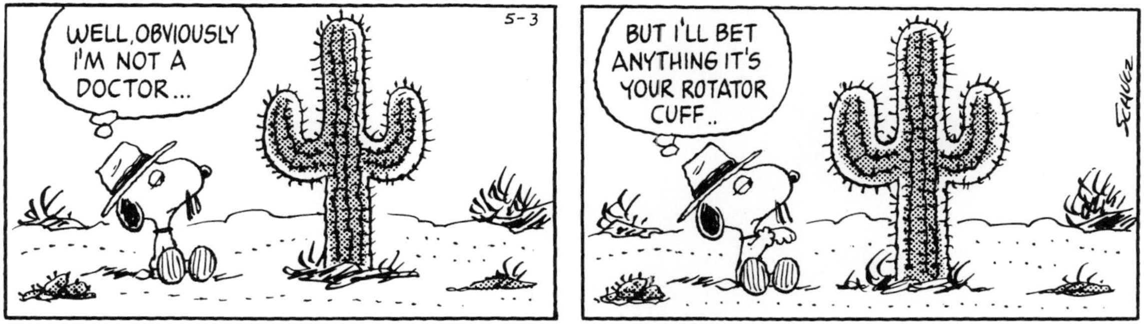
WELL, OBVIOUSLY I'M NOT A DOCTOR...
BUT I'LL BET ANYTHING IT'S YOUR ROTATOR CUFF..

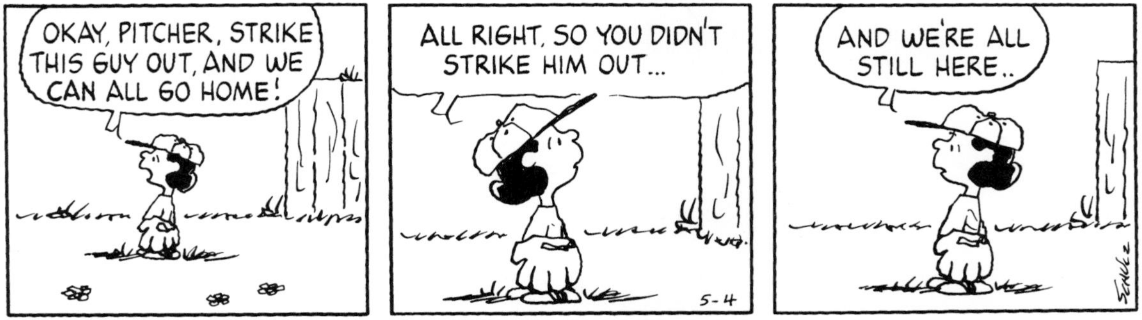
OKAY, PITCHER, STRIKE THIS GUY OUT, AND WE CAN ALL GO HOME!
ALL RIGHT, SO YOU DIDN'T STRIKE HIM OUT...
AND WE'RE ALL STILL HERE..

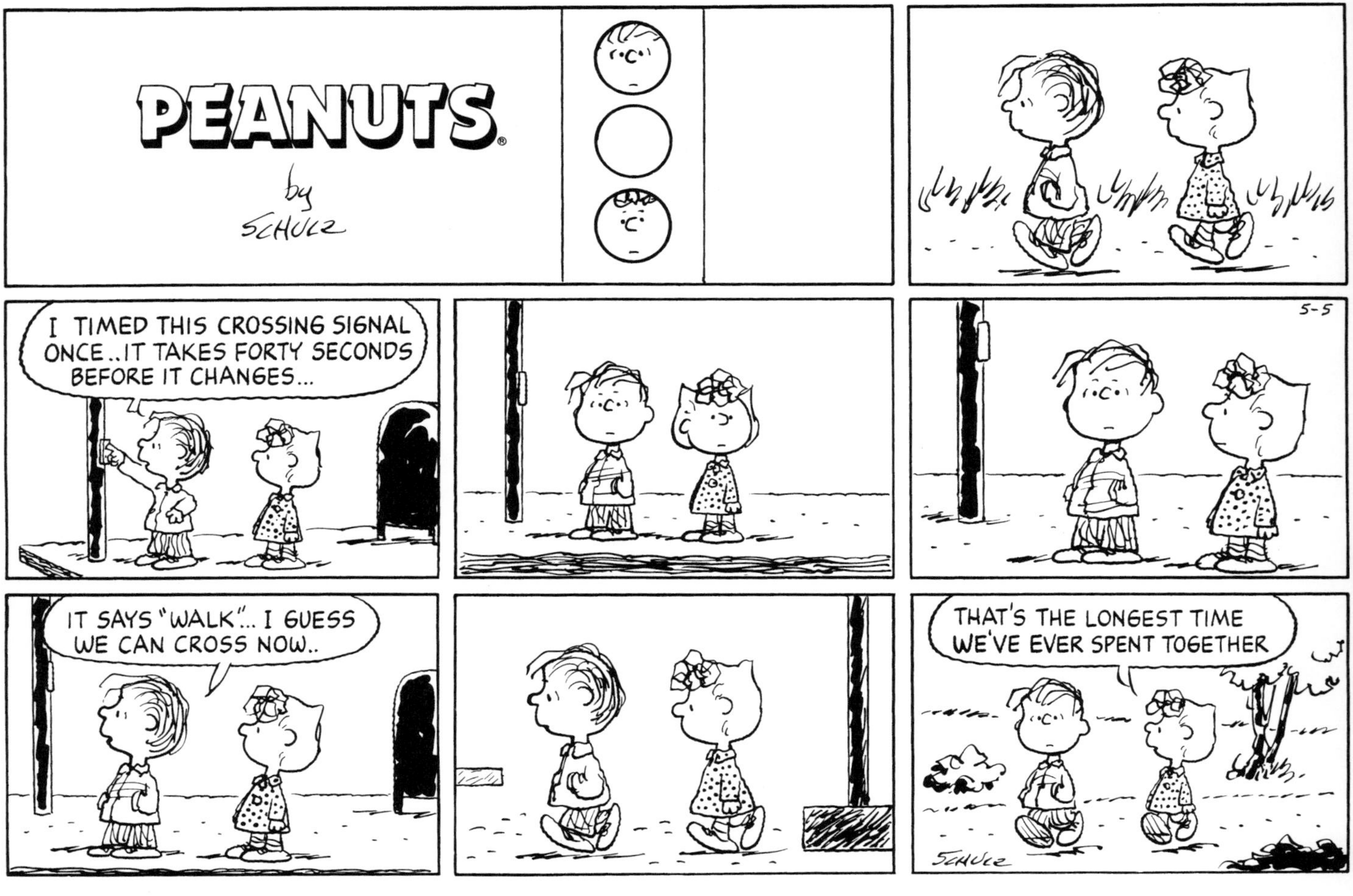
PEANUTS
by SCHULZ
I TIMED THIS CROSSING SIGNAL ONCE..IT TAKES FORTY SECONDS BEFORE IT CHANGES...
5-5
IT SAYS "WALK"... I GUESS WE CAN CROSS NOW..
THAT'S THE LONGEST TIME WE'VE EVER SPENT TOGETHER
SCHULZ

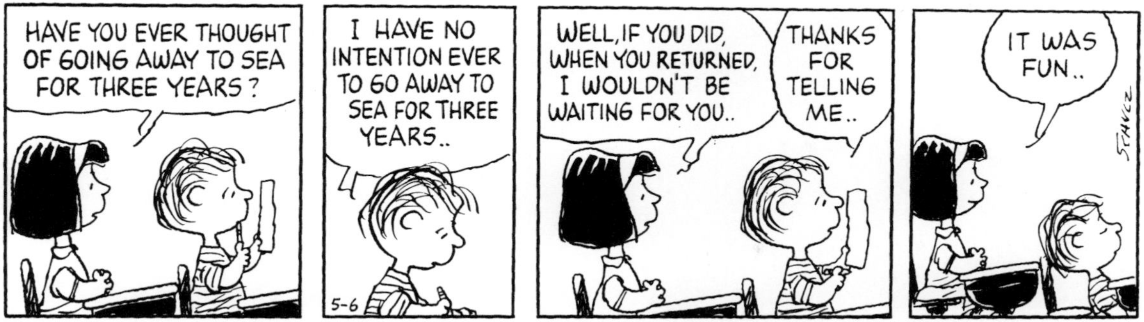
HAVE YOU EVER THOUGHT OF GOING AWAY TO SEA FOR THREE YEARS?
I HAVE NO INTENTION EVER TO GO AWAY TO SEA FOR THREE YEARS..
5-6
WELL, IF YOU DID, WHEN YOU RETURNED, I WOULDN'T BE WAITING FOR YOU..
THANKS FOR TELLING ME..
IT WAS FUN..

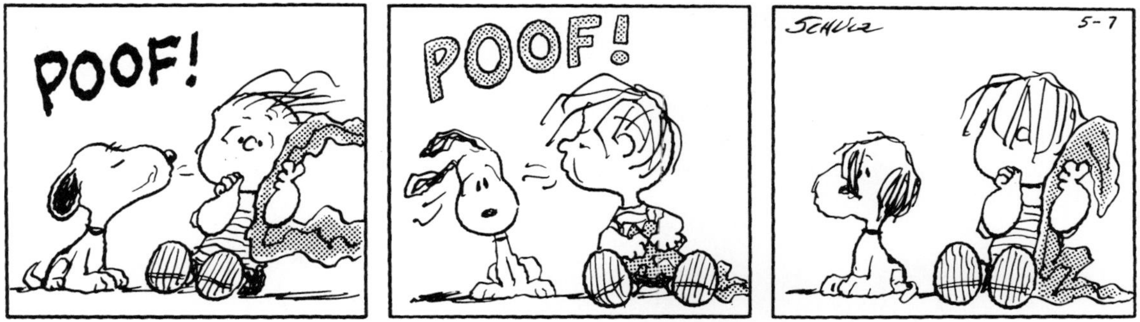
POOF!
POOF!
5-7

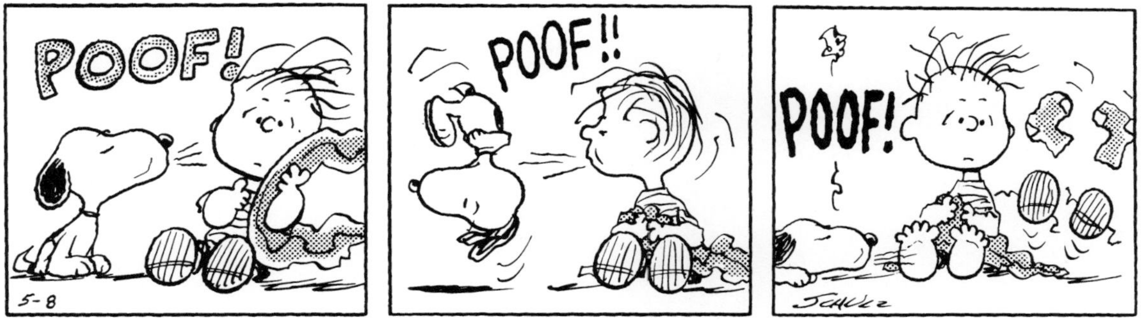
POOF!
POOF!!
POOF!
5-8

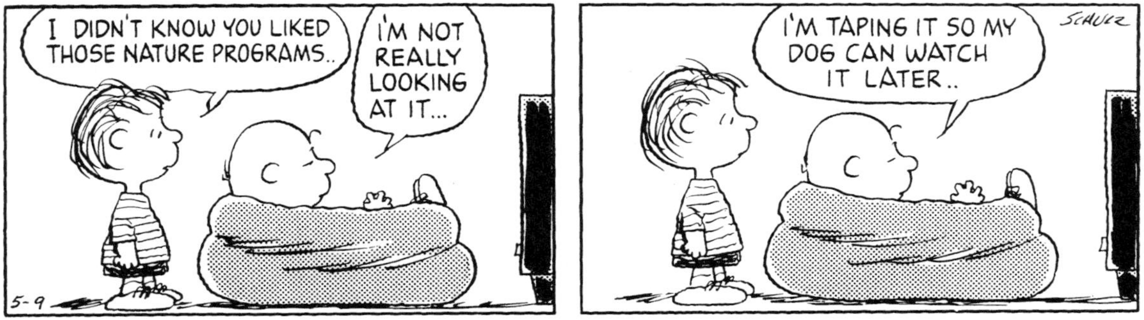
5-9
I DIDN'T KNOW YOU LIKED THOSE NATURE PROGRAMS..
I'M NOT REALLY LOOKING AT IT...
I'M TAPING IT SO MY DOG CAN WATCH IT LATER..

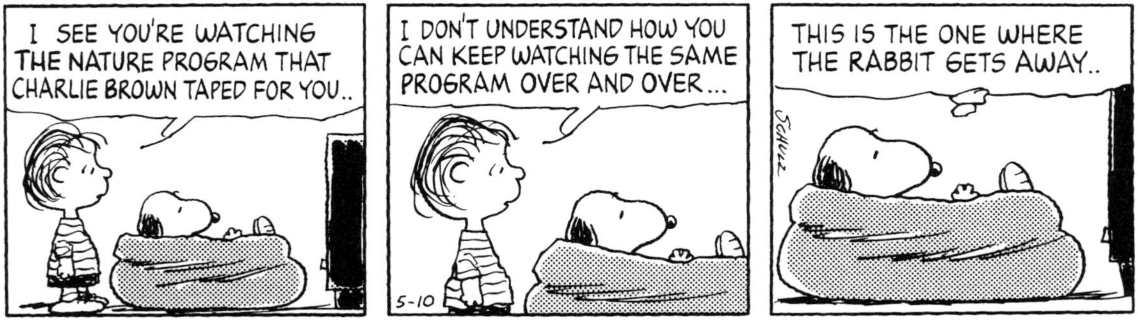
I SEE YOU'RE WATCHING THE NATURE PROGRAM THAT CHARLIE BROWN TAPED FOR YOU..
5-10
I DON'T UNDERSTAND HOW YOU CAN KEEP WATCHING THE SAME PROGRAM OVER AND OVER...
THIS IS THE ONE WHERE THE RABBIT GETS AWAY..

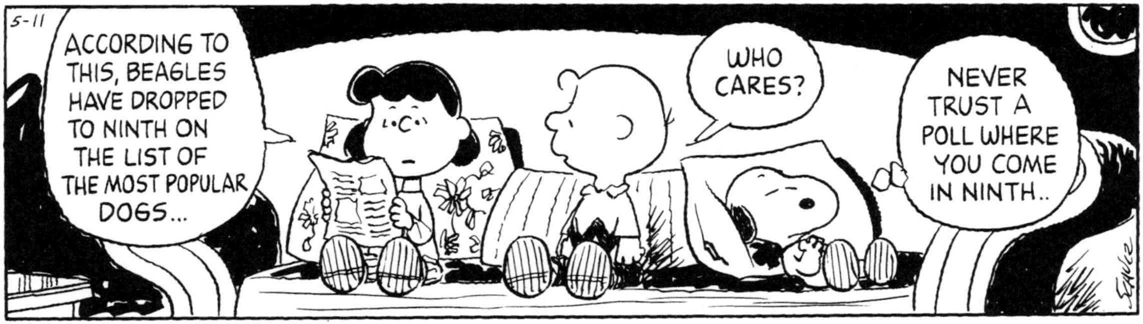
5-11
ACCORDING TO THIS, BEAGLES HAVE DROPPED TO NINTH ON THE LIST OF THE MOST POPULAR DOGS...
WHO CARES?
NEVER TRUST A POLL WHERE YOU COME IN NINTH..

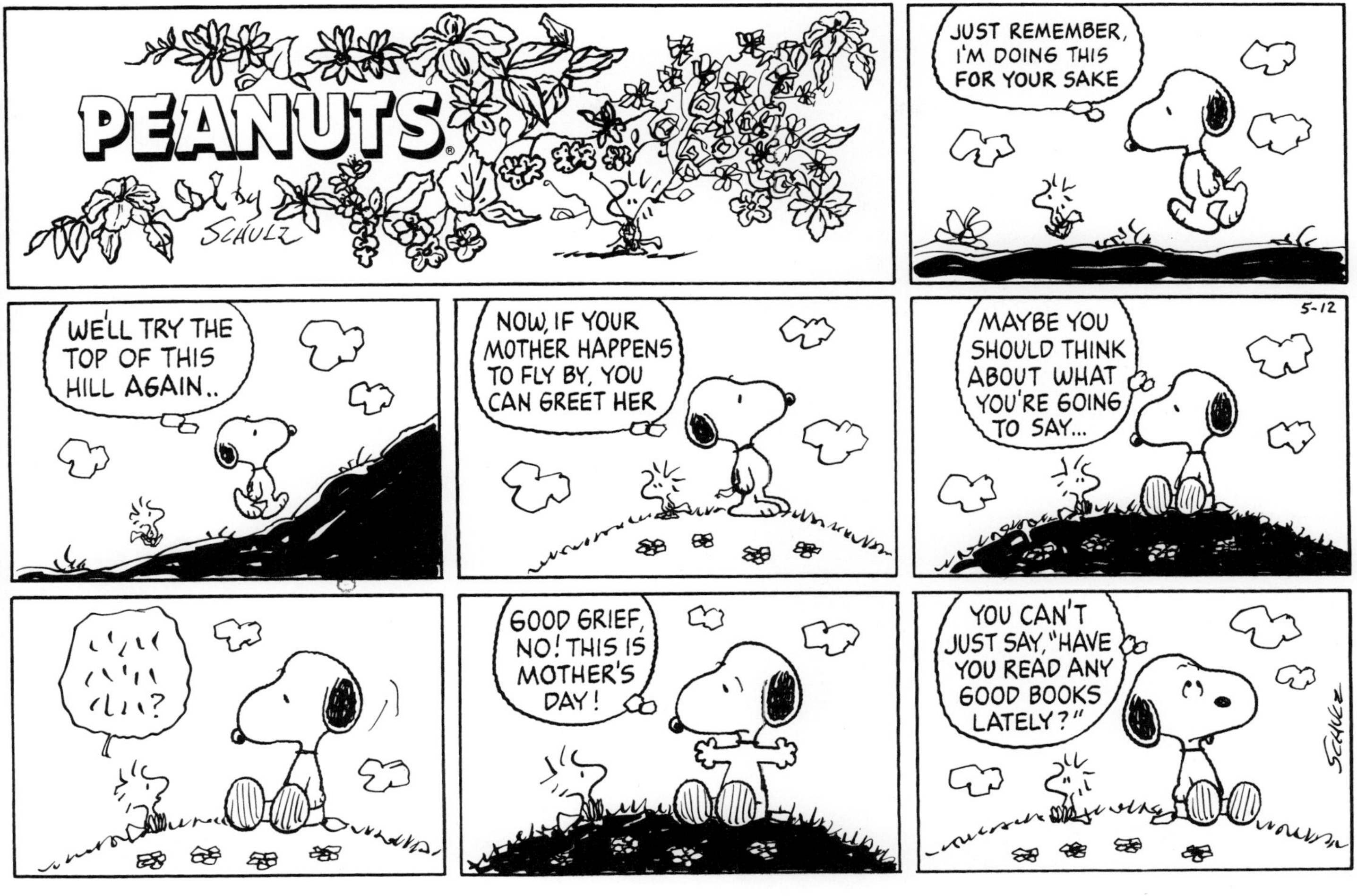
PEANUTS®
by SCHULZ
JUST REMEMBER, I'M DOING THIS FOR YOUR SAKE
WE'LL TRY THE TOP OF THIS HILL AGAIN..
NOW, IF YOUR MOTHER HAPPENS TO FLY BY, YOU CAN GREET HER
5-12
MAYBE YOU SHOULD THINK ABOUT WHAT YOU'RE GOING TO SAY...
?
GOOD GRIEF, NO! THIS IS MOTHER'S DAY!
YOU CAN'T JUST SAY, "HAVE YOU READ ANY GOOD BOOKS LATELY?"
SCHULZ

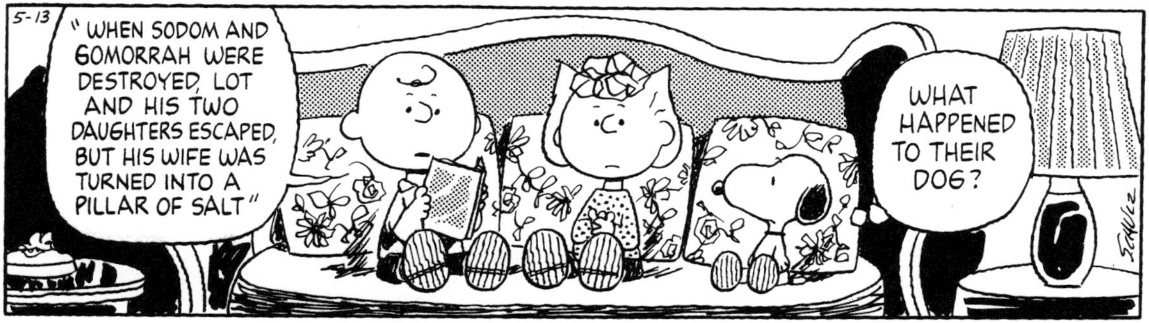
5-13
"WHEN SODOM AND GOMORRAH WERE DESTROYED, LOT AND HIS TWO DAUGHTERS ESCAPED, BUT HIS WIFE WAS TURNED INTO A PILLAR OF SALT"
WHAT HAPPENED TO THEIR DOG?
SCHULZ

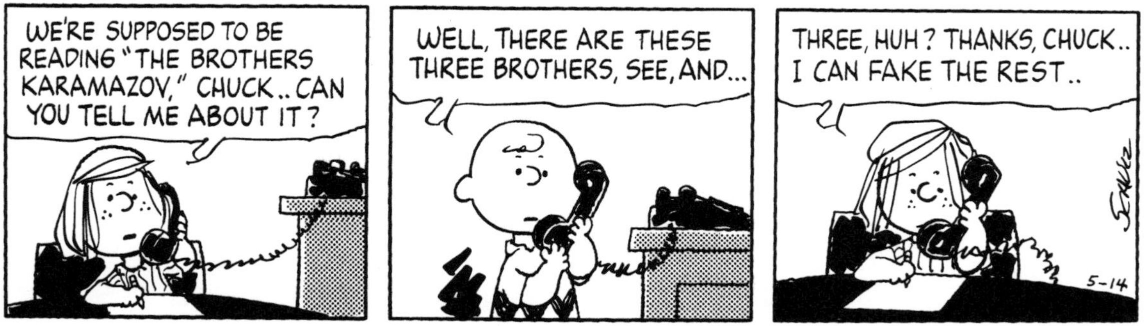
WE'RE SUPPOSED TO BE READING "THE BROTHERS KARAMAZOV," CHUCK.. CAN YOU TELL ME ABOUT IT?
WELL, THERE ARE THESE THREE BROTHERS, SEE, AND...
THREE, HUH? THANKS, CHUCK.. I CAN FAKE THE REST..
SCHULZ
5-14

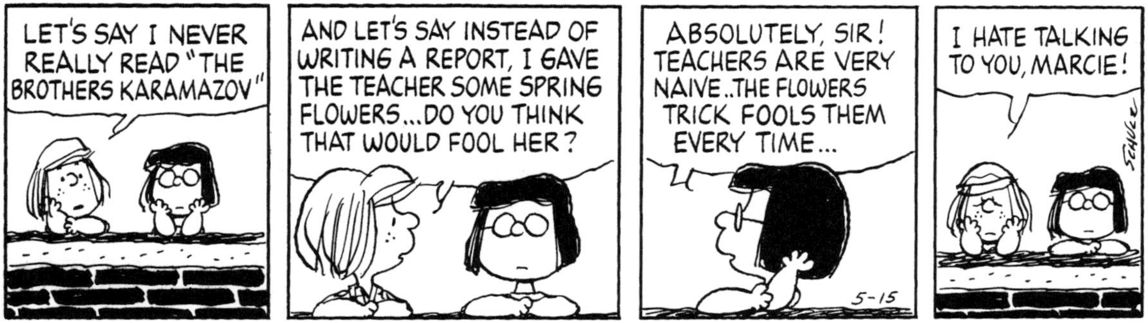
LET'S SAY I NEVER REALLY READ "THE BROTHERS KARAMAZOV"
AND LET'S SAY INSTEAD OF WRITING A REPORT, I GAVE THE TEACHER SOME SPRING FLOWERS...DO YOU THINK THAT WOULD FOOL HER?
ABSOLUTELY, SIR! TEACHERS ARE VERY NAIVE..THE FLOWERS TRICK FOOLS THEM EVERY TIME...
5-15
I HATE TALKING TO YOU, MARCIE!
SCHULZ

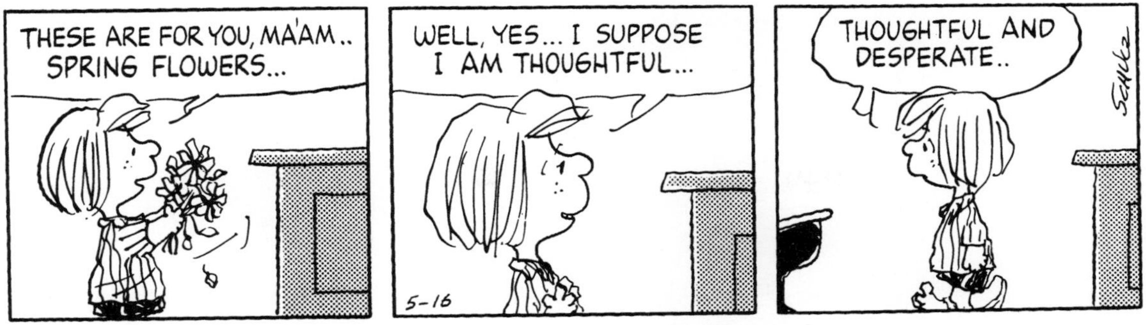
THESE ARE FOR YOU, MA'AM.. SPRING FLOWERS...
WELL, YES... I SUPPOSE I AM THOUGHTFUL...
5-16
THOUGHTFUL AND DESPERATE..
SCHULZ

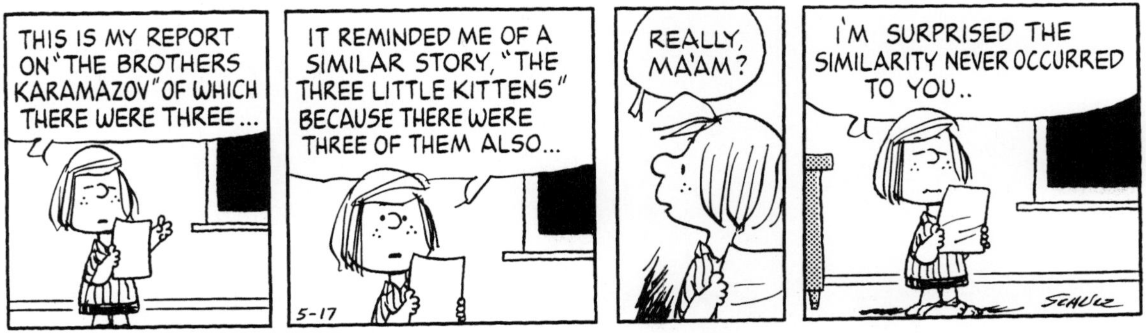
THIS IS MY REPORT ON "THE BROTHERS KARAMAZOV" OF WHICH THERE WERE THREE...
IT REMINDED ME OF A SIMILAR STORY, "THE THREE LITTLE KITTENS" BECAUSE THERE WERE THREE OF THEM ALSO...
5-17
REALLY, MA'AM?
I'M SURPRISED THE SIMILARITY NEVER OCCURRED TO YOU..
SCHULZ

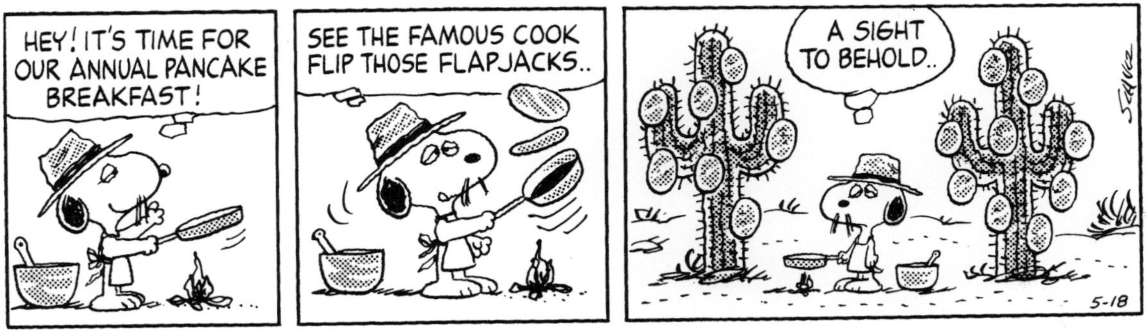
HEY! IT'S TIME FOR OUR ANNUAL PANCAKE BREAKFAST!
SEE THE FAMOUS COOK FLIP THOSE FLAPJACKS..
A SIGHT TO BEHOLD..
SCHULZ
5-18

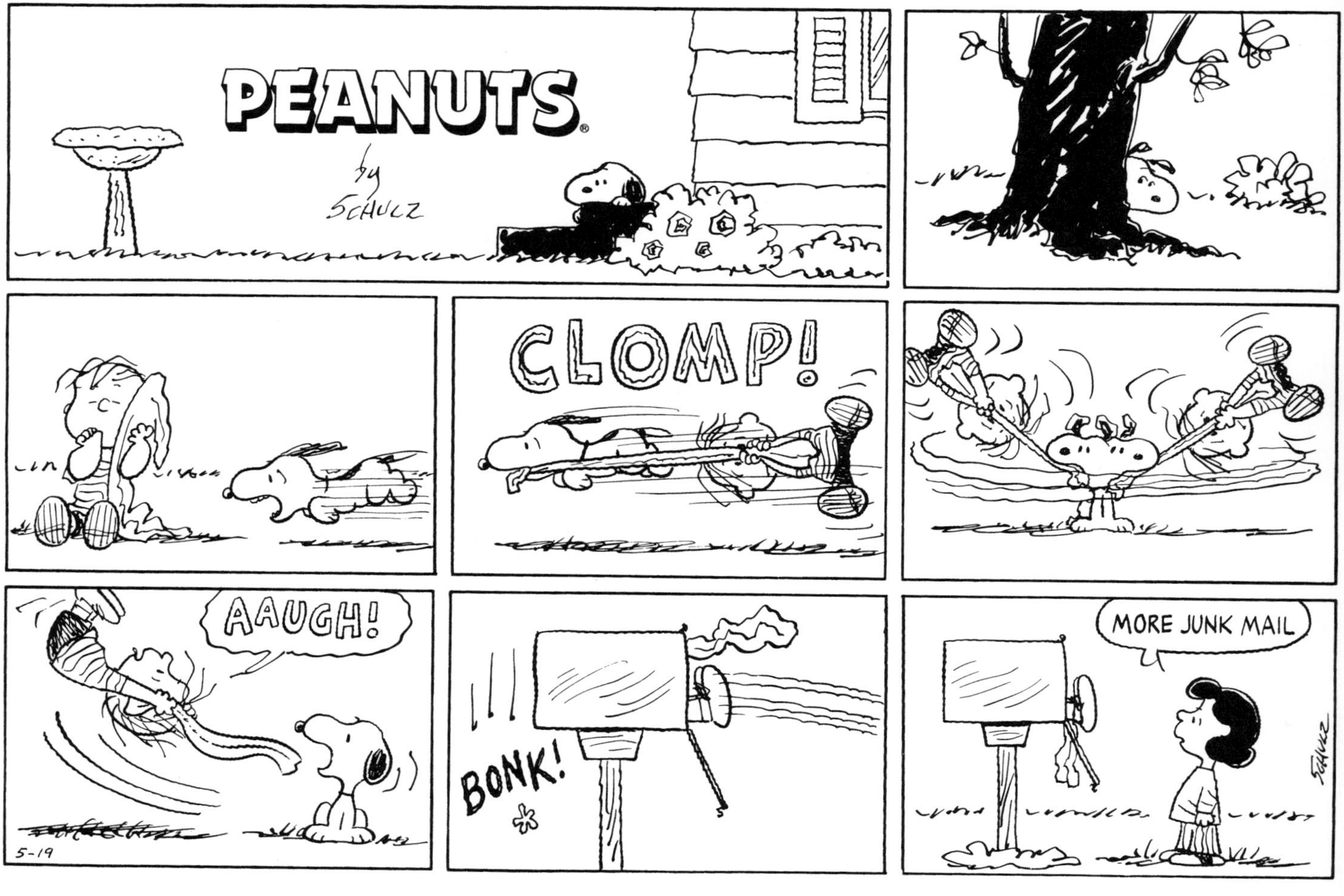
PEANUTS
by SCHULZ
CLOMP!
AAUGH!
5-19
BONK!
MORE JUNK MAIL
SCHULZ

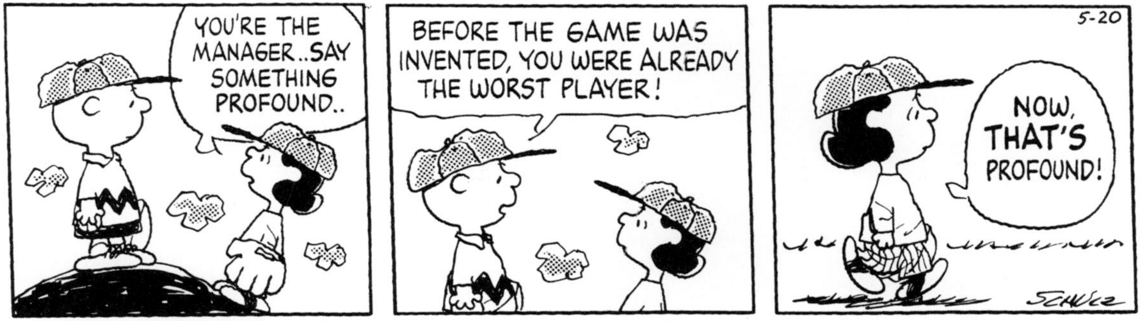
YOU'RE THE MANAGER..SAY SOMETHING PROFOUND..
BEFORE THE GAME WAS INVENTED, YOU WERE ALREADY THE WORST PLAYER!
5-20
NOW, THAT'S PROFOUND!
SCHULZ

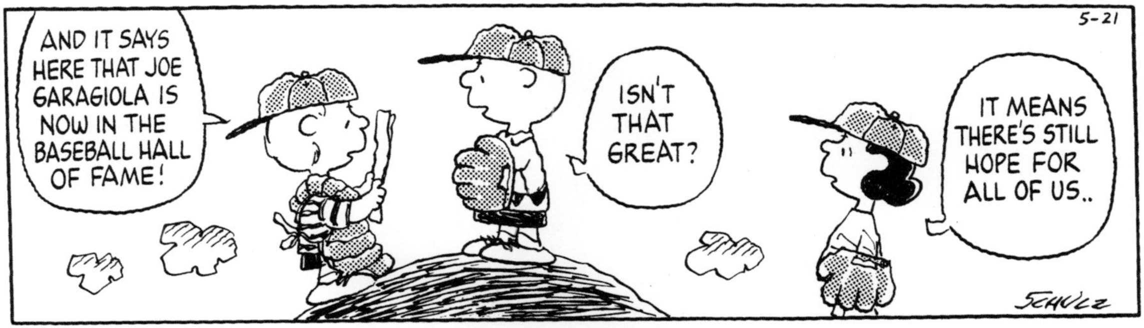
5-21
AND IT SAYS HERE THAT JOE GARAGIOLA IS NOW IN THE BASEBALL HALL OF FAME!
ISN'T THAT GREAT?
IT MEANS THERE'S STILL HOPE FOR ALL OF US..
SCHULZ

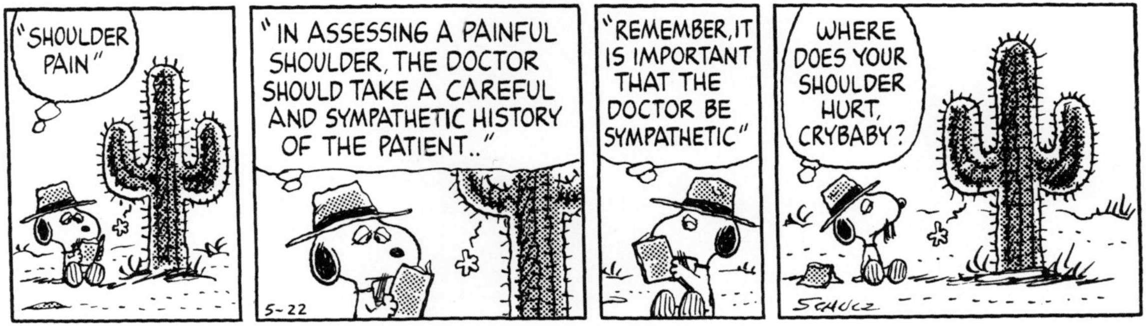
"SHOULDER PAIN"
"IN ASSESSING A PAINFUL SHOULDER, THE DOCTOR SHOULD TAKE A CAREFUL AND SYMPATHETIC HISTORY OF THE PATIENT.."
5-22
"REMEMBER, IT IS IMPORTANT THAT THE DOCTOR BE SYMPATHETIC"
WHERE DOES YOUR SHOULDER HURT, CRYBABY?
SCHULZ

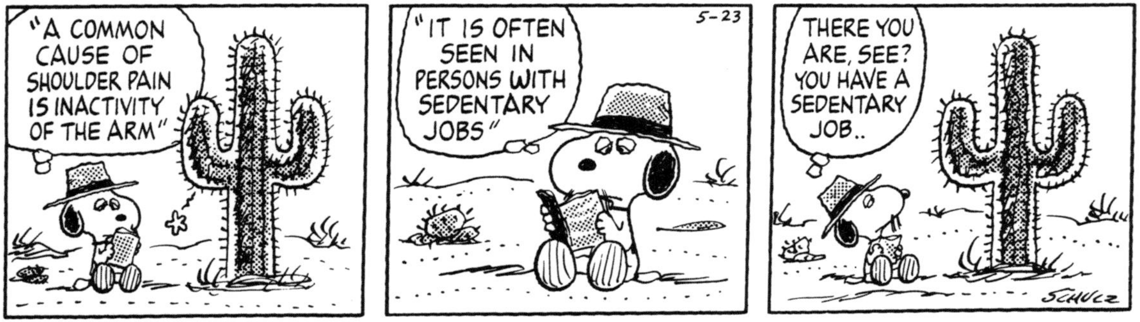
"A COMMON CAUSE OF SHOULDER PAIN IS INACTIVITY OF THE ARM"
5-23
"IT IS OFTEN SEEN IN PERSONS WITH SEDENTARY JOBS"
THERE YOU ARE, SEE? YOU HAVE A SEDENTARY JOB..
SCHULZ

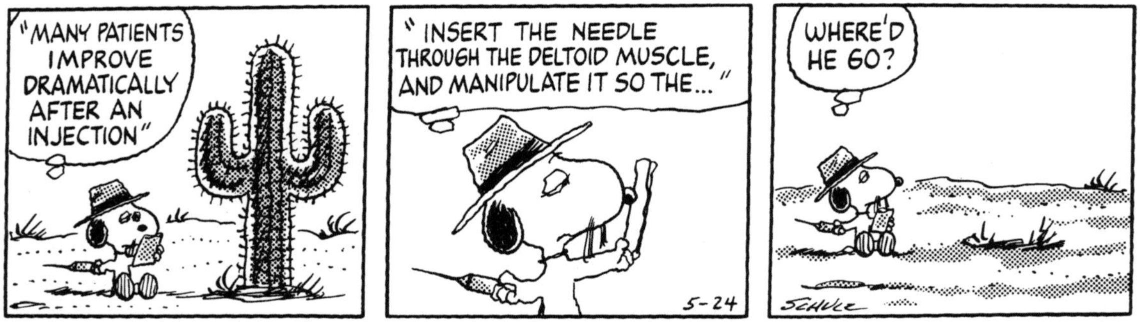
"MANY PATIENTS IMPROVE DRAMATICALLY AFTER AN INJECTION"
"INSERT THE NEEDLE THROUGH THE DELTOID MUSCLE, AND MANIPULATE IT SO THE..."
5-24
WHERE'D HE GO?
SCHULZ

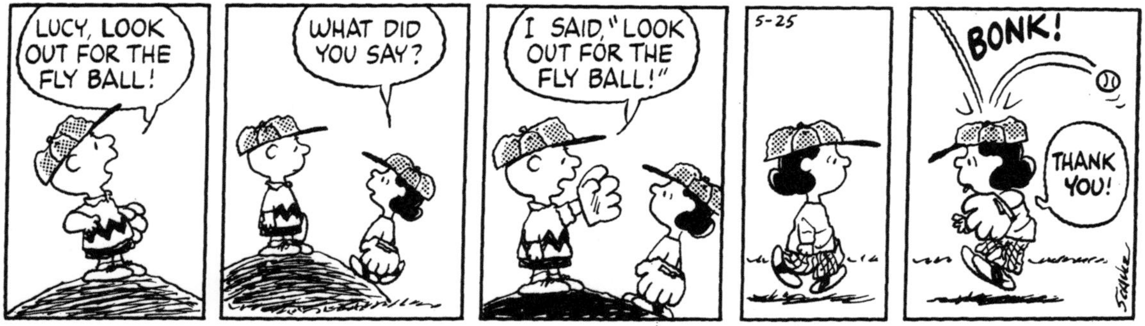
LUCY, LOOK OUT FOR THE FLY BALL!
WHAT DID YOU SAY?
I SAID, "LOOK OUT FOR THE FLY BALL!"
5-25
BONK!
THANK YOU!
SCHULZ

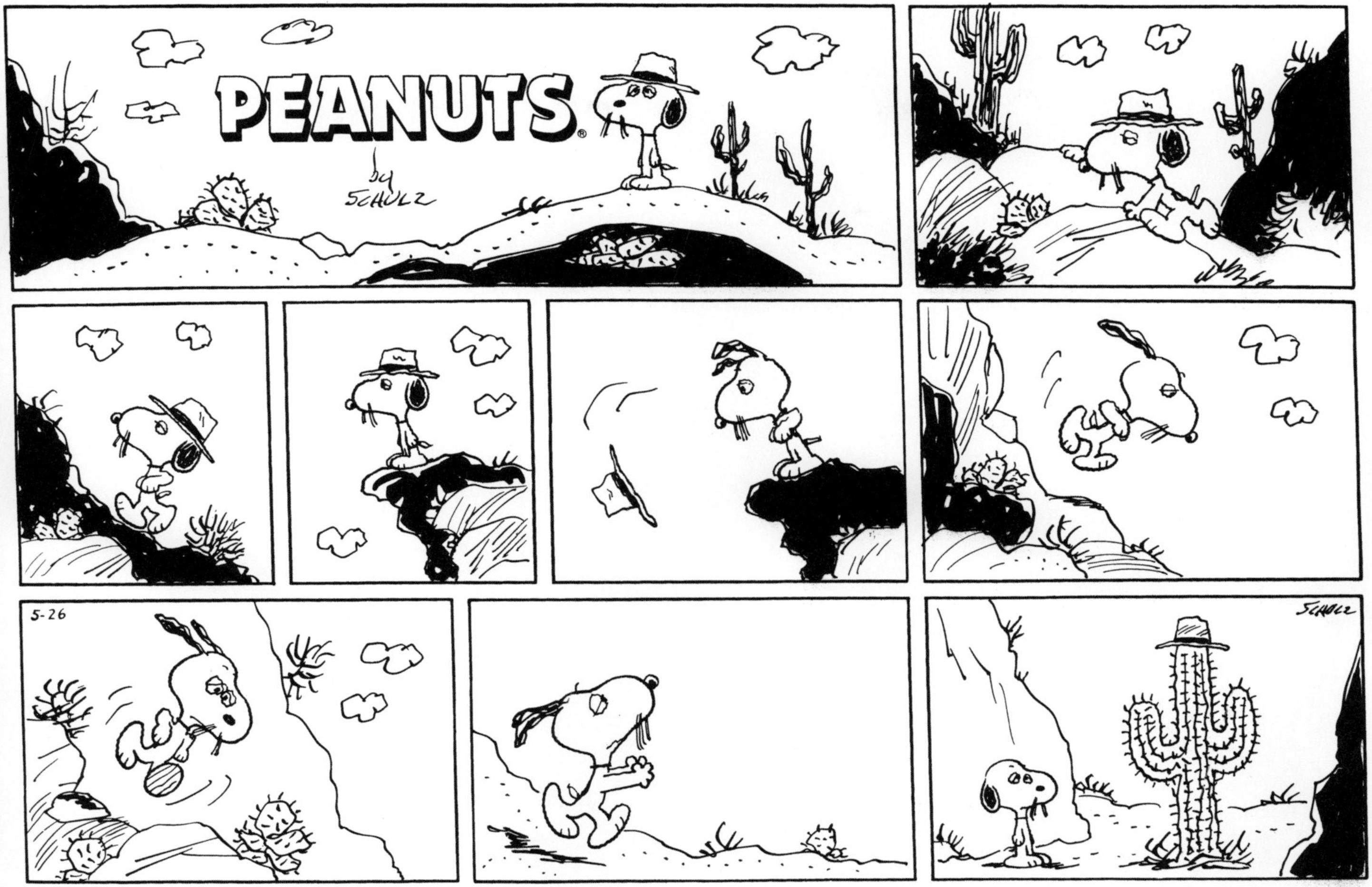
PEANUTS®
by SCHULZ
5-26
SCHULZ

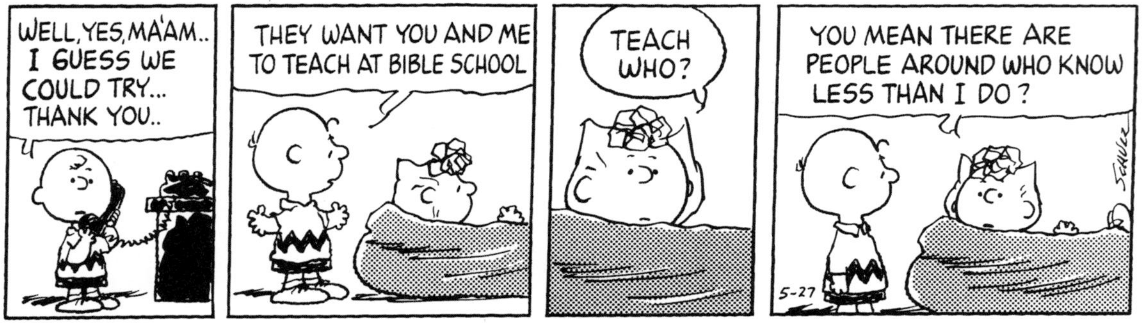
WELL, YES, MA'AM.. I GUESS WE COULD TRY... THANK YOU..
THEY WANT YOU AND ME TO TEACH AT BIBLE SCHOOL
TEACH WHO?
YOU MEAN THERE ARE PEOPLE AROUND WHO KNOW LESS THAN I DO?
5-27

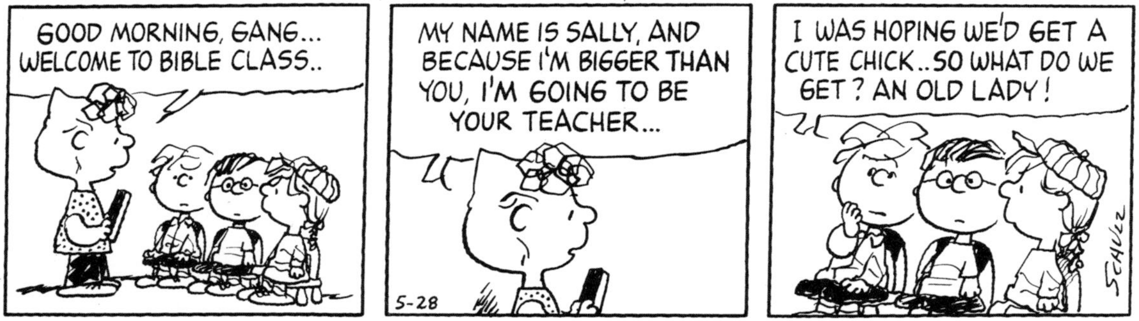
GOOD MORNING, GANG... WELCOME TO BIBLE CLASS..
MY NAME IS SALLY, AND BECAUSE I'M BIGGER THAN YOU, I'M GOING TO BE YOUR TEACHER...
5-28
I WAS HOPING WE'D GET A CUTE CHICK.. SO WHAT DO WE GET? AN OLD LADY!

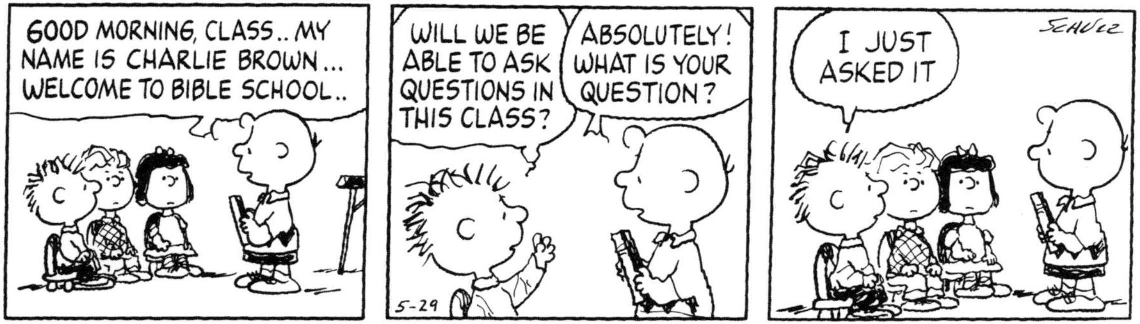
GOOD MORNING, CLASS.. MY NAME IS CHARLIE BROWN... WELCOME TO BIBLE SCHOOL..
WILL WE BE ABLE TO ASK QUESTIONS IN THIS CLASS?
ABSOLUTELY! WHAT IS YOUR QUESTION?
5-29
I JUST ASKED IT

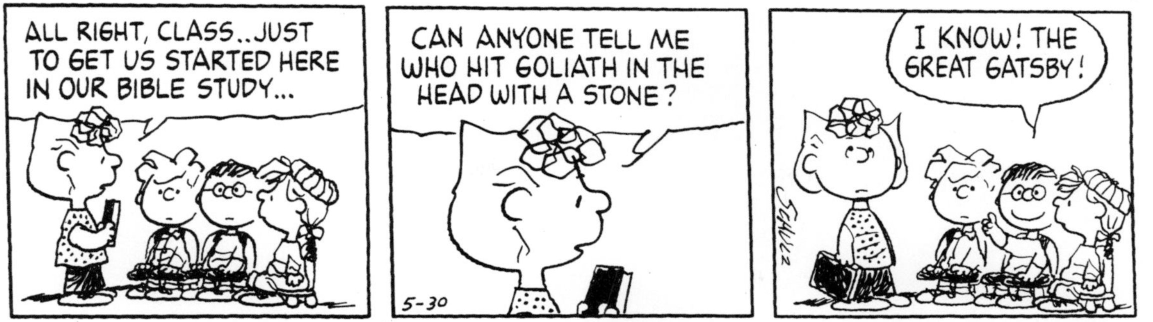
ALL RIGHT, CLASS..JUST TO GET US STARTED HERE IN OUR BIBLE STUDY...
CAN ANYONE TELL ME WHO HIT GOLIATH IN THE HEAD WITH A STONE?
5-30
I KNOW! THE GREAT GATSBY!
SCHULZ

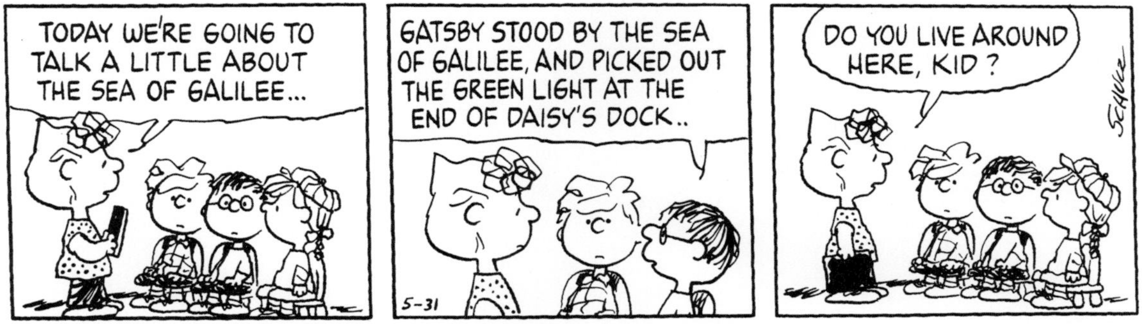
TODAY WE'RE GOING TO TALK A LITTLE ABOUT THE SEA OF GALILEE...
GATSBY STOOD BY THE SEA OF GALILEE, AND PICKED OUT THE GREEN LIGHT AT THE END OF DAISY'S DOCK..
5-31
DO YOU LIVE AROUND HERE, KID?
SCHULZ

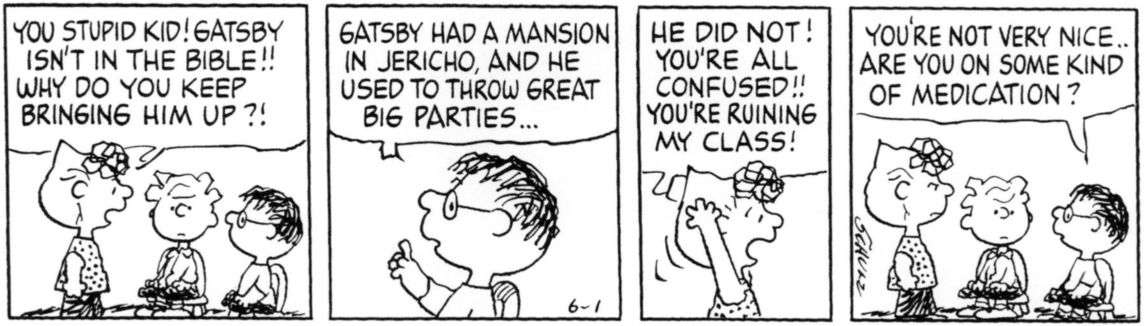
YOU STUPID KID! GATSBY ISN'T IN THE BIBLE!! WHY DO YOU KEEP BRINGING HIM UP?!
GATSBY HAD A MANSION IN JERICHO, AND HE USED TO THROW GREAT BIG PARTIES...
6-1
HE DID NOT! YOU'RE ALL CONFUSED!! YOU'RE RUINING MY CLASS!
YOU'RE NOT VERY NICE.. ARE YOU ON SOME KIND OF MEDICATION?
SCHULZ

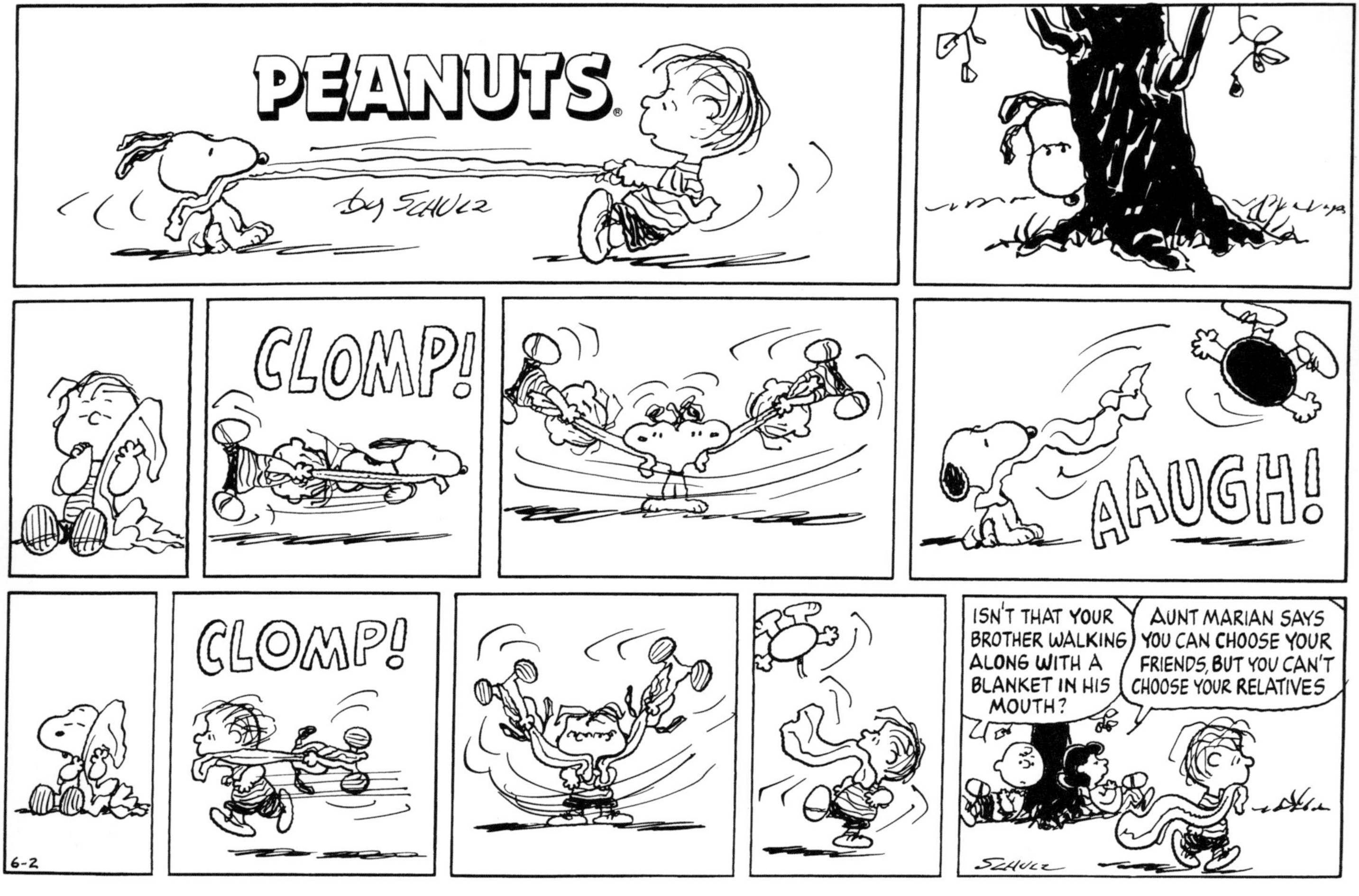
PEANUTS
by SCHULZ
CLOMP!
AAUGH!
6-2
CLOMP!
ISN'T THAT YOUR BROTHER WALKING ALONG WITH A BLANKET IN HIS MOUTH?
AUNT MARIAN SAYS YOU CAN CHOOSE YOUR FRIENDS, BUT YOU CAN'T CHOOSE YOUR RELATIVES
SCHULZ

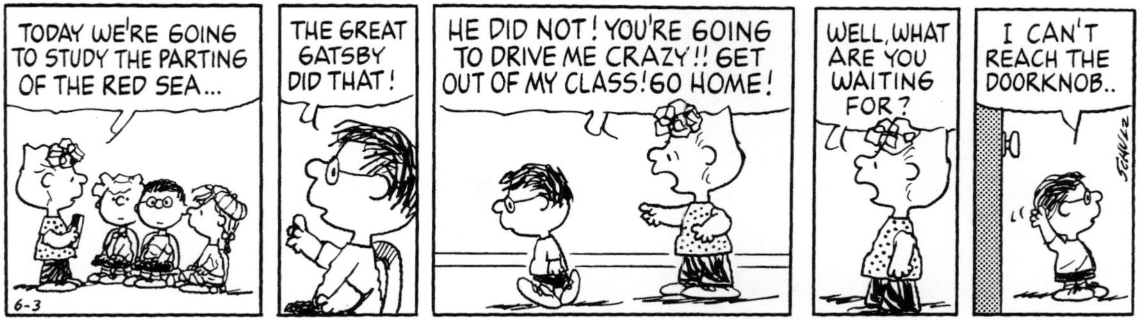
TODAY WE'RE GOING TO STUDY THE PARTING OF THE RED SEA...
6-3
THE GREAT GATSBY DID THAT!
HE DID NOT! YOU'RE GOING TO DRIVE ME CRAZY!! GET OUT OF MY CLASS! GO HOME!
WELL, WHAT ARE YOU WAITING FOR?
I CAN'T REACH THE DOORKNOB..
SCHULZ

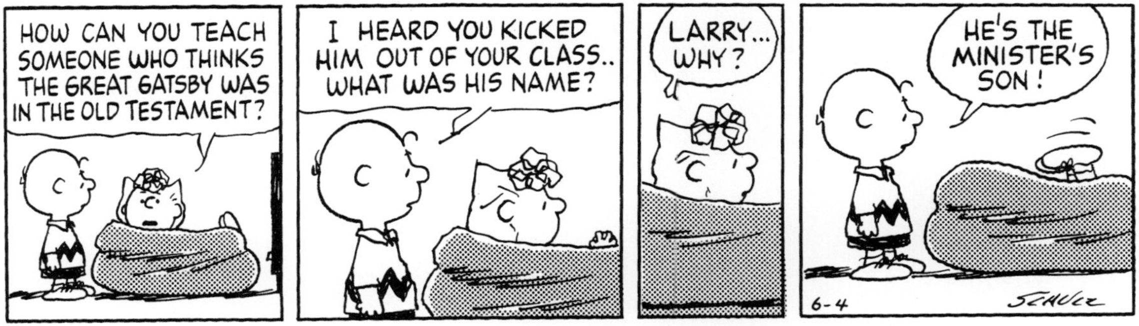
HOW CAN YOU TEACH SOMEONE WHO THINKS THE GREAT GATSBY WAS IN THE OLD TESTAMENT?
I HEARD YOU KICKED HIM OUT OF YOUR CLASS.. WHAT WAS HIS NAME?
LARRY... WHY?
HE'S THE MINISTER'S SON!
6-4
SCHULZ

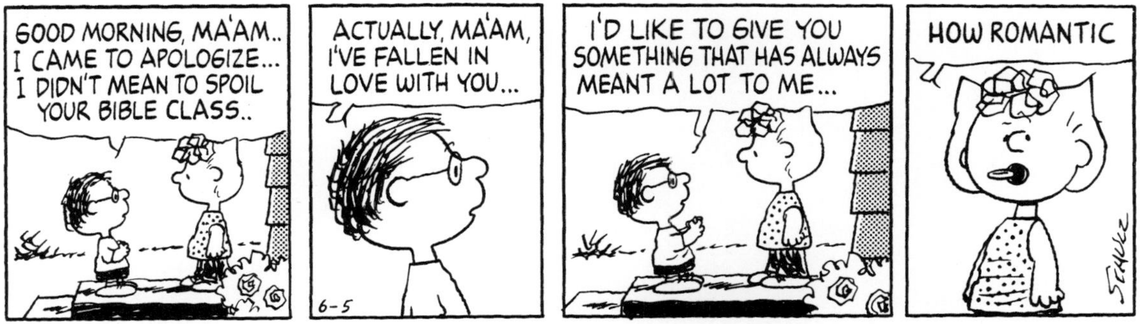
GOOD MORNING, MA'AM.. I CAME TO APOLOGIZE... I DIDN'T MEAN TO SPOIL YOUR BIBLE CLASS..
ACTUALLY, MA'AM, I'VE FALLEN IN LOVE WITH YOU...
6-5
I'D LIKE TO GIVE YOU SOMETHING THAT HAS ALWAYS MEANT A LOT TO ME...
HOW ROMANTIC
SCHULZ

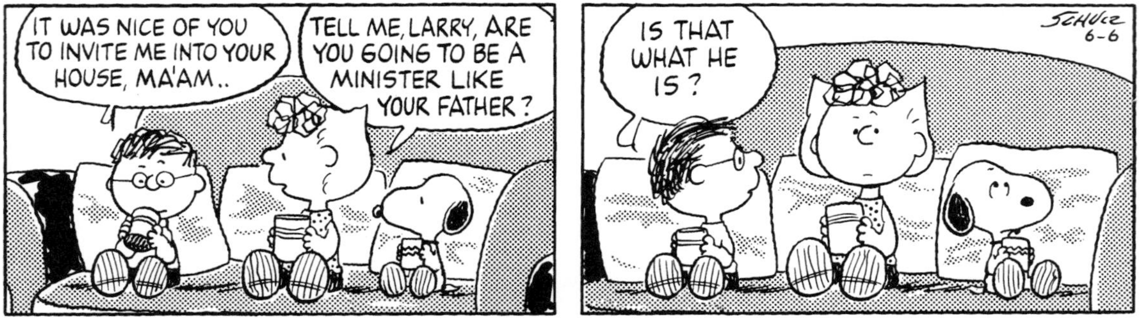
IT WAS NICE OF YOU TO INVITE ME INTO YOUR HOUSE, MA'AM..
TELL ME, LARRY, ARE YOU GOING TO BE A MINISTER LIKE YOUR FATHER?
IS THAT WHAT HE IS?

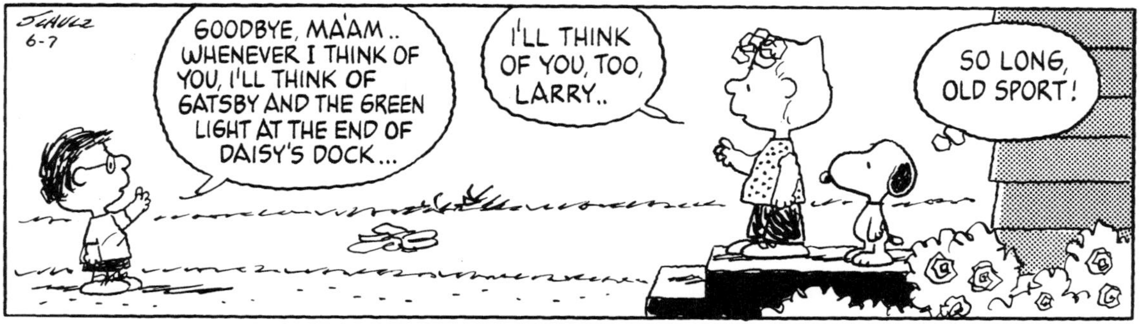
GOODBYE, MA'AM.. WHENEVER I THINK OF YOU, I'LL THINK OF GATSBY AND THE GREEN LIGHT AT THE END OF DAISY'S DOCK...
I'LL THINK OF YOU, TOO, LARRY..
SO LONG, OLD SPORT!

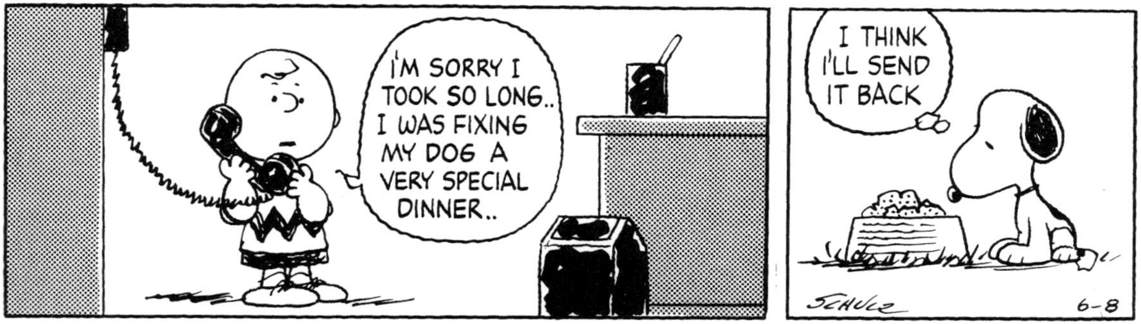
I'M SORRY I TOOK SO LONG.. I WAS FIXING MY DOG A VERY SPECIAL DINNER..
I THINK I'LL SEND IT BACK

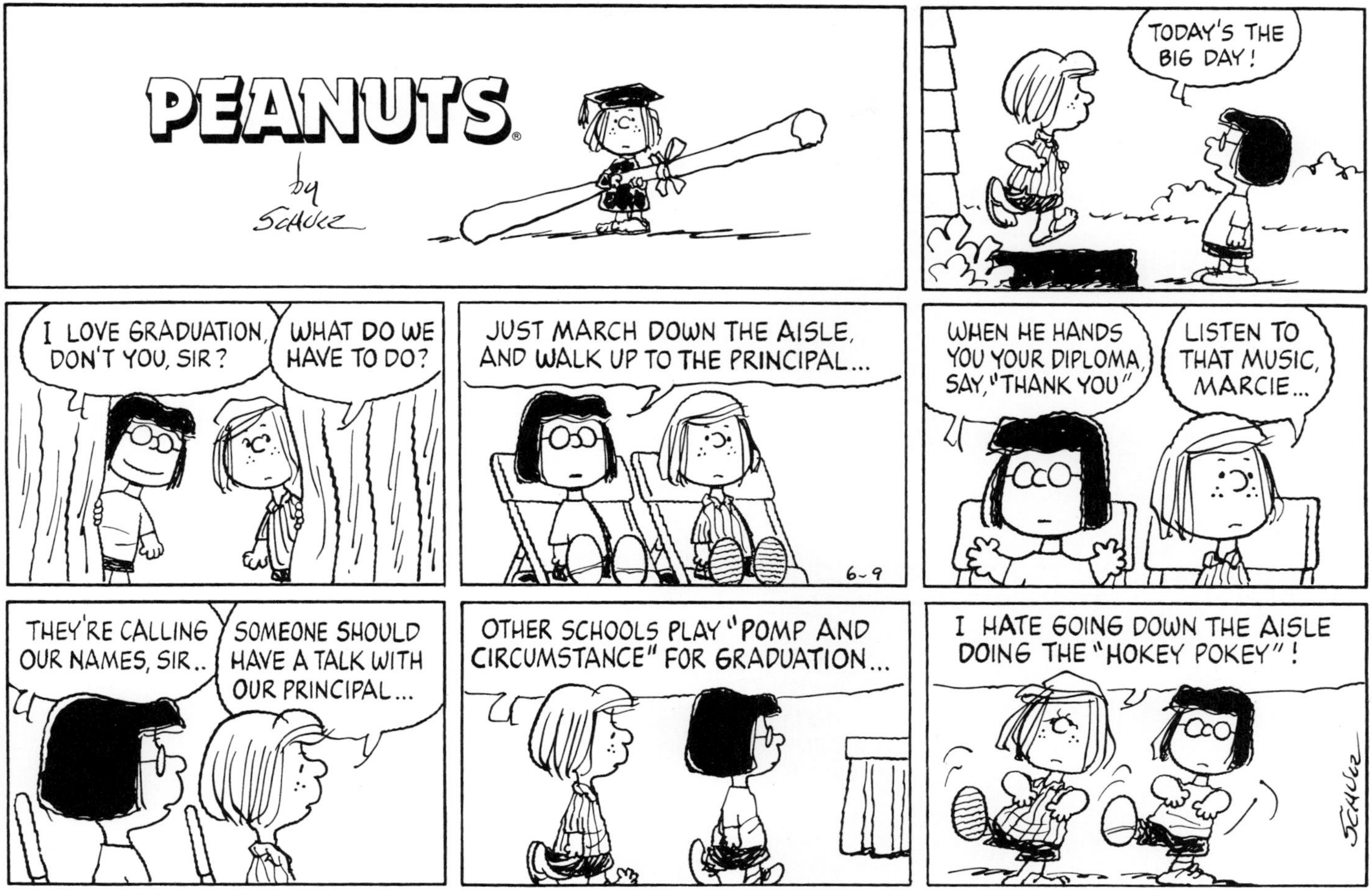
PEANUTS
by SCHULZ
TODAY'S THE BIG DAY!
I LOVE GRADUATION, DON'T YOU, SIR?
WHAT DO WE HAVE TO DO?
JUST MARCH DOWN THE AISLE, AND WALK UP TO THE PRINCIPAL...
6-9
WHEN HE HANDS YOU YOUR DIPLOMA, SAY, "THANK YOU"
LISTEN TO THAT MUSIC, MARCIE...
THEY'RE CALLING OUR NAMES, SIR..
SOMEONE SHOULD HAVE A TALK WITH OUR PRINCIPAL...
OTHER SCHOOLS PLAY "POMP AND CIRCUMSTANCE" FOR GRADUATION...
I HATE GOING DOWN THE AISLE DOING THE "HOKEY POKEY"!
SCHULZ

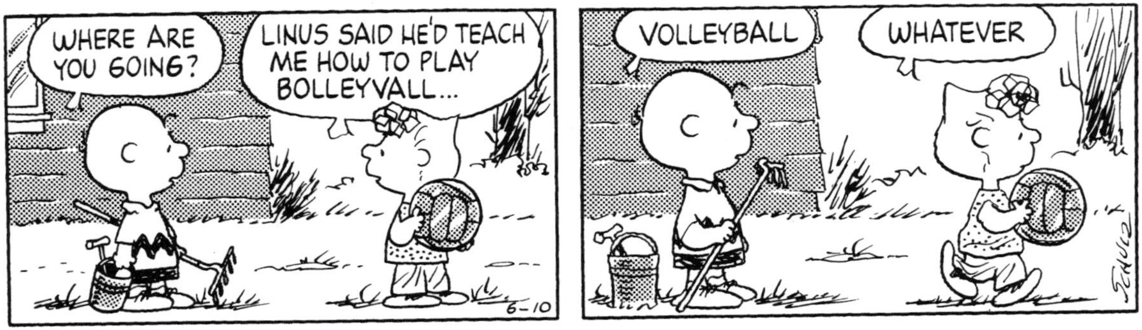
WHERE ARE YOU GOING?
LINUS SAID HE'D TEACH ME HOW TO PLAY BOLLEYVALL...
VOLLEYBALL
WHATEVER
6-10
SCHULZ

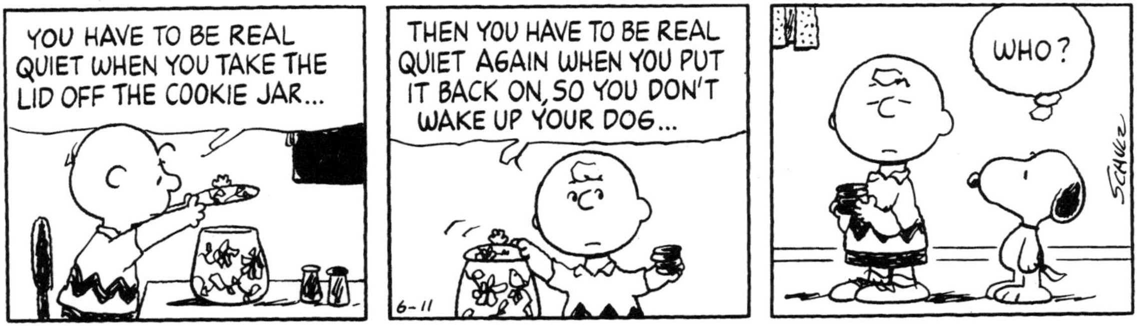
YOU HAVE TO BE REAL QUIET WHEN YOU TAKE THE LID OFF THE COOKIE JAR...
THEN YOU HAVE TO BE REAL QUIET AGAIN WHEN YOU PUT IT BACK ON, SO YOU DON'T WAKE UP YOUR DOG...
6-11
WHO?
SCHULZ

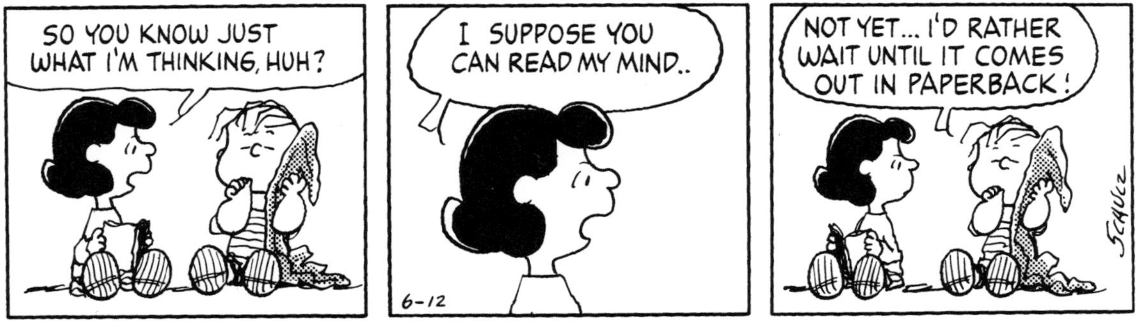
SO YOU KNOW JUST WHAT I'M THINKING, HUH?
I SUPPOSE YOU CAN READ MY MIND..
6-12
NOT YET... I'D RATHER WAIT UNTIL IT COMES OUT IN PAPERBACK!
SCHULZ

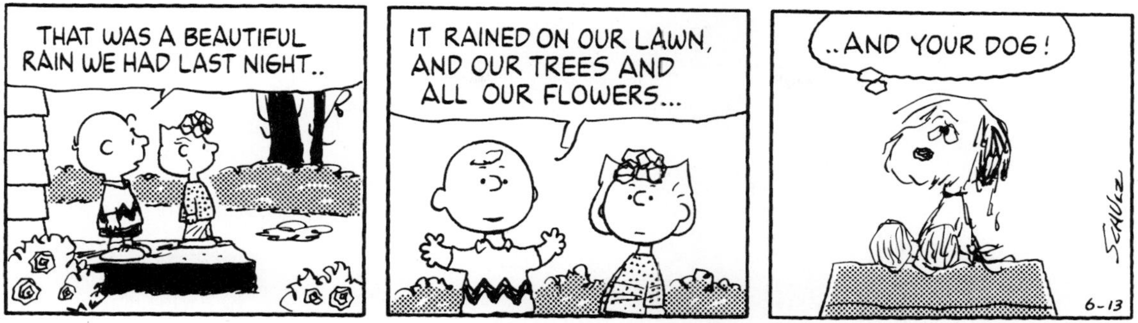
THAT WAS A BEAUTIFUL RAIN WE HAD LAST NIGHT..
IT RAINED ON OUR LAWN, AND OUR TREES AND ALL OUR FLOWERS...
..AND YOUR DOG!
SCHULZ
6-13

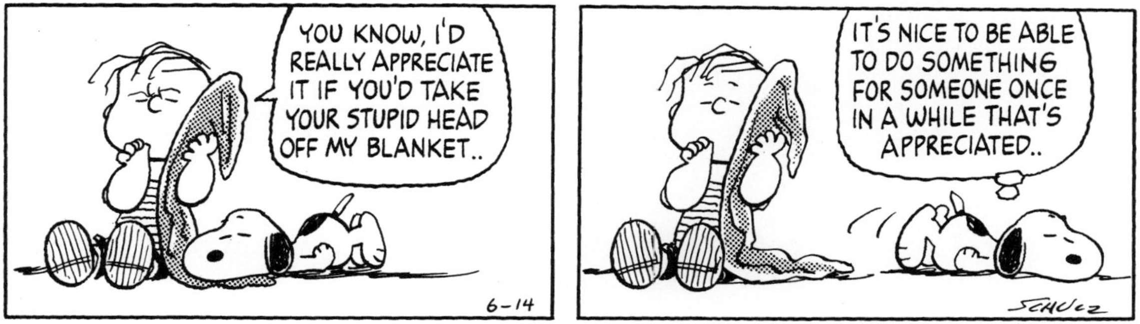
YOU KNOW, I'D REALLY APPRECIATE IT IF YOU'D TAKE YOUR STUPID HEAD OFF MY BLANKET..
6-14
IT'S NICE TO BE ABLE TO DO SOMETHING FOR SOMEONE ONCE IN A WHILE THAT'S APPRECIATED..
SCHULZ

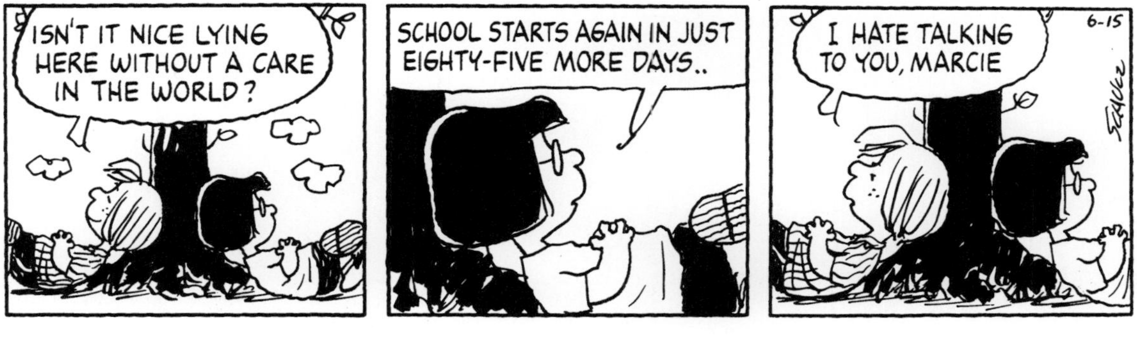
ISN'T IT NICE LYING HERE WITHOUT A CARE IN THE WORLD?
SCHOOL STARTS AGAIN IN JUST EIGHTY-FIVE MORE DAYS..
6-15
I HATE TALKING TO YOU, MARCIE
SCHULZ

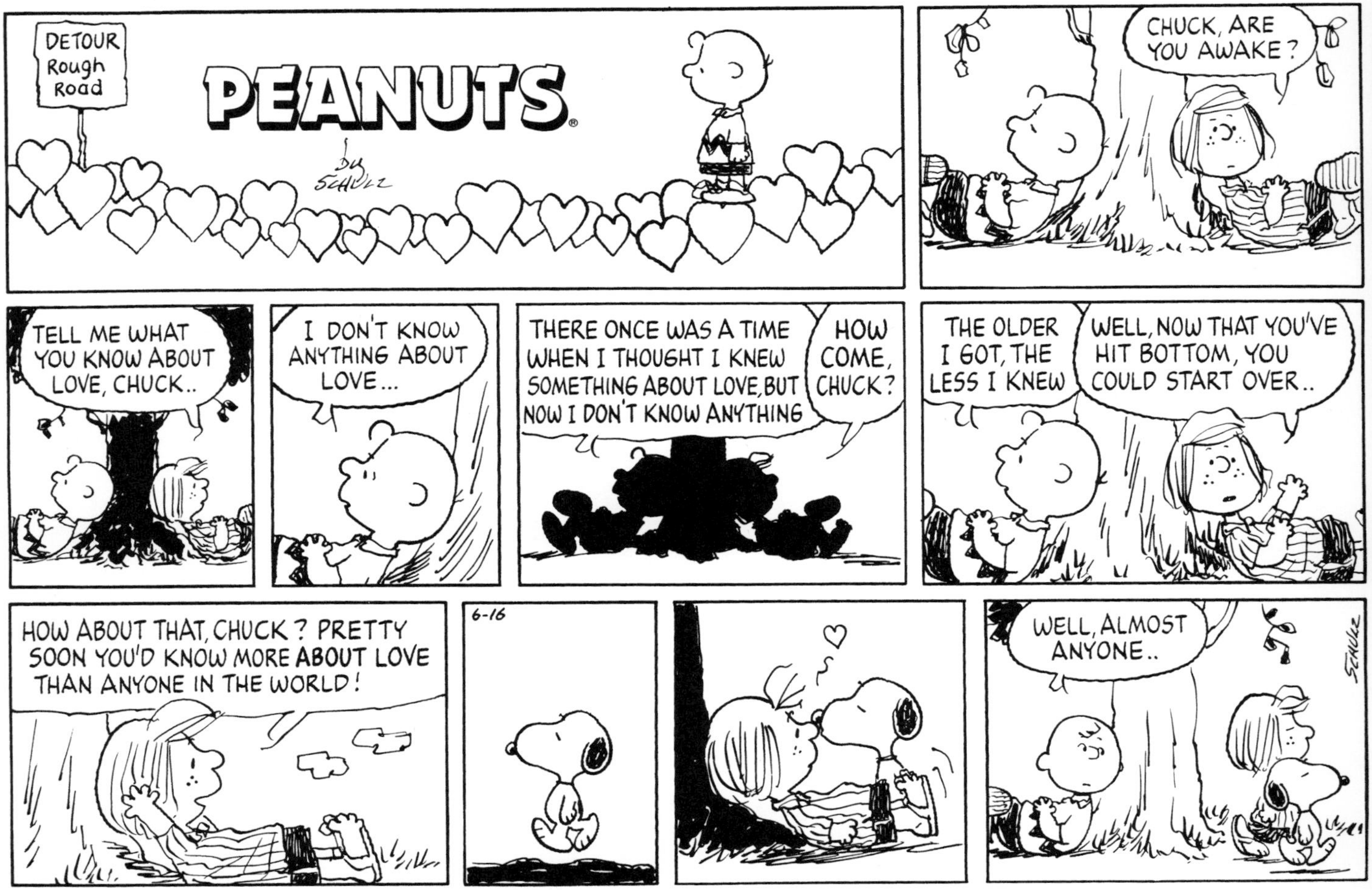
DETOUR Rough Road
PEANUTS
by SCHULZ
CHUCK, ARE YOU AWAKE?
TELL ME WHAT YOU KNOW ABOUT LOVE, CHUCK..
I DON'T KNOW ANYTHING ABOUT LOVE...
THERE ONCE WAS A TIME WHEN I THOUGHT I KNEW SOMETHING ABOUT LOVE, BUT NOW I DON'T KNOW ANYTHING
HOW COME, CHUCK?
THE OLDER I GOT, THE LESS I KNEW
WELL, NOW THAT YOU'VE HIT BOTTOM, YOU COULD START OVER..
HOW ABOUT THAT, CHUCK? PRETTY SOON YOU'D KNOW MORE ABOUT LOVE THAN ANYONE IN THE WORLD!
6-16
WELL, ALMOST ANYONE..
SCHULZ

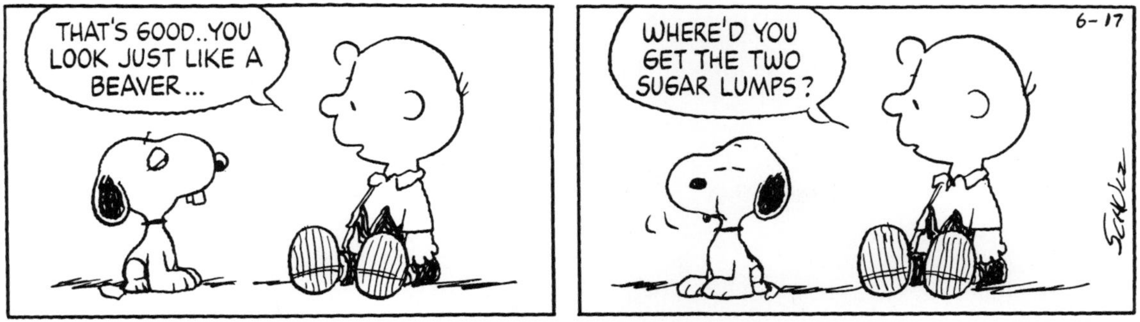
THAT'S GOOD..YOU LOOK JUST LIKE A BEAVER...
WHERE'D YOU GET THE TWO SUGAR LUMPS?
6-17

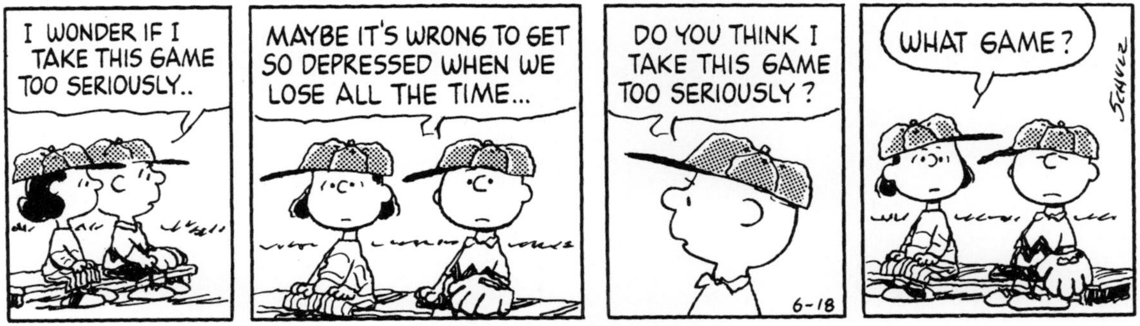
I WONDER IF I TAKE THIS GAME TOO SERIOUSLY..
MAYBE IT'S WRONG TO GET SO DEPRESSED WHEN WE LOSE ALL THE TIME...
DO YOU THINK I TAKE THIS GAME TOO SERIOUSLY?
6-18
WHAT GAME?

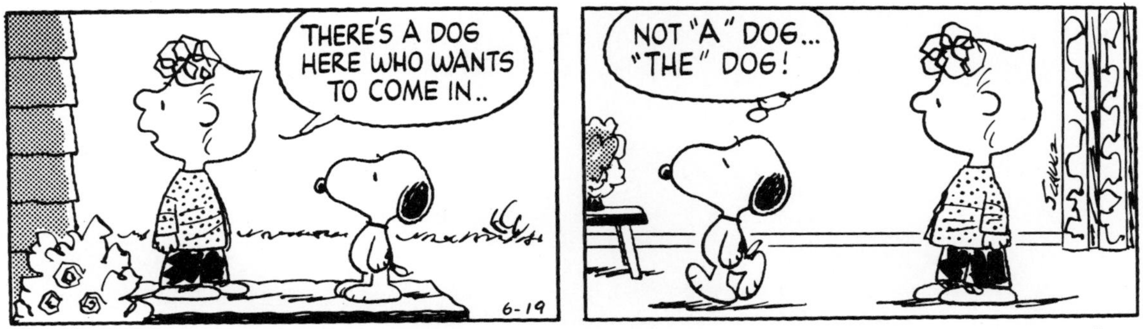
THERE'S A DOG HERE WHO WANTS TO COME IN..
6-19
NOT "A" DOG... "THE" DOG!

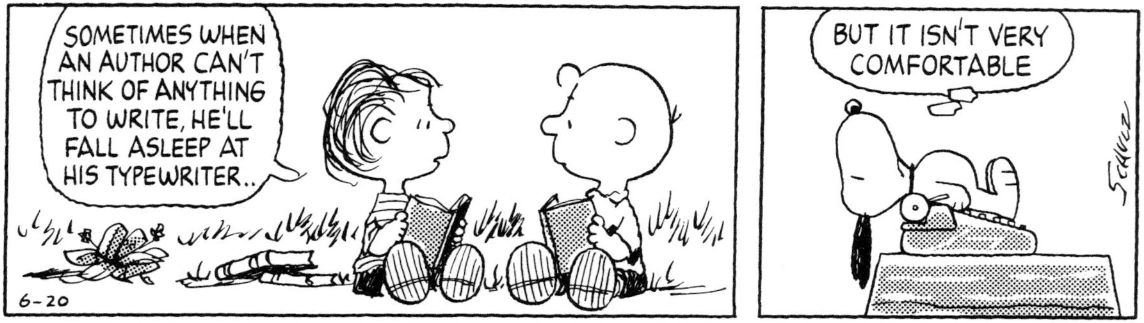
SOMETIMES WHEN AN AUTHOR CAN'T THINK OF ANYTHING TO WRITE, HE'LL FALL ASLEEP AT HIS TYPEWRITER..
6-20
BUT IT ISN'T VERY COMFORTABLE
SCHULZ

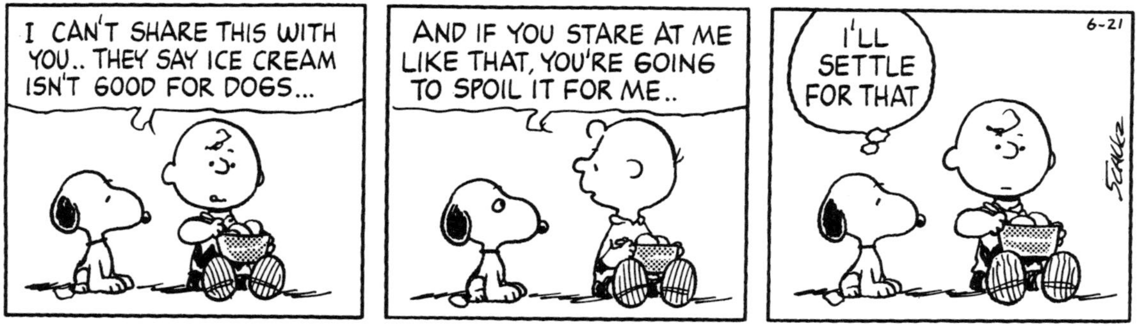
I CAN'T SHARE THIS WITH YOU.. THEY SAY ICE CREAM ISN'T GOOD FOR DOGS...
AND IF YOU STARE AT ME LIKE THAT, YOU'RE GOING TO SPOIL IT FOR ME..
6-21
I'LL SETTLE FOR THAT
SCHULZ

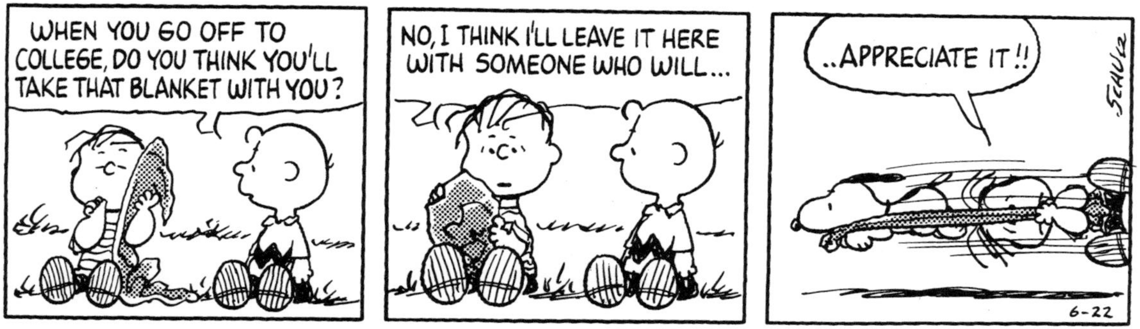
WHEN YOU GO OFF TO COLLEGE, DO YOU THINK YOU'LL TAKE THAT BLANKET WITH YOU?
NO, I THINK I'LL LEAVE IT HERE WITH SOMEONE WHO WILL...
..APPRECIATE IT!!
SCHULZ
6-22

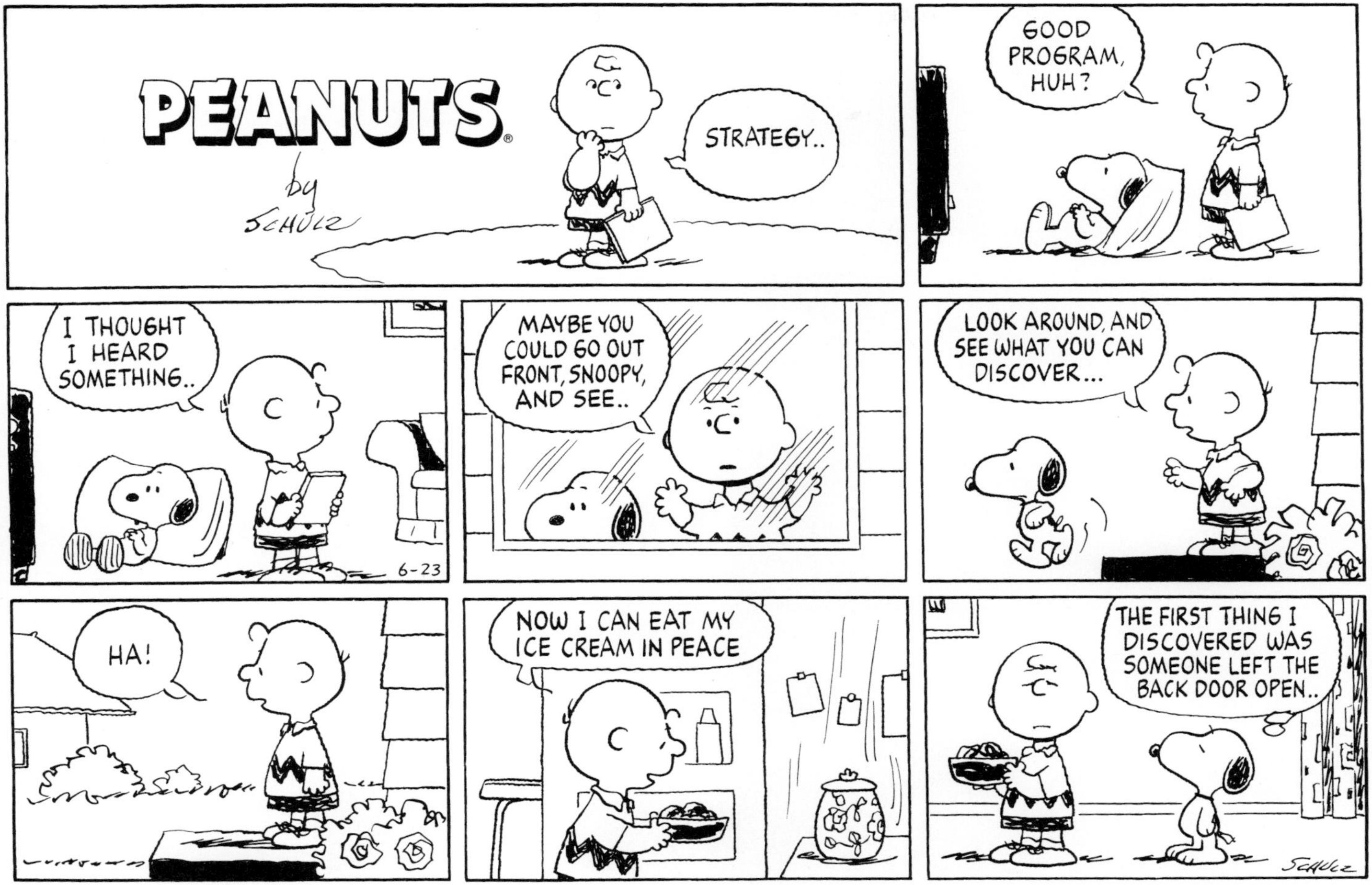
PEANUTS®
by SCHULZ
STRATEGY..
GOOD PROGRAM, HUH?
I THOUGHT I HEARD SOMETHING..
6-23
MAYBE YOU COULD GO OUT FRONT, SNOOPY, AND SEE..
LOOK AROUND, AND SEE WHAT YOU CAN DISCOVER...
HA!
NOW I CAN EAT MY ICE CREAM IN PEACE
THE FIRST THING I DISCOVERED WAS SOMEONE LEFT THE BACK DOOR OPEN..
SCHULZ

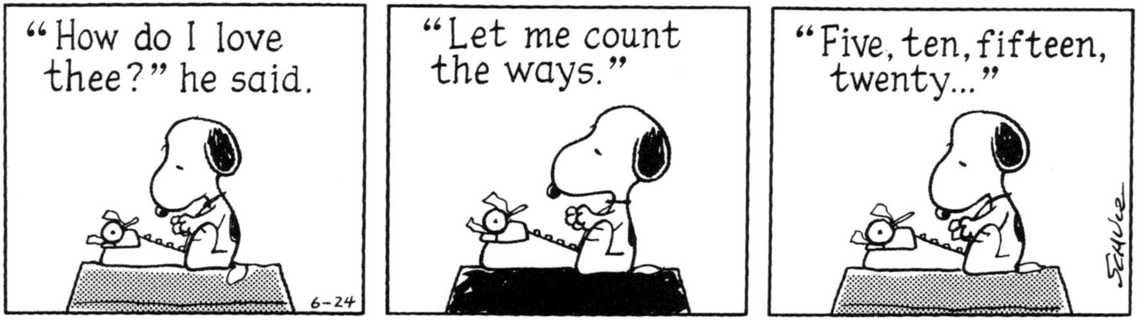
"How do I love thee?" he said.
"Let me count the ways."
"Five, ten, fifteen, twenty..."

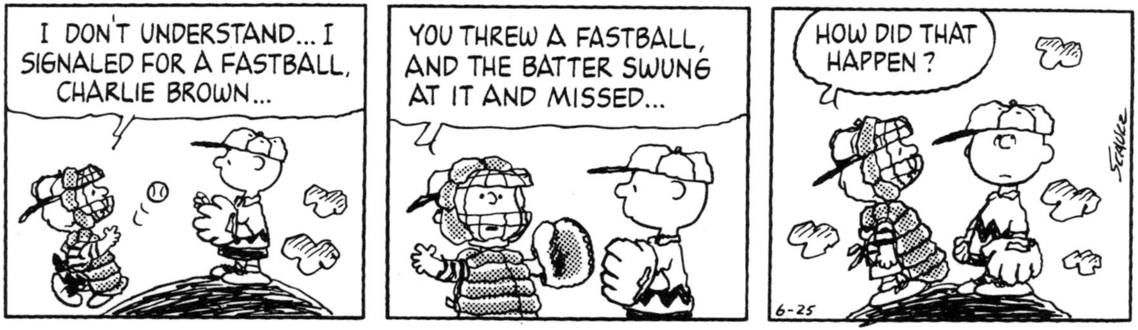
I DON'T UNDERSTAND... I SIGNALED FOR A FASTBALL, CHARLIE BROWN...
YOU THREW A FASTBALL, AND THE BATTER SWUNG AT IT AND MISSED...
HOW DID THAT HAPPEN?

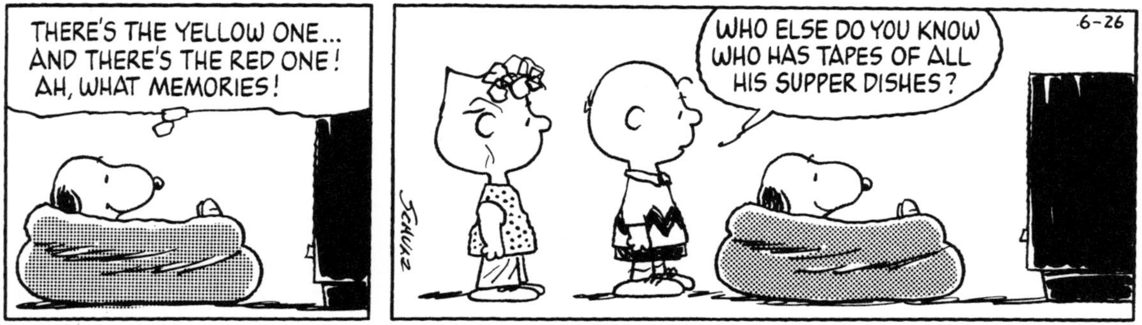
THERE'S THE YELLOW ONE... AND THERE'S THE RED ONE! AH, WHAT MEMORIES!
WHO ELSE DO YOU KNOW WHO HAS TAPES OF ALL HIS SUPPER DISHES?

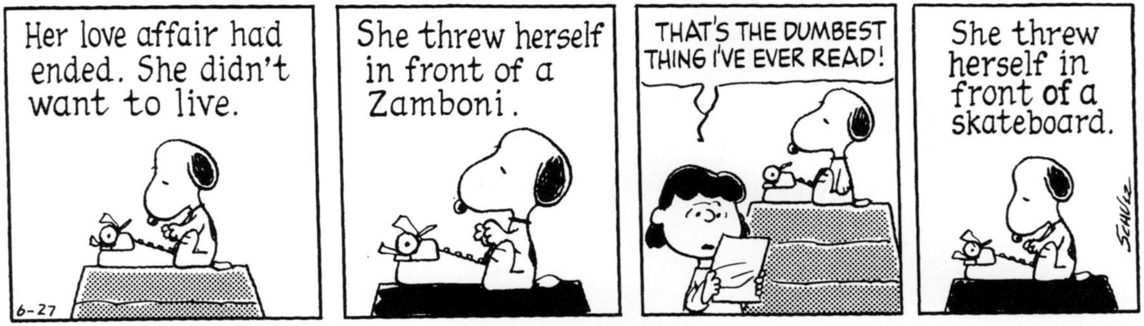
Her love affair had ended. She didn't want to live.
She threw herself in front of a Zamboni.
THAT'S THE DUMBEST THING I'VE EVER READ!
She threw herself in front of a skateboard.
6-27
SCHULZ

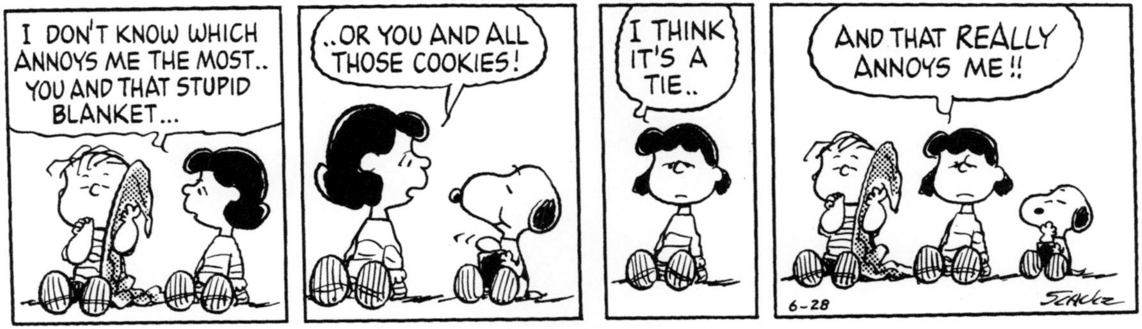
I DON'T KNOW WHICH ANNOYS ME THE MOST.. YOU AND THAT STUPID BLANKET...
..OR YOU AND ALL THOSE COOKIES!
I THINK IT'S A TIE..
AND THAT REALLY ANNOYS ME!!
6-28
SCHULZ

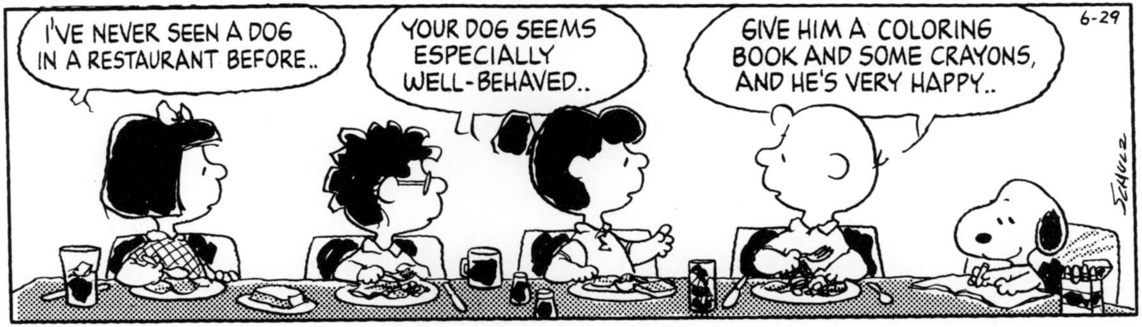
I'VE NEVER SEEN A DOG IN A RESTAURANT BEFORE..
YOUR DOG SEEMS ESPECIALLY WELL-BEHAVED..
GIVE HIM A COLORING BOOK AND SOME CRAYONS, AND HE'S VERY HAPPY..
6-29
SCHULZ

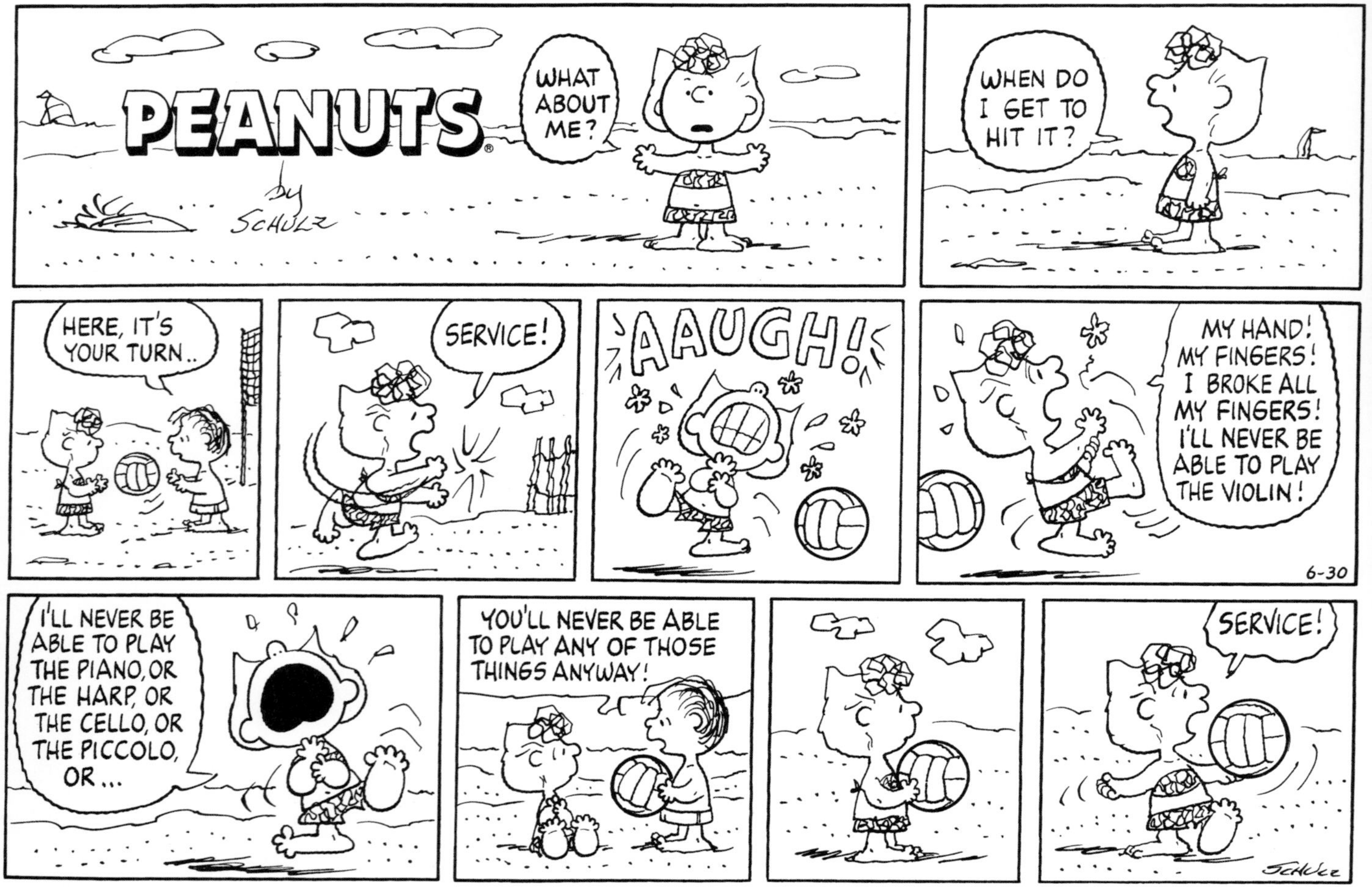
PEANUTS®
by SCHULZ
WHAT ABOUT ME?
WHEN DO I GET TO HIT IT?
HERE, IT'S YOUR TURN..
SERVICE!
AAUGH!
MY HAND! MY FINGERS! I BROKE ALL MY FINGERS! I'LL NEVER BE ABLE TO PLAY THE VIOLIN!
6-30
I'LL NEVER BE ABLE TO PLAY THE PIANO, OR THE HARP, OR THE CELLO, OR THE PICCOLO, OR...
YOU'LL NEVER BE ABLE TO PLAY ANY OF THOSE THINGS ANYWAY!
SERVICE!
SCHULZ

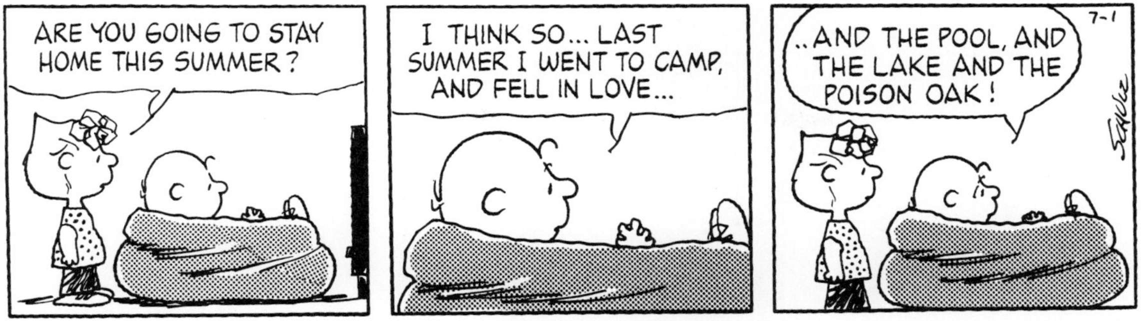
ARE YOU GOING TO STAY HOME THIS SUMMER?
I THINK SO... LAST SUMMER I WENT TO CAMP, AND FELL IN LOVE...
..AND THE POOL, AND THE LAKE AND THE POISON OAK!
7-1
SCHULZ

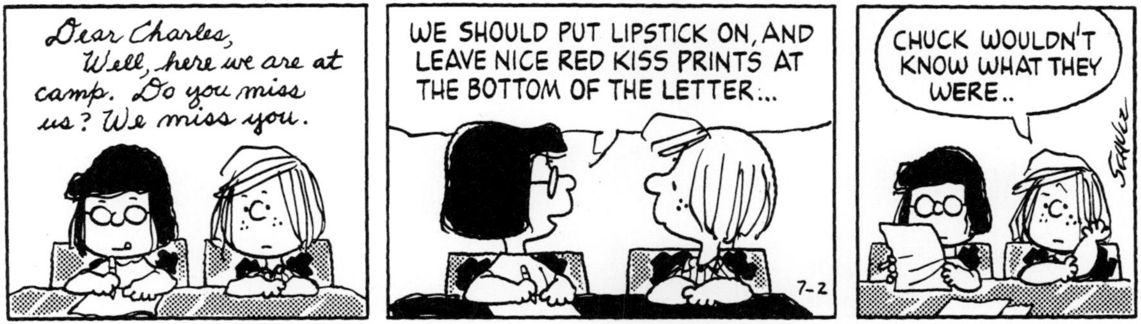
Dear Charles,
Well, here we are at camp. Do you miss us? We miss you.
WE SHOULD PUT LIPSTICK ON, AND LEAVE NICE RED KISS PRINTS AT THE BOTTOM OF THE LETTER...
7-2
CHUCK WOULDN'T KNOW WHAT THEY WERE..
SCHULZ

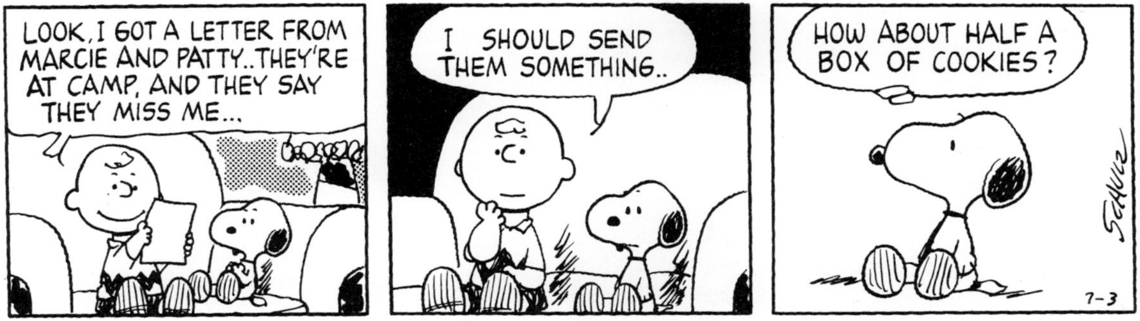
LOOK, I GOT A LETTER FROM MARCIE AND PATTY..THEY'RE AT CAMP, AND THEY SAY THEY MISS ME...
I SHOULD SEND THEM SOMETHING..
HOW ABOUT HALF A BOX OF COOKIES?
SCHULZ
7-3

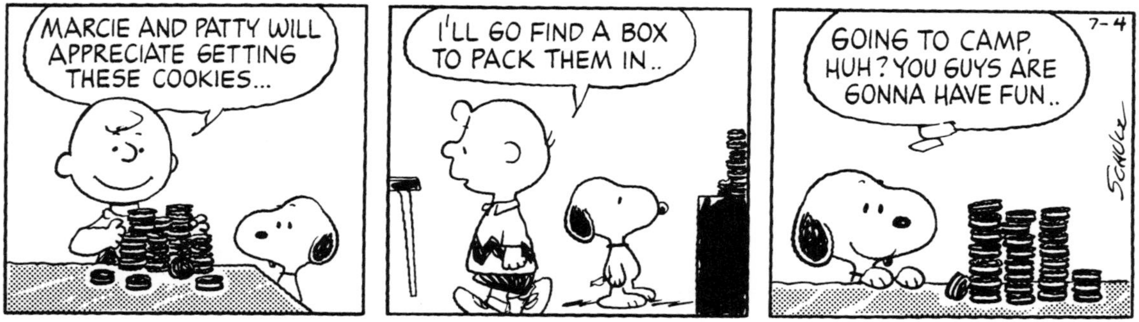
MARCIE AND PATTY WILL APPRECIATE GETTING THESE COOKIES...
I'LL GO FIND A BOX TO PACK THEM IN..
7-4
GOING TO CAMP, HUH? YOU GUYS ARE GONNA HAVE FUN..

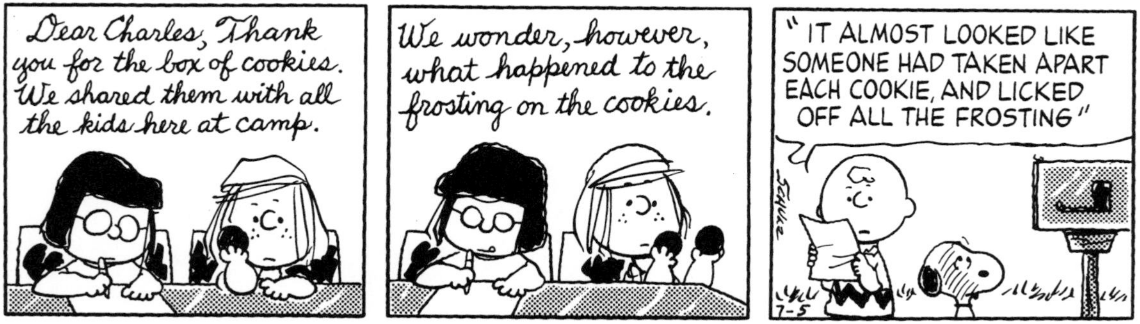
Dear Charles, Thank you for the box of cookies. We shared them with all the kids here at camp.
We wonder, however, what happened to the frosting on the cookies.
" IT ALMOST LOOKED LIKE SOMEONE HAD TAKEN APART EACH COOKIE, AND LICKED OFF ALL THE FROSTING"
7-5

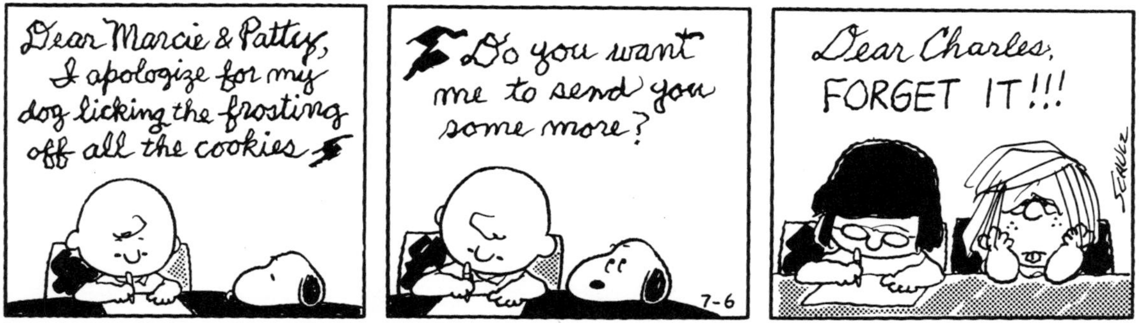
Dear Marcie & Patty, I apologize for my dog licking the frosting off all the cookies
Do you want me to send you some more?
7-6
Dear Charles, FORGET IT!!!

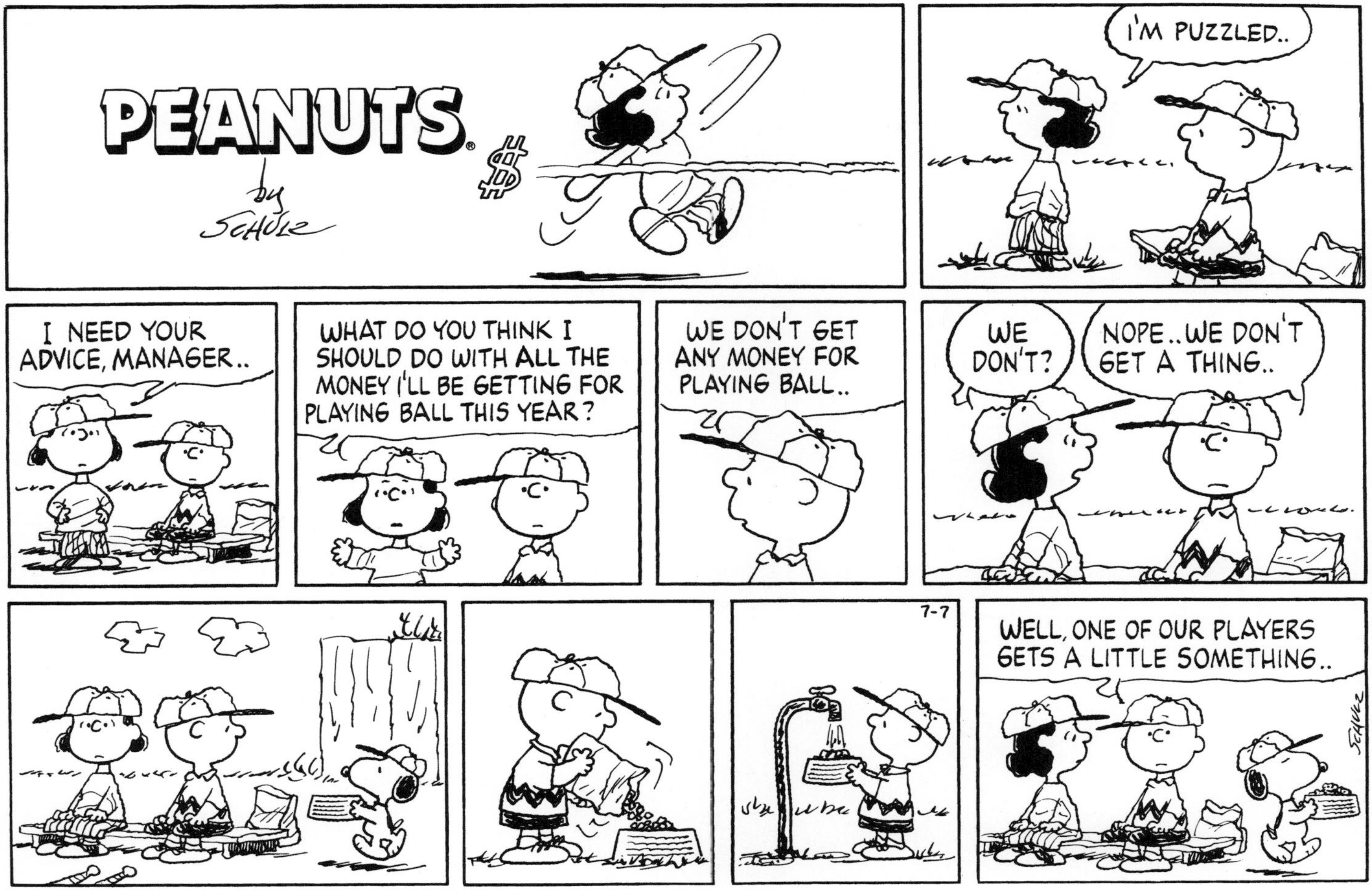
PEANUTS
by SCHULZ
I'M PUZZLED..
I NEED YOUR ADVICE, MANAGER..
WHAT DO YOU THINK I SHOULD DO WITH ALL THE MONEY I'LL BE GETTING FOR PLAYING BALL THIS YEAR?
WE DON'T GET ANY MONEY FOR PLAYING BALL..
WE DON'T?
NOPE..WE DON'T GET A THING..
7-7
WELL, ONE OF OUR PLAYERS GETS A LITTLE SOMETHING..
SCHULZ

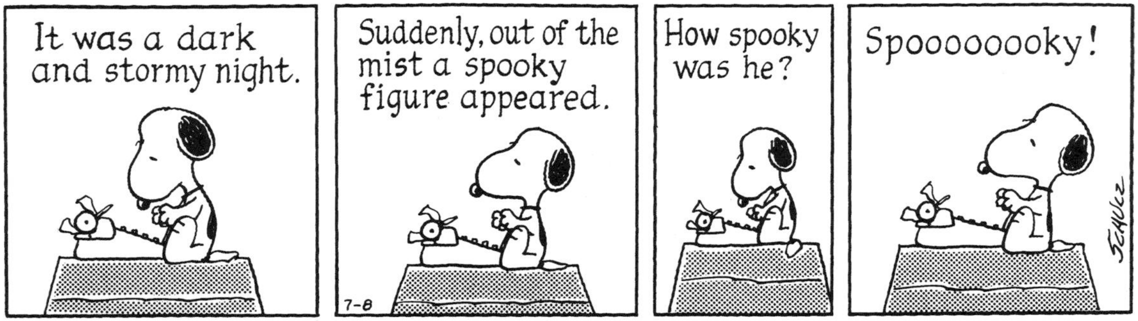
It was a dark and stormy night.
Suddenly, out of the mist a spooky figure appeared.
7-8
How spooky was he?
Spoooooooky!

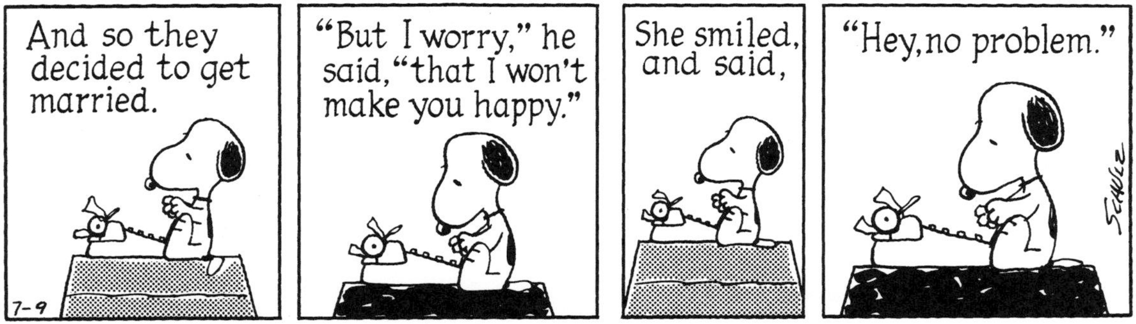
And so they decided to get married.
7-9
"But I worry," he said, "that I won't make you happy."
She smiled, and said,
"Hey, no problem."

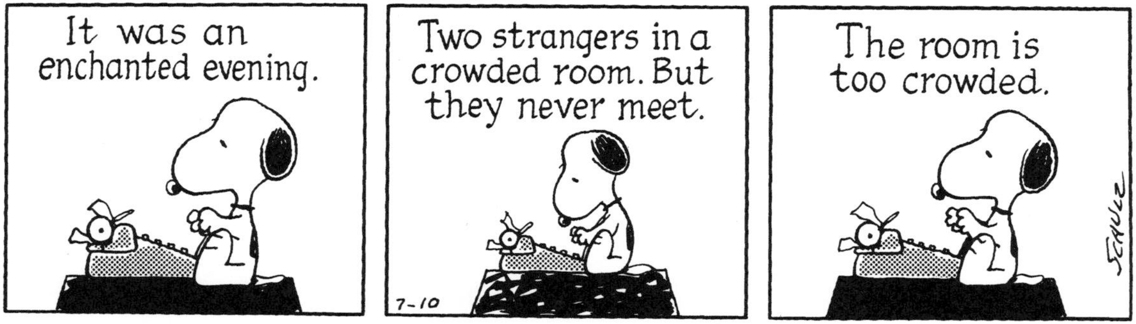
It was an enchanted evening.
Two strangers in a crowded room. But they never meet.
7-10
The room is too crowded.

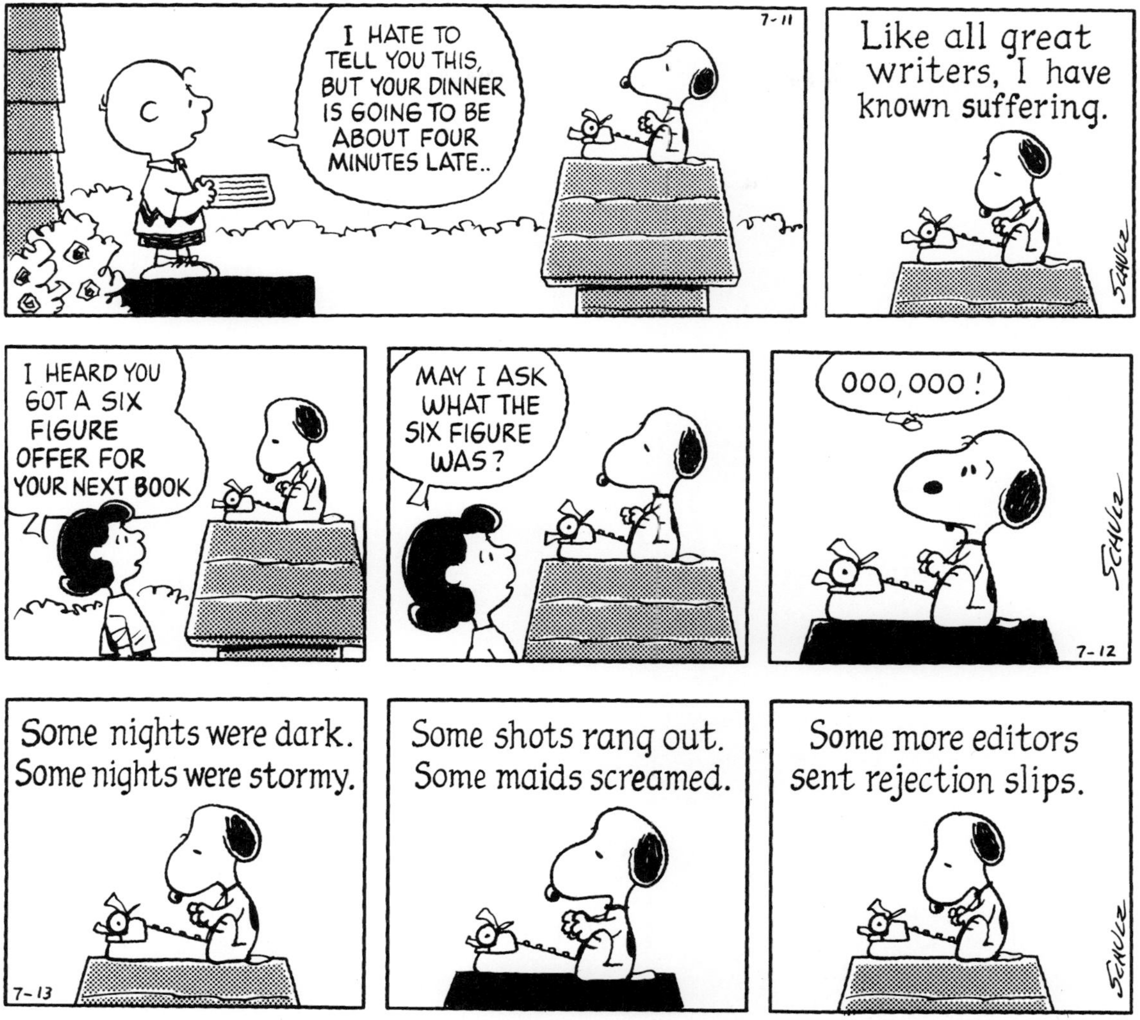
7-11
I HATE TO TELL YOU THIS, BUT YOUR DINNER IS GOING TO BE ABOUT FOUR MINUTES LATE..
Like all great writers, I have known suffering.
SCHULZ
I HEARD YOU GOT A SIX FIGURE OFFER FOR YOUR NEXT BOOK
MAY I ASK WHAT THE SIX FIGURE WAS?
000,000!
SCHULZ
7-12
Some nights were dark. Some nights were stormy.
7-13
Some shots rang out. Some maids screamed.
Some more editors sent rejection slips.
SCHULZ

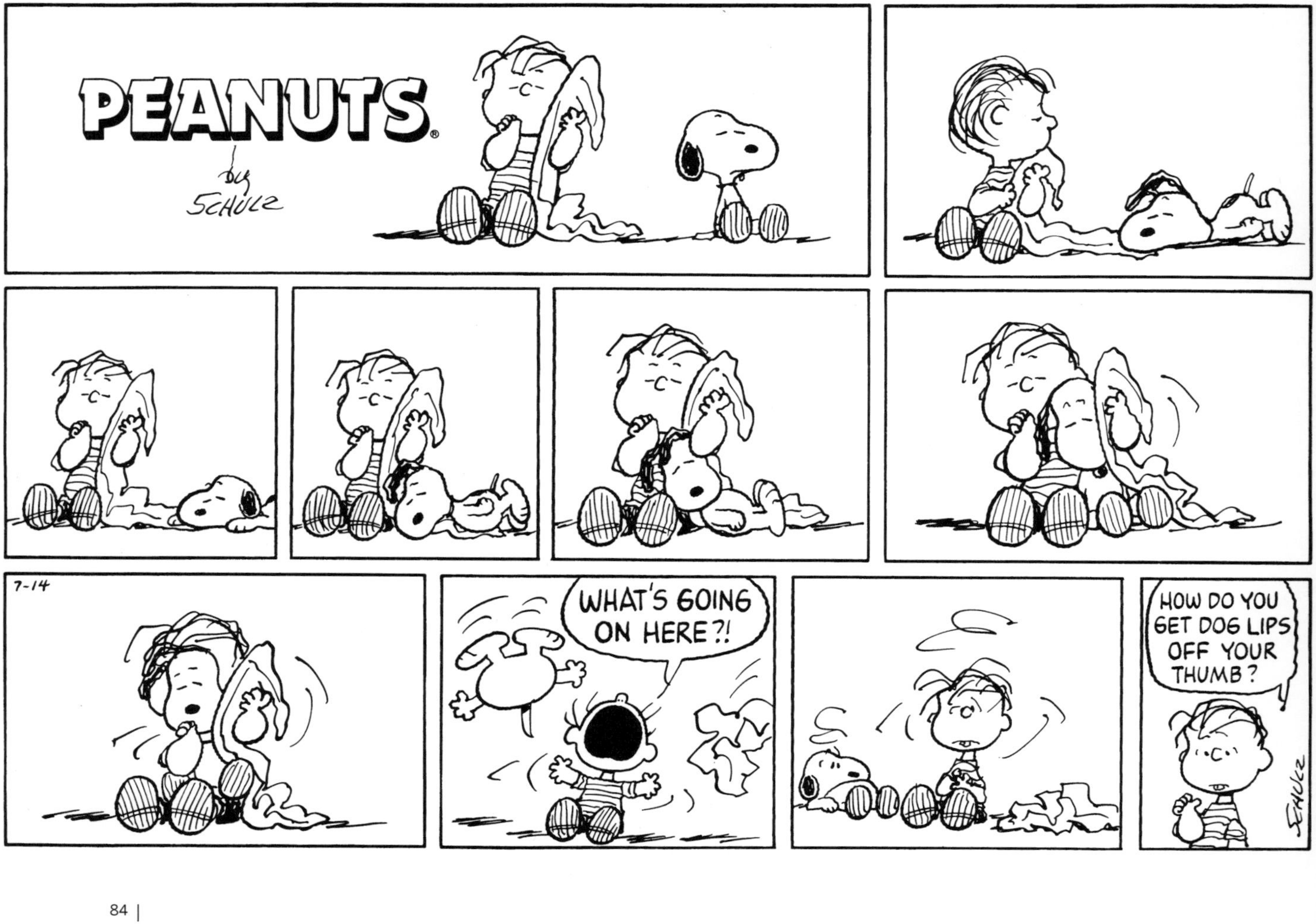
PEANUTS
SCHULZ
7-14
WHAT'S GOING ON HERE?!
HOW DO YOU GET DOG LIPS OFF YOUR THUMB?
SCHULZ

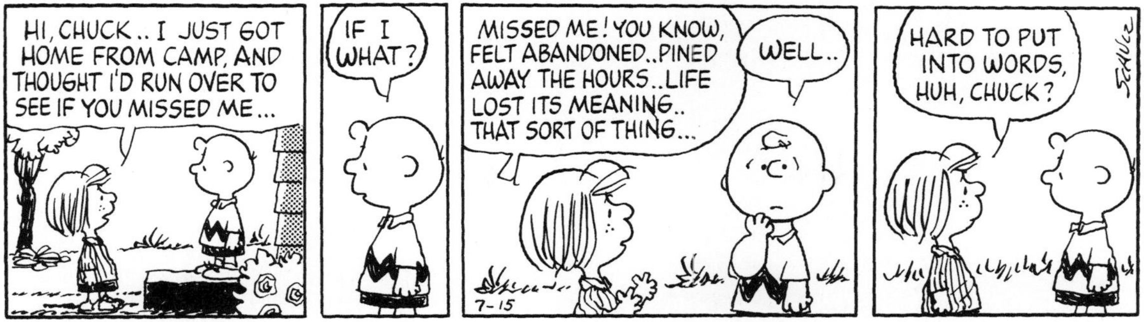
HI, CHUCK.. I JUST GOT HOME FROM CAMP, AND THOUGHT I'D RUN OVER TO SEE IF YOU MISSED ME...
IF I WHAT?
MISSED ME! YOU KNOW, FELT ABANDONED..PINED AWAY THE HOURS..LIFE LOST ITS MEANING.. THAT SORT OF THING...
WELL..
7-15
HARD TO PUT INTO WORDS, HUH, CHUCK?

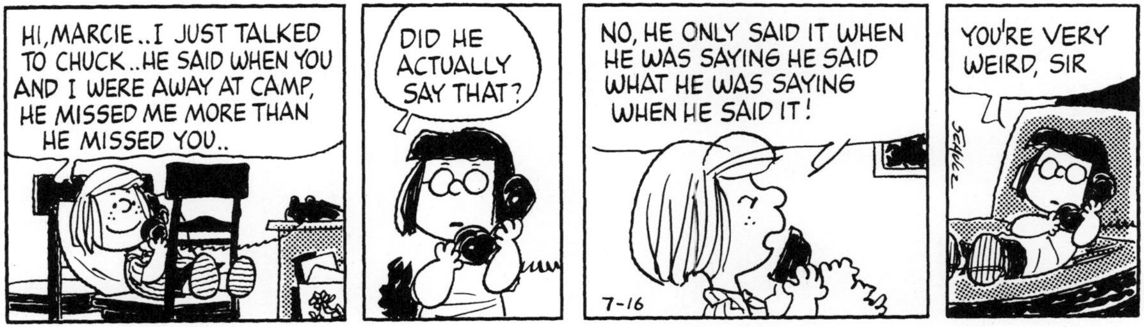
HI, MARCIE..I JUST TALKED TO CHUCK..HE SAID WHEN YOU AND I WERE AWAY AT CAMP, HE MISSED ME MORE THAN HE MISSED YOU..
DID HE ACTUALLY SAY THAT?
NO, HE ONLY SAID IT WHEN HE WAS SAYING HE SAID WHAT HE WAS SAYING WHEN HE SAID IT!
7-16
YOU'RE VERY WEIRD, SIR

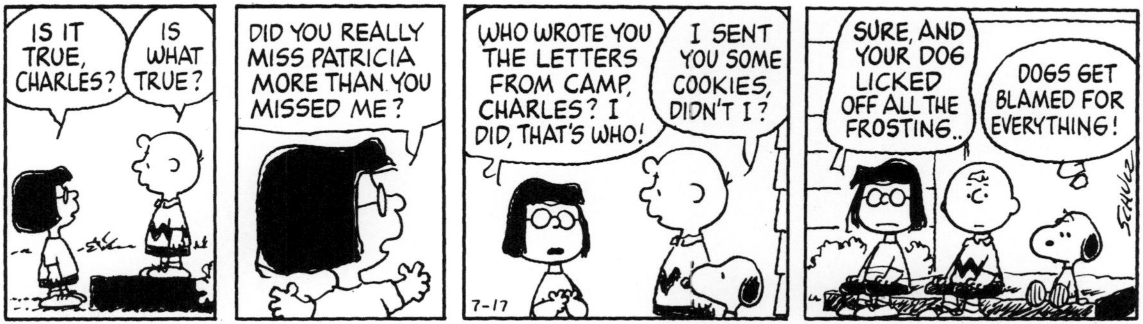
IS IT TRUE, CHARLES?
IS WHAT TRUE?
DID YOU REALLY MISS PATRICIA MORE THAN YOU MISSED ME?
WHO WROTE YOU THE LETTERS FROM CAMP, CHARLES? I DID, THAT'S WHO!
I SENT YOU SOME COOKIES, DIDN'T I?
7-17
SURE, AND YOUR DOG LICKED OFF ALL THE FROSTING..
DOGS GET BLAMED FOR EVERYTHING!

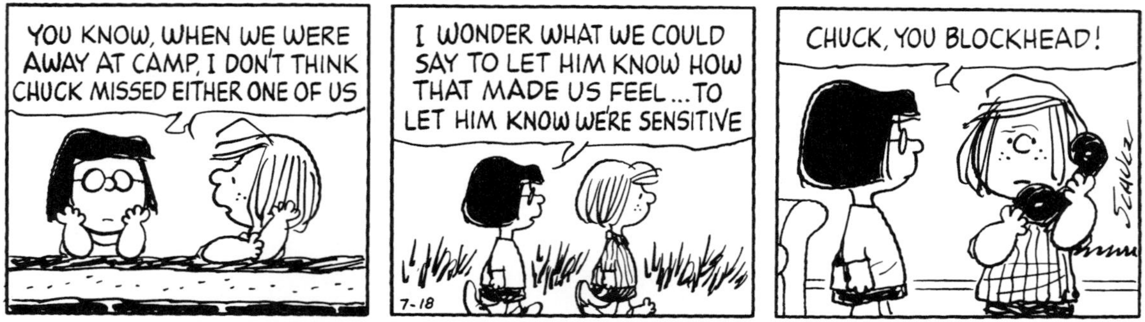
YOU KNOW, WHEN WE WERE AWAY AT CAMP, I DON'T THINK CHUCK MISSED EITHER ONE OF US
I WONDER WHAT WE COULD SAY TO LET HIM KNOW HOW THAT MADE US FEEL...TO LET HIM KNOW WE'RE SENSITIVE
7-18
CHUCK, YOU BLOCKHEAD!
SCHULZ

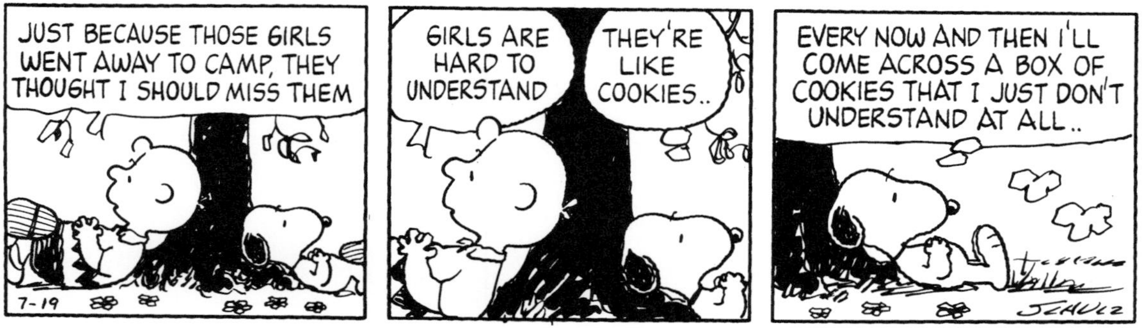
JUST BECAUSE THOSE GIRLS WENT AWAY TO CAMP, THEY THOUGHT I SHOULD MISS THEM
7-19
GIRLS ARE HARD TO UNDERSTAND
THEY'RE LIKE COOKIES..
EVERY NOW AND THEN I'LL COME ACROSS A BOX OF COOKIES THAT I JUST DON'T UNDERSTAND AT ALL..
SCHULZ

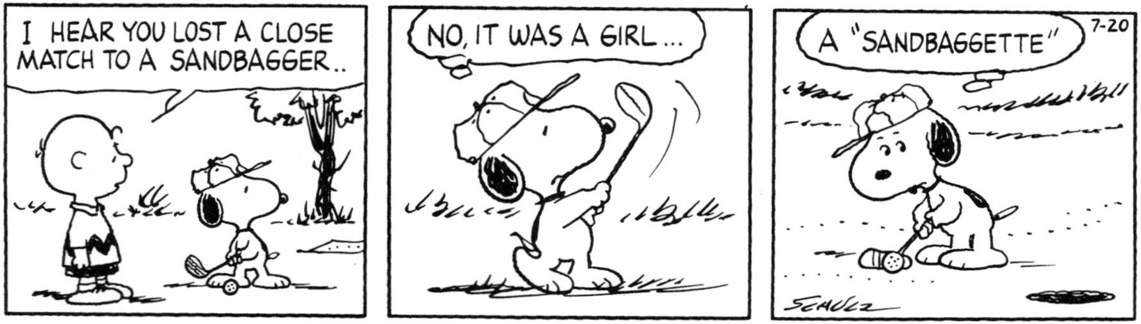
I HEAR YOU LOST A CLOSE MATCH TO A SANDBAGGER..
NO, IT WAS A GIRL...
A "SANDBAGGETTE"
7-20
SCHULZ

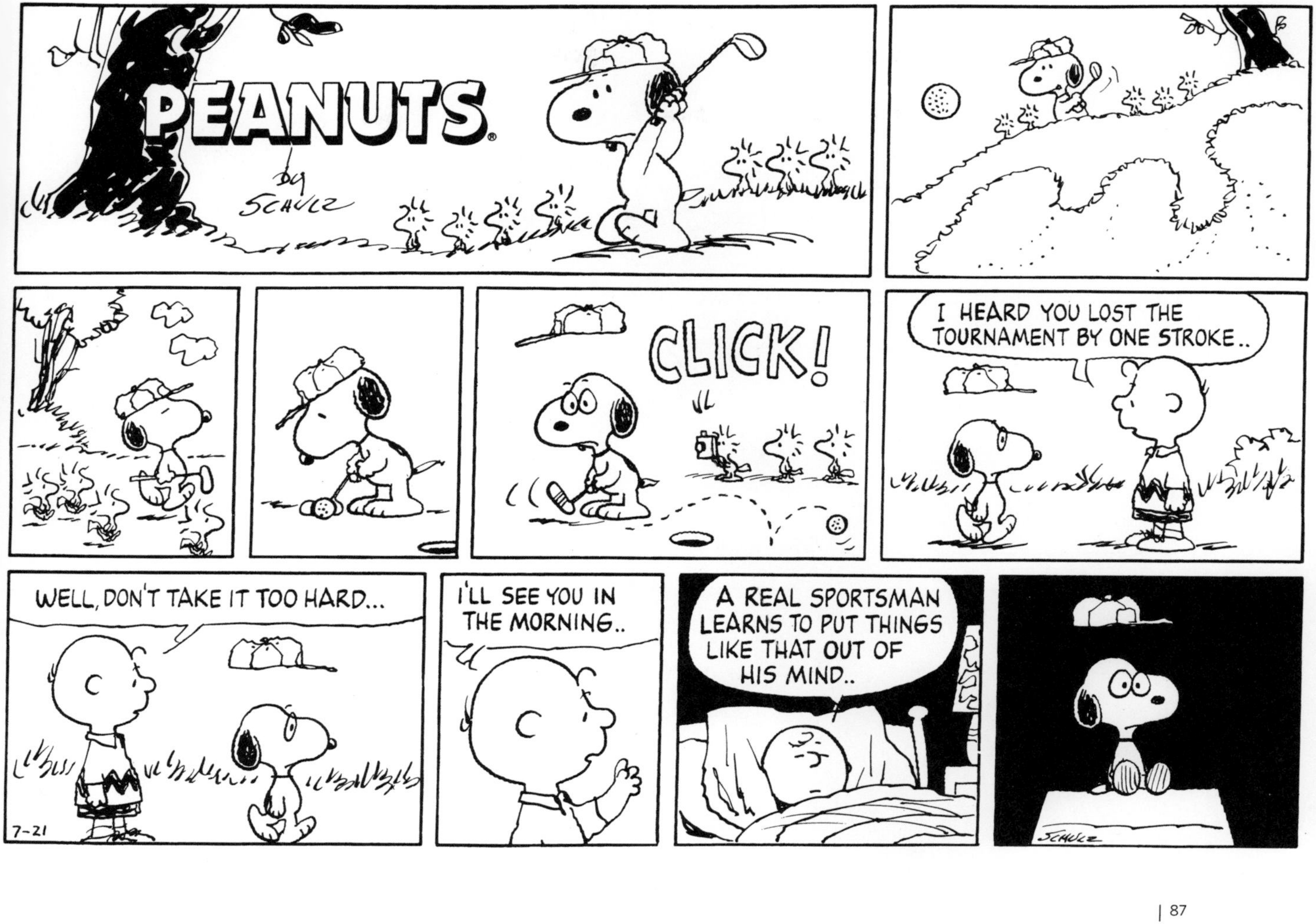
PEANUTS
by SCHULZ
CLICK!
I HEARD YOU LOST THE TOURNAMENT BY ONE STROKE..
WELL, DON'T TAKE IT TOO HARD...
I'LL SEE YOU IN THE MORNING..
A REAL SPORTSMAN LEARNS TO PUT THINGS LIKE THAT OUT OF HIS MIND..
7-21
SCHULZ

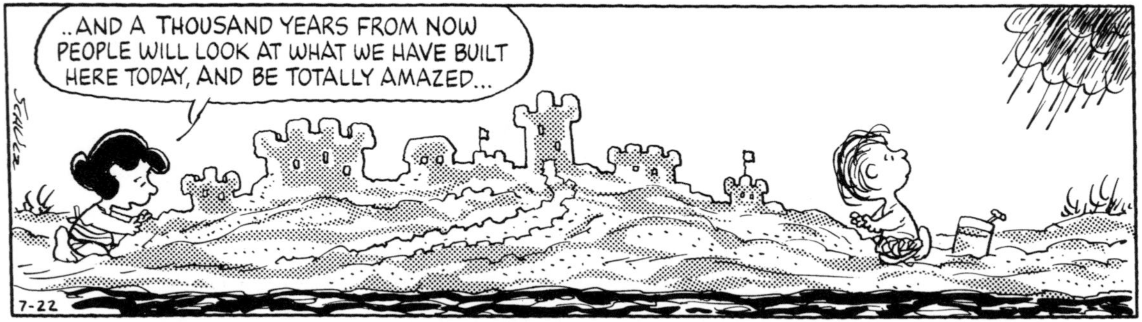
..AND A THOUSAND YEARS FROM NOW PEOPLE WILL LOOK AT WHAT WE HAVE BUILT HERE TODAY, AND BE TOTALLY AMAZED...
7-22

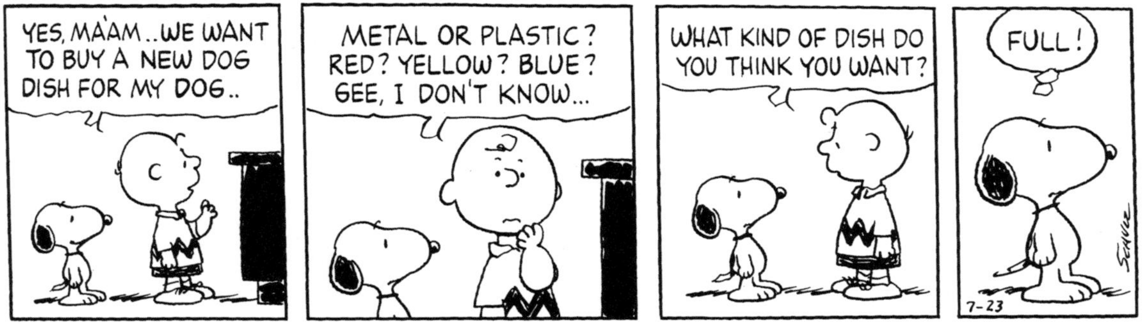
YES, MA'AM..WE WANT TO BUY A NEW DOG DISH FOR MY DOG..
METAL OR PLASTIC? RED? YELLOW? BLUE? GEE, I DON'T KNOW...
WHAT KIND OF DISH DO YOU THINK YOU WANT?
FULL!
7-23

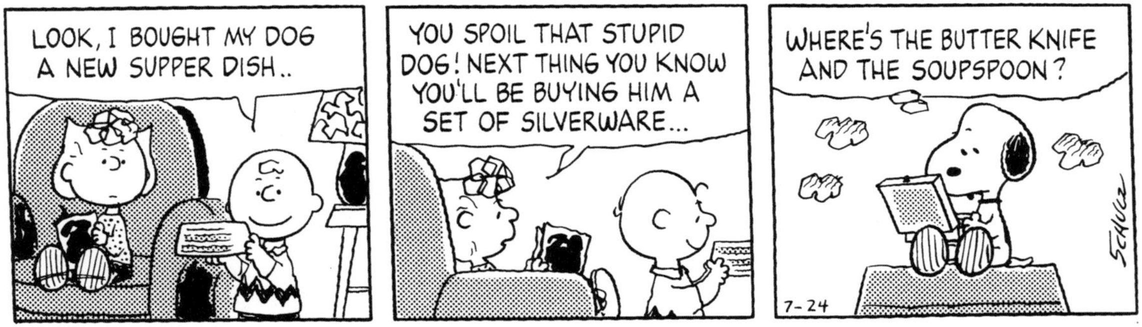
LOOK, I BOUGHT MY DOG A NEW SUPPER DISH..
YOU SPOIL THAT STUPID DOG! NEXT THING YOU KNOW YOU'LL BE BUYING HIM A SET OF SILVERWARE...
WHERE'S THE BUTTER KNIFE AND THE SOUPSPOON?
7-24

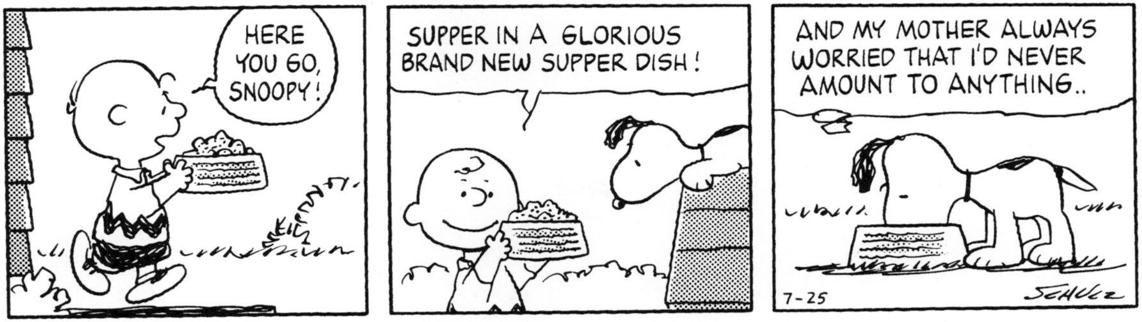
HERE YOU GO, SNOOPY!
SUPPER IN A GLORIOUS BRAND NEW SUPPER DISH!
AND MY MOTHER ALWAYS WORRIED THAT I'D NEVER AMOUNT TO ANYTHING..
7-25

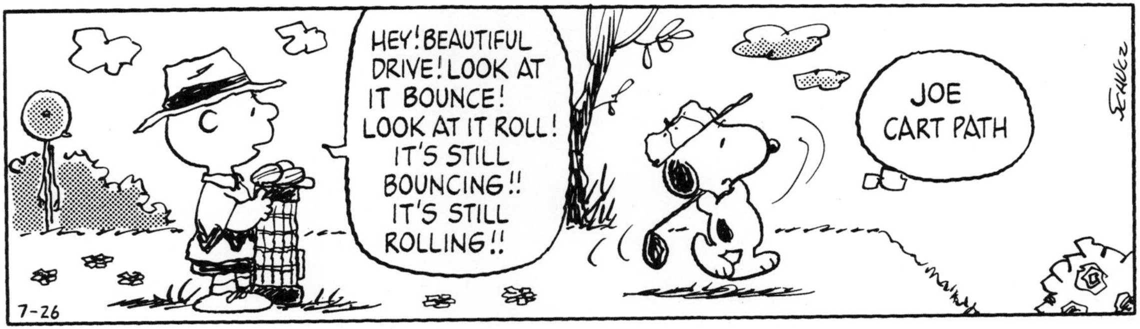
HEY! BEAUTIFUL DRIVE! LOOK AT IT BOUNCE! LOOK AT IT ROLL! IT'S STILL BOUNCING!! IT'S STILL ROLLING!!
JOE CART PATH
7-26

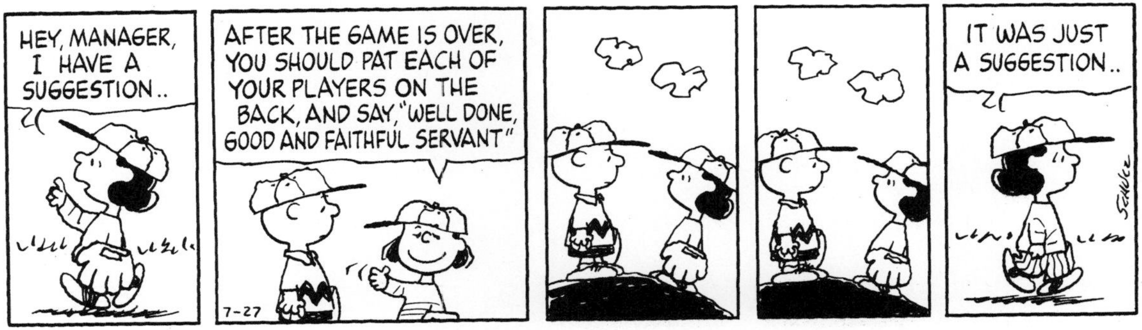
HEY, MANAGER, I HAVE A SUGGESTION..
AFTER THE GAME IS OVER, YOU SHOULD PAT EACH OF YOUR PLAYERS ON THE BACK, AND SAY, "WELL DONE, GOOD AND FAITHFUL SERVANT"
IT WAS JUST A SUGGESTION..
7-27

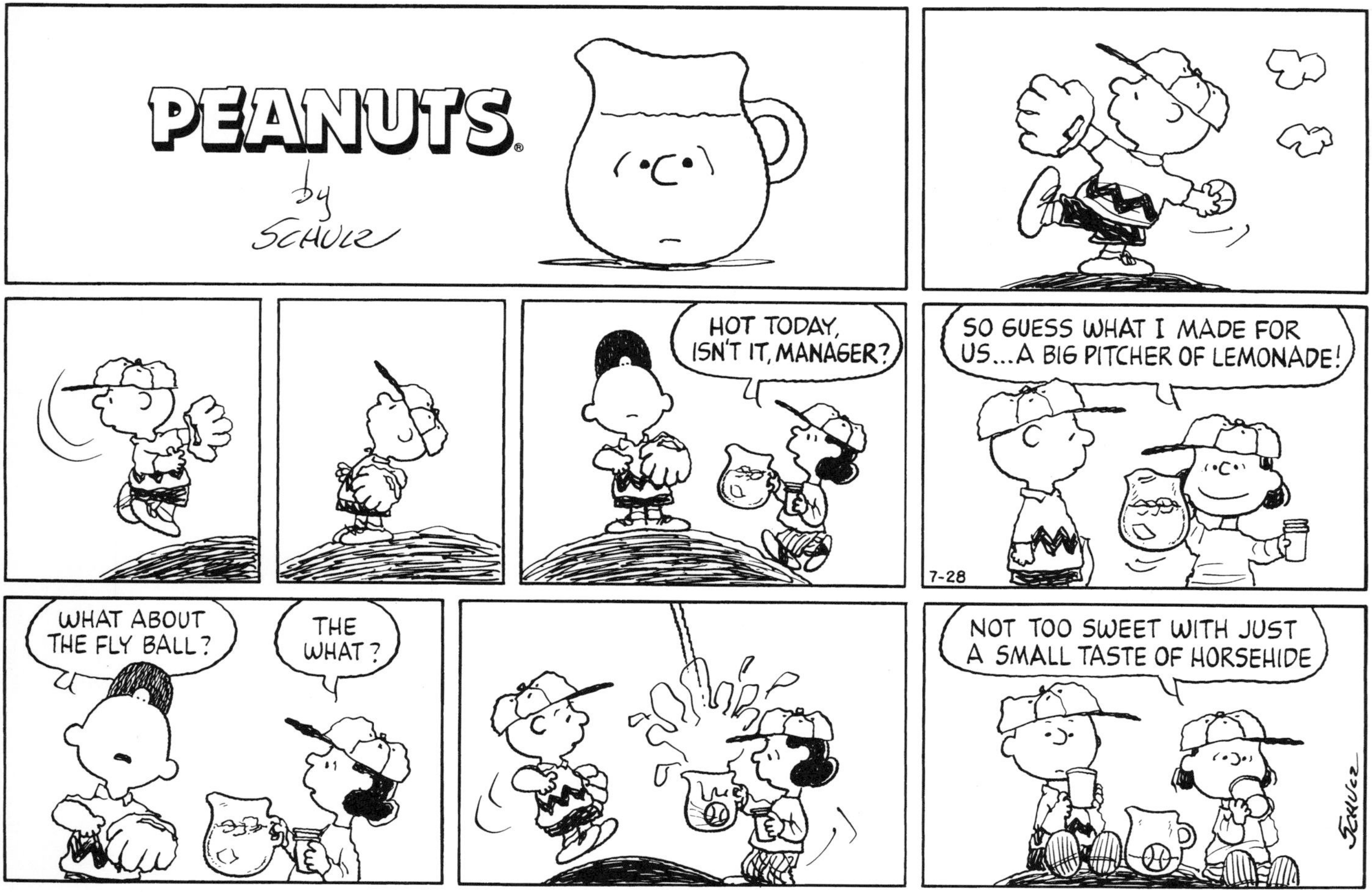
PEANUTS
by SCHULZ
HOT TODAY, ISN'T IT, MANAGER?
SO GUESS WHAT I MADE FOR US... A BIG PITCHER OF LEMONADE!
7-28
WHAT ABOUT THE FLY BALL?
THE WHAT?
NOT TOO SWEET WITH JUST A SMALL TASTE OF HORSEHIDE
SCHULZ

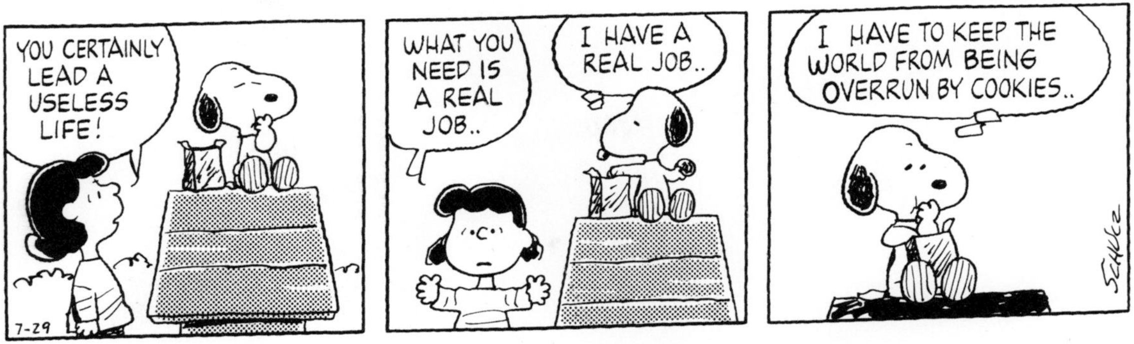
YOU CERTAINLY LEAD A USELESS LIFE!
WHAT YOU NEED IS A REAL JOB..
I HAVE A REAL JOB..
I HAVE TO KEEP THE WORLD FROM BEING OVERRUN BY COOKIES..
7-29
SCHULZ

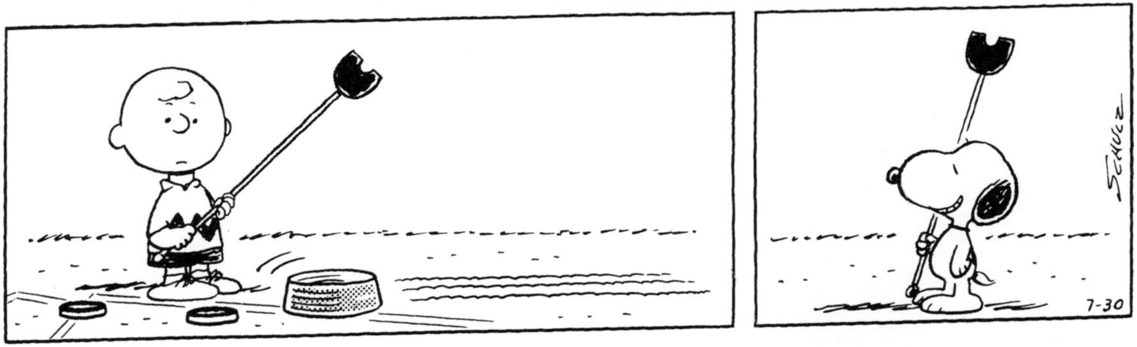
SCHULZ
7-30

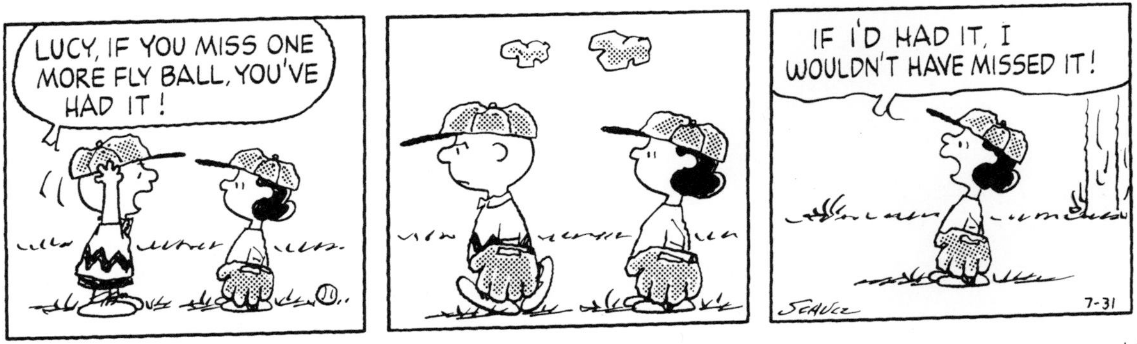
LUCY, IF YOU MISS ONE MORE FLY BALL, YOU'VE HAD IT!
IF I'D HAD IT, I WOULDN'T HAVE MISSED IT!
SCHULZ
7-31

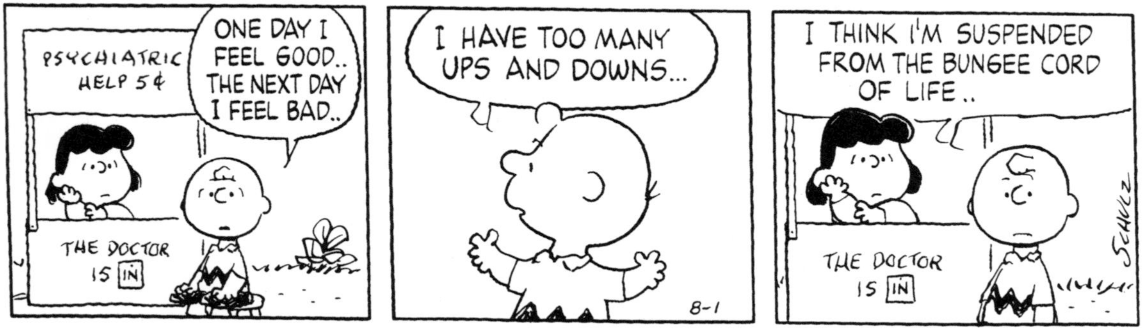
PSYCHIATRIC HELP 5¢
THE DOCTOR IS IN
ONE DAY I FEEL GOOD.. THE NEXT DAY I FEEL BAD..
I HAVE TOO MANY UPS AND DOWNS...
8-1
I THINK I'M SUSPENDED FROM THE BUNGEE CORD OF LIFE..
THE DOCTOR IS IN
SCHULZ

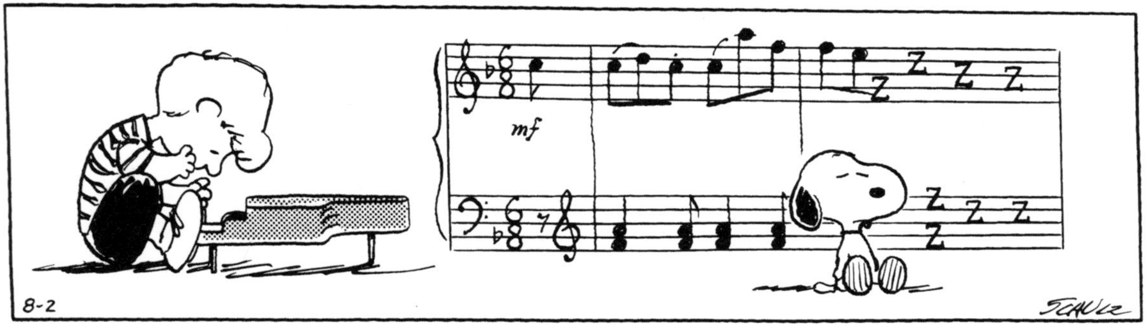
mf
8-2
SCHULZ

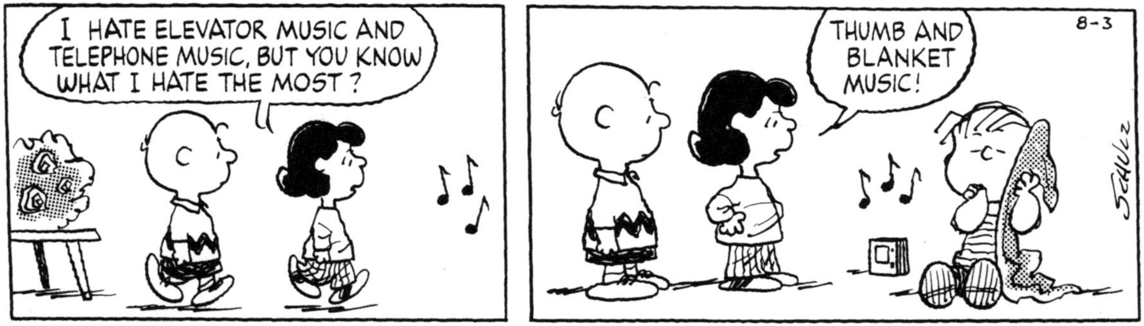
I HATE ELEVATOR MUSIC AND TELEPHONE MUSIC, BUT YOU KNOW WHAT I HATE THE MOST?
8-3
THUMB AND BLANKET MUSIC!
SCHULZ

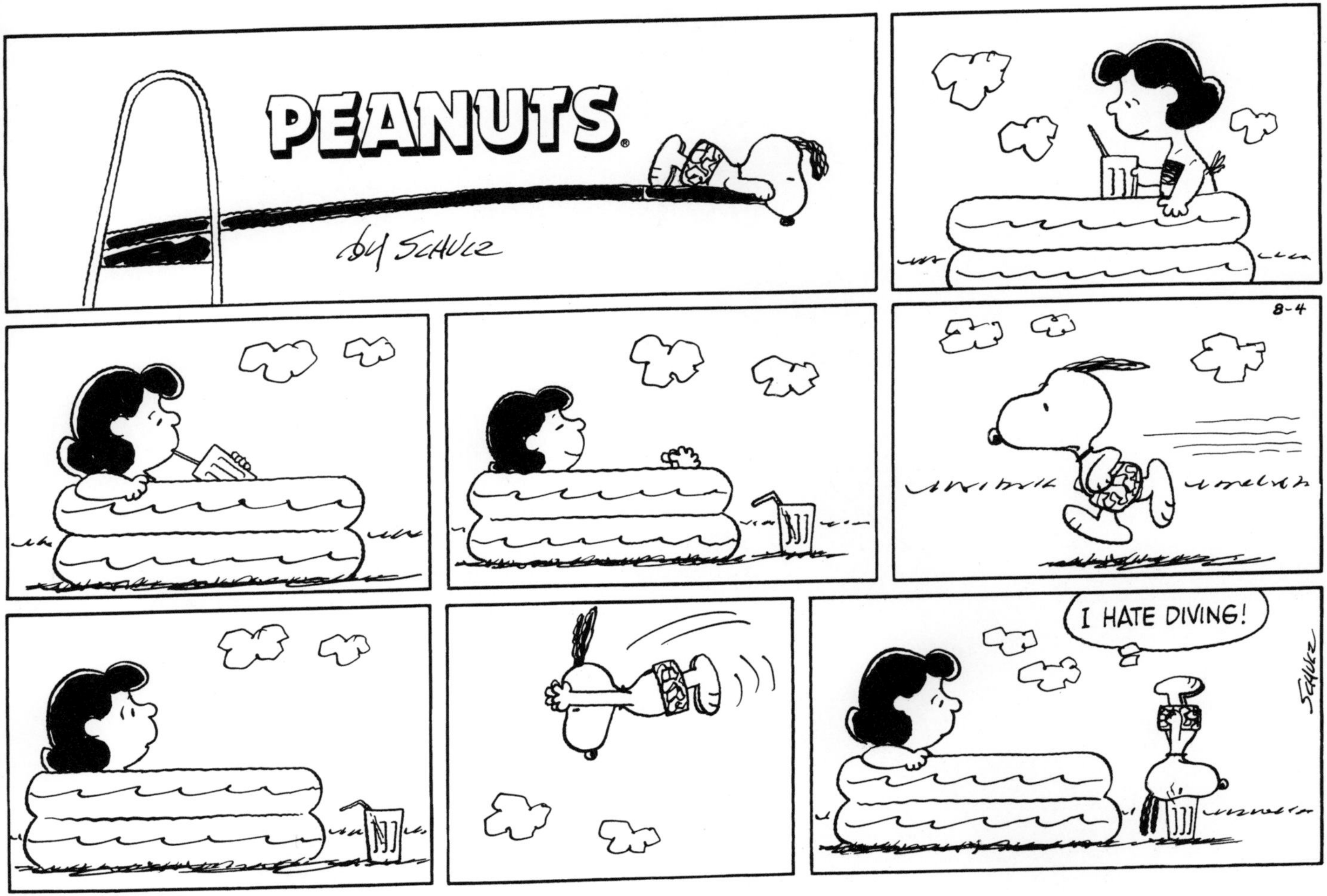
PEANUTS
by SCHULZ
8-4
I HATE DIVING!
SCHULZ

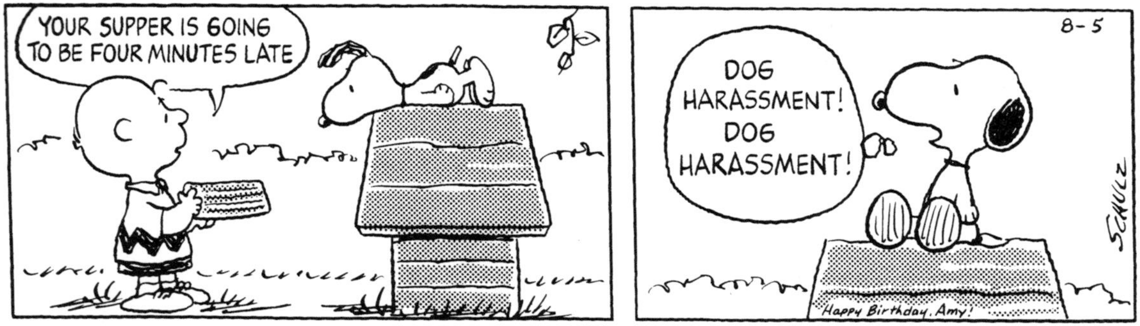
YOUR SUPPER IS GOING TO BE FOUR MINUTES LATE
DOG HARASSMENT! DOG HARASSMENT!
8-5
SCHULZ
Happy Birthday, Amy!

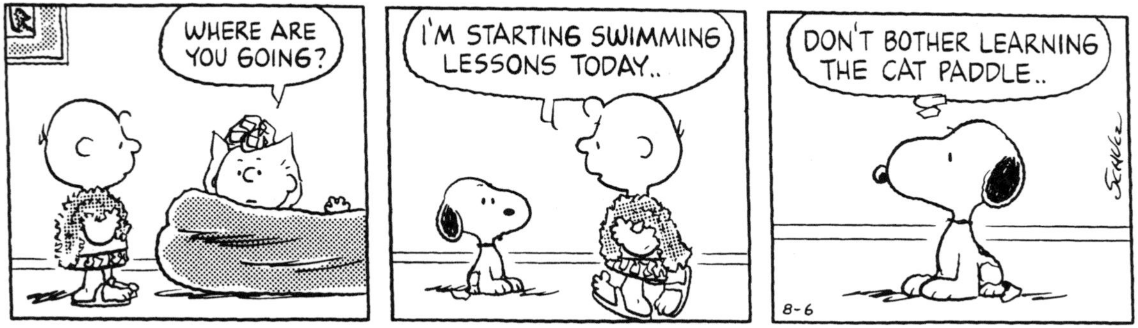
WHERE ARE YOU GOING?
I'M STARTING SWIMMING LESSONS TODAY..
DON'T BOTHER LEARNING THE CAT PADDLE..
SCHULZ
8-6

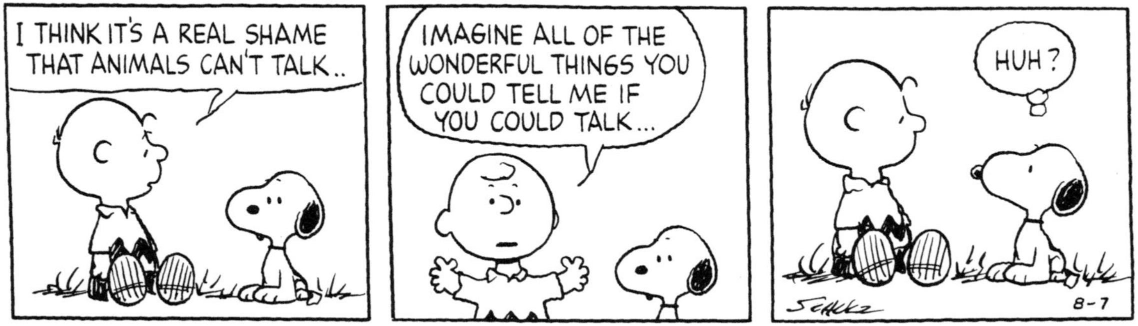
I THINK IT'S A REAL SHAME THAT ANIMALS CAN'T TALK..
IMAGINE ALL OF THE WONDERFUL THINGS YOU COULD TELL ME IF YOU COULD TALK...
HUH?
SCHULZ
8-7

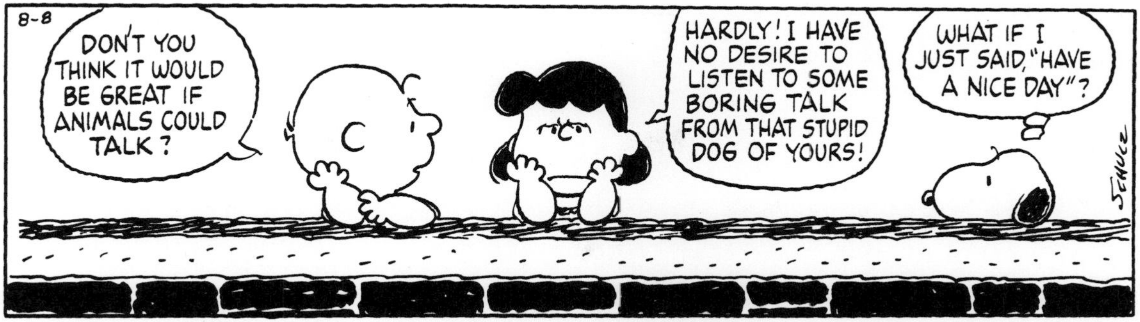
8-8
DON'T YOU THINK IT WOULD BE GREAT IF ANIMALS COULD TALK ?
HARDLY! I HAVE NO DESIRE TO LISTEN TO SOME BORING TALK FROM THAT STUPID DOG OF YOURS!
WHAT IF I JUST SAID, "HAVE A NICE DAY"?

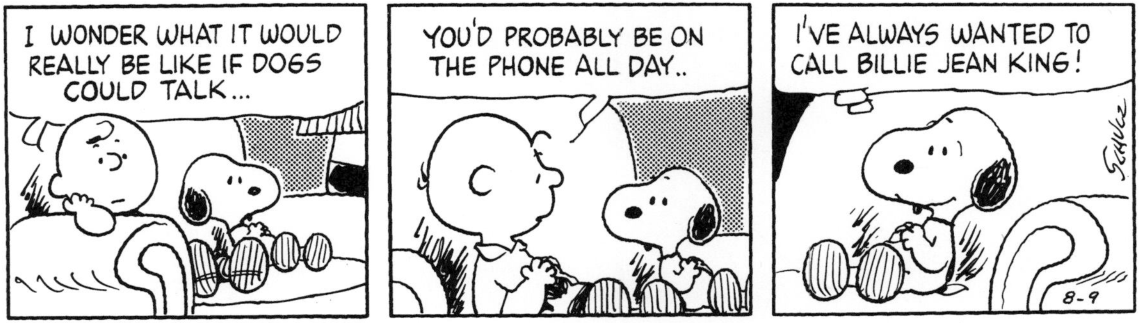
I WONDER WHAT IT WOULD REALLY BE LIKE IF DOGS COULD TALK...
YOU'D PROBABLY BE ON THE PHONE ALL DAY..
I'VE ALWAYS WANTED TO CALL BILLIE JEAN KING!
8-9

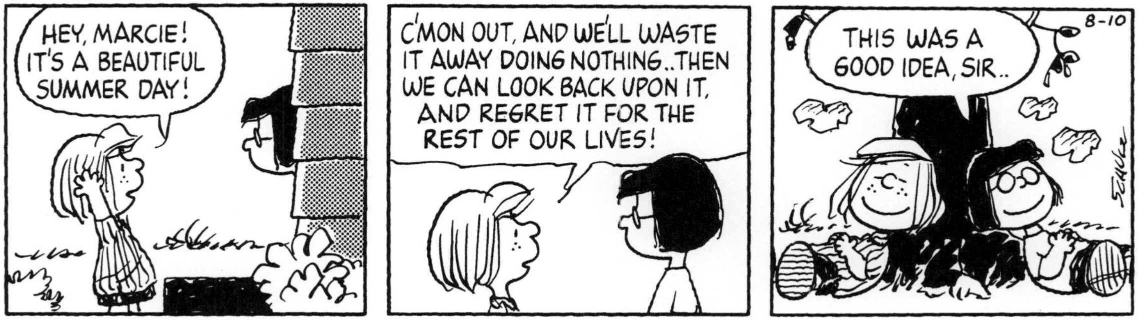
HEY, MARCIE! IT'S A BEAUTIFUL SUMMER DAY!
C'MON OUT, AND WE'LL WASTE IT AWAY DOING NOTHING..THEN WE CAN LOOK BACK UPON IT, AND REGRET IT FOR THE REST OF OUR LIVES!
8-10
THIS WAS A GOOD IDEA, SIR..

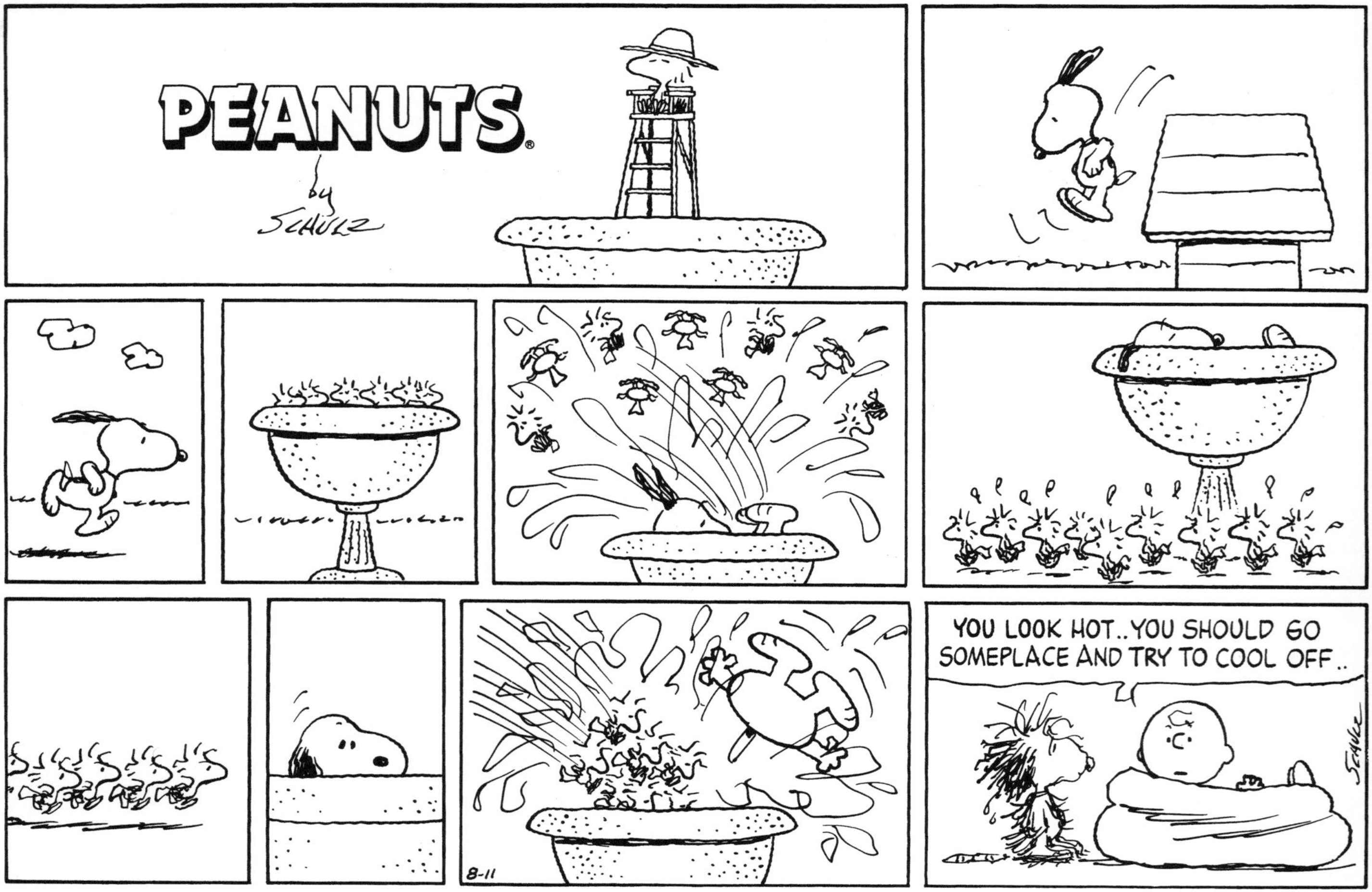
PEANUTS
by SCHULZ
8-11
YOU LOOK HOT..YOU SHOULD GO SOMEPLACE AND TRY TO COOL OFF..
SCHULZ

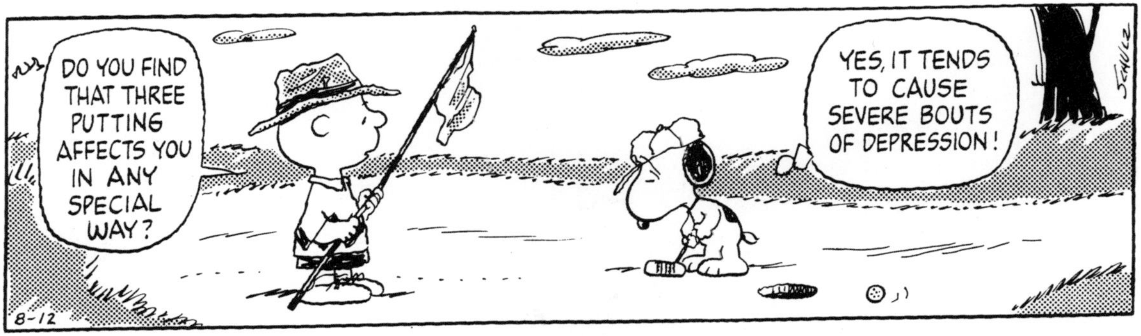
DO YOU FIND THAT THREE PUTTING AFFECTS YOU IN ANY SPECIAL WAY?
YES, IT TENDS TO CAUSE SEVERE BOUTS OF DEPRESSION!
8-12

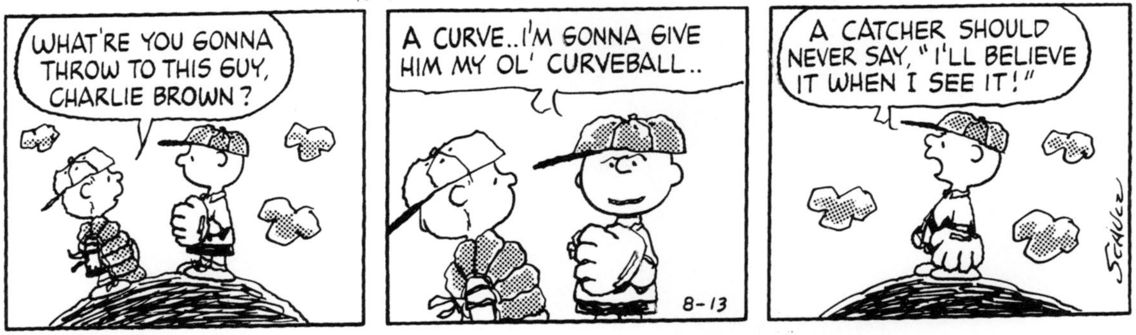
WHAT'RE YOU GONNA THROW TO THIS GUY, CHARLIE BROWN?
A CURVE..I'M GONNA GIVE HIM MY OL' CURVEBALL..
A CATCHER SHOULD NEVER SAY, "I'LL BELIEVE IT WHEN I SEE IT!"
8-13

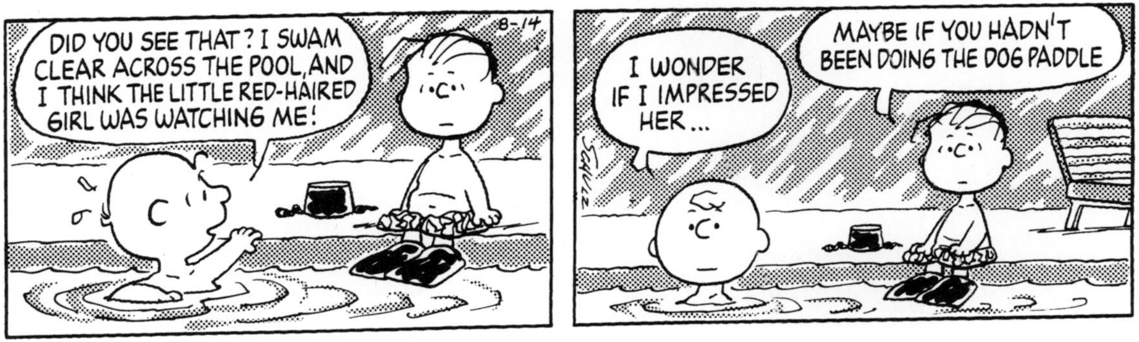
8-14
DID YOU SEE THAT? I SWAM CLEAR ACROSS THE POOL, AND I THINK THE LITTLE RED-HAIRED GIRL WAS WATCHING ME!
I WONDER IF I IMPRESSED HER...
MAYBE IF YOU HADN'T BEEN DOING THE DOG PADDLE

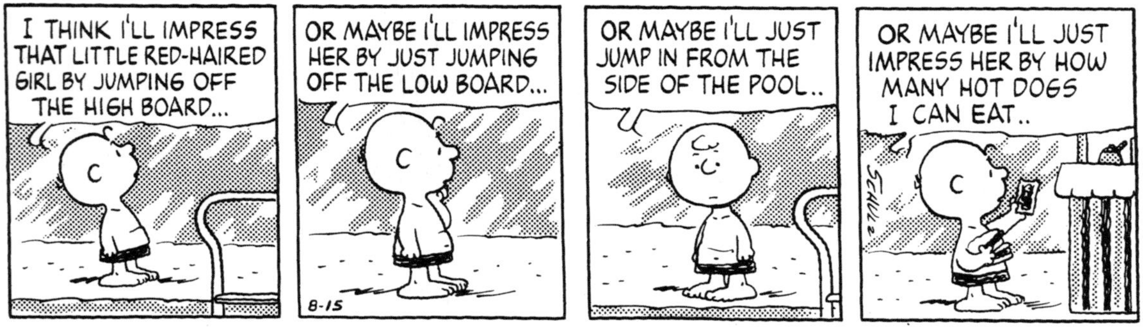
I THINK I'LL IMPRESS THAT LITTLE RED-HAIRED GIRL BY JUMPING OFF THE HIGH BOARD...
OR MAYBE I'LL IMPRESS HER BY JUST JUMPING OFF THE LOW BOARD...
8-15
OR MAYBE I'LL JUST JUMP IN FROM THE SIDE OF THE POOL..
OR MAYBE I'LL JUST IMPRESS HER BY HOW MANY HOT DOGS I CAN EAT..
SCHULZ

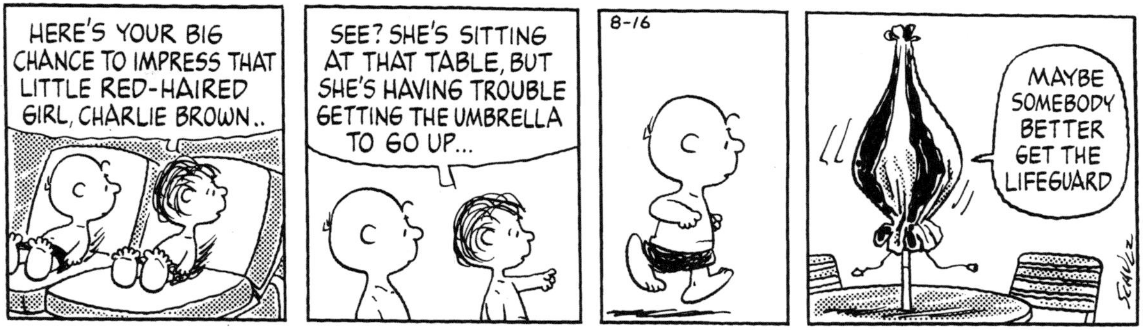
HERE'S YOUR BIG CHANCE TO IMPRESS THAT LITTLE RED-HAIRED GIRL, CHARLIE BROWN..
SEE? SHE'S SITTING AT THAT TABLE, BUT SHE'S HAVING TROUBLE GETTING THE UMBRELLA TO GO UP...
8-16
MAYBE SOMEBODY BETTER GET THE LIFEGUARD
SCHULZ

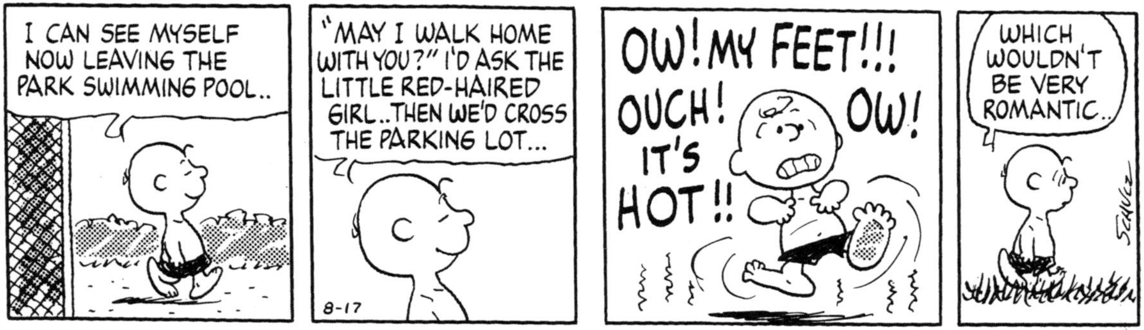
I CAN SEE MYSELF NOW LEAVING THE PARK SWIMMING POOL..
"MAY I WALK HOME WITH YOU?" I'D ASK THE LITTLE RED-HAIRED GIRL..THEN WE'D CROSS THE PARKING LOT...
8-17
OW! MY FEET!!!
OUCH!
OW!
IT'S HOT!!
WHICH WOULDN'T BE VERY ROMANTIC..
SCHULZ

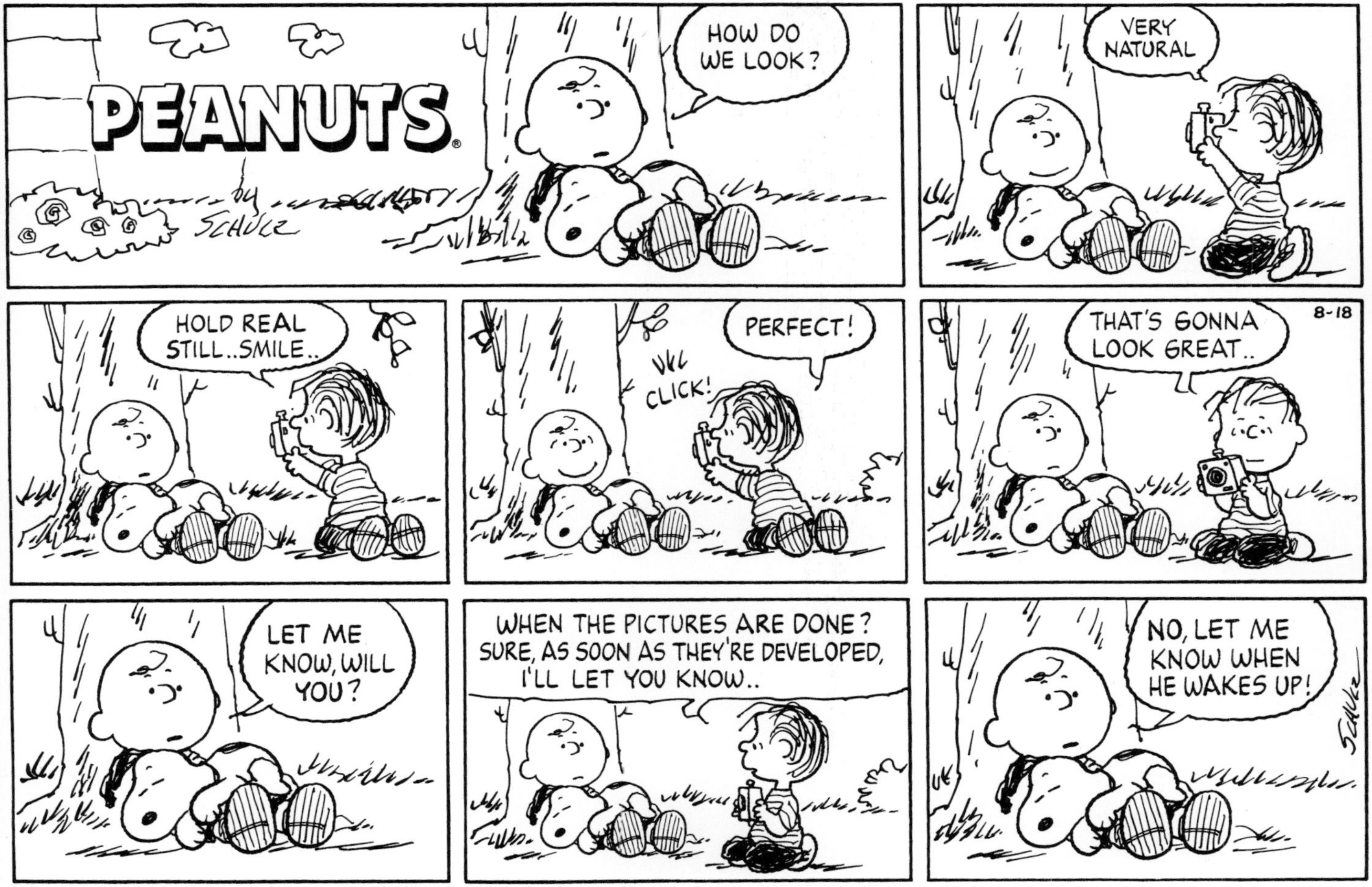
PEANUTS
by SCHULZ
HOW DO WE LOOK?
VERY NATURAL
HOLD REAL STILL..SMILE..
CLICK!
PERFECT!
8-18
THAT'S GONNA LOOK GREAT..
LET ME KNOW, WILL YOU?
WHEN THE PICTURES ARE DONE? SURE, AS SOON AS THEY'RE DEVELOPED, I'LL LET YOU KNOW..
NO, LET ME KNOW WHEN HE WAKES UP!
SCHULZ

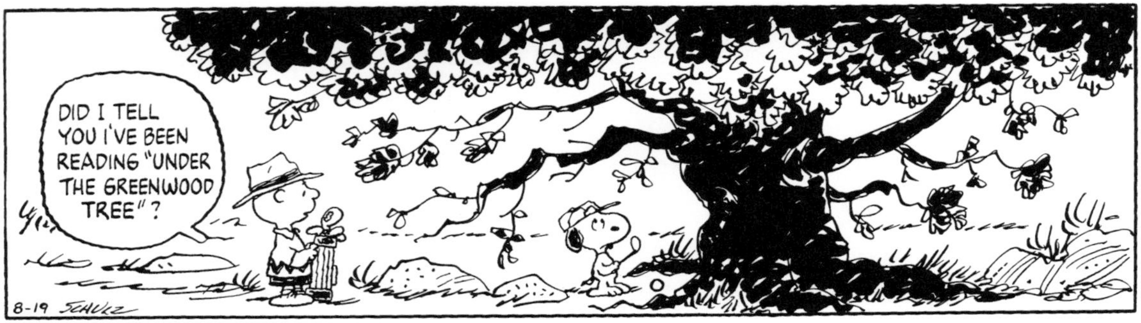
DID I TELL YOU I'VE BEEN READING "UNDER THE GREENWOOD TREE"?
8-19 SCHULZ

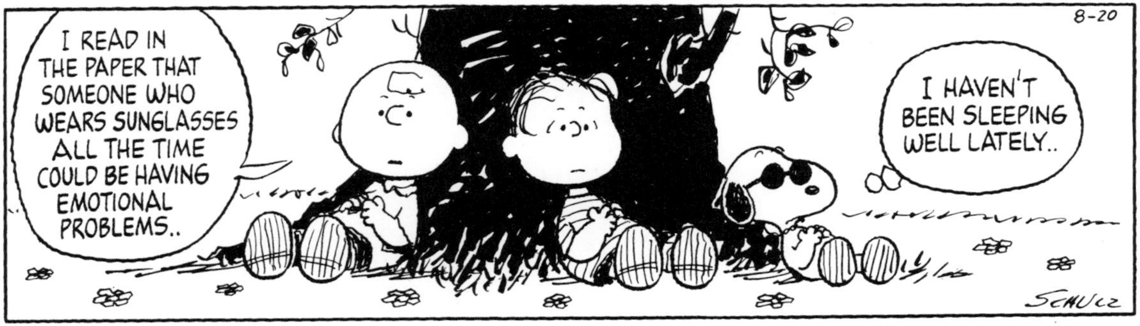
8-20
I READ IN THE PAPER THAT SOMEONE WHO WEARS SUNGLASSES ALL THE TIME COULD BE HAVING EMOTIONAL PROBLEMS..
I HAVEN'T BEEN SLEEPING WELL LATELY..
SCHULZ

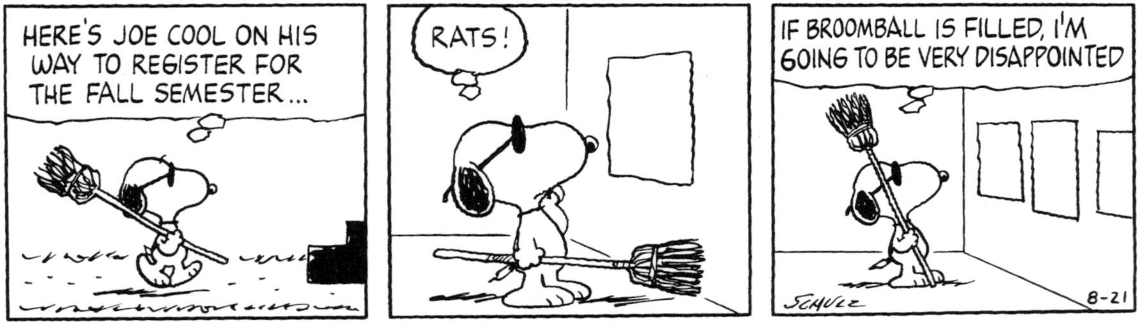
HERE'S JOE COOL ON HIS WAY TO REGISTER FOR THE FALL SEMESTER...
RATS!
IF BROOMBALL IS FILLED, I'M GOING TO BE VERY DISAPPOINTED
SCHULZ
8-21

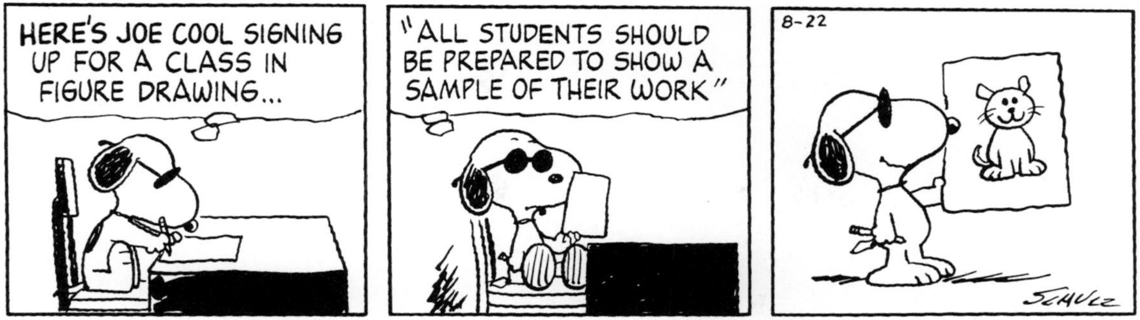
HERE'S JOE COOL SIGNING UP FOR A CLASS IN FIGURE DRAWING...
"ALL STUDENTS SHOULD BE PREPARED TO SHOW A SAMPLE OF THEIR WORK"
8-22

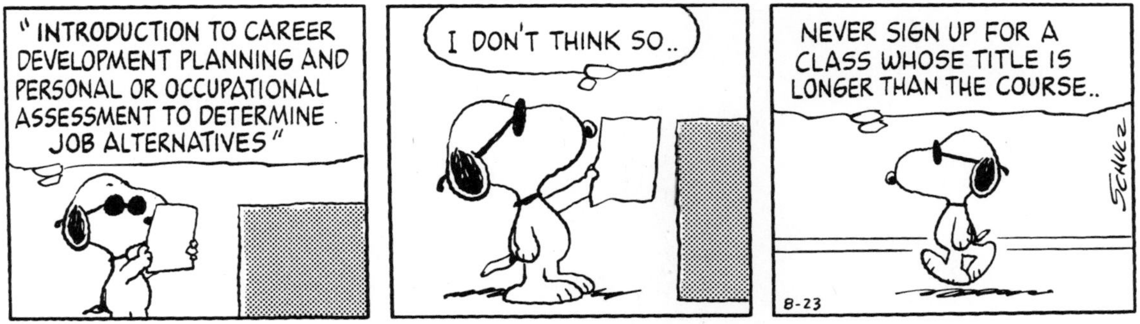
"INTRODUCTION TO CAREER DEVELOPMENT PLANNING AND PERSONAL OR OCCUPATIONAL ASSESSMENT TO DETERMINE JOB ALTERNATIVES"
I DON'T THINK SO..
NEVER SIGN UP FOR A CLASS WHOSE TITLE IS LONGER THAN THE COURSE..
8-23

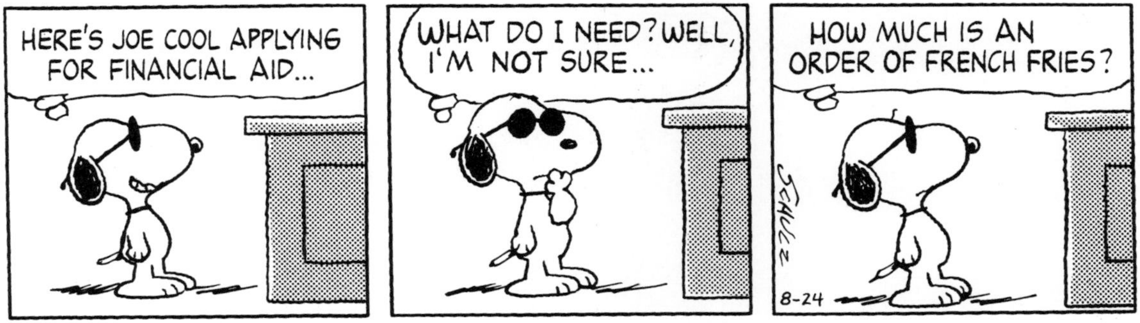
HERE'S JOE COOL APPLYING FOR FINANCIAL AID...
WHAT DO I NEED? WELL, I'M NOT SURE...
HOW MUCH IS AN ORDER OF FRENCH FRIES?
8-24

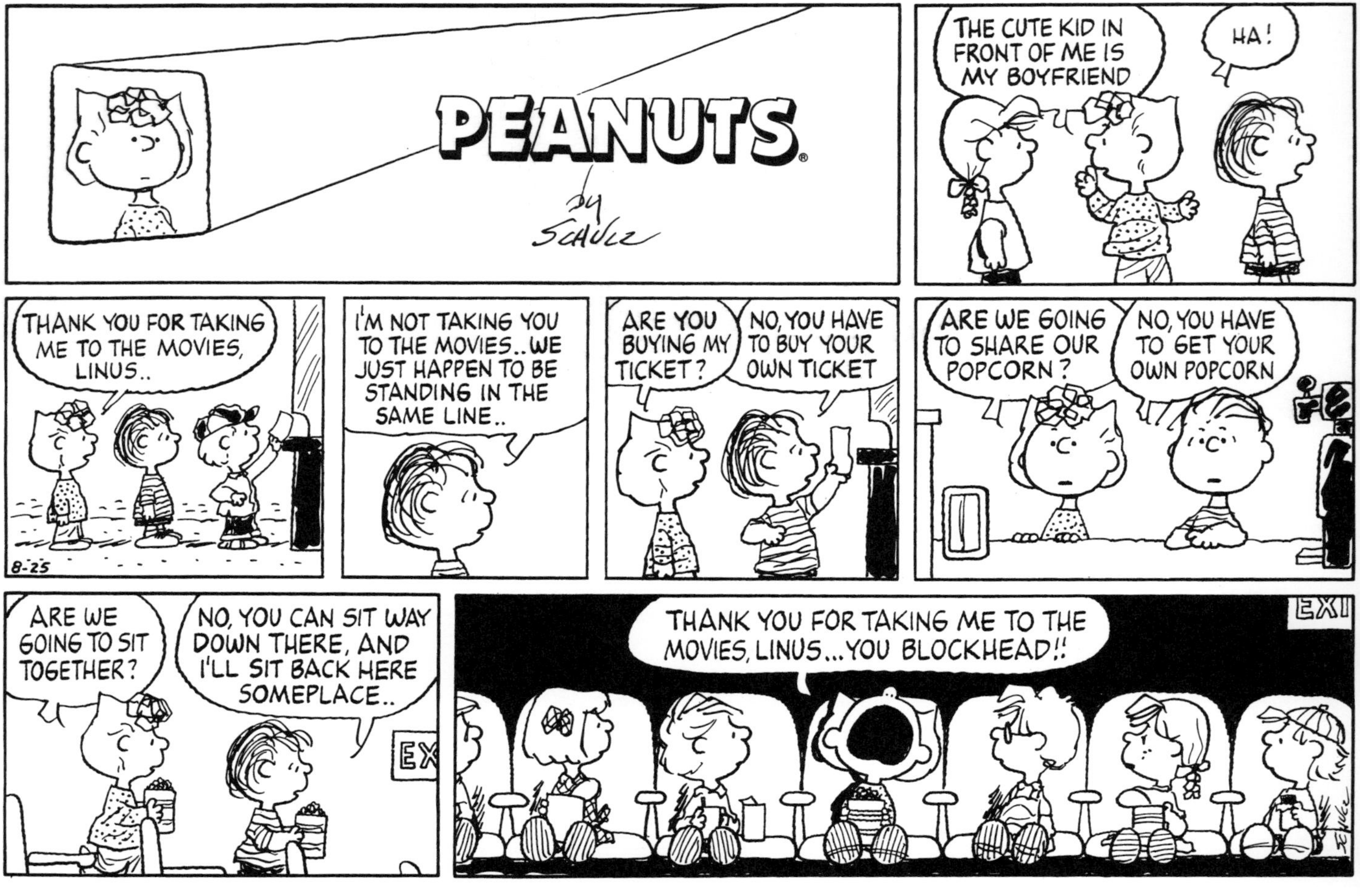
PEANUTS
by SCHULZ
THE CUTE KID IN FRONT OF ME IS MY BOYFRIEND
HA!
THANK YOU FOR TAKING ME TO THE MOVIES, LINUS..
8-25
I'M NOT TAKING YOU TO THE MOVIES..WE JUST HAPPEN TO BE STANDING IN THE SAME LINE..
ARE YOU BUYING MY TICKET?
NO, YOU HAVE TO BUY YOUR OWN TICKET
ARE WE GOING TO SHARE OUR POPCORN?
NO, YOU HAVE TO GET YOUR OWN POPCORN
ARE WE GOING TO SIT TOGETHER?
NO, YOU CAN SIT WAY DOWN THERE, AND I'LL SIT BACK HERE SOMEPLACE..
EX
EXI
THANK YOU FOR TAKING ME TO THE MOVIES, LINUS...YOU BLOCKHEAD!!

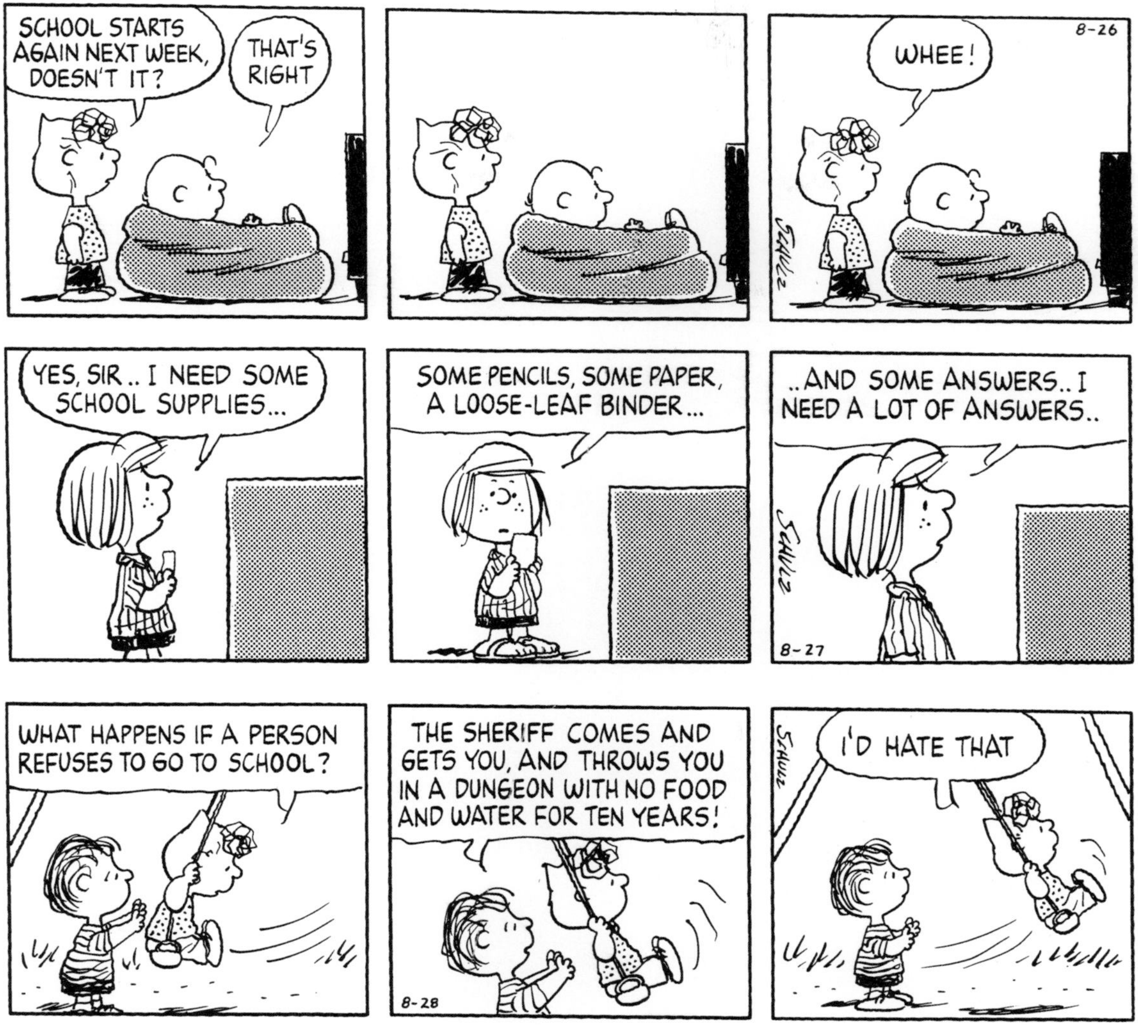
SCHOOL STARTS AGAIN NEXT WEEK, DOESN'T IT?
THAT'S RIGHT
8-26
WHEE!
SCHULZ
YES, SIR.. I NEED SOME SCHOOL SUPPLIES...
SOME PENCILS, SOME PAPER, A LOOSE-LEAF BINDER...
..AND SOME ANSWERS.. I NEED A LOT OF ANSWERS..
SCHULZ
8-27
WHAT HAPPENS IF A PERSON REFUSES TO GO TO SCHOOL?
THE SHERIFF COMES AND GETS YOU, AND THROWS YOU IN A DUNGEON WITH NO FOOD AND WATER FOR TEN YEARS!
8-28
SCHULZ
I'D HATE THAT

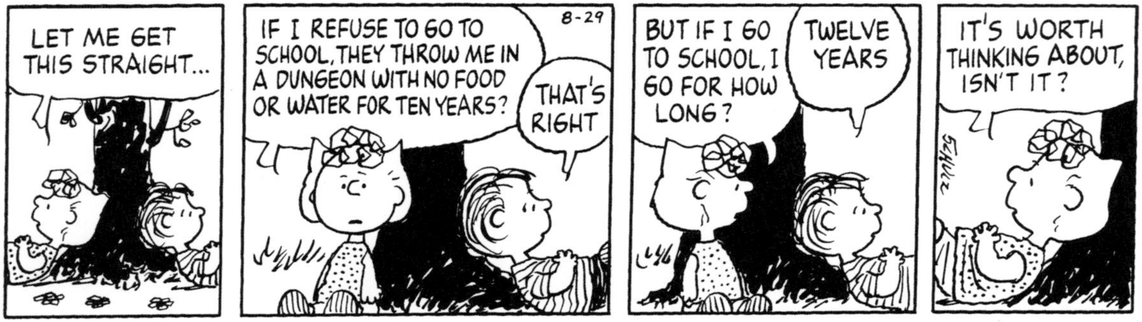
LET ME GET THIS STRAIGHT...
IF I REFUSE TO GO TO SCHOOL, THEY THROW ME IN A DUNGEON WITH NO FOOD OR WATER FOR TEN YEARS?
8-29
THAT'S RIGHT
BUT IF I GO TO SCHOOL, I GO FOR HOW LONG?
TWELVE YEARS
IT'S WORTH THINKING ABOUT, ISN'T IT?

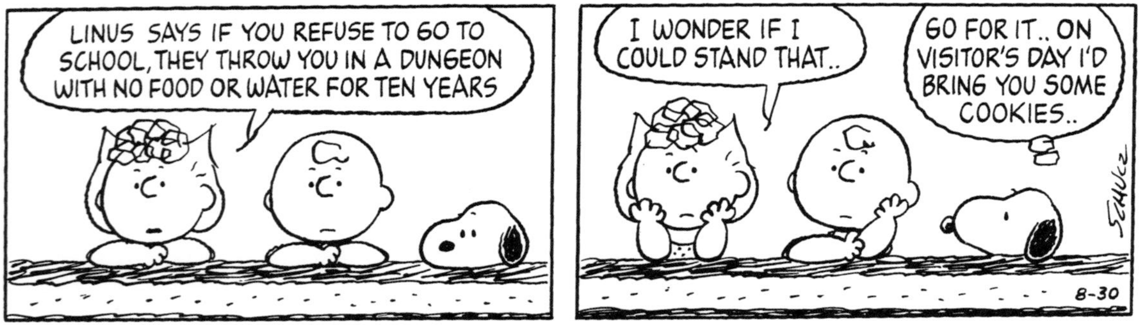
LINUS SAYS IF YOU REFUSE TO GO TO SCHOOL, THEY THROW YOU IN A DUNGEON WITH NO FOOD OR WATER FOR TEN YEARS
I WONDER IF I COULD STAND THAT..
GO FOR IT.. ON VISITOR'S DAY I'D BRING YOU SOME COOKIES..
8-30

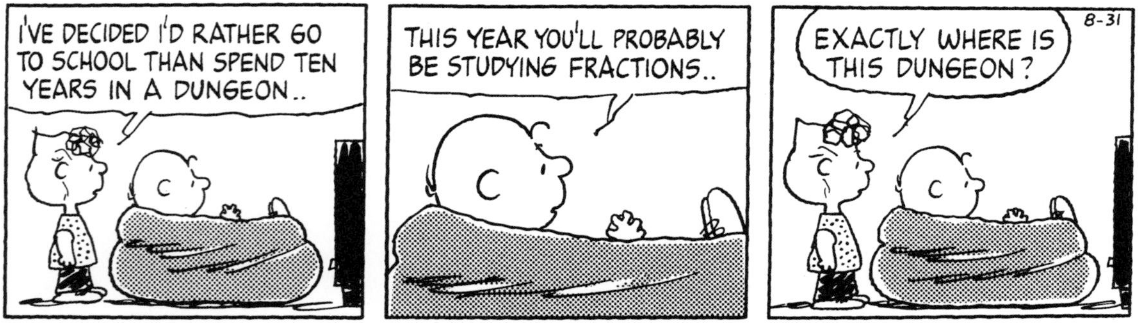
I'VE DECIDED I'D RATHER GO TO SCHOOL THAN SPEND TEN YEARS IN A DUNGEON..
THIS YEAR YOU'LL PROBABLY BE STUDYING FRACTIONS..
8-31
EXACTLY WHERE IS THIS DUNGEON?

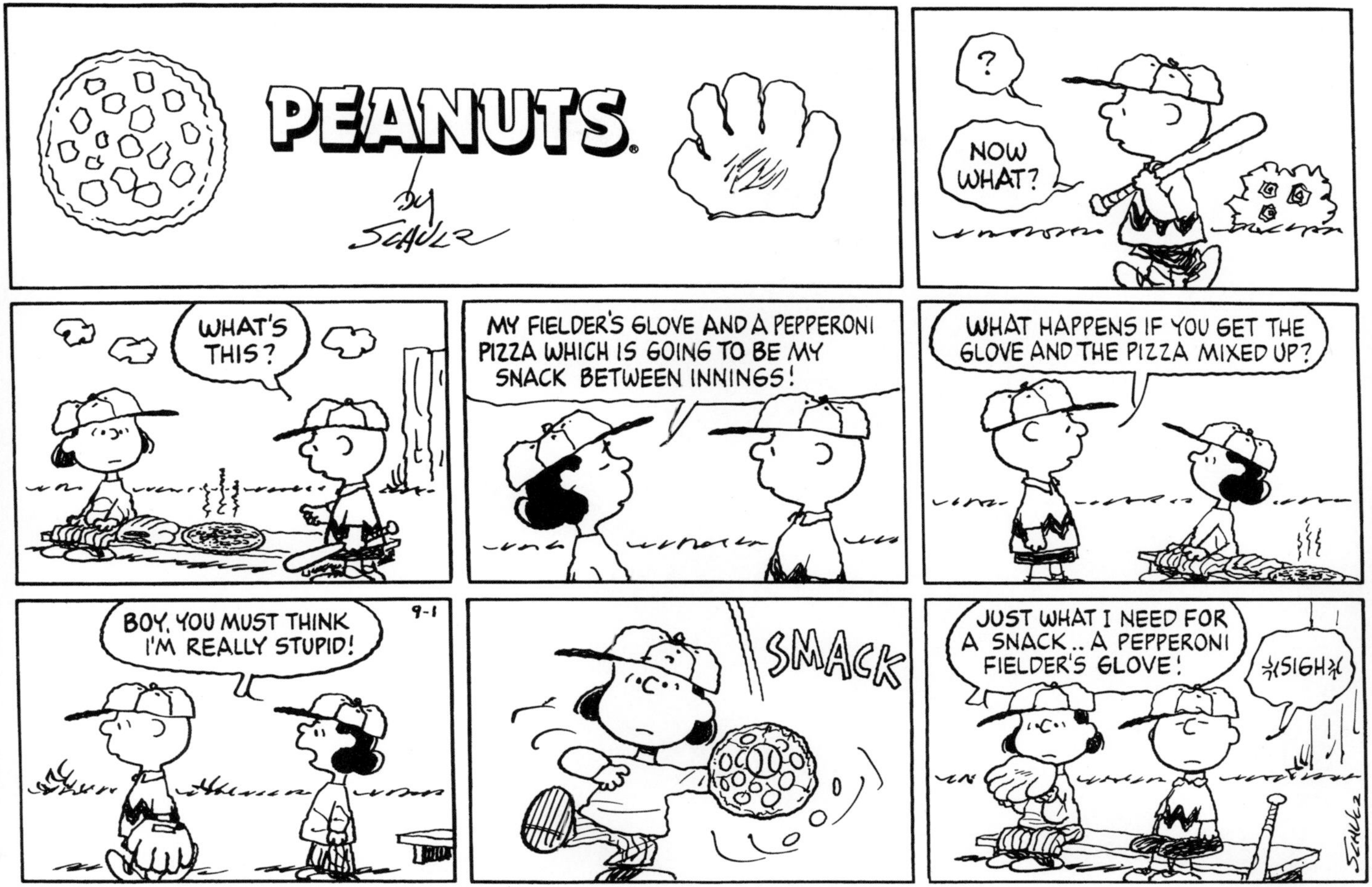
PEANUTS
by SCHULZ
?
NOW WHAT?
WHAT'S THIS?
MY FIELDER'S GLOVE AND A PEPPERONI PIZZA WHICH IS GOING TO BE MY SNACK BETWEEN INNINGS!
WHAT HAPPENS IF YOU GET THE GLOVE AND THE PIZZA MIXED UP?
9-1
BOY, YOU MUST THINK I'M REALLY STUPID!
SMACK
JUST WHAT I NEED FOR A SNACK.. A PEPPERONI FIELDER'S GLOVE!
SIGH
SCHULZ

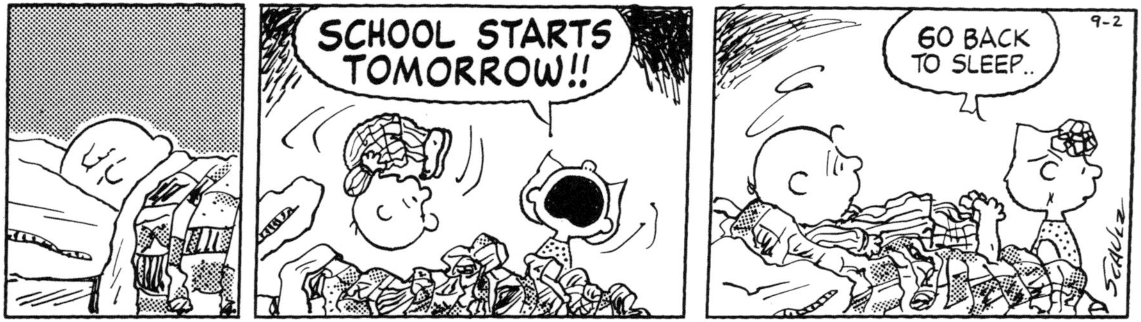
SCHOOL STARTS TOMORROW!!
GO BACK TO SLEEP..

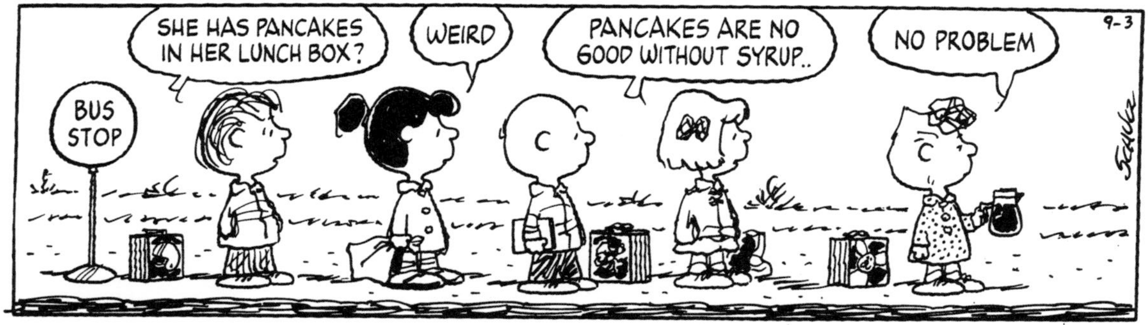
BUS STOP
SHE HAS PANCAKES IN HER LUNCH BOX?
WEIRD
PANCAKES ARE NO GOOD WITHOUT SYRUP..
NO PROBLEM

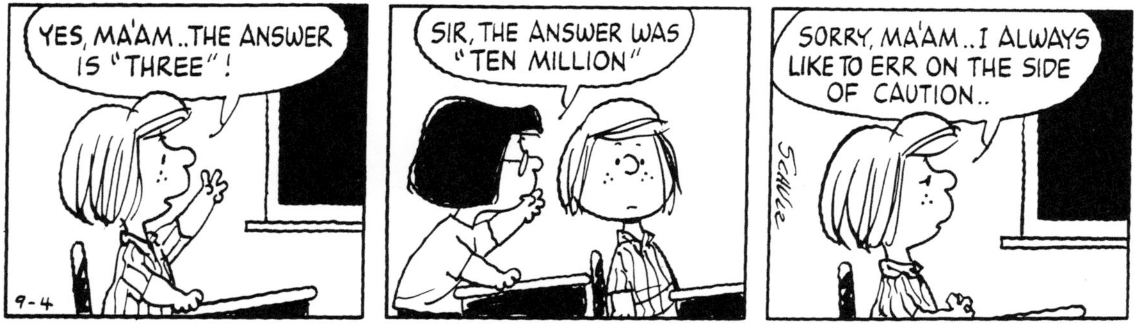
YES, MA'AM..THE ANSWER IS "THREE"!
SIR, THE ANSWER WAS "TEN MILLION"
SORRY, MA'AM..I ALWAYS LIKE TO ERR ON THE SIDE OF CAUTION..

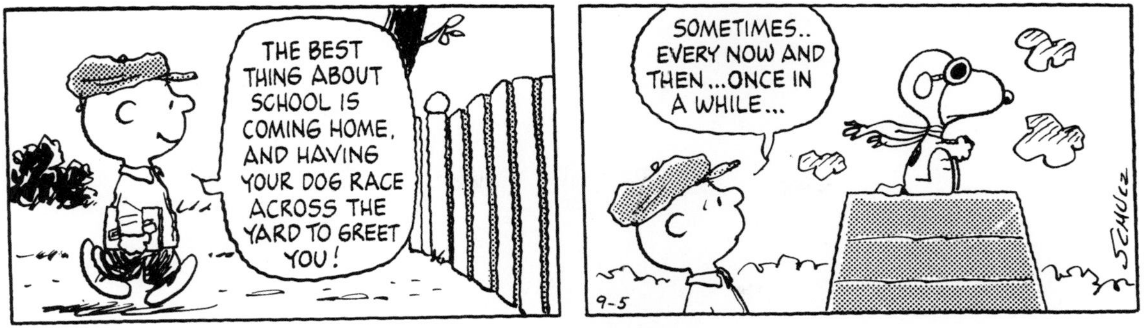
THE BEST THING ABOUT SCHOOL IS COMING HOME, AND HAVING YOUR DOG RACE ACROSS THE YARD TO GREET YOU!
SOMETIMES.. EVERY NOW AND THEN...ONCE IN A WHILE...

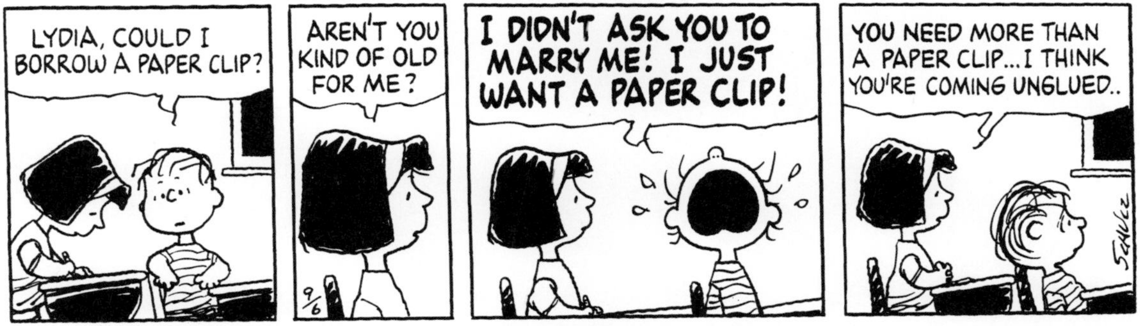
LYDIA, COULD I BORROW A PAPER CLIP?
AREN'T YOU KIND OF OLD FOR ME?
I DIDN'T ASK YOU TO MARRY ME! I JUST WANT A PAPER CLIP!
YOU NEED MORE THAN A PAPER CLIP...I THINK YOU'RE COMING UNGLUED..

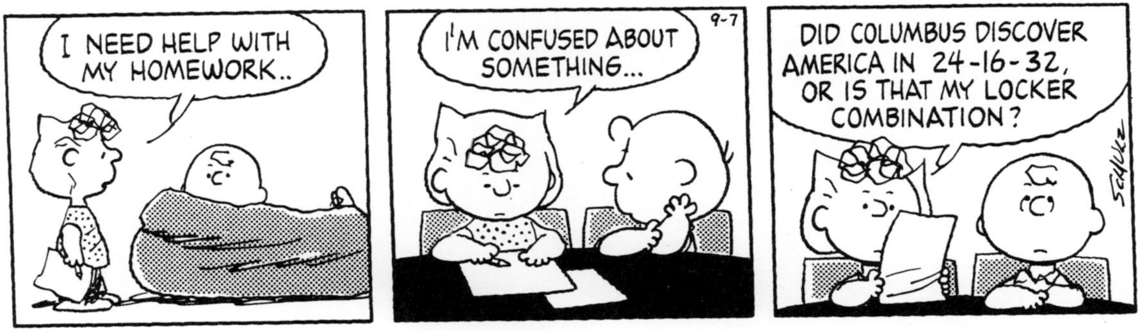
I NEED HELP WITH MY HOMEWORK..
I'M CONFUSED ABOUT SOMETHING...
DID COLUMBUS DISCOVER AMERICA IN 24-16-32, OR IS THAT MY LOCKER COMBINATION?

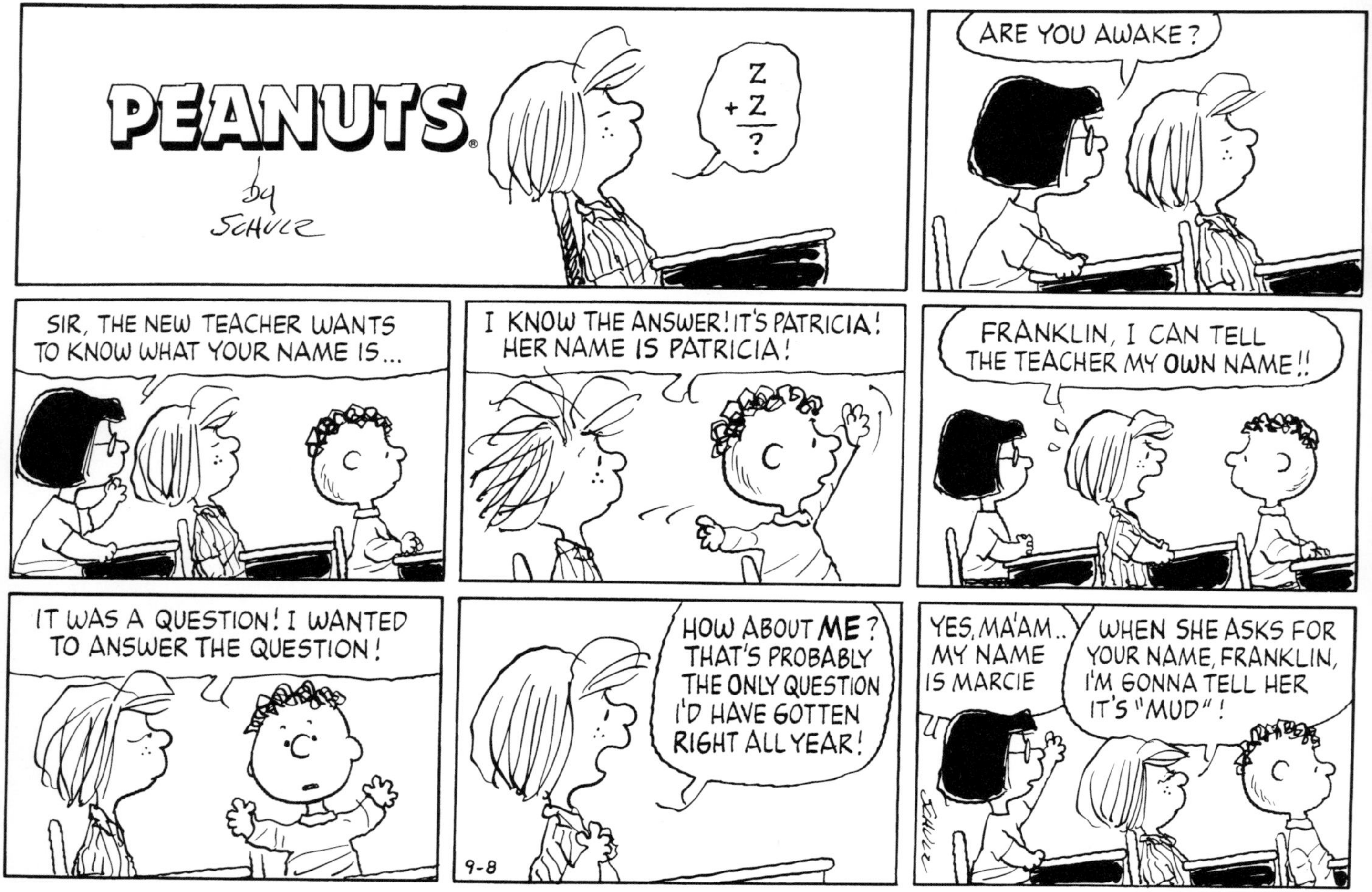
PEANUTS
by SCHULZ
Z
+ Z
?
ARE YOU AWAKE?
SIR, THE NEW TEACHER WANTS TO KNOW WHAT YOUR NAME IS...
I KNOW THE ANSWER! IT'S PATRICIA! HER NAME IS PATRICIA!
FRANKLIN, I CAN TELL THE TEACHER MY OWN NAME!!
IT WAS A QUESTION! I WANTED TO ANSWER THE QUESTION!
HOW ABOUT ME? THAT'S PROBABLY THE ONLY QUESTION I'D HAVE GOTTEN RIGHT ALL YEAR!
9-8
YES, MA'AM.. MY NAME IS MARCIE
WHEN SHE ASKS FOR YOUR NAME, FRANKLIN, I'M GONNA TELL HER IT'S "MUD"!
SCHULZ

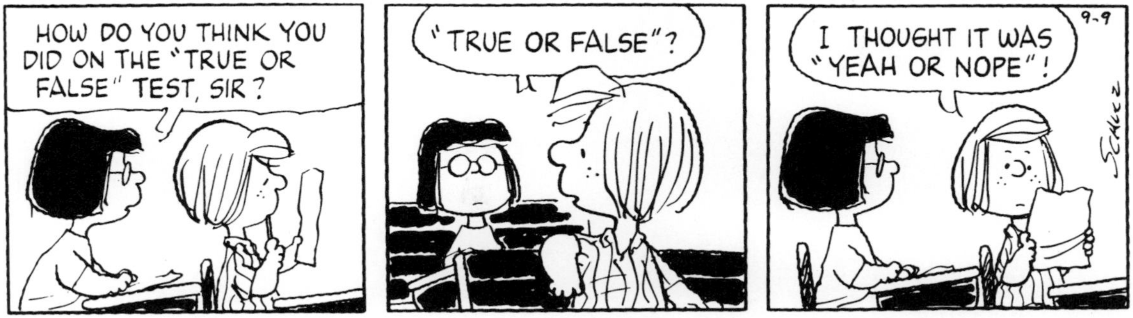
HOW DO YOU THINK YOU DID ON THE "TRUE OR FALSE" TEST, SIR?
"TRUE OR FALSE"?
I THOUGHT IT WAS "YEAH OR NOPE"!
9-9

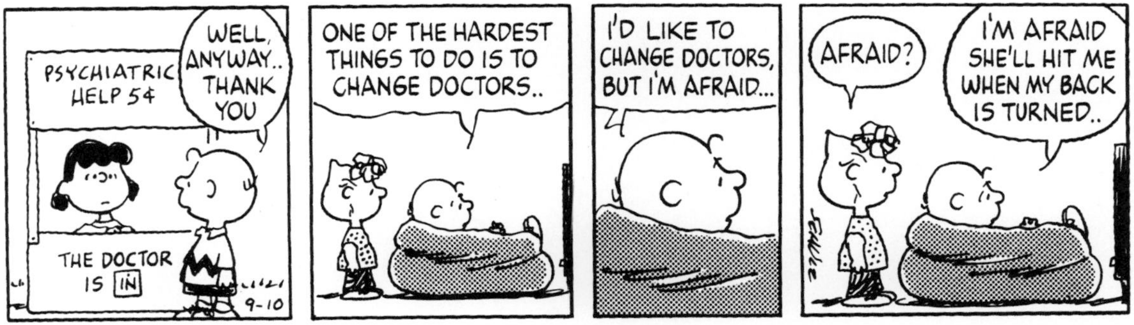
PSYCHIATRIC HELP 5¢
THE DOCTOR IS IN
WELL, ANYWAY.. THANK YOU
9-10
ONE OF THE HARDEST THINGS TO DO IS TO CHANGE DOCTORS..
I'D LIKE TO CHANGE DOCTORS, BUT I'M AFRAID...
AFRAID?
I'M AFRAID SHE'LL HIT ME WHEN MY BACK IS TURNED..

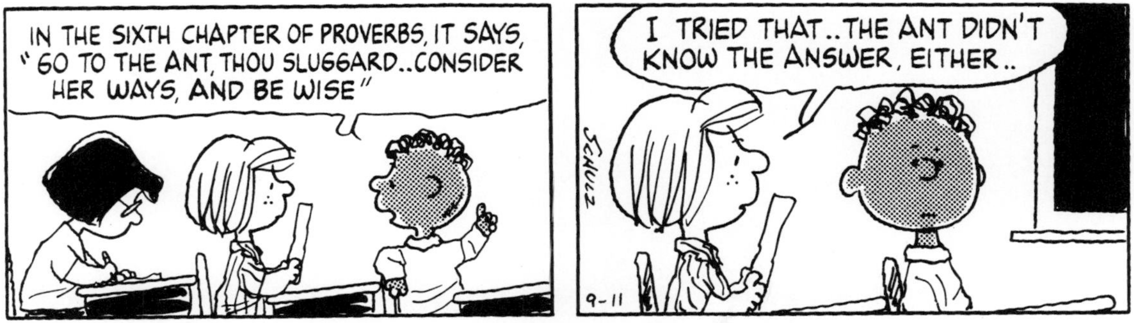
IN THE SIXTH CHAPTER OF PROVERBS, IT SAYS, "GO TO THE ANT, THOU SLUGGARD..CONSIDER HER WAYS, AND BE WISE"
I TRIED THAT..THE ANT DIDN'T KNOW THE ANSWER, EITHER..
9-11

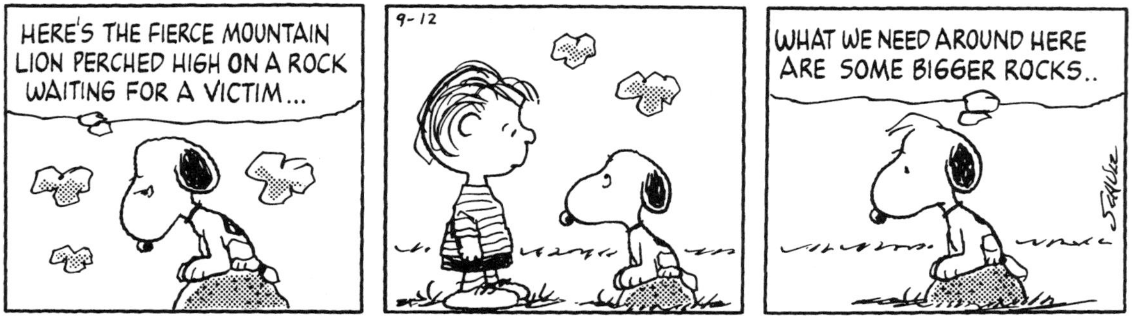
HERE'S THE FIERCE MOUNTAIN LION PERCHED HIGH ON A ROCK WAITING FOR A VICTIM...
9-12
WHAT WE NEED AROUND HERE ARE SOME BIGGER ROCKS..

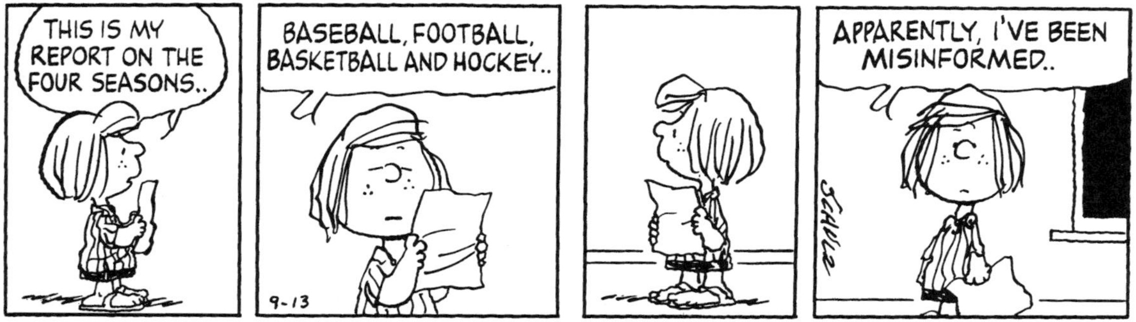
THIS IS MY REPORT ON THE FOUR SEASONS..
BASEBALL, FOOTBALL, BASKETBALL AND HOCKEY..
9-13
APPARENTLY, I'VE BEEN MISINFORMED..

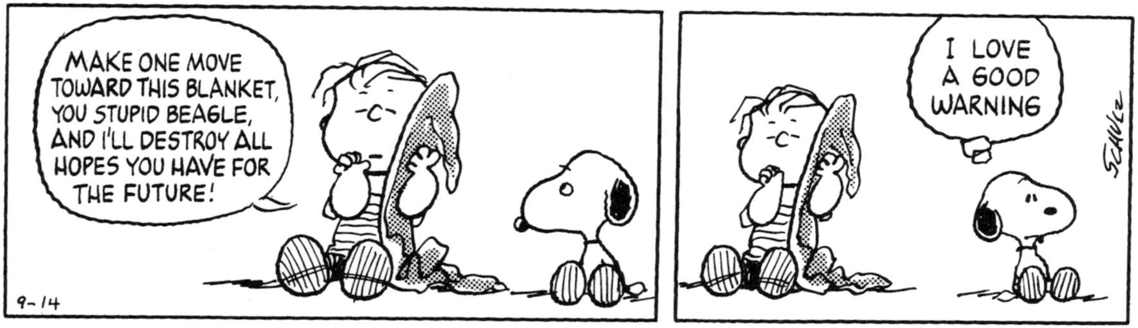
MAKE ONE MOVE TOWARD THIS BLANKET, YOU STUPID BEAGLE, AND I'LL DESTROY ALL HOPES YOU HAVE FOR THE FUTURE!
9-14
I LOVE A GOOD WARNING

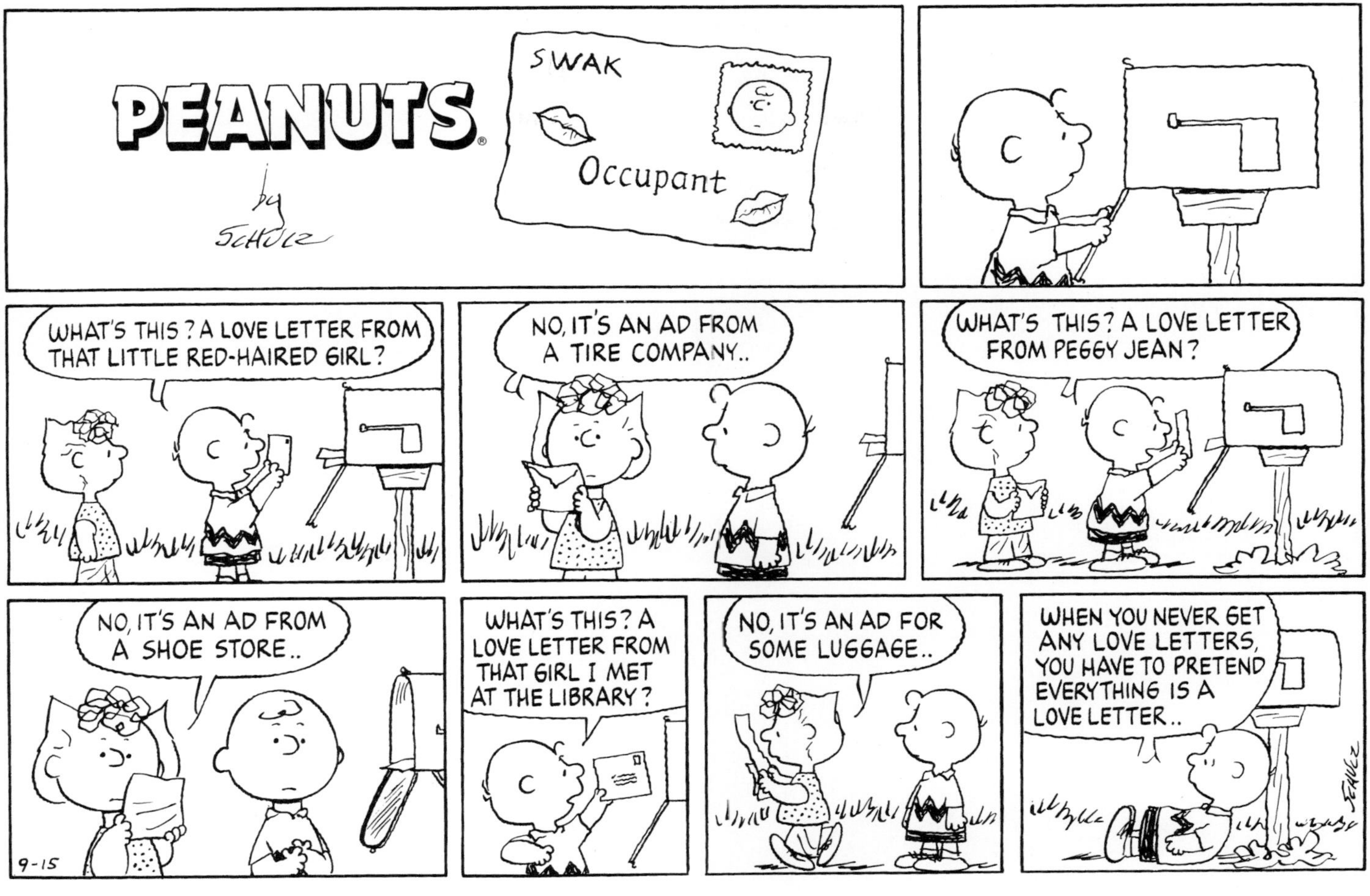
PEANUTS
by SCHULZ
SWAK
Occupant
WHAT'S THIS? A LOVE LETTER FROM THAT LITTLE RED-HAIRED GIRL?
NO, IT'S AN AD FROM A TIRE COMPANY..
WHAT'S THIS? A LOVE LETTER FROM PEGGY JEAN?
NO, IT'S AN AD FROM A SHOE STORE..
9-15
WHAT'S THIS? A LOVE LETTER FROM THAT GIRL I MET AT THE LIBRARY?
NO, IT'S AN AD FOR SOME LUGGAGE..
WHEN YOU NEVER GET ANY LOVE LETTERS, YOU HAVE TO PRETEND EVERYTHING IS A LOVE LETTER..
SCHULZ

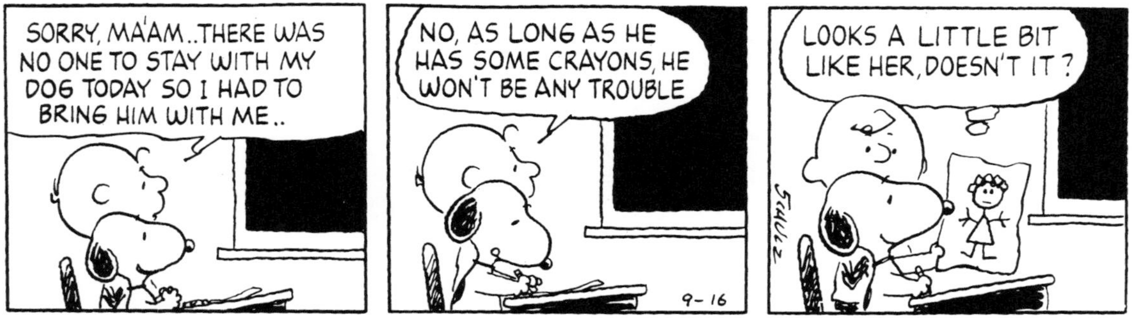
SORRY, MA'AM..THERE WAS NO ONE TO STAY WITH MY DOG TODAY SO I HAD TO BRING HIM WITH ME..
NO, AS LONG AS HE HAS SOME CRAYONS, HE WON'T BE ANY TROUBLE
9-16
LOOKS A LITTLE BIT LIKE HER, DOESN'T IT?
SCHULZ

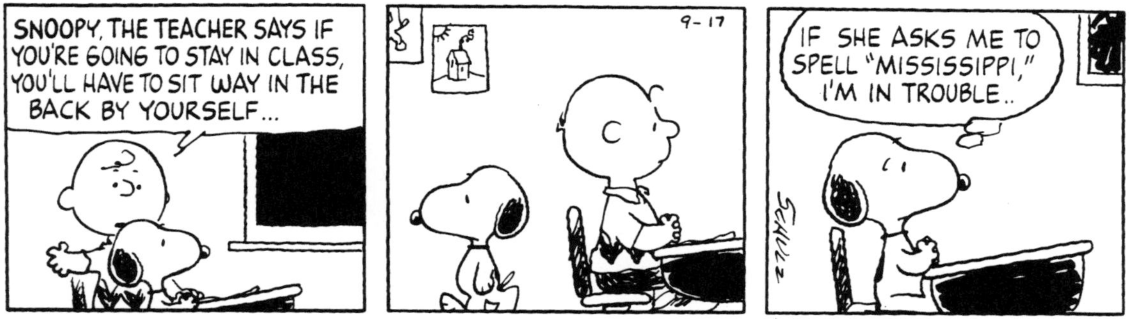
SNOOPY, THE TEACHER SAYS IF YOU'RE GOING TO STAY IN CLASS, YOU'LL HAVE TO SIT WAY IN THE BACK BY YOURSELF...
9-17
IF SHE ASKS ME TO SPELL "MISSISSIPPI," I'M IN TROUBLE..
SCHULZ

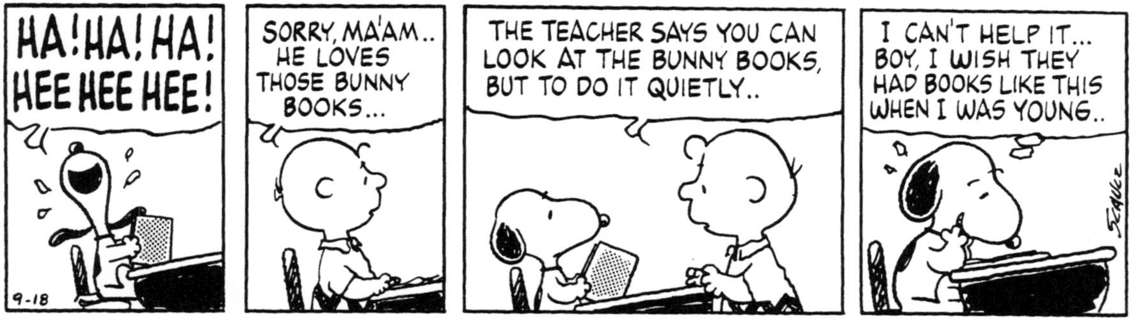
HA! HA! HA! HEE HEE HEE!
9-18
SORRY, MA'AM.. HE LOVES THOSE BUNNY BOOKS...
THE TEACHER SAYS YOU CAN LOOK AT THE BUNNY BOOKS, BUT TO DO IT QUIETLY..
I CAN'T HELP IT... BOY, I WISH THEY HAD BOOKS LIKE THIS WHEN I WAS YOUNG..
SCHULZ

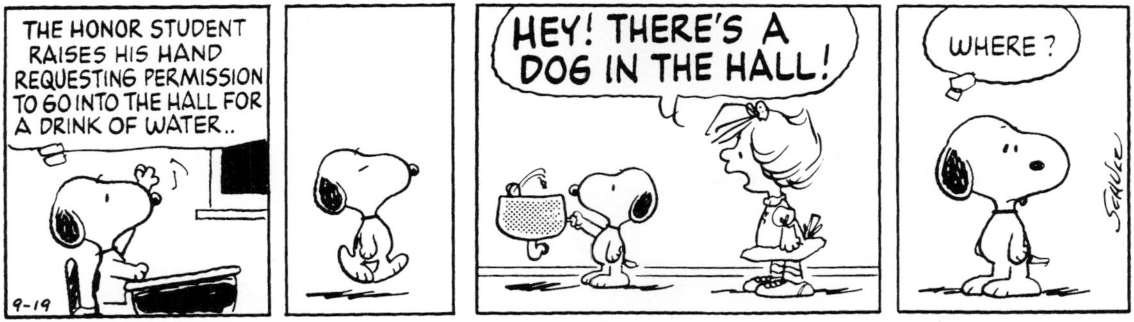
THE HONOR STUDENT RAISES HIS HAND REQUESTING PERMISSION TO GO INTO THE HALL FOR A DRINK OF WATER..
HEY! THERE'S A DOG IN THE HALL!
WHERE?
9-19

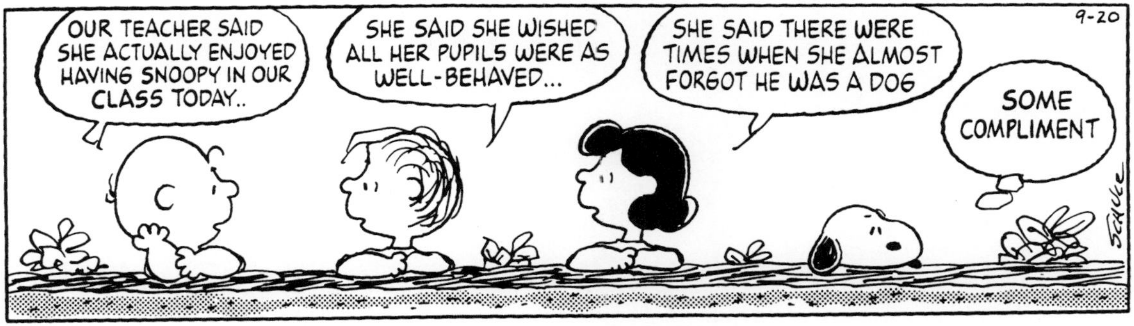
OUR TEACHER SAID SHE ACTUALLY ENJOYED HAVING SNOOPY IN OUR CLASS TODAY..
SHE SAID SHE WISHED ALL HER PUPILS WERE AS WELL-BEHAVED...
SHE SAID THERE WERE TIMES WHEN SHE ALMOST FORGOT HE WAS A DOG
SOME COMPLIMENT
9-20

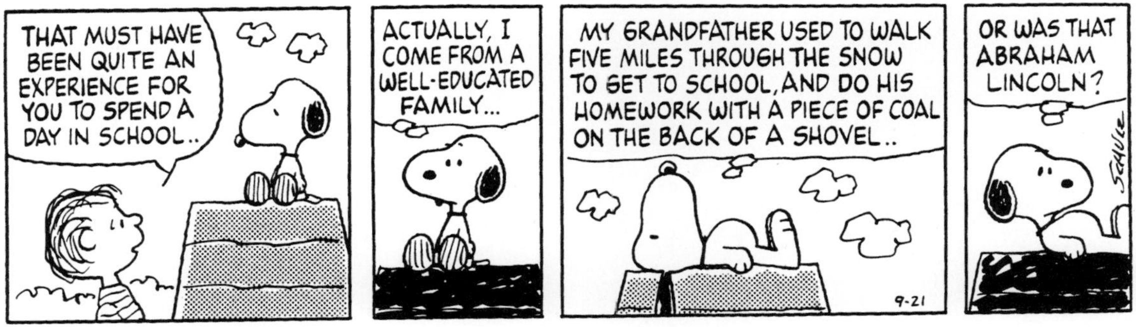
THAT MUST HAVE BEEN QUITE AN EXPERIENCE FOR YOU TO SPEND A DAY IN SCHOOL..
ACTUALLY, I COME FROM A WELL-EDUCATED FAMILY...
MY GRANDFATHER USED TO WALK FIVE MILES THROUGH THE SNOW TO GET TO SCHOOL, AND DO HIS HOMEWORK WITH A PIECE OF COAL ON THE BACK OF A SHOVEL..
OR WAS THAT ABRAHAM LINCOLN?
9-21

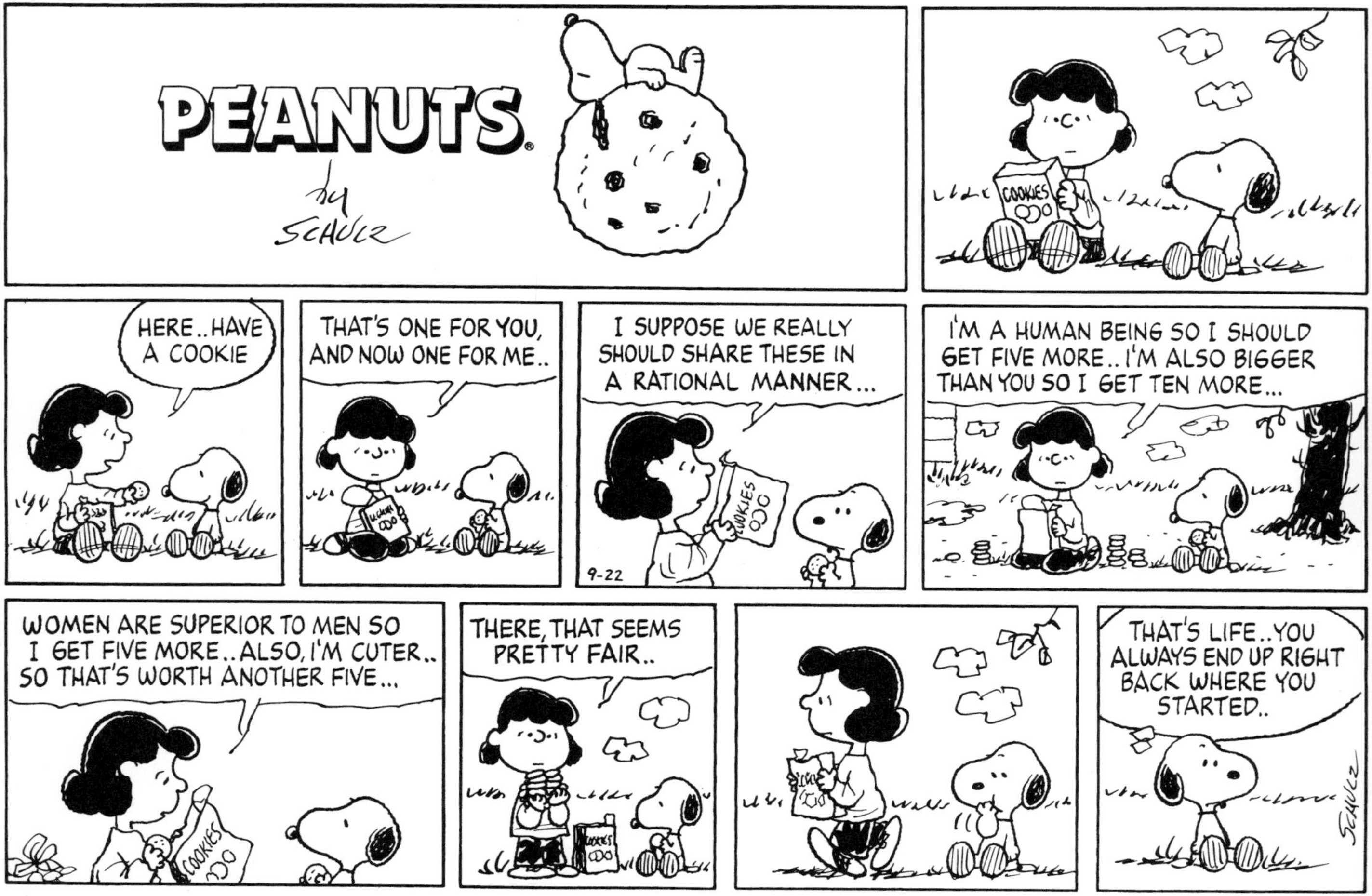
PEANUTS
by SCHULZ
COOKIES
HERE..HAVE A COOKIE
THAT'S ONE FOR YOU, AND NOW ONE FOR ME..
I SUPPOSE WE REALLY SHOULD SHARE THESE IN A RATIONAL MANNER...
9-22
I'M A HUMAN BEING SO I SHOULD GET FIVE MORE..I'M ALSO BIGGER THAN YOU SO I GET TEN MORE...
WOMEN ARE SUPERIOR TO MEN SO I GET FIVE MORE..ALSO, I'M CUTER.. SO THAT'S WORTH ANOTHER FIVE...
THERE, THAT SEEMS PRETTY FAIR..
THAT'S LIFE..YOU ALWAYS END UP RIGHT BACK WHERE YOU STARTED..
SCHULZ

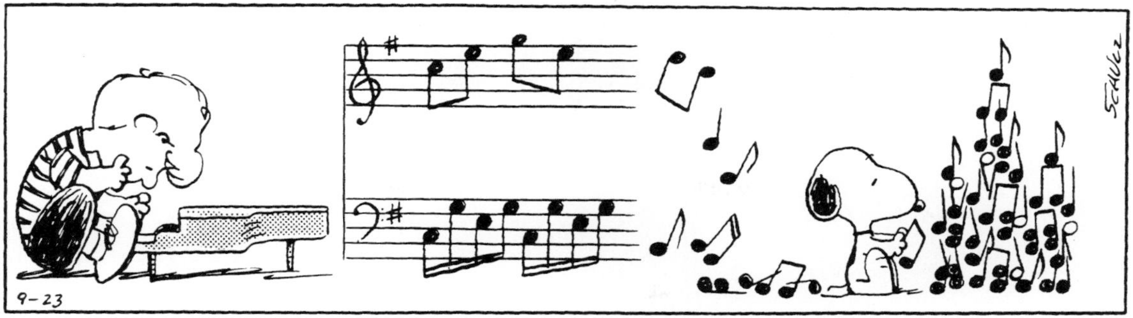
9-23

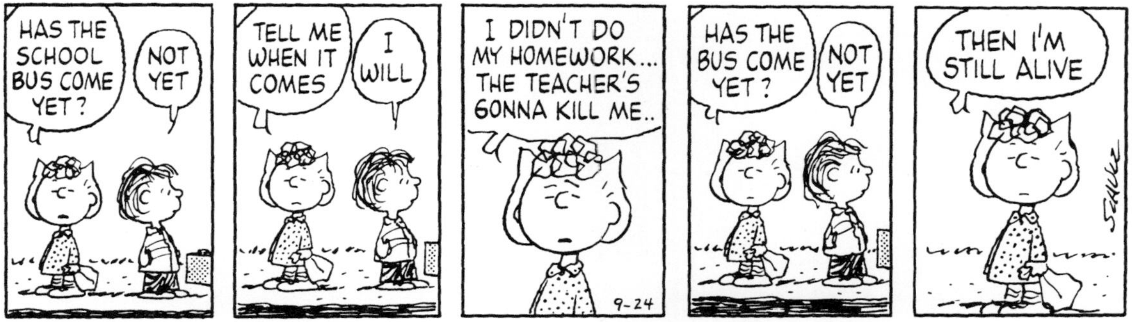
HAS THE SCHOOL BUS COME YET?
NOT YET
TELL ME WHEN IT COMES
I WILL
I DIDN'T DO MY HOMEWORK... THE TEACHER'S GONNA KILL ME..
9-24
HAS THE BUS COME YET?
NOT YET
THEN I'M STILL ALIVE

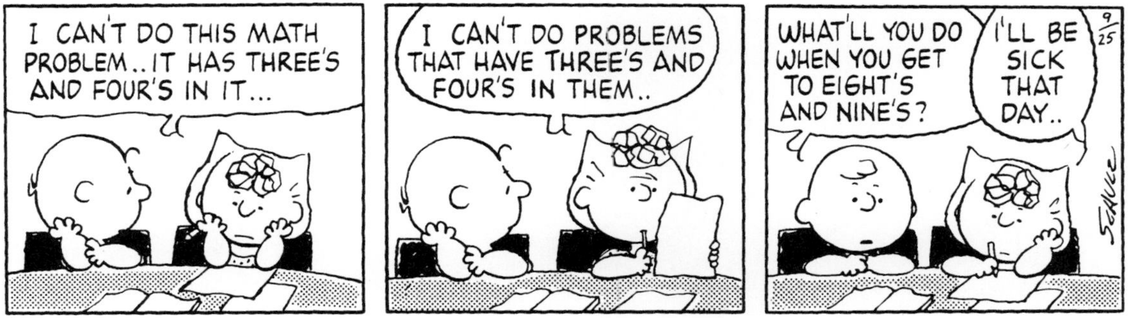
I CAN'T DO THIS MATH PROBLEM.. IT HAS THREE'S AND FOUR'S IN IT...
I CAN'T DO PROBLEMS THAT HAVE THREE'S AND FOUR'S IN THEM..
WHAT'LL YOU DO WHEN YOU GET TO EIGHT'S AND NINE'S?
I'LL BE SICK THAT DAY..
9/25

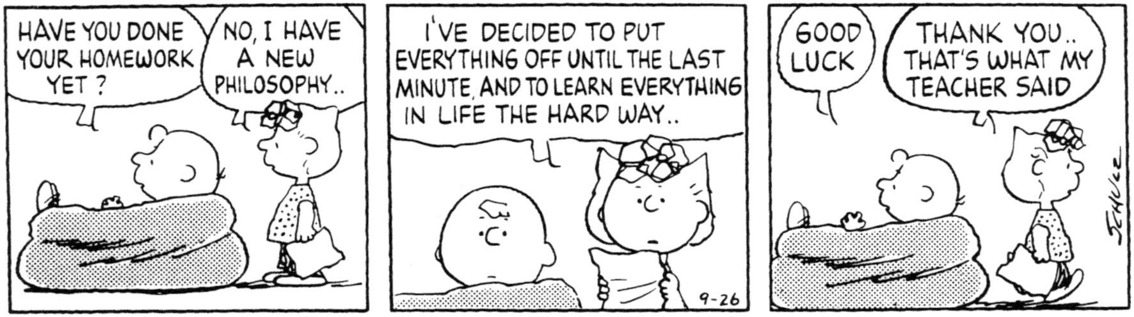
HAVE YOU DONE YOUR HOMEWORK YET ?
NO, I HAVE A NEW PHILOSOPHY..
I'VE DECIDED TO PUT EVERYTHING OFF UNTIL THE LAST MINUTE, AND TO LEARN EVERYTHING IN LIFE THE HARD WAY..
9-26
GOOD LUCK
THANK YOU.. THAT'S WHAT MY TEACHER SAID
SCHULZ

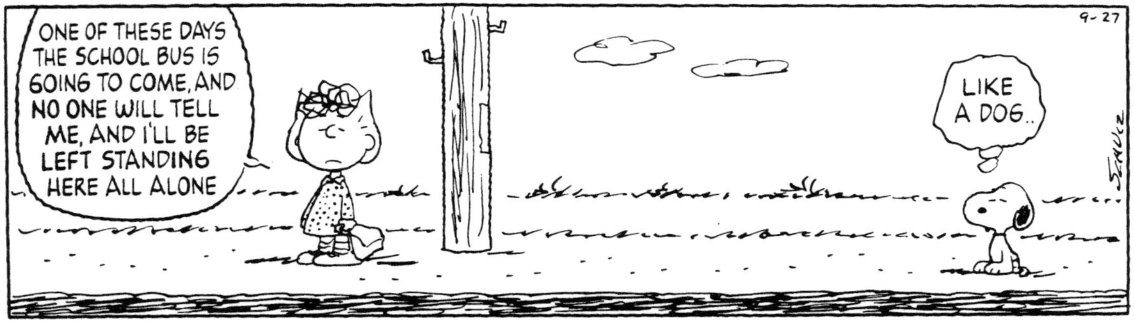
9-27
ONE OF THESE DAYS THE SCHOOL BUS IS GOING TO COME, AND NO ONE WILL TELL ME, AND I'LL BE LEFT STANDING HERE ALL ALONE
LIKE A DOG..
SCHULZ

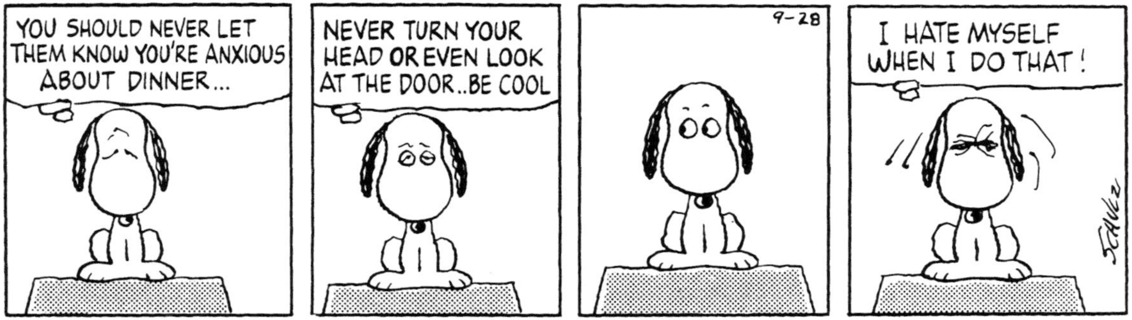
YOU SHOULD NEVER LET THEM KNOW YOU'RE ANXIOUS ABOUT DINNER...
NEVER TURN YOUR HEAD OR EVEN LOOK AT THE DOOR..BE COOL
9-28
I HATE MYSELF WHEN I DO THAT !
SCHULZ

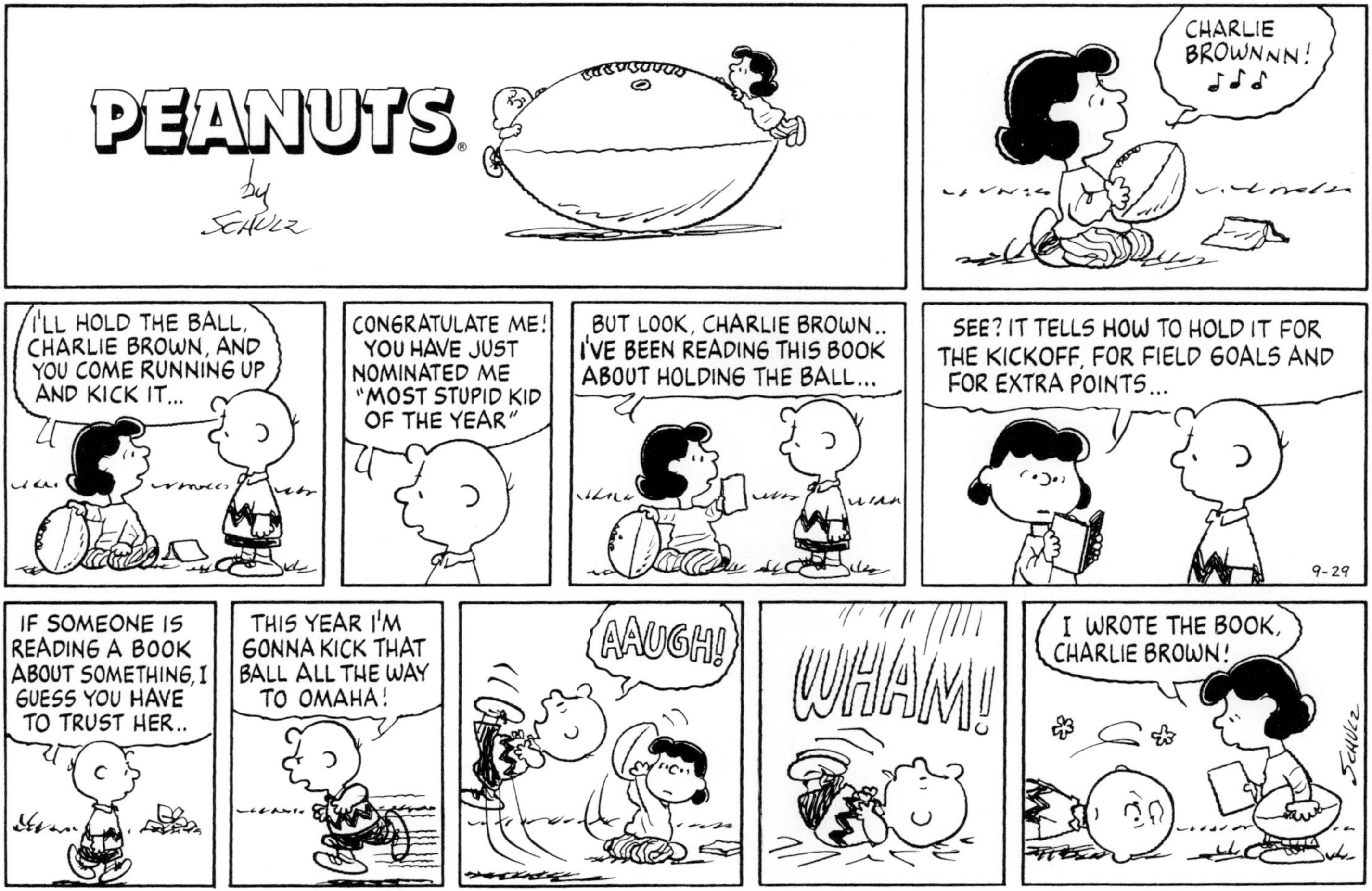
PEANUTS
by SCHULZ
CHARLIE BROWNNN!
I'LL HOLD THE BALL, CHARLIE BROWN, AND YOU COME RUNNING UP AND KICK IT...
CONGRATULATE ME! YOU HAVE JUST NOMINATED ME "MOST STUPID KID OF THE YEAR"
BUT LOOK, CHARLIE BROWN.. I'VE BEEN READING THIS BOOK ABOUT HOLDING THE BALL...
SEE? IT TELLS HOW TO HOLD IT FOR THE KICKOFF, FOR FIELD GOALS AND FOR EXTRA POINTS...
9-29
IF SOMEONE IS READING A BOOK ABOUT SOMETHING, I GUESS YOU HAVE TO TRUST HER..
THIS YEAR I'M GONNA KICK THAT BALL ALL THE WAY TO OMAHA!
AAUGH!
WHAM!
I WROTE THE BOOK, CHARLIE BROWN!
SCHULZ

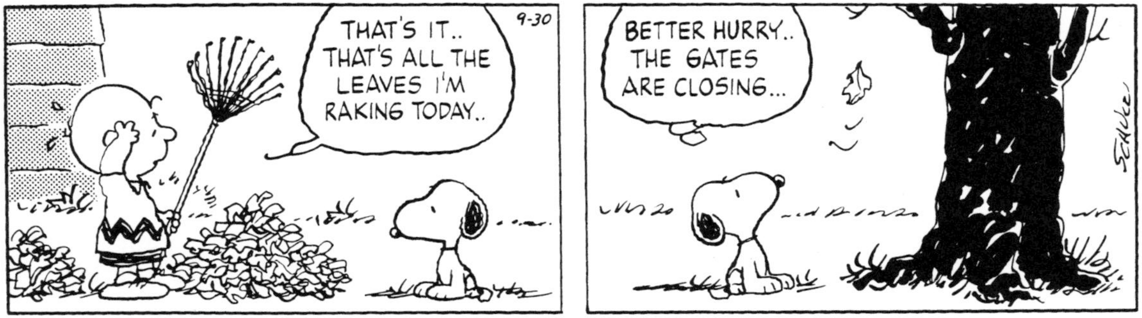
THAT'S IT..
THAT'S ALL THE LEAVES I'M RAKING TODAY..
9-30
BETTER HURRY.. THE GATES ARE CLOSING...

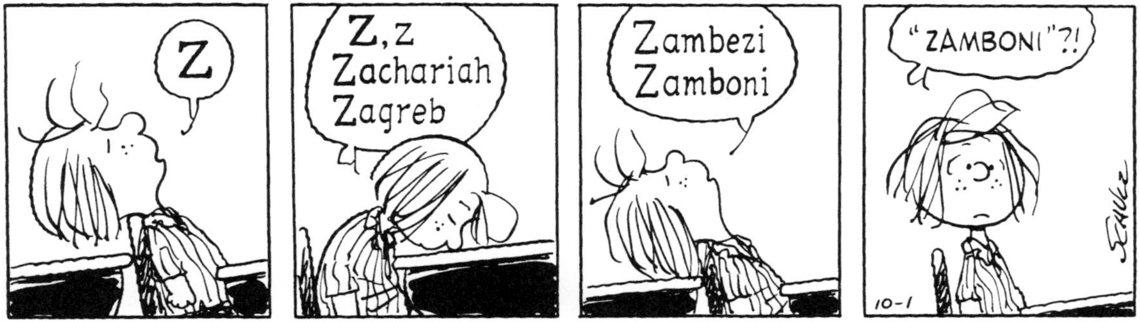
Z
Z, z Zachariah Zagreb
Zambezi Zamboni
"ZAMBONI"?!
10-1

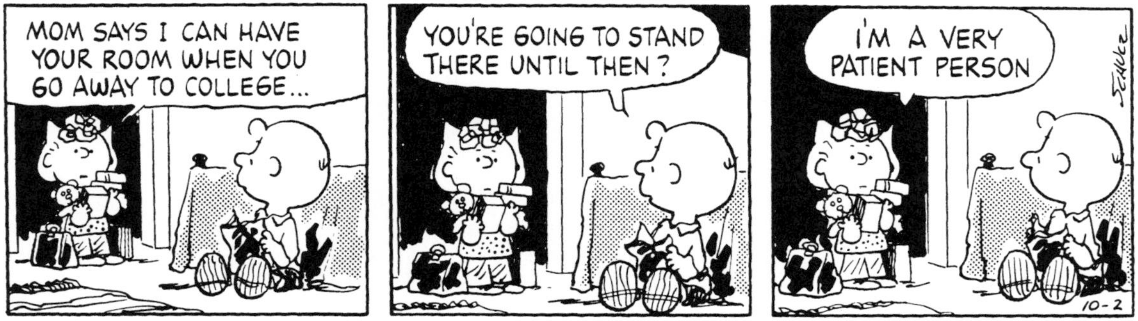
MOM SAYS I CAN HAVE YOUR ROOM WHEN YOU GO AWAY TO COLLEGE...
YOU'RE GOING TO STAND THERE UNTIL THEN?
I'M A VERY PATIENT PERSON
10-2

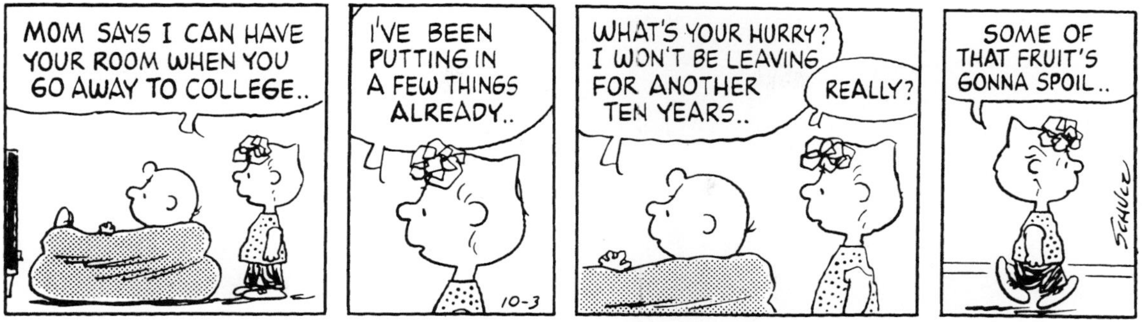
MOM SAYS I CAN HAVE YOUR ROOM WHEN YOU GO AWAY TO COLLEGE..
I'VE BEEN PUTTING IN A FEW THINGS ALREADY..
10-3
WHAT'S YOUR HURRY? I WON'T BE LEAVING FOR ANOTHER TEN YEARS..
REALLY?
SOME OF THAT FRUIT'S GONNA SPOIL..

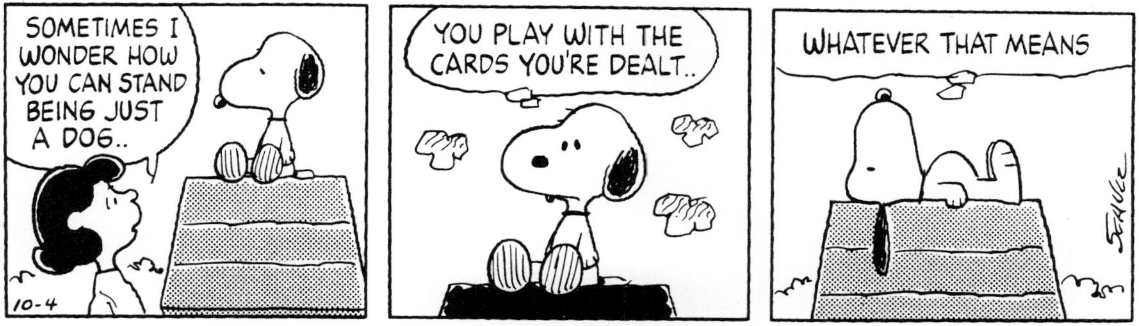
SOMETIMES I WONDER HOW YOU CAN STAND BEING JUST A DOG..
10-4
YOU PLAY WITH THE CARDS YOU'RE DEALT..
WHATEVER THAT MEANS

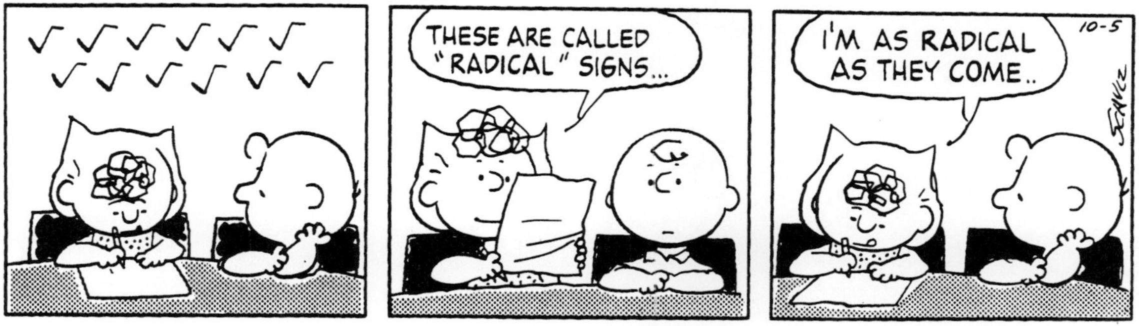
THESE ARE CALLED "RADICAL" SIGNS...
I'M AS RADICAL AS THEY COME..
10-5

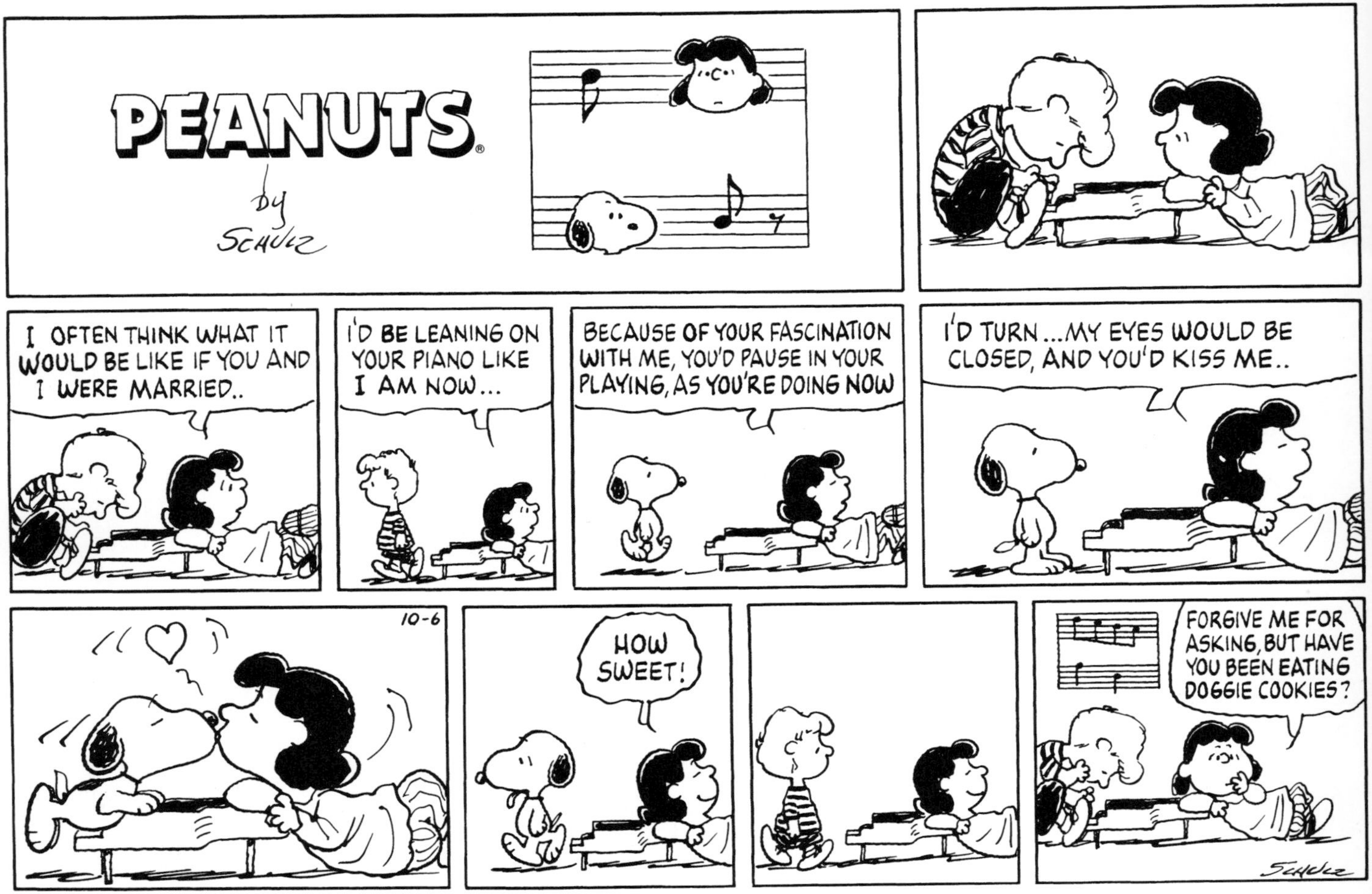
PEANUTS
by SCHULZ
I OFTEN THINK WHAT IT WOULD BE LIKE IF YOU AND I WERE MARRIED..
I'D BE LEANING ON YOUR PIANO LIKE I AM NOW...
BECAUSE OF YOUR FASCINATION WITH ME, YOU'D PAUSE IN YOUR PLAYING, AS YOU'RE DOING NOW
I'D TURN ...MY EYES WOULD BE CLOSED, AND YOU'D KISS ME..
10-6
HOW SWEET!
FORGIVE ME FOR ASKING, BUT HAVE YOU BEEN EATING DOGGIE COOKIES?
SCHULZ

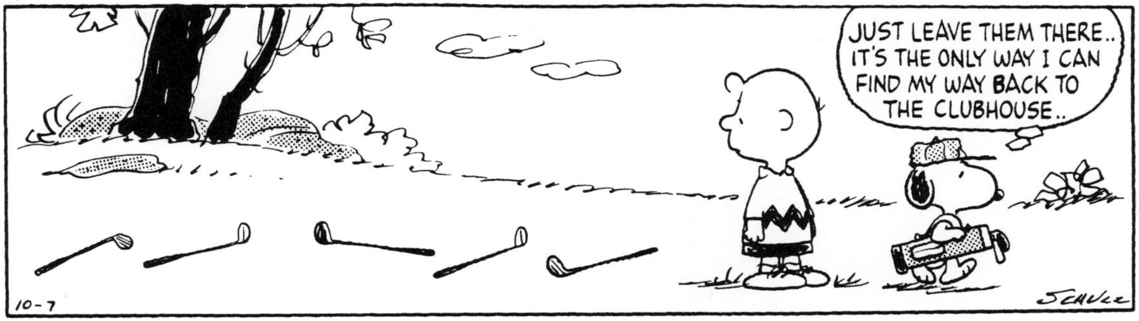
JUST LEAVE THEM THERE.. IT'S THE ONLY WAY I CAN FIND MY WAY BACK TO THE CLUBHOUSE..

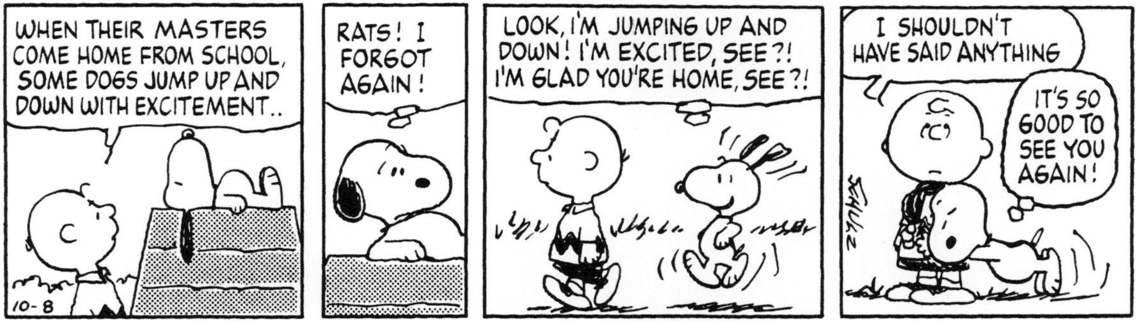
WHEN THEIR MASTERS COME HOME FROM SCHOOL, SOME DOGS JUMP UP AND DOWN WITH EXCITEMENT..
RATS! I FORGOT AGAIN!
LOOK, I'M JUMPING UP AND DOWN! I'M EXCITED, SEE?! I'M GLAD YOU'RE HOME, SEE?!
I SHOULDN'T HAVE SAID ANYTHING
IT'S SO GOOD TO SEE YOU AGAIN!

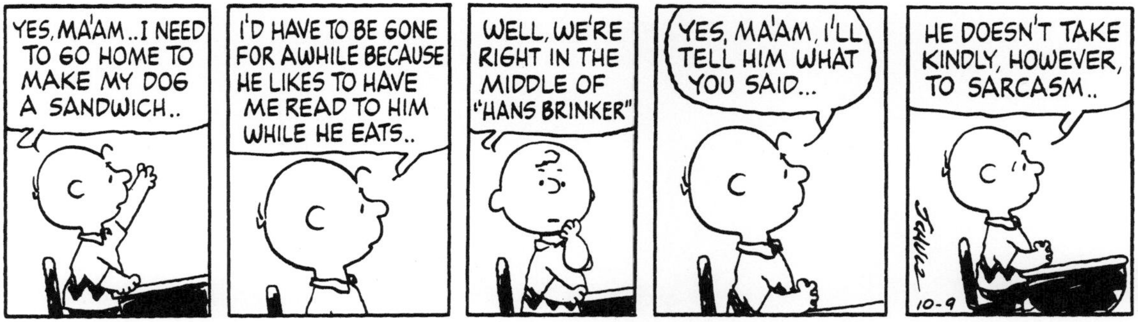
YES, MA'AM..I NEED TO GO HOME TO MAKE MY DOG A SANDWICH..
I'D HAVE TO BE GONE FOR AWHILE BECAUSE HE LIKES TO HAVE ME READ TO HIM WHILE HE EATS..
WELL, WE'RE RIGHT IN THE MIDDLE OF "HANS BRINKER"
YES, MA'AM, I'LL TELL HIM WHAT YOU SAID...
HE DOESN'T TAKE KINDLY, HOWEVER, TO SARCASM..

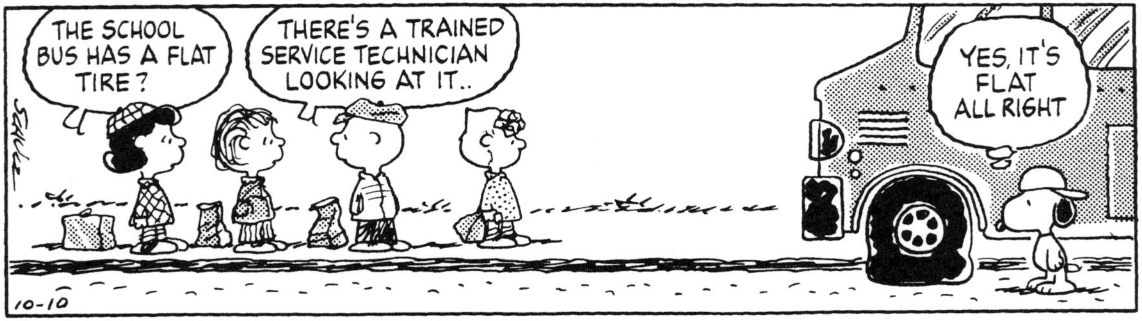
THE SCHOOL BUS HAS A FLAT TIRE?
THERE'S A TRAINED SERVICE TECHNICIAN LOOKING AT IT..
YES, IT'S FLAT ALL RIGHT
10-10

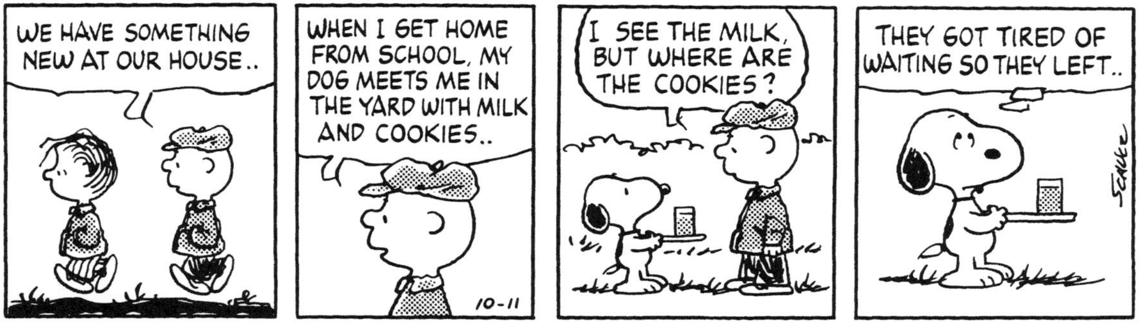
WE HAVE SOMETHING NEW AT OUR HOUSE..
WHEN I GET HOME FROM SCHOOL, MY DOG MEETS ME IN THE YARD WITH MILK AND COOKIES..
10-11
I SEE THE MILK, BUT WHERE ARE THE COOKIES?
THEY GOT TIRED OF WAITING SO THEY LEFT..

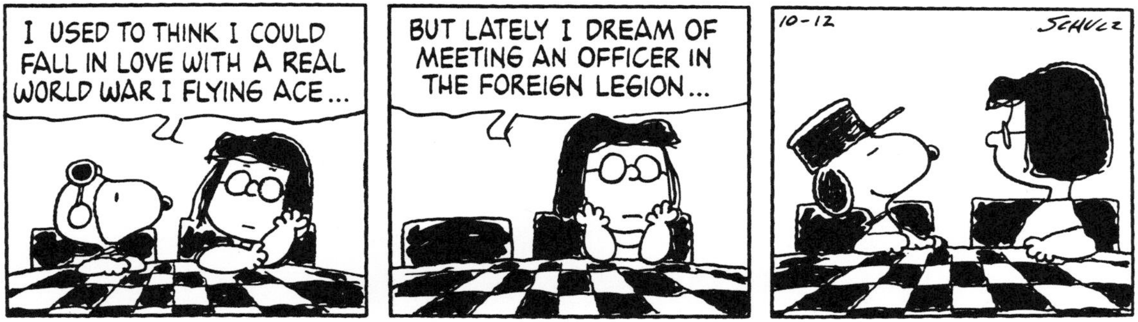
I USED TO THINK I COULD FALL IN LOVE WITH A REAL WORLD WAR I FLYING ACE...
BUT LATELY I DREAM OF MEETING AN OFFICER IN THE FOREIGN LEGION...
10-12
SCHULZ

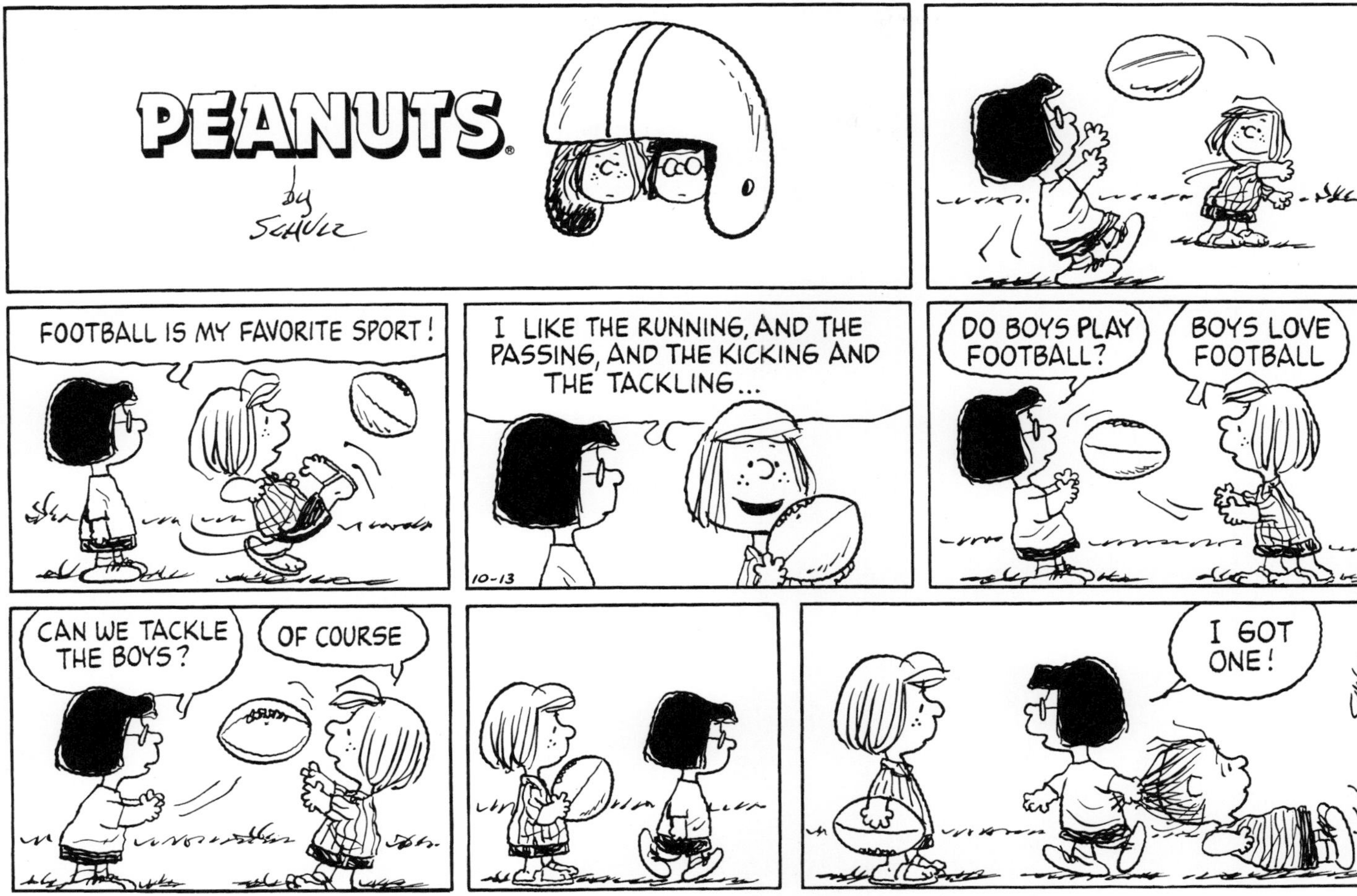
PEANUTS
by SCHULZ
FOOTBALL IS MY FAVORITE SPORT!
I LIKE THE RUNNING, AND THE PASSING, AND THE KICKING AND THE TACKLING...
10-13
DO BOYS PLAY FOOTBALL?
BOYS LOVE FOOTBALL
CAN WE TACKLE THE BOYS?
OF COURSE
I GOT ONE!
SCHULZ

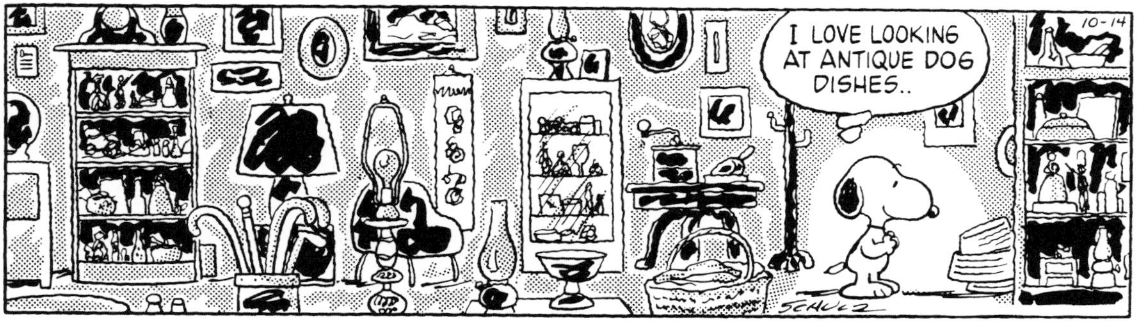
10-14
I LOVE LOOKING AT ANTIQUE DOG DISHES..
SCHULZ

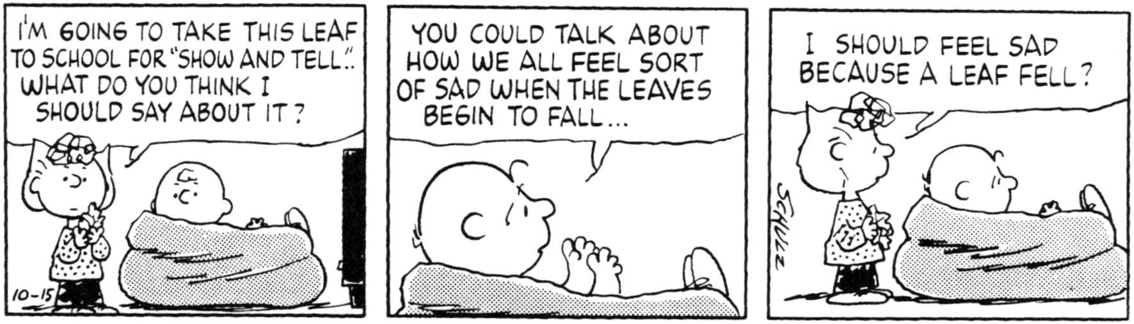
I'M GOING TO TAKE THIS LEAF TO SCHOOL FOR "SHOW AND TELL".. WHAT DO YOU THINK I SHOULD SAY ABOUT IT?
10-15
YOU COULD TALK ABOUT HOW WE ALL FEEL SORT OF SAD WHEN THE LEAVES BEGIN TO FALL...
I SHOULD FEEL SAD BECAUSE A LEAF FELL?
SCHULZ

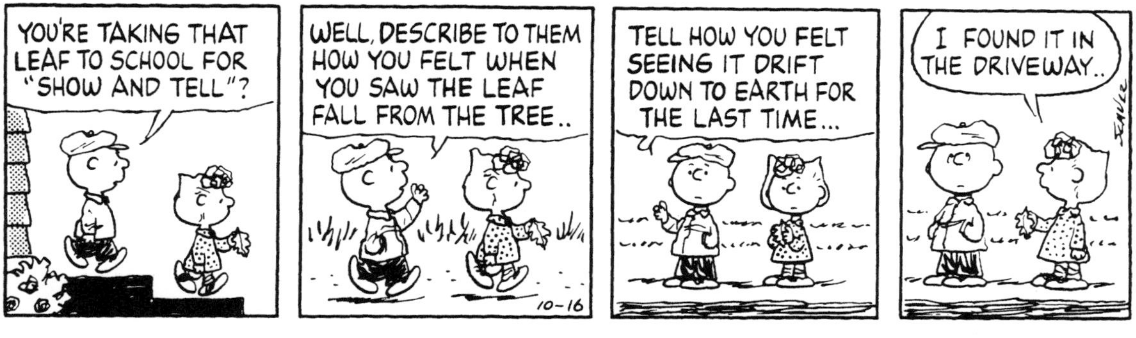
YOU'RE TAKING THAT LEAF TO SCHOOL FOR "SHOW AND TELL"?
WELL, DESCRIBE TO THEM HOW YOU FELT WHEN YOU SAW THE LEAF FALL FROM THE TREE..
10-16
TELL HOW YOU FELT SEEING IT DRIFT DOWN TO EARTH FOR THE LAST TIME...
I FOUND IT IN THE DRIVEWAY..
SCHULZ

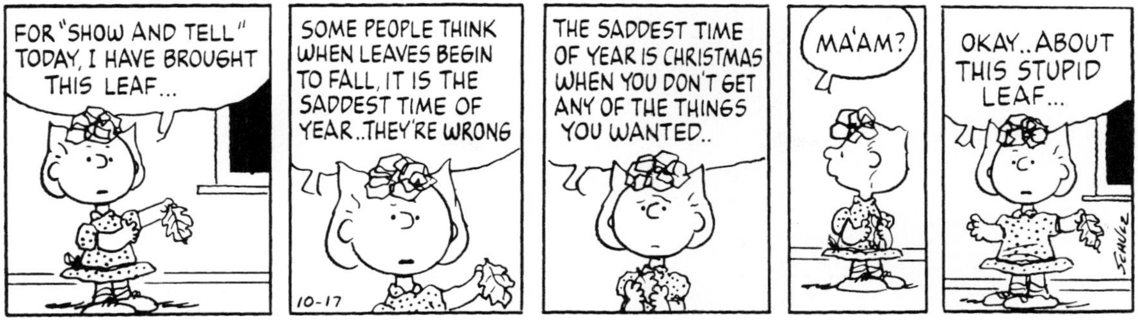
FOR "SHOW AND TELL" TODAY, I HAVE BROUGHT THIS LEAF...
SOME PEOPLE THINK WHEN LEAVES BEGIN TO FALL, IT IS THE SADDEST TIME OF YEAR..THEY'RE WRONG
10-17
THE SADDEST TIME OF YEAR IS CHRISTMAS WHEN YOU DON'T GET ANY OF THE THINGS YOU WANTED..
MA'AM?
OKAY..ABOUT THIS STUPID LEAF...
SCHULZ

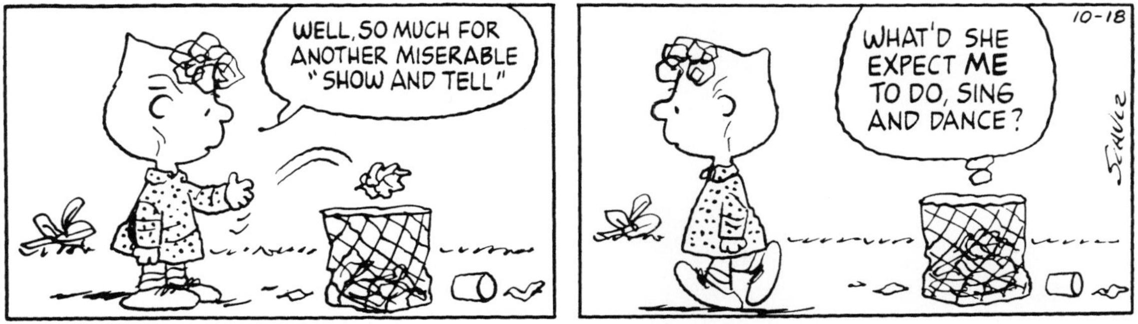
WELL, SO MUCH FOR ANOTHER MISERABLE "SHOW AND TELL"
10-18
WHAT'D SHE EXPECT **ME** TO DO, SING AND DANCE?
SCHULZ

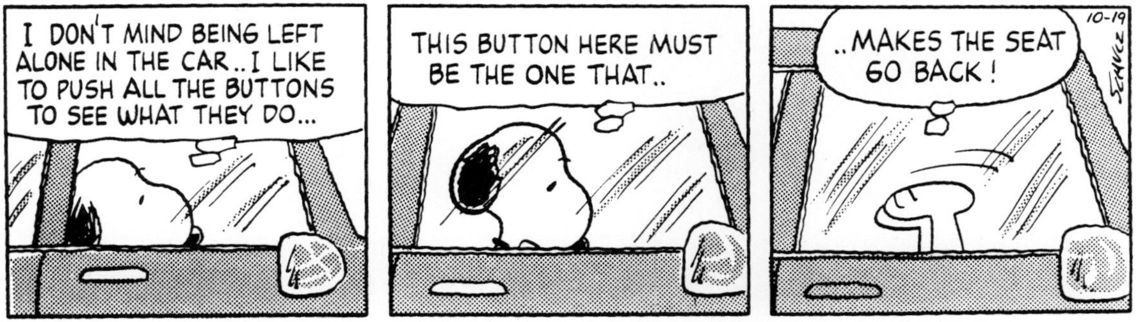
I DON'T MIND BEING LEFT ALONE IN THE CAR..I LIKE TO PUSH ALL THE BUTTONS TO SEE WHAT THEY DO...
THIS BUTTON HERE MUST BE THE ONE THAT..
10-19
..MAKES THE SEAT GO BACK!
SCHULZ

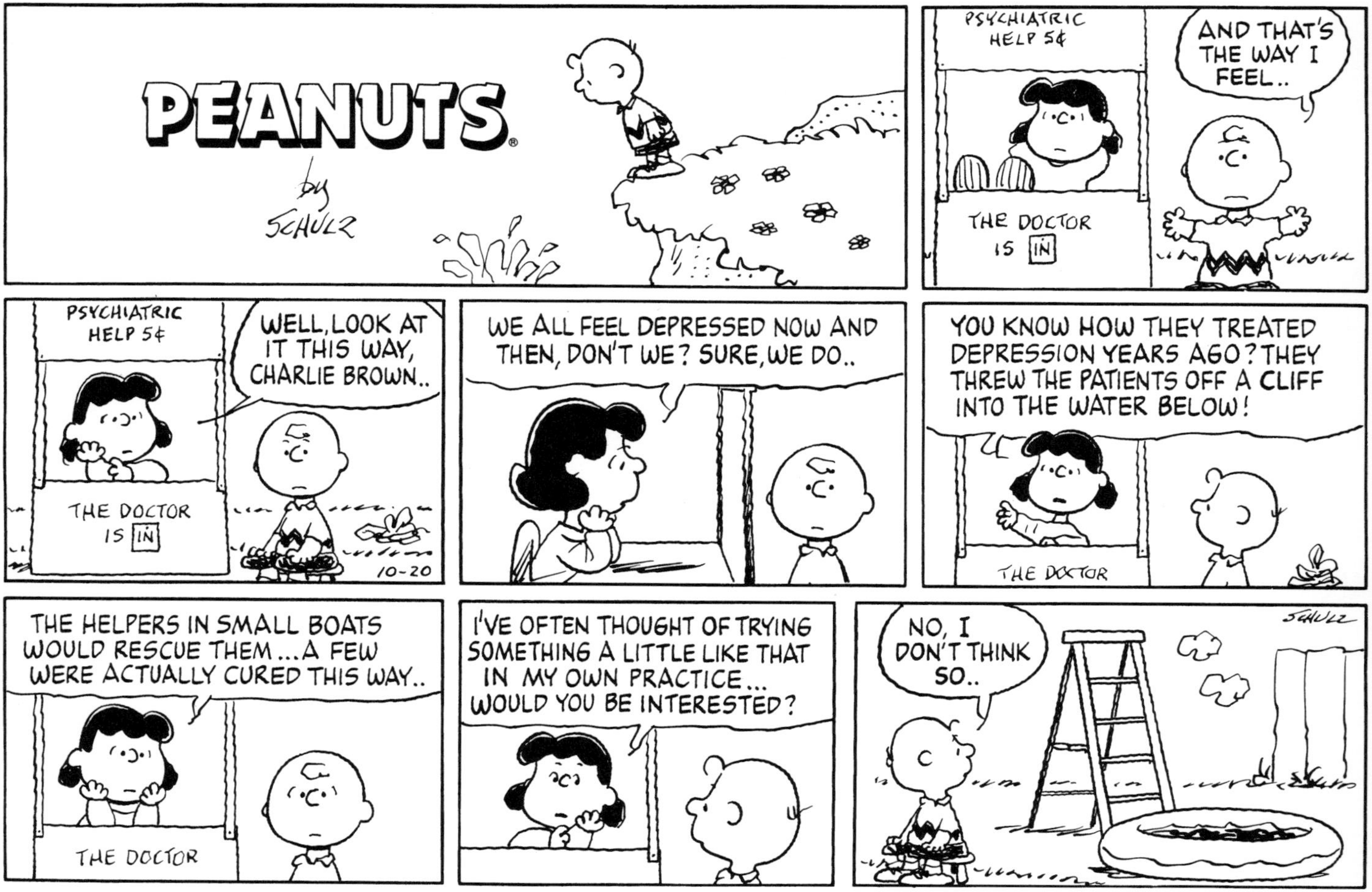
PEANUTS
by SCHULZ
PSYCHIATRIC HELP 5¢
THE DOCTOR IS IN
AND THAT'S THE WAY I FEEL..
PSYCHIATRIC HELP 5¢
THE DOCTOR IS IN
WELL, LOOK AT IT THIS WAY, CHARLIE BROWN..
10-20
WE ALL FEEL DEPRESSED NOW AND THEN, DON'T WE? SURE, WE DO..
YOU KNOW HOW THEY TREATED DEPRESSION YEARS AGO? THEY THREW THE PATIENTS OFF A CLIFF INTO THE WATER BELOW!
THE DOCTOR
THE HELPERS IN SMALL BOATS WOULD RESCUE THEM ...A FEW WERE ACTUALLY CURED THIS WAY..
THE DOCTOR
I'VE OFTEN THOUGHT OF TRYING SOMETHING A LITTLE LIKE THAT IN MY OWN PRACTICE... WOULD YOU BE INTERESTED?
NO, I DON'T THINK SO..
SCHULZ

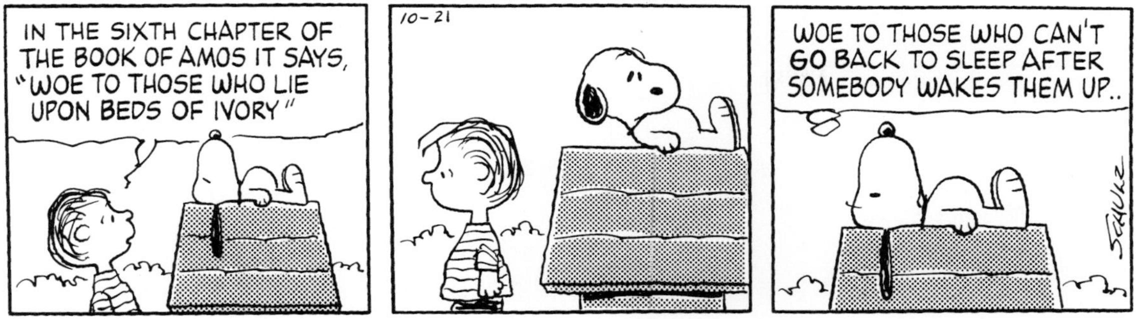
IN THE SIXTH CHAPTER OF THE BOOK OF AMOS IT SAYS, "WOE TO THOSE WHO LIE UPON BEDS OF IVORY"
10-21
WOE TO THOSE WHO CAN'T GO BACK TO SLEEP AFTER SOMEBODY WAKES THEM UP..
SCHULZ

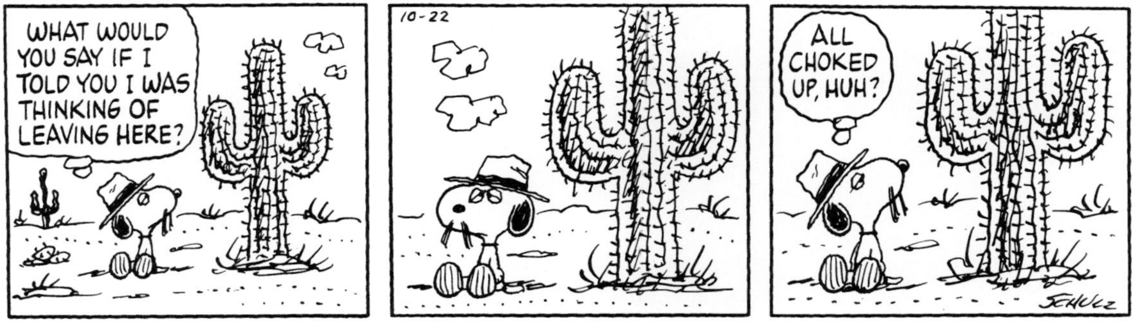
WHAT WOULD YOU SAY IF I TOLD YOU I WAS THINKING OF LEAVING HERE?
10-22
ALL CHOKED UP, HUH?
SCHULZ

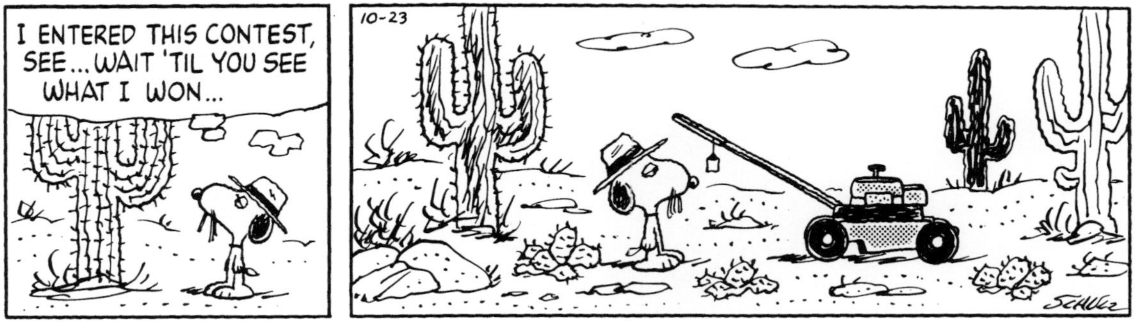
I ENTERED THIS CONTEST, SEE... WAIT 'TIL YOU SEE WHAT I WON...
10-23
SCHULZ

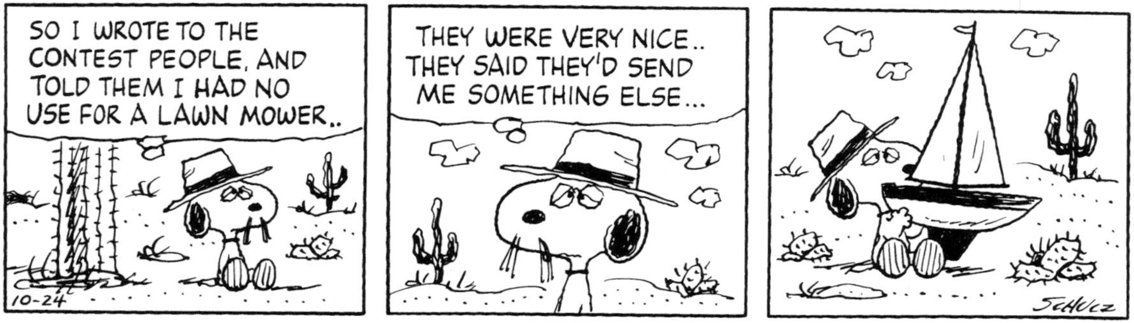
SO I WROTE TO THE CONTEST PEOPLE, AND TOLD THEM I HAD NO USE FOR A LAWN MOWER..
10-24
THEY WERE VERY NICE.. THEY SAID THEY'D SEND ME SOMETHING ELSE...

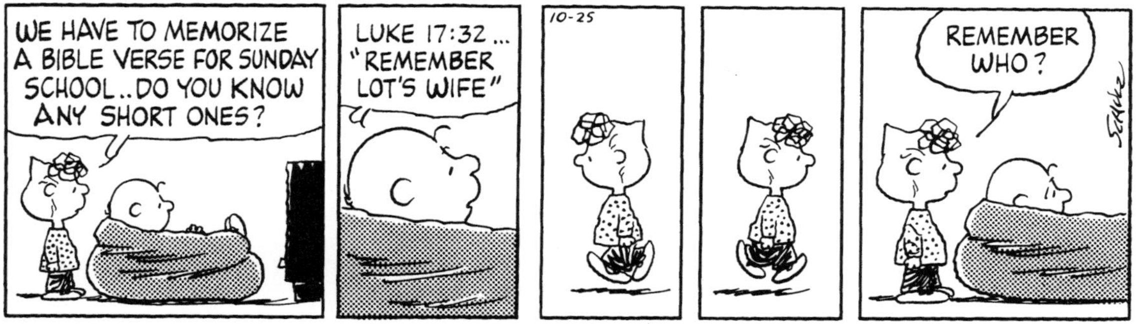
WE HAVE TO MEMORIZE A BIBLE VERSE FOR SUNDAY SCHOOL..DO YOU KNOW ANY SHORT ONES?
LUKE 17:32... "REMEMBER LOT'S WIFE"
10-25
REMEMBER WHO?

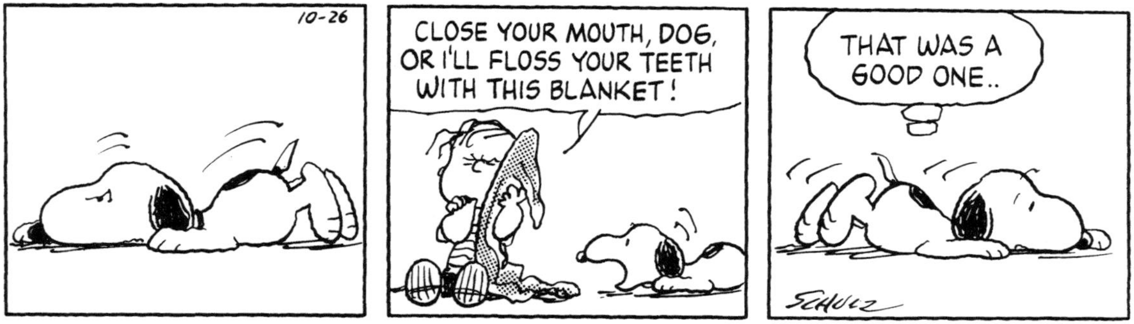
10-26
CLOSE YOUR MOUTH, DOG, OR I'LL FLOSS YOUR TEETH WITH THIS BLANKET!
THAT WAS A GOOD ONE..

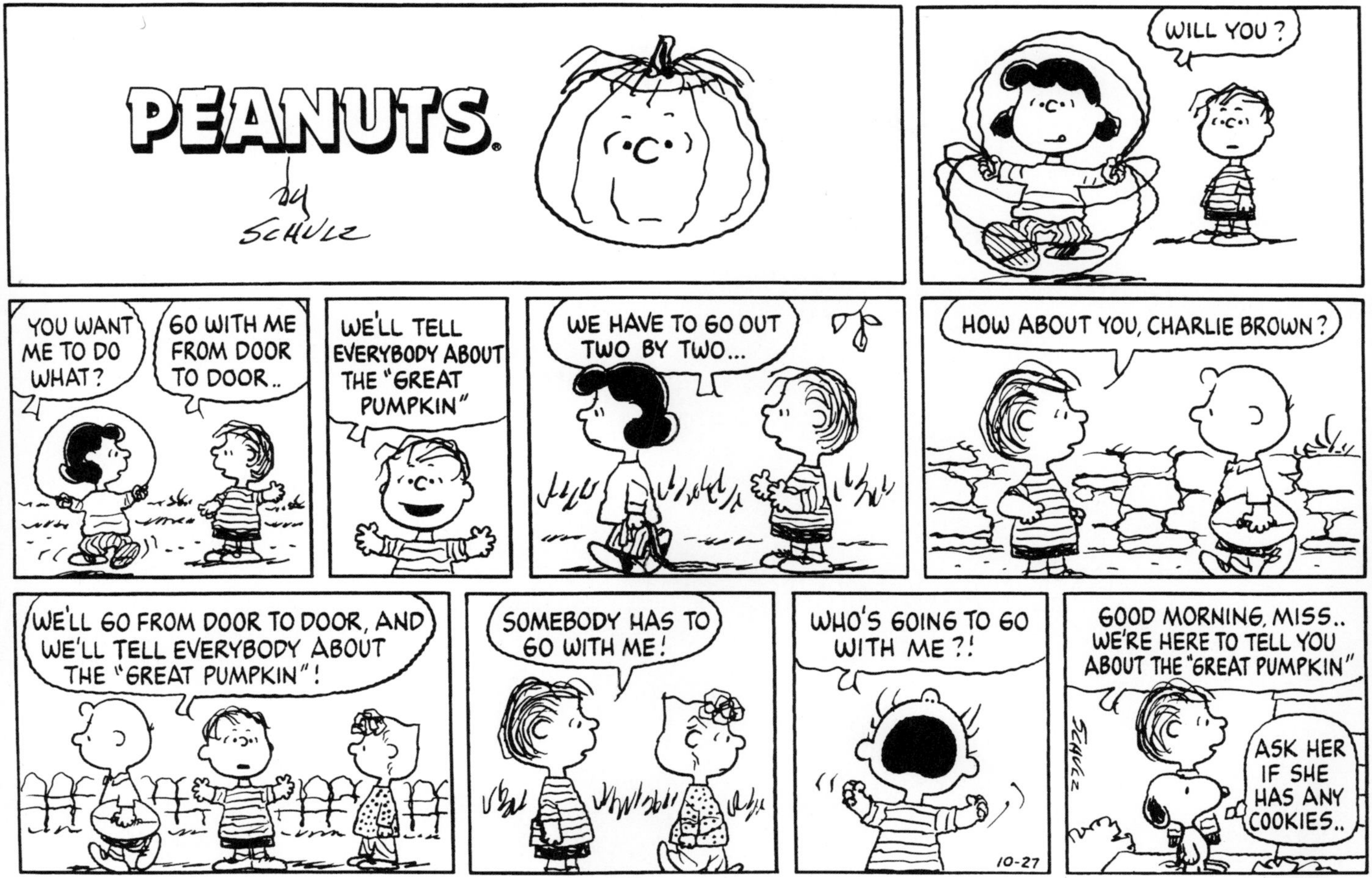
PEANUTS
by SCHULZ
WILL YOU?
YOU WANT ME TO DO WHAT?
GO WITH ME FROM DOOR TO DOOR..
WE'LL TELL EVERYBODY ABOUT THE "GREAT PUMPKIN"
WE HAVE TO GO OUT TWO BY TWO...
HOW ABOUT YOU, CHARLIE BROWN?
WE'LL GO FROM DOOR TO DOOR, AND WE'LL TELL EVERYBODY ABOUT THE "GREAT PUMPKIN"!
SOMEBODY HAS TO GO WITH ME!
WHO'S GOING TO GO WITH ME?!
10-27
GOOD MORNING, MISS.. WE'RE HERE TO TELL YOU ABOUT THE "GREAT PUMPKIN"
SCHULZ
ASK HER IF SHE HAS ANY COOKIES..

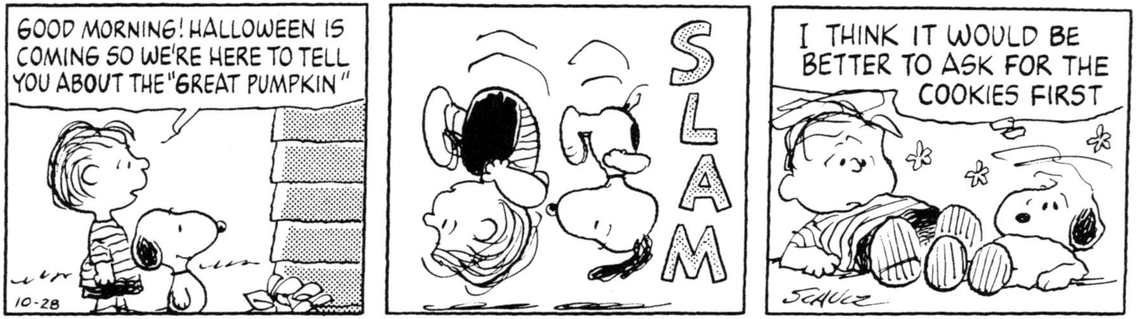
GOOD MORNING! HALLOWEEN IS COMING SO WE'RE HERE TO TELL YOU ABOUT THE "GREAT PUMPKIN"
10-28
SLAM
I THINK IT WOULD BE BETTER TO ASK FOR THE COOKIES FIRST
SCHULZ

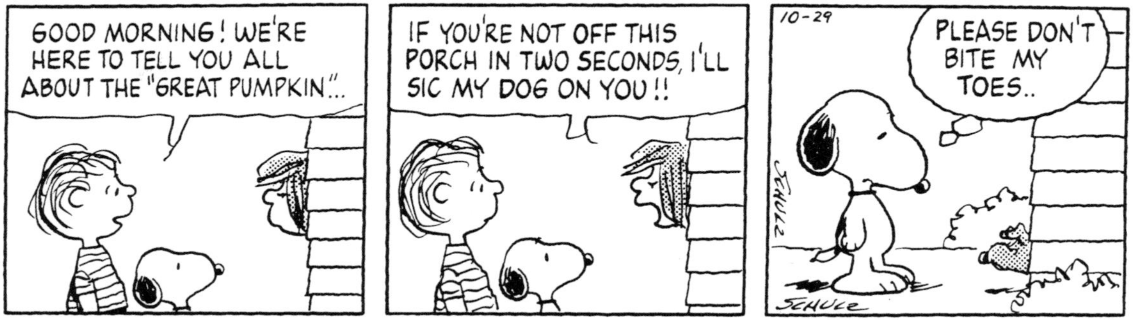
GOOD MORNING! WE'RE HERE TO TELL YOU ALL ABOUT THE "GREAT PUMPKIN"...
IF YOU'RE NOT OFF THIS PORCH IN TWO SECONDS, I'LL SIC MY DOG ON YOU!!
10-29
PLEASE DON'T BITE MY TOES..
SCHULZ

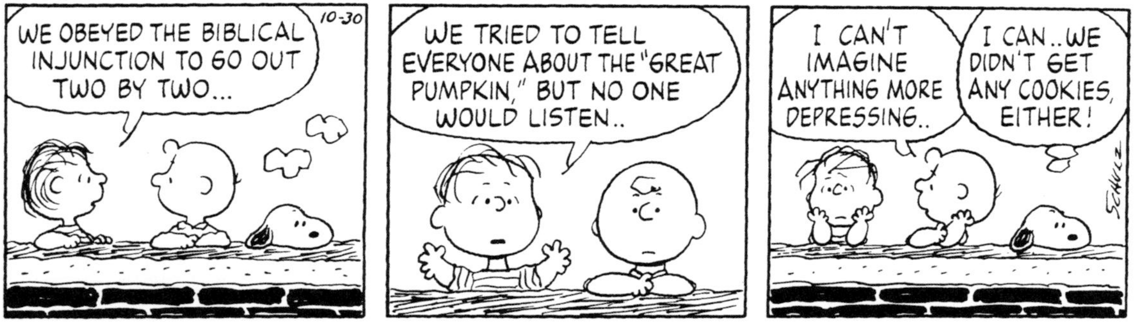
10-30
WE OBEYED THE BIBLICAL INJUNCTION TO GO OUT TWO BY TWO...
WE TRIED TO TELL EVERYONE ABOUT THE "GREAT PUMPKIN," BUT NO ONE WOULD LISTEN..
I CAN'T IMAGINE ANYTHING MORE DEPRESSING..
I CAN..WE DIDN'T GET ANY COOKIES, EITHER!
SCHULZ

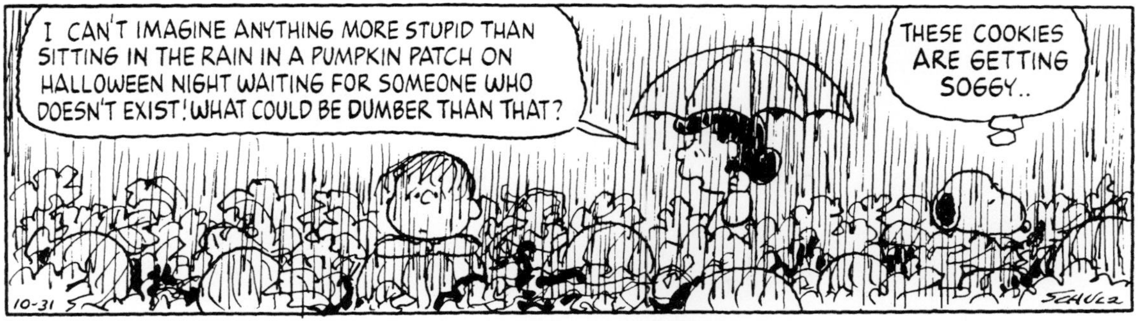
I CAN'T IMAGINE ANYTHING MORE STUPID THAN SITTING IN THE RAIN IN A PUMPKIN PATCH ON HALLOWEEN NIGHT WAITING FOR SOMEONE WHO DOESN'T EXIST! WHAT COULD BE DUMBER THAN THAT?
THESE COOKIES ARE GETTING SOGGY..

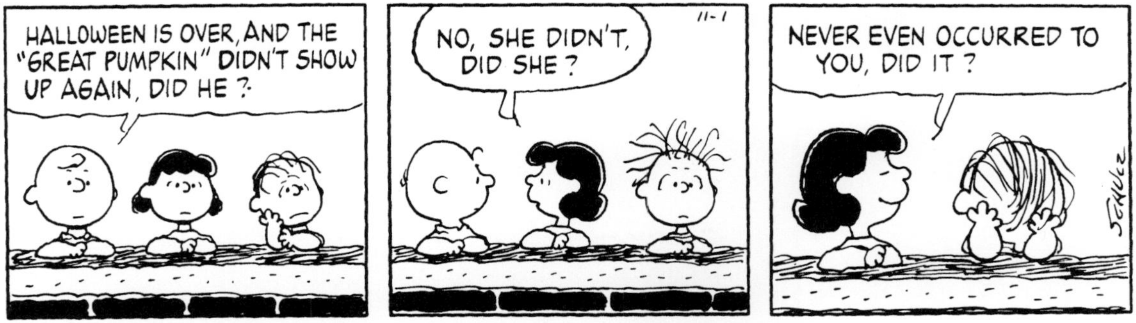
HALLOWEEN IS OVER, AND THE "GREAT PUMPKIN" DIDN'T SHOW UP AGAIN, DID HE ?
NO, SHE DIDN'T, DID SHE ?
NEVER EVEN OCCURRED TO YOU, DID IT ?

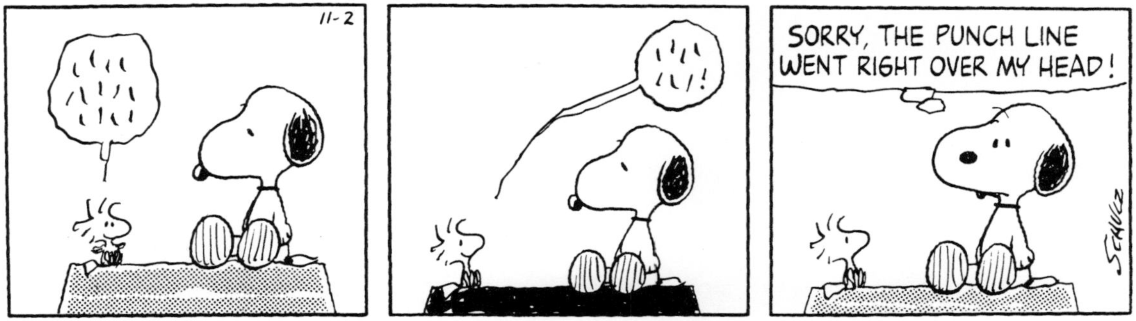
SORRY, THE PUNCH LINE WENT RIGHT OVER MY HEAD!

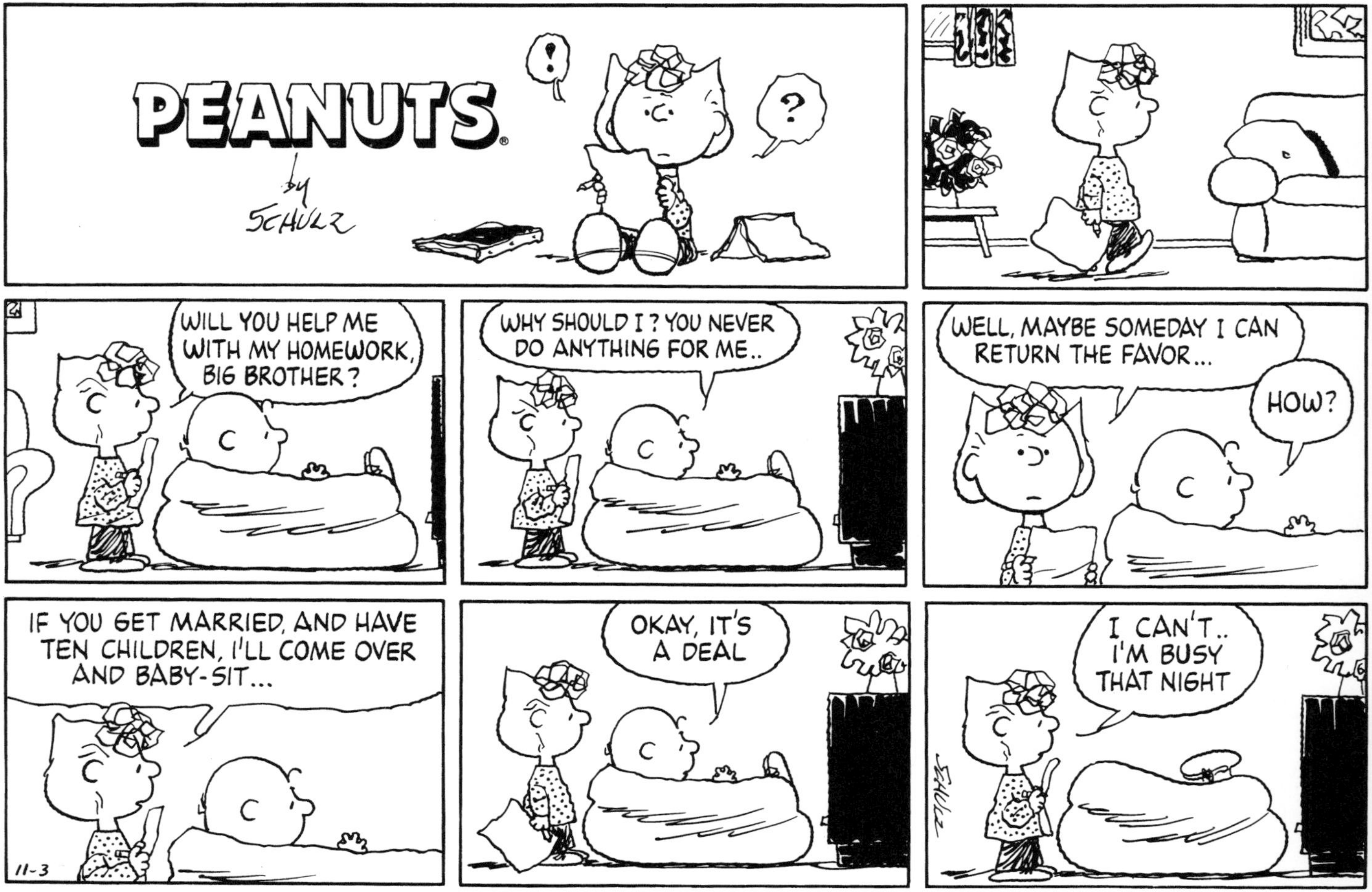
PEANUTS
by SCHULZ
!
?
WILL YOU HELP ME WITH MY HOMEWORK, BIG BROTHER?
WHY SHOULD I? YOU NEVER DO ANYTHING FOR ME..
WELL, MAYBE SOMEDAY I CAN RETURN THE FAVOR...
HOW?
IF YOU GET MARRIED, AND HAVE TEN CHILDREN, I'LL COME OVER AND BABY-SIT...
11-3
OKAY, IT'S A DEAL
I CAN'T.. I'M BUSY THAT NIGHT
SCHULZ

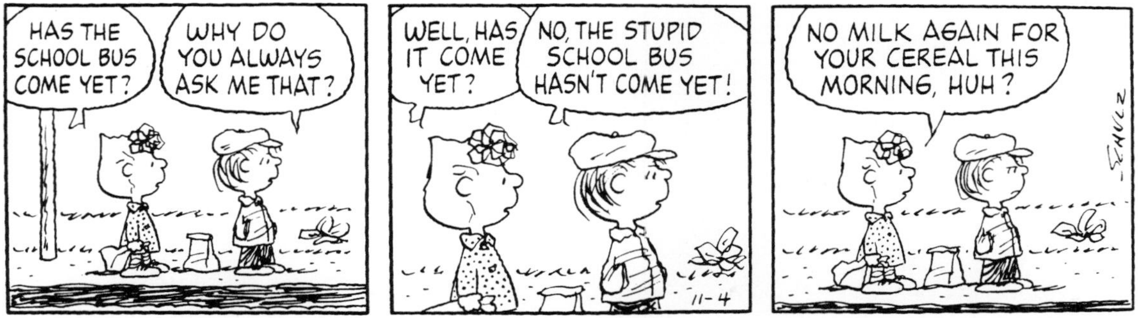
HAS THE SCHOOL BUS COME YET?
WHY DO YOU ALWAYS ASK ME THAT?
WELL, HAS IT COME YET?
NO, THE STUPID SCHOOL BUS HASN'T COME YET!
11-4
NO MILK AGAIN FOR YOUR CEREAL THIS MORNING, HUH?
SCHULZ

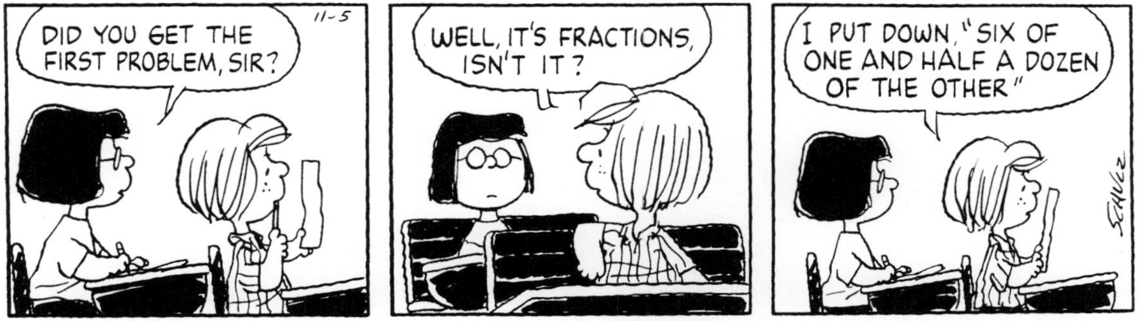
11-5
DID YOU GET THE FIRST PROBLEM, SIR?
WELL, IT'S FRACTIONS, ISN'T IT?
I PUT DOWN, "SIX OF ONE AND HALF A DOZEN OF THE OTHER"
SCHULZ

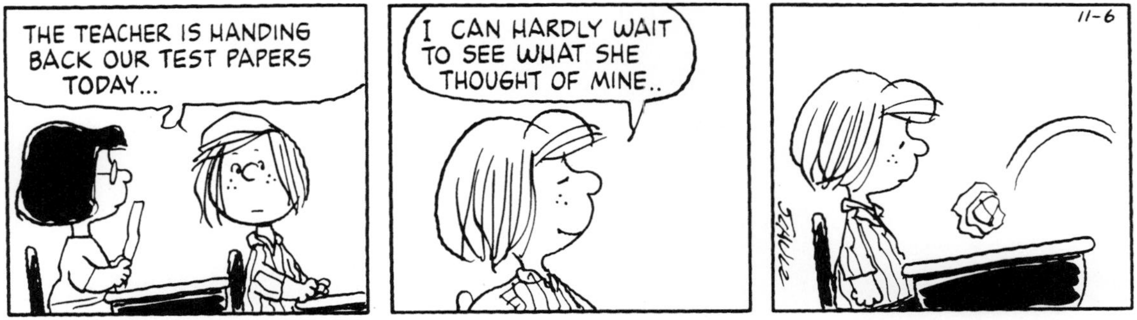
THE TEACHER IS HANDING BACK OUR TEST PAPERS TODAY...
I CAN HARDLY WAIT TO SEE WHAT SHE THOUGHT OF MINE..
11-6
SCHULZ

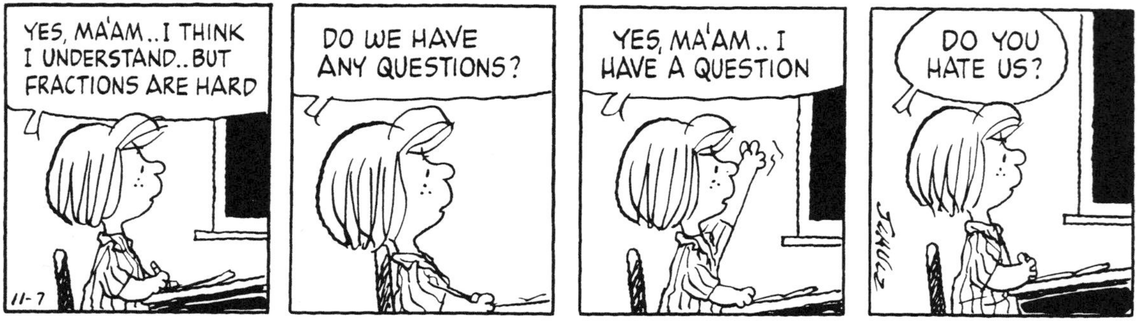
YES, MA'AM.. I THINK I UNDERSTAND.. BUT FRACTIONS ARE HARD
11-7
DO WE HAVE ANY QUESTIONS?
YES, MA'AM.. I HAVE A QUESTION
DO YOU HATE US?

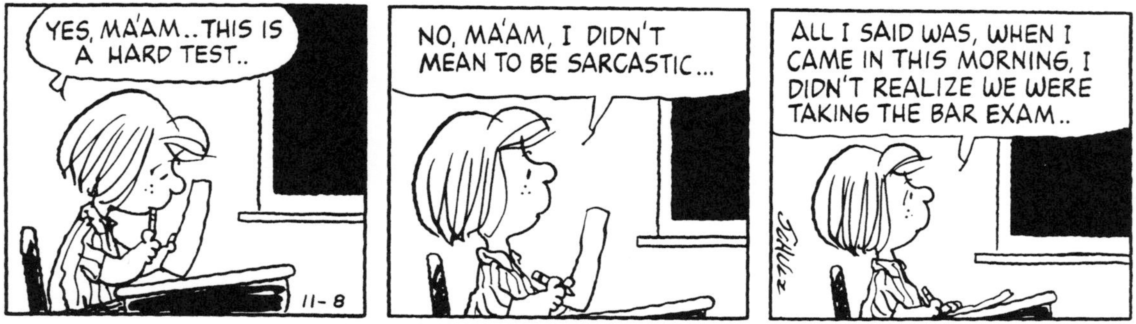
YES, MA'AM..THIS IS A HARD TEST..
11-8
NO, MA'AM, I DIDN'T MEAN TO BE SARCASTIC...
ALL I SAID WAS, WHEN I CAME IN THIS MORNING, I DIDN'T REALIZE WE WERE TAKING THE BAR EXAM..

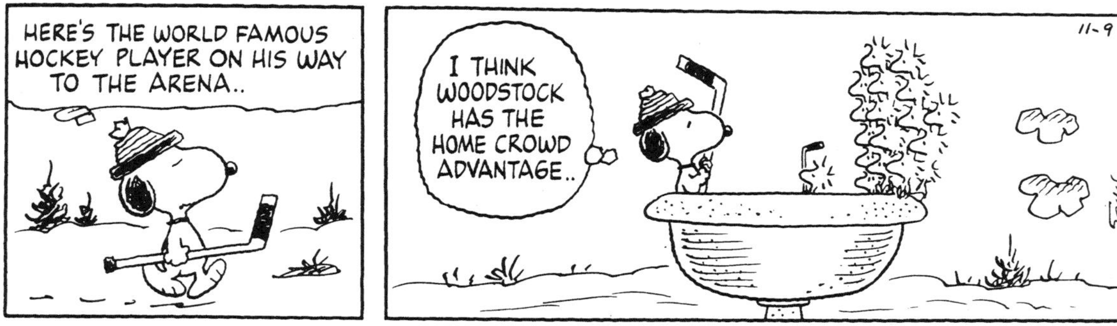
HERE'S THE WORLD FAMOUS HOCKEY PLAYER ON HIS WAY TO THE ARENA..
11-9
I THINK WOODSTOCK HAS THE HOME CROWD ADVANTAGE..

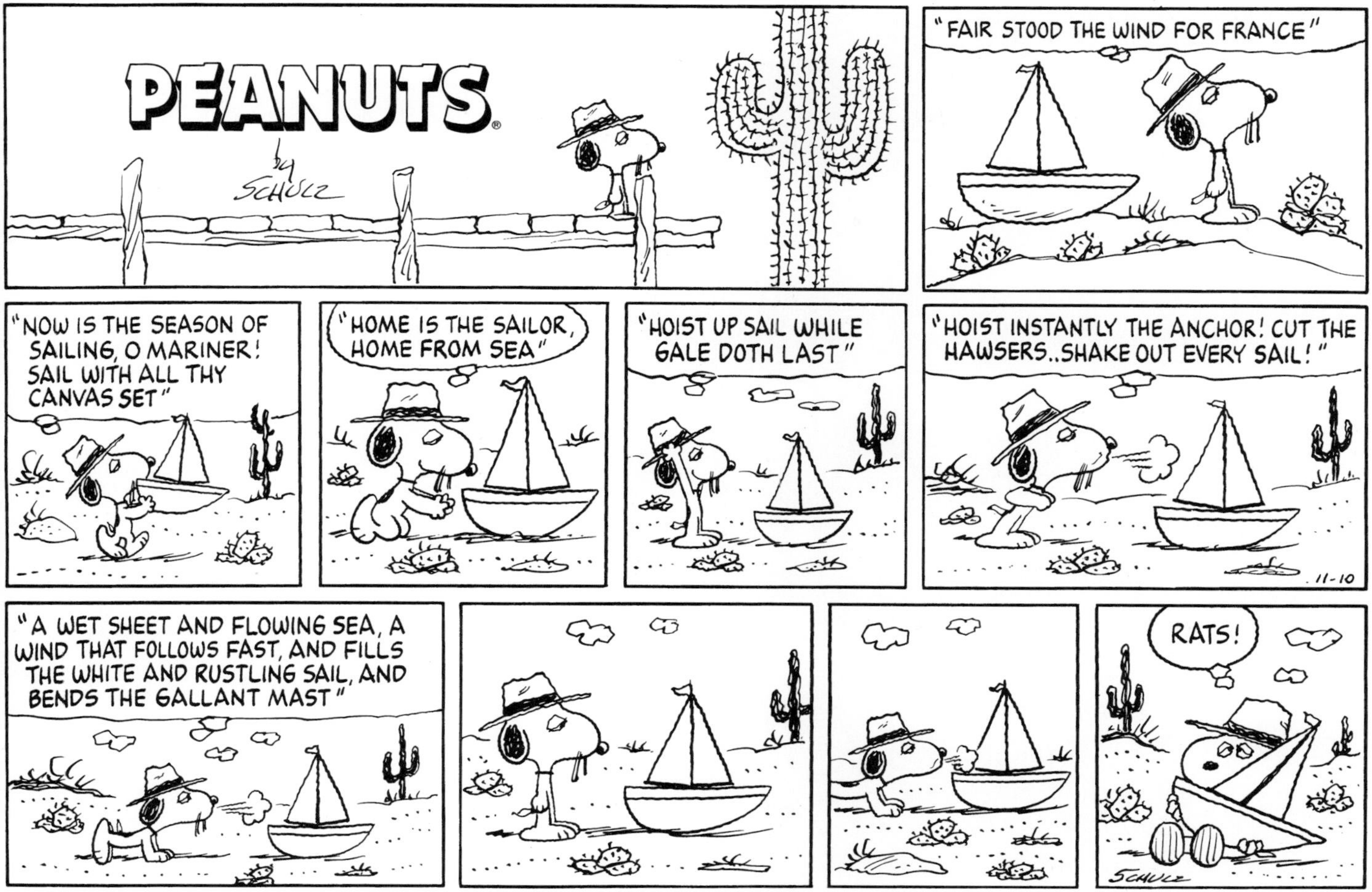
PEANUTS®
by SCHULZ
"FAIR STOOD THE WIND FOR FRANCE"
"NOW IS THE SEASON OF SAILING, O MARINER! SAIL WITH ALL THY CANVAS SET"
"HOME IS THE SAILOR, HOME FROM SEA"
"HOIST UP SAIL WHILE GALE DOTH LAST"
"HOIST INSTANTLY THE ANCHOR! CUT THE HAWSERS..SHAKE OUT EVERY SAIL!"
11-10
"A WET SHEET AND FLOWING SEA, A WIND THAT FOLLOWS FAST, AND FILLS THE WHITE AND RUSTLING SAIL, AND BENDS THE GALLANT MAST"
RATS!
SCHULZ

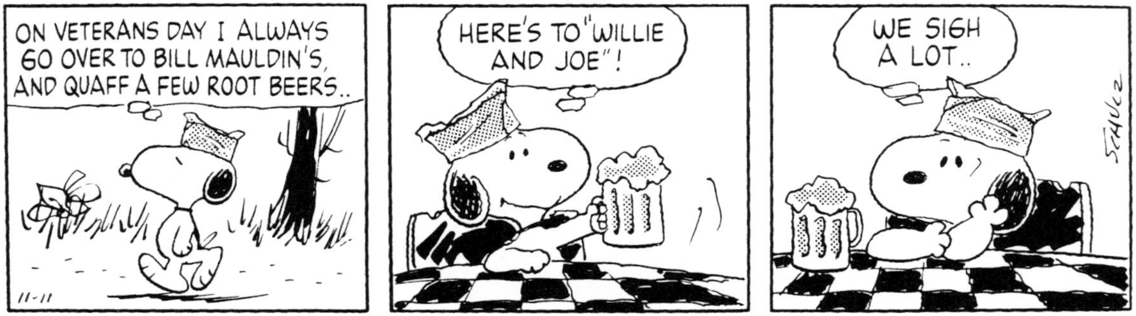
ON VETERANS DAY I ALWAYS GO OVER TO BILL MAULDIN'S, AND QUAFF A FEW ROOT BEERS..
HERE'S TO "WILLIE AND JOE"!
WE SIGH A LOT..

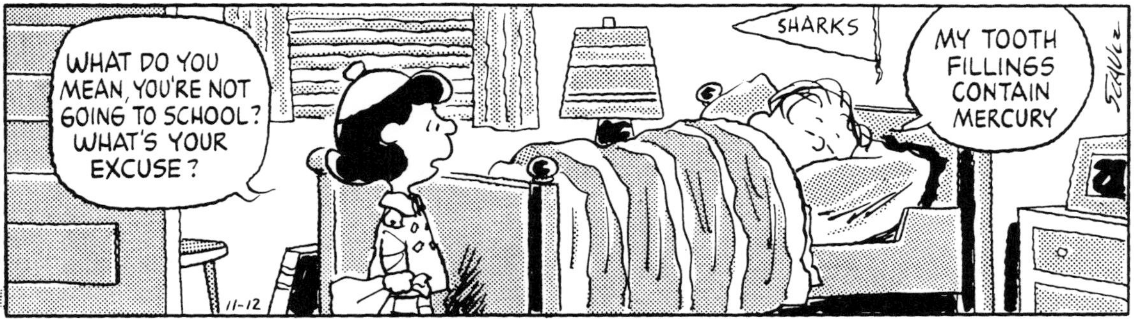
WHAT DO YOU MEAN, YOU'RE NOT GOING TO SCHOOL? WHAT'S YOUR EXCUSE?
SHARKS
MY TOOTH FILLINGS CONTAIN MERCURY

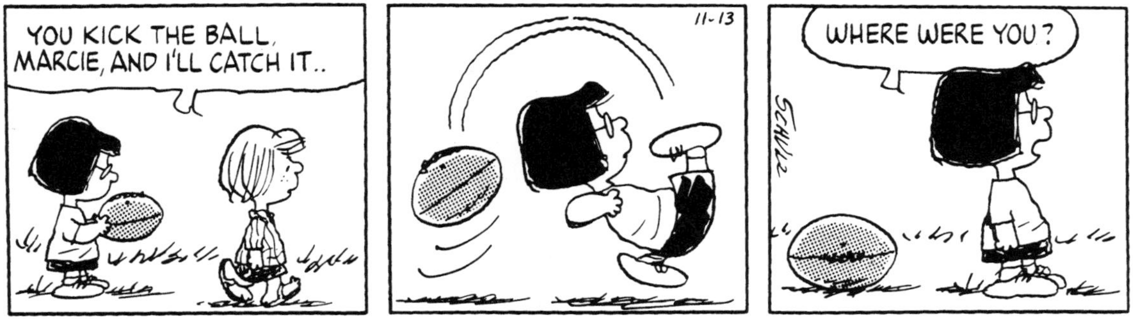
YOU KICK THE BALL, MARCIE, AND I'LL CATCH IT..
WHERE WERE YOU?

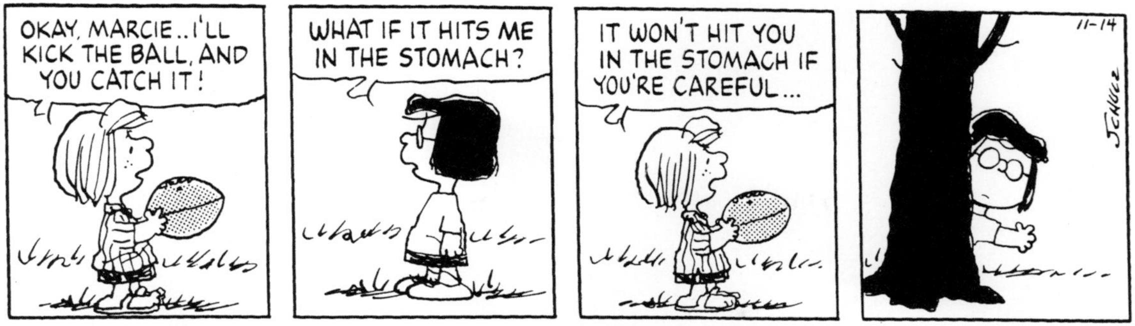
OKAY, MARCIE.. I'LL KICK THE BALL, AND YOU CATCH IT!
WHAT IF IT HITS ME IN THE STOMACH?
IT WON'T HIT YOU IN THE STOMACH IF YOU'RE CAREFUL...
11-14
SCHULZ

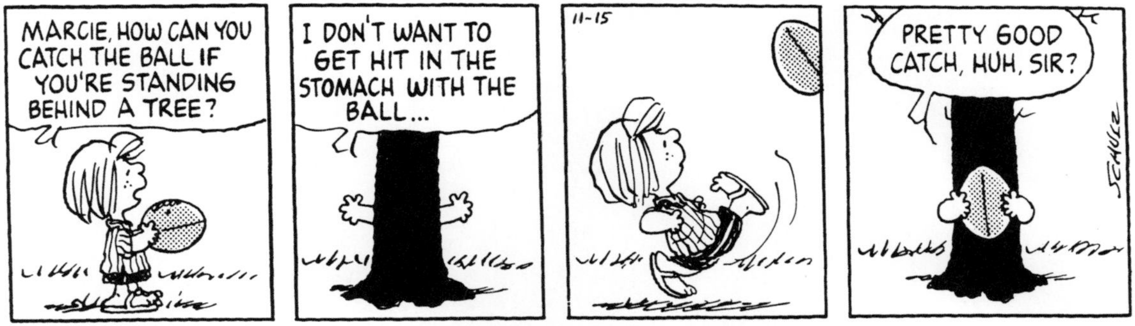
MARCIE, HOW CAN YOU CATCH THE BALL IF YOU'RE STANDING BEHIND A TREE?
I DON'T WANT TO GET HIT IN THE STOMACH WITH THE BALL...
11-15
PRETTY GOOD CATCH, HUH, SIR?
SCHULZ

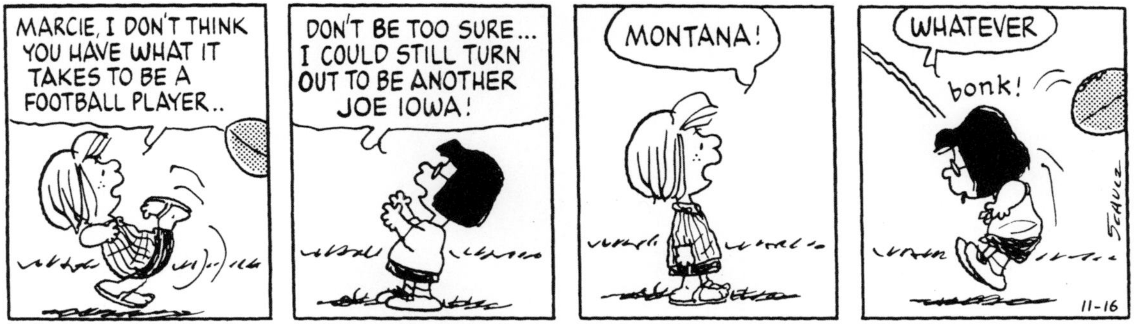
MARCIE, I DON'T THINK YOU HAVE WHAT IT TAKES TO BE A FOOTBALL PLAYER..
DON'T BE TOO SURE... I COULD STILL TURN OUT TO BE ANOTHER JOE IOWA!
MONTANA!
WHATEVER
bonk!
SCHULZ
11-16

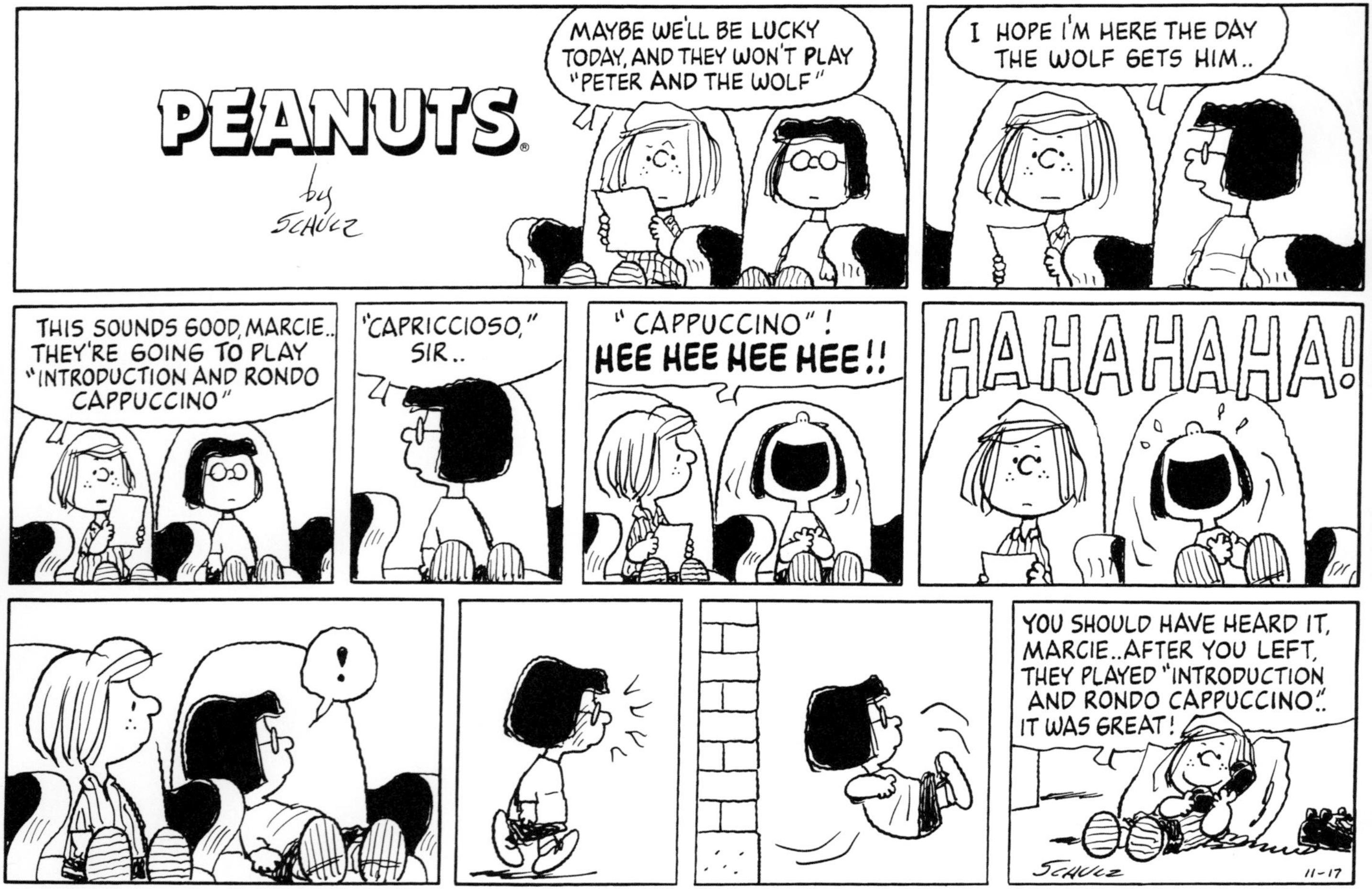
PEANUTS
by SCHULZ
MAYBE WE'LL BE LUCKY TODAY, AND THEY WON'T PLAY "PETER AND THE WOLF"
I HOPE I'M HERE THE DAY THE WOLF GETS HIM..
THIS SOUNDS GOOD, MARCIE.. THEY'RE GOING TO PLAY "INTRODUCTION AND RONDO CAPPUCCINO"
"CAPRICCIOSO," SIR..
"CAPPUCCINO"! HEE HEE HEE HEE!!
HAHAHAHA!
!
YOU SHOULD HAVE HEARD IT, MARCIE..AFTER YOU LEFT, THEY PLAYED "INTRODUCTION AND RONDO CAPPUCCINO".. IT WAS GREAT!
SCHULZ
11-17

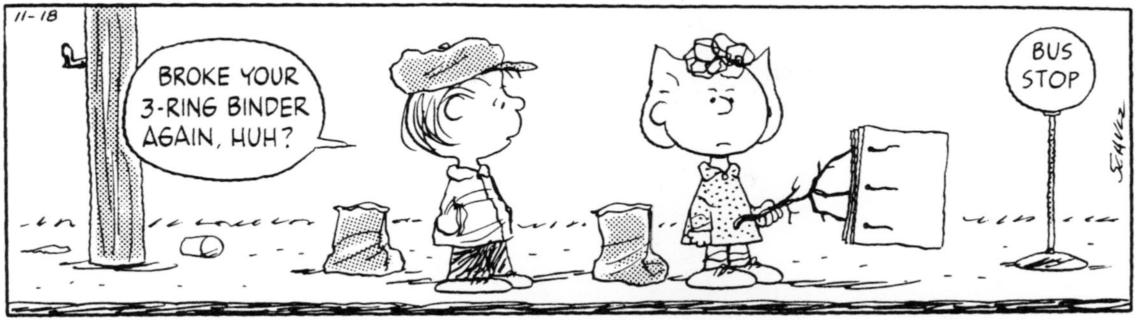
11-18
BROKE YOUR 3-RING BINDER AGAIN, HUH?
BUS STOP
SCHULZ

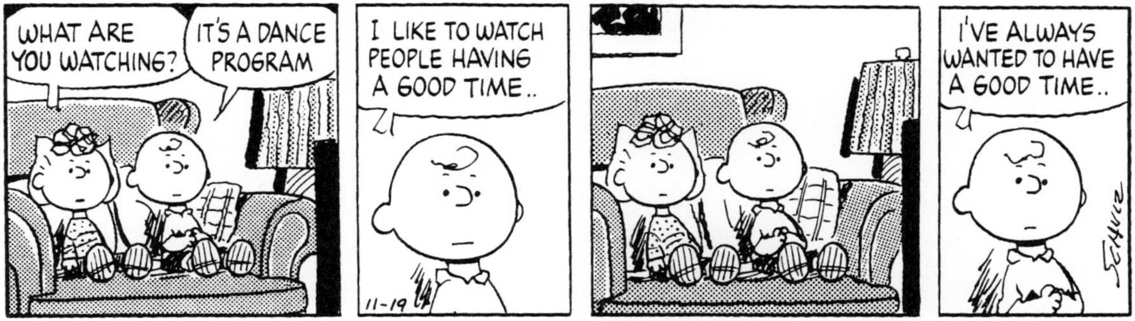
WHAT ARE YOU WATCHING?
IT'S A DANCE PROGRAM
I LIKE TO WATCH PEOPLE HAVING A GOOD TIME..
11-19
I'VE ALWAYS WANTED TO HAVE A GOOD TIME..
SCHULZ

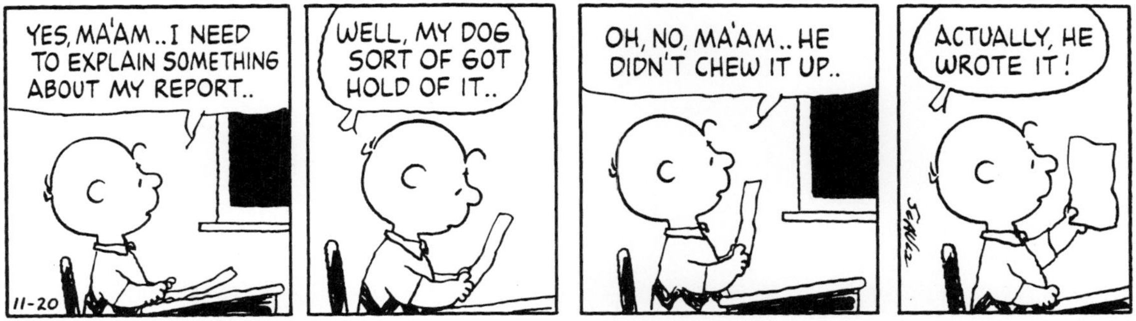
YES, MA'AM..I NEED TO EXPLAIN SOMETHING ABOUT MY REPORT..
11-20
WELL, MY DOG SORT OF GOT HOLD OF IT..
OH, NO, MA'AM.. HE DIDN'T CHEW IT UP..
SCHULZ
ACTUALLY, HE WROTE IT!

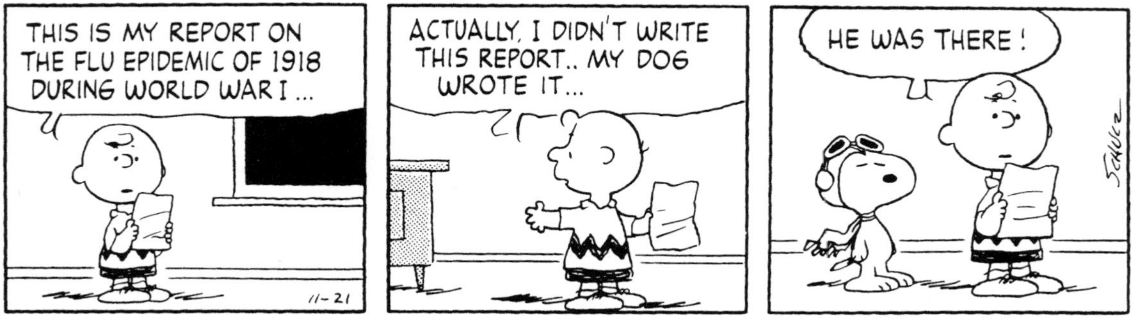
THIS IS MY REPORT ON THE FLU EPIDEMIC OF 1918 DURING WORLD WAR I ...
ACTUALLY, I DIDN'T WRITE THIS REPORT.. MY DOG WROTE IT...
HE WAS THERE!

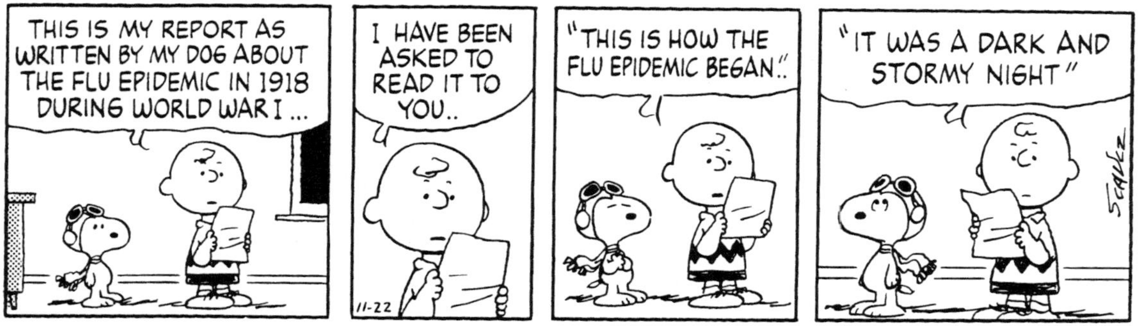
THIS IS MY REPORT AS WRITTEN BY MY DOG ABOUT THE FLU EPIDEMIC IN 1918 DURING WORLD WAR I ...
I HAVE BEEN ASKED TO READ IT TO YOU..
"THIS IS HOW THE FLU EPIDEMIC BEGAN."
"IT WAS A DARK AND STORMY NIGHT"

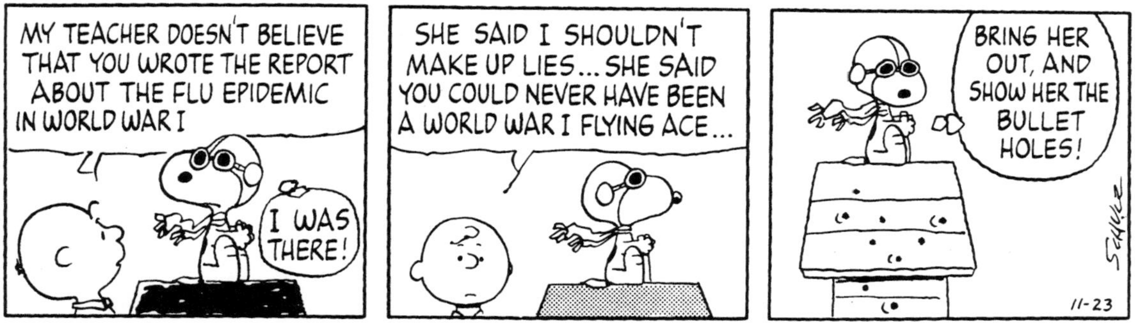
MY TEACHER DOESN'T BELIEVE THAT YOU WROTE THE REPORT ABOUT THE FLU EPIDEMIC IN WORLD WAR I
I WAS THERE!
SHE SAID I SHOULDN'T MAKE UP LIES... SHE SAID YOU COULD NEVER HAVE BEEN A WORLD WAR I FLYING ACE...
BRING HER OUT, AND SHOW HER THE BULLET HOLES!

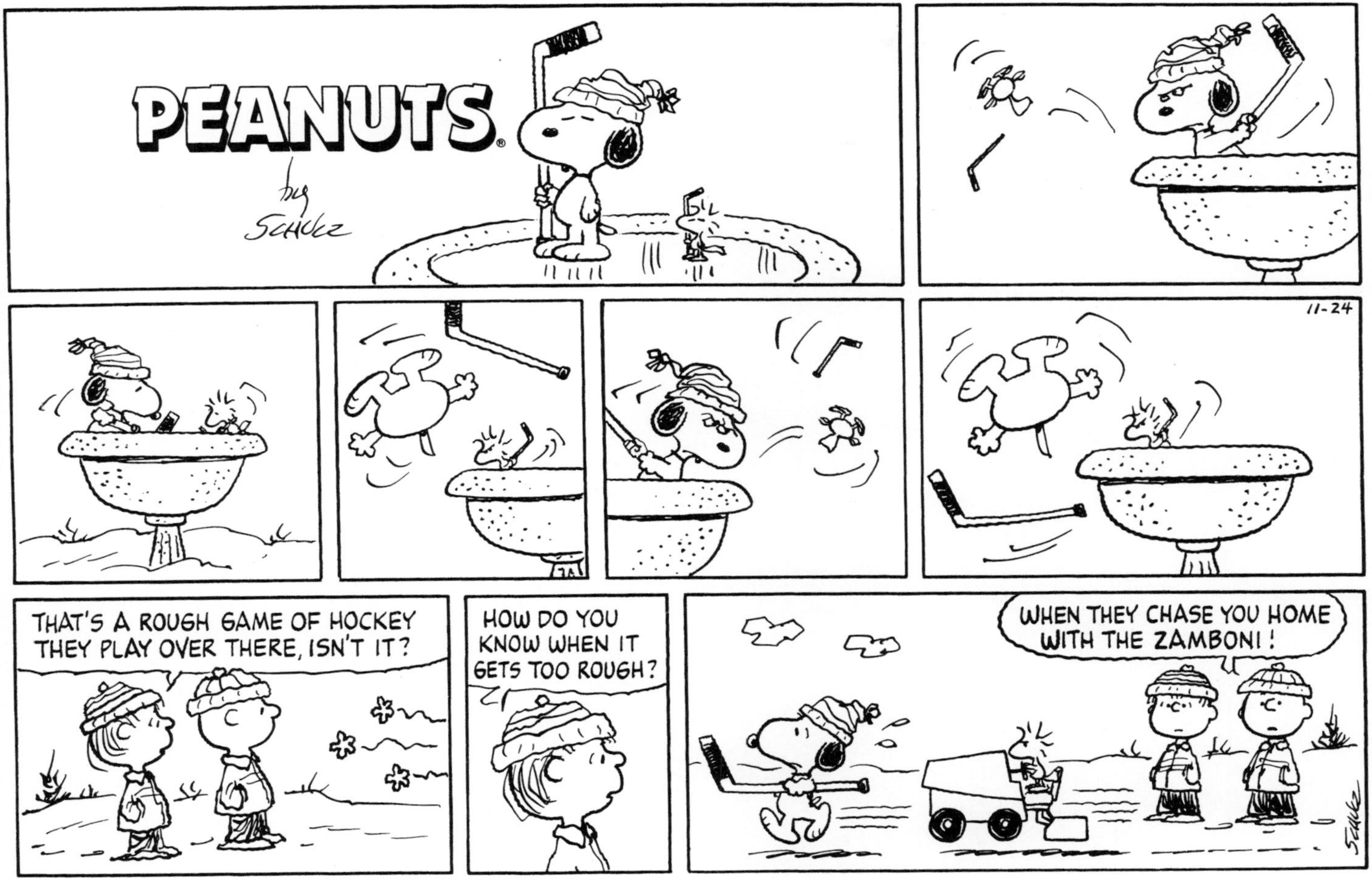
PEANUTS®
by SCHULZ
11-24
THAT'S A ROUGH GAME OF HOCKEY THEY PLAY OVER THERE, ISN'T IT?
HOW DO YOU KNOW WHEN IT GETS TOO ROUGH?
WHEN THEY CHASE YOU HOME WITH THE ZAMBONI!
SCHULZ

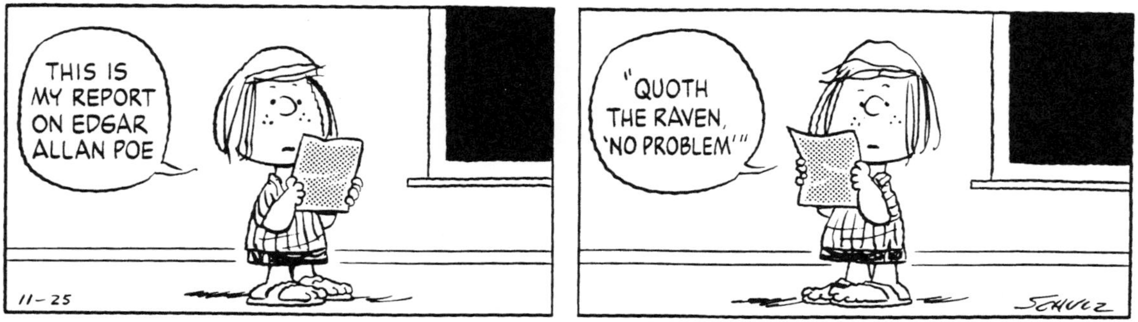
THIS IS MY REPORT ON EDGAR ALLAN POE
"QUOTH THE RAVEN, 'NO PROBLEM'"
11-25
SCHULZ

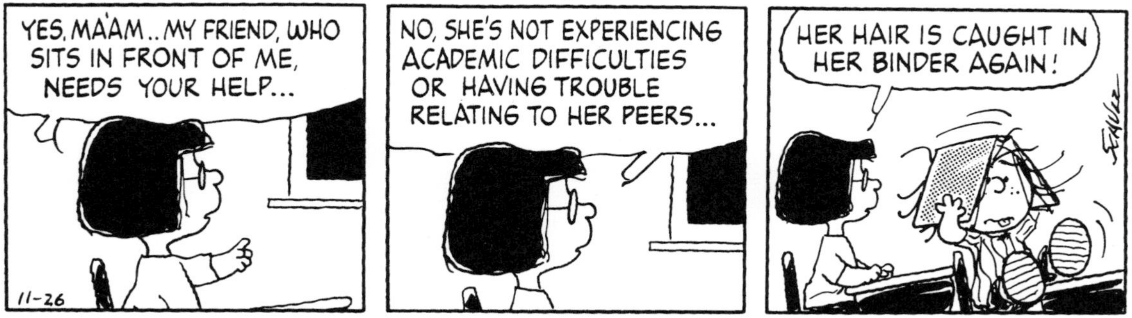
YES, MA'AM.. MY FRIEND, WHO SITS IN FRONT OF ME, NEEDS YOUR HELP...
NO, SHE'S NOT EXPERIENCING ACADEMIC DIFFICULTIES OR HAVING TROUBLE RELATING TO HER PEERS...
HER HAIR IS CAUGHT IN HER BINDER AGAIN!
11-26
SCHULZ

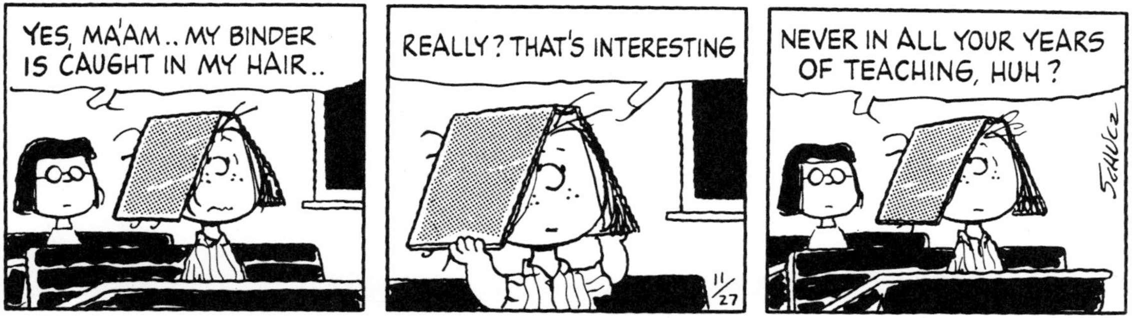
YES, MA'AM.. MY BINDER IS CAUGHT IN MY HAIR..
REALLY? THAT'S INTERESTING
NEVER IN ALL YOUR YEARS OF TEACHING, HUH?
11/27
SCHULZ

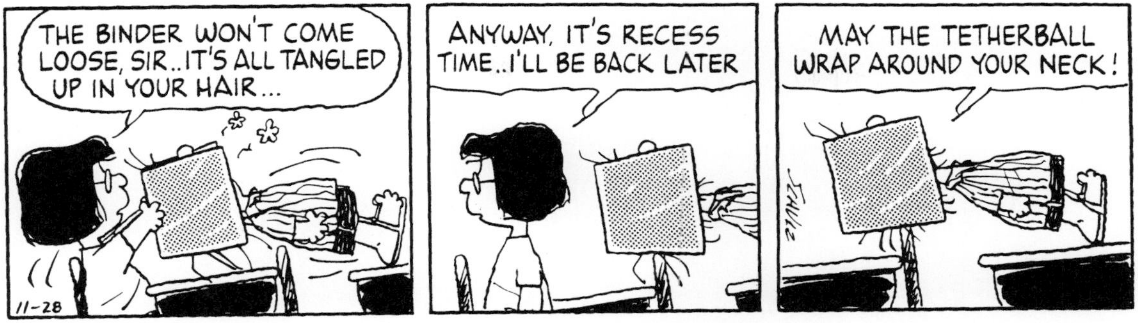
THE BINDER WON'T COME LOOSE, SIR..IT'S ALL TANGLED UP IN YOUR HAIR...
11-28
ANYWAY, IT'S RECESS TIME..I'LL BE BACK LATER
MAY THE TETHERBALL WRAP AROUND YOUR NECK!

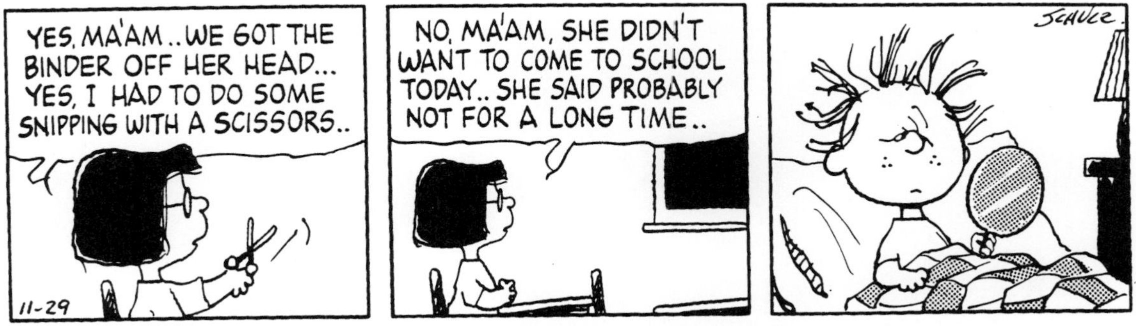
YES, MA'AM..WE GOT THE BINDER OFF HER HEAD... YES, I HAD TO DO SOME SNIPPING WITH A SCISSORS..
11-29
NO, MA'AM, SHE DIDN'T WANT TO COME TO SCHOOL TODAY.. SHE SAID PROBABLY NOT FOR A LONG TIME..

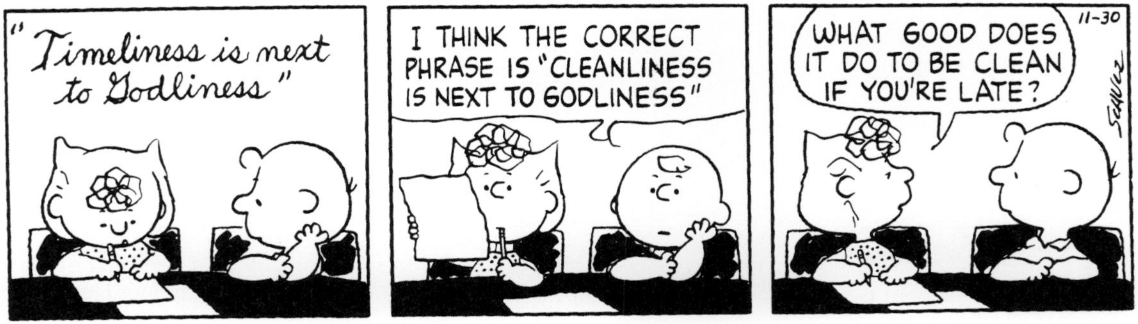
"Timeliness is next to Godliness"
I THINK THE CORRECT PHRASE IS "CLEANLINESS IS NEXT TO GODLINESS"
11-30
WHAT GOOD DOES IT DO TO BE CLEAN IF YOU'RE LATE?

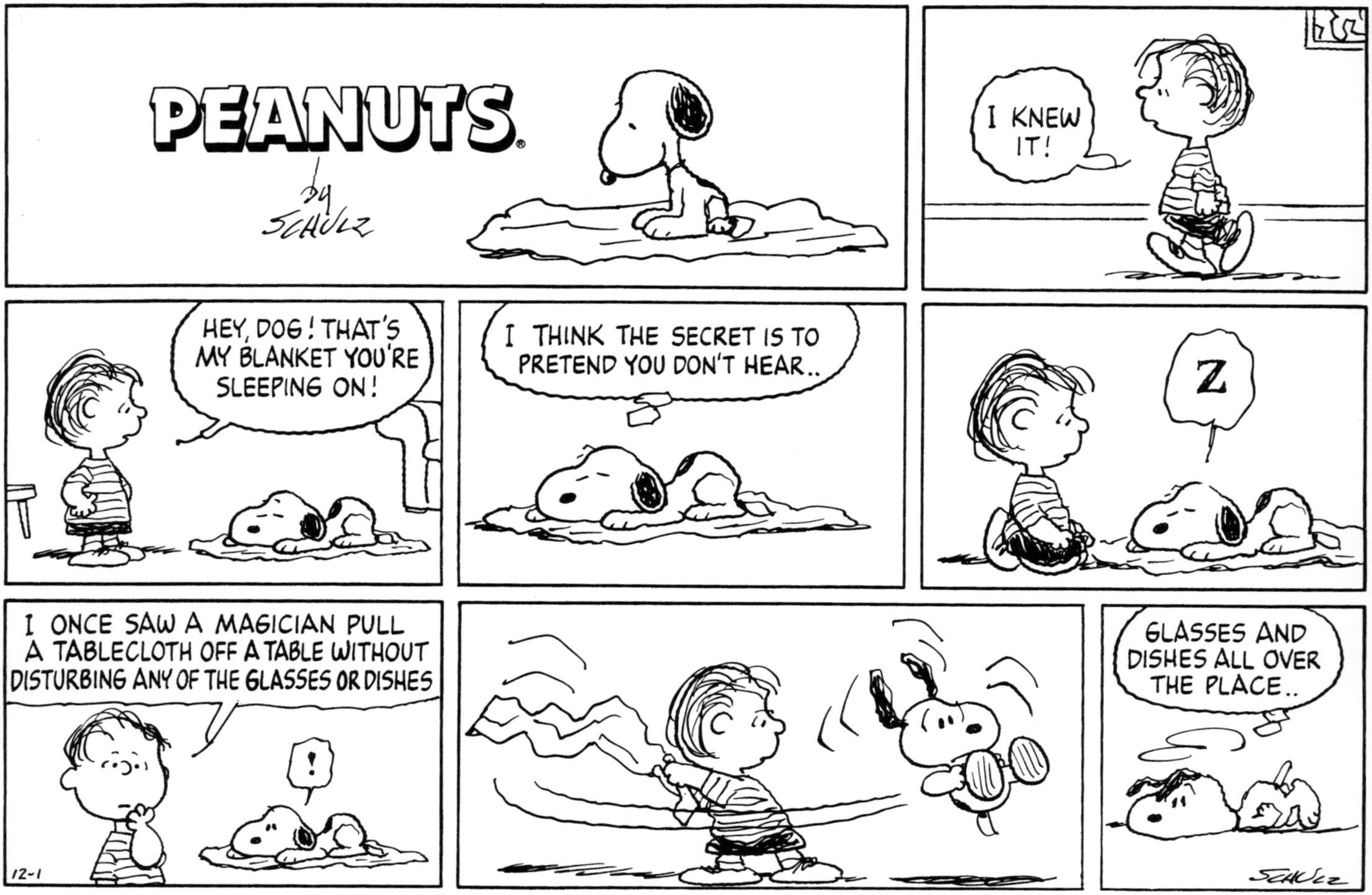
PEANUTS
by SCHULZ
I KNEW IT!
HEY, DOG! THAT'S MY BLANKET YOU'RE SLEEPING ON!
I THINK THE SECRET IS TO PRETEND YOU DON'T HEAR..
Z
I ONCE SAW A MAGICIAN PULL A TABLECLOTH OFF A TABLE WITHOUT DISTURBING ANY OF THE GLASSES OR DISHES
!
12-1
GLASSES AND DISHES ALL OVER THE PLACE..
SCHULZ

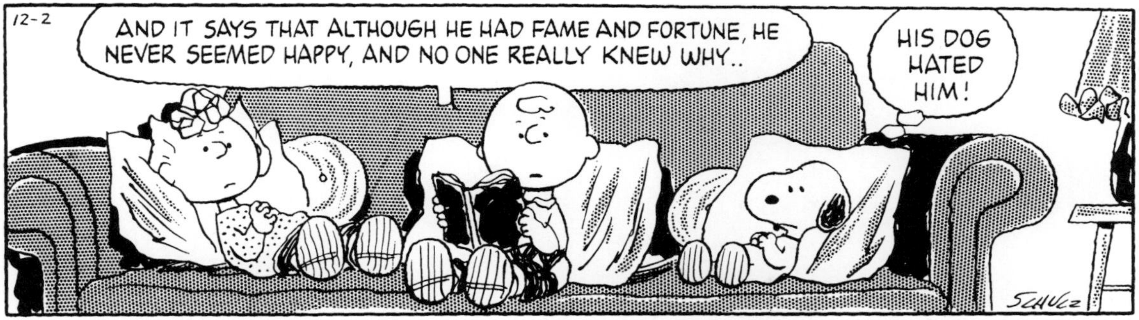
12-2
AND IT SAYS THAT ALTHOUGH HE HAD FAME AND FORTUNE, HE NEVER SEEMED HAPPY, AND NO ONE REALLY KNEW WHY..
HIS DOG HATED HIM!
SCHULZ

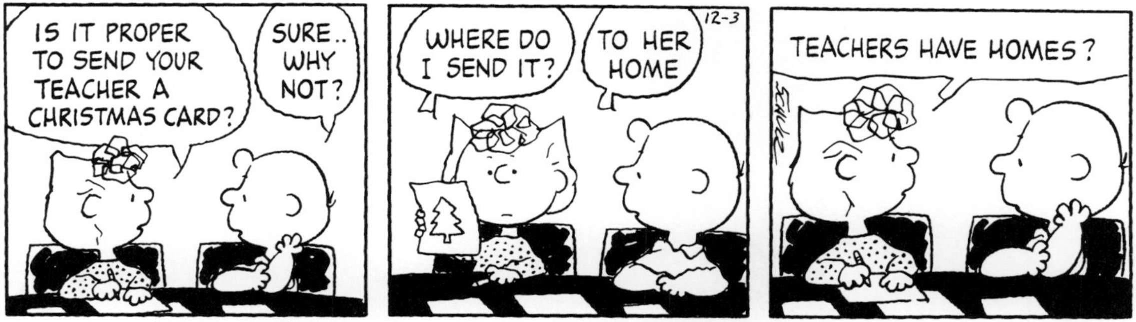
IS IT PROPER TO SEND YOUR TEACHER A CHRISTMAS CARD?
SURE.. WHY NOT?
12-3
WHERE DO I SEND IT?
TO HER HOME
TEACHERS HAVE HOMES?
SCHULZ

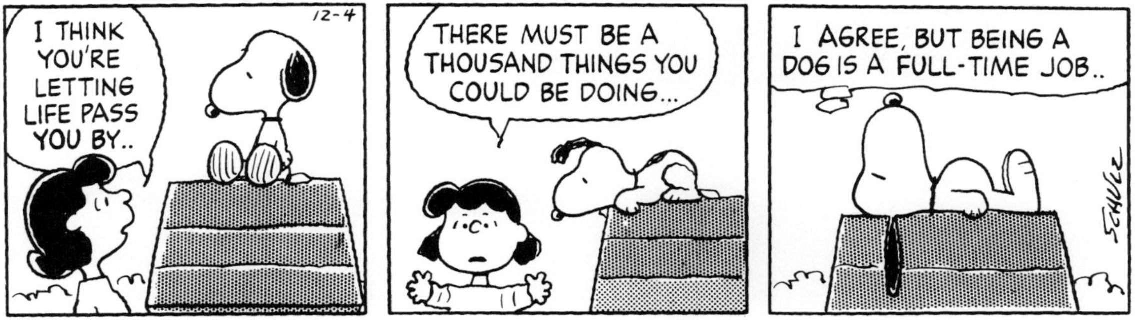
12-4
I THINK YOU'RE LETTING LIFE PASS YOU BY..
THERE MUST BE A THOUSAND THINGS YOU COULD BE DOING...
I AGREE, BUT BEING A DOG IS A FULL-TIME JOB..
SCHULZ

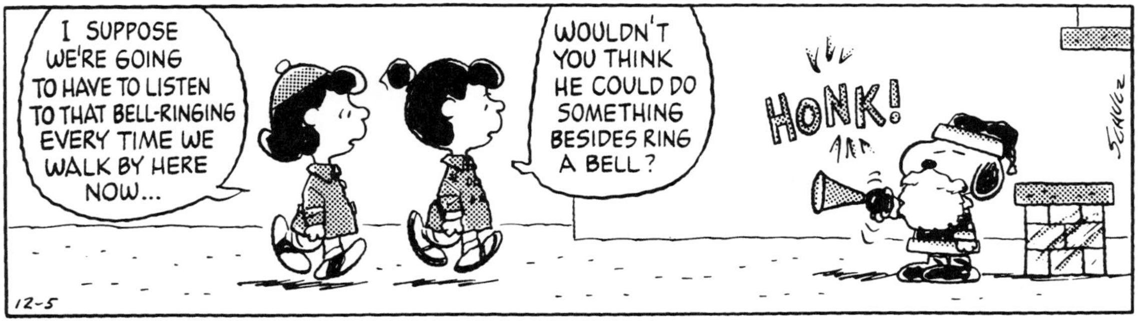
I SUPPOSE WE'RE GOING TO HAVE TO LISTEN TO THAT BELL-RINGING EVERY TIME WE WALK BY HERE NOW...
WOULDN'T YOU THINK HE COULD DO SOMETHING BESIDES RING A BELL?
HONK!
12-5

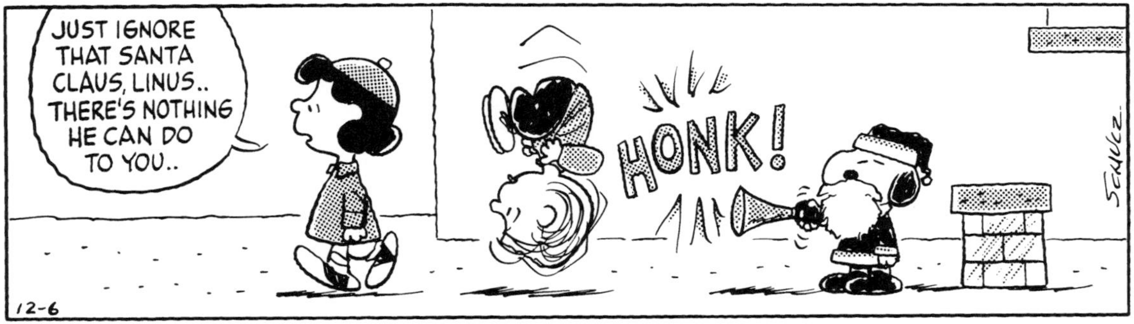
JUST IGNORE THAT SANTA CLAUS, LINUS.. THERE'S NOTHING HE CAN DO TO YOU..
HONK!
12-6

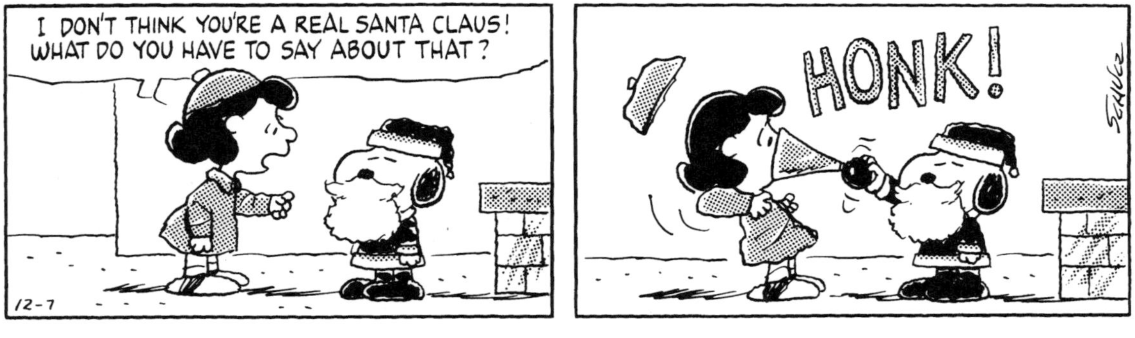
I DON'T THINK YOU'RE A REAL SANTA CLAUS! WHAT DO YOU HAVE TO SAY ABOUT THAT?
HONK!
12-7

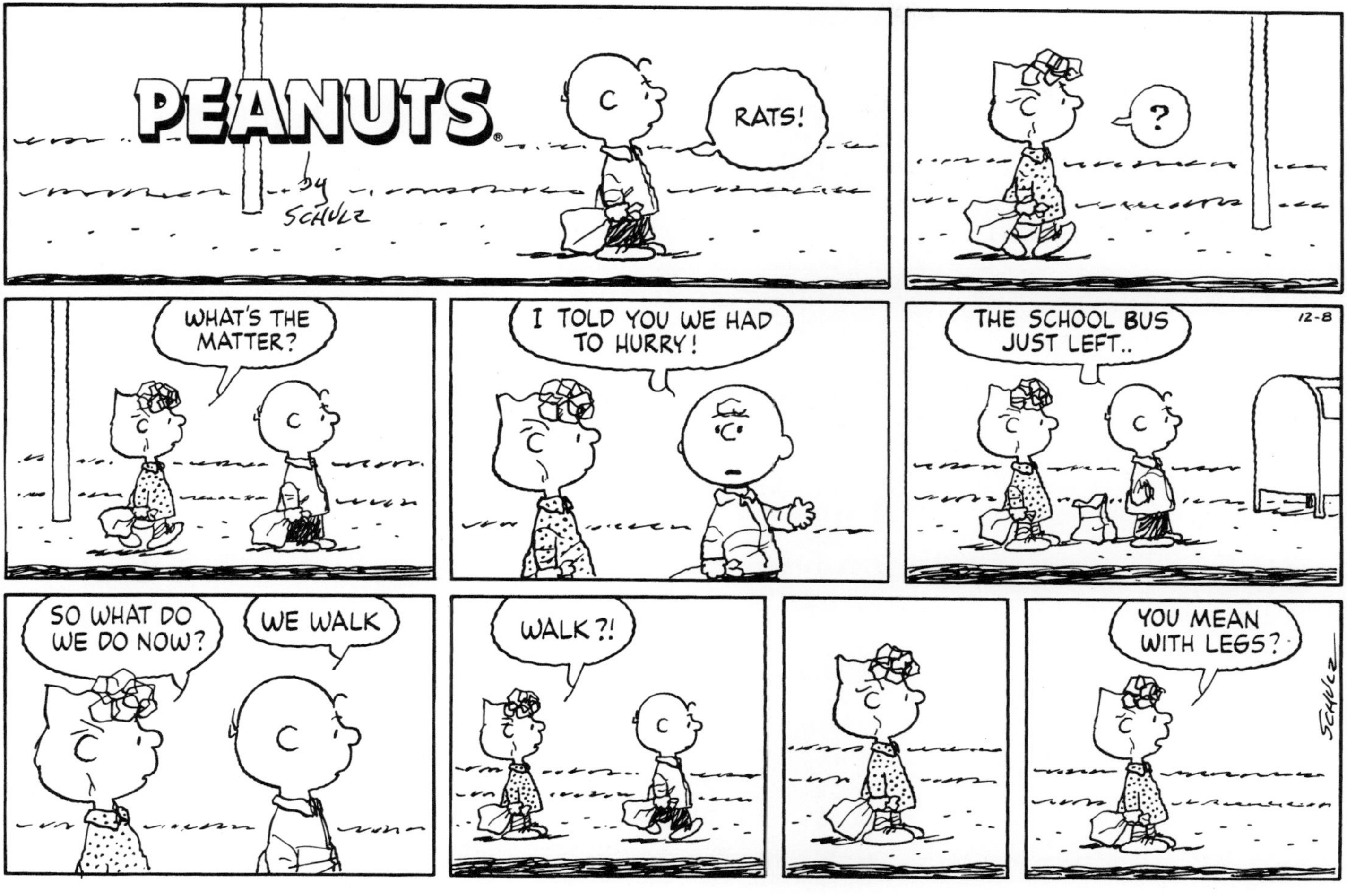
PEANUTS
by SCHULZ
RATS!
?
WHAT'S THE MATTER?
I TOLD YOU WE HAD TO HURRY!
THE SCHOOL BUS JUST LEFT..
12-8
SO WHAT DO WE DO NOW?
WE WALK
WALK?!
YOU MEAN WITH LEGS?
SCHULZ

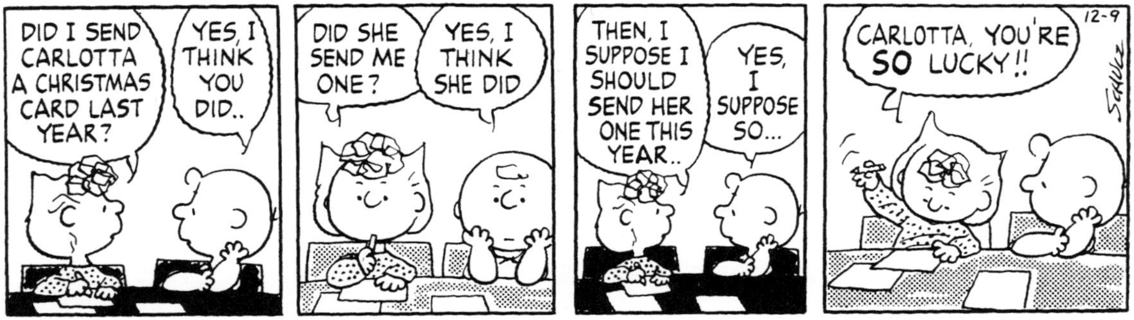
DID I SEND CARLOTTA A CHRISTMAS CARD LAST YEAR?
YES, I THINK YOU DID..
DID SHE SEND ME ONE?
YES, I THINK SHE DID
THEN, I SUPPOSE I SHOULD SEND HER ONE THIS YEAR..
YES, I SUPPOSE SO...
12-9
CARLOTTA, YOU'RE SO LUCKY!!
SCHULZ

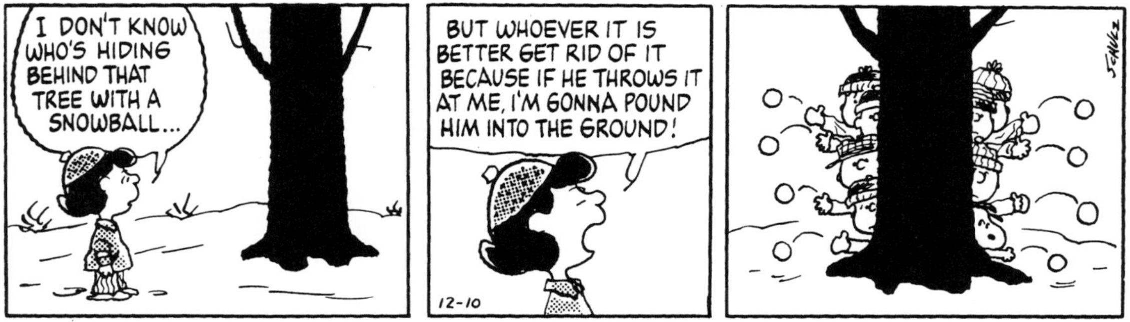
I DON'T KNOW WHO'S HIDING BEHIND THAT TREE WITH A SNOWBALL...
BUT WHOEVER IT IS BETTER GET RID OF IT BECAUSE IF HE THROWS IT AT ME, I'M GONNA POUND HIM INTO THE GROUND!
12-10
SCHULZ

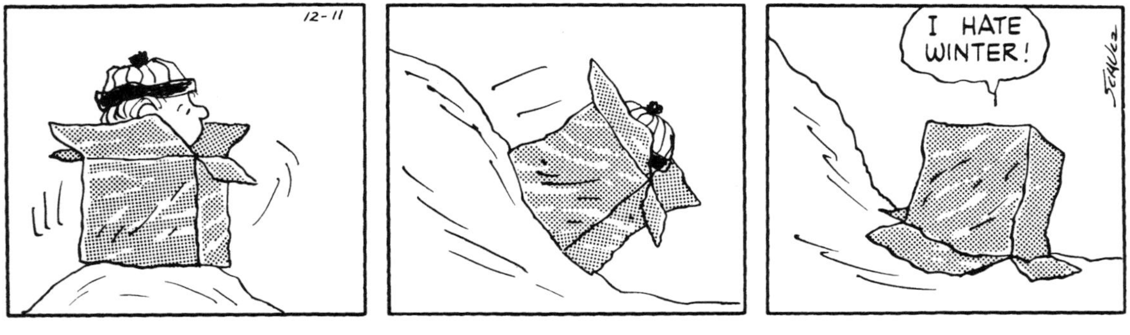
12-11
I HATE WINTER!
SCHULZ

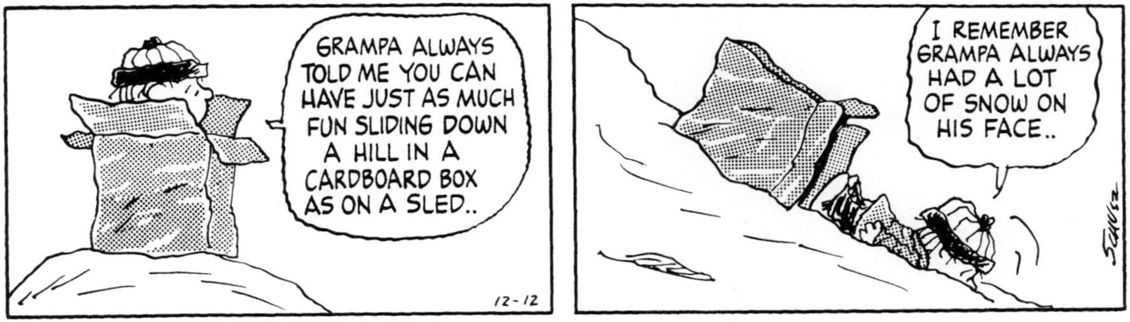
GRAMPA ALWAYS TOLD ME YOU CAN HAVE JUST AS MUCH FUN SLIDING DOWN A HILL IN A CARDBOARD BOX AS ON A SLED..
12-12
I REMEMBER GRAMPA ALWAYS HAD A LOT OF SNOW ON HIS FACE..
SCHULZ

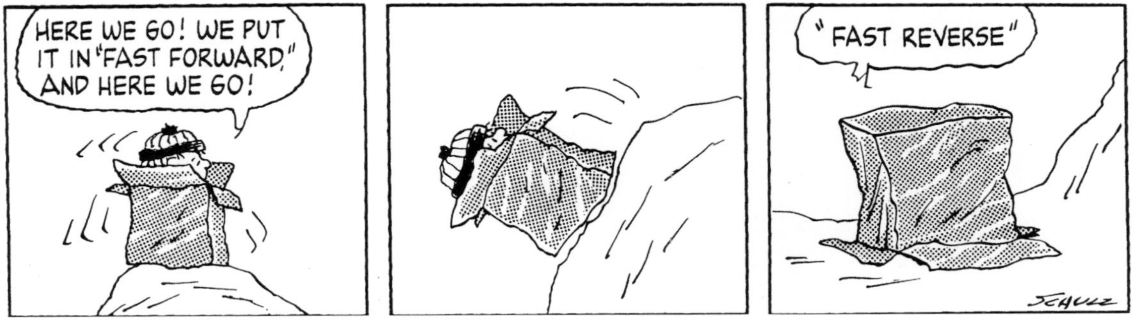
HERE WE GO! WE PUT IT IN "FAST FORWARD," AND HERE WE GO!
"FAST REVERSE"
SCHULZ

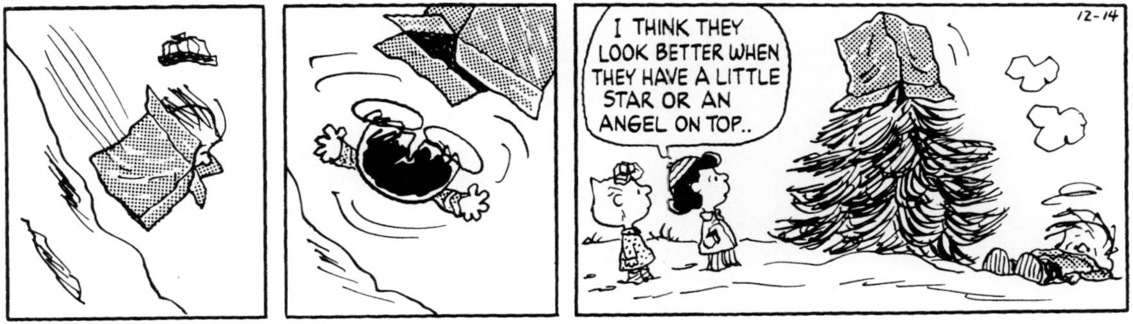
12-14
I THINK THEY LOOK BETTER WHEN THEY HAVE A LITTLE STAR OR AN ANGEL ON TOP..

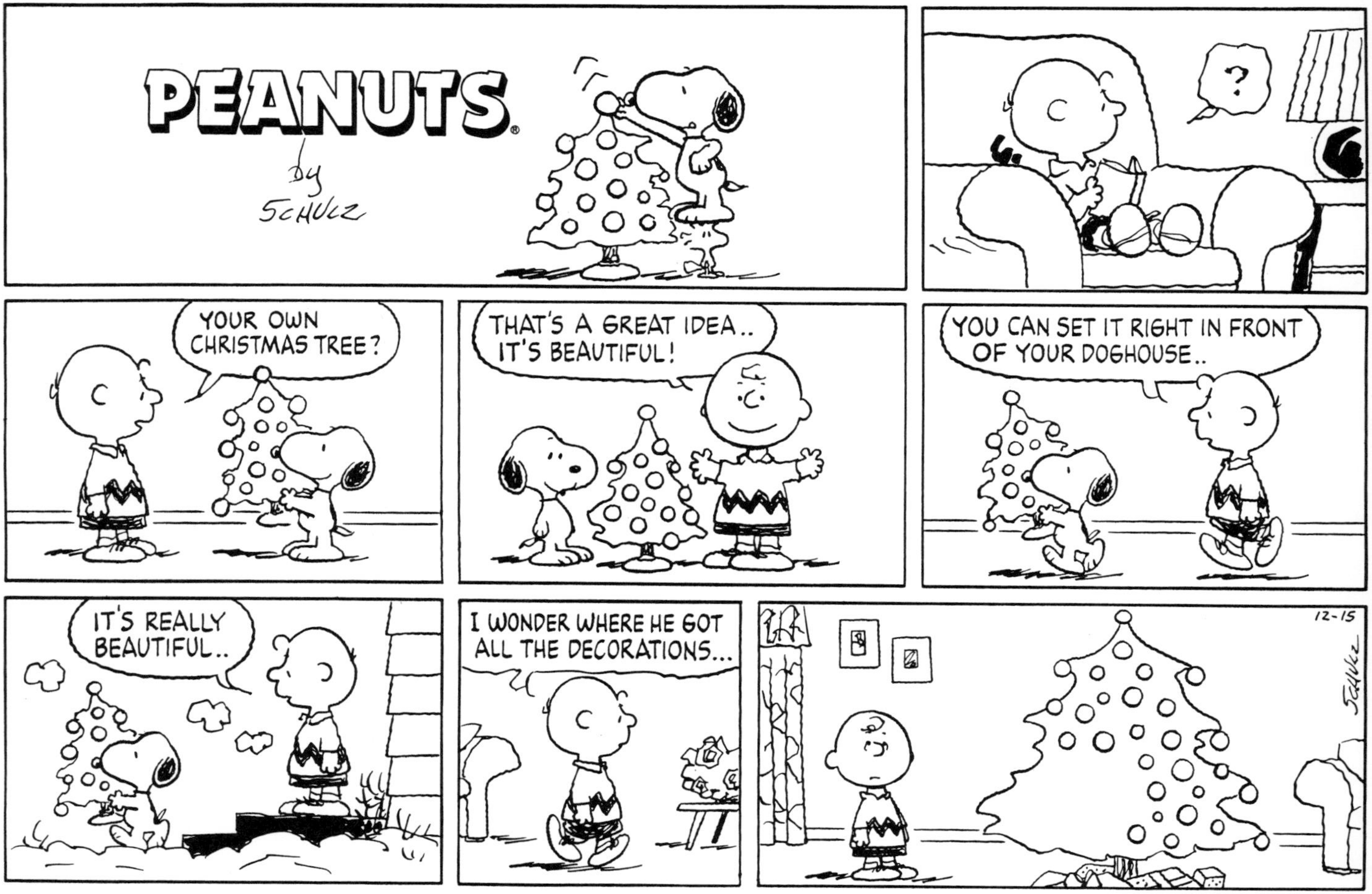
PEANUTS
by SCHULZ
?
YOUR OWN CHRISTMAS TREE?
THAT'S A GREAT IDEA.. IT'S BEAUTIFUL!
YOU CAN SET IT RIGHT IN FRONT OF YOUR DOGHOUSE..
IT'S REALLY BEAUTIFUL..
I WONDER WHERE HE GOT ALL THE DECORATIONS...
12-15
SCHULZ

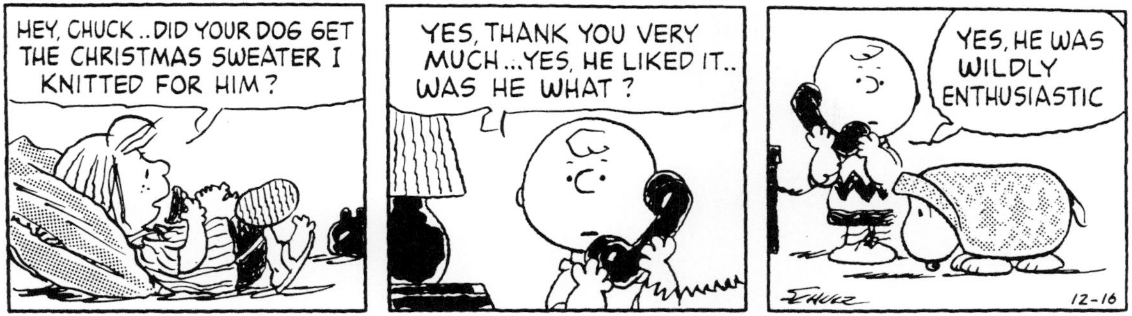
HEY, CHUCK..DID YOUR DOG GET THE CHRISTMAS SWEATER I KNITTED FOR HIM?
YES, THANK YOU VERY MUCH...YES, HE LIKED IT.. WAS HE WHAT?
YES, HE WAS WILDLY ENTHUSIASTIC
12-16

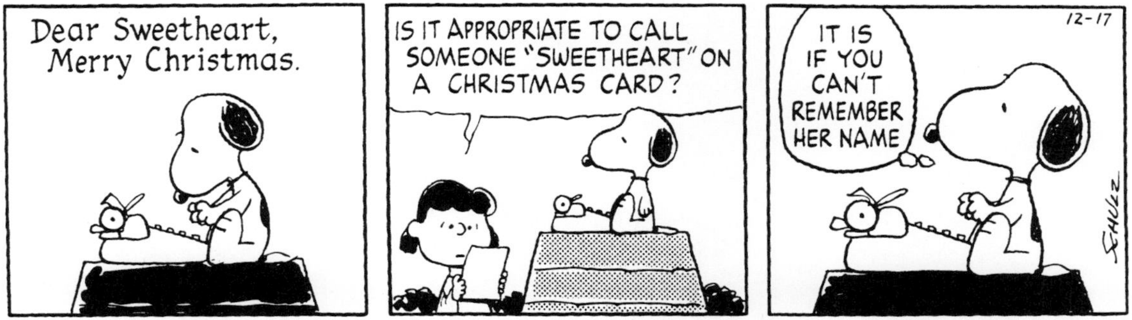
Dear Sweetheart,
Merry Christmas.
IS IT APPROPRIATE TO CALL SOMEONE "SWEETHEART" ON A CHRISTMAS CARD?
IT IS IF YOU CAN'T REMEMBER HER NAME
12-17

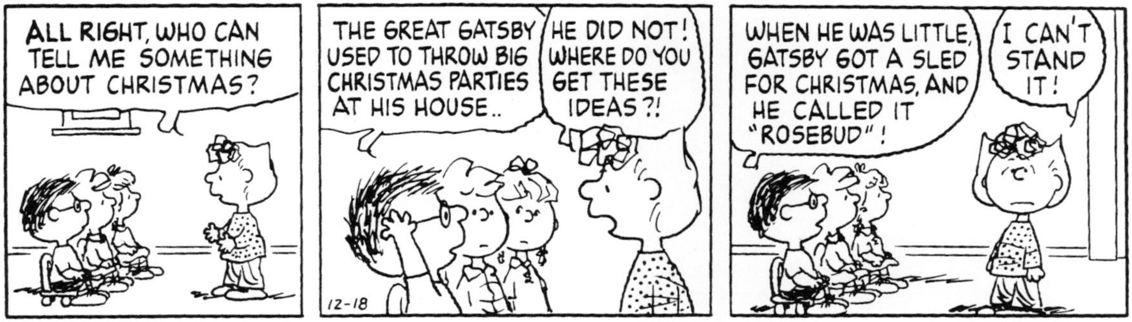
ALL RIGHT, WHO CAN TELL ME SOMETHING ABOUT CHRISTMAS?
THE GREAT GATSBY USED TO THROW BIG CHRISTMAS PARTIES AT HIS HOUSE..
HE DID NOT! WHERE DO YOU GET THESE IDEAS?!
12-18
WHEN HE WAS LITTLE, GATSBY GOT A SLED FOR CHRISTMAS, AND HE CALLED IT "ROSEBUD"!
I CAN'T STAND IT!

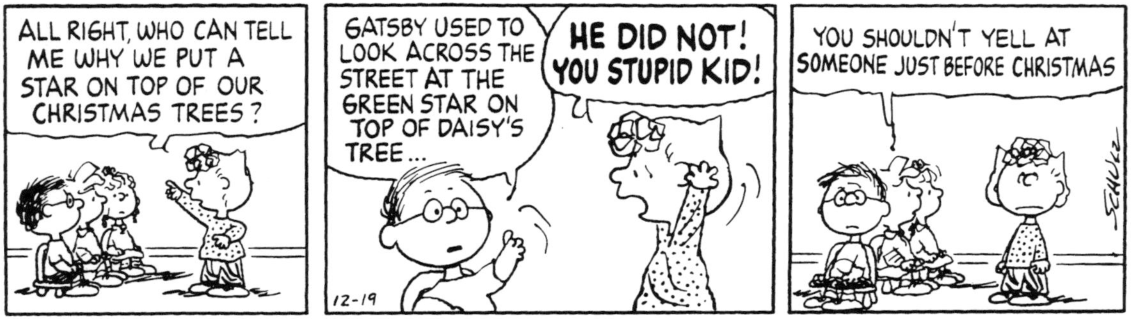
ALL RIGHT, WHO CAN TELL ME WHY WE PUT A STAR ON TOP OF OUR CHRISTMAS TREES ?
GATSBY USED TO LOOK ACROSS THE STREET AT THE GREEN STAR ON TOP OF DAISY'S TREE...
HE DID NOT! YOU STUPID KID!
12-19
YOU SHOULDN'T YELL AT SOMEONE JUST BEFORE CHRISTMAS
SCHULZ

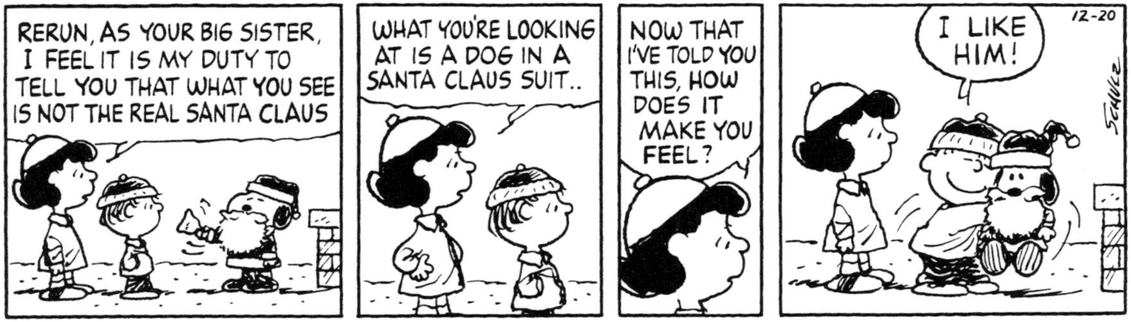
RERUN, AS YOUR BIG SISTER, I FEEL IT IS MY DUTY TO TELL YOU THAT WHAT YOU SEE IS NOT THE REAL SANTA CLAUS
WHAT YOU'RE LOOKING AT IS A DOG IN A SANTA CLAUS SUIT..
NOW THAT I'VE TOLD YOU THIS, HOW DOES IT MAKE YOU FEEL?
12-20
I LIKE HIM!
SCHULZ

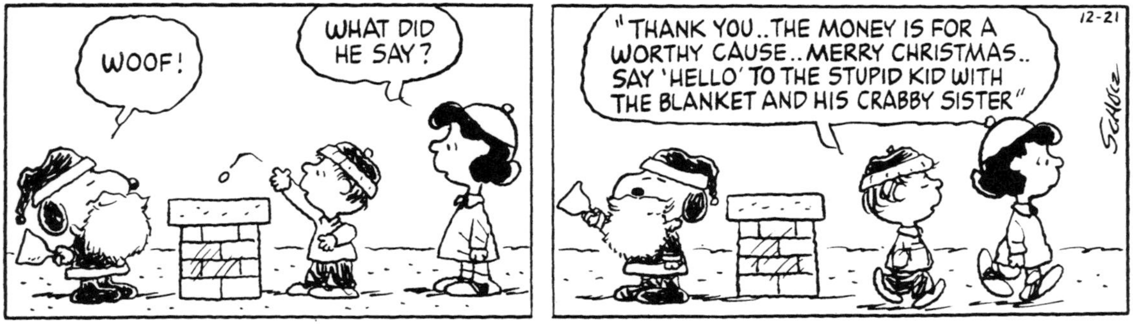
WOOF!
WHAT DID HE SAY?
12-21
"THANK YOU..THE MONEY IS FOR A WORTHY CAUSE..MERRY CHRISTMAS.. SAY 'HELLO' TO THE STUPID KID WITH THE BLANKET AND HIS CRABBY SISTER"
SCHULZ

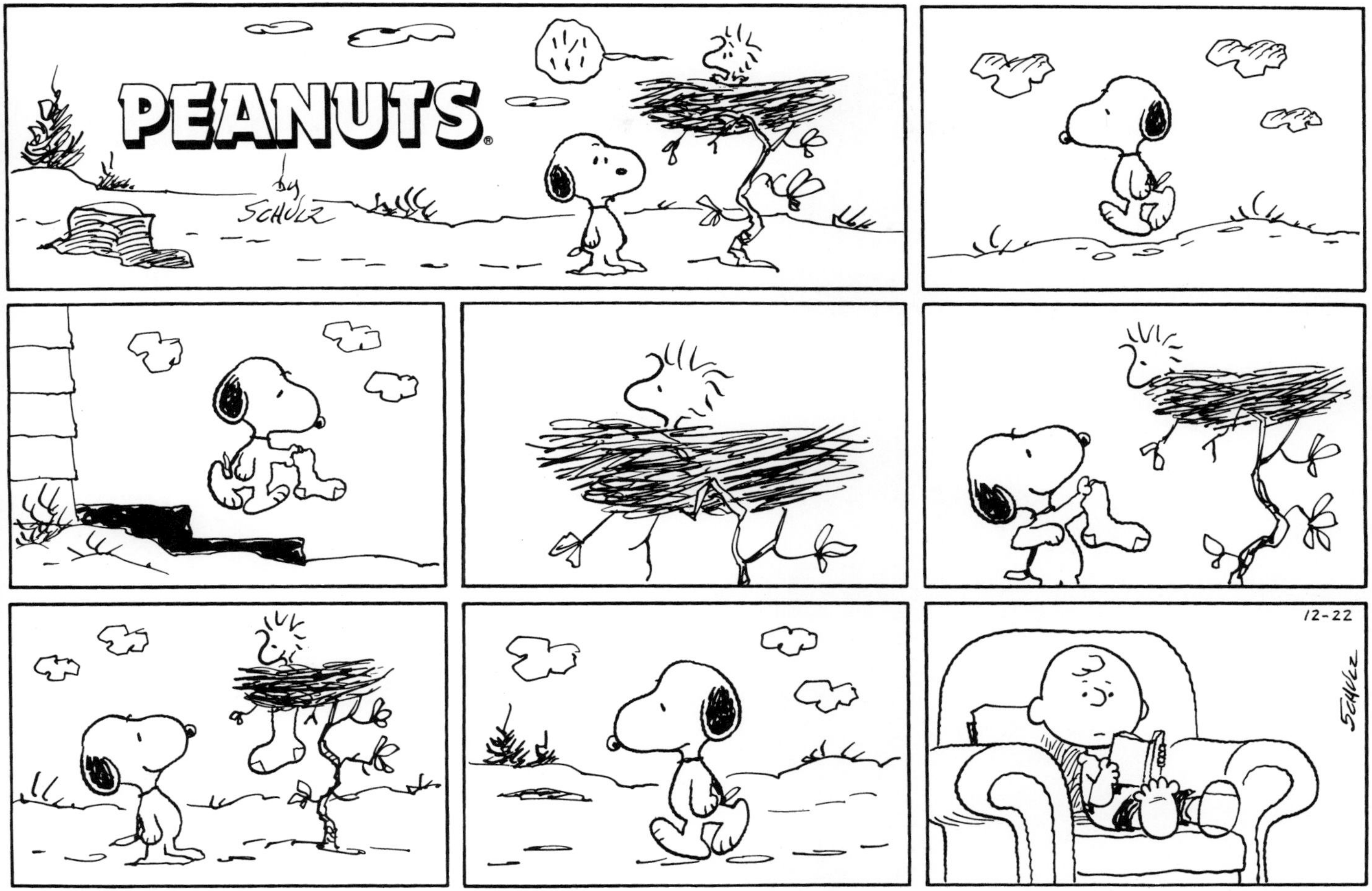
PEANUTS®
by SCHULZ
12-22
SCHULZ

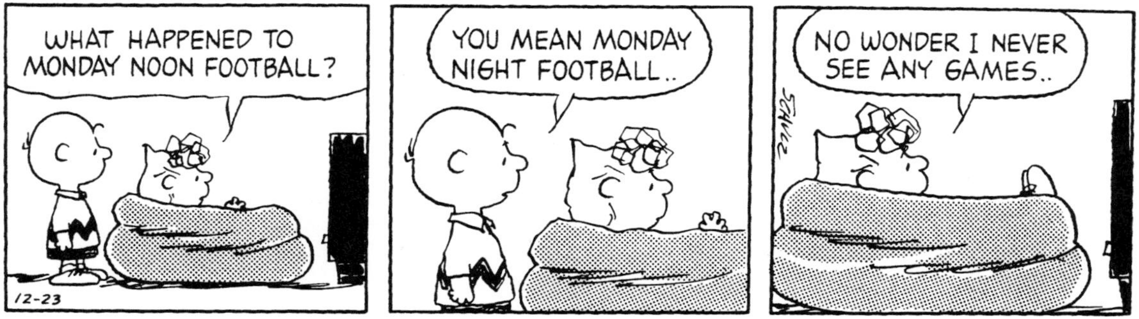
WHAT HAPPENED TO MONDAY NOON FOOTBALL?
12-23
YOU MEAN MONDAY NIGHT FOOTBALL..
NO WONDER I NEVER SEE ANY GAMES..
SCHULZ

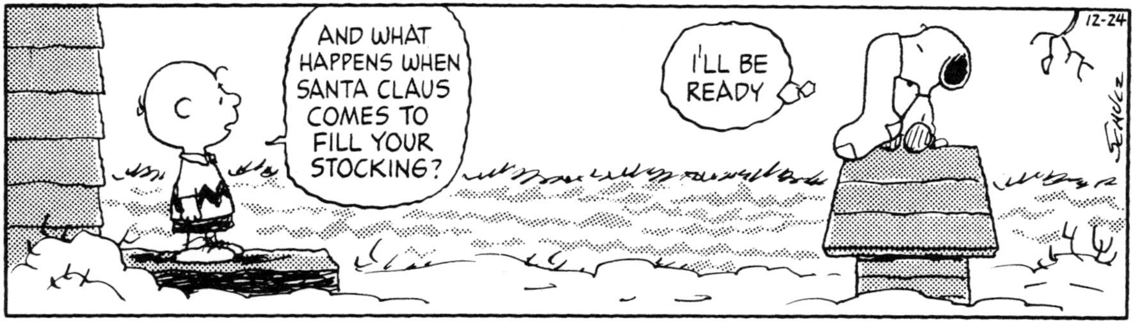
AND WHAT HAPPENS WHEN SANTA CLAUS COMES TO FILL YOUR STOCKING?
I'LL BE READY
12-24
SCHULZ

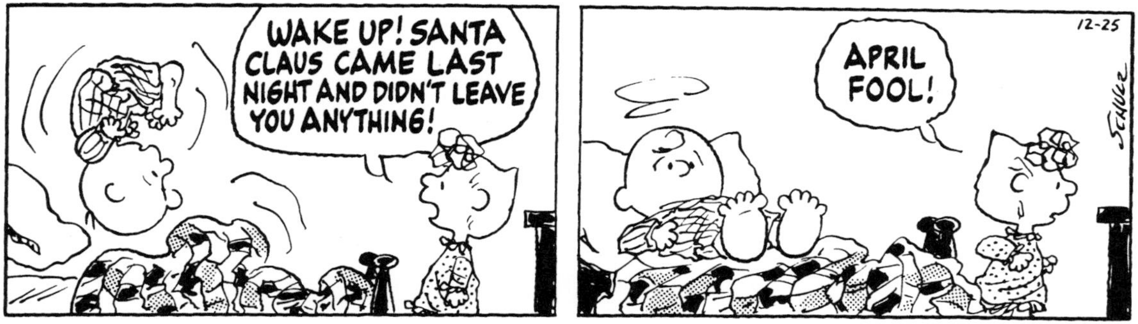
WAKE UP! SANTA CLAUS CAME LAST NIGHT AND DIDN'T LEAVE YOU ANYTHING!
12-25
APRIL FOOL!
SCHULZ

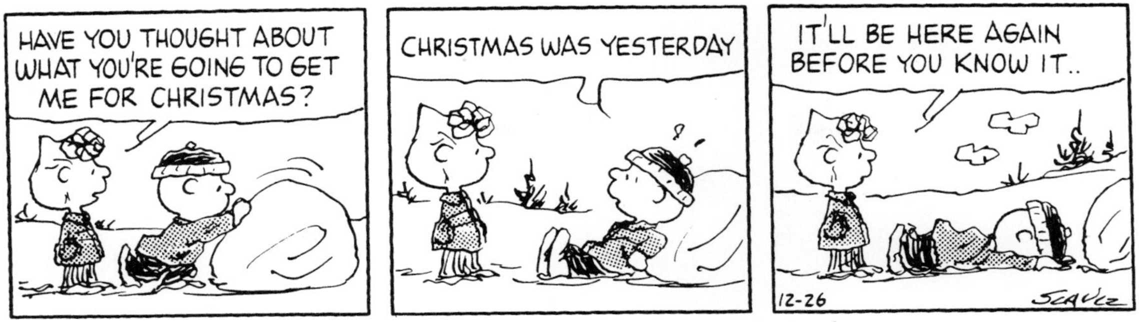
HAVE YOU THOUGHT ABOUT WHAT YOU'RE GOING TO GET ME FOR CHRISTMAS?
CHRISTMAS WAS YESTERDAY
?
IT'LL BE HERE AGAIN BEFORE YOU KNOW IT..
12-26
SCHULZ

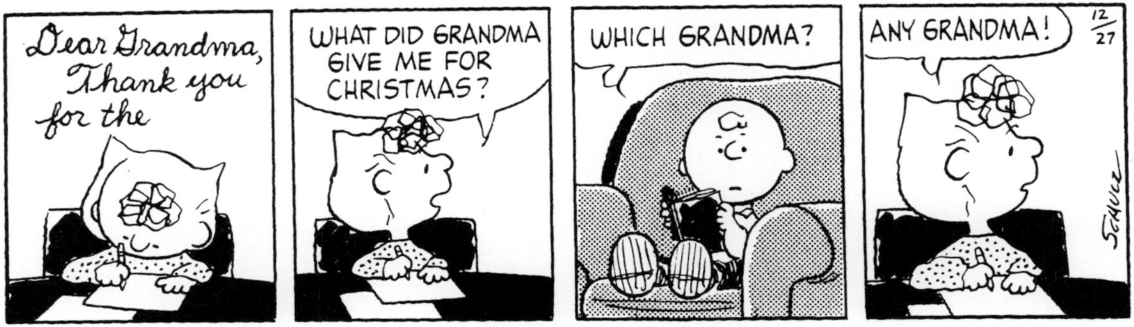
Dear Grandma, Thank you for the
WHAT DID GRANDMA GIVE ME FOR CHRISTMAS?
WHICH GRANDMA?
ANY GRANDMA!
12/27
SCHULZ

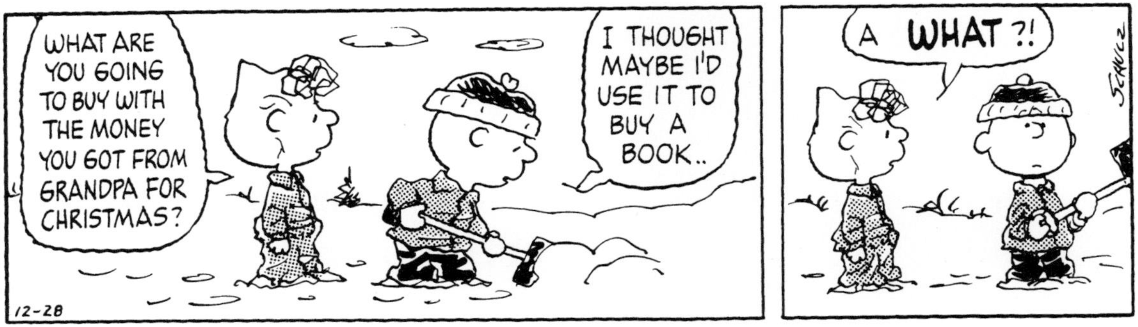
WHAT ARE YOU GOING TO BUY WITH THE MONEY YOU GOT FROM GRANDPA FOR CHRISTMAS?
I THOUGHT MAYBE I'D USE IT TO BUY A BOOK..
A WHAT?!
12-28
SCHULZ

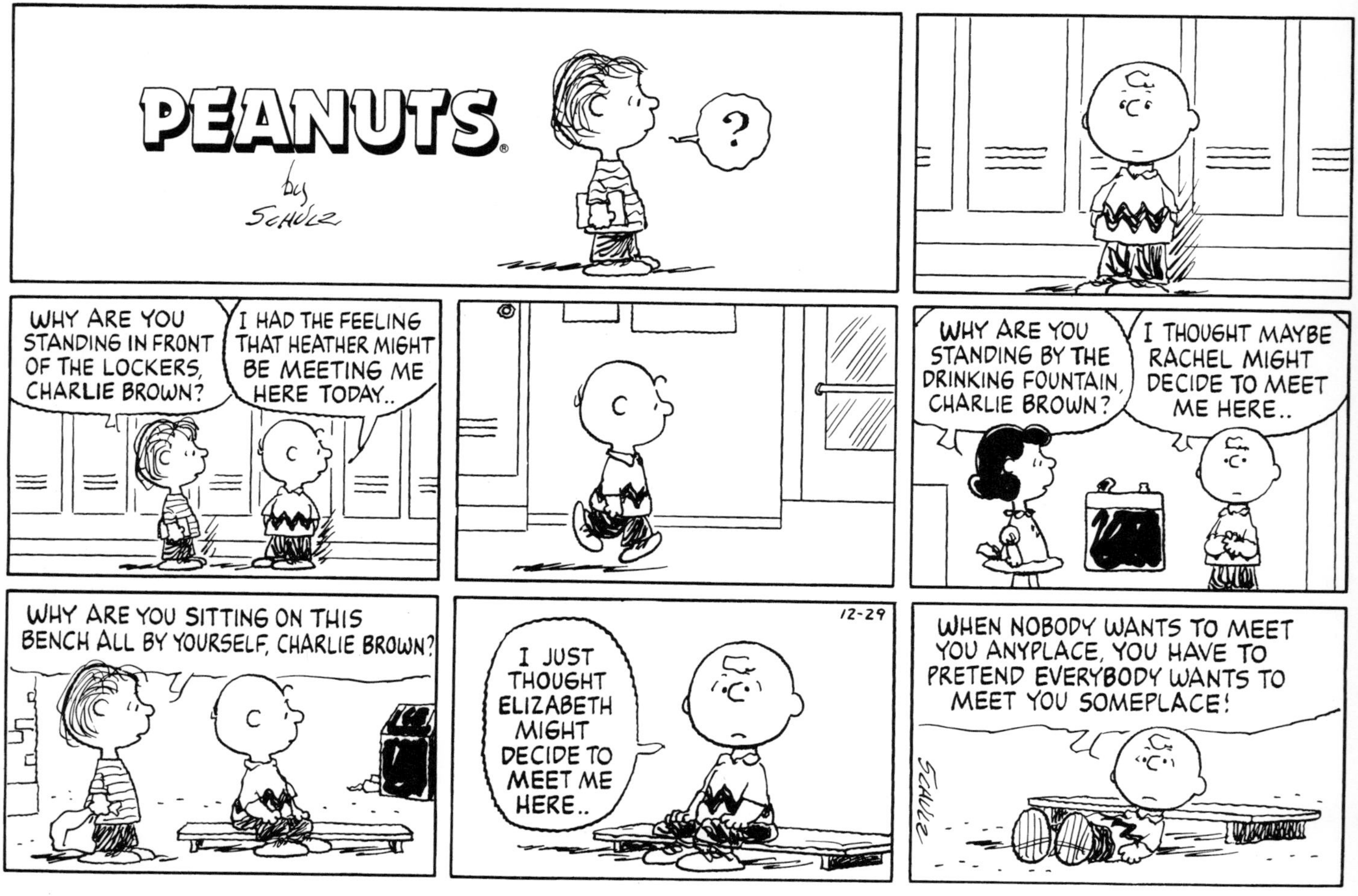
PEANUTS
by SCHULZ
?
WHY ARE YOU STANDING IN FRONT OF THE LOCKERS, CHARLIE BROWN?
I HAD THE FEELING THAT HEATHER MIGHT BE MEETING ME HERE TODAY..
WHY ARE YOU STANDING BY THE DRINKING FOUNTAIN, CHARLIE BROWN?
I THOUGHT MAYBE RACHEL MIGHT DECIDE TO MEET ME HERE..
WHY ARE YOU SITTING ON THIS BENCH ALL BY YOURSELF, CHARLIE BROWN?
12-29
I JUST THOUGHT ELIZABETH MIGHT DECIDE TO MEET ME HERE..
WHEN NOBODY WANTS TO MEET YOU ANYPLACE, YOU HAVE TO PRETEND EVERYBODY WANTS TO MEET YOU SOMEPLACE!
SCHULZ

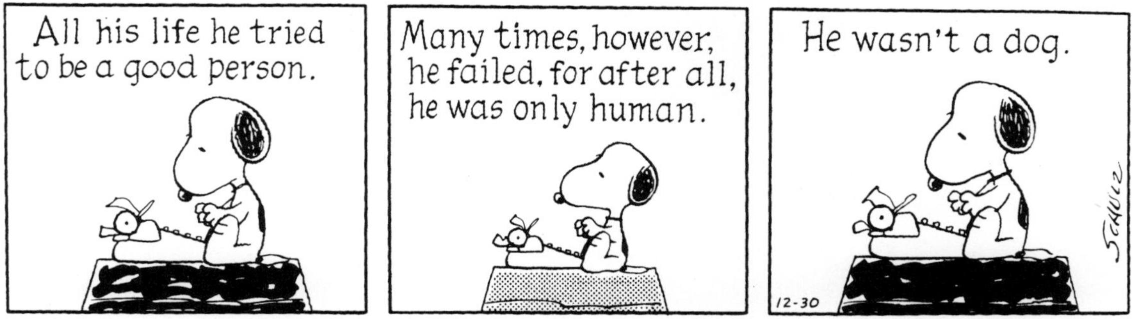
All his life he tried to be a good person.
Many times, however, he failed, for after all, he was only human.
He wasn't a dog.
SCHULZ
12-30

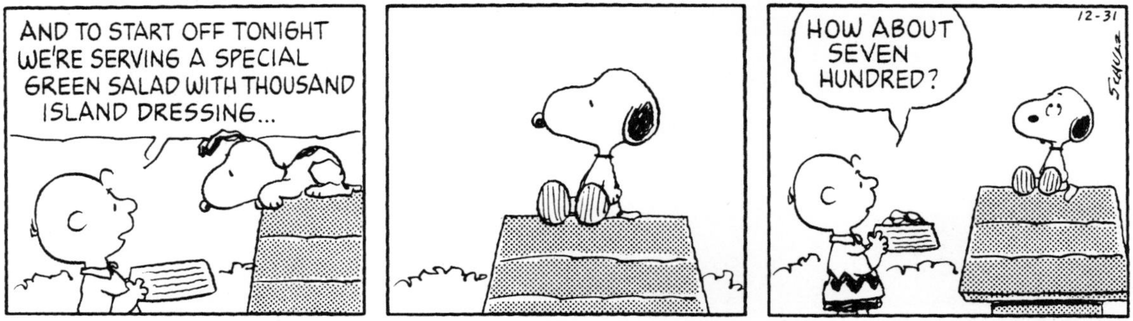
AND TO START OFF TONIGHT WE'RE SERVING A SPECIAL GREEN SALAD WITH THOUSAND ISLAND DRESSING...
HOW ABOUT SEVEN HUNDRED?
12-31
SCHULZ

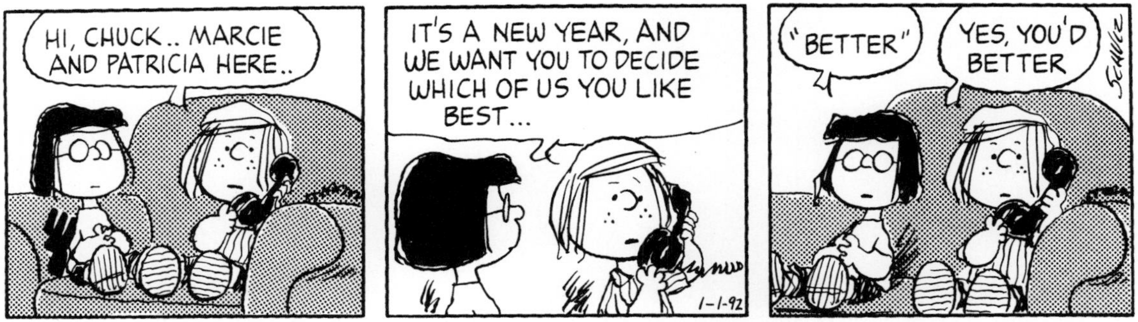
HI, CHUCK.. MARCIE AND PATRICIA HERE..
IT'S A NEW YEAR, AND WE WANT YOU TO DECIDE WHICH OF US YOU LIKE BEST...
1-1-92
"BETTER"
YES, YOU'D BETTER
SCHULZ

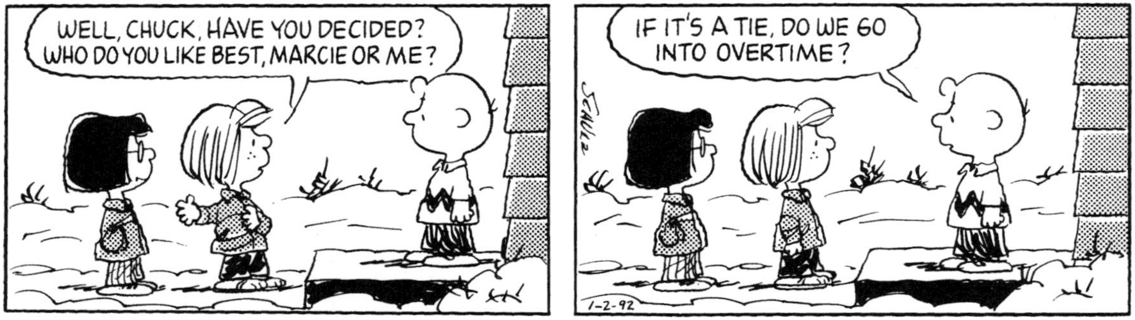
WELL, CHUCK, HAVE YOU DECIDED? WHO DO YOU LIKE BEST, MARCIE OR ME?
IF IT'S A TIE, DO WE GO INTO OVERTIME?
1-2-92

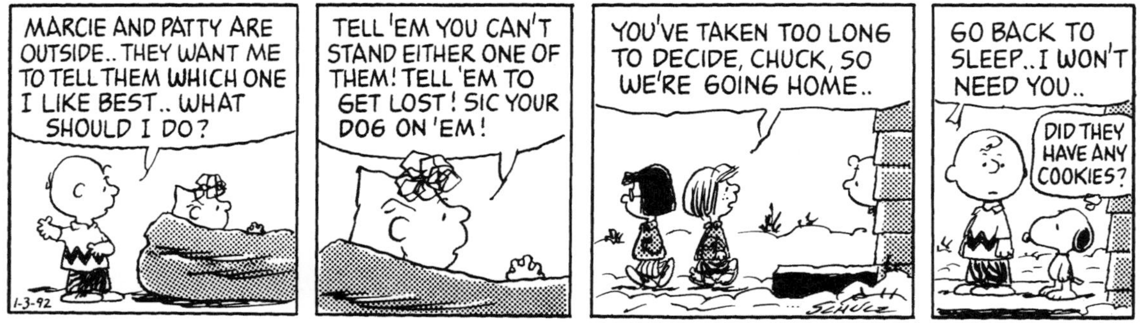
MARCIE AND PATTY ARE OUTSIDE.. THEY WANT ME TO TELL THEM WHICH ONE I LIKE BEST.. WHAT SHOULD I DO?
TELL 'EM YOU CAN'T STAND EITHER ONE OF THEM! TELL 'EM TO GET LOST! SIC YOUR DOG ON 'EM!
YOU'VE TAKEN TOO LONG TO DECIDE, CHUCK, SO WE'RE GOING HOME..
GO BACK TO SLEEP.. I WON'T NEED YOU..
DID THEY HAVE ANY COOKIES?
1-3-92

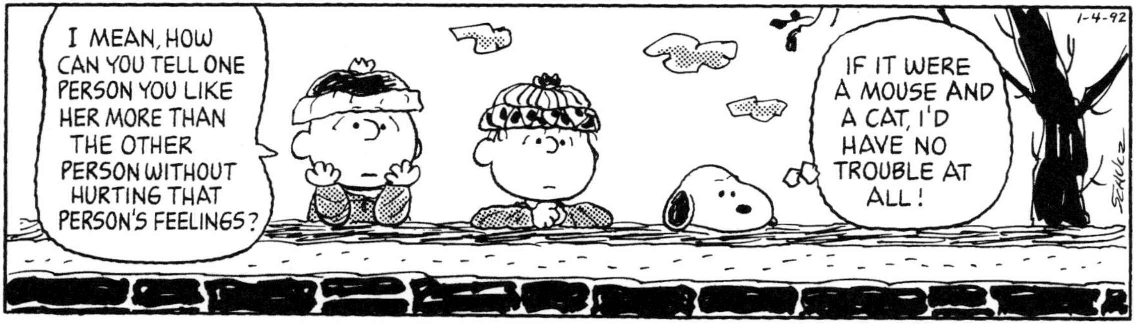
I MEAN, HOW CAN YOU TELL ONE PERSON YOU LIKE HER MORE THAN THE OTHER PERSON WITHOUT HURTING THAT PERSON'S FEELINGS?
IF IT WERE A MOUSE AND A CAT, I'D HAVE NO TROUBLE AT ALL!
1-4-92

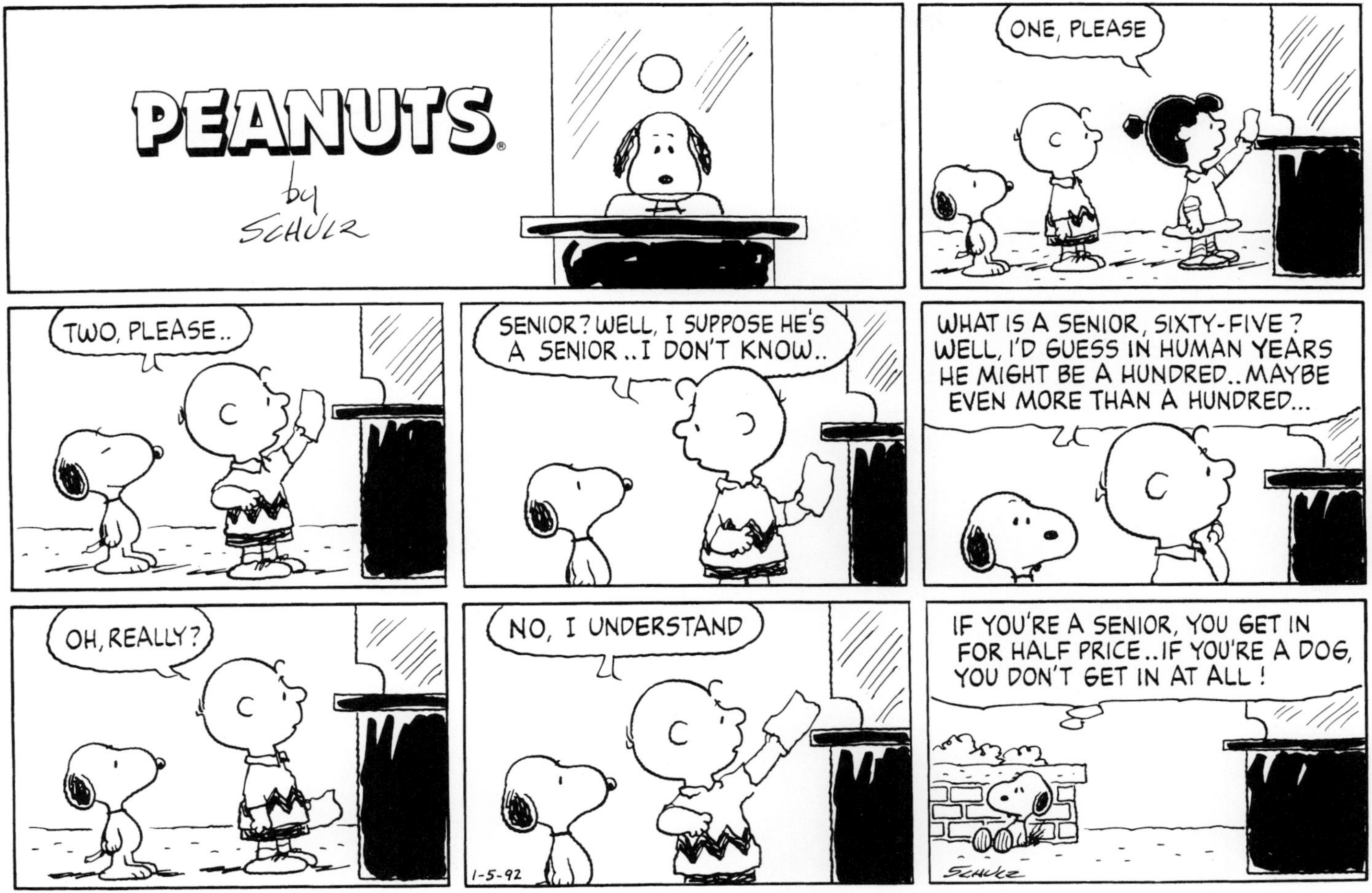
PEANUTS
by SCHULZ
ONE, PLEASE
TWO, PLEASE..
SENIOR? WELL, I SUPPOSE HE'S A SENIOR..I DON'T KNOW..
WHAT IS A SENIOR, SIXTY-FIVE? WELL, I'D GUESS IN HUMAN YEARS HE MIGHT BE A HUNDRED..MAYBE EVEN MORE THAN A HUNDRED...
OH, REALLY?
NO, I UNDERSTAND
1-5-92
IF YOU'RE A SENIOR, YOU GET IN FOR HALF PRICE..IF YOU'RE A DOG, YOU DON'T GET IN AT ALL!
SCHULZ

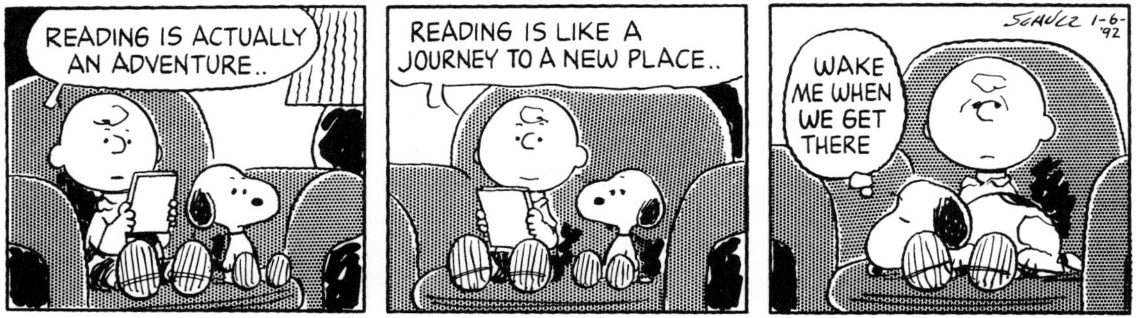
READING IS ACTUALLY AN ADVENTURE..
READING IS LIKE A JOURNEY TO A NEW PLACE..
SCHULZ 1-6-'92
WAKE ME WHEN WE GET THERE

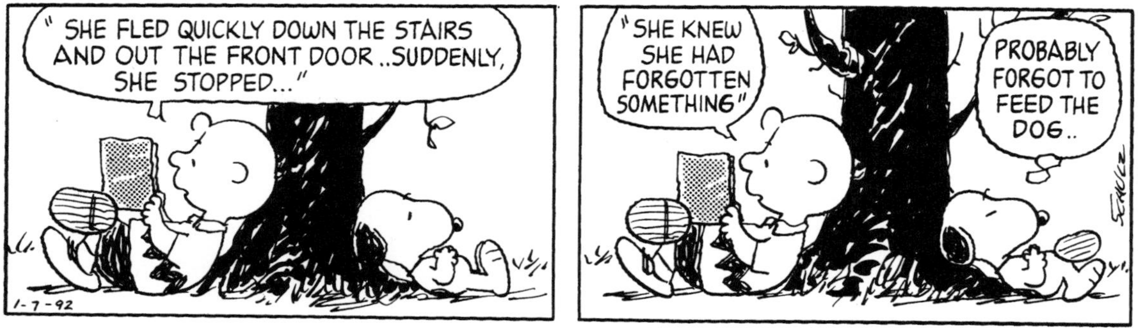
" SHE FLED QUICKLY DOWN THE STAIRS AND OUT THE FRONT DOOR..SUDDENLY, SHE STOPPED..."
1-7-92
"SHE KNEW SHE HAD FORGOTTEN SOMETHING"
PROBABLY FORGOT TO FEED THE DOG..
SCHULZ

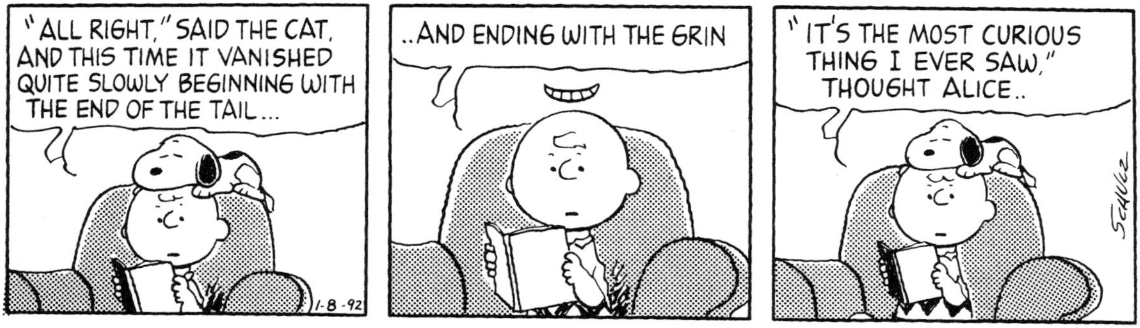
"ALL RIGHT," SAID THE CAT, AND THIS TIME IT VANISHED QUITE SLOWLY BEGINNING WITH THE END OF THE TAIL...
1-8-92
..AND ENDING WITH THE GRIN
"IT'S THE MOST CURIOUS THING I EVER SAW," THOUGHT ALICE..
SCHULZ

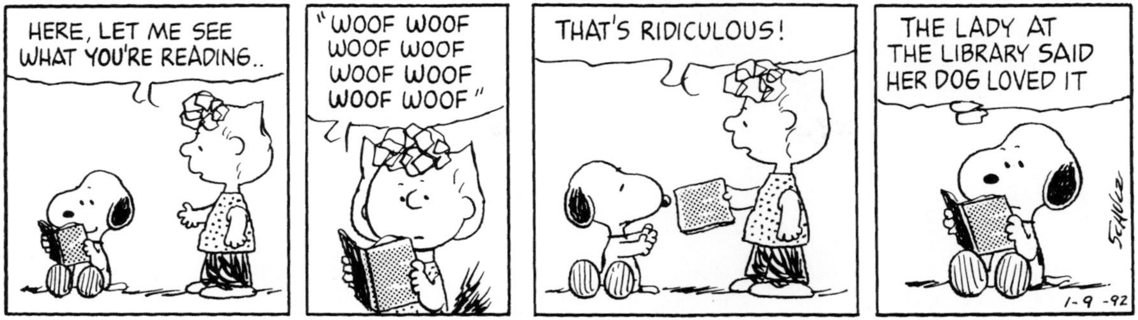
HERE, LET ME SEE WHAT YOU'RE READING..
"WOOF WOOF WOOF WOOF WOOF WOOF WOOF WOOF"
THAT'S RIDICULOUS!
THE LADY AT THE LIBRARY SAID HER DOG LOVED IT
1-9-92

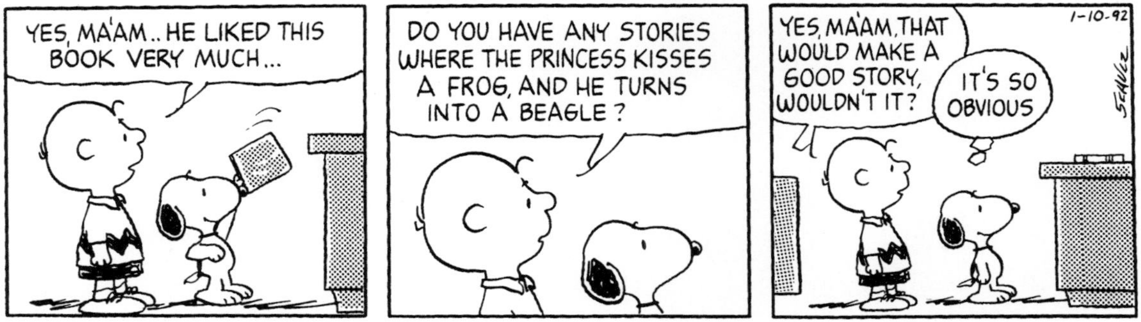
YES, MA'AM.. HE LIKED THIS BOOK VERY MUCH...
DO YOU HAVE ANY STORIES WHERE THE PRINCESS KISSES A FROG, AND HE TURNS INTO A BEAGLE?
1-10-92
YES, MA'AM, THAT WOULD MAKE A GOOD STORY, WOULDN'T IT?
IT'S SO OBVIOUS

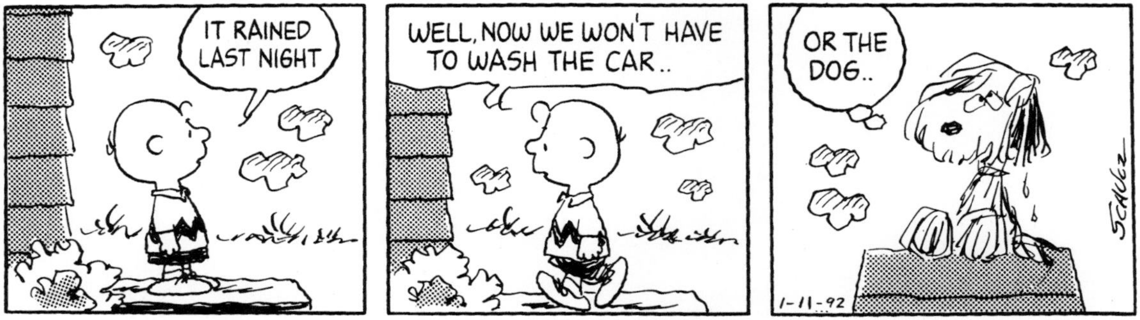
IT RAINED LAST NIGHT
WELL, NOW WE WON'T HAVE TO WASH THE CAR..
OR THE DOG..
1-11-92

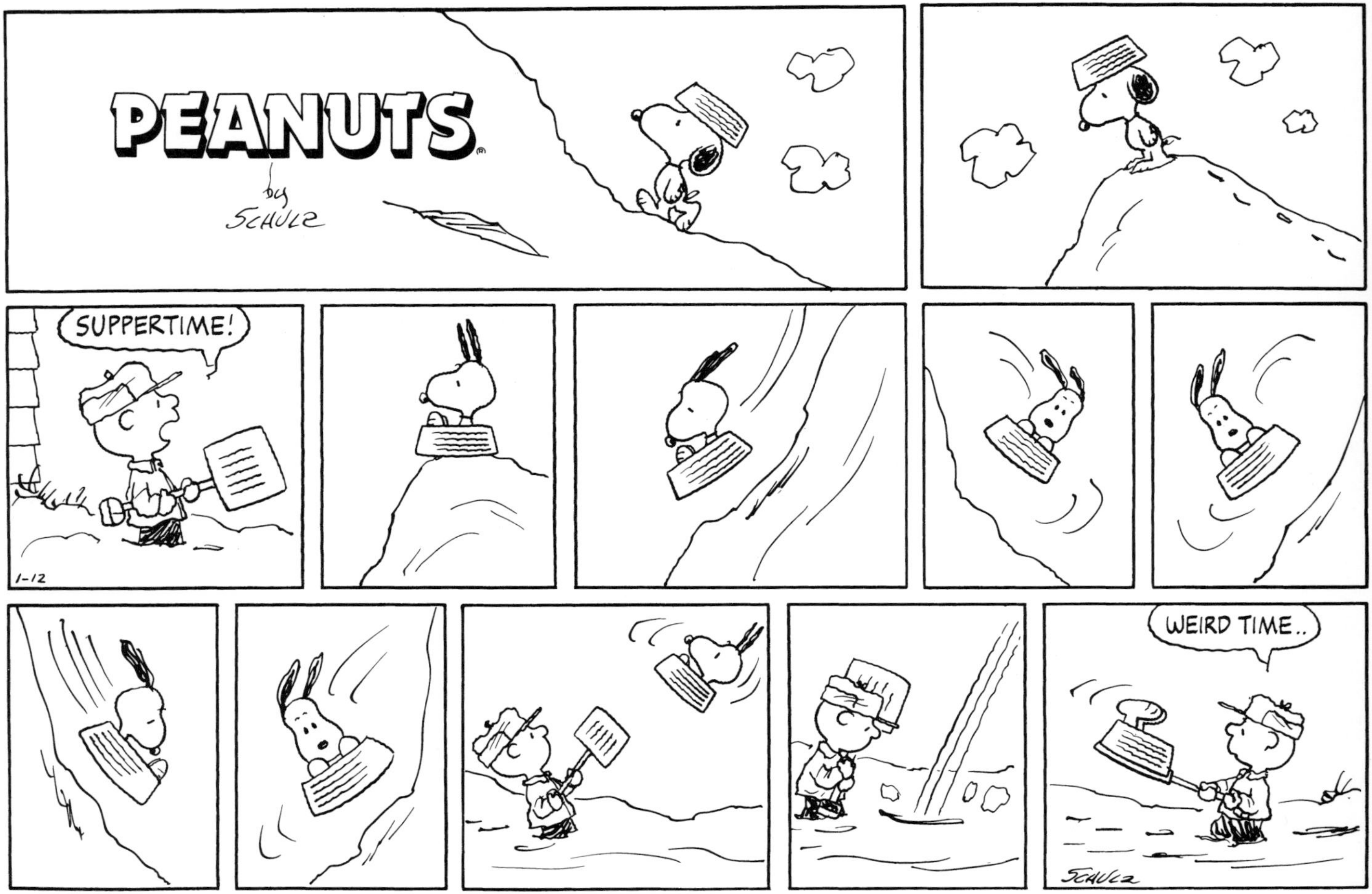
PEANUTS
by SCHULZ
SUPPERTIME!
1-12
WEIRD TIME..
SCHULZ

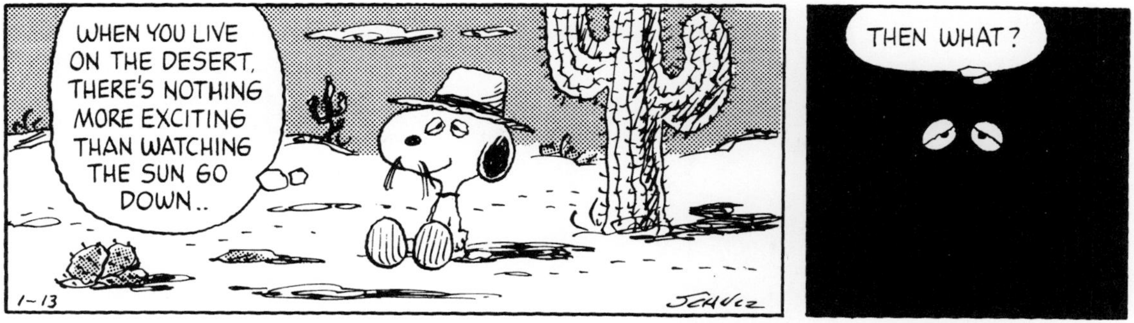
WHEN YOU LIVE ON THE DESERT, THERE'S NOTHING MORE EXCITING THAN WATCHING THE SUN GO DOWN..
1-13
THEN WHAT?

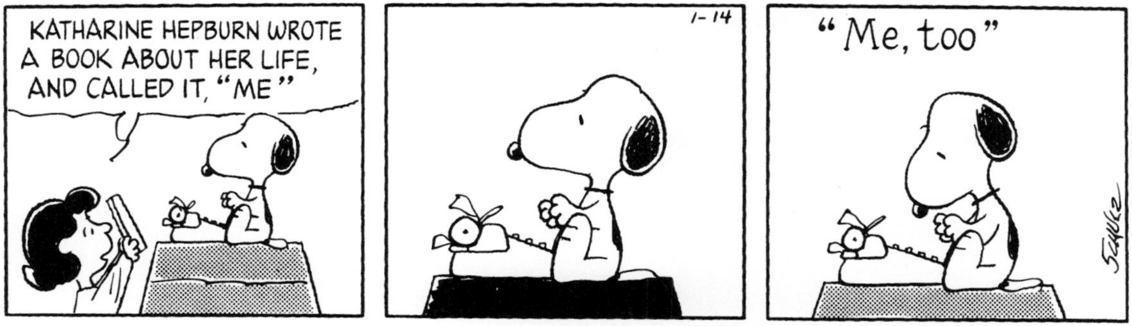
KATHARINE HEPBURN WROTE A BOOK ABOUT HER LIFE, AND CALLED IT, "ME"
1-14
"Me, too"

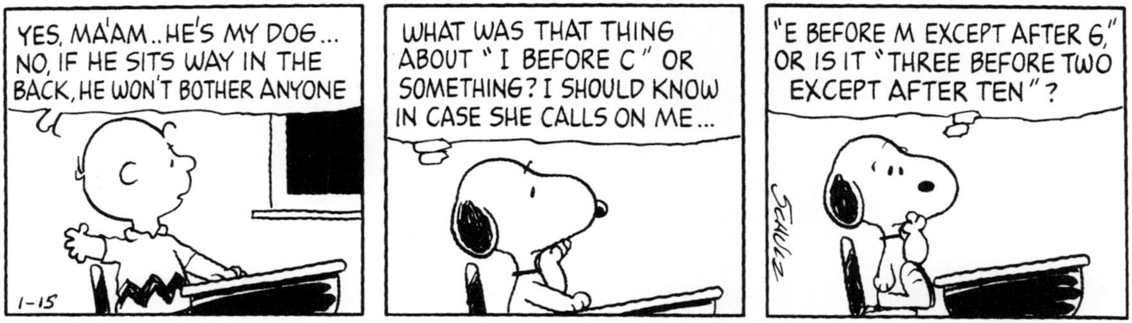
YES, MA'AM..HE'S MY DOG... NO, IF HE SITS WAY IN THE BACK, HE WON'T BOTHER ANYONE
1-15
WHAT WAS THAT THING ABOUT "I BEFORE C" OR SOMETHING? I SHOULD KNOW IN CASE SHE CALLS ON ME...
"E BEFORE M EXCEPT AFTER G," OR IS IT "THREE BEFORE TWO EXCEPT AFTER TEN"?

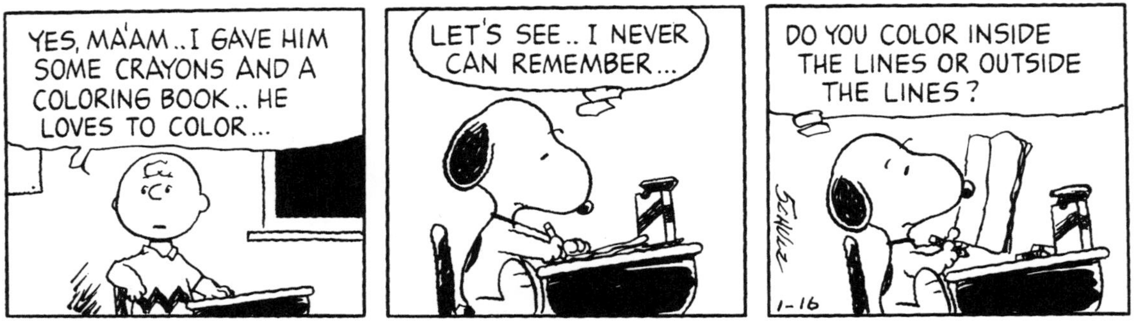
YES, MA'AM.. I GAVE HIM SOME CRAYONS AND A COLORING BOOK.. HE LOVES TO COLOR...
LET'S SEE.. I NEVER CAN REMEMBER...
DO YOU COLOR INSIDE THE LINES OR OUTSIDE THE LINES?
SCHULZ
1-16

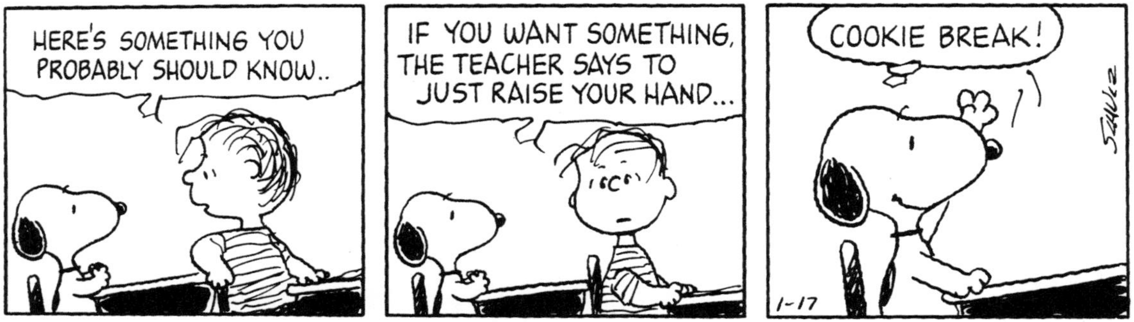
HERE'S SOMETHING YOU PROBABLY SHOULD KNOW..
IF YOU WANT SOMETHING, THE TEACHER SAYS TO JUST RAISE YOUR HAND...
COOKIE BREAK!
SCHULZ
1-17

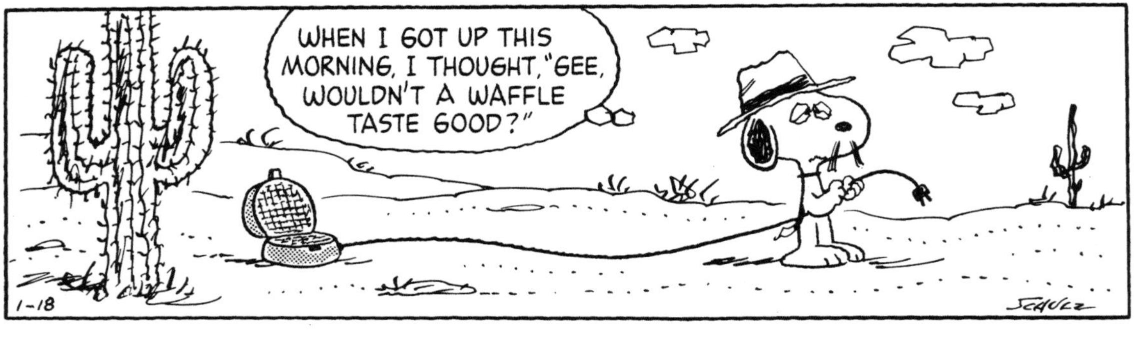
WHEN I GOT UP THIS MORNING, I THOUGHT, "GEE, WOULDN'T A WAFFLE TASTE GOOD?"
1-18
SCHULZ

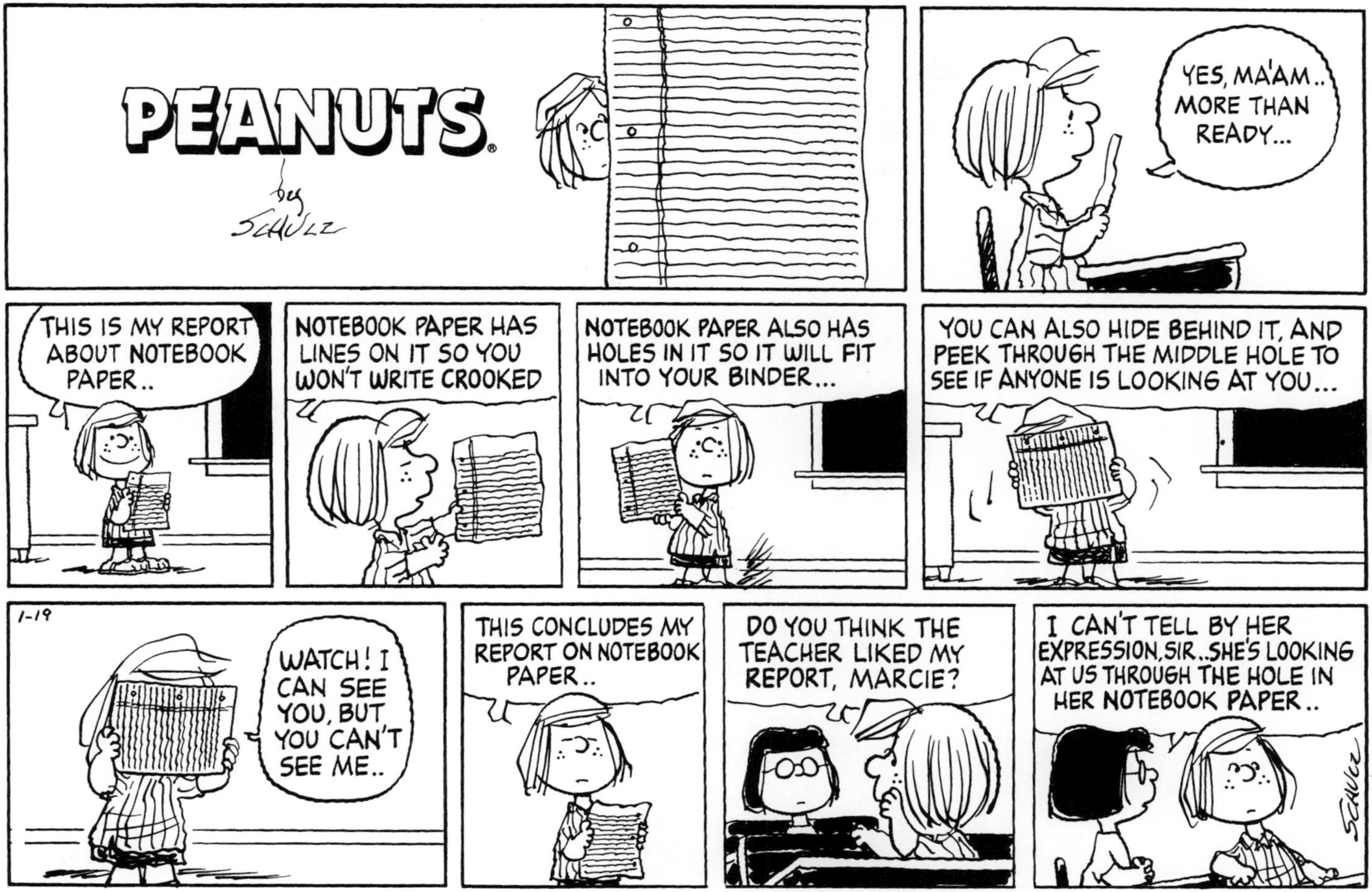
PEANUTS
by SCHULZ
YES, MA'AM.. MORE THAN READY...
THIS IS MY REPORT ABOUT NOTEBOOK PAPER..
NOTEBOOK PAPER HAS LINES ON IT SO YOU WON'T WRITE CROOKED
NOTEBOOK PAPER ALSO HAS HOLES IN IT SO IT WILL FIT INTO YOUR BINDER...
YOU CAN ALSO HIDE BEHIND IT, AND PEEK THROUGH THE MIDDLE HOLE TO SEE IF ANYONE IS LOOKING AT YOU...
1-19
WATCH! I CAN SEE YOU, BUT YOU CAN'T SEE ME..
THIS CONCLUDES MY REPORT ON NOTEBOOK PAPER..
DO YOU THINK THE TEACHER LIKED MY REPORT, MARCIE?
I CAN'T TELL BY HER EXPRESSION, SIR..SHE'S LOOKING AT US THROUGH THE HOLE IN HER NOTEBOOK PAPER..
SCHULZ

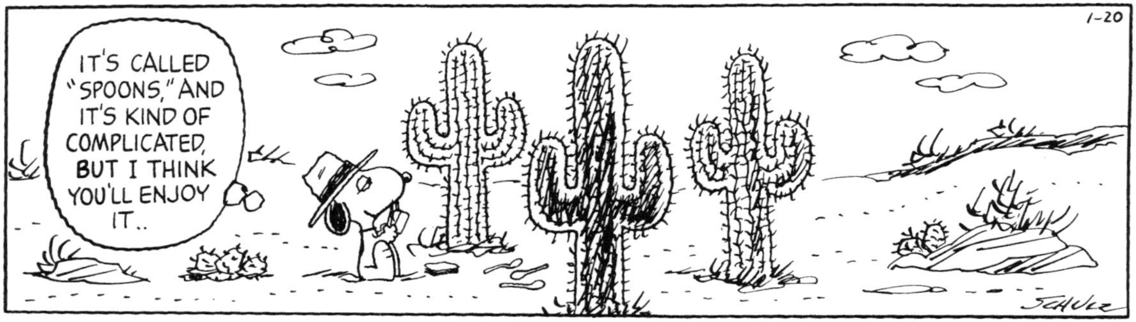
1-20
IT'S CALLED "SPOONS," AND IT'S KIND OF COMPLICATED, BUT I THINK YOU'LL ENJOY IT..
SCHULZ

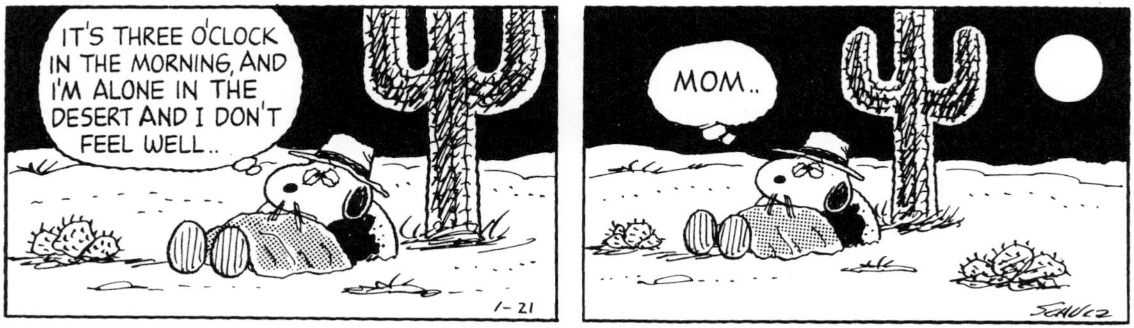
IT'S THREE O'CLOCK IN THE MORNING, AND I'M ALONE IN THE DESERT AND I DON'T FEEL WELL..
1-21
MOM..
SCHULZ

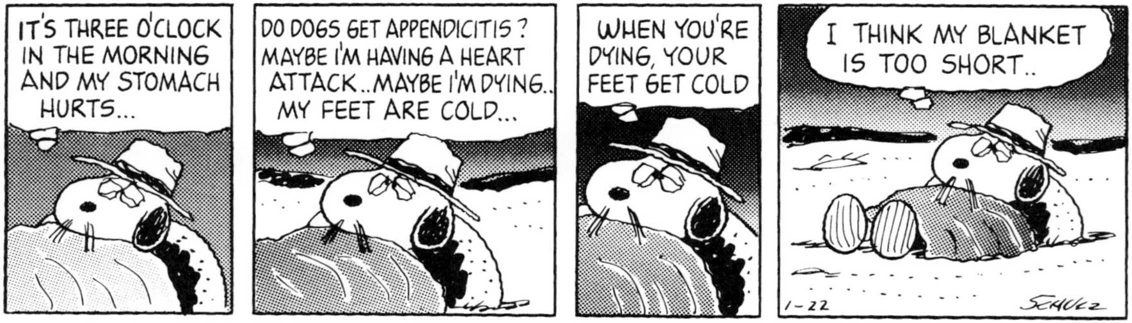
IT'S THREE O'CLOCK IN THE MORNING AND MY STOMACH HURTS...
DO DOGS GET APPENDICITIS? MAYBE I'M HAVING A HEART ATTACK..MAYBE I'M DYING.. MY FEET ARE COLD...
WHEN YOU'RE DYING, YOUR FEET GET COLD
I THINK MY BLANKET IS TOO SHORT..
1-22
SCHULZ

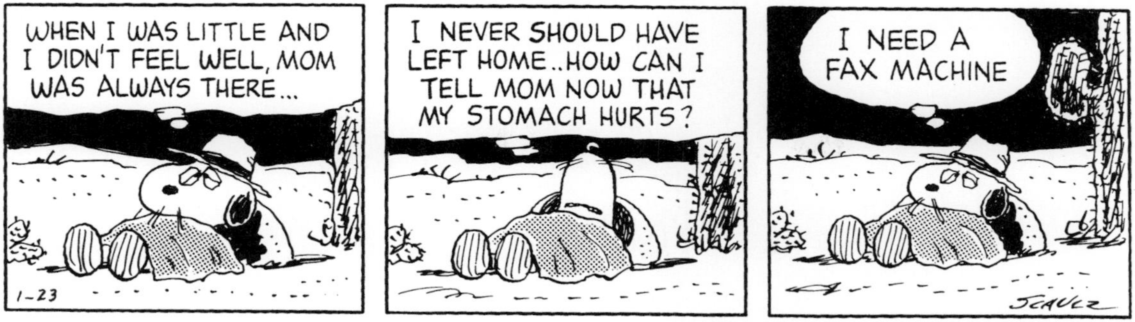
WHEN I WAS LITTLE AND I DIDN'T FEEL WELL, MOM WAS ALWAYS THERE...
I NEVER SHOULD HAVE LEFT HOME..HOW CAN I TELL MOM NOW THAT MY STOMACH HURTS?
I NEED A FAX MACHINE
1-23
SCHULZ

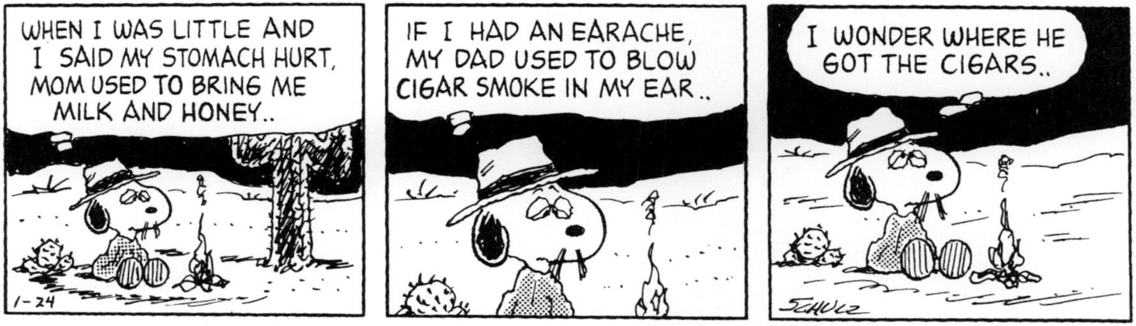
WHEN I WAS LITTLE AND I SAID MY STOMACH HURT, MOM USED TO BRING ME MILK AND HONEY..
IF I HAD AN EARACHE, MY DAD USED TO BLOW CIGAR SMOKE IN MY EAR..
I WONDER WHERE HE GOT THE CIGARS..
1-24
SCHULZ

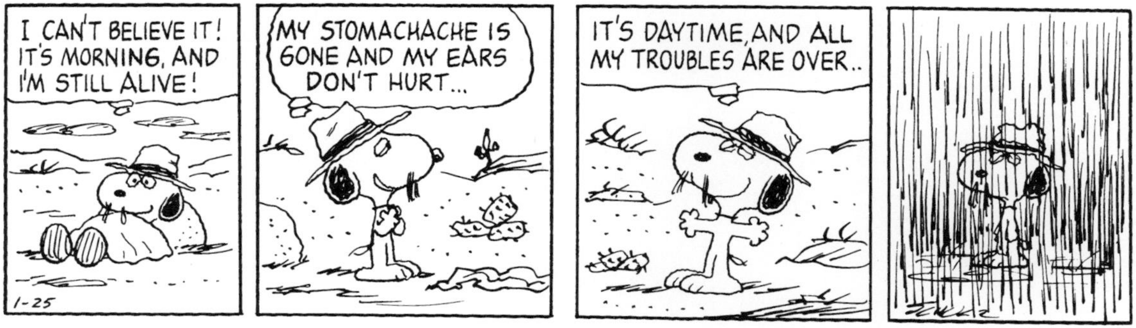
I CAN'T BELIEVE IT! IT'S MORNING, AND I'M STILL ALIVE!
MY STOMACHACHE IS GONE AND MY EARS DON'T HURT...
IT'S DAYTIME, AND ALL MY TROUBLES ARE OVER..
1-25
SCHULZ

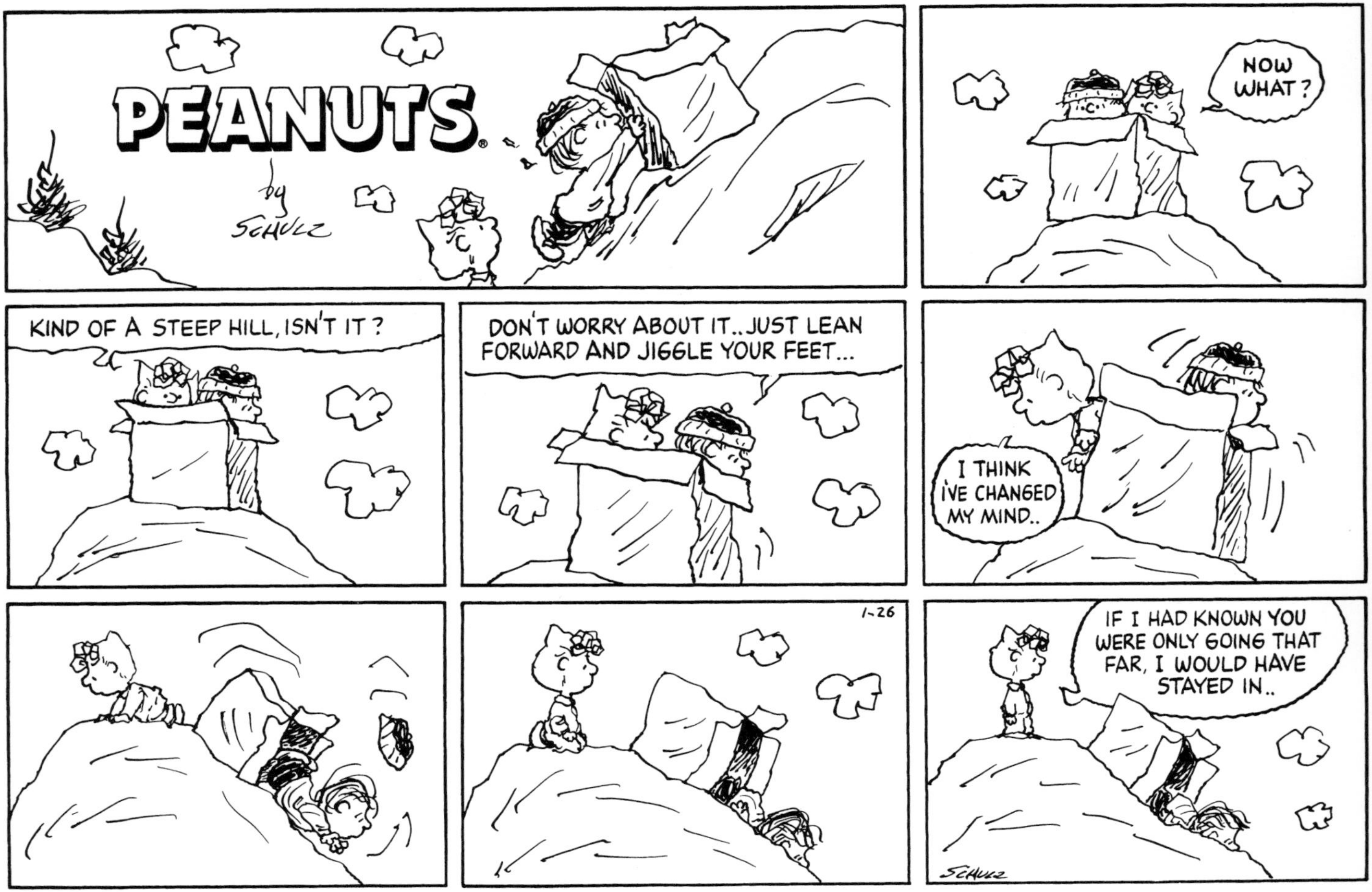
PEANUTS
by SCHULZ
NOW WHAT?
KIND OF A STEEP HILL, ISN'T IT?
DON'T WORRY ABOUT IT.. JUST LEAN FORWARD AND JIGGLE YOUR FEET...
I THINK I'VE CHANGED MY MIND..
1-26
IF I HAD KNOWN YOU WERE ONLY GOING THAT FAR, I WOULD HAVE STAYED IN..
SCHULZ

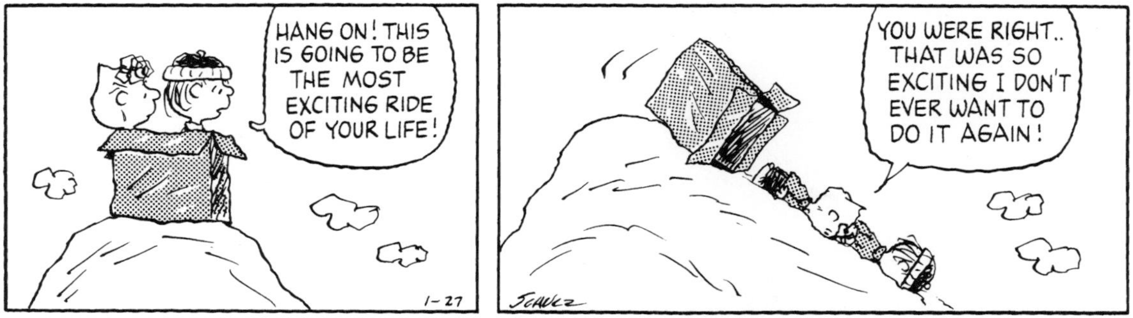
HANG ON! THIS IS GOING TO BE THE MOST EXCITING RIDE OF YOUR LIFE!
1-27
YOU WERE RIGHT.. THAT WAS SO EXCITING I DON'T EVER WANT TO DO IT AGAIN!
SCHULZ

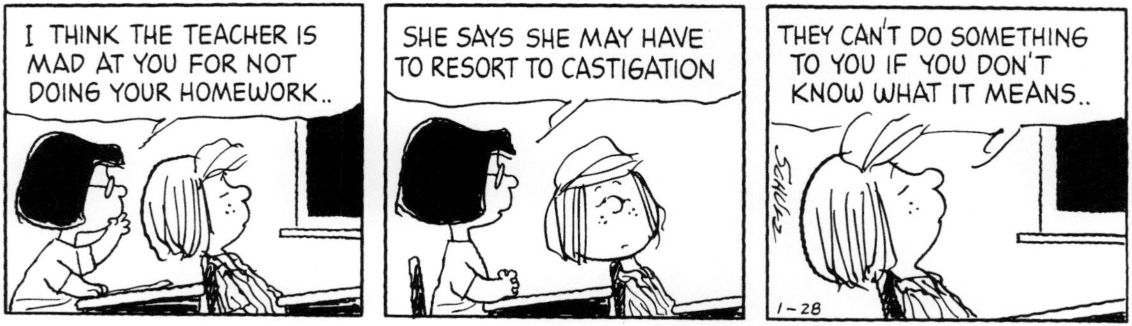
I THINK THE TEACHER IS MAD AT YOU FOR NOT DOING YOUR HOMEWORK..
SHE SAYS SHE MAY HAVE TO RESORT TO CASTIGATION
THEY CAN'T DO SOMETHING TO YOU IF YOU DON'T KNOW WHAT IT MEANS..
SCHULZ
1-28

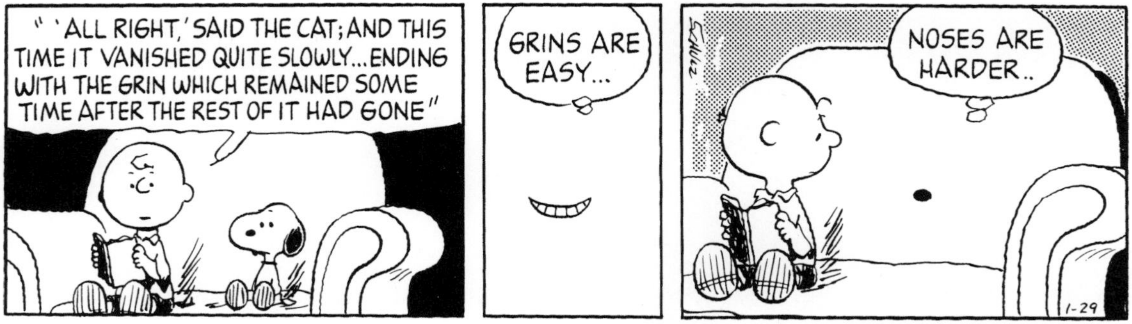
" 'ALL RIGHT,' SAID THE CAT; AND THIS TIME IT VANISHED QUITE SLOWLY...ENDING WITH THE GRIN WHICH REMAINED SOME TIME AFTER THE REST OF IT HAD GONE"
GRINS ARE EASY...
SCHULZ
NOSES ARE HARDER..
1-29

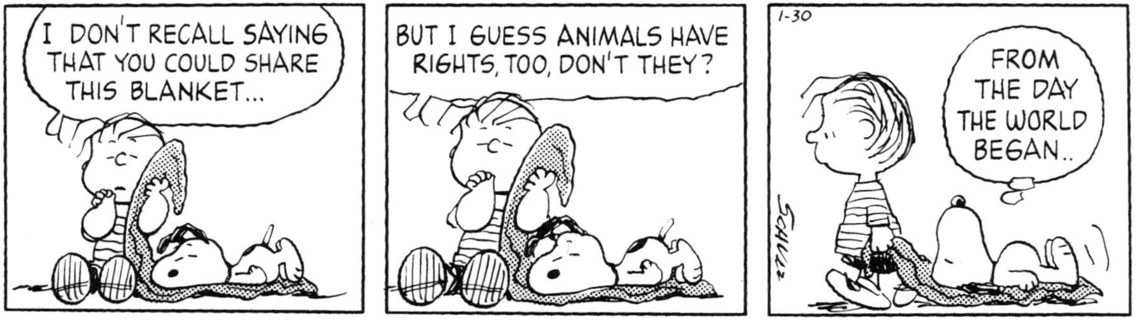
I DON'T RECALL SAYING THAT YOU COULD SHARE THIS BLANKET...
BUT I GUESS ANIMALS HAVE RIGHTS, TOO, DON'T THEY?
1-30
FROM THE DAY THE WORLD BEGAN..

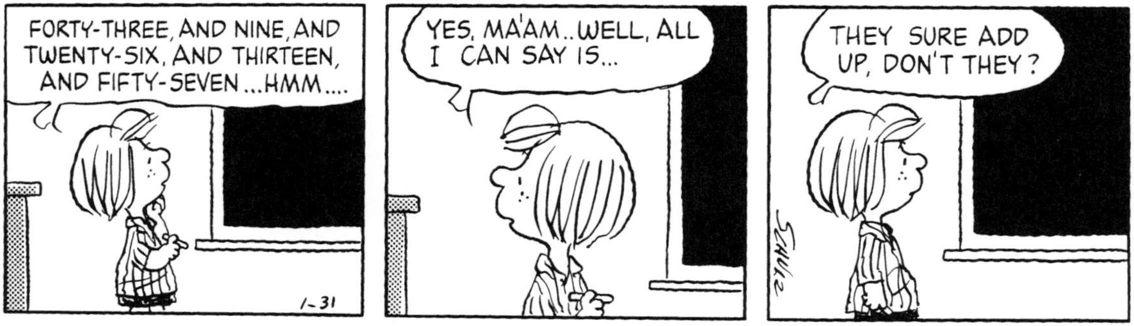
FORTY-THREE, AND NINE, AND TWENTY-SIX, AND THIRTEEN, AND FIFTY-SEVEN ...HMM....
1-31
YES, MA'AM..WELL, ALL I CAN SAY IS...
THEY SURE ADD UP, DON'T THEY?

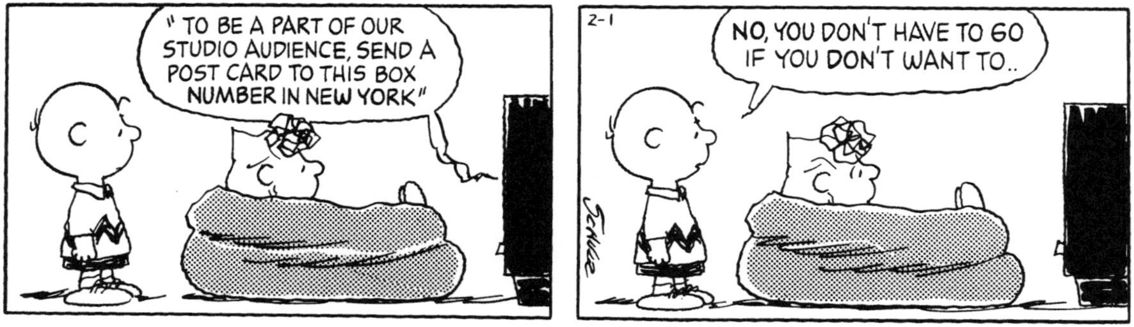
"TO BE A PART OF OUR STUDIO AUDIENCE, SEND A POST CARD TO THIS BOX NUMBER IN NEW YORK"
2-1
NO, YOU DON'T HAVE TO GO IF YOU DON'T WANT TO..

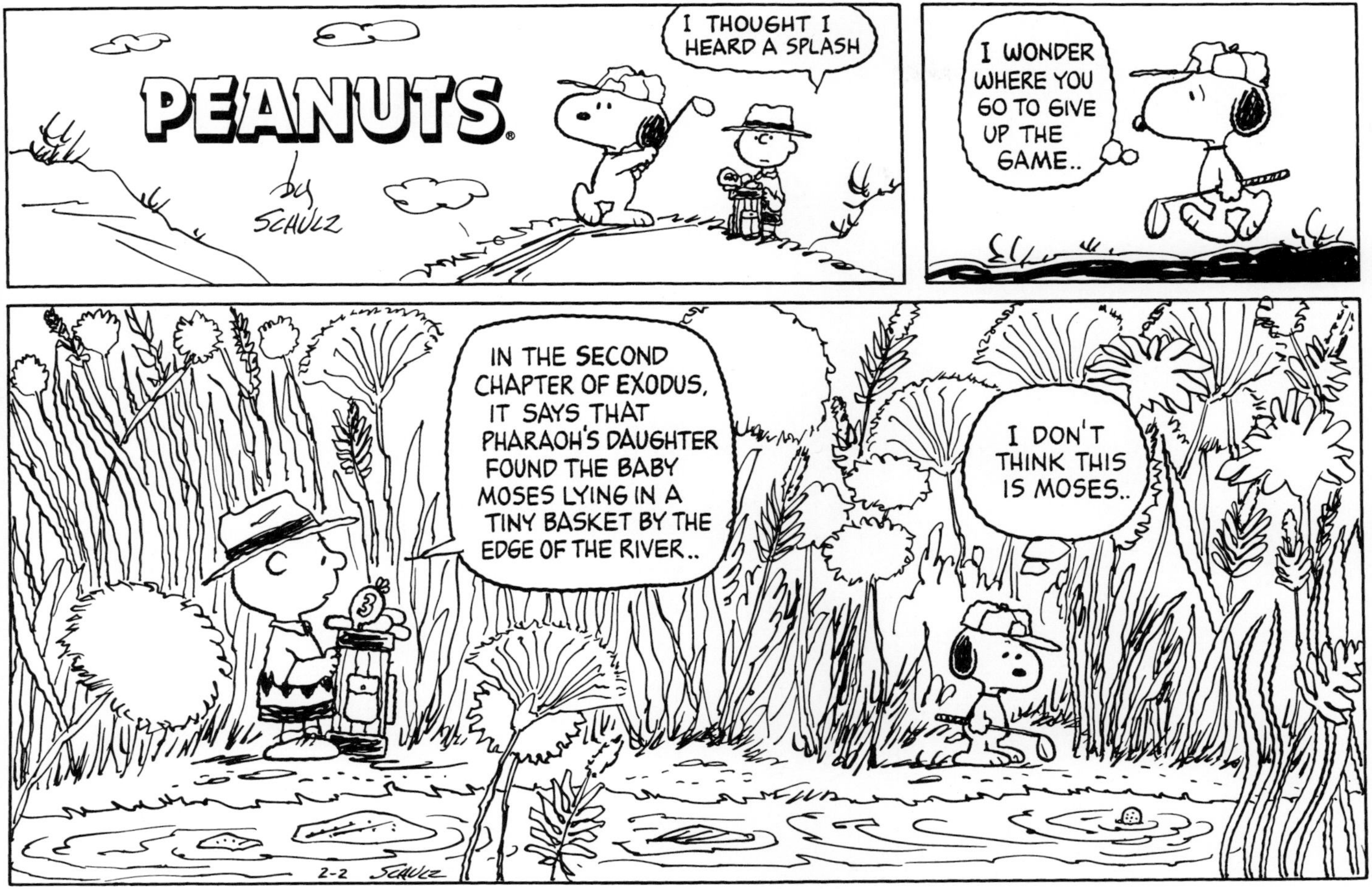
PEANUTS
by SCHULZ
I THOUGHT I HEARD A SPLASH
I WONDER WHERE YOU GO TO GIVE UP THE GAME..
IN THE SECOND CHAPTER OF EXODUS, IT SAYS THAT PHARAOH'S DAUGHTER FOUND THE BABY MOSES LYING IN A TINY BASKET BY THE EDGE OF THE RIVER..
I DON'T THINK THIS IS MOSES..
2-2 SCHULZ

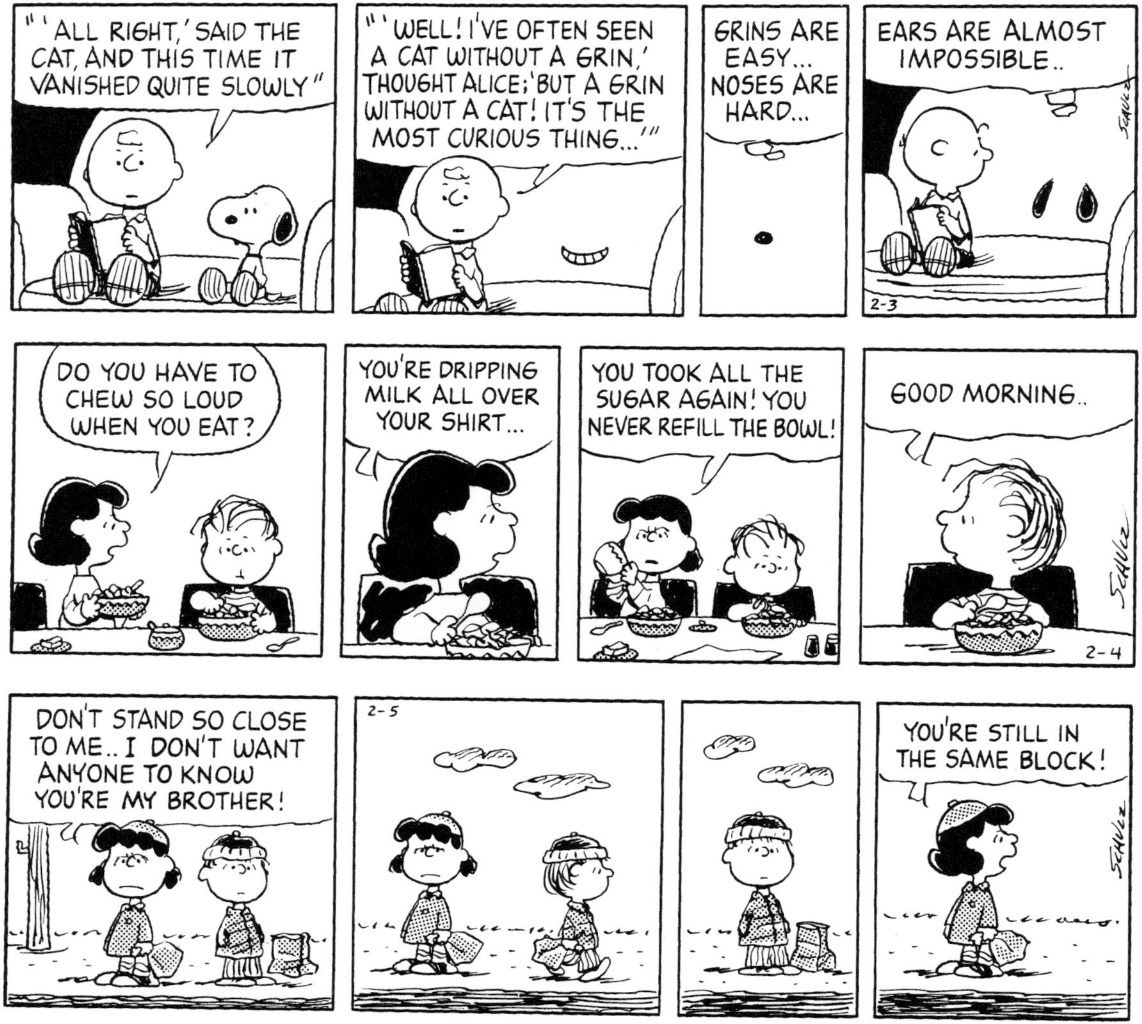
"'ALL RIGHT,' SAID THE CAT, AND THIS TIME IT VANISHED QUITE SLOWLY"
"'WELL! I'VE OFTEN SEEN A CAT WITHOUT A GRIN,' THOUGHT ALICE; 'BUT A GRIN WITHOUT A CAT! IT'S THE MOST CURIOUS THING...'"
GRINS ARE EASY... NOSES ARE HARD...
EARS ARE ALMOST IMPOSSIBLE..
SCHULZ
2-3
DO YOU HAVE TO CHEW SO LOUD WHEN YOU EAT?
YOU'RE DRIPPING MILK ALL OVER YOUR SHIRT...
YOU TOOK ALL THE SUGAR AGAIN! YOU NEVER REFILL THE BOWL!
GOOD MORNING..
SCHULZ
2-4
DON'T STAND SO CLOSE TO ME.. I DON'T WANT ANYONE TO KNOW YOU'RE MY BROTHER!
2-5
YOU'RE STILL IN THE SAME BLOCK!
SCHULZ

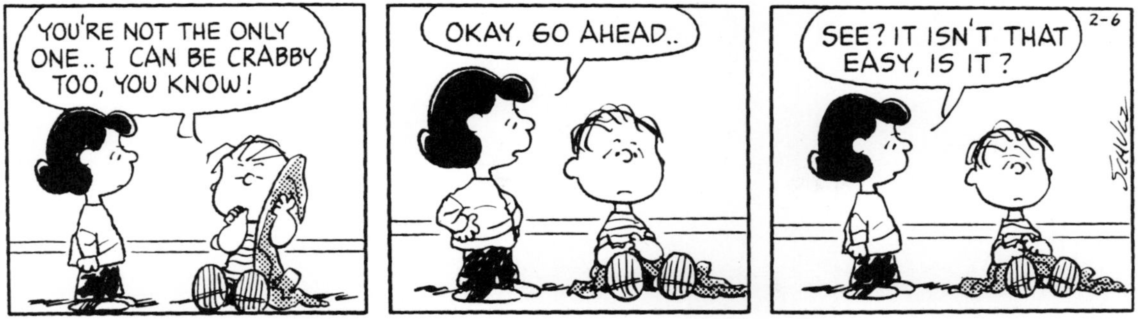
YOU'RE NOT THE ONLY ONE.. I CAN BE CRABBY TOO, YOU KNOW!
OKAY, GO AHEAD..
SEE? IT ISN'T THAT EASY, IS IT?
2-6

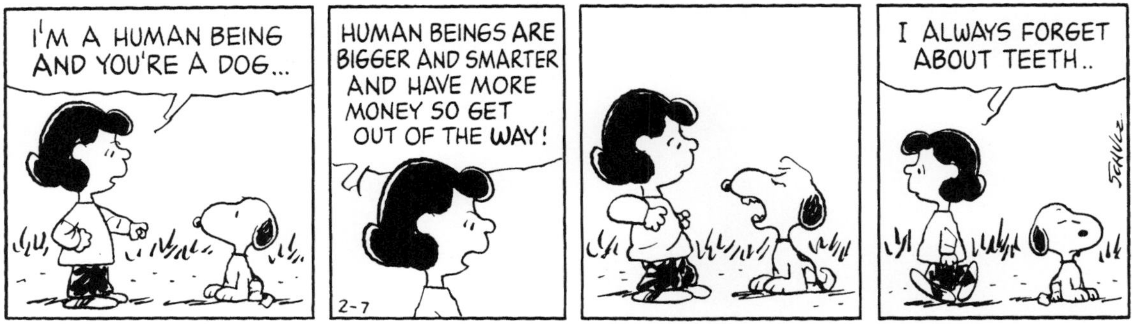
I'M A HUMAN BEING AND YOU'RE A DOG...
HUMAN BEINGS ARE BIGGER AND SMARTER AND HAVE MORE MONEY SO GET OUT OF THE WAY!
2-7
I ALWAYS FORGET ABOUT TEETH..

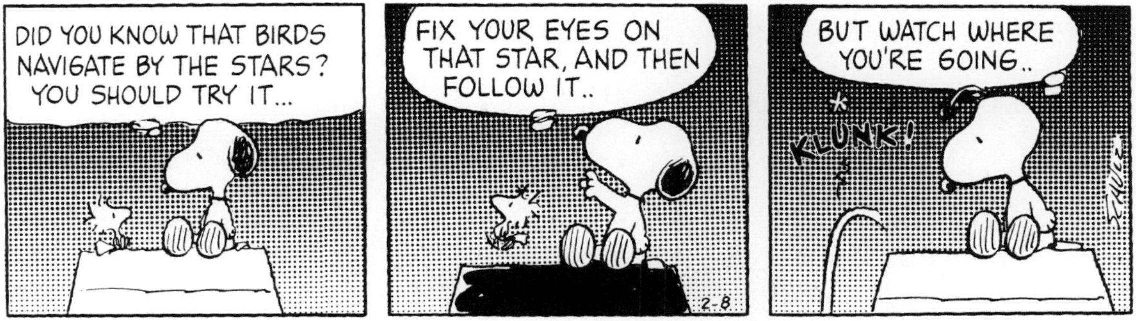
DID YOU KNOW THAT BIRDS NAVIGATE BY THE STARS? YOU SHOULD TRY IT...
FIX YOUR EYES ON THAT STAR, AND THEN FOLLOW IT..
2-8
BUT WATCH WHERE YOU'RE GOING..
KLUNK!

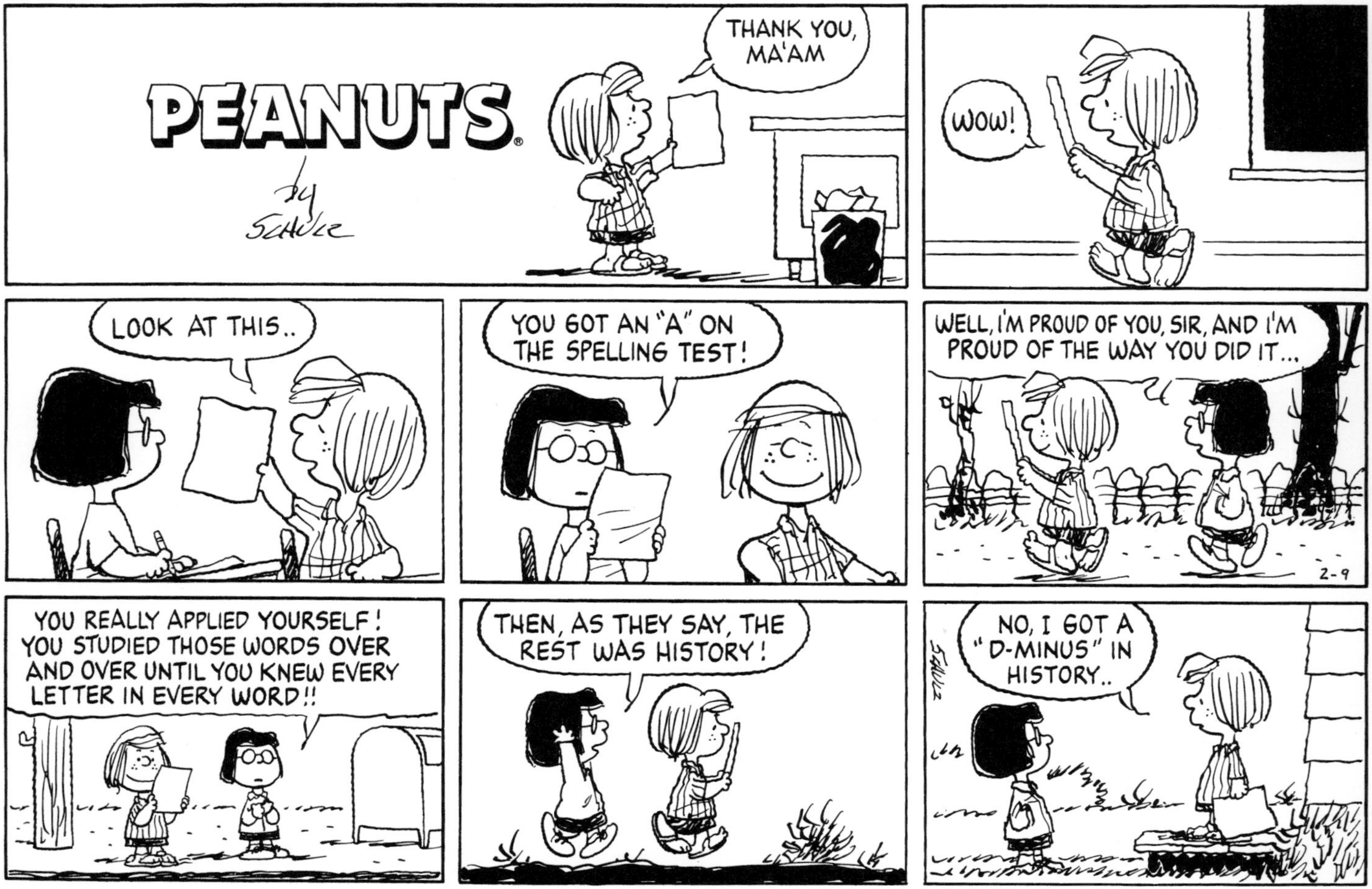
PEANUTS
by SCHULZ
THANK YOU, MA'AM
WOW!
LOOK AT THIS..
YOU GOT AN "A" ON THE SPELLING TEST!
WELL, I'M PROUD OF YOU, SIR, AND I'M PROUD OF THE WAY YOU DID IT...
2-9
YOU REALLY APPLIED YOURSELF! YOU STUDIED THOSE WORDS OVER AND OVER UNTIL YOU KNEW EVERY LETTER IN EVERY WORD!!
THEN, AS THEY SAY, THE REST WAS HISTORY!
SCHULZ
NO, I GOT A "D-MINUS" IN HISTORY..

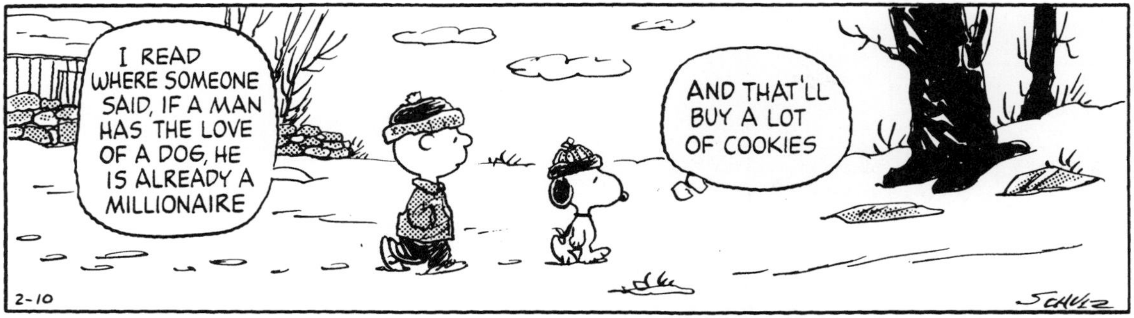
I READ WHERE SOMEONE SAID, IF A MAN HAS THE LOVE OF A DOG, HE IS ALREADY A MILLIONAIRE
AND THAT'LL BUY A LOT OF COOKIES
2-10

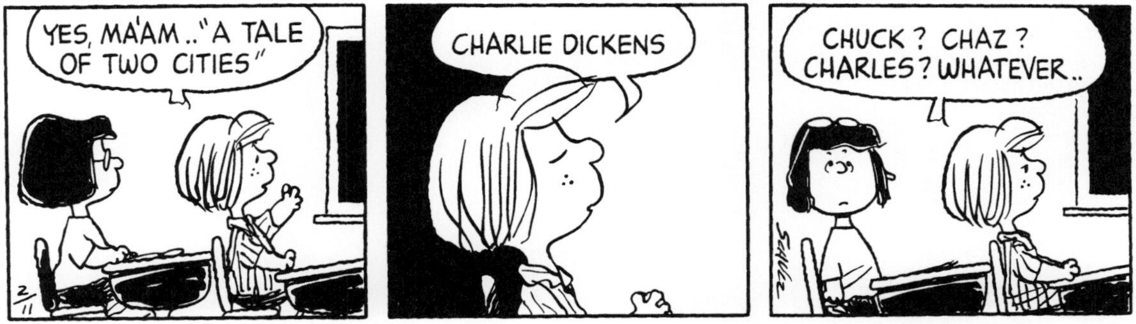
YES, MA'AM.."A TALE OF TWO CITIES"
CHARLIE DICKENS
CHUCK ? CHAZ ? CHARLES ? WHATEVER..
2/11

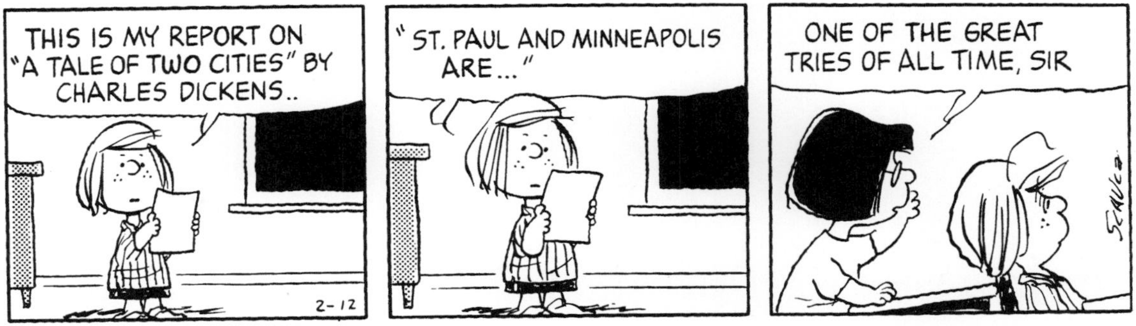
THIS IS MY REPORT ON "A TALE OF TWO CITIES" BY CHARLES DICKENS..
"ST. PAUL AND MINNEAPOLIS ARE..."
ONE OF THE GREAT TRIES OF ALL TIME, SIR
2-12

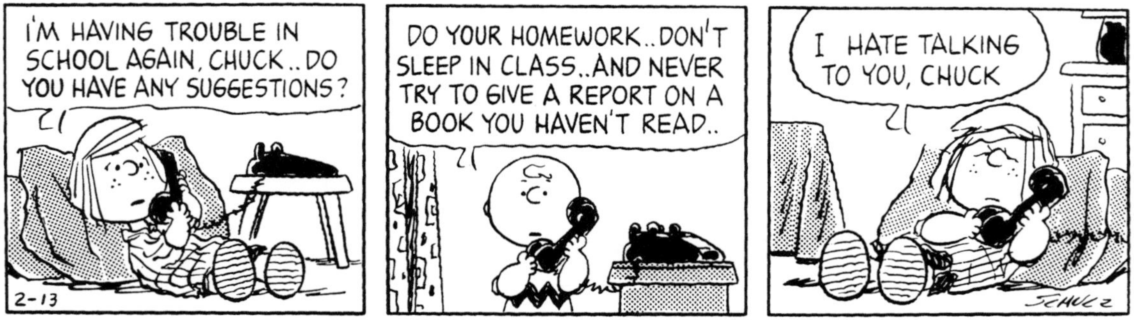
I'M HAVING TROUBLE IN SCHOOL AGAIN, CHUCK.. DO YOU HAVE ANY SUGGESTIONS?
2-13
DO YOUR HOMEWORK.. DON'T SLEEP IN CLASS.. AND NEVER TRY TO GIVE A REPORT ON A BOOK YOU HAVEN'T READ..
I HATE TALKING TO YOU, CHUCK
SCHULZ

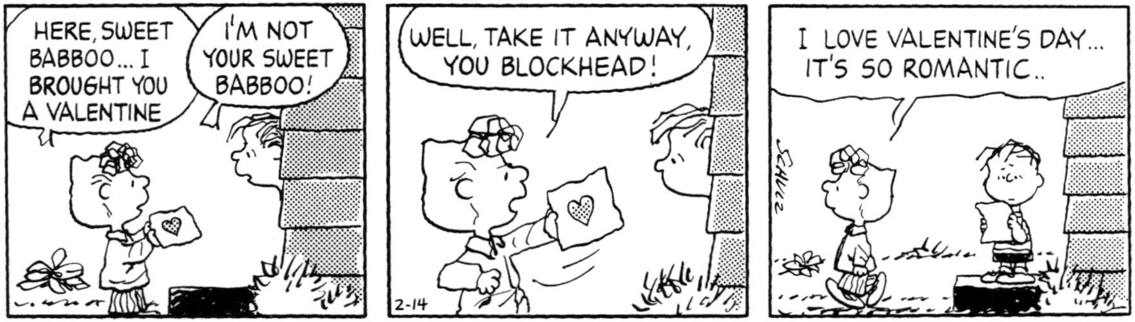
HERE, SWEET BABBOO... I BROUGHT YOU A VALENTINE
I'M NOT YOUR SWEET BABBOO!
WELL, TAKE IT ANYWAY, YOU BLOCKHEAD!
2-14
I LOVE VALENTINE'S DAY... IT'S SO ROMANTIC..
SCHULZ

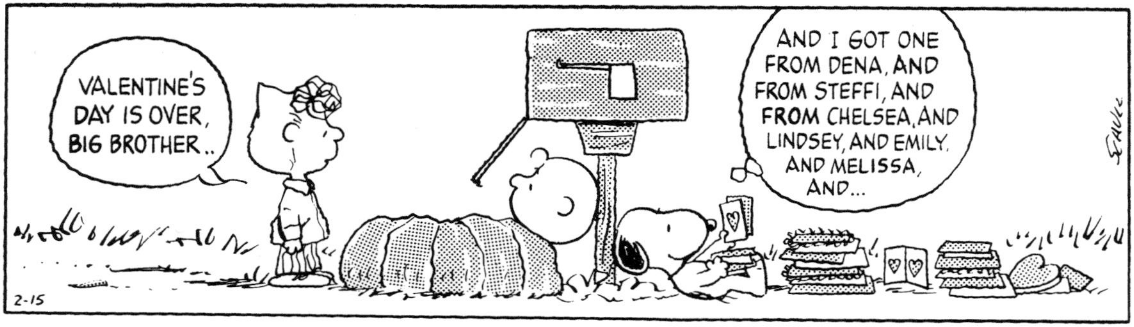
VALENTINE'S DAY IS OVER, BIG BROTHER..
AND I GOT ONE FROM DENA, AND FROM STEFFI, AND FROM CHELSEA, AND LINDSEY, AND EMILY, AND MELISSA, AND...
2-15
SCHULZ

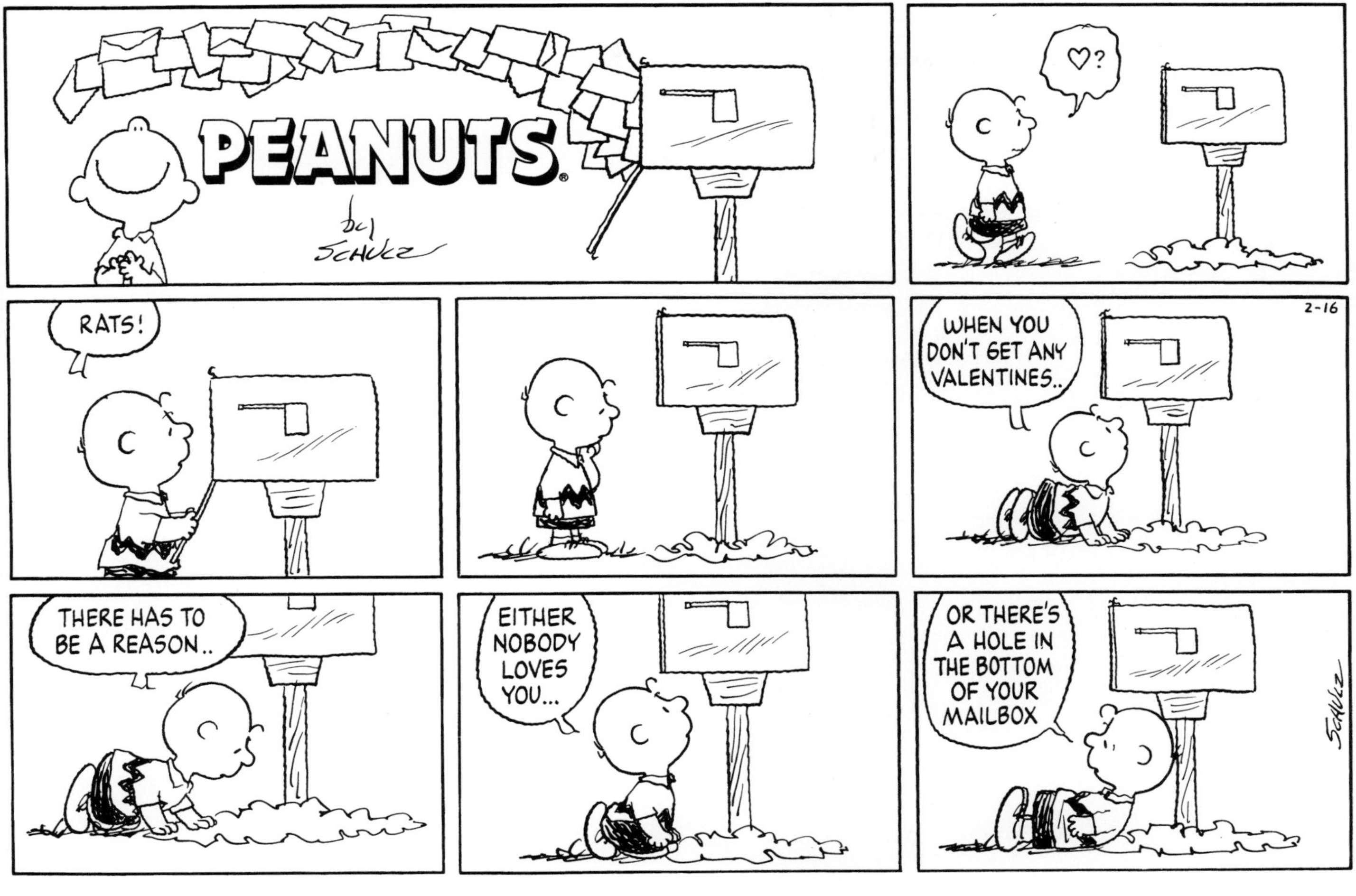
PEANUTS
by SCHULZ
♡?
RATS!
2-16
WHEN YOU DON'T GET ANY VALENTINES..
THERE HAS TO BE A REASON..
EITHER NOBODY LOVES YOU...
OR THERE'S A HOLE IN THE BOTTOM OF YOUR MAILBOX
SCHULZ

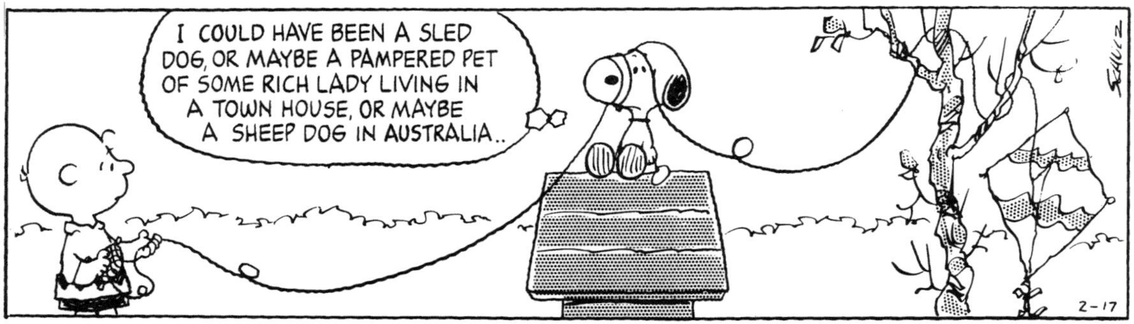
I COULD HAVE BEEN A SLED DOG, OR MAYBE A PAMPERED PET OF SOME RICH LADY LIVING IN A TOWN HOUSE, OR MAYBE A SHEEP DOG IN AUSTRALIA..
SCHULZ
2-17

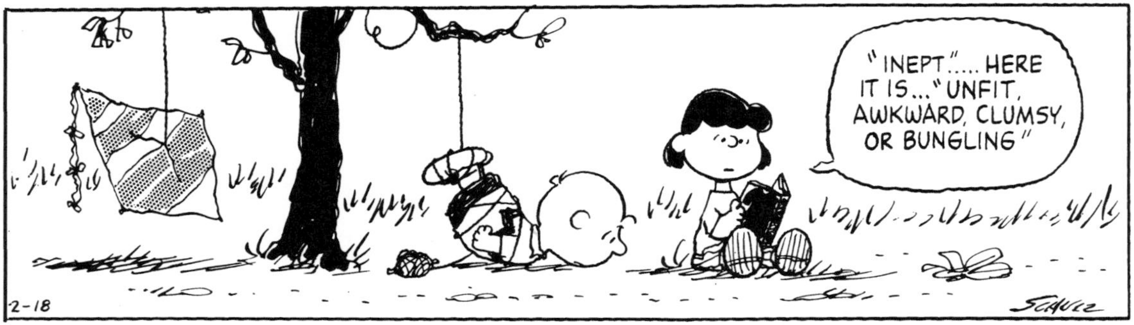
"INEPT"..... HERE IT IS..."UNFIT, AWKWARD, CLUMSY, OR BUNGLING"
2-18
SCHULZ

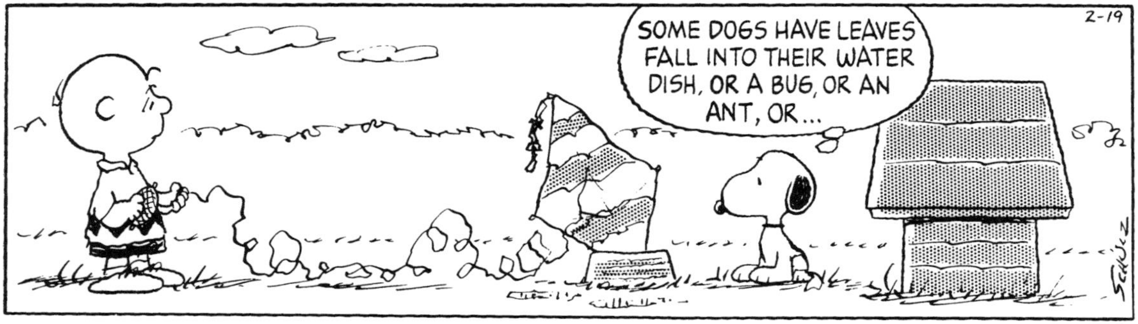
2-19
SOME DOGS HAVE LEAVES FALL INTO THEIR WATER DISH, OR A BUG, OR AN ANT, OR...
SCHULZ

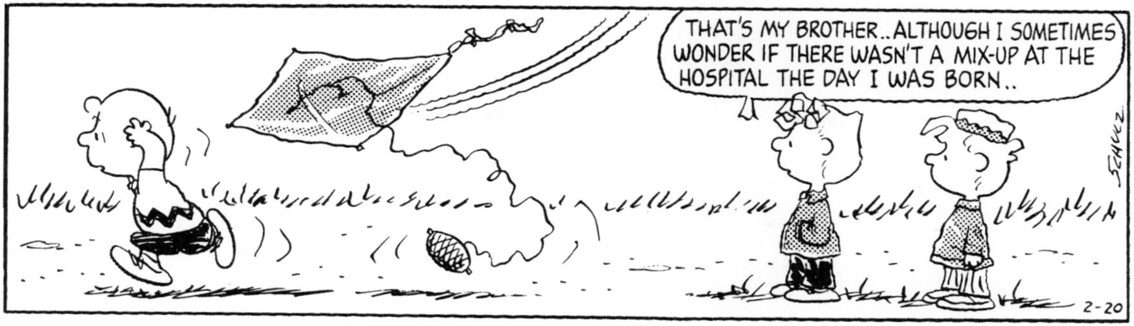
THAT'S MY BROTHER..ALTHOUGH I SOMETIMES WONDER IF THERE WASN'T A MIX-UP AT THE HOSPITAL THE DAY I WAS BORN..
SCHULZ
2-20

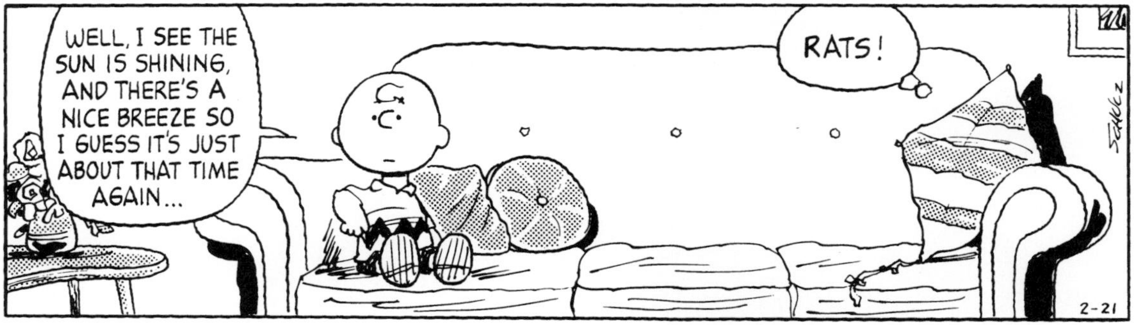
WELL, I SEE THE SUN IS SHINING, AND THERE'S A NICE BREEZE SO I GUESS IT'S JUST ABOUT THAT TIME AGAIN...
RATS!
SCHULZ
2-21

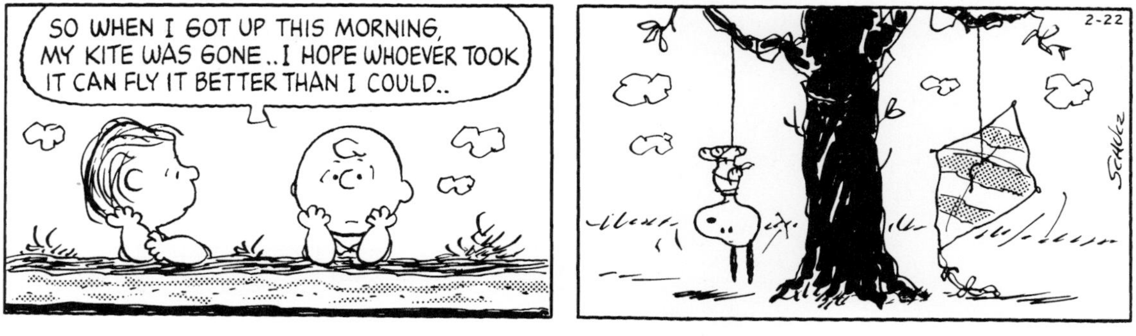
SO WHEN I GOT UP THIS MORNING, MY KITE WAS GONE..I HOPE WHOEVER TOOK IT CAN FLY IT BETTER THAN I COULD..
2-22
SCHULZ

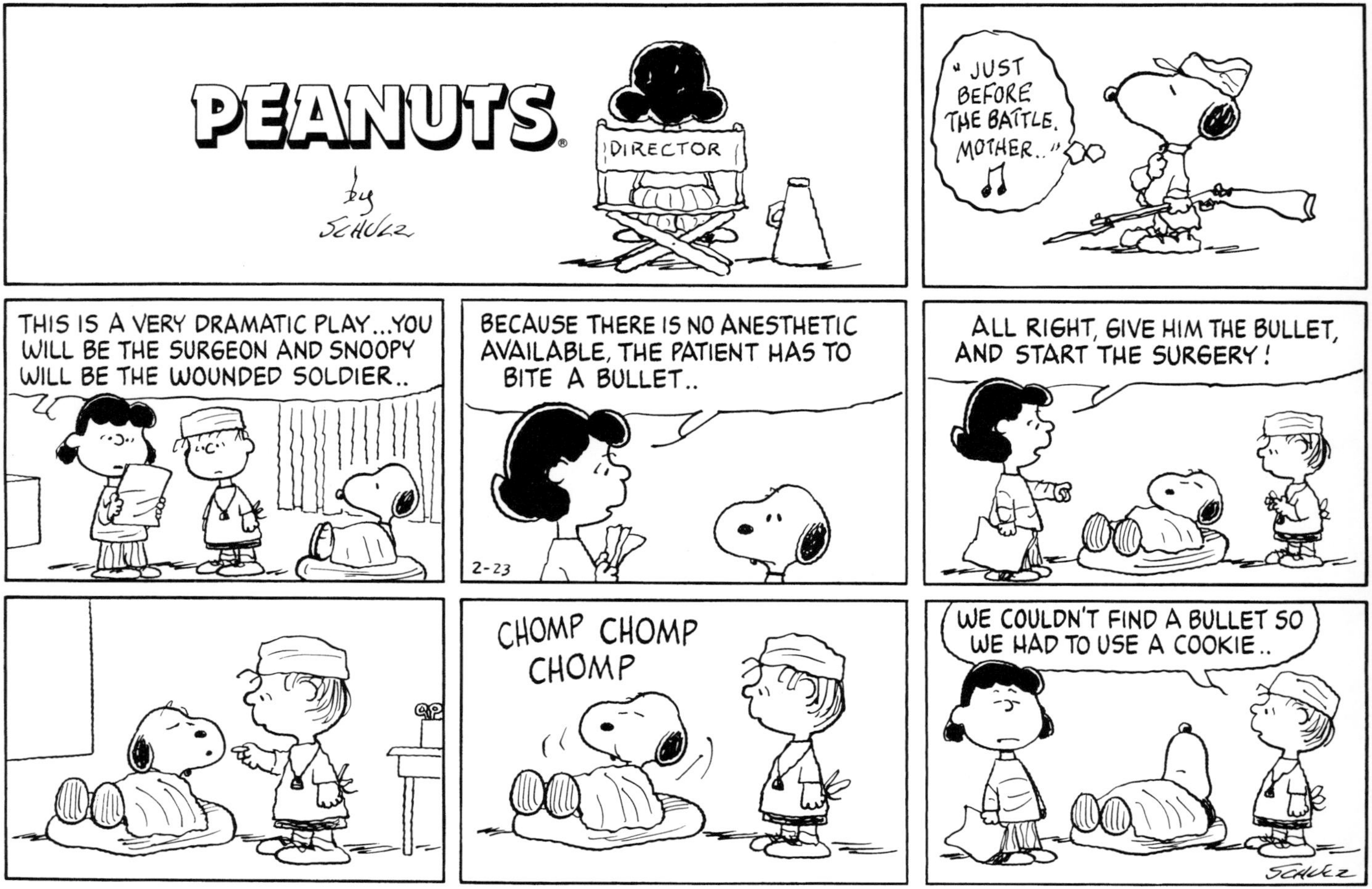
PEANUTS
by SCHULZ
DIRECTOR
" JUST BEFORE THE BATTLE, MOTHER.. "
THIS IS A VERY DRAMATIC PLAY...YOU WILL BE THE SURGEON AND SNOOPY WILL BE THE WOUNDED SOLDIER..
BECAUSE THERE IS NO ANESTHETIC AVAILABLE, THE PATIENT HAS TO BITE A BULLET..
2-23
ALL RIGHT, GIVE HIM THE BULLET, AND START THE SURGERY!
CHOMP CHOMP
CHOMP
WE COULDN'T FIND A BULLET SO WE HAD TO USE A COOKIE..
SCHULZ

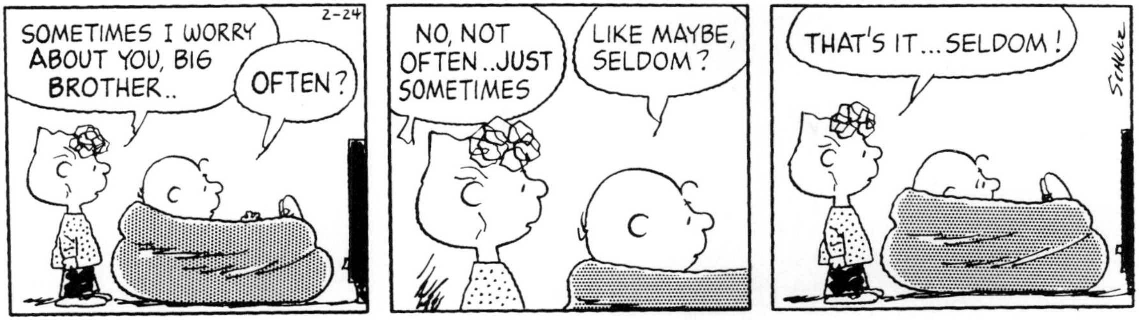
2-24
SOMETIMES I WORRY ABOUT YOU, BIG BROTHER..
OFTEN?
NO, NOT OFTEN..JUST SOMETIMES
LIKE MAYBE, SELDOM?
THAT'S IT...SELDOM!
SCHULZ

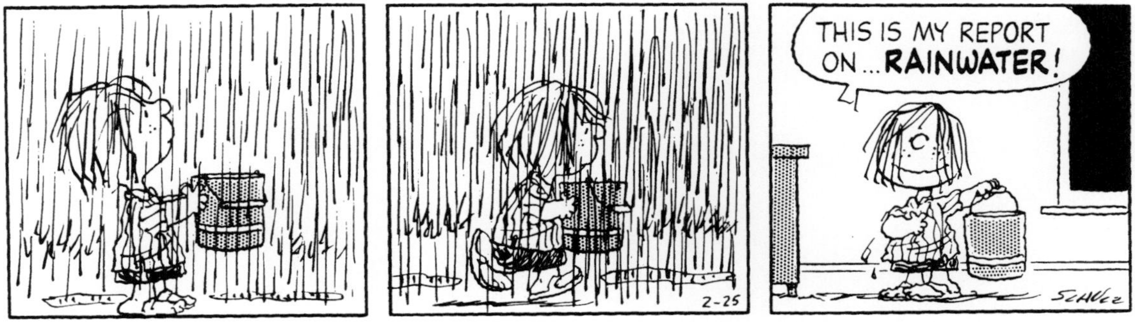
2-25
THIS IS MY REPORT ON...**RAINWATER**!
SCHULZ

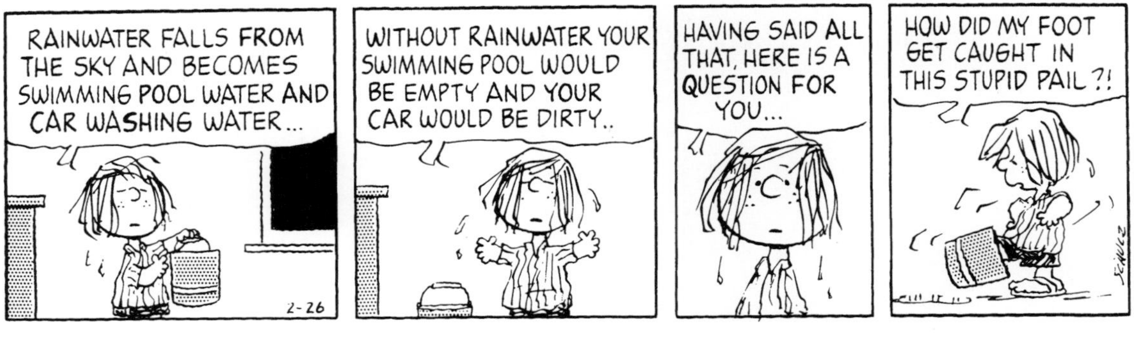
RAINWATER FALLS FROM THE SKY AND BECOMES SWIMMING POOL WATER AND CAR WASHING WATER...
2-26
WITHOUT RAINWATER YOUR SWIMMING POOL WOULD BE EMPTY AND YOUR CAR WOULD BE DIRTY..
HAVING SAID ALL THAT, HERE IS A QUESTION FOR YOU...
HOW DID MY FOOT GET CAUGHT IN THIS STUPID PAIL?!
SCHULZ

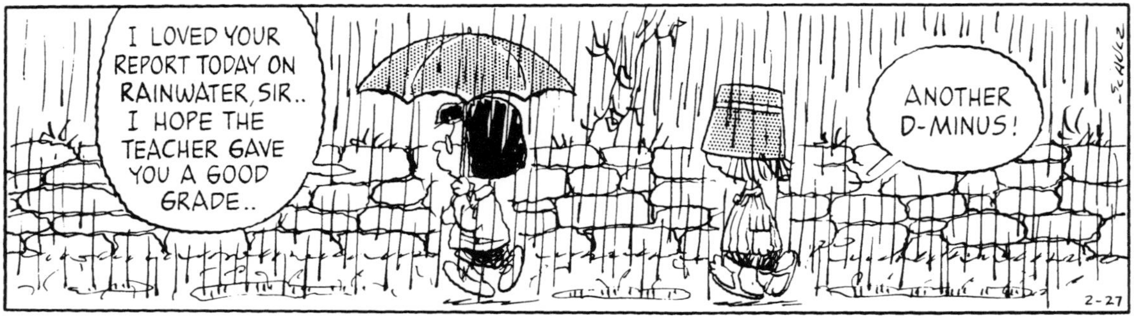
I LOVED YOUR REPORT TODAY ON RAINWATER, SIR.. I HOPE THE TEACHER GAVE YOU A GOOD GRADE..
ANOTHER D-MINUS!
SCHULZ
2-27

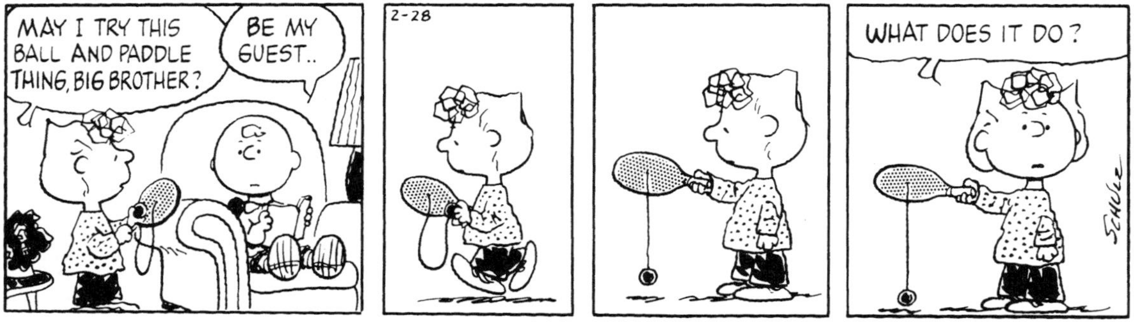
MAY I TRY THIS BALL AND PADDLE THING, BIG BROTHER?
BE MY GUEST..
2-28
WHAT DOES IT DO?
SCHULZ

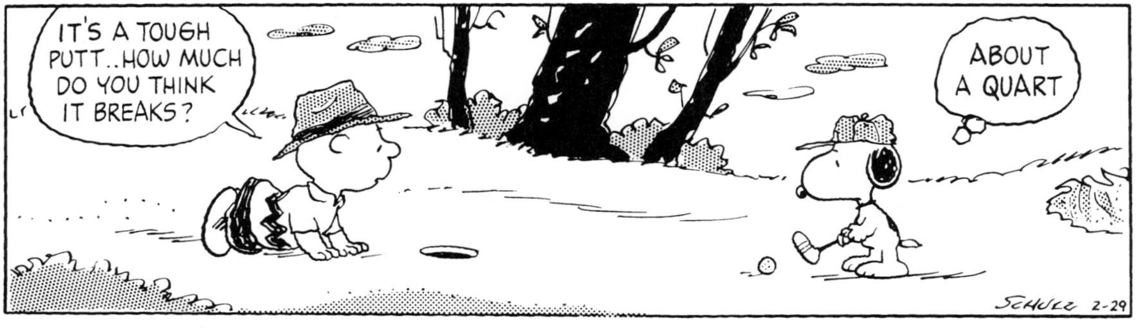
IT'S A TOUGH PUTT..HOW MUCH DO YOU THINK IT BREAKS?
ABOUT A QUART
SCHULZ 2-29

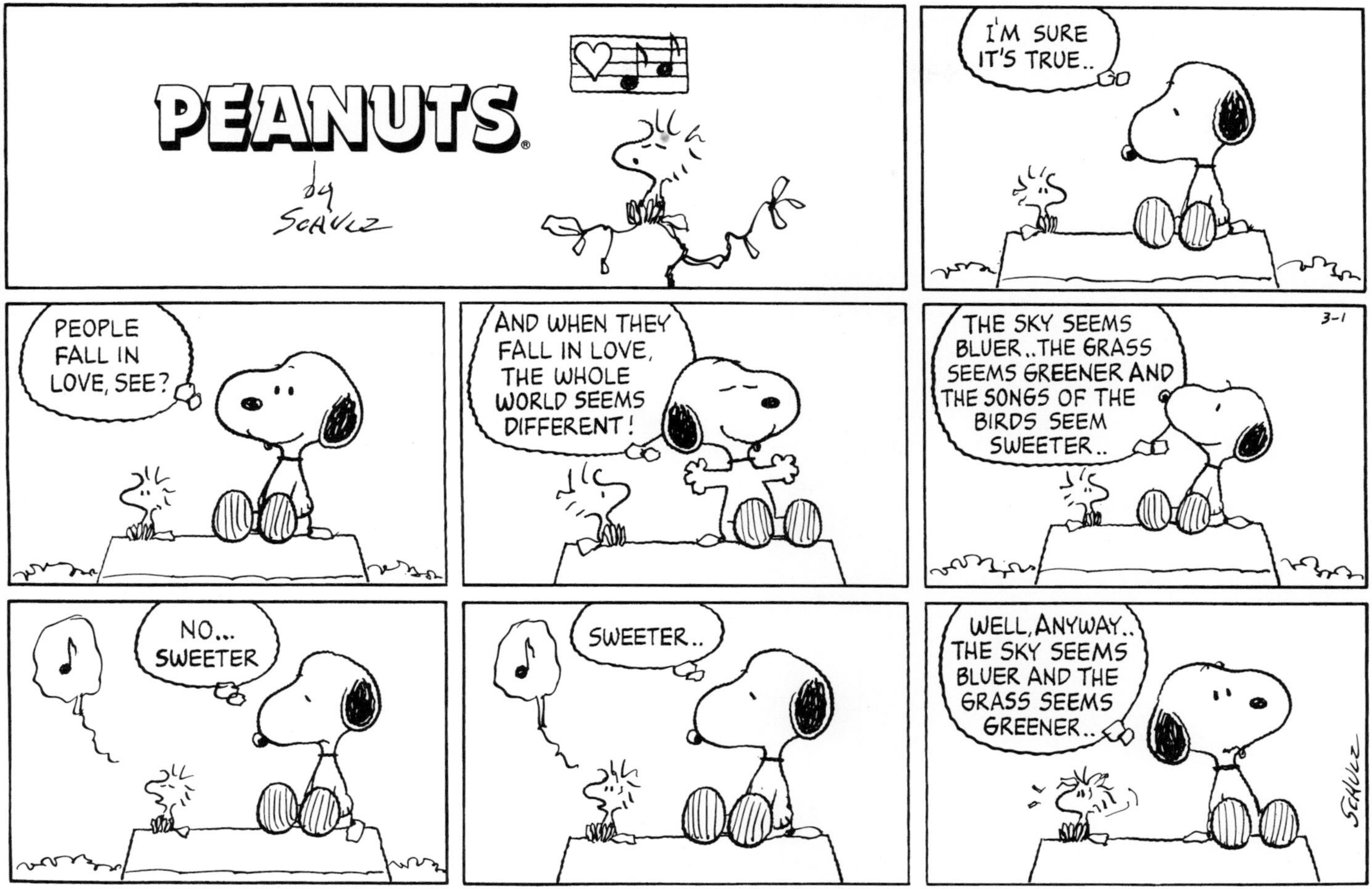
PEANUTS
by SCHULZ
I'M SURE IT'S TRUE..
PEOPLE FALL IN LOVE, SEE?
AND WHEN THEY FALL IN LOVE, THE WHOLE WORLD SEEMS DIFFERENT!
THE SKY SEEMS BLUER..THE GRASS SEEMS GREENER AND THE SONGS OF THE BIRDS SEEM SWEETER..
3-1
NO... SWEETER
SWEETER..
WELL, ANYWAY.. THE SKY SEEMS BLUER AND THE GRASS SEEMS GREENER..
SCHULZ

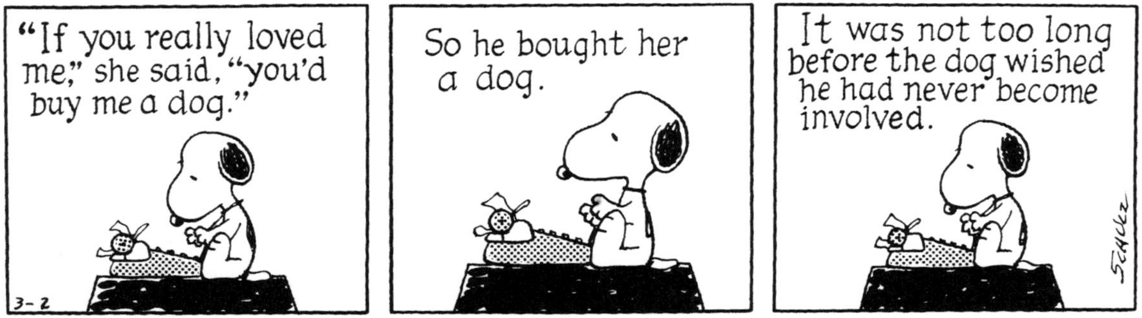
"If you really loved me," she said, "you'd buy me a dog."
3-2
So he bought her a dog.
It was not too long before the dog wished he had never become involved.
SCHULZ

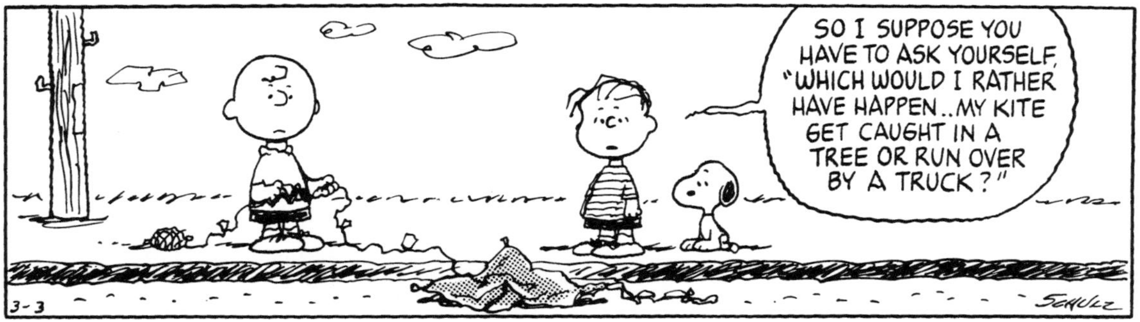
SO I SUPPOSE YOU HAVE TO ASK YOURSELF, "WHICH WOULD I RATHER HAVE HAPPEN..MY KITE GET CAUGHT IN A TREE OR RUN OVER BY A TRUCK?"
3-3
SCHULZ

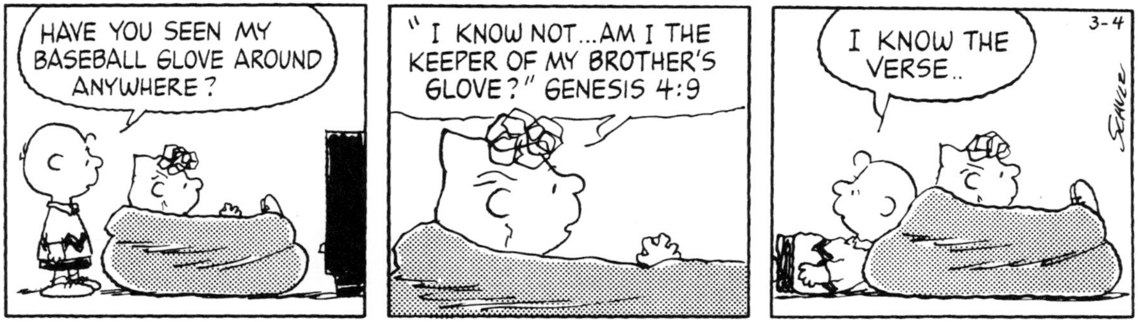
HAVE YOU SEEN MY BASEBALL GLOVE AROUND ANYWHERE?
"I KNOW NOT...AM I THE KEEPER OF MY BROTHER'S GLOVE?" GENESIS 4:9
3-4
I KNOW THE VERSE..
SCHULZ

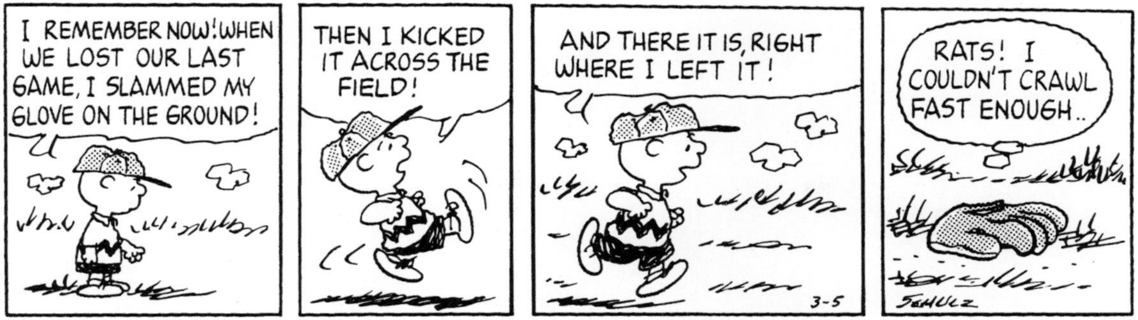
I REMEMBER NOW! WHEN WE LOST OUR LAST GAME, I SLAMMED MY GLOVE ON THE GROUND!
THEN I KICKED IT ACROSS THE FIELD!
AND THERE IT IS, RIGHT WHERE I LEFT IT!
3-5
RATS! I COULDN'T CRAWL FAST ENOUGH..
SCHULZ

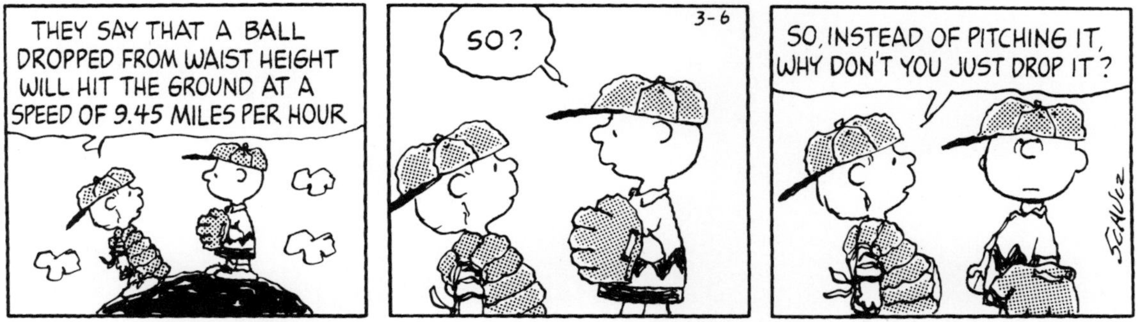
THEY SAY THAT A BALL DROPPED FROM WAIST HEIGHT WILL HIT THE GROUND AT A SPEED OF 9.45 MILES PER HOUR
3-6
SO?
SO, INSTEAD OF PITCHING IT, WHY DON'T YOU JUST DROP IT?
SCHULZ

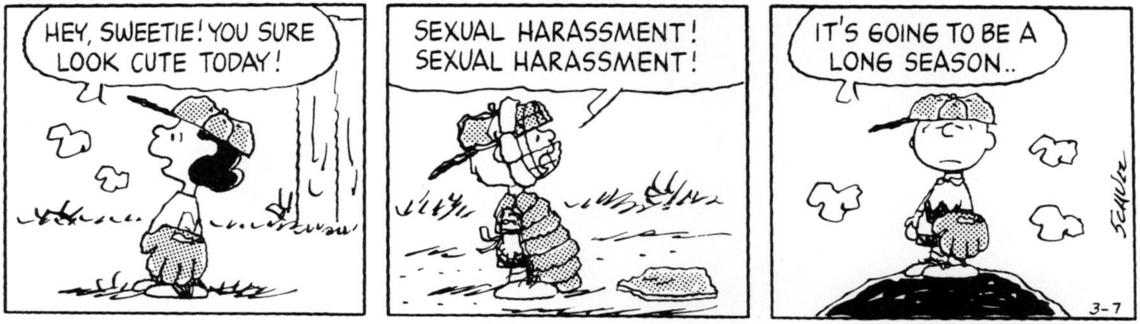
HEY, SWEETIE! YOU SURE LOOK CUTE TODAY!
SEXUAL HARASSMENT! SEXUAL HARASSMENT!
IT'S GOING TO BE A LONG SEASON..
SCHULZ
3-7

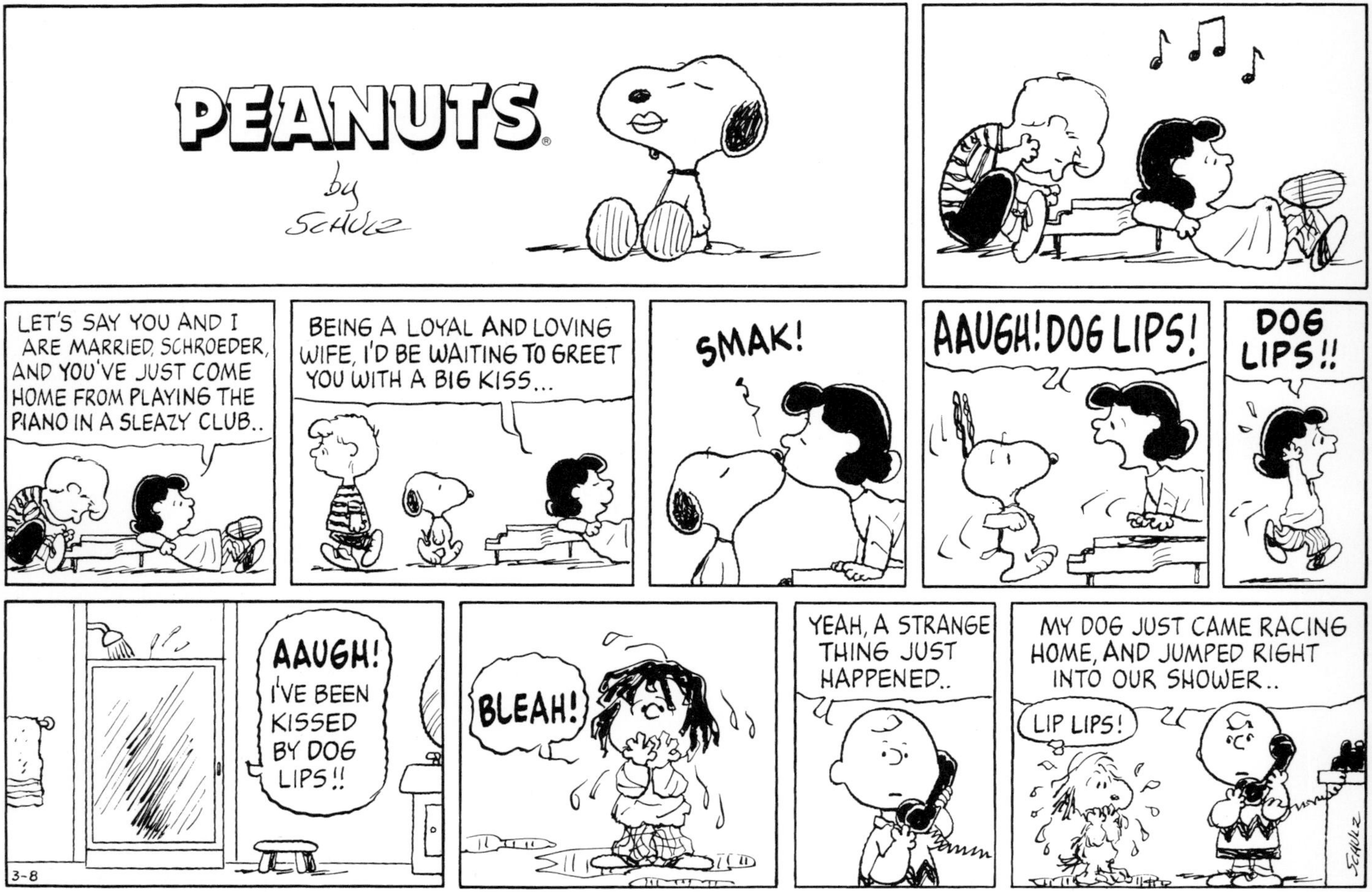
PEANUTS
by SCHULZ
LET'S SAY YOU AND I ARE MARRIED, SCHROEDER, AND YOU'VE JUST COME HOME FROM PLAYING THE PIANO IN A SLEAZY CLUB..
BEING A LOYAL AND LOVING WIFE, I'D BE WAITING TO GREET YOU WITH A BIG KISS...
SMAK!
AAUGH! DOG LIPS!
DOG LIPS!!
AAUGH! I'VE BEEN KISSED BY DOG LIPS!!
BLEAH!
YEAH, A STRANGE THING JUST HAPPENED..
MY DOG JUST CAME RACING HOME, AND JUMPED RIGHT INTO OUR SHOWER..
LIP LIPS!
3-8
SCHULZ

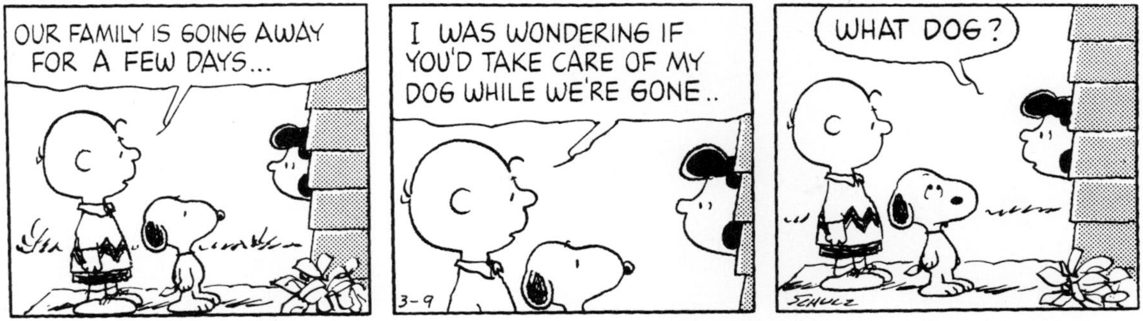
OUR FAMILY IS GOING AWAY FOR A FEW DAYS...
I WAS WONDERING IF YOU'D TAKE CARE OF MY DOG WHILE WE'RE GONE..
WHAT DOG?

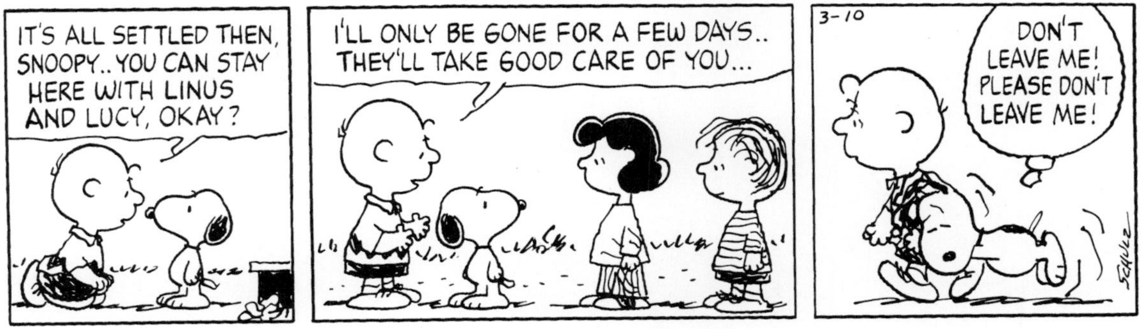
IT'S ALL SETTLED THEN, SNOOPY.. YOU CAN STAY HERE WITH LINUS AND LUCY, OKAY?
I'LL ONLY BE GONE FOR A FEW DAYS.. THEY'LL TAKE GOOD CARE OF YOU...
DON'T LEAVE ME! PLEASE DON'T LEAVE ME!

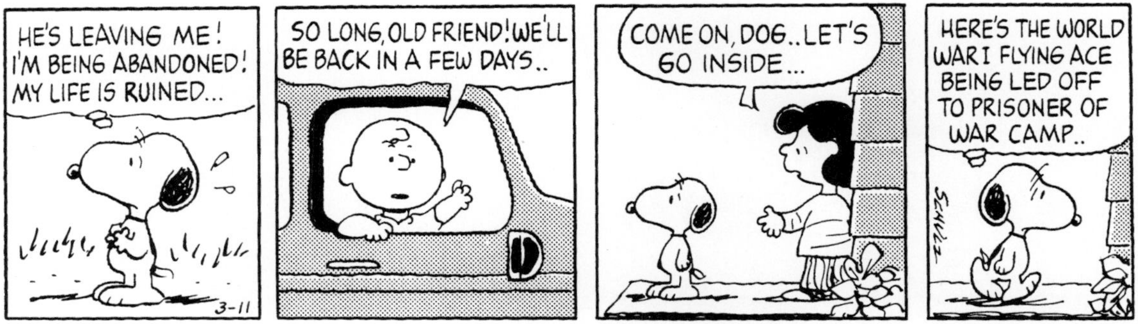
HE'S LEAVING ME! I'M BEING ABANDONED! MY LIFE IS RUINED...
SO LONG, OLD FRIEND! WE'LL BE BACK IN A FEW DAYS..
COME ON, DOG.. LET'S GO INSIDE...
HERE'S THE WORLD WAR I FLYING ACE BEING LED OFF TO PRISONER OF WAR CAMP..

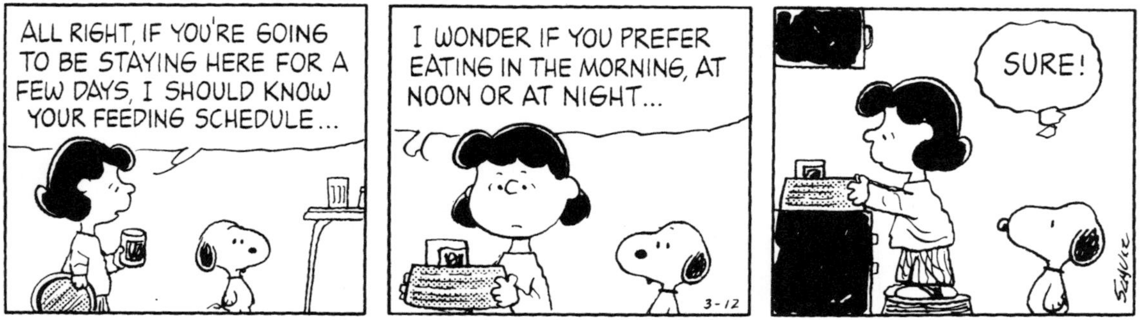
ALL RIGHT, IF YOU'RE GOING TO BE STAYING HERE FOR A FEW DAYS, I SHOULD KNOW YOUR FEEDING SCHEDULE...
I WONDER IF YOU PREFER EATING IN THE MORNING, AT NOON OR AT NIGHT...
3-12
SURE!
SCHULZ

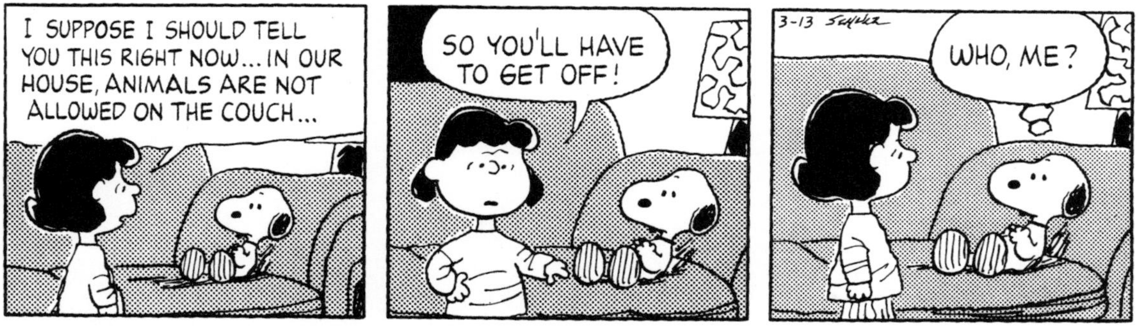
I SUPPOSE I SHOULD TELL YOU THIS RIGHT NOW... IN OUR HOUSE, ANIMALS ARE NOT ALLOWED ON THE COUCH...
SO YOU'LL HAVE TO GET OFF!
3-13 SCHULZ
WHO, ME?

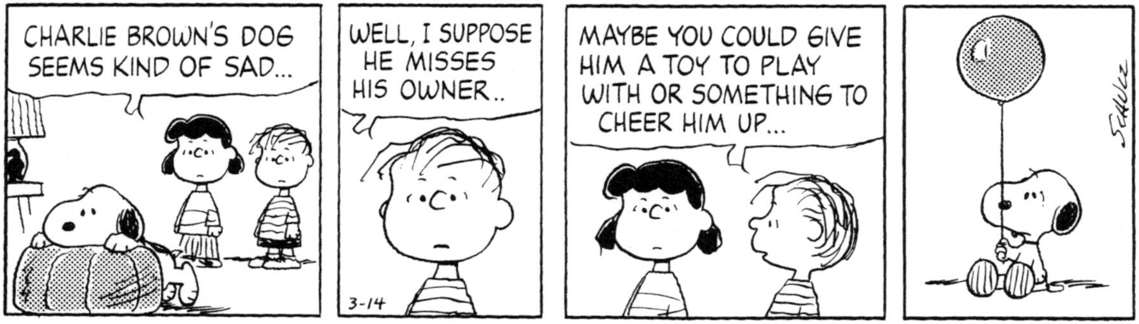
CHARLIE BROWN'S DOG SEEMS KIND OF SAD...
WELL, I SUPPOSE HE MISSES HIS OWNER..
3-14
MAYBE YOU COULD GIVE HIM A TOY TO PLAY WITH OR SOMETHING TO CHEER HIM UP...
SCHULZ

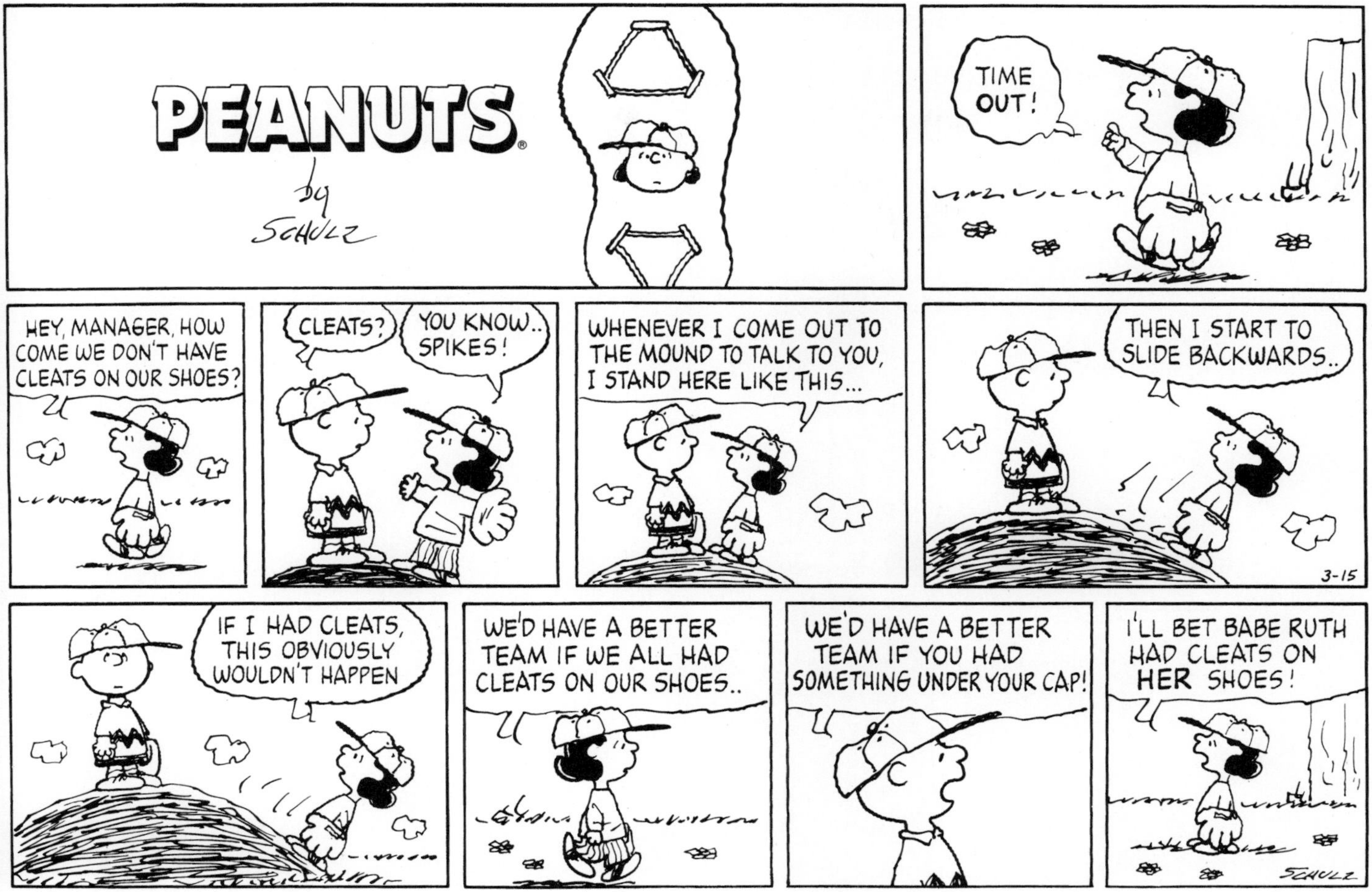
PEANUTS
by SCHULZ
TIME OUT!
HEY, MANAGER, HOW COME WE DON'T HAVE CLEATS ON OUR SHOES?
CLEATS?
YOU KNOW.. SPIKES!
WHENEVER I COME OUT TO THE MOUND TO TALK TO YOU, I STAND HERE LIKE THIS...
THEN I START TO SLIDE BACKWARDS..
3-15
IF I HAD CLEATS, THIS OBVIOUSLY WOULDN'T HAPPEN
WE'D HAVE A BETTER TEAM IF WE ALL HAD CLEATS ON OUR SHOES..
WE'D HAVE A BETTER TEAM IF YOU HAD SOMETHING UNDER YOUR CAP!
I'LL BET BABE RUTH HAD CLEATS ON HER SHOES!
SCHULZ

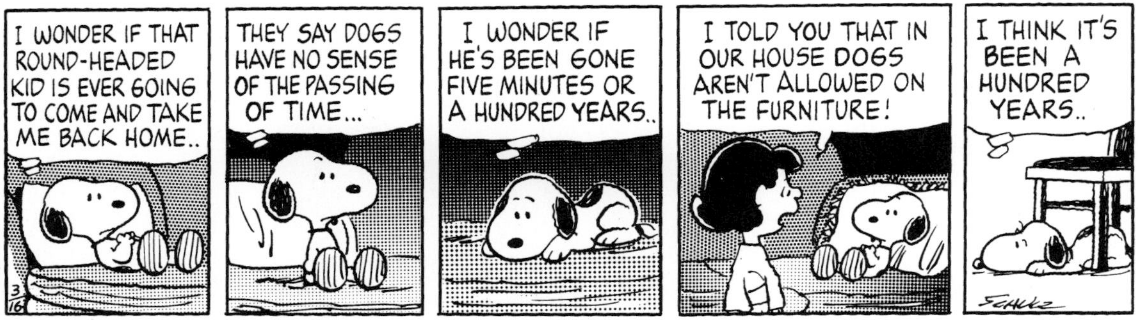
I WONDER IF THAT ROUND-HEADED KID IS EVER GOING TO COME AND TAKE ME BACK HOME..
THEY SAY DOGS HAVE NO SENSE OF THE PASSING OF TIME...
I WONDER IF HE'S BEEN GONE FIVE MINUTES OR A HUNDRED YEARS..
I TOLD YOU THAT IN OUR HOUSE DOGS AREN'T ALLOWED ON THE FURNITURE!
I THINK IT'S BEEN A HUNDRED YEARS..
3/16
SCHULZ

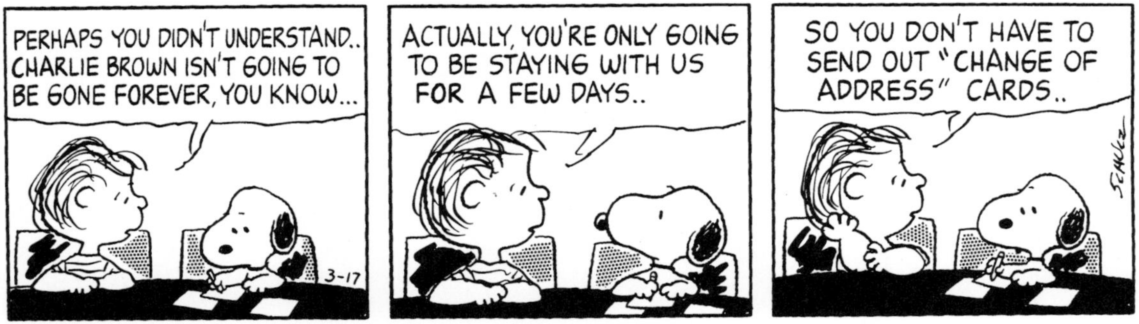
PERHAPS YOU DIDN'T UNDERSTAND.. CHARLIE BROWN ISN'T GOING TO BE GONE FOREVER, YOU KNOW...
3-17
ACTUALLY, YOU'RE ONLY GOING TO BE STAYING WITH US FOR A FEW DAYS..
SO YOU DON'T HAVE TO SEND OUT "CHANGE OF ADDRESS" CARDS..
SCHULZ

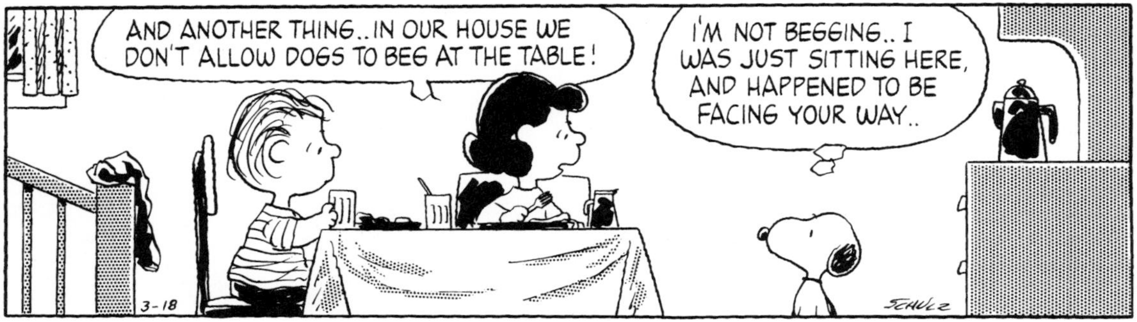
AND ANOTHER THING..IN OUR HOUSE WE DON'T ALLOW DOGS TO BEG AT THE TABLE!
I'M NOT BEGGING.. I WAS JUST SITTING HERE, AND HAPPENED TO BE FACING YOUR WAY..
3-18
SCHULZ

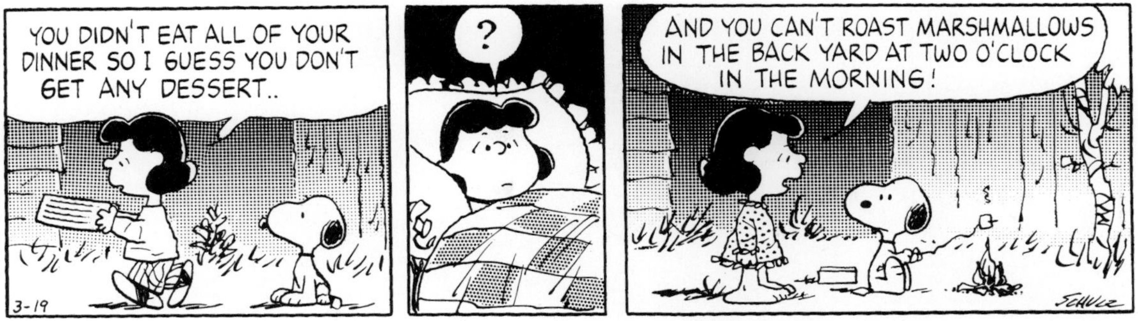
YOU DIDN'T EAT ALL OF YOUR DINNER SO I GUESS YOU DON'T GET ANY DESSERT..
3-19
?
AND YOU CAN'T ROAST MARSHMALLOWS IN THE BACK YARD AT TWO O'CLOCK IN THE MORNING!
SCHULZ

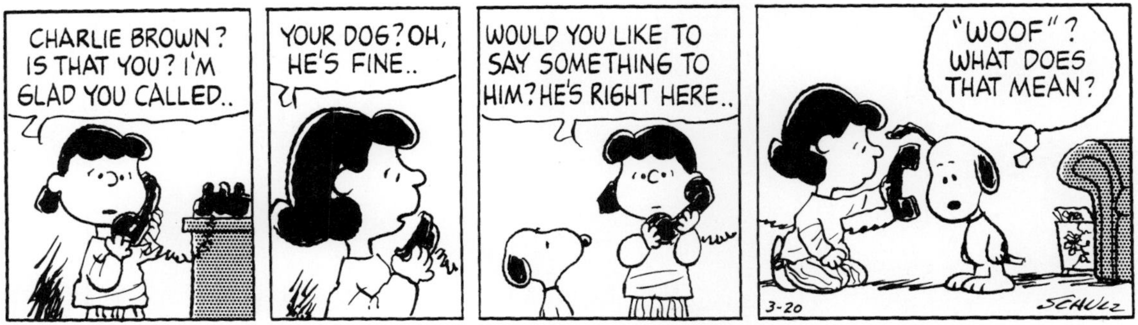
CHARLIE BROWN? IS THAT YOU? I'M GLAD YOU CALLED..
YOUR DOG? OH, HE'S FINE..
WOULD YOU LIKE TO SAY SOMETHING TO HIM? HE'S RIGHT HERE..
"WOOF"? WHAT DOES THAT MEAN?
3-20
SCHULZ

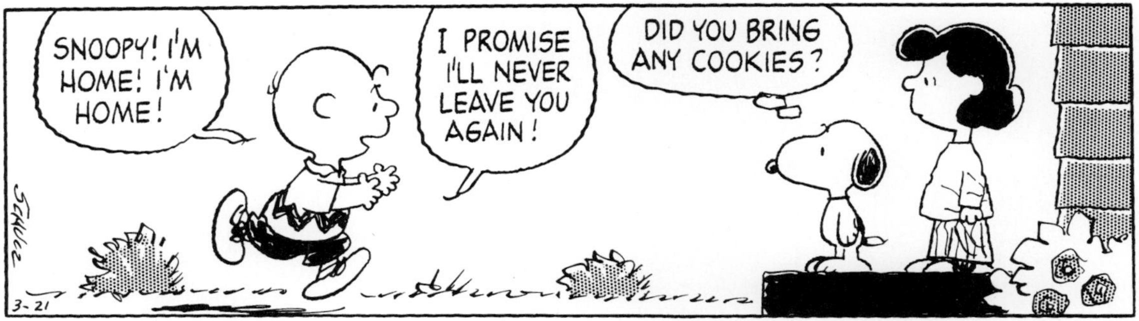
SNOOPY! I'M HOME! I'M HOME!
I PROMISE I'LL NEVER LEAVE YOU AGAIN!
DID YOU BRING ANY COOKIES?
SCHULZ
3-21

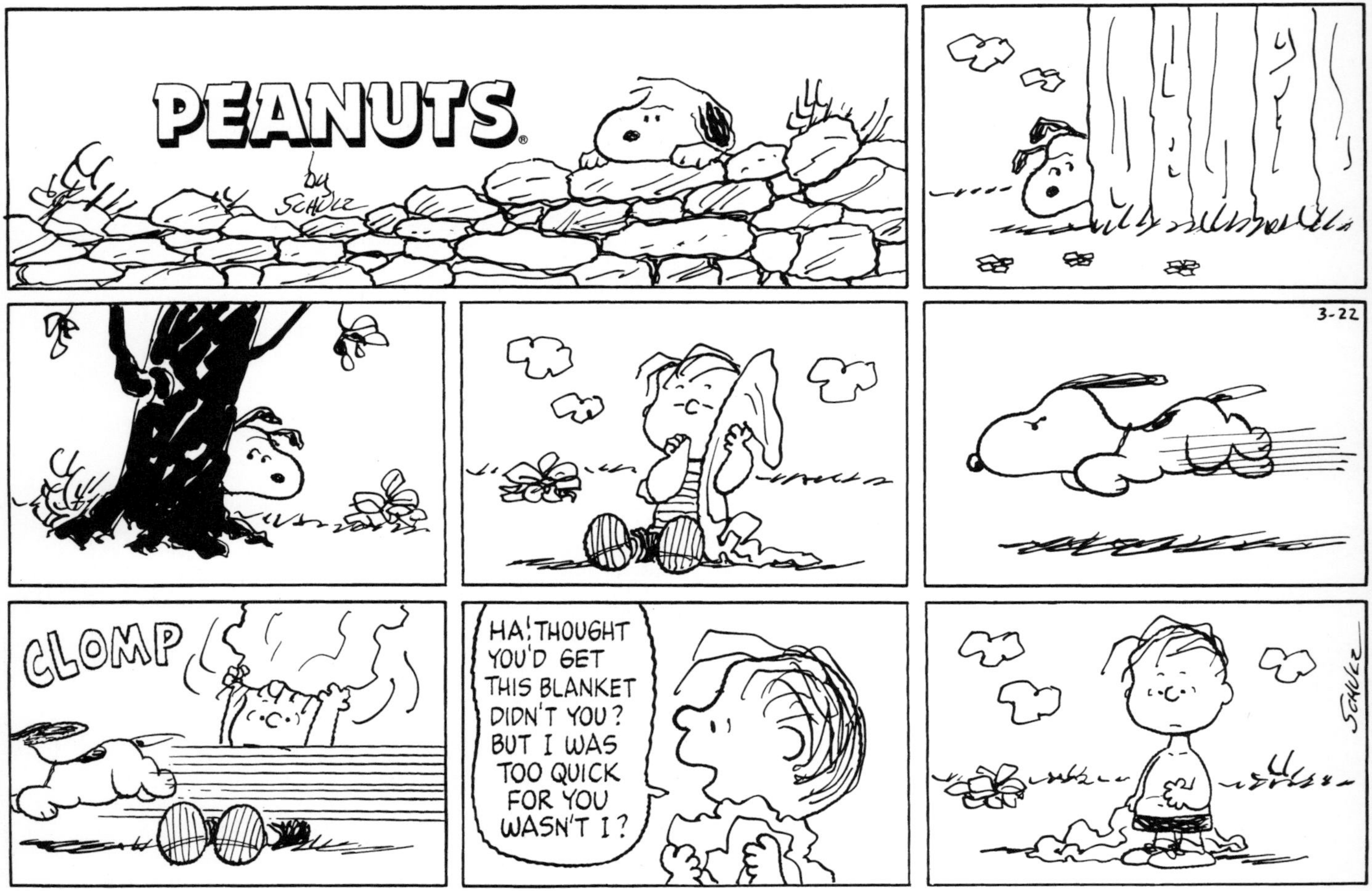
PEANUTS
by SCHULZ
3-22
CLOMP
HA! THOUGHT YOU'D GET THIS BLANKET DIDN'T YOU? BUT I WAS TOO QUICK FOR YOU WASN'T I?
SCHULZ

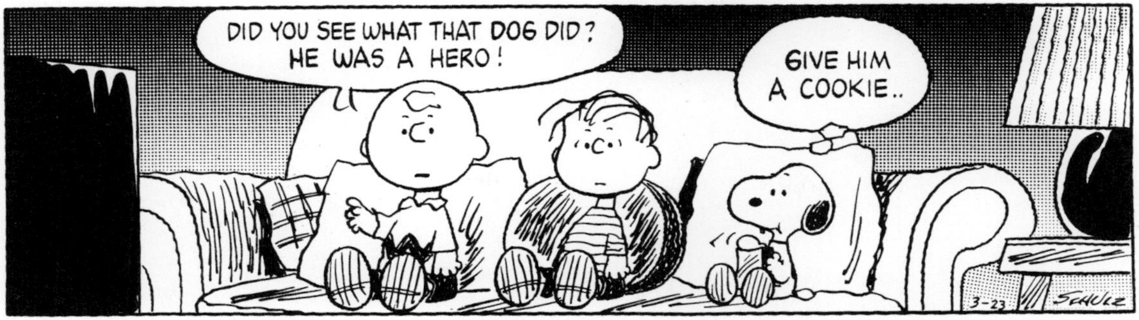
DID YOU SEE WHAT THAT DOG DID? HE WAS A HERO!
GIVE HIM A COOKIE..

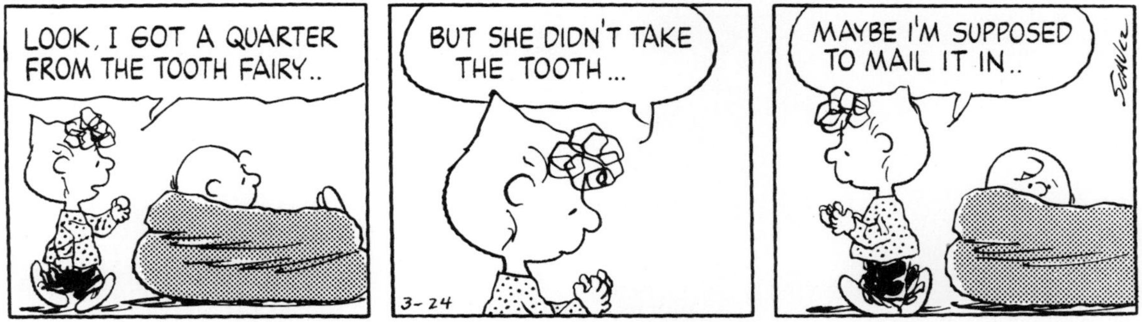
LOOK, I GOT A QUARTER FROM THE TOOTH FAIRY..
BUT SHE DIDN'T TAKE THE TOOTH...
MAYBE I'M SUPPOSED TO MAIL IT IN..

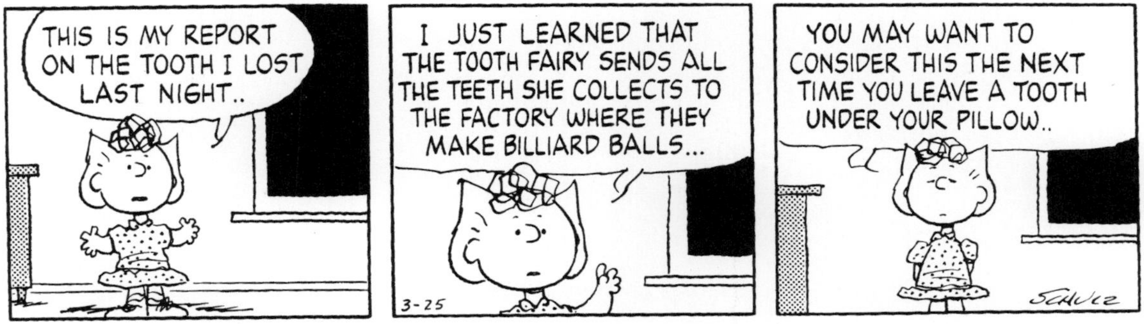
THIS IS MY REPORT ON THE TOOTH I LOST LAST NIGHT..
I JUST LEARNED THAT THE TOOTH FAIRY SENDS ALL THE TEETH SHE COLLECTS TO THE FACTORY WHERE THEY MAKE BILLIARD BALLS...
YOU MAY WANT TO CONSIDER THIS THE NEXT TIME YOU LEAVE A TOOTH UNDER YOUR PILLOW..

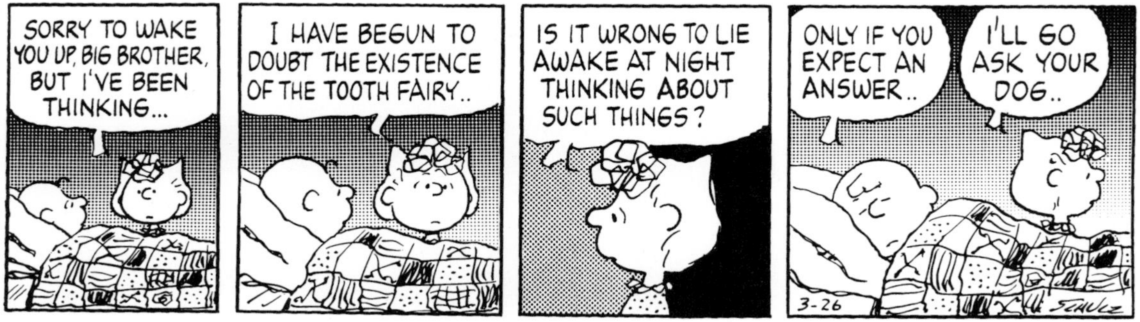
SORRY TO WAKE YOU UP, BIG BROTHER, BUT I'VE BEEN THINKING...
I HAVE BEGUN TO DOUBT THE EXISTENCE OF THE TOOTH FAIRY..
IS IT WRONG TO LIE AWAKE AT NIGHT THINKING ABOUT SUCH THINGS?
ONLY IF YOU EXPECT AN ANSWER..
I'LL GO ASK YOUR DOG..
3-26

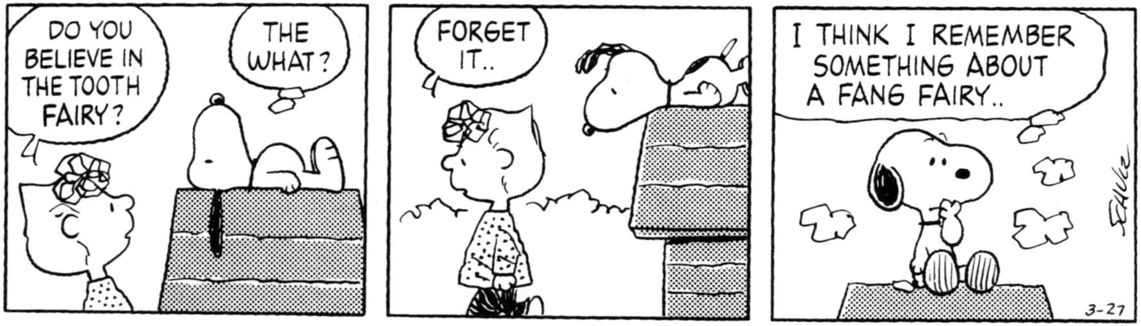
DO YOU BELIEVE IN THE TOOTH FAIRY?
THE WHAT?
FORGET IT..
I THINK I REMEMBER SOMETHING ABOUT A FANG FAIRY..
3-27

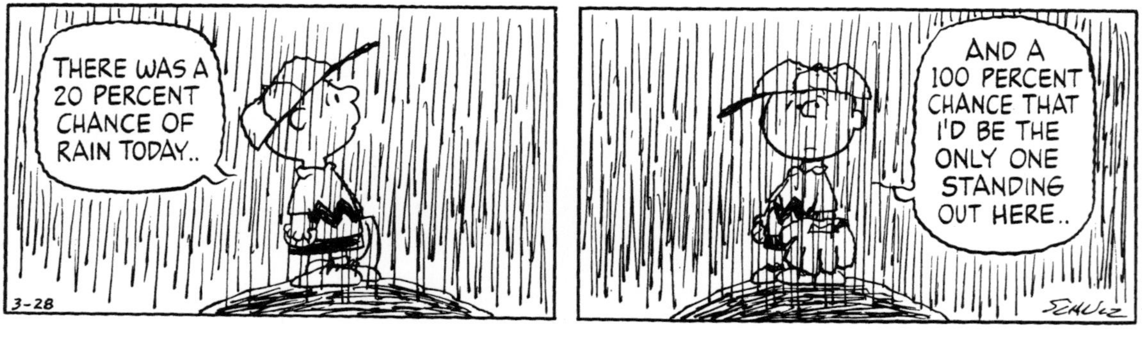
THERE WAS A 20 PERCENT CHANCE OF RAIN TODAY..
AND A 100 PERCENT CHANCE THAT I'D BE THE ONLY ONE STANDING OUT HERE..
3-28

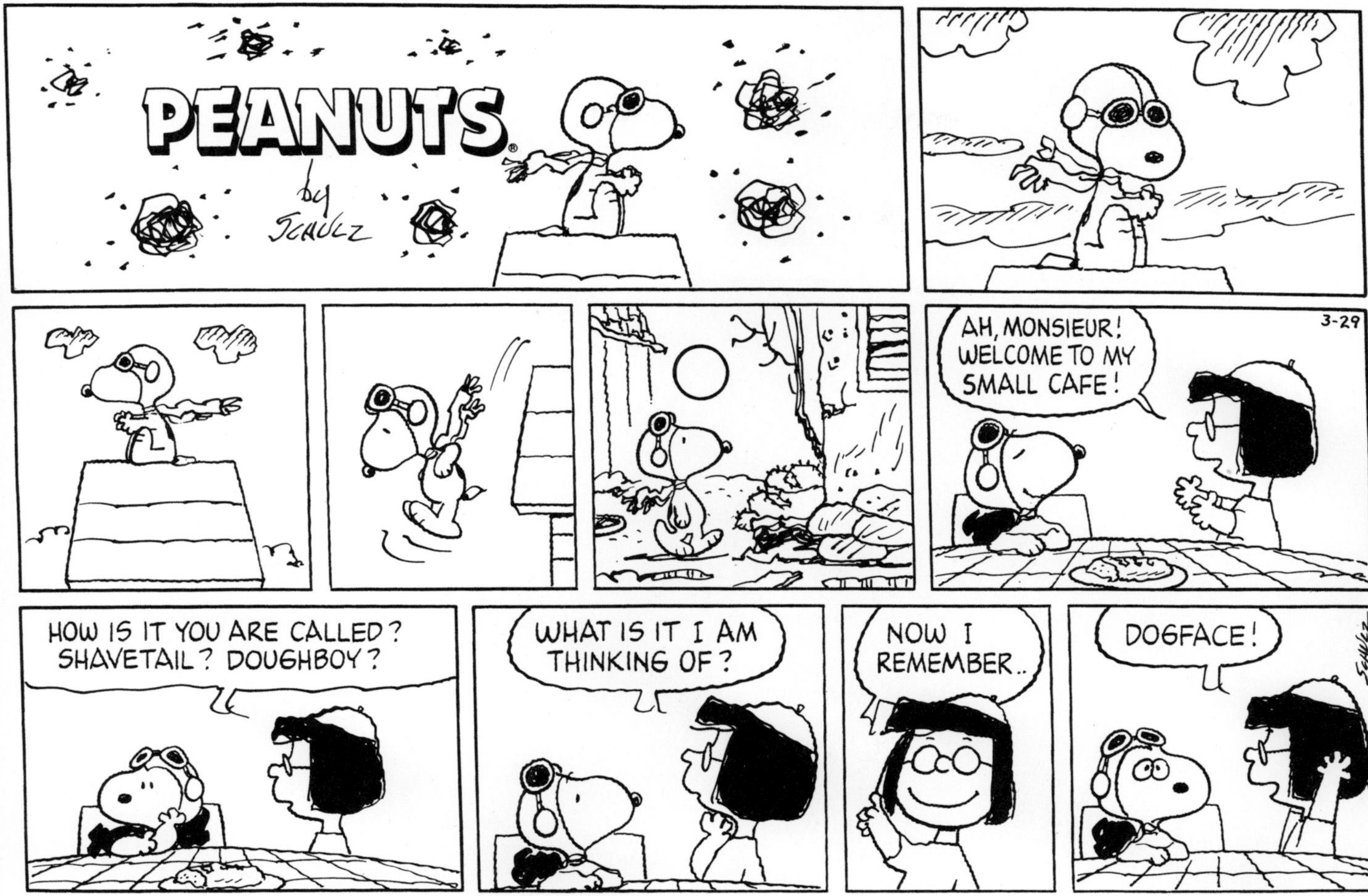
PEANUTS
by SCHULZ
3-29
AH, MONSIEUR! WELCOME TO MY SMALL CAFE!
HOW IS IT YOU ARE CALLED? SHAVETAIL? DOUGHBOY?
WHAT IS IT I AM THINKING OF?
NOW I REMEMBER..
DOGFACE!
SCHULZ

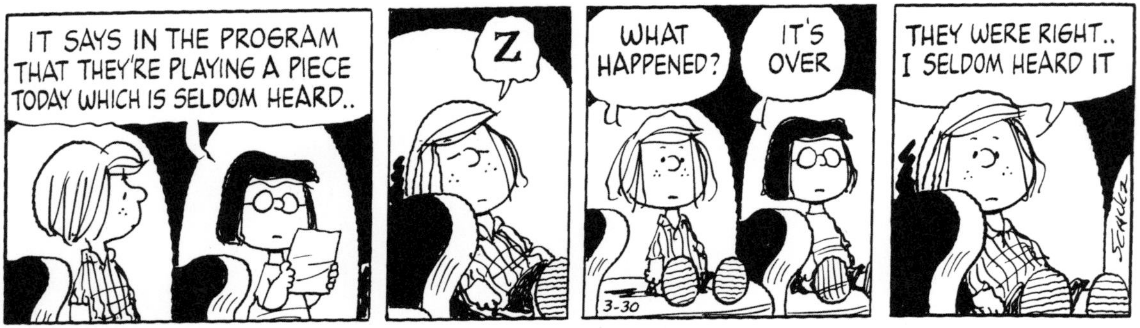
IT SAYS IN THE PROGRAM THAT THEY'RE PLAYING A PIECE TODAY WHICH IS SELDOM HEARD..
Z
WHAT HAPPENED?
IT'S OVER
THEY WERE RIGHT.. I SELDOM HEARD IT

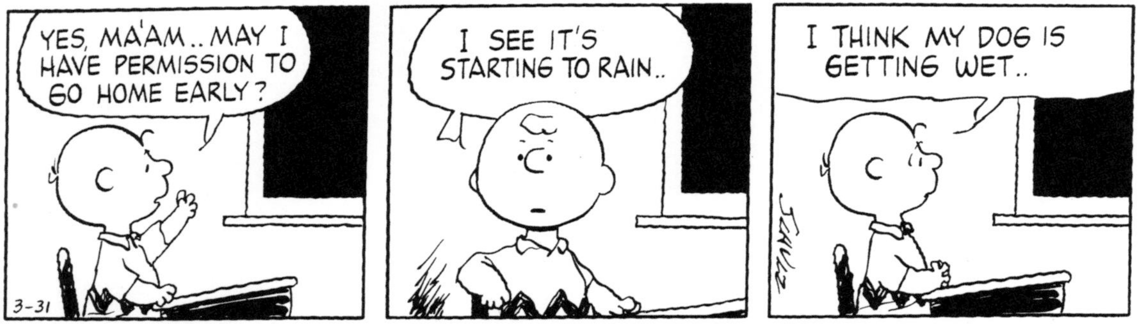
YES, MA'AM.. MAY I HAVE PERMISSION TO GO HOME EARLY?
I SEE IT'S STARTING TO RAIN..
I THINK MY DOG IS GETTING WET..

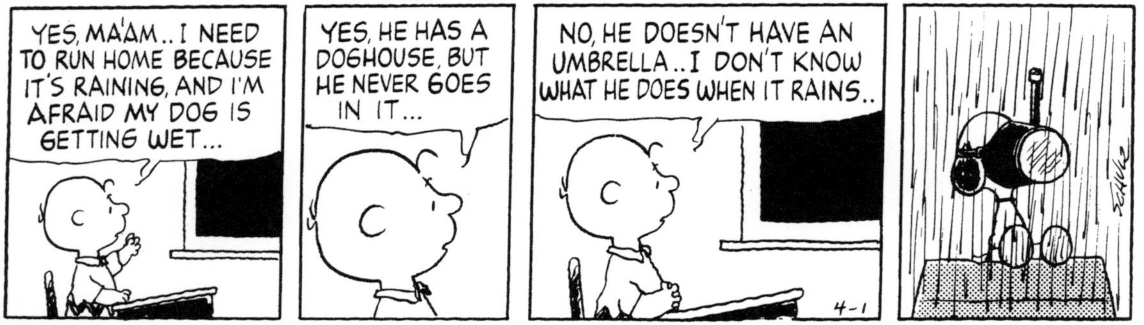
YES, MA'AM.. I NEED TO RUN HOME BECAUSE IT'S RAINING, AND I'M AFRAID MY DOG IS GETTING WET...
YES, HE HAS A DOGHOUSE, BUT HE NEVER GOES IN IT...
NO, HE DOESN'T HAVE AN UMBRELLA.. I DON'T KNOW WHAT HE DOES WHEN IT RAINS..

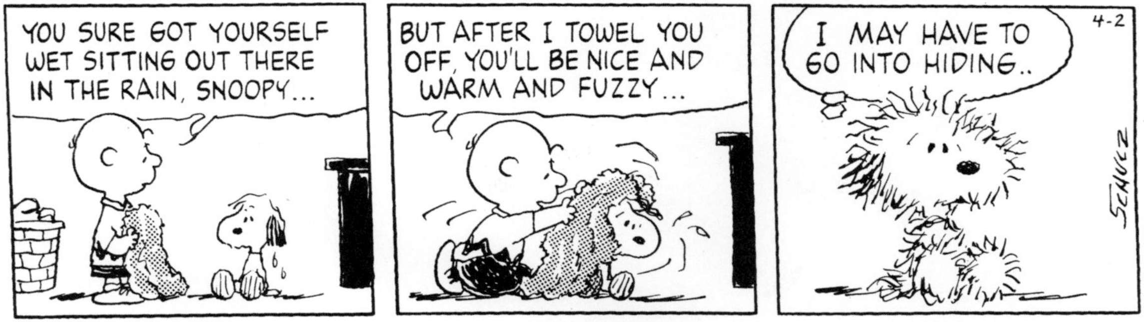
YOU SURE GOT YOURSELF WET SITTING OUT THERE IN THE RAIN, SNOOPY...
BUT AFTER I TOWEL YOU OFF, YOU'LL BE NICE AND WARM AND FUZZY...
I MAY HAVE TO GO INTO HIDING..

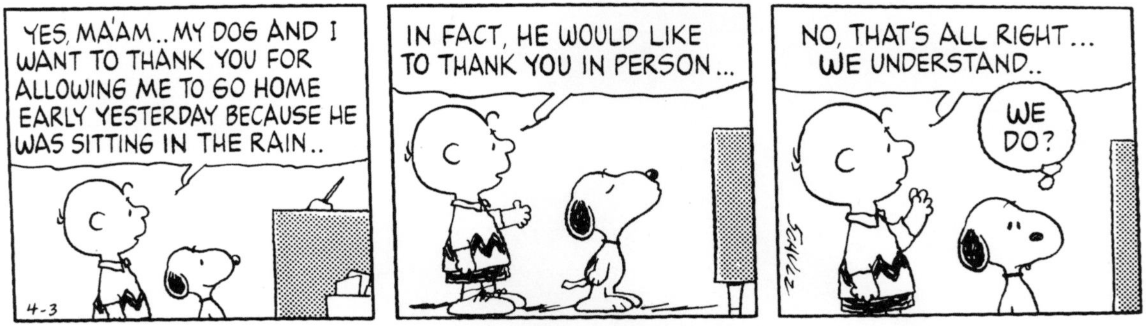
YES, MA'AM..MY DOG AND I WANT TO THANK YOU FOR ALLOWING ME TO GO HOME EARLY YESTERDAY BECAUSE HE WAS SITTING IN THE RAIN..
IN FACT, HE WOULD LIKE TO THANK YOU IN PERSON...
NO, THAT'S ALL RIGHT... WE UNDERSTAND..
WE DO?

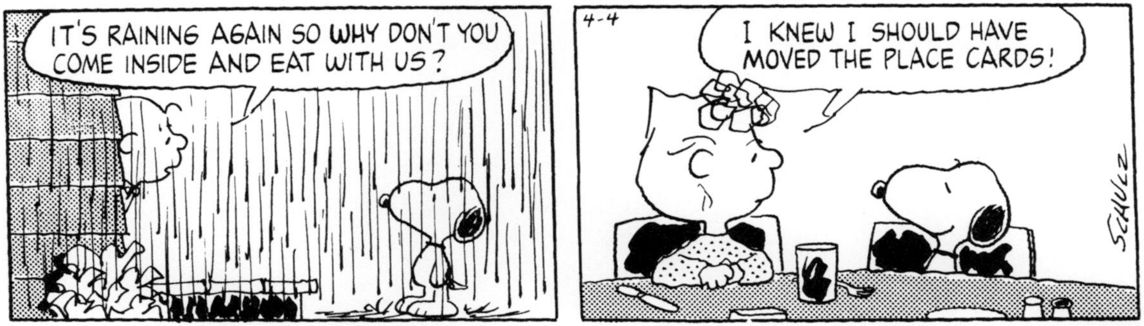
IT'S RAINING AGAIN SO WHY DON'T YOU COME INSIDE AND EAT WITH US?
I KNEW I SHOULD HAVE MOVED THE PLACE CARDS!

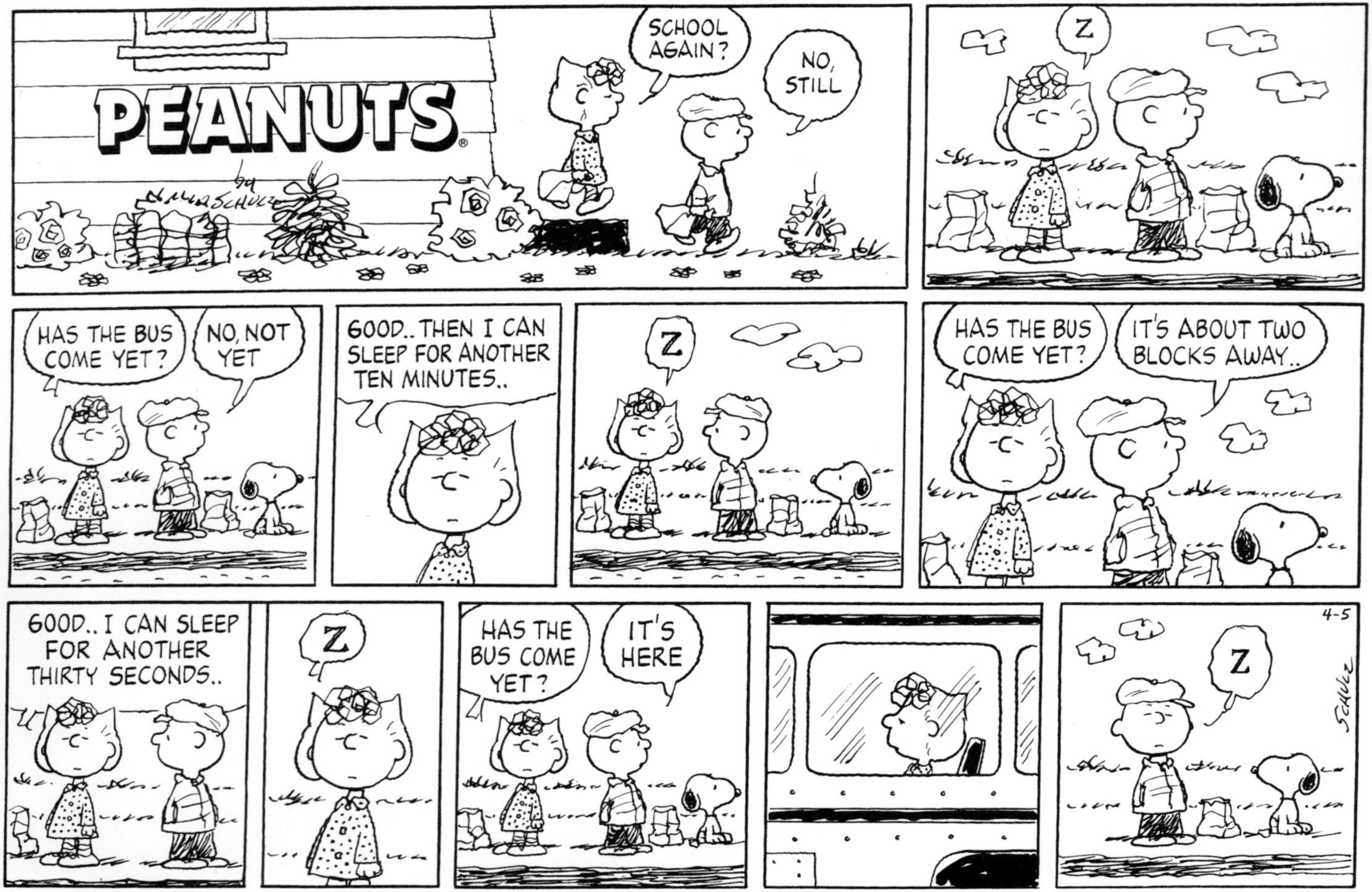
PEANUTS
by SCHULZ
SCHOOL AGAIN?
NO, STILL
Z
HAS THE BUS COME YET?
NO, NOT YET
GOOD.. THEN I CAN SLEEP FOR ANOTHER TEN MINUTES..
Z
HAS THE BUS COME YET?
IT'S ABOUT TWO BLOCKS AWAY..
GOOD.. I CAN SLEEP FOR ANOTHER THIRTY SECONDS..
Z
HAS THE BUS COME YET?
IT'S HERE
4-5
SCHULZ
Z

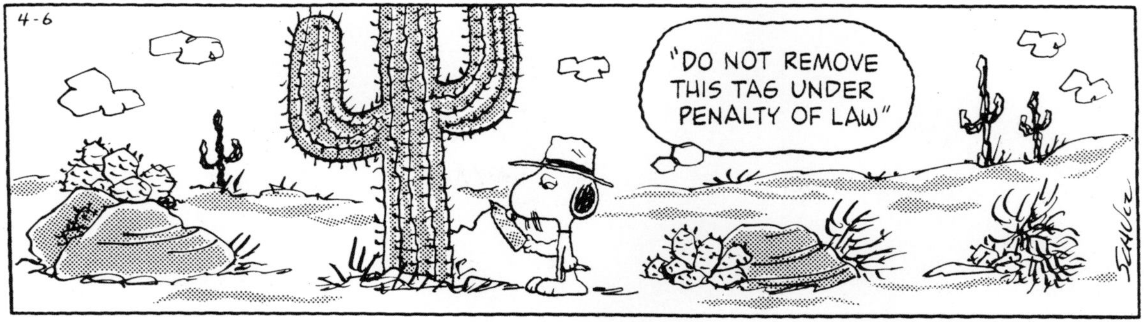
4-6
"DO NOT REMOVE THIS TAG UNDER PENALTY OF LAW"

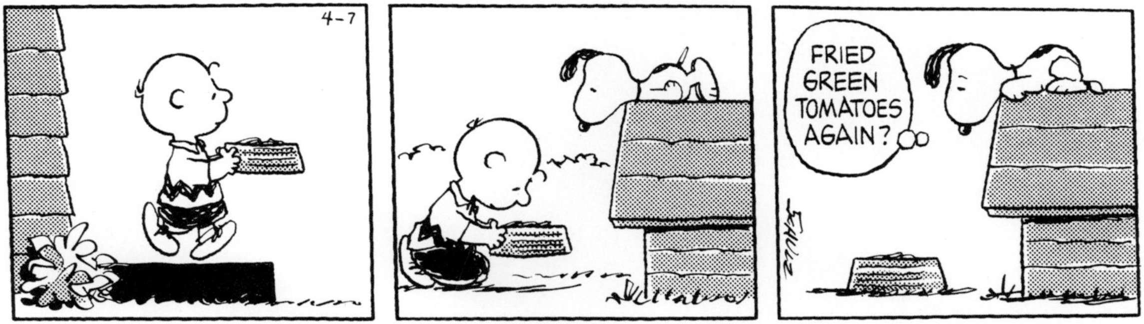
4-7
FRIED GREEN TOMATOES AGAIN?

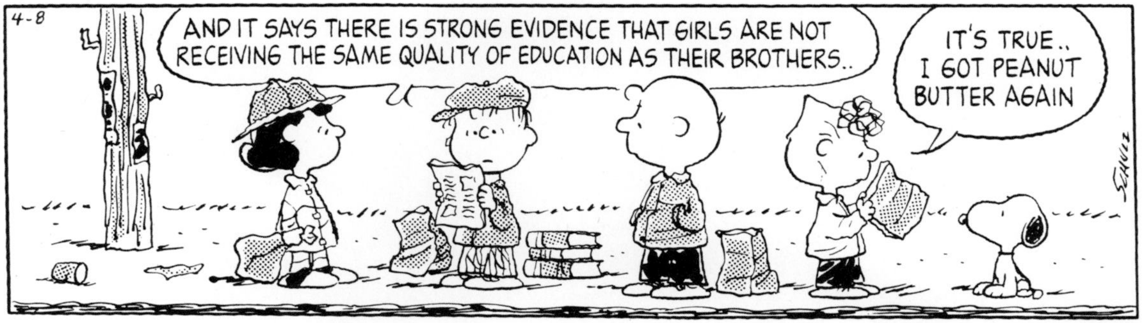
4-8
AND IT SAYS THERE IS STRONG EVIDENCE THAT GIRLS ARE NOT RECEIVING THE SAME QUALITY OF EDUCATION AS THEIR BROTHERS..
IT'S TRUE.. I GOT PEANUT BUTTER AGAIN

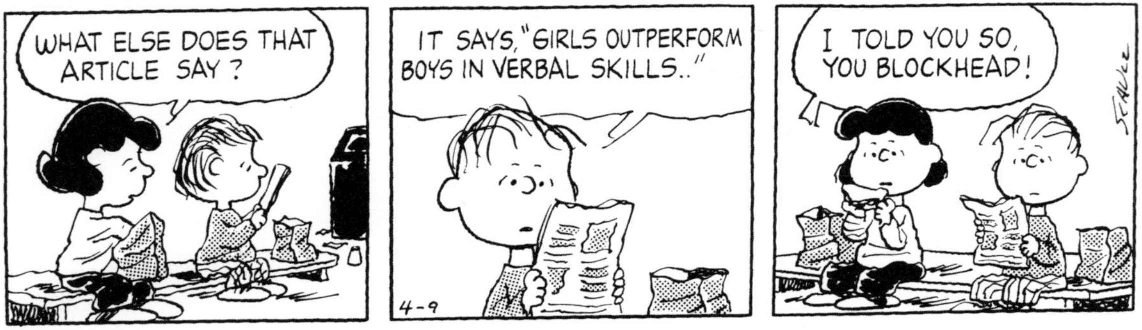
WHAT ELSE DOES THAT ARTICLE SAY ?
IT SAYS, "GIRLS OUTPERFORM BOYS IN VERBAL SKILLS.."
I TOLD YOU SO, YOU BLOCKHEAD!
4-9
SCHULZ

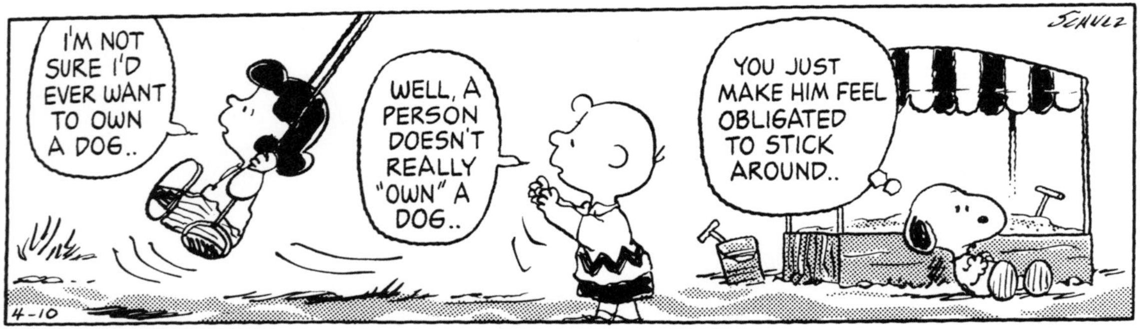
I'M NOT SURE I'D EVER WANT TO OWN A DOG..
WELL, A PERSON DOESN'T REALLY "OWN" A DOG..
YOU JUST MAKE HIM FEEL OBLIGATED TO STICK AROUND..
4-10
SCHULZ

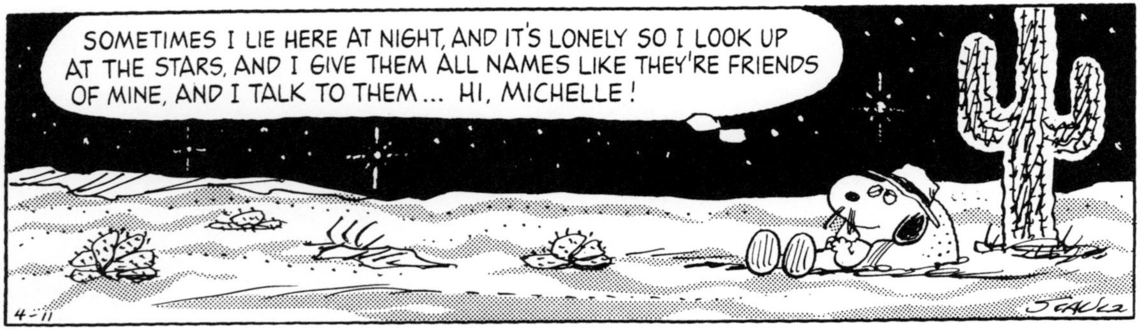
SOMETIMES I LIE HERE AT NIGHT, AND IT'S LONELY SO I LOOK UP AT THE STARS, AND I GIVE THEM ALL NAMES LIKE THEY'RE FRIENDS OF MINE, AND I TALK TO THEM... HI, MICHELLE!
4-11
SCHULZ

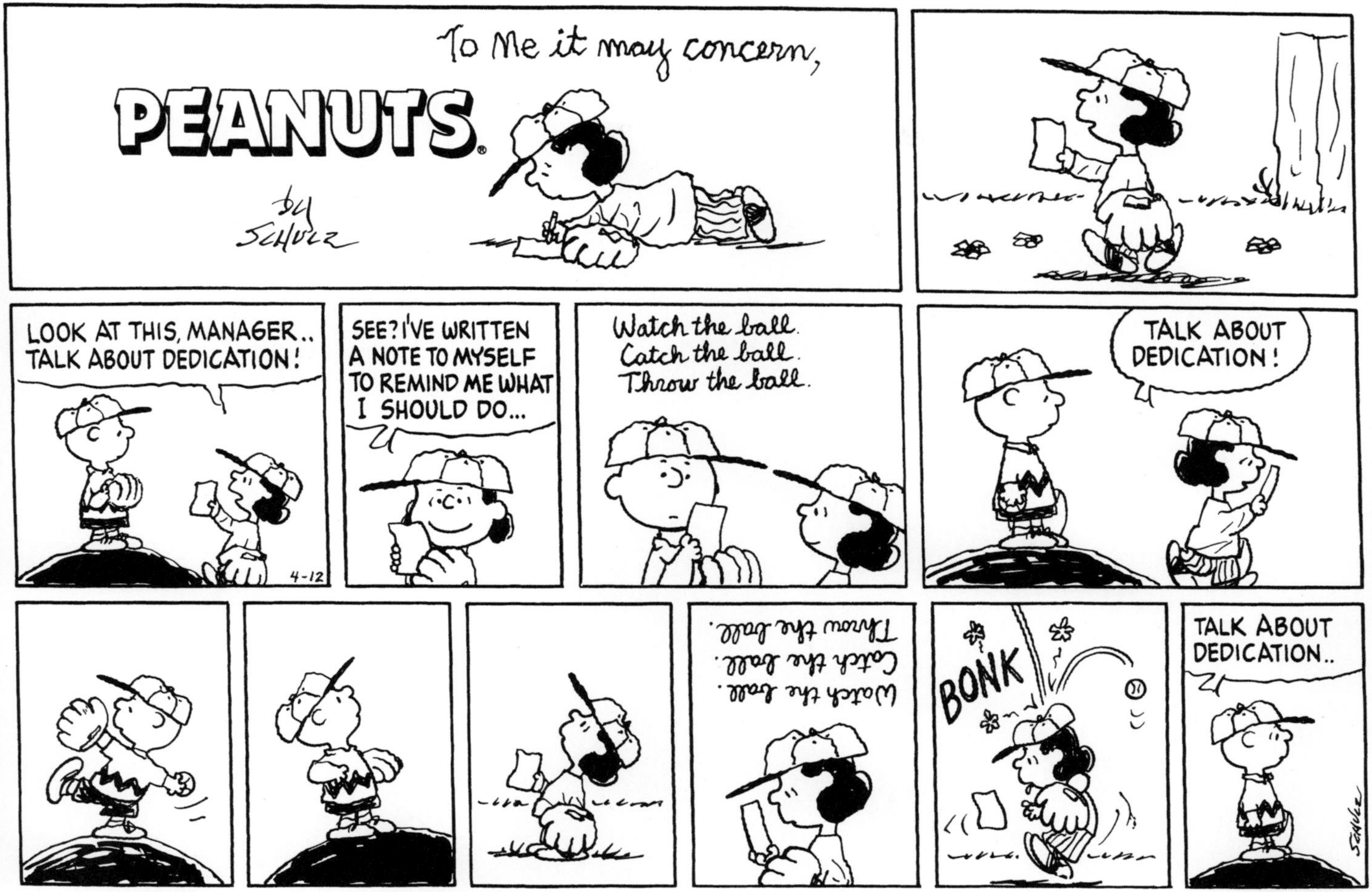

PEANUTS
by SCHULZ
To Me it may concern,
LOOK AT THIS, MANAGER.. TALK ABOUT DEDICATION!
4-12
SEE? I'VE WRITTEN A NOTE TO MYSELF TO REMIND ME WHAT I SHOULD DO...
Watch the ball. Catch the ball. Throw the ball.
TALK ABOUT DEDICATION!
Watch the ball. Catch the ball. Throw the ball.
BONK
TALK ABOUT DEDICATION..
SCHULZ

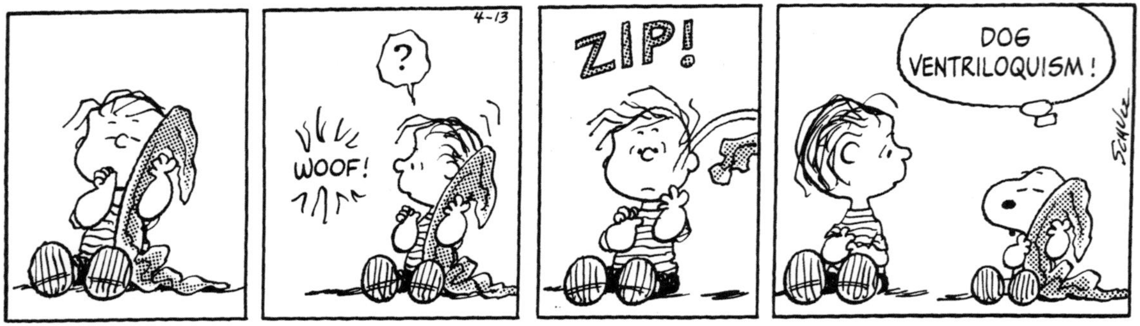
4-13
?
WOOF!
ZIP!
DOG VENTRILOQUISM!
SCHULZ

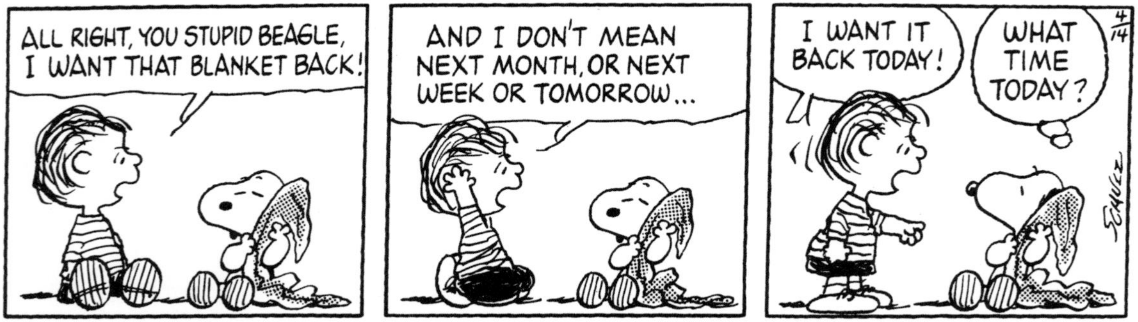
ALL RIGHT, YOU STUPID BEAGLE, I WANT THAT BLANKET BACK!
AND I DON'T MEAN NEXT MONTH, OR NEXT WEEK OR TOMORROW...
4/14
I WANT IT BACK TODAY!
WHAT TIME TODAY?
SCHULZ

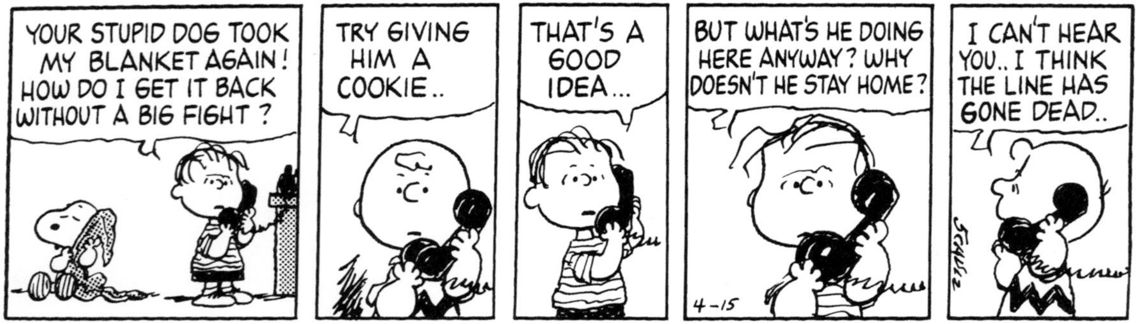
YOUR STUPID DOG TOOK MY BLANKET AGAIN! HOW DO I GET IT BACK WITHOUT A BIG FIGHT?
TRY GIVING HIM A COOKIE..
THAT'S A GOOD IDEA...
BUT WHAT'S HE DOING HERE ANYWAY? WHY DOESN'T HE STAY HOME?
4-15
SCHULZ
I CAN'T HEAR YOU.. I THINK THE LINE HAS GONE DEAD..

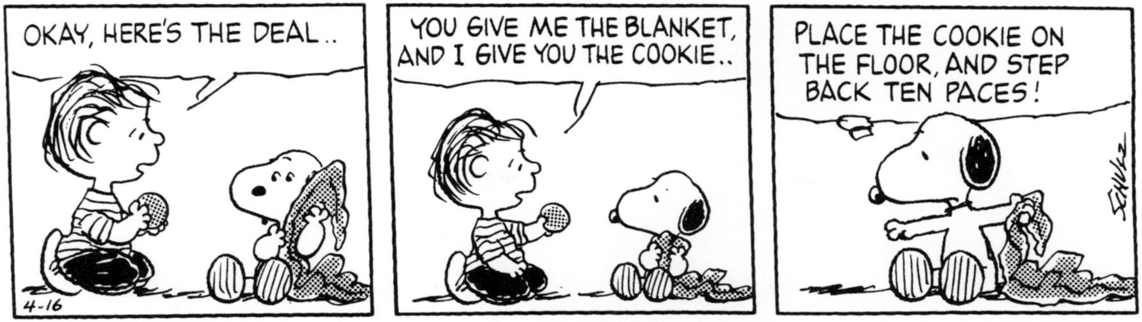
OKAY, HERE'S THE DEAL..
YOU GIVE ME THE BLANKET, AND I GIVE YOU THE COOKIE..
PLACE THE COOKIE ON THE FLOOR, AND STEP BACK TEN PACES!
4-16

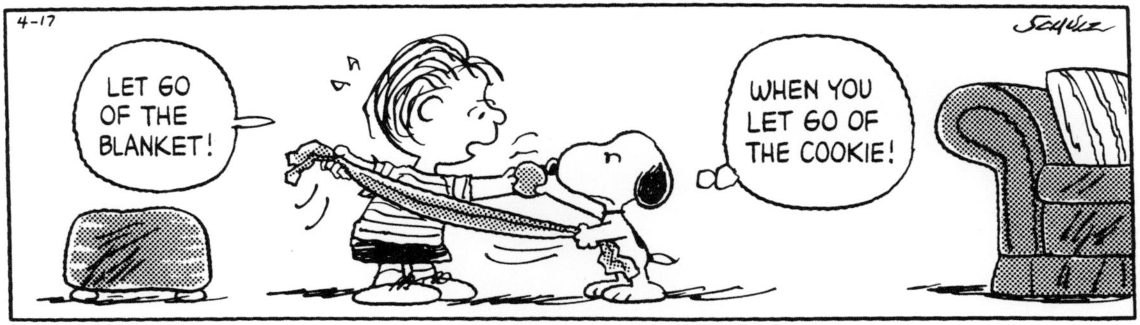
4-17
LET GO OF THE BLANKET!
WHEN YOU LET GO OF THE COOKIE!

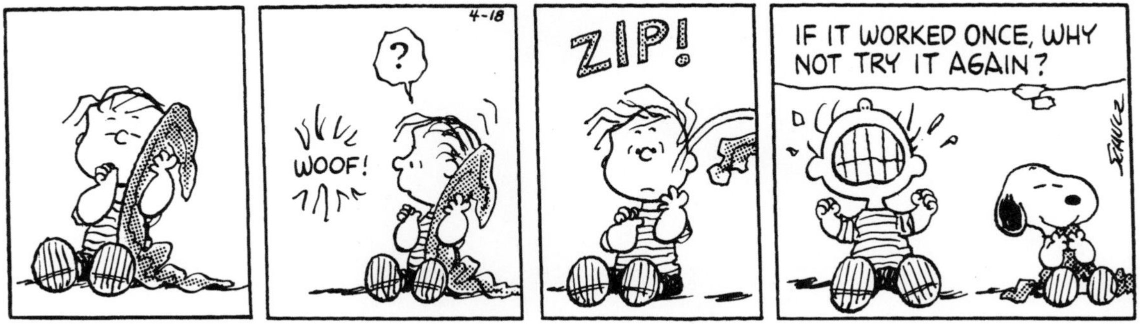
4-18
?
WOOF!
ZIP!
IF IT WORKED ONCE, WHY NOT TRY IT AGAIN?

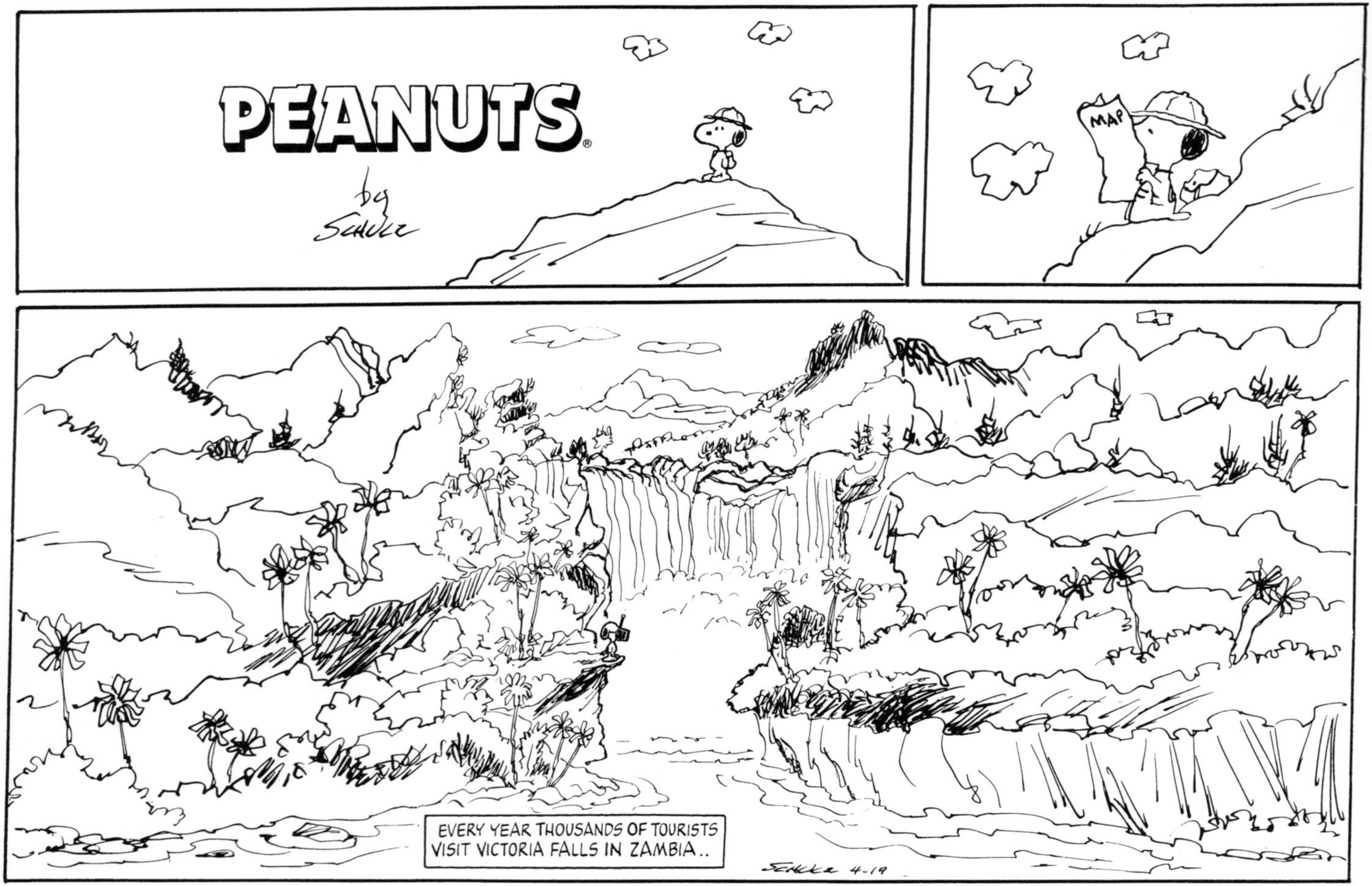
PEANUTS
by SCHULZ
MAP
EVERY YEAR THOUSANDS OF TOURISTS VISIT VICTORIA FALLS IN ZAMBIA..
SCHULZ 4-19

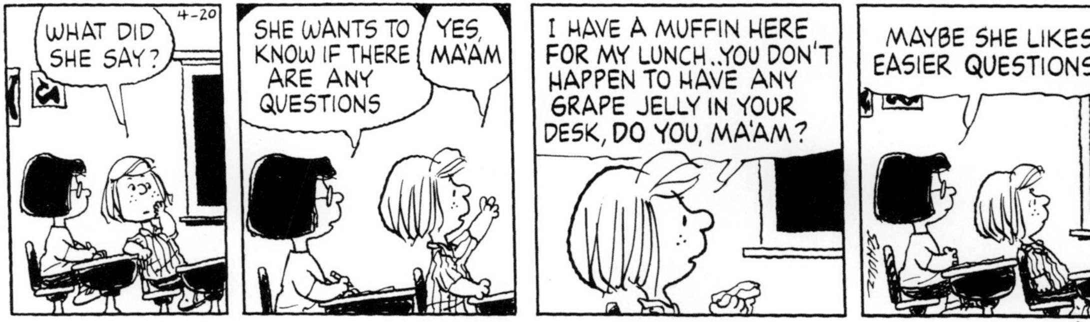
4-20
WHAT DID SHE SAY?
SHE WANTS TO KNOW IF THERE ARE ANY QUESTIONS
YES, MA'AM
I HAVE A MUFFIN HERE FOR MY LUNCH..YOU DON'T HAPPEN TO HAVE ANY GRAPE JELLY IN YOUR DESK, DO YOU, MA'AM?
MAYBE SHE LIKES EASIER QUESTIONS

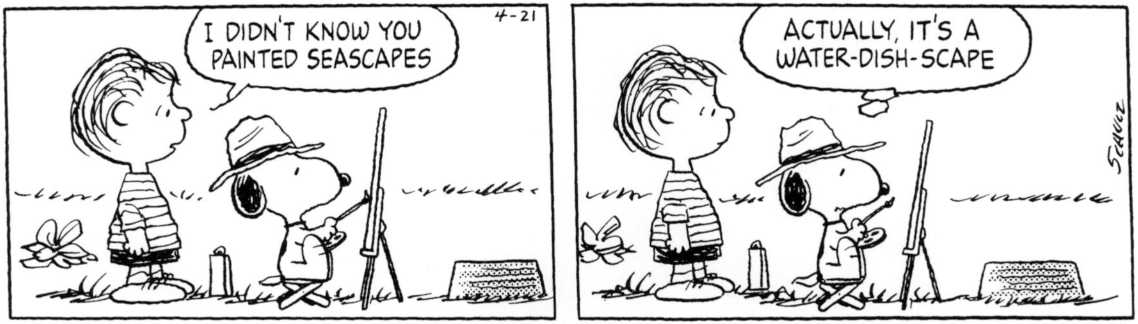
4-21
I DIDN'T KNOW YOU PAINTED SEASCAPES
ACTUALLY, IT'S A WATER-DISH-SCAPE

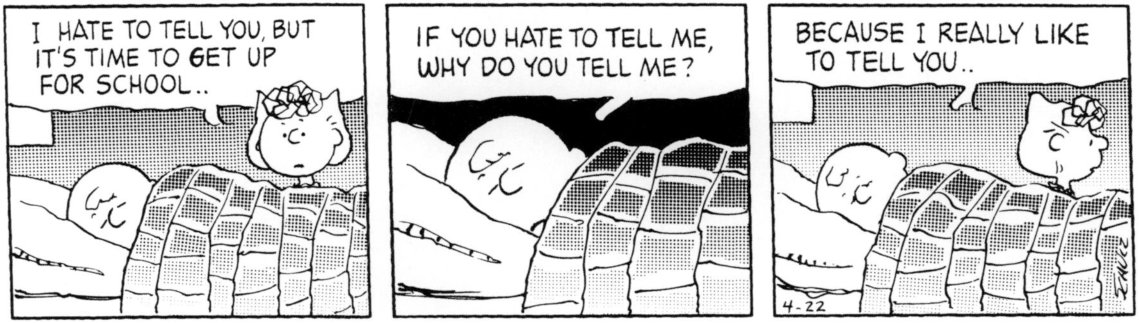
I HATE TO TELL YOU, BUT IT'S TIME TO GET UP FOR SCHOOL..
IF YOU HATE TO TELL ME, WHY DO YOU TELL ME?
BECAUSE I REALLY LIKE TO TELL YOU..
4-22

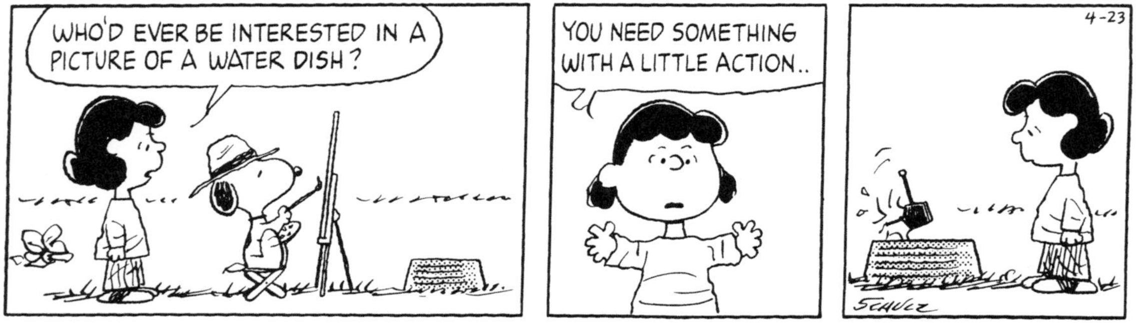
WHO'D EVER BE INTERESTED IN A PICTURE OF A WATER DISH?
YOU NEED SOMETHING WITH A LITTLE ACTION..
4-23

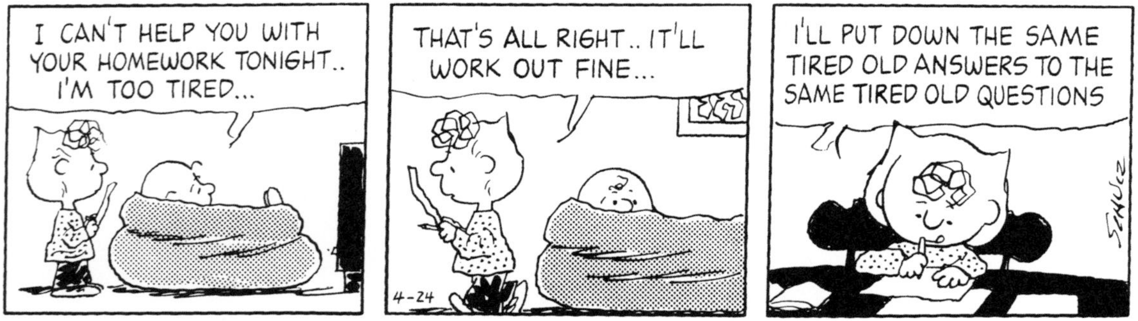
I CAN'T HELP YOU WITH YOUR HOMEWORK TONIGHT.. I'M TOO TIRED...
THAT'S ALL RIGHT.. IT'LL WORK OUT FINE...
4-24
I'LL PUT DOWN THE SAME TIRED OLD ANSWERS TO THE SAME TIRED OLD QUESTIONS

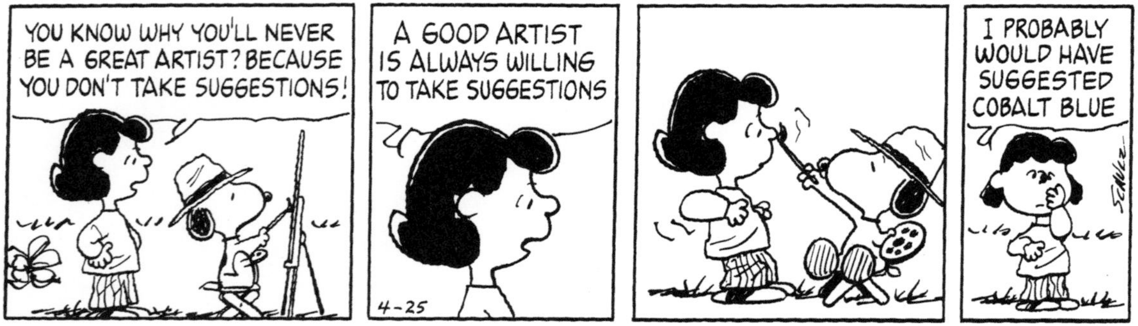
YOU KNOW WHY YOU'LL NEVER BE A GREAT ARTIST? BECAUSE YOU DON'T TAKE SUGGESTIONS!
A GOOD ARTIST IS ALWAYS WILLING TO TAKE SUGGESTIONS
4-25
I PROBABLY WOULD HAVE SUGGESTED COBALT BLUE

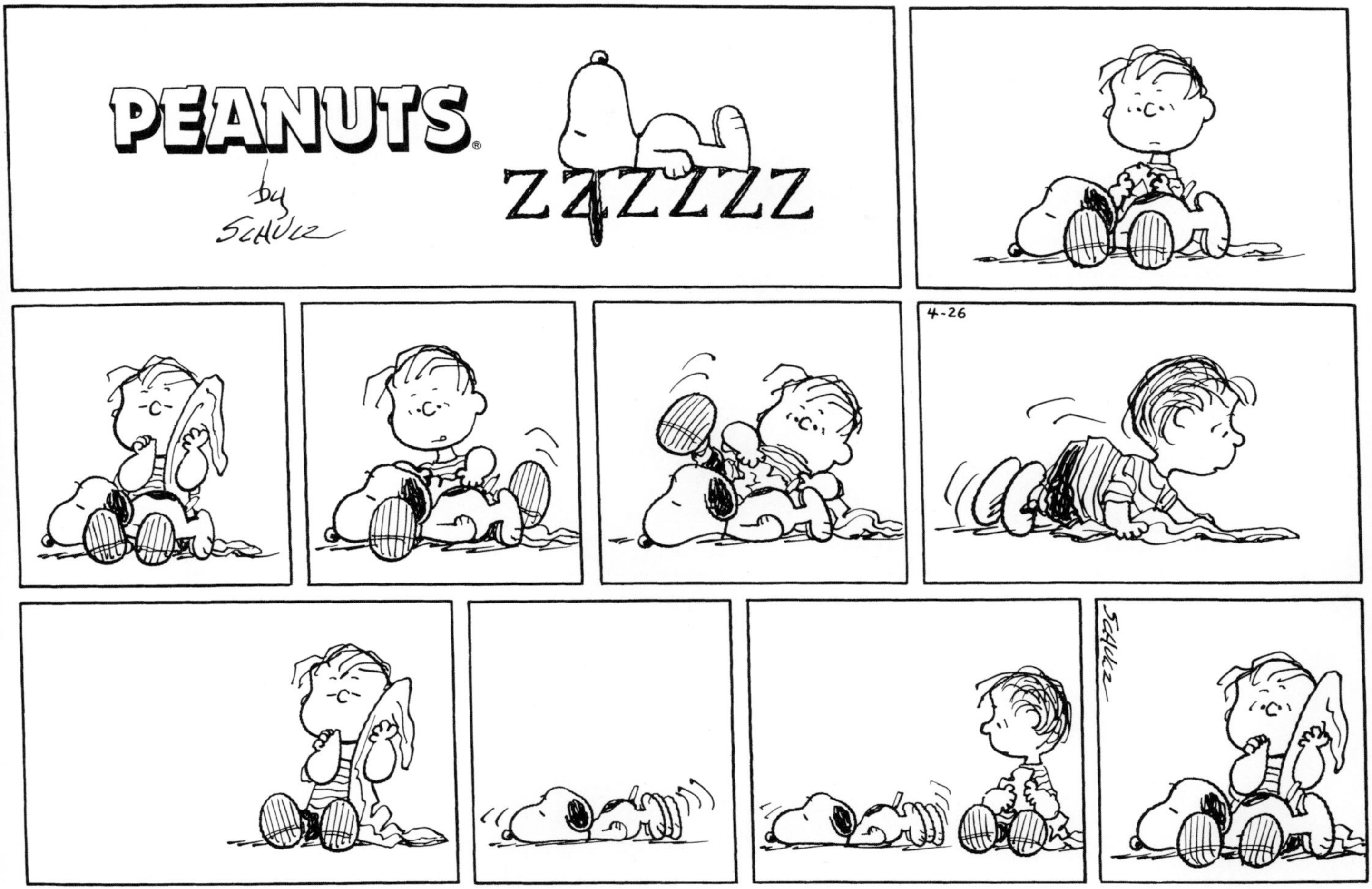
PEANUTS
by Schulz
ZZZZZZ
4-26
SCHULZ

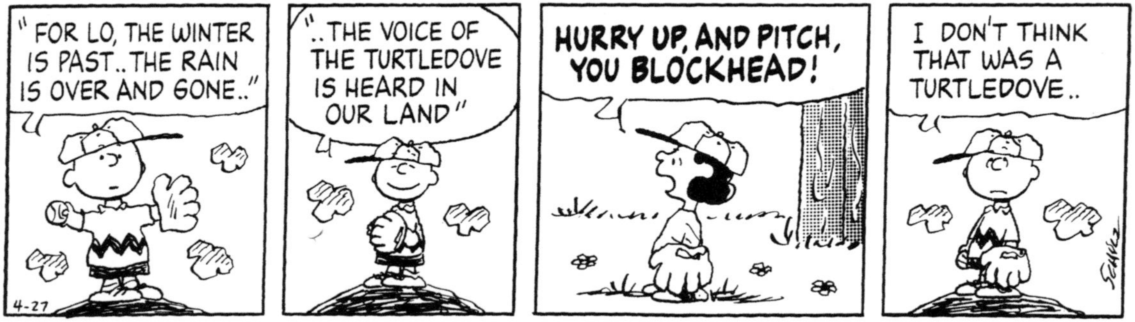
" FOR LO, THE WINTER IS PAST.. THE RAIN IS OVER AND GONE.."
"..THE VOICE OF THE TURTLEDOVE IS HEARD IN OUR LAND"
HURRY UP, AND PITCH, YOU BLOCKHEAD!
I DON'T THINK THAT WAS A TURTLEDOVE..
4-27
SCHULZ

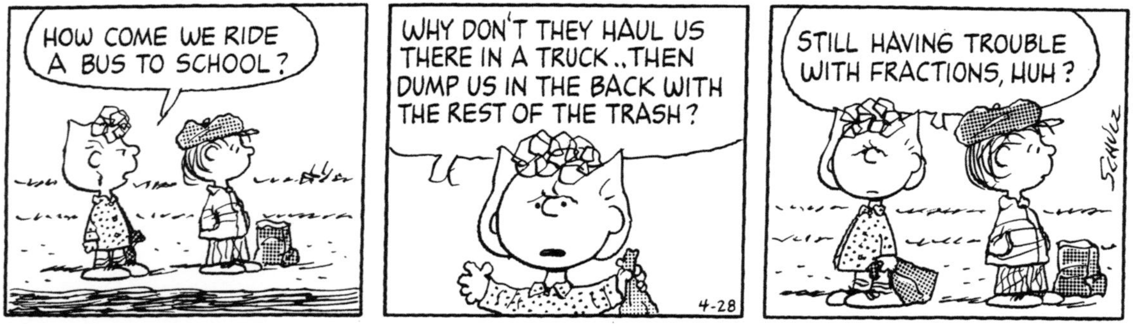
HOW COME WE RIDE A BUS TO SCHOOL?
WHY DON'T THEY HAUL US THERE IN A TRUCK..THEN DUMP US IN THE BACK WITH THE REST OF THE TRASH?
STILL HAVING TROUBLE WITH FRACTIONS, HUH?
4-28
SCHULZ

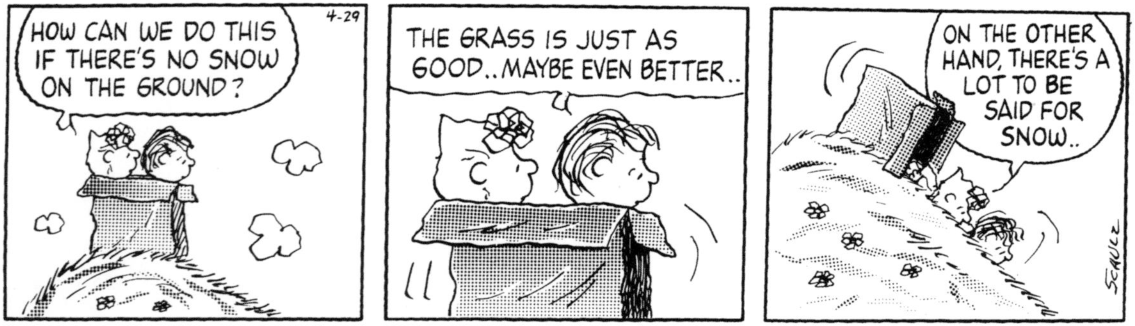
HOW CAN WE DO THIS IF THERE'S NO SNOW ON THE GROUND?
THE GRASS IS JUST AS GOOD..MAYBE EVEN BETTER..
ON THE OTHER HAND, THERE'S A LOT TO BE SAID FOR SNOW..
4-29
SCHULZ

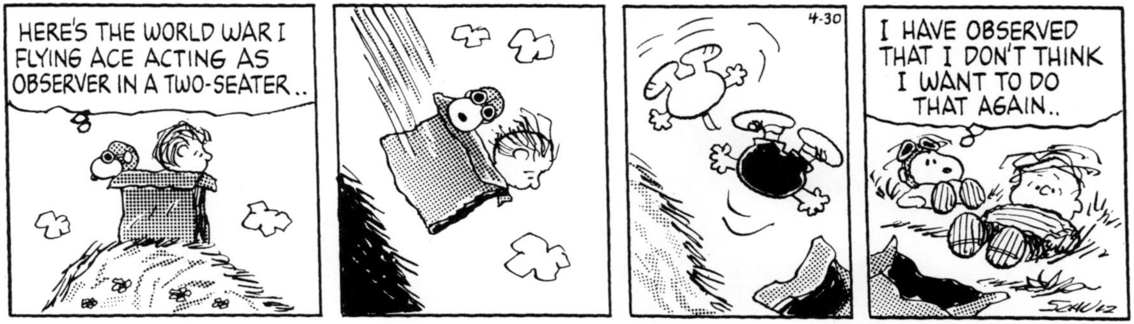
HERE'S THE WORLD WAR I FLYING ACE ACTING AS OBSERVER IN A TWO-SEATER..
4-30
I HAVE OBSERVED THAT I DON'T THINK I WANT TO DO THAT AGAIN..
SCHULZ

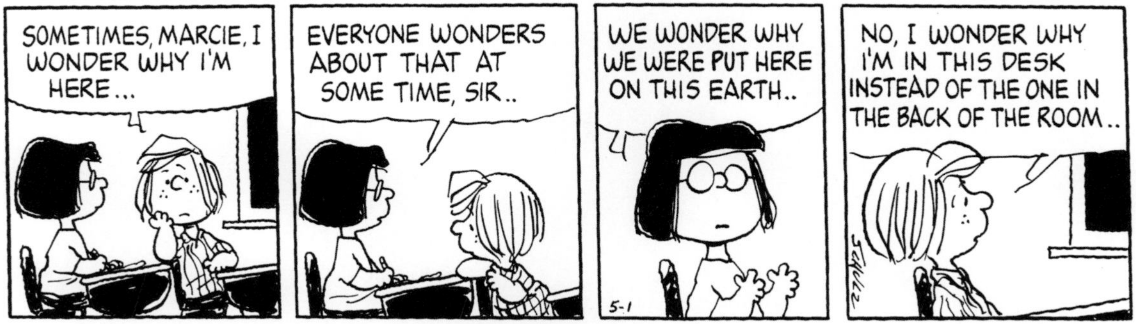
SOMETIMES, MARCIE, I WONDER WHY I'M HERE...
EVERYONE WONDERS ABOUT THAT AT SOME TIME, SIR..
WE WONDER WHY WE WERE PUT HERE ON THIS EARTH..
5-1
SCHULZ
NO, I WONDER WHY I'M IN THIS DESK INSTEAD OF THE ONE IN THE BACK OF THE ROOM..

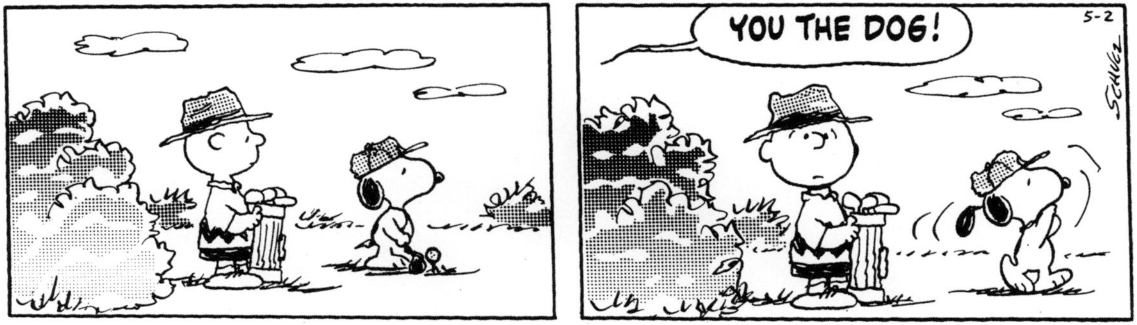
YOU THE DOG!
5-2
SCHULZ

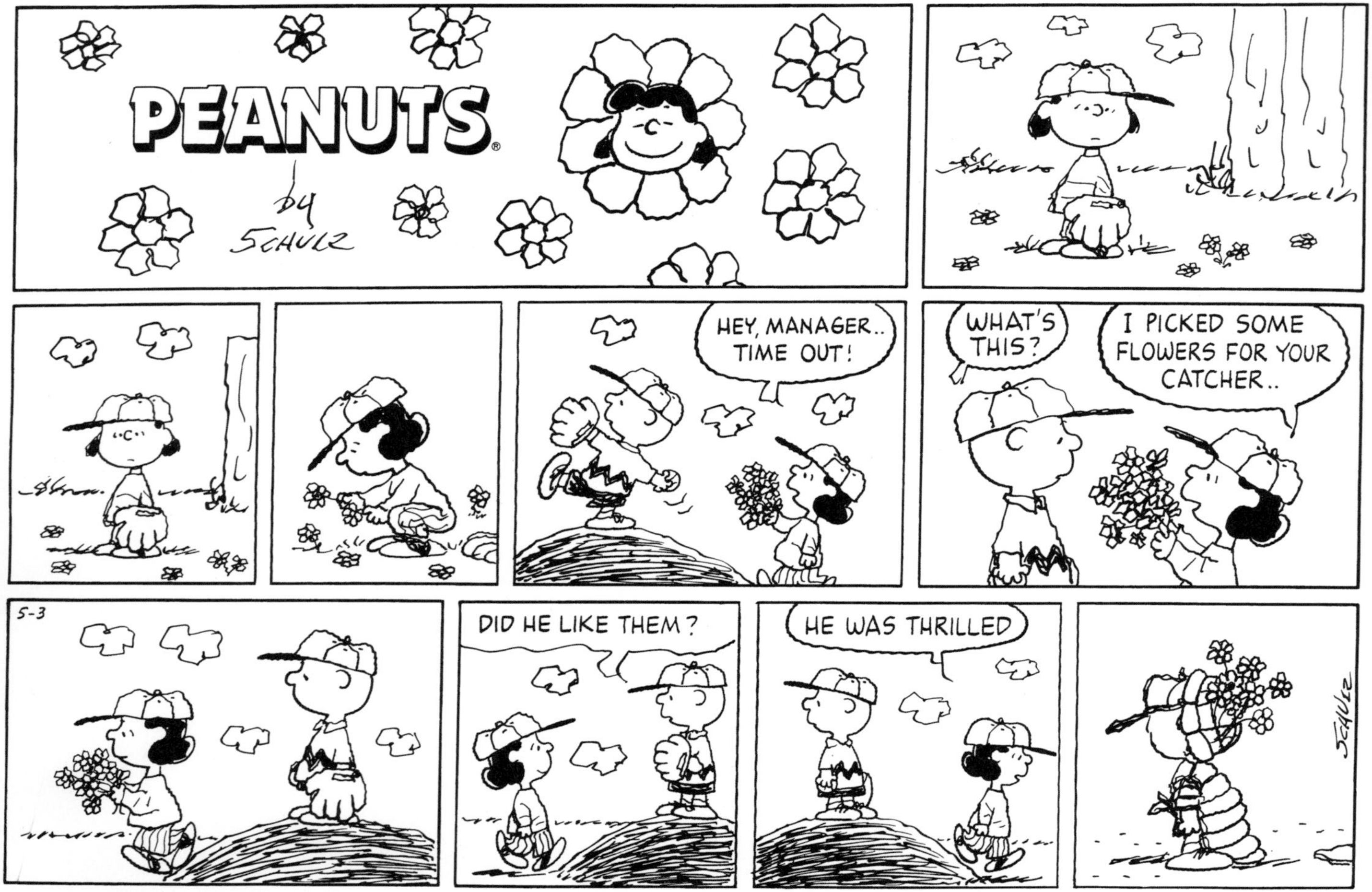
PEANUTS
by SCHULZ
HEY, MANAGER.. TIME OUT!
WHAT'S THIS?
I PICKED SOME FLOWERS FOR YOUR CATCHER..
5-3
DID HE LIKE THEM?
HE WAS THRILLED
SCHULZ

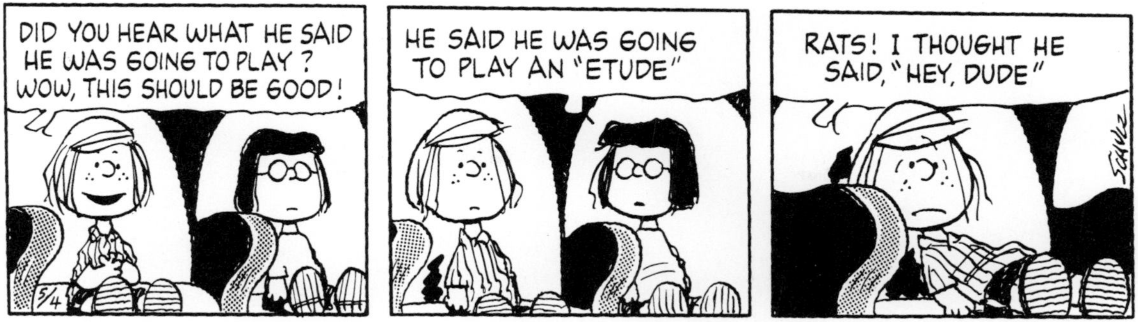
DID YOU HEAR WHAT HE SAID HE WAS GOING TO PLAY ? WOW, THIS SHOULD BE GOOD !
HE SAID HE WAS GOING TO PLAY AN "ETUDE"
RATS ! I THOUGHT HE SAID, "HEY, DUDE"
SCHULZ
5/4

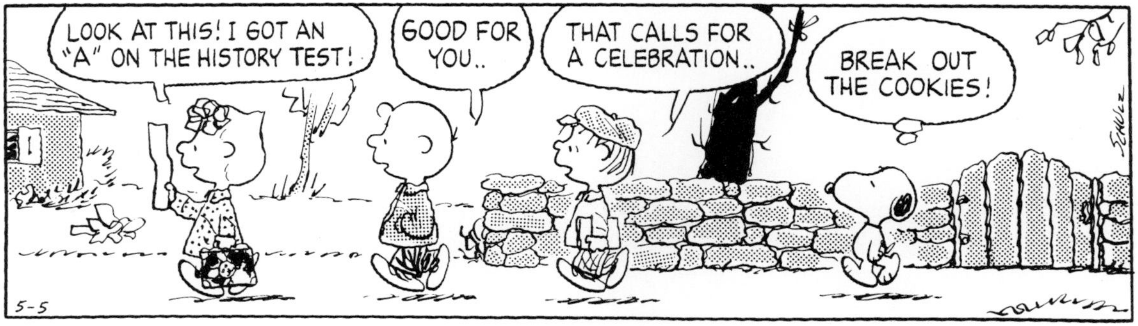
LOOK AT THIS ! I GOT AN "A" ON THE HISTORY TEST !
GOOD FOR YOU..
THAT CALLS FOR A CELEBRATION..
BREAK OUT THE COOKIES !
SCHULZ
5-5

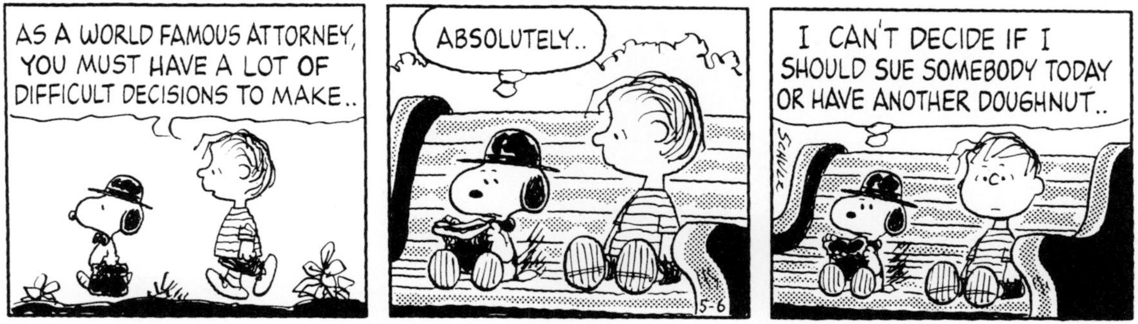
AS A WORLD FAMOUS ATTORNEY, YOU MUST HAVE A LOT OF DIFFICULT DECISIONS TO MAKE..
ABSOLUTELY..
I CAN'T DECIDE IF I SHOULD SUE SOMEBODY TODAY OR HAVE ANOTHER DOUGHNUT..
SCHULZ
5-6

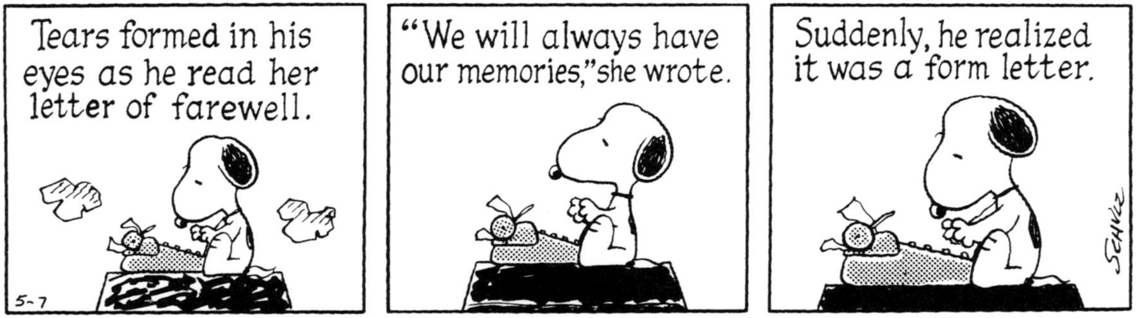
Tears formed in his eyes as he read her letter of farewell.
"We will always have our memories," she wrote.
Suddenly, he realized it was a form letter.
SCHULZ
5-7

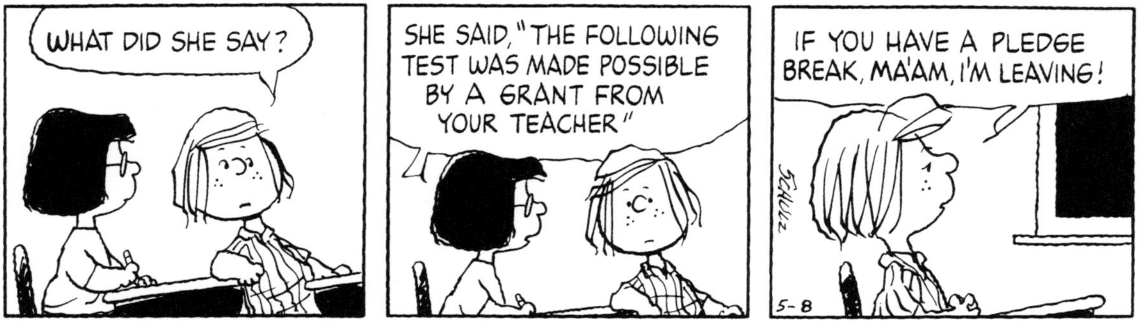
WHAT DID SHE SAY?
SHE SAID, "THE FOLLOWING TEST WAS MADE POSSIBLE BY A GRANT FROM YOUR TEACHER"
IF YOU HAVE A PLEDGE BREAK, MA'AM, I'M LEAVING!
SCHULZ
5-8

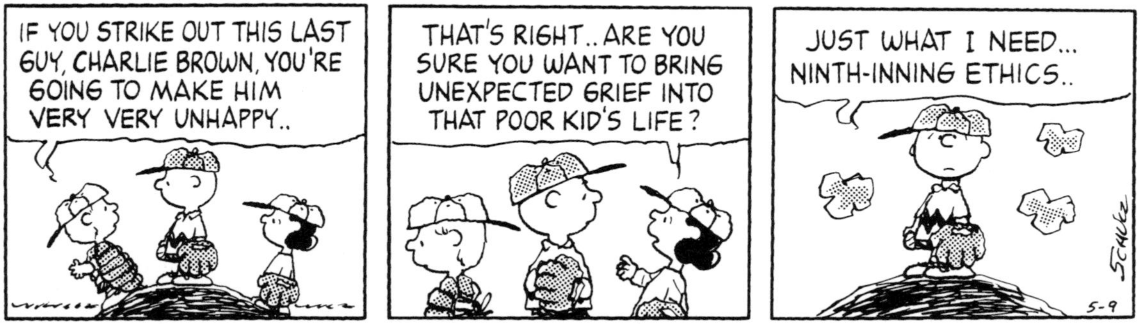
IF YOU STRIKE OUT THIS LAST GUY, CHARLIE BROWN, YOU'RE GOING TO MAKE HIM VERY VERY UNHAPPY..
THAT'S RIGHT.. ARE YOU SURE YOU WANT TO BRING UNEXPECTED GRIEF INTO THAT POOR KID'S LIFE?
JUST WHAT I NEED... NINTH-INNING ETHICS..
SCHULZ
5-9

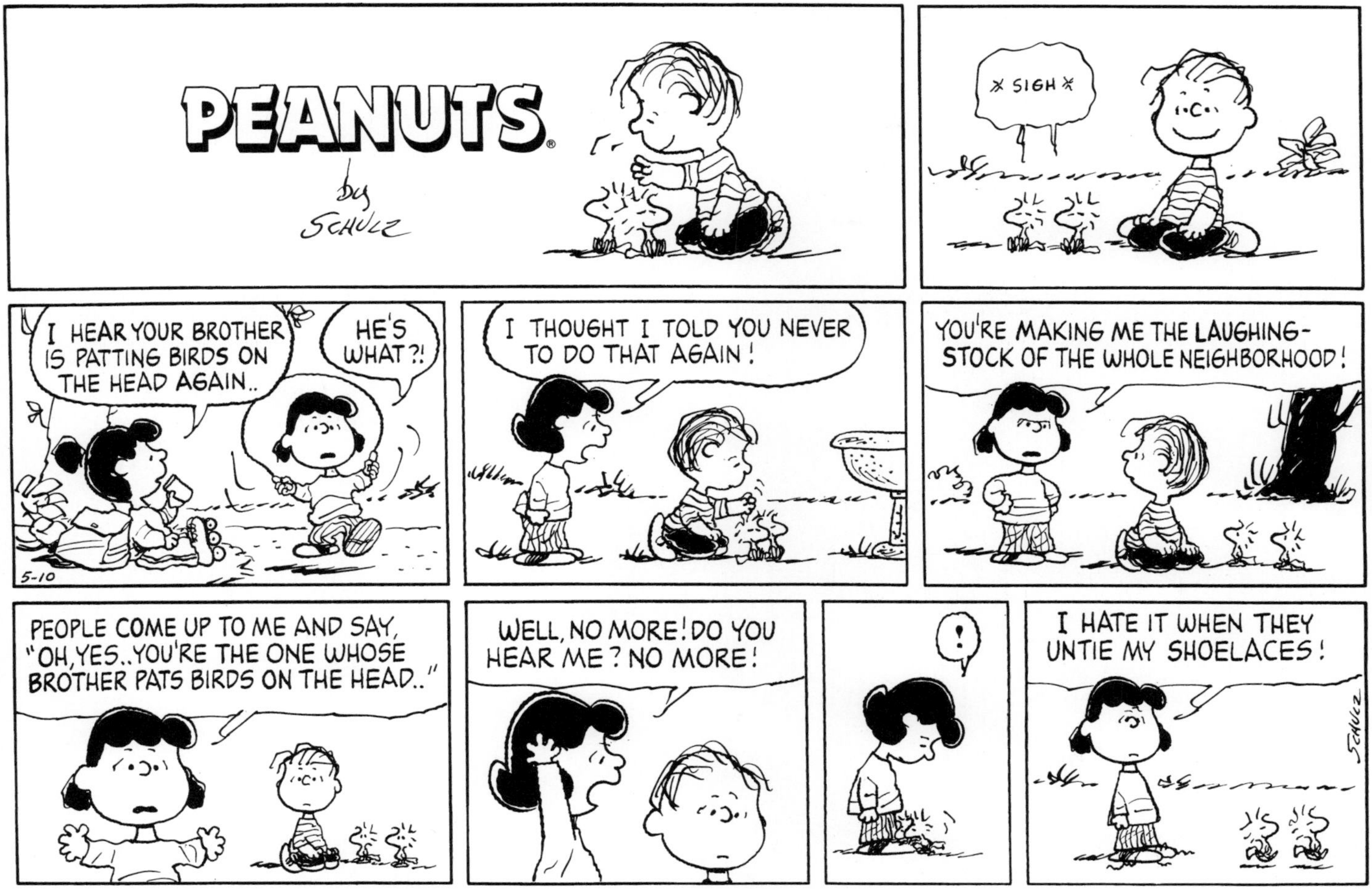
PEANUTS
by SCHULZ
* SIGH *
5-10
I HEAR YOUR BROTHER IS PATTING BIRDS ON THE HEAD AGAIN..
HE'S WHAT?!
I THOUGHT I TOLD YOU NEVER TO DO THAT AGAIN!
YOU'RE MAKING ME THE LAUGHING-STOCK OF THE WHOLE NEIGHBORHOOD!
PEOPLE COME UP TO ME AND SAY, "OH, YES..YOU'RE THE ONE WHOSE BROTHER PATS BIRDS ON THE HEAD.."
WELL, NO MORE! DO YOU HEAR ME? NO MORE!
!
I HATE IT WHEN THEY UNTIE MY SHOELACES!
SCHULZ

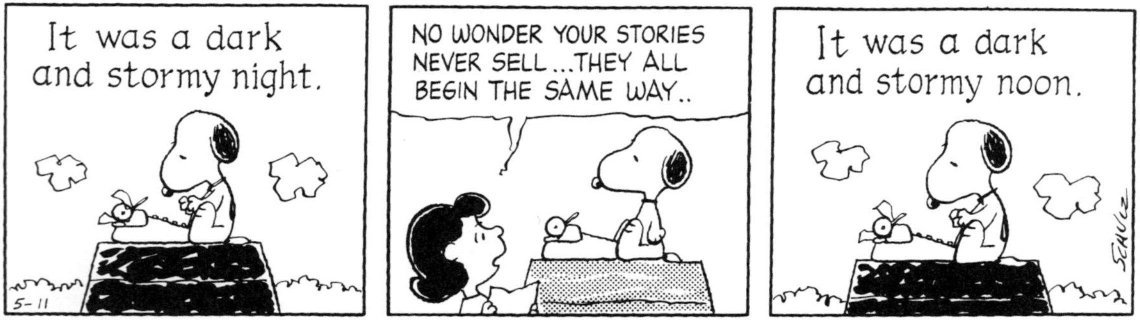
It was a dark and stormy night.
NO WONDER YOUR STORIES NEVER SELL ...THEY ALL BEGIN THE SAME WAY..
It was a dark and stormy noon.
5-11
SCHULZ

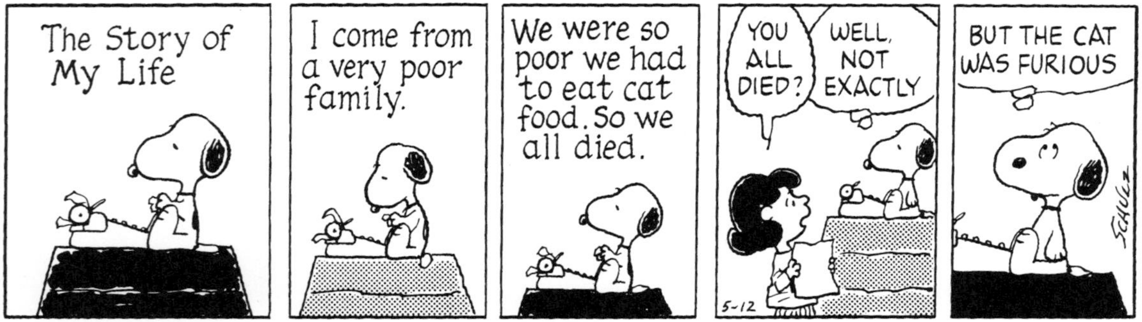
The Story of My Life
I come from a very poor family.
We were so poor we had to eat cat food. So we all died.
YOU ALL DIED?
WELL, NOT EXACTLY
BUT THE CAT WAS FURIOUS
5-12
SCHULZ

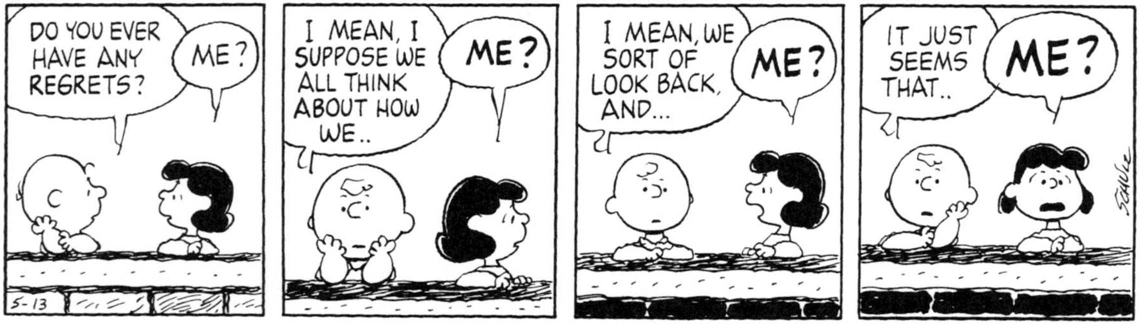
DO YOU EVER HAVE ANY REGRETS?
ME?
I MEAN, I SUPPOSE WE ALL THINK ABOUT HOW WE..
ME?
I MEAN, WE SORT OF LOOK BACK, AND...
ME?
IT JUST SEEMS THAT..
ME?
5-13
SCHULZ

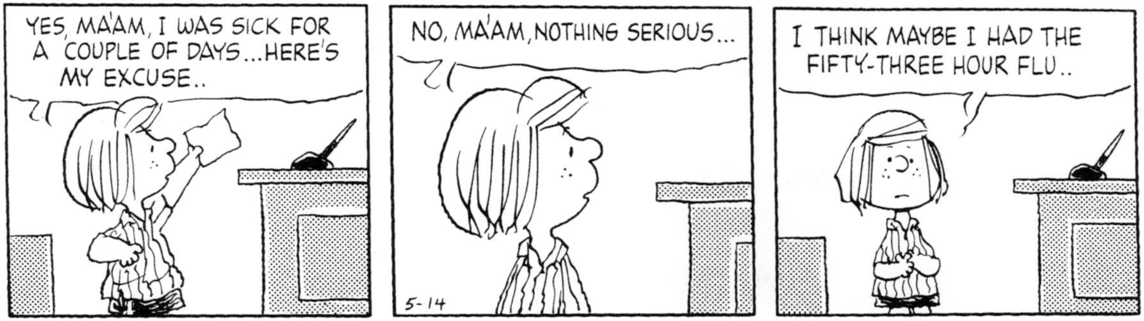
YES, MA'AM, I WAS SICK FOR A COUPLE OF DAYS...HERE'S MY EXCUSE..
NO, MA'AM, NOTHING SERIOUS...
5-14
I THINK MAYBE I HAD THE FIFTY-THREE HOUR FLU..

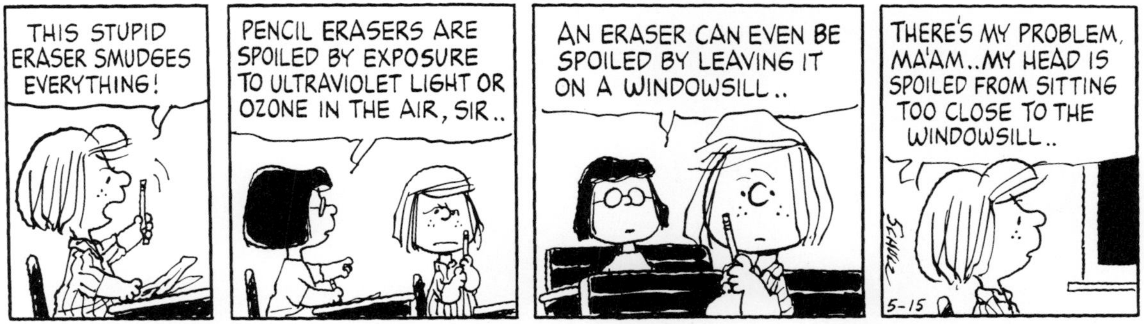
THIS STUPID ERASER SMUDGES EVERYTHING!
PENCIL ERASERS ARE SPOILED BY EXPOSURE TO ULTRAVIOLET LIGHT OR OZONE IN THE AIR, SIR..
AN ERASER CAN EVEN BE SPOILED BY LEAVING IT ON A WINDOWSILL..
THERE'S MY PROBLEM, MA'AM..MY HEAD IS SPOILED FROM SITTING TOO CLOSE TO THE WINDOWSILL..
SCHULZ
5-15

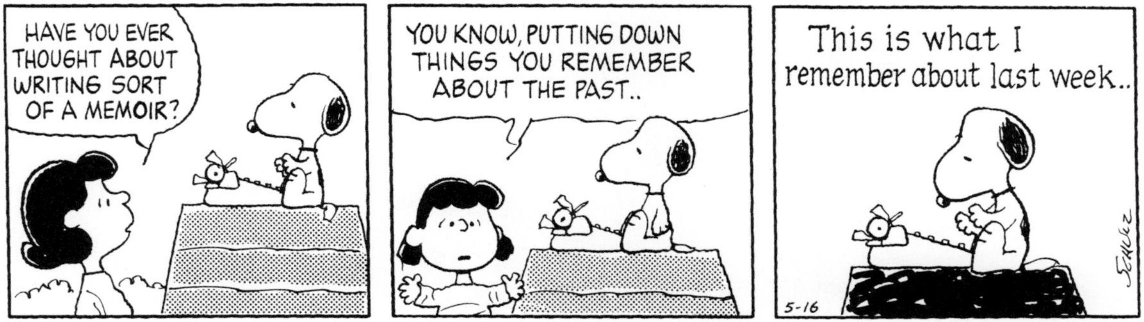
HAVE YOU EVER THOUGHT ABOUT WRITING SORT OF A MEMOIR?
YOU KNOW, PUTTING DOWN THINGS YOU REMEMBER ABOUT THE PAST..
This is what I remember about last week..
SCHULZ
5-16

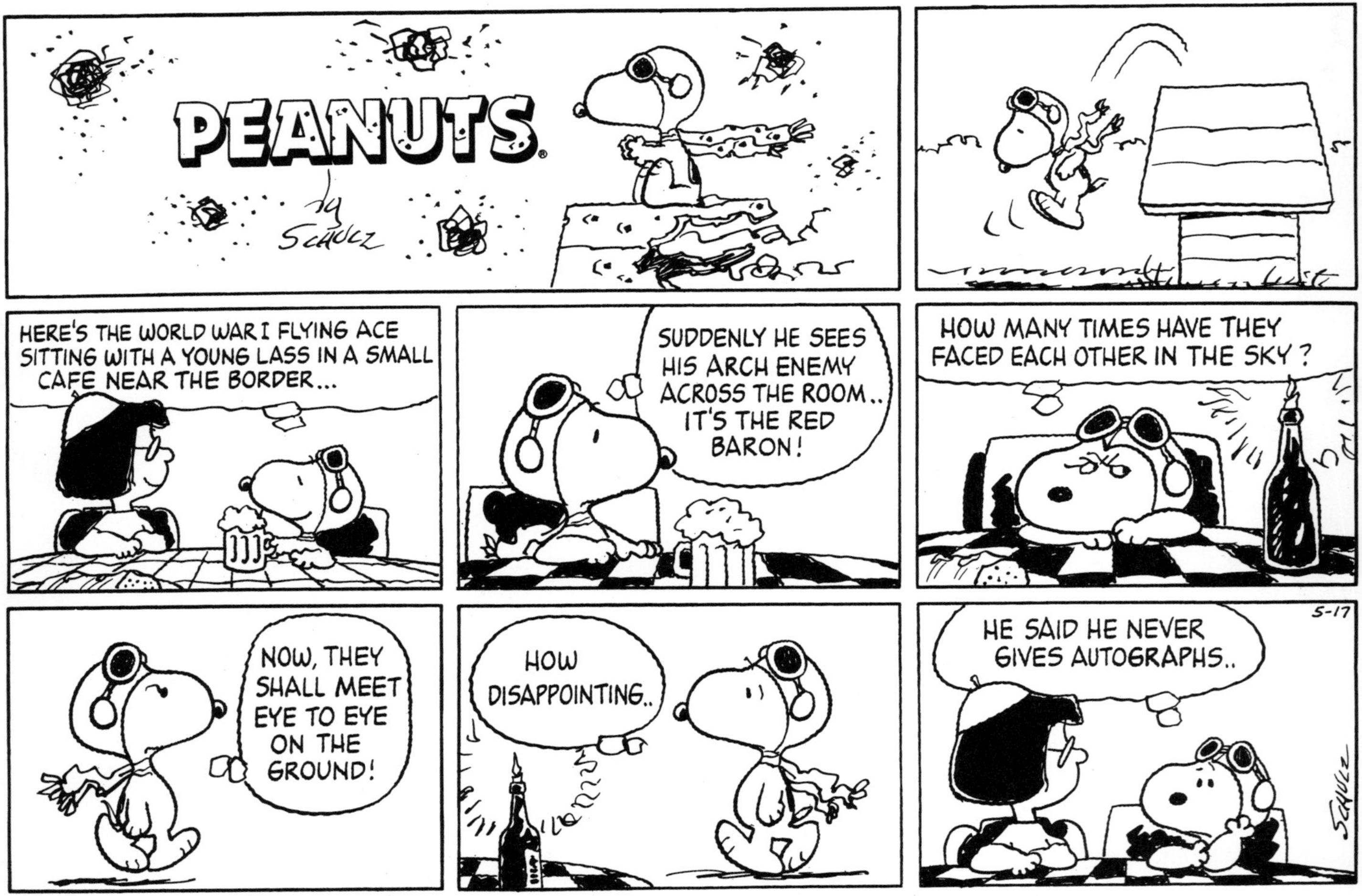
PEANUTS
by SCHULZ
HERE'S THE WORLD WAR I FLYING ACE SITTING WITH A YOUNG LASS IN A SMALL CAFE NEAR THE BORDER...
SUDDENLY HE SEES HIS ARCH ENEMY ACROSS THE ROOM.. IT'S THE RED BARON!
HOW MANY TIMES HAVE THEY FACED EACH OTHER IN THE SKY?
NOW, THEY SHALL MEET EYE TO EYE ON THE GROUND!
HOW DISAPPOINTING..
5-17
HE SAID HE NEVER GIVES AUTOGRAPHS..
SCHULZ

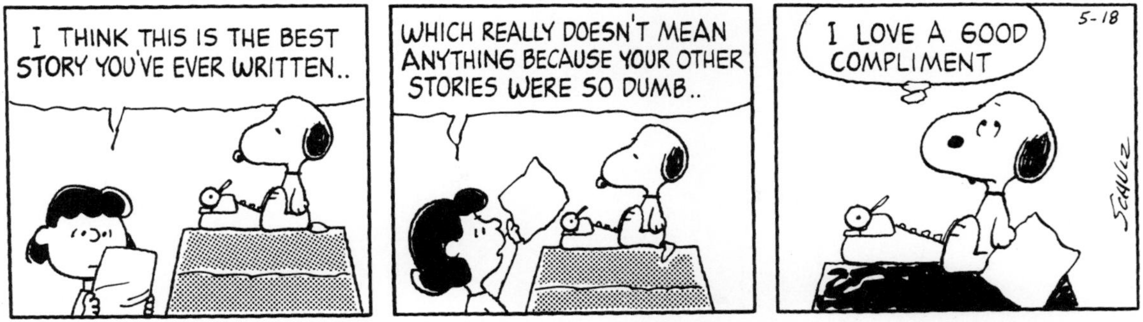
I THINK THIS IS THE BEST STORY YOU'VE EVER WRITTEN..
WHICH REALLY DOESN'T MEAN ANYTHING BECAUSE YOUR OTHER STORIES WERE SO DUMB..
I LOVE A GOOD COMPLIMENT
5-18
SCHULZ

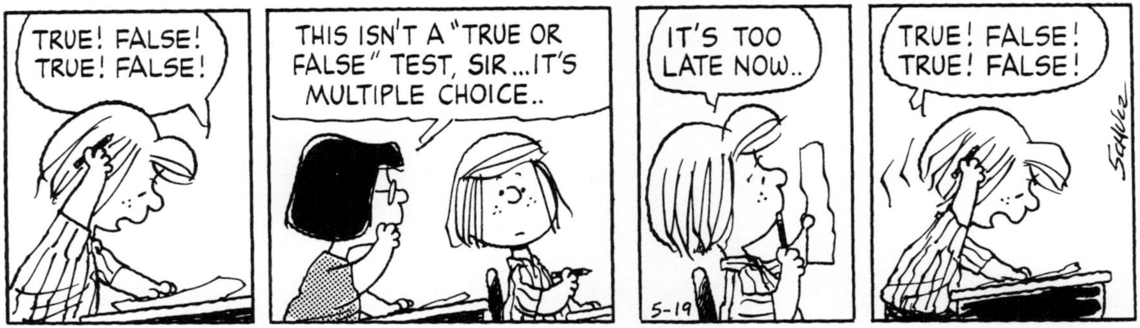
TRUE! FALSE! TRUE! FALSE!
THIS ISN'T A "TRUE OR FALSE" TEST, SIR...IT'S MULTIPLE CHOICE..
IT'S TOO LATE NOW..
5-19
TRUE! FALSE! TRUE! FALSE!
SCHULZ

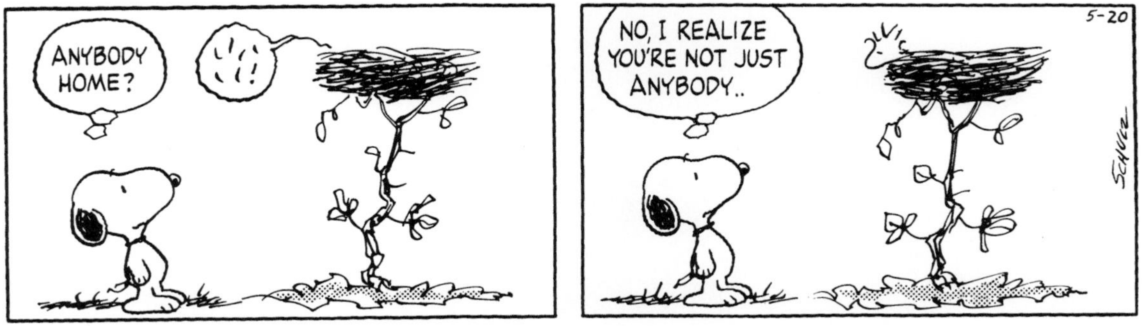
ANYBODY HOME?
NO, I REALIZE YOU'RE NOT JUST ANYBODY..
5-20
SCHULZ

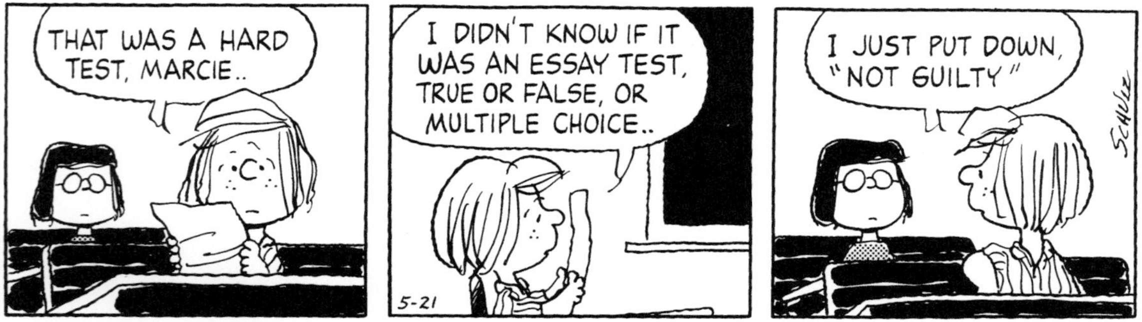
THAT WAS A HARD TEST, MARCIE..
I DIDN'T KNOW IF IT WAS AN ESSAY TEST, TRUE OR FALSE, OR MULTIPLE CHOICE..
5-21
I JUST PUT DOWN, "NOT GUILTY"

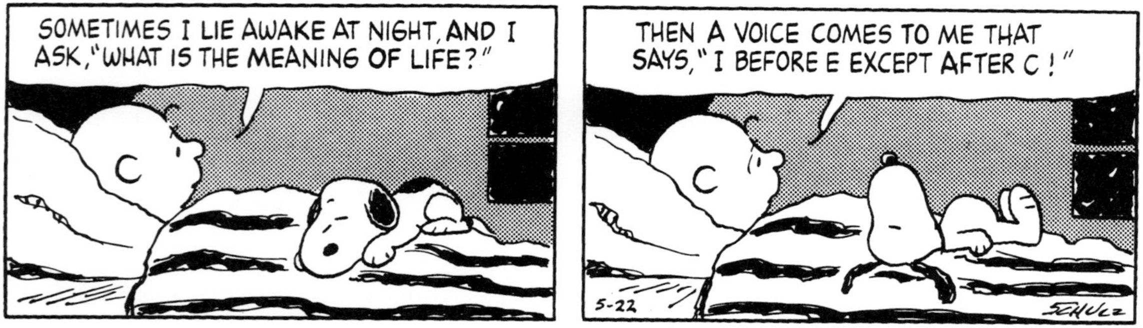
SOMETIMES I LIE AWAKE AT NIGHT, AND I ASK, "WHAT IS THE MEANING OF LIFE?"
THEN A VOICE COMES TO ME THAT SAYS, "I BEFORE E EXCEPT AFTER C!"
5-22

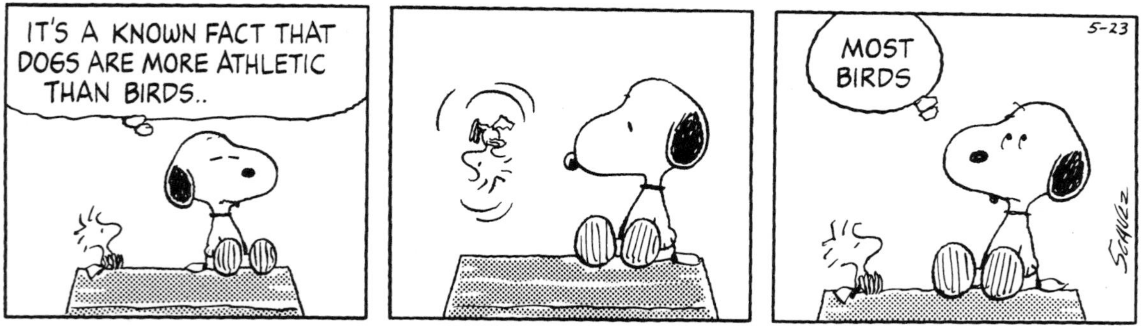
IT'S A KNOWN FACT THAT DOGS ARE MORE ATHLETIC THAN BIRDS..
5-23
MOST BIRDS

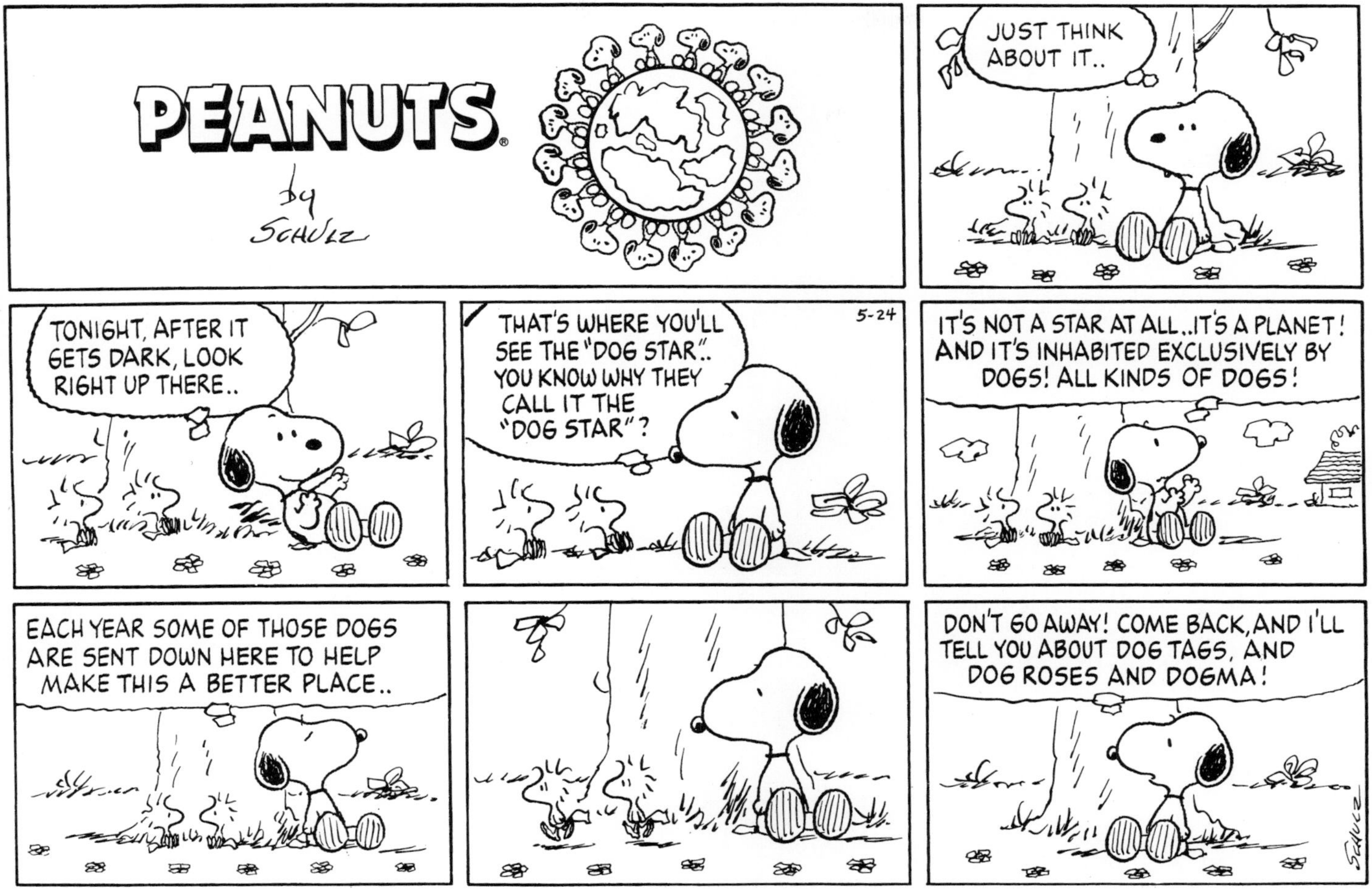
PEANUTS
by SCHULZ
JUST THINK ABOUT IT..
TONIGHT, AFTER IT GETS DARK, LOOK RIGHT UP THERE..
5-24
THAT'S WHERE YOU'LL SEE THE "DOG STAR".. YOU KNOW WHY THEY CALL IT THE "DOG STAR"?
IT'S NOT A STAR AT ALL..IT'S A PLANET! AND IT'S INHABITED EXCLUSIVELY BY DOGS! ALL KINDS OF DOGS!
EACH YEAR SOME OF THOSE DOGS ARE SENT DOWN HERE TO HELP MAKE THIS A BETTER PLACE..
DON'T GO AWAY! COME BACK, AND I'LL TELL YOU ABOUT DOG TAGS, AND DOG ROSES AND DOGMA!
SCHULZ

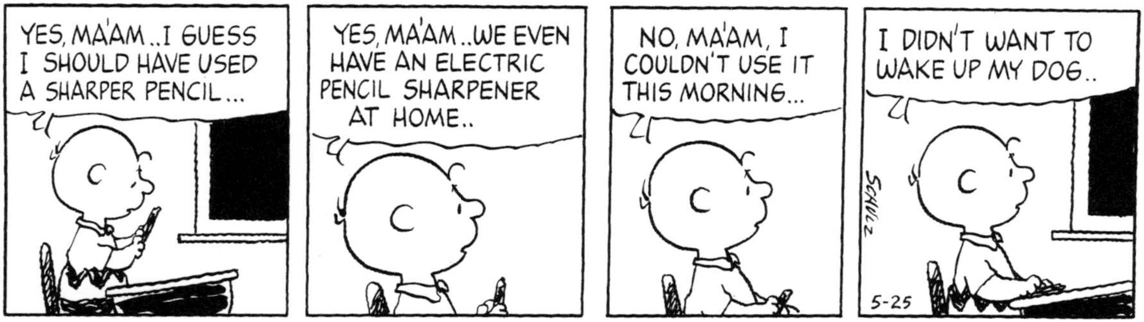
YES, MA'AM..I GUESS I SHOULD HAVE USED A SHARPER PENCIL...
YES, MA'AM..WE EVEN HAVE AN ELECTRIC PENCIL SHARPENER AT HOME..
NO, MA'AM, I COULDN'T USE IT THIS MORNING...
I DIDN'T WANT TO WAKE UP MY DOG..
SCHULZ
5-25

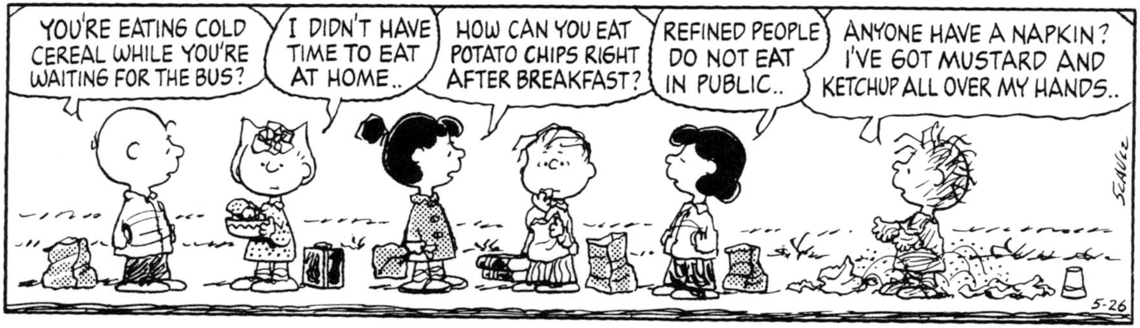
YOU'RE EATING COLD CEREAL WHILE YOU'RE WAITING FOR THE BUS?
I DIDN'T HAVE TIME TO EAT AT HOME..
HOW CAN YOU EAT POTATO CHIPS RIGHT AFTER BREAKFAST?
REFINED PEOPLE DO NOT EAT IN PUBLIC..
ANYONE HAVE A NAPKIN? I'VE GOT MUSTARD AND KETCHUP ALL OVER MY HANDS..
SCHULZ
5-26

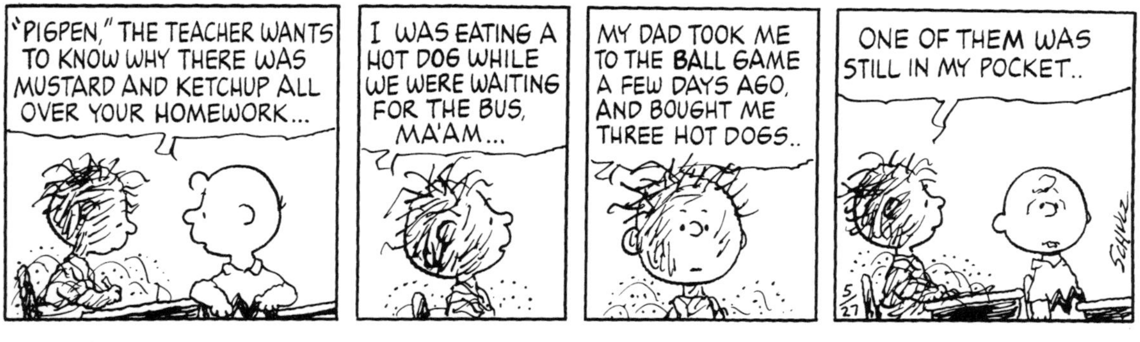
"PIGPEN," THE TEACHER WANTS TO KNOW WHY THERE WAS MUSTARD AND KETCHUP ALL OVER YOUR HOMEWORK...
I WAS EATING A HOT DOG WHILE WE WERE WAITING FOR THE BUS, MA'AM...
MY DAD TOOK ME TO THE BALL GAME A FEW DAYS AGO, AND BOUGHT ME THREE HOT DOGS..
ONE OF THEM WAS STILL IN MY POCKET..
SCHULZ
5/27

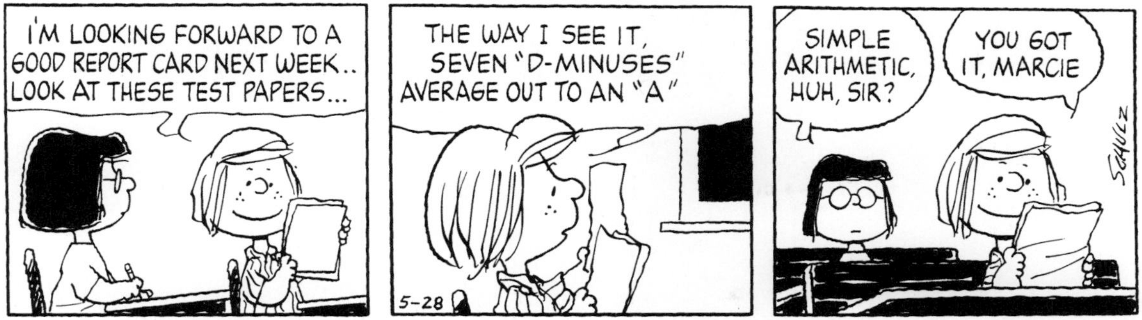
I'M LOOKING FORWARD TO A GOOD REPORT CARD NEXT WEEK.. LOOK AT THESE TEST PAPERS...
THE WAY I SEE IT, SEVEN "D-MINUSES" AVERAGE OUT TO AN "A"
5-28
SIMPLE ARITHMETIC, HUH, SIR?
YOU GOT IT, MARCIE
SCHULZ

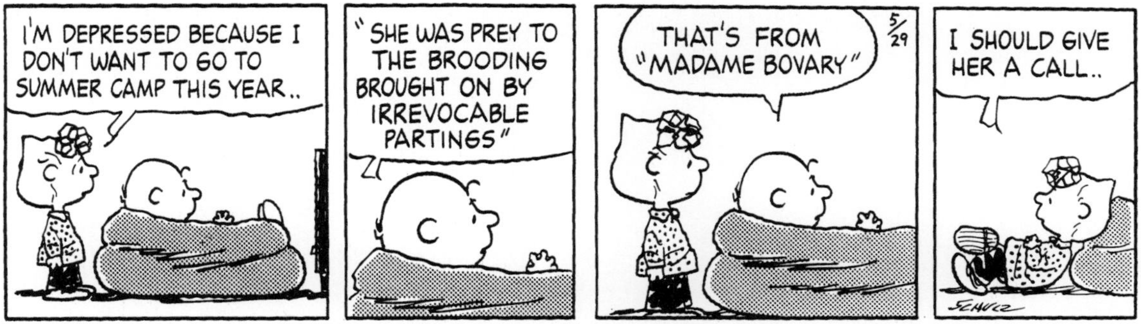
I'M DEPRESSED BECAUSE I DON'T WANT TO GO TO SUMMER CAMP THIS YEAR..
"SHE WAS PREY TO THE BROODING BROUGHT ON BY IRREVOCABLE PARTINGS"
5/29
THAT'S FROM "MADAME BOVARY"
I SHOULD GIVE HER A CALL..
SCHULZ

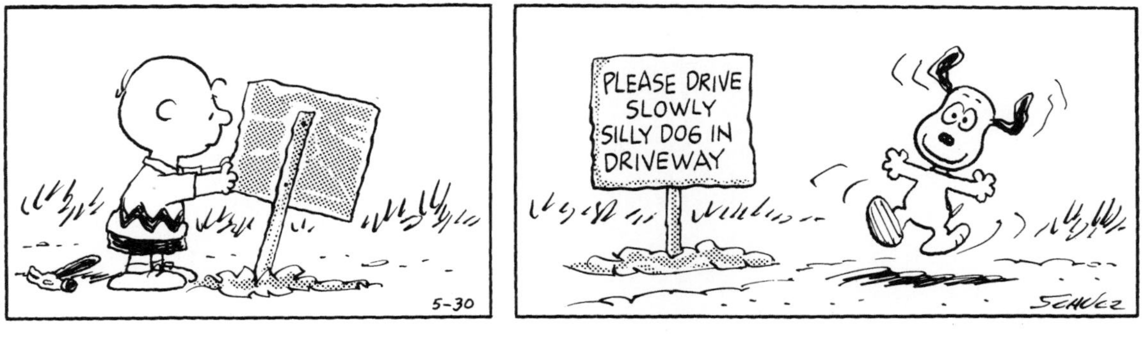
5-30
PLEASE DRIVE SLOWLY SILLY DOG IN DRIVEWAY
SCHULZ

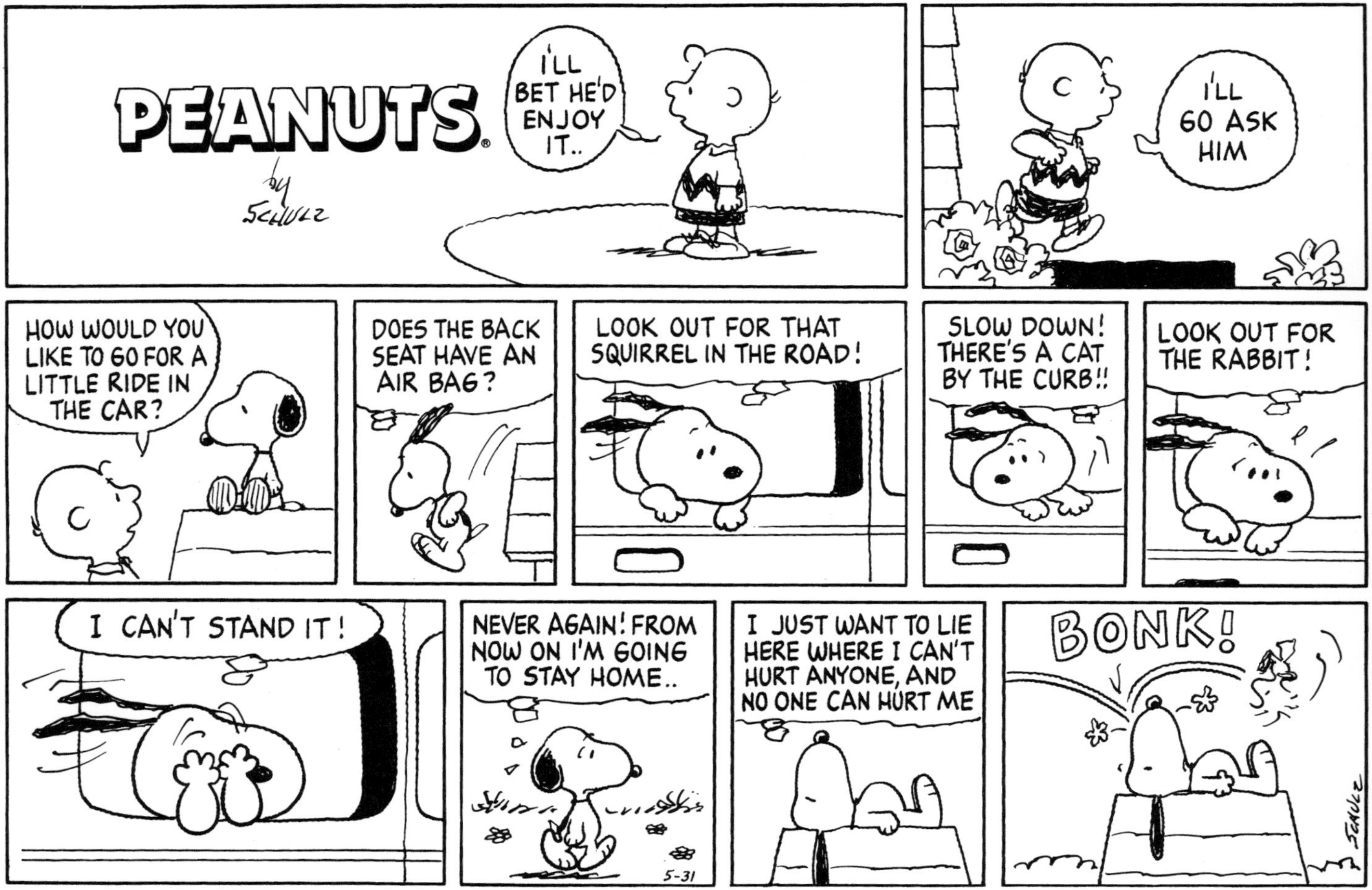
PEANUTS
by SCHULZ
I'LL BET HE'D ENJOY IT..
I'LL GO ASK HIM
HOW WOULD YOU LIKE TO GO FOR A LITTLE RIDE IN THE CAR?
DOES THE BACK SEAT HAVE AN AIR BAG?
LOOK OUT FOR THAT SQUIRREL IN THE ROAD!
SLOW DOWN! THERE'S A CAT BY THE CURB!!
LOOK OUT FOR THE RABBIT!
I CAN'T STAND IT!
NEVER AGAIN! FROM NOW ON I'M GOING TO STAY HOME..
5-31
I JUST WANT TO LIE HERE WHERE I CAN'T HURT ANYONE, AND NO ONE CAN HURT ME
BONK!
SCHULZ

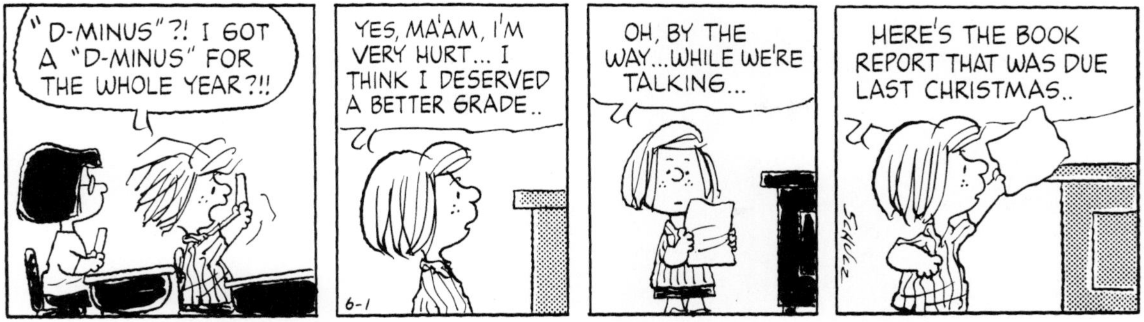
"D-MINUS"?! I GOT A "D-MINUS" FOR THE WHOLE YEAR?!!
YES, MA'AM, I'M VERY HURT... I THINK I DESERVED A BETTER GRADE..
6-1
OH, BY THE WAY...WHILE WE'RE TALKING...
HERE'S THE BOOK REPORT THAT WAS DUE LAST CHRISTMAS..
SCHULZ

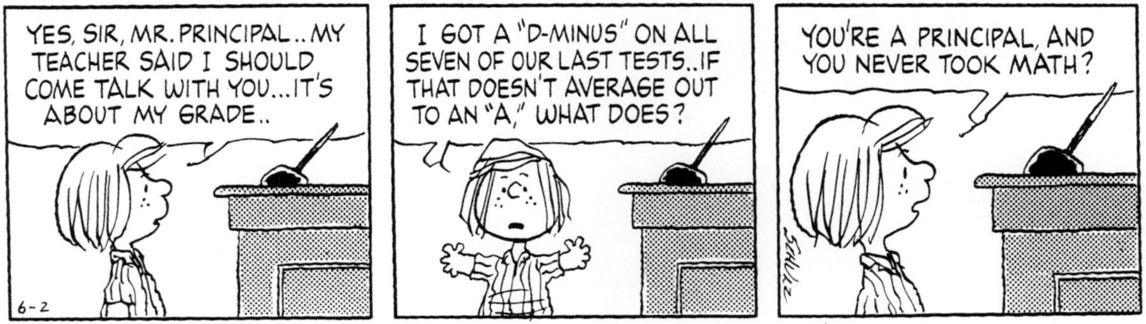
YES, SIR, MR. PRINCIPAL.. MY TEACHER SAID I SHOULD COME TALK WITH YOU...IT'S ABOUT MY GRADE..
6-2
I GOT A "D-MINUS" ON ALL SEVEN OF OUR LAST TESTS..IF THAT DOESN'T AVERAGE OUT TO AN "A," WHAT DOES?
YOU'RE A PRINCIPAL, AND YOU NEVER TOOK MATH?
SCHULZ

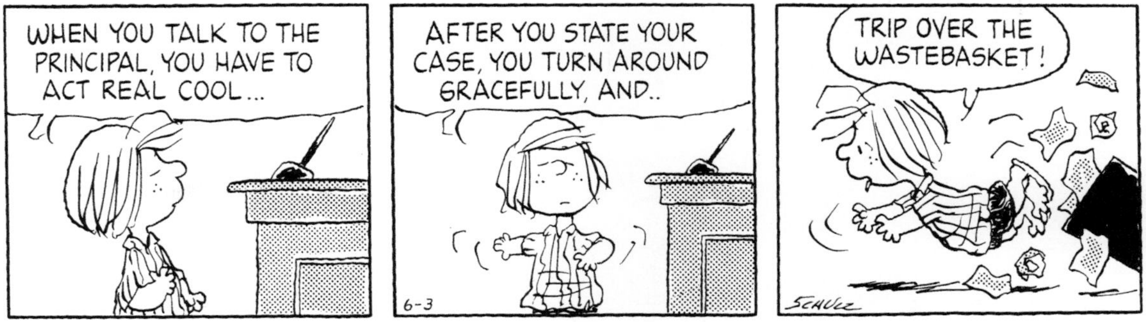
WHEN YOU TALK TO THE PRINCIPAL, YOU HAVE TO ACT REAL COOL...
AFTER YOU STATE YOUR CASE, YOU TURN AROUND GRACEFULLY, AND..
6-3
TRIP OVER THE WASTEBASKET!
SCHULZ

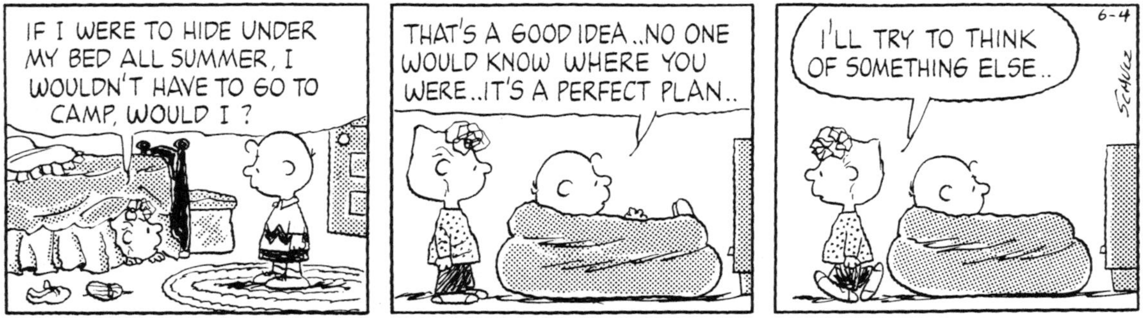
IF I WERE TO HIDE UNDER MY BED ALL SUMMER, I WOULDN'T HAVE TO GO TO CAMP, WOULD I ?
THAT'S A GOOD IDEA..NO ONE WOULD KNOW WHERE YOU WERE..IT'S A PERFECT PLAN..
I'LL TRY TO THINK OF SOMETHING ELSE..
6-4
SCHULZ

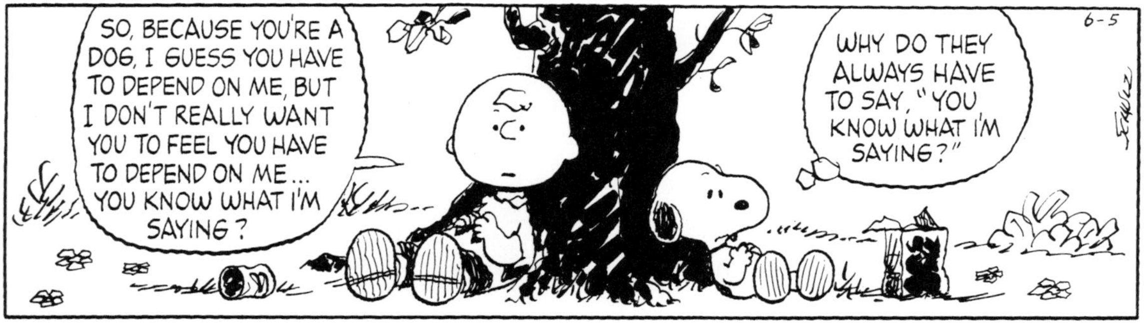
SO, BECAUSE YOU'RE A DOG, I GUESS YOU HAVE TO DEPEND ON ME, BUT I DON'T REALLY WANT YOU TO FEEL YOU HAVE TO DEPEND ON ME... YOU KNOW WHAT I'M SAYING ?
6-5
WHY DO THEY ALWAYS HAVE TO SAY, "YOU KNOW WHAT I'M SAYING?"
SCHULZ

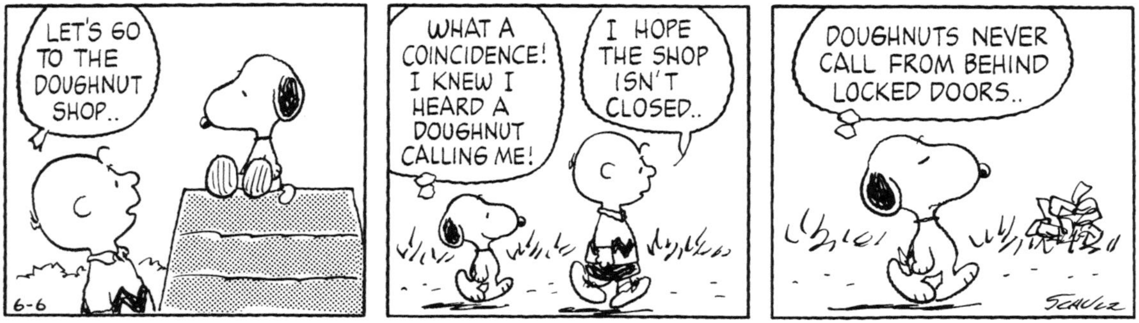
LET'S GO TO THE DOUGHNUT SHOP..
6-6
WHAT A COINCIDENCE! I KNEW I HEARD A DOUGHNUT CALLING ME!
I HOPE THE SHOP ISN'T CLOSED..
DOUGHNUTS NEVER CALL FROM BEHIND LOCKED DOORS..
SCHULZ

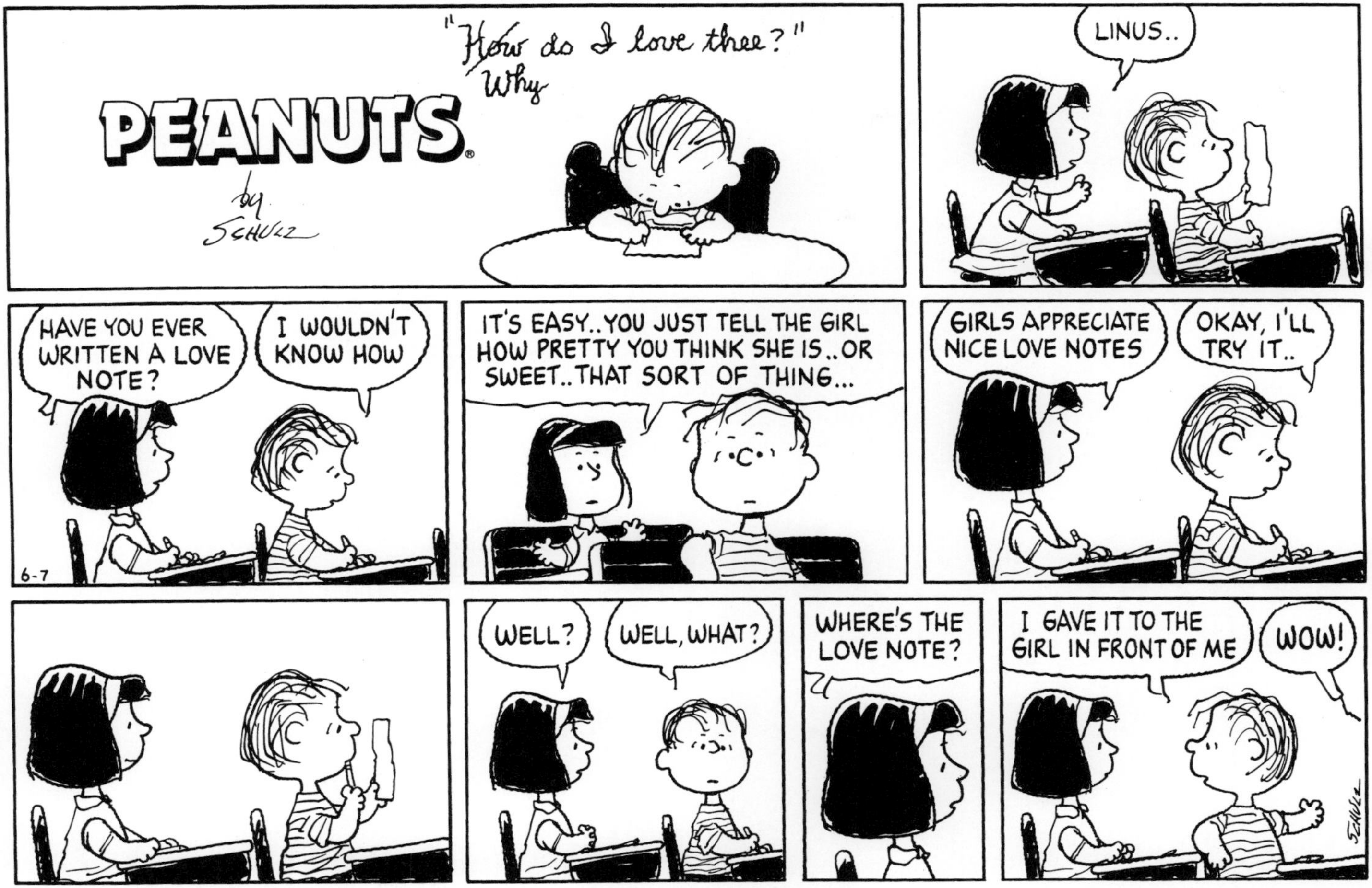
"How do I love thee?"
Why
PEANUTS
by SCHULZ
LINUS..
HAVE YOU EVER WRITTEN A LOVE NOTE?
I WOULDN'T KNOW HOW
6-7
IT'S EASY..YOU JUST TELL THE GIRL HOW PRETTY YOU THINK SHE IS..OR SWEET..THAT SORT OF THING...
GIRLS APPRECIATE NICE LOVE NOTES
OKAY, I'LL TRY IT..
WELL?
WELL, WHAT?
WHERE'S THE LOVE NOTE?
I GAVE IT TO THE GIRL IN FRONT OF ME
WOW!
SCHULZ

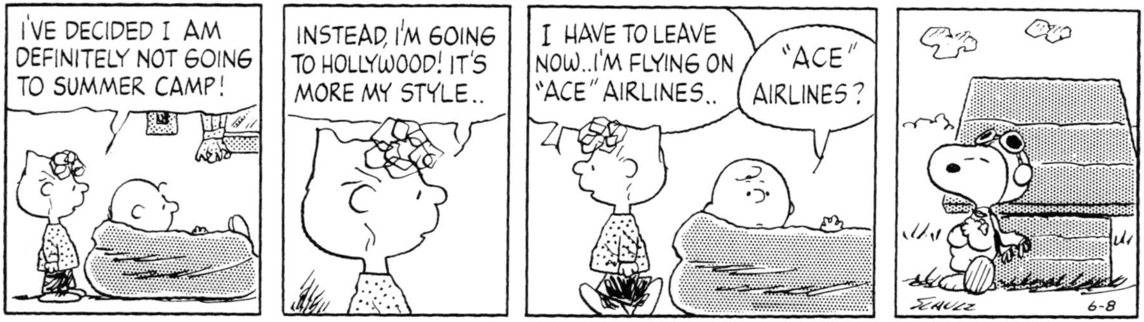
I'VE DECIDED I AM DEFINITELY NOT GOING TO SUMMER CAMP!
INSTEAD, I'M GOING TO HOLLYWOOD! IT'S MORE MY STYLE..
I HAVE TO LEAVE NOW..I'M FLYING ON "ACE" AIRLINES..
"ACE" AIRLINES?
SCHULZ
6-8

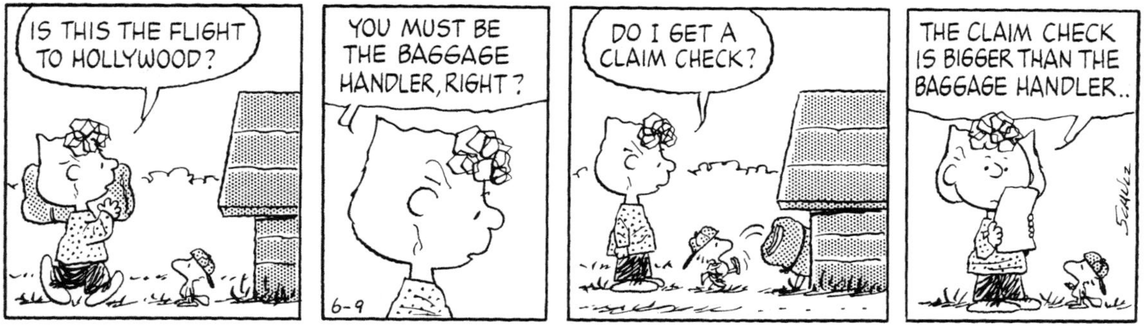
IS THIS THE FLIGHT TO HOLLYWOOD?
YOU MUST BE THE BAGGAGE HANDLER, RIGHT?
6-9
DO I GET A CLAIM CHECK?
THE CLAIM CHECK IS BIGGER THAN THE BAGGAGE HANDLER..
SCHULZ

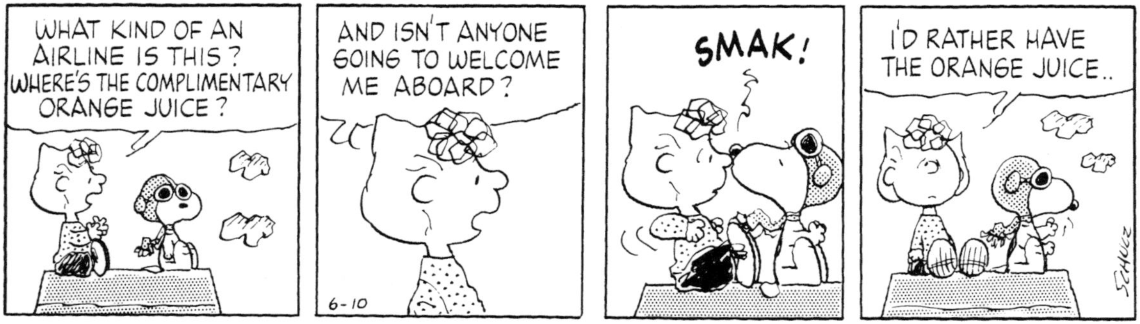
WHAT KIND OF AN AIRLINE IS THIS? WHERE'S THE COMPLIMENTARY ORANGE JUICE?
AND ISN'T ANYONE GOING TO WELCOME ME ABOARD?
6-10
SMAK!
I'D RATHER HAVE THE ORANGE JUICE..
SCHULZ

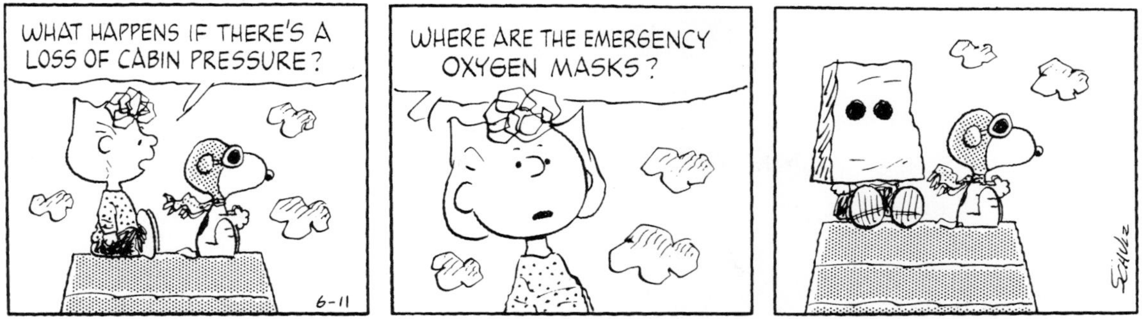
WHAT HAPPENS IF THERE'S A LOSS OF CABIN PRESSURE?
WHERE ARE THE EMERGENCY OXYGEN MASKS?

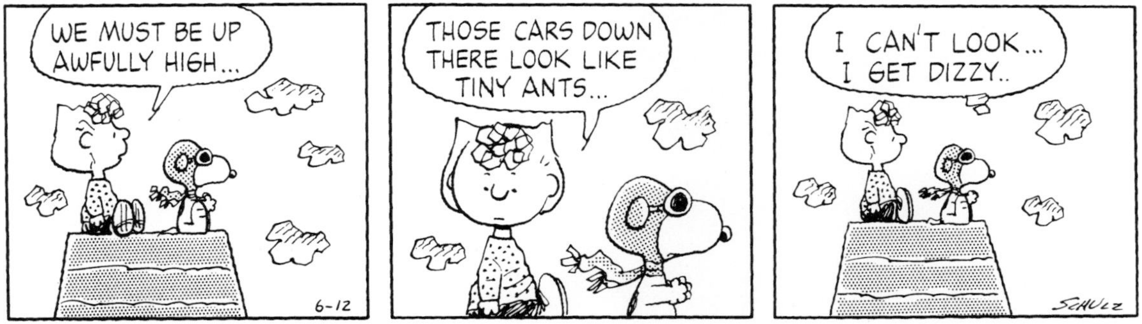
WE MUST BE UP AWFULLY HIGH...
THOSE CARS DOWN THERE LOOK LIKE TINY ANTS...
I CAN'T LOOK... I GET DIZZY..

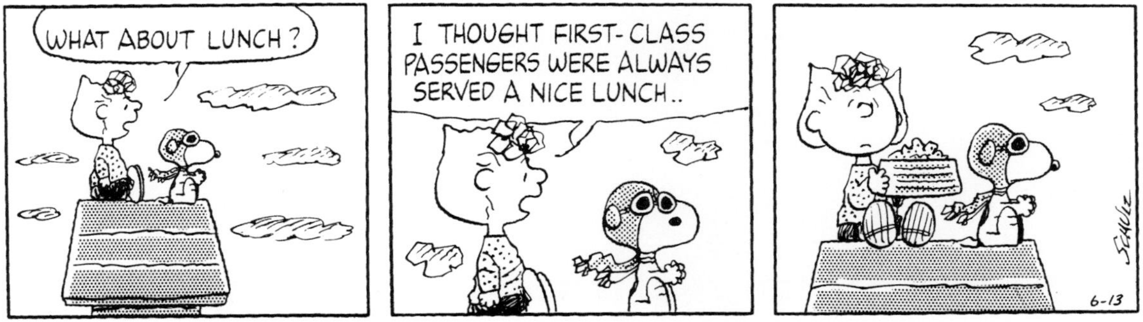
WHAT ABOUT LUNCH?
I THOUGHT FIRST-CLASS PASSENGERS WERE ALWAYS SERVED A NICE LUNCH..

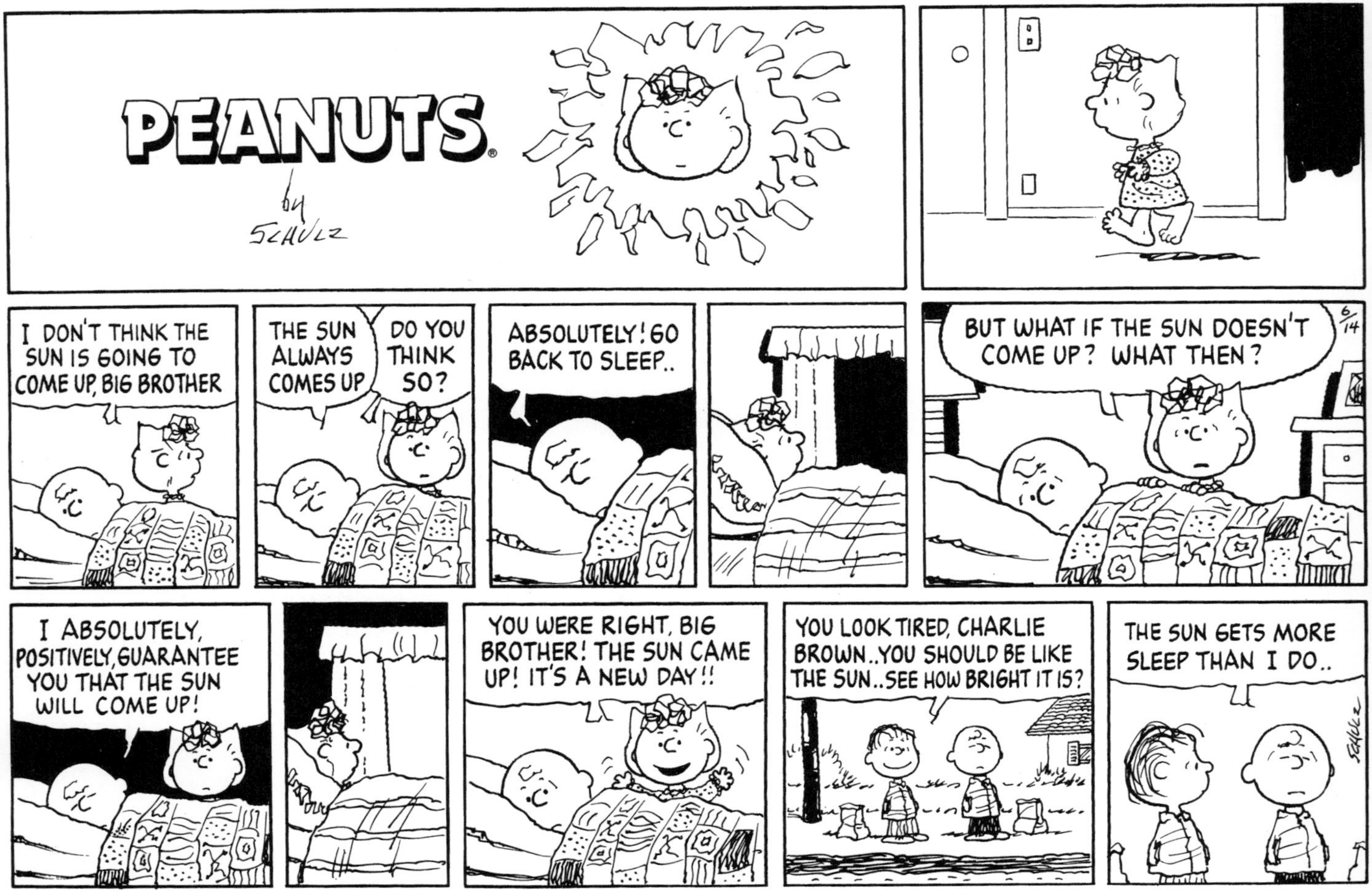
PEANUTS
by SCHULZ
I DON'T THINK THE SUN IS GOING TO COME UP, BIG BROTHER
THE SUN ALWAYS COMES UP
DO YOU THINK SO?
ABSOLUTELY! GO BACK TO SLEEP..
BUT WHAT IF THE SUN DOESN'T COME UP? WHAT THEN?
6/14
I ABSOLUTELY, POSITIVELY, GUARANTEE YOU THAT THE SUN WILL COME UP!
YOU WERE RIGHT, BIG BROTHER! THE SUN CAME UP! IT'S A NEW DAY!!
YOU LOOK TIRED, CHARLIE BROWN..YOU SHOULD BE LIKE THE SUN..SEE HOW BRIGHT IT IS?
THE SUN GETS MORE SLEEP THAN I DO..
SCHULZ

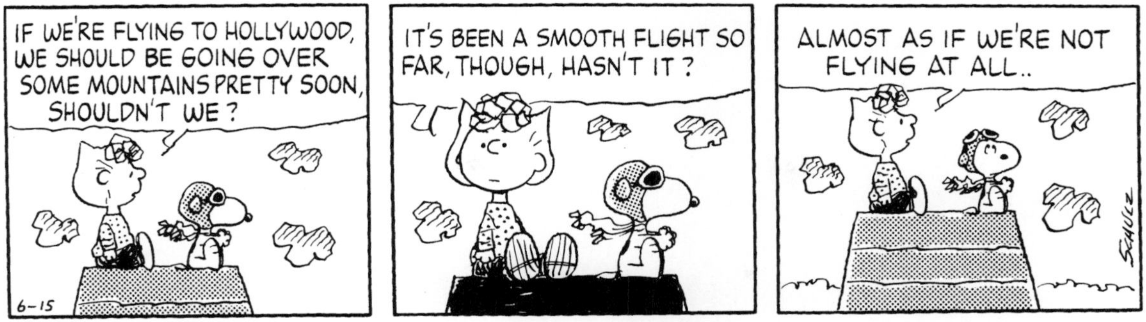
IF WE'RE FLYING TO HOLLYWOOD, WE SHOULD BE GOING OVER SOME MOUNTAINS PRETTY SOON, SHOULDN'T WE?
6-15
IT'S BEEN A SMOOTH FLIGHT SO FAR, THOUGH, HASN'T IT?
ALMOST AS IF WE'RE NOT FLYING AT ALL..
SCHULZ

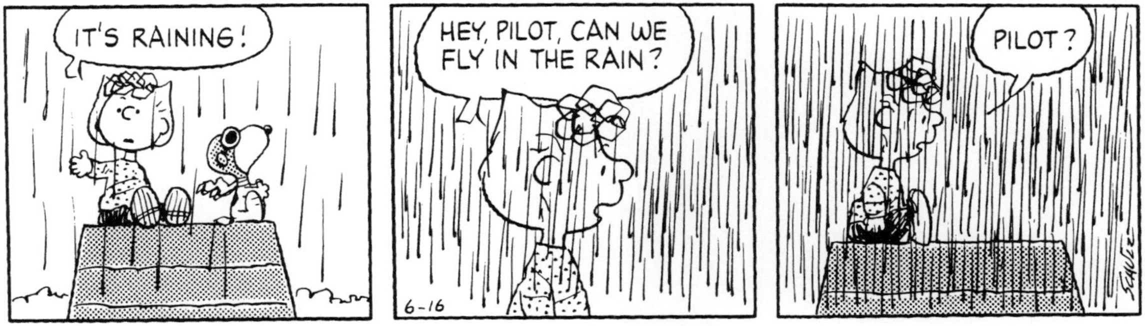
IT'S RAINING!
HEY, PILOT, CAN WE FLY IN THE RAIN?
6-16
PILOT?
SCHULZ

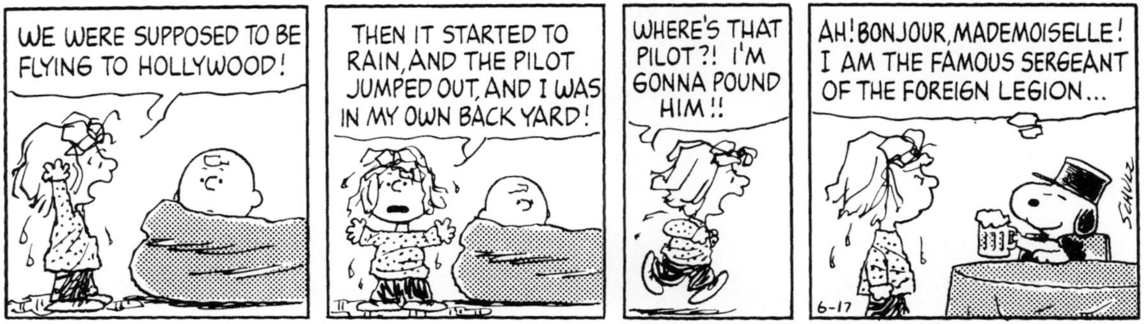
WE WERE SUPPOSED TO BE FLYING TO HOLLYWOOD!
THEN IT STARTED TO RAIN, AND THE PILOT JUMPED OUT, AND I WAS IN MY OWN BACK YARD!
WHERE'S THAT PILOT?! I'M GONNA POUND HIM!!
AH! BONJOUR, MADEMOISELLE! I AM THE FAMOUS SERGEANT OF THE FOREIGN LEGION...
6-17
SCHULZ

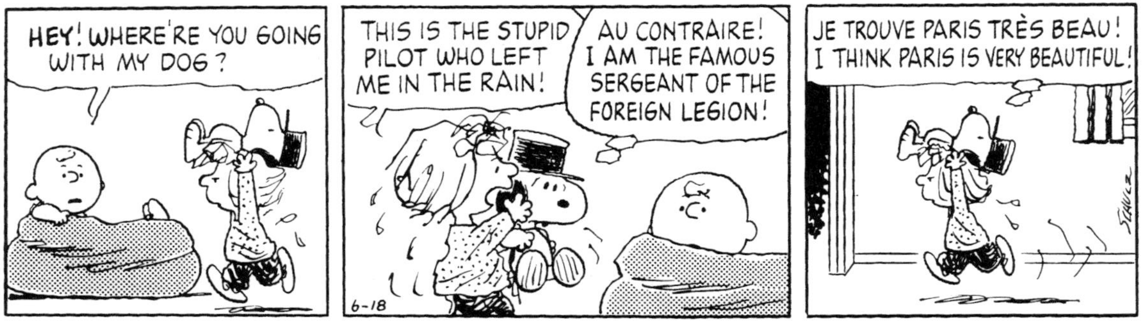
HEY! WHERE'RE YOU GOING WITH MY DOG?
THIS IS THE STUPID PILOT WHO LEFT ME IN THE RAIN!
AU CONTRAIRE! I AM THE FAMOUS SERGEANT OF THE FOREIGN LEGION!
JE TROUVE PARIS TRÈS BEAU! I THINK PARIS IS VERY BEAUTIFUL!
6-18
SCHULZ

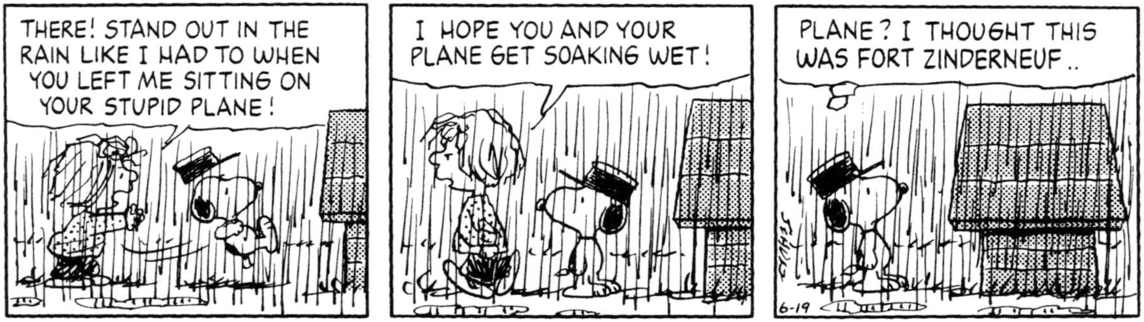
THERE! STAND OUT IN THE RAIN LIKE I HAD TO WHEN YOU LEFT ME SITTING ON YOUR STUPID PLANE!
I HOPE YOU AND YOUR PLANE GET SOAKING WET!
PLANE? I THOUGHT THIS WAS FORT ZINDERNEUF..
SCHULZ
6-19

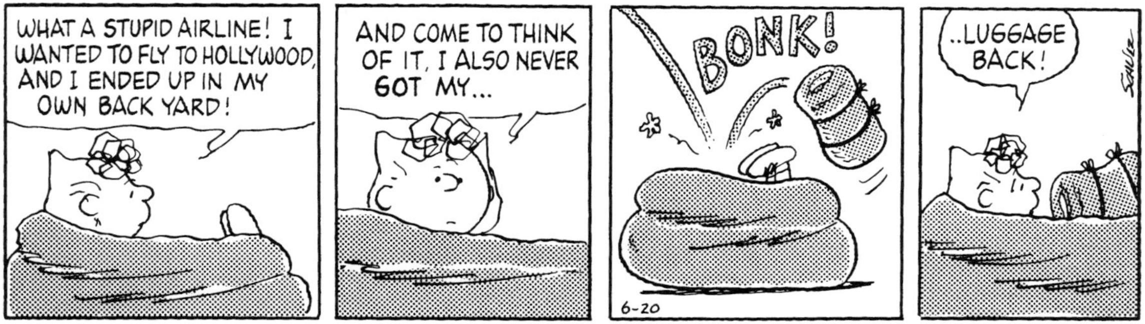
WHAT A STUPID AIRLINE! I WANTED TO FLY TO HOLLYWOOD, AND I ENDED UP IN MY OWN BACK YARD!
AND COME TO THINK OF IT, I ALSO NEVER GOT MY...
BONK!
6-20
..LUGGAGE BACK!
SCHULZ

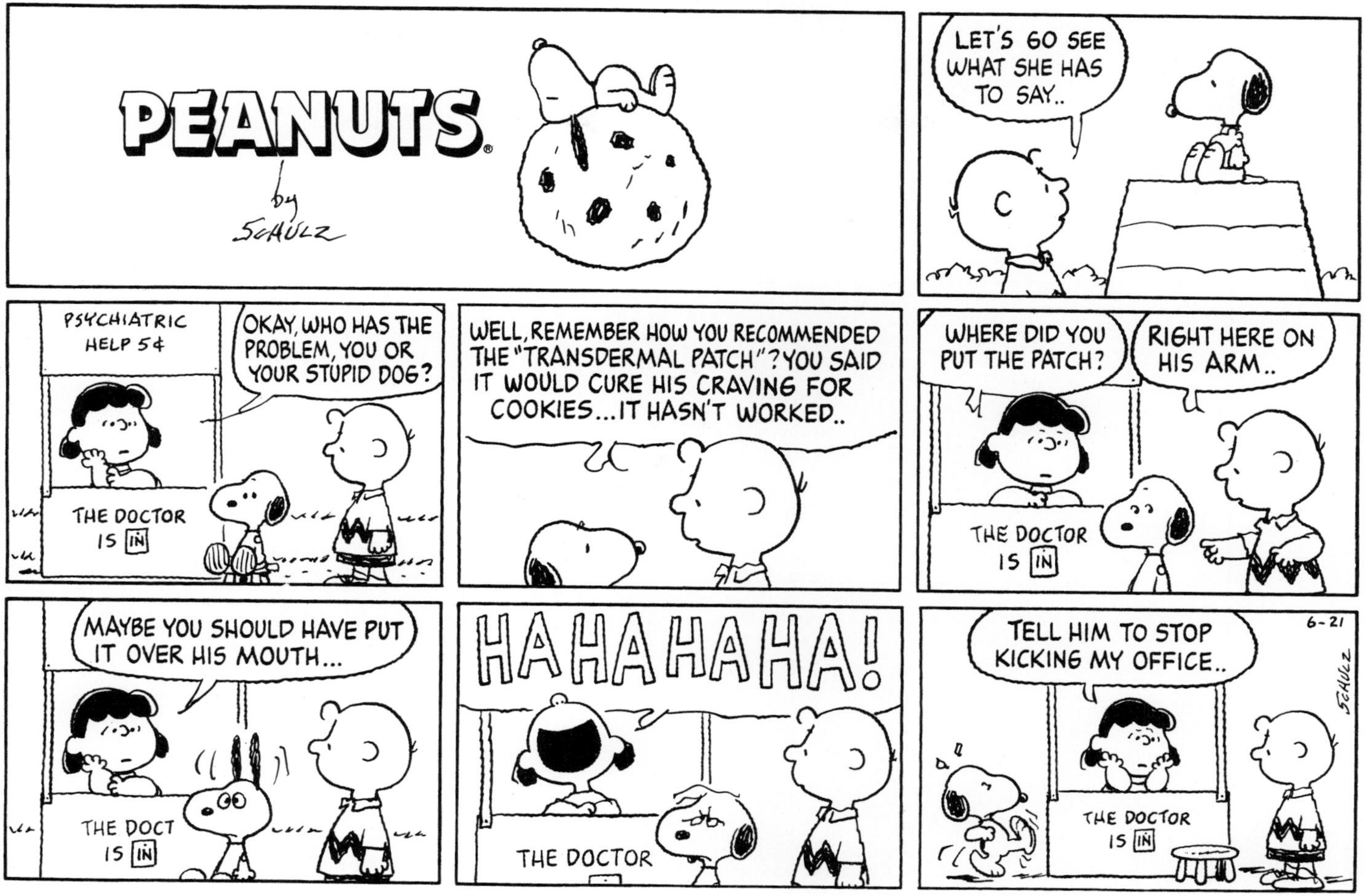
PEANUTS
by SCHULZ
LET'S GO SEE WHAT SHE HAS TO SAY..
PSYCHIATRIC HELP 5¢
OKAY, WHO HAS THE PROBLEM, YOU OR YOUR STUPID DOG?
THE DOCTOR IS IN
WELL, REMEMBER HOW YOU RECOMMENDED THE "TRANSDERMAL PATCH"? YOU SAID IT WOULD CURE HIS CRAVING FOR COOKIES...IT HASN'T WORKED..
WHERE DID YOU PUT THE PATCH?
RIGHT HERE ON HIS ARM..
THE DOCTOR IS IN
MAYBE YOU SHOULD HAVE PUT IT OVER HIS MOUTH...
THE DOCT IS IN
HAHAHAHA!
THE DOCTOR
TELL HIM TO STOP KICKING MY OFFICE..
6-21
SCHULZ
THE DOCTOR IS IN

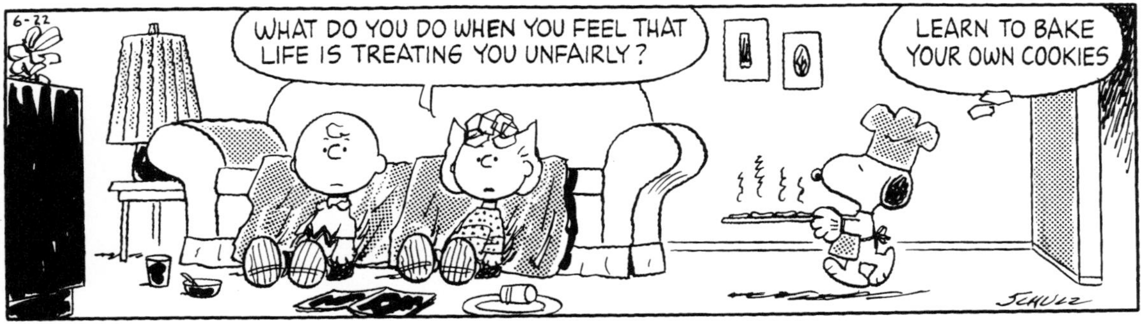
6-22
WHAT DO YOU DO WHEN YOU FEEL THAT LIFE IS TREATING YOU UNFAIRLY?
LEARN TO BAKE YOUR OWN COOKIES
SCHULZ

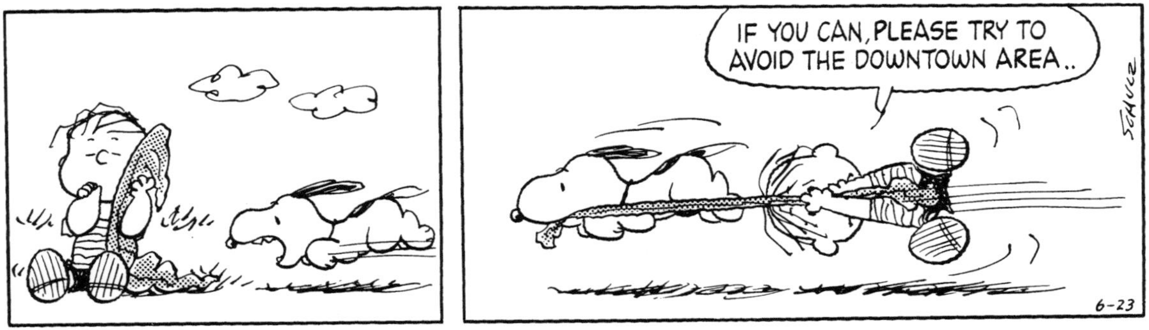
IF YOU CAN, PLEASE TRY TO AVOID THE DOWNTOWN AREA..
SCHULZ
6-23

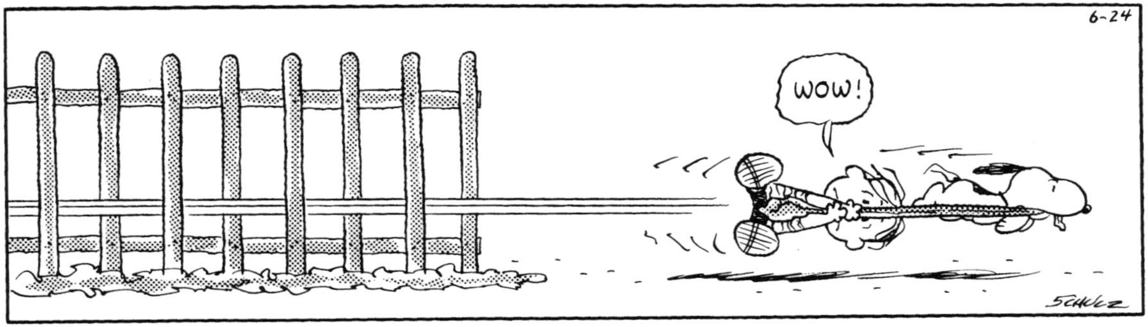
6-24
WOW!
SCHULZ

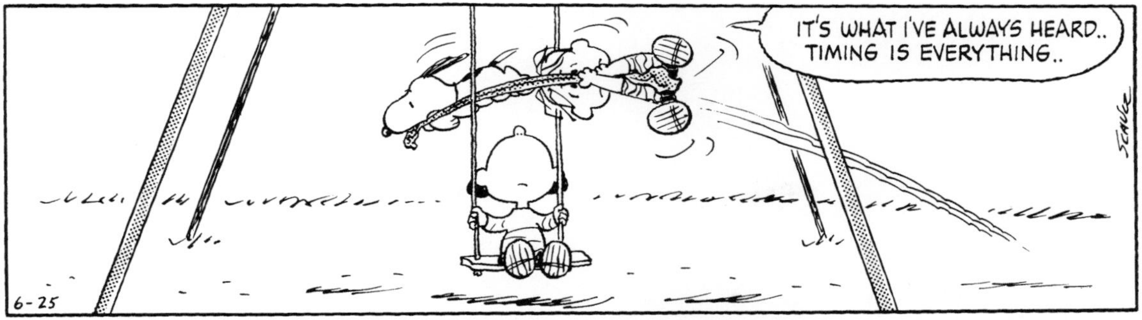
IT'S WHAT I'VE ALWAYS HEARD..
TIMING IS EVERYTHING..
SCHULZ
6-25

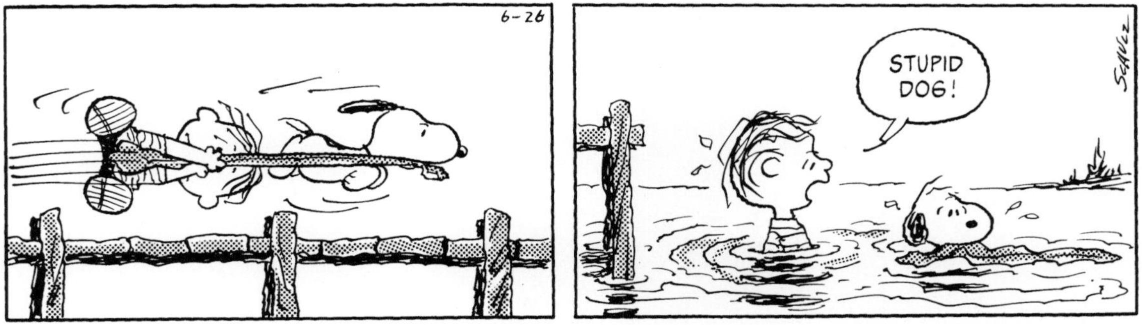
6-26
STUPID DOG!
SCHULZ

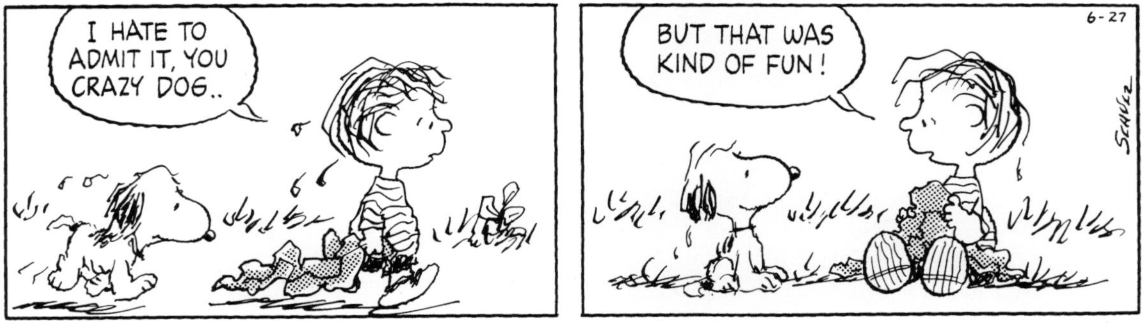
I HATE TO ADMIT IT, YOU CRAZY DOG..
BUT THAT WAS KIND OF FUN!
6-27
SCHULZ

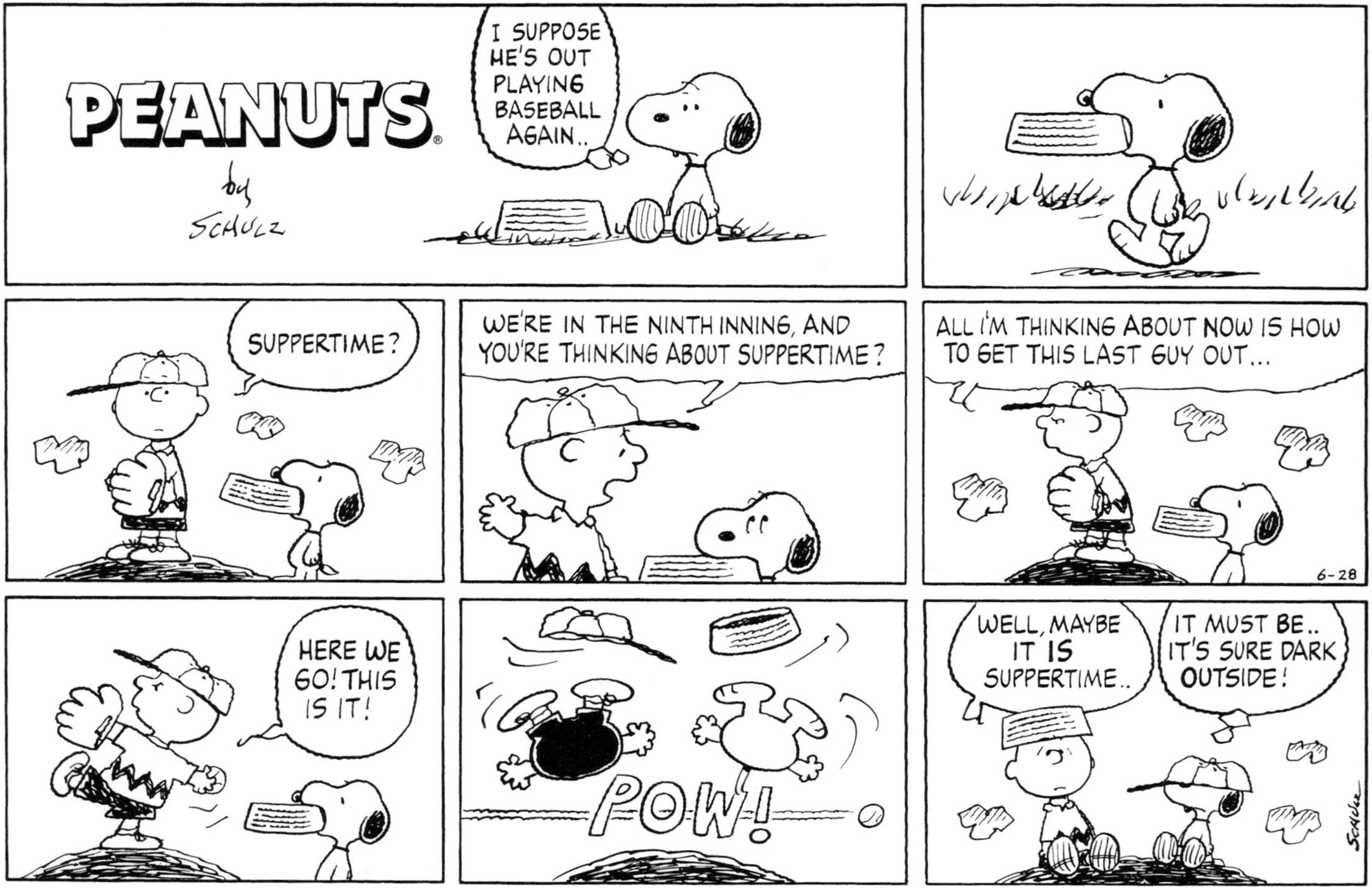
PEANUTS
by SCHULZ
I SUPPOSE HE'S OUT PLAYING BASEBALL AGAIN..
SUPPERTIME?
WE'RE IN THE NINTH INNING, AND YOU'RE THINKING ABOUT SUPPERTIME?
ALL I'M THINKING ABOUT NOW IS HOW TO GET THIS LAST GUY OUT...
6-28
HERE WE GO! THIS IS IT!
POW!
WELL, MAYBE IT IS SUPPERTIME..
IT MUST BE.. IT'S SURE DARK OUTSIDE!
SCHULZ

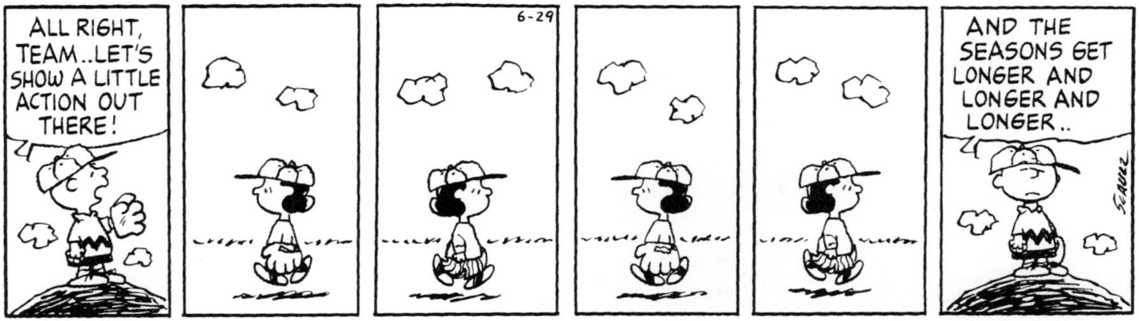
ALL RIGHT, TEAM..LET'S SHOW A LITTLE ACTION OUT THERE!
6-29
AND THE SEASONS GET LONGER AND LONGER AND LONGER..

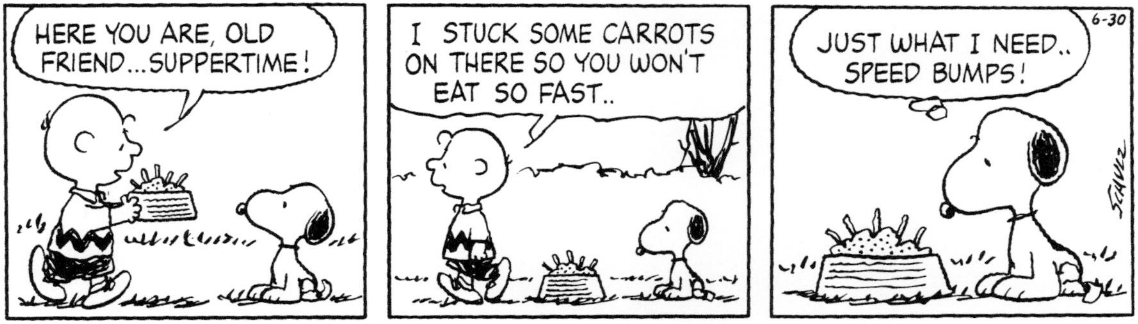
HERE YOU ARE, OLD FRIEND...SUPPERTIME!
I STUCK SOME CARROTS ON THERE SO YOU WON'T EAT SO FAST..
6-30
JUST WHAT I NEED.. SPEED BUMPS!

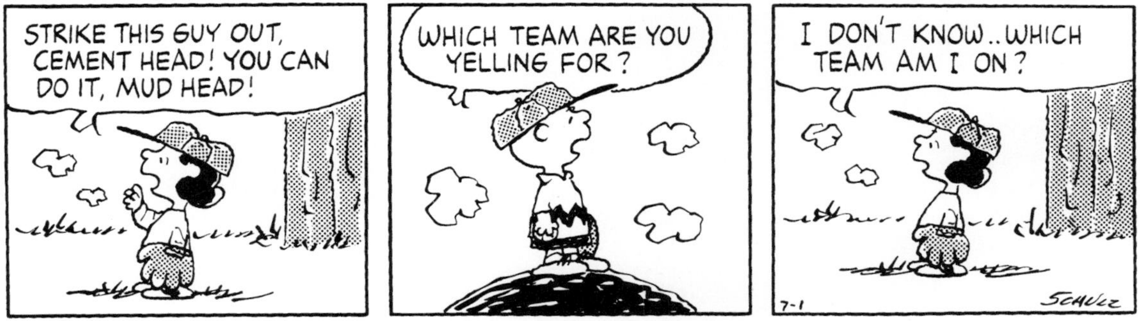
STRIKE THIS GUY OUT, CEMENT HEAD! YOU CAN DO IT, MUD HEAD!
WHICH TEAM ARE YOU YELLING FOR?
I DON'T KNOW..WHICH TEAM AM I ON?
7-1

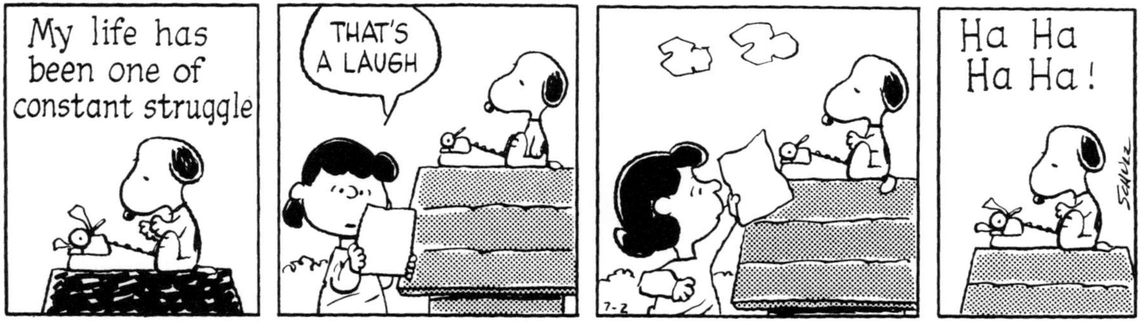
My life has been one of constant struggle
THAT'S A LAUGH
Ha Ha Ha Ha!

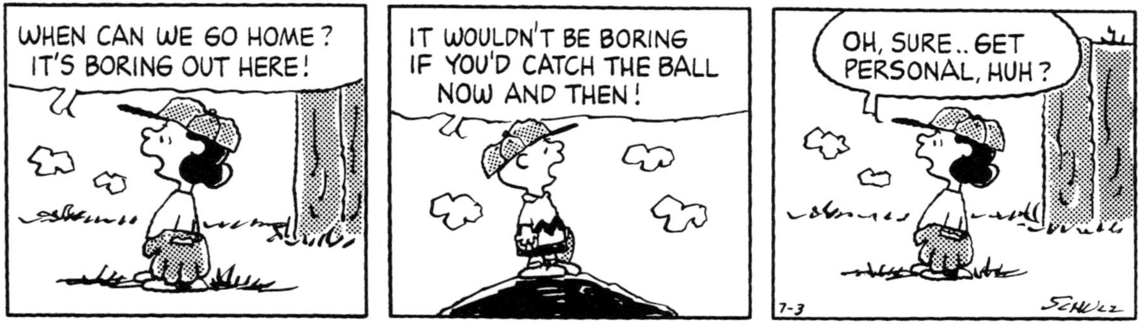
WHEN CAN WE GO HOME? IT'S BORING OUT HERE!
IT WOULDN'T BE BORING IF YOU'D CATCH THE BALL NOW AND THEN!
OH, SURE.. GET PERSONAL, HUH?

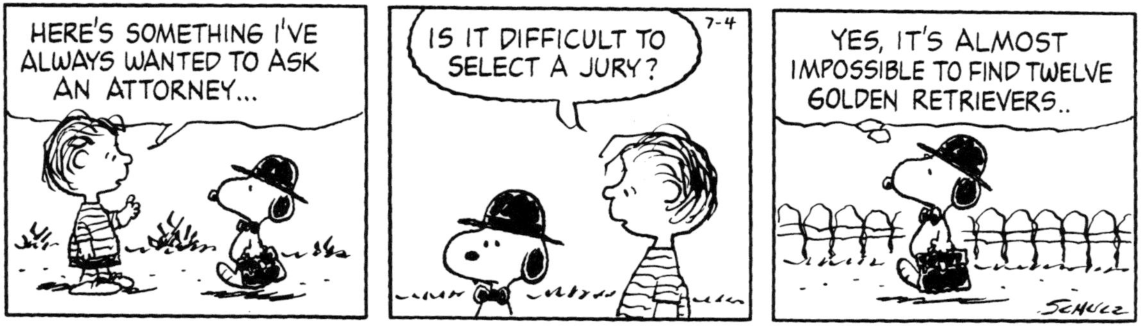
HERE'S SOMETHING I'VE ALWAYS WANTED TO ASK AN ATTORNEY...
IS IT DIFFICULT TO SELECT A JURY?
YES, IT'S ALMOST IMPOSSIBLE TO FIND TWELVE GOLDEN RETRIEVERS..

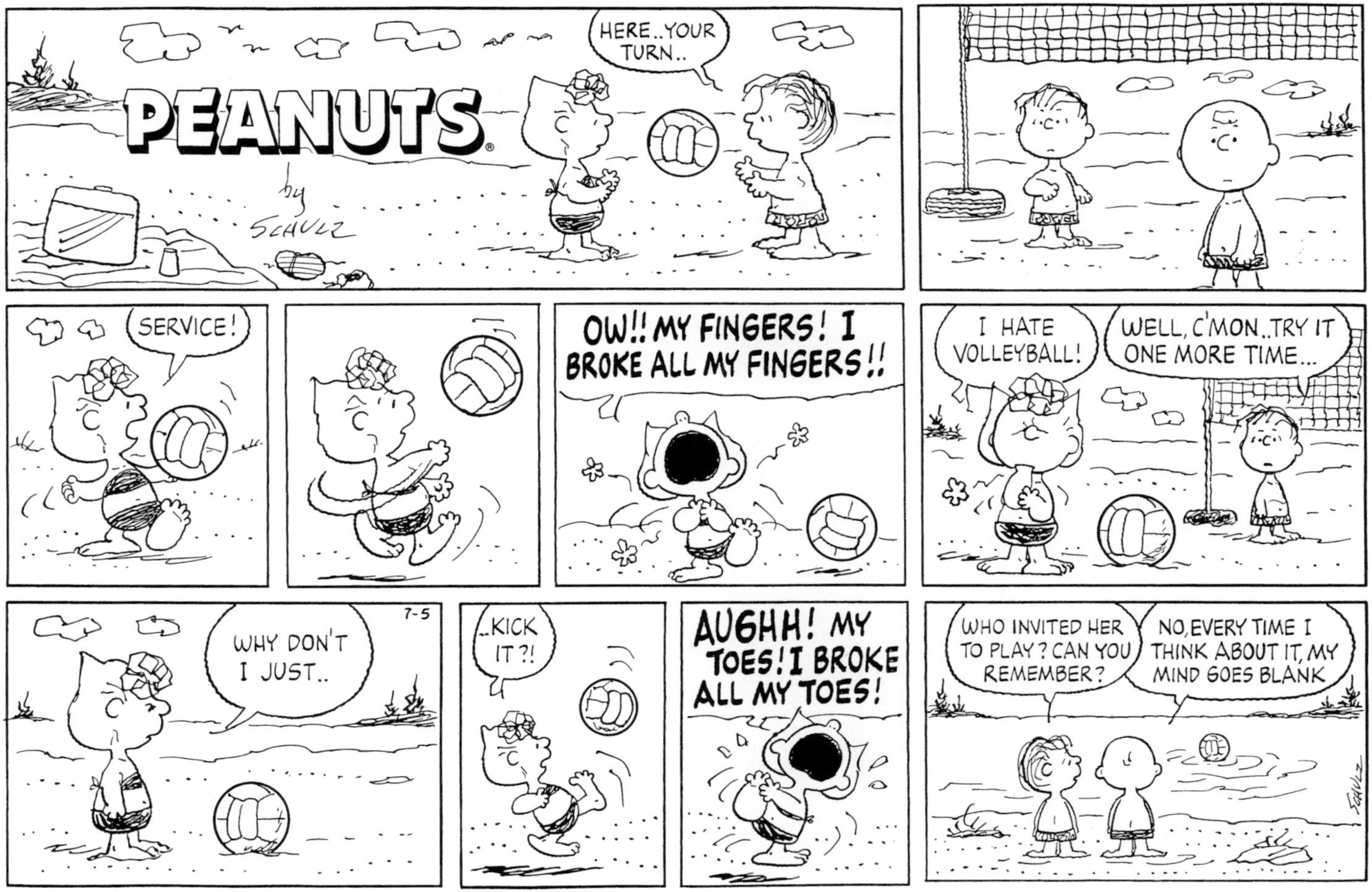
PEANUTS
by SCHULZ
HERE..YOUR TURN..
SERVICE!
OW!! MY FINGERS! I BROKE ALL MY FINGERS!!
I HATE VOLLEYBALL!
WELL, C'MON..TRY IT ONE MORE TIME...
7-5
WHY DON'T I JUST..
..KICK IT?!
AUGHH! MY TOES! I BROKE ALL MY TOES!
WHO INVITED HER TO PLAY? CAN YOU REMEMBER?
NO, EVERY TIME I THINK ABOUT IT, MY MIND GOES BLANK
SCHULZ

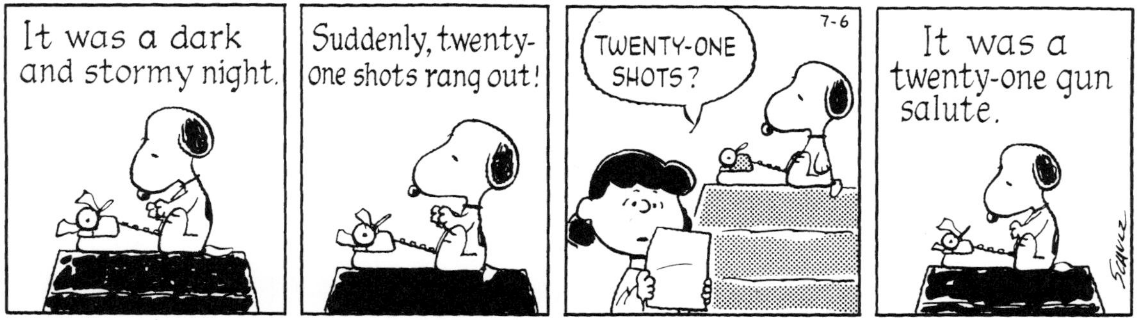
It was a dark and stormy night.
Suddenly, twenty-one shots rang out!
7-6
TWENTY-ONE SHOTS?
It was a twenty-one gun salute.

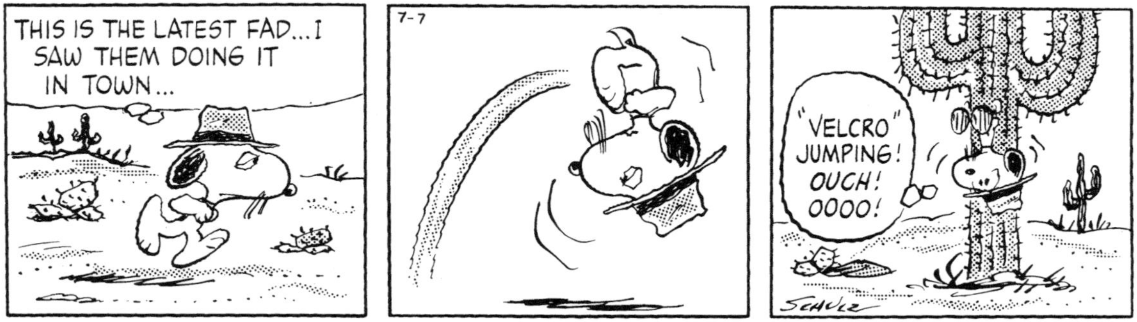
THIS IS THE LATEST FAD...I SAW THEM DOING IT IN TOWN...
7-7
"VELCRO" JUMPING! OUCH! OOOO!

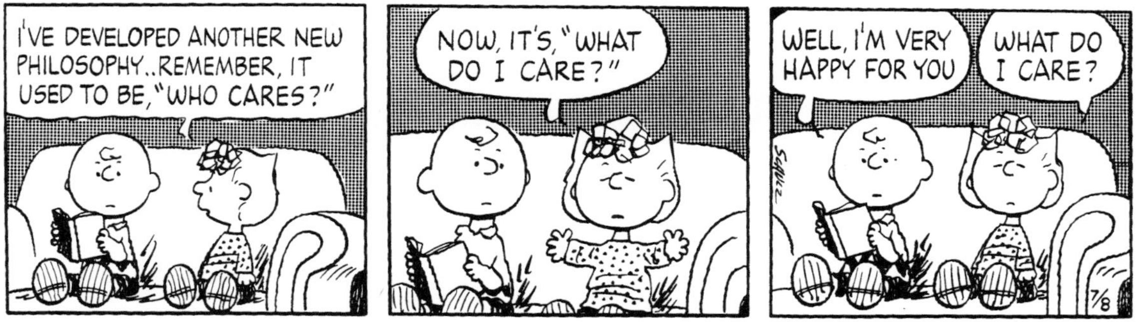
I'VE DEVELOPED ANOTHER NEW PHILOSOPHY..REMEMBER, IT USED TO BE, "WHO CARES?"
NOW, IT'S, "WHAT DO I CARE?"
WELL, I'M VERY HAPPY FOR YOU
WHAT DO I CARE?
7/8

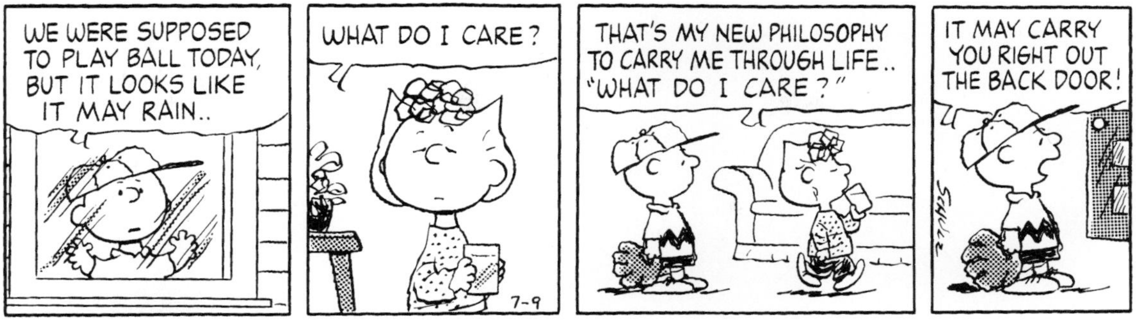
WE WERE SUPPOSED TO PLAY BALL TODAY, BUT IT LOOKS LIKE IT MAY RAIN..
WHAT DO I CARE?
THAT'S MY NEW PHILOSOPHY TO CARRY ME THROUGH LIFE.. "WHAT DO I CARE?"
IT MAY CARRY YOU RIGHT OUT THE BACK DOOR!

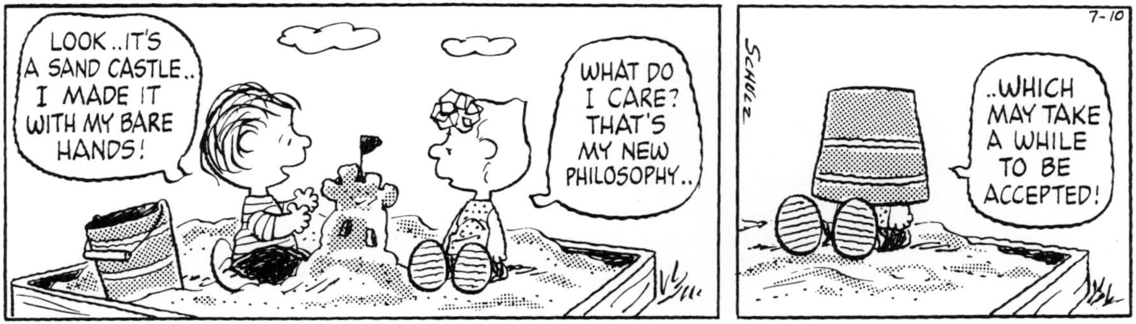
LOOK..IT'S A SAND CASTLE.. I MADE IT WITH MY BARE HANDS!
WHAT DO I CARE? THAT'S MY NEW PHILOSOPHY..
..WHICH MAY TAKE A WHILE TO BE ACCEPTED!

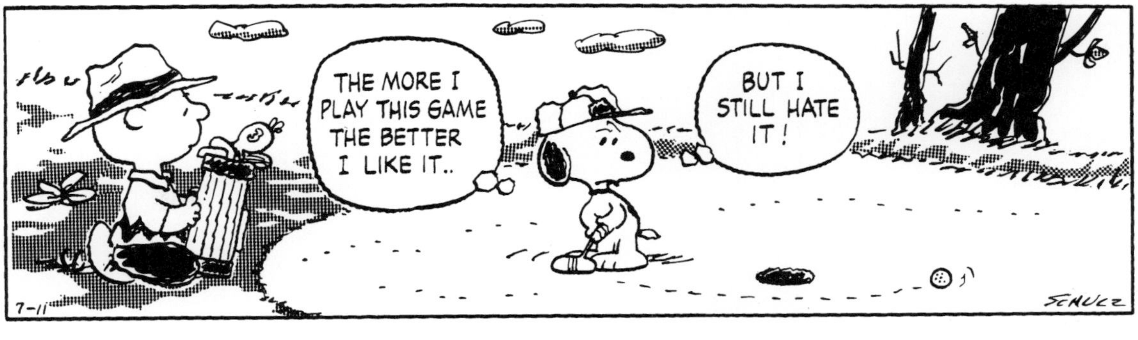
THE MORE I PLAY THIS GAME THE BETTER I LIKE IT..
BUT I STILL HATE IT!

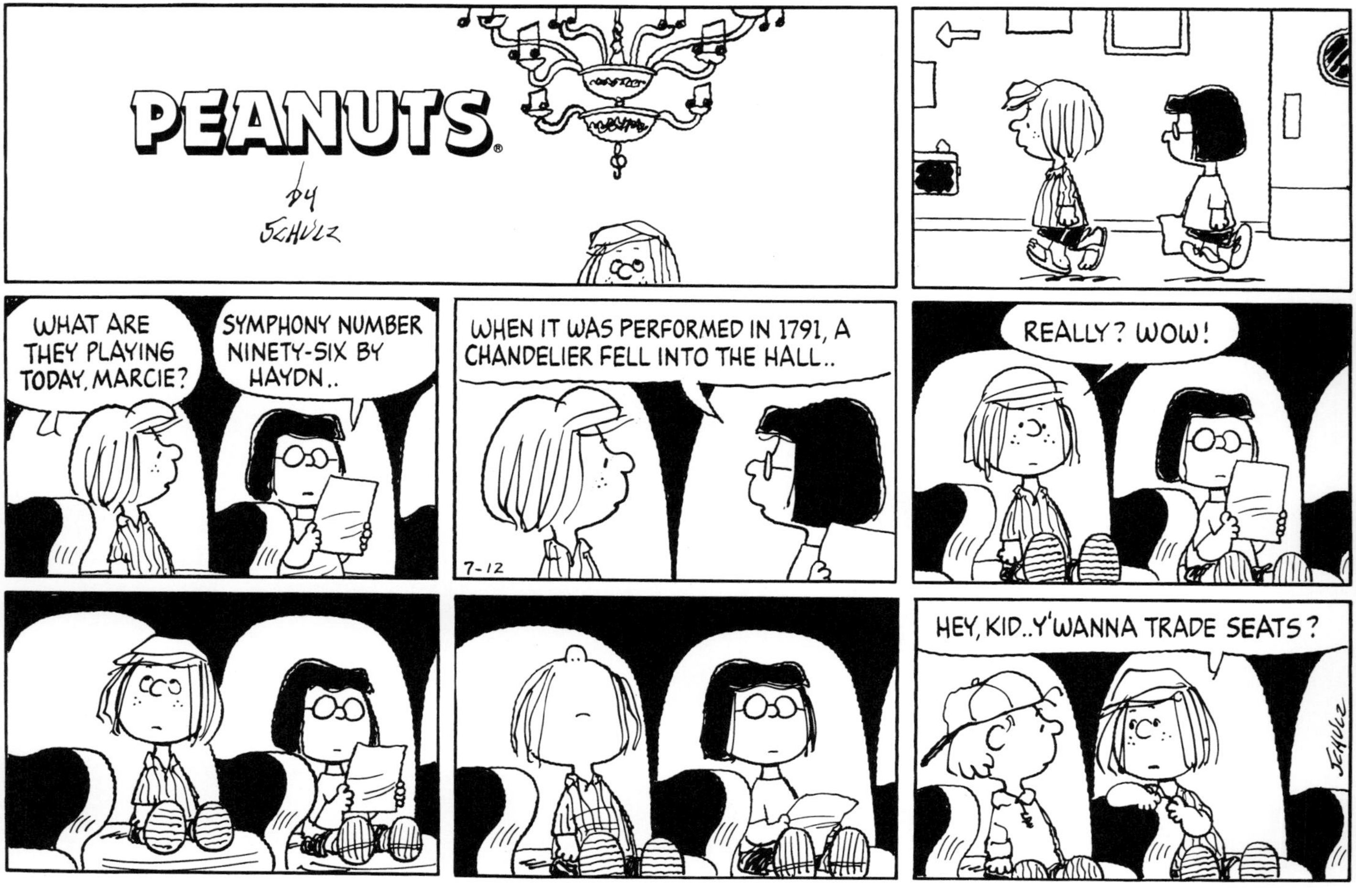
PEANUTS
by SCHULZ
WHAT ARE THEY PLAYING TODAY, MARCIE?
SYMPHONY NUMBER NINETY-SIX BY HAYDN..
WHEN IT WAS PERFORMED IN 1791, A CHANDELIER FELL INTO THE HALL..
7-12
REALLY? WOW!
HEY, KID..Y'WANNA TRADE SEATS?
SCHULZ

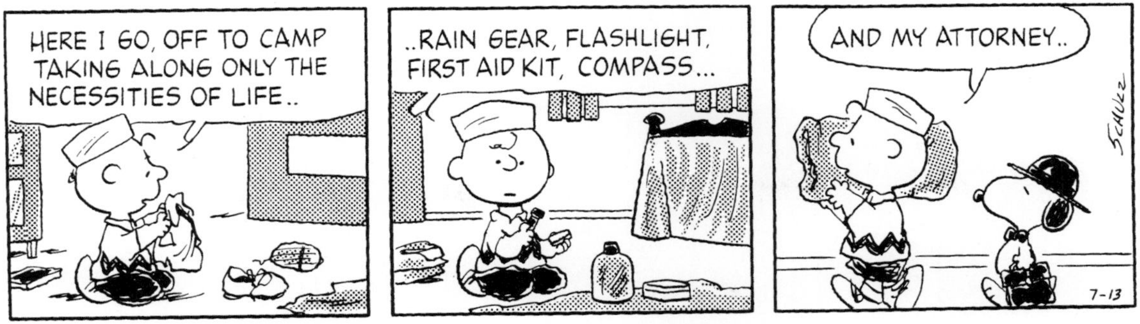
HERE I GO, OFF TO CAMP TAKING ALONG ONLY THE NECESSITIES OF LIFE..
..RAIN GEAR, FLASHLIGHT, FIRST AID KIT, COMPASS...
AND MY ATTORNEY..
SCHULZ
7-13

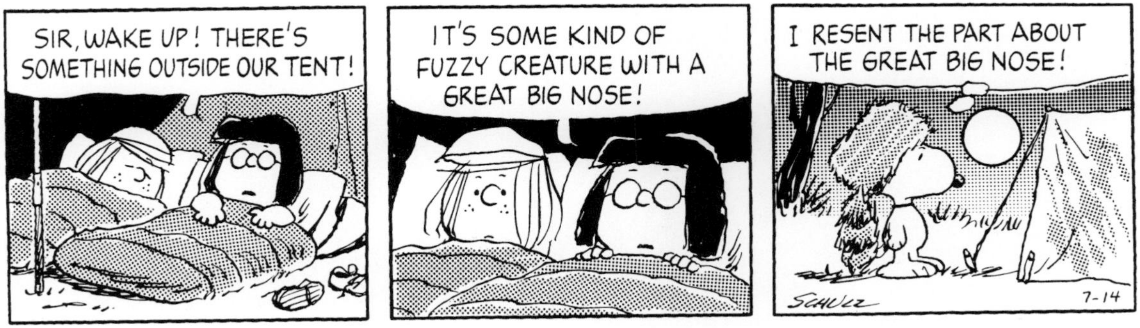
SIR, WAKE UP! THERE'S SOMETHING OUTSIDE OUR TENT!
IT'S SOME KIND OF FUZZY CREATURE WITH A GREAT BIG NOSE!
I RESENT THE PART ABOUT THE GREAT BIG NOSE!
SCHULZ
7-14

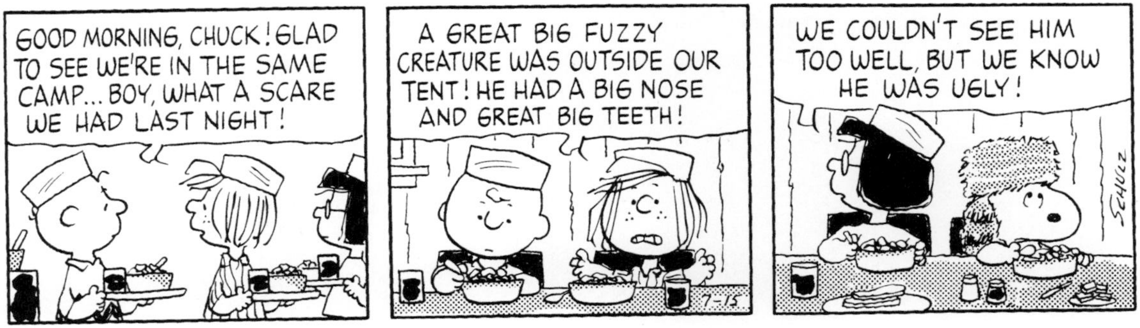
GOOD MORNING, CHUCK! GLAD TO SEE WE'RE IN THE SAME CAMP... BOY, WHAT A SCARE WE HAD LAST NIGHT!
A GREAT BIG FUZZY CREATURE WAS OUTSIDE OUR TENT! HE HAD A BIG NOSE AND GREAT BIG TEETH!
WE COULDN'T SEE HIM TOO WELL, BUT WE KNOW HE WAS UGLY!
7-15
SCHULZ

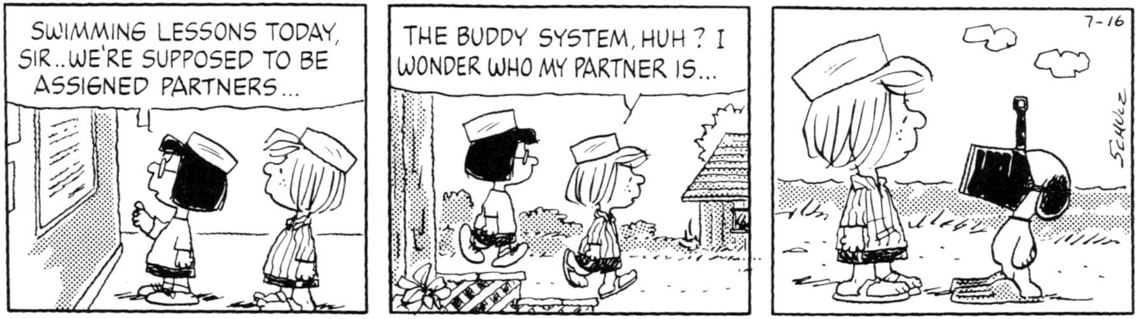
SWIMMING LESSONS TODAY, SIR..WE'RE SUPPOSED TO BE ASSIGNED PARTNERS...
THE BUDDY SYSTEM, HUH? I WONDER WHO MY PARTNER IS...
7-16
SCHULZ

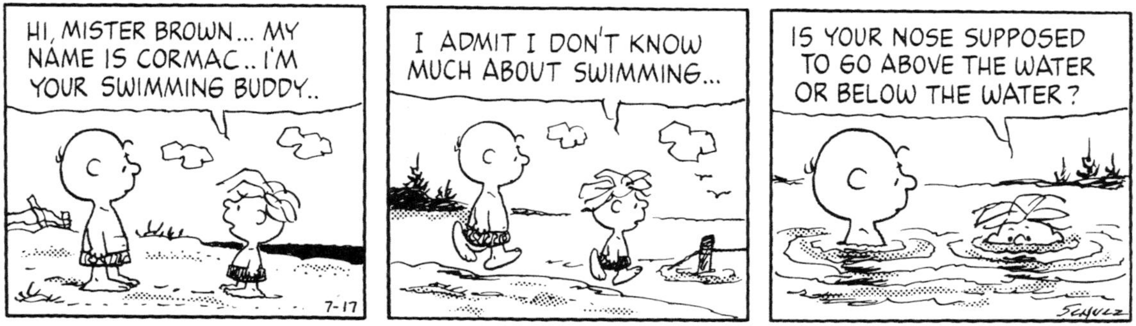
HI, MISTER BROWN... MY NAME IS CORMAC..I'M YOUR SWIMMING BUDDY..
7-17
I ADMIT I DON'T KNOW MUCH ABOUT SWIMMING...
IS YOUR NOSE SUPPOSED TO GO ABOVE THE WATER OR BELOW THE WATER?
SCHULZ

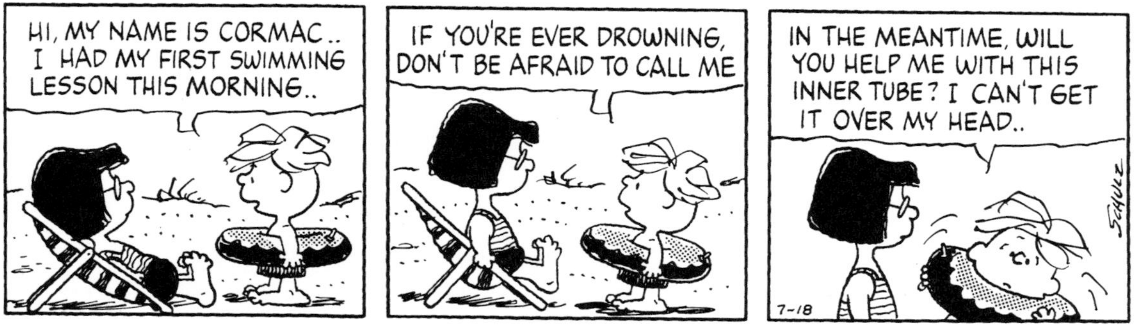
HI, MY NAME IS CORMAC.. I HAD MY FIRST SWIMMING LESSON THIS MORNING..
IF YOU'RE EVER DROWNING, DON'T BE AFRAID TO CALL ME
IN THE MEANTIME, WILL YOU HELP ME WITH THIS INNER TUBE? I CAN'T GET IT OVER MY HEAD..
SCHULZ
7-18

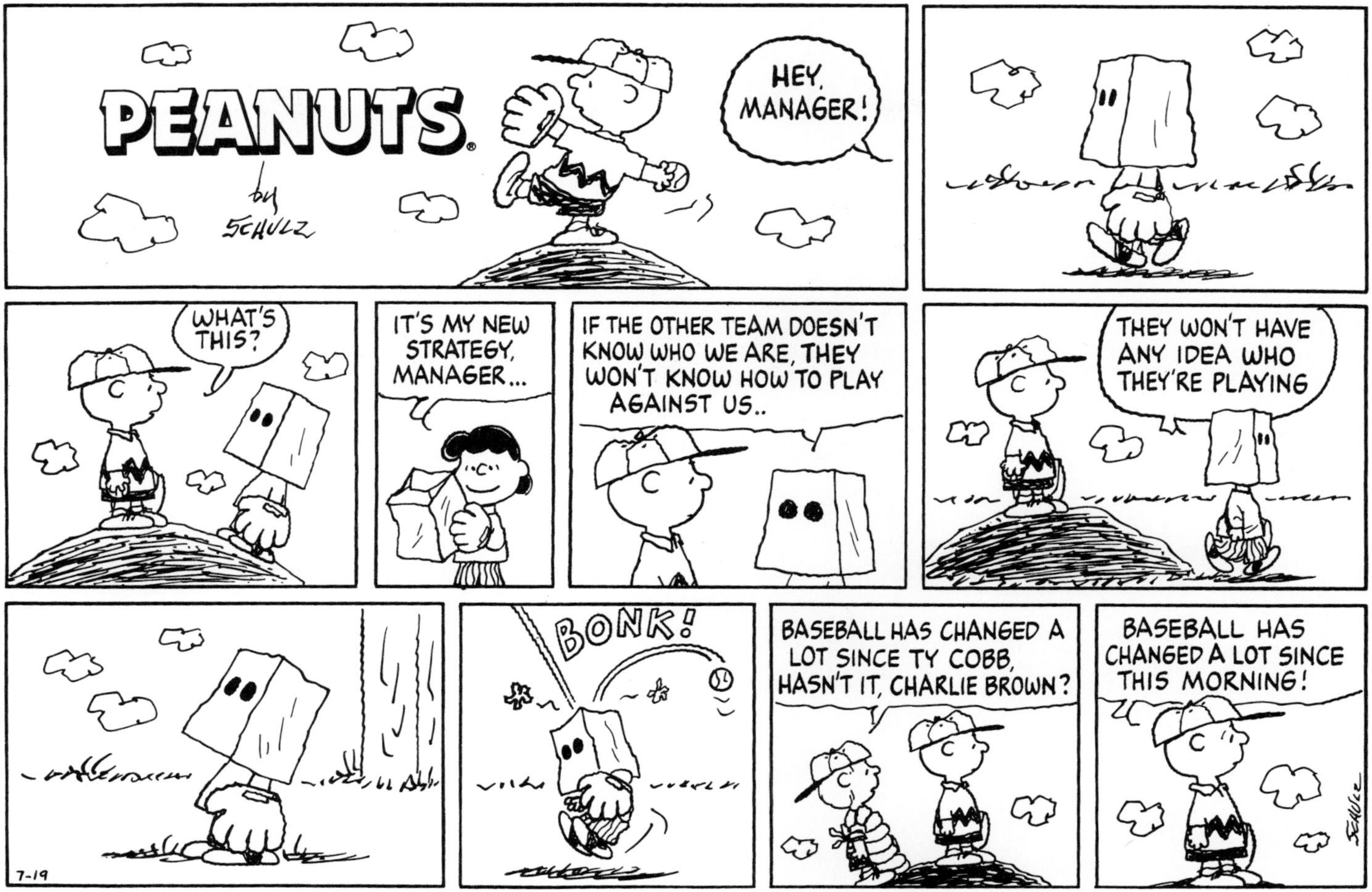
PEANUTS
by SCHULZ
HEY, MANAGER!
WHAT'S THIS?
IT'S MY NEW STRATEGY, MANAGER...
IF THE OTHER TEAM DOESN'T KNOW WHO WE ARE, THEY WON'T KNOW HOW TO PLAY AGAINST US..
THEY WON'T HAVE ANY IDEA WHO THEY'RE PLAYING
7-19
BONK!
BASEBALL HAS CHANGED A LOT SINCE TY COBB, HASN'T IT, CHARLIE BROWN?
BASEBALL HAS CHANGED A LOT SINCE THIS MORNING!
SCHULZ

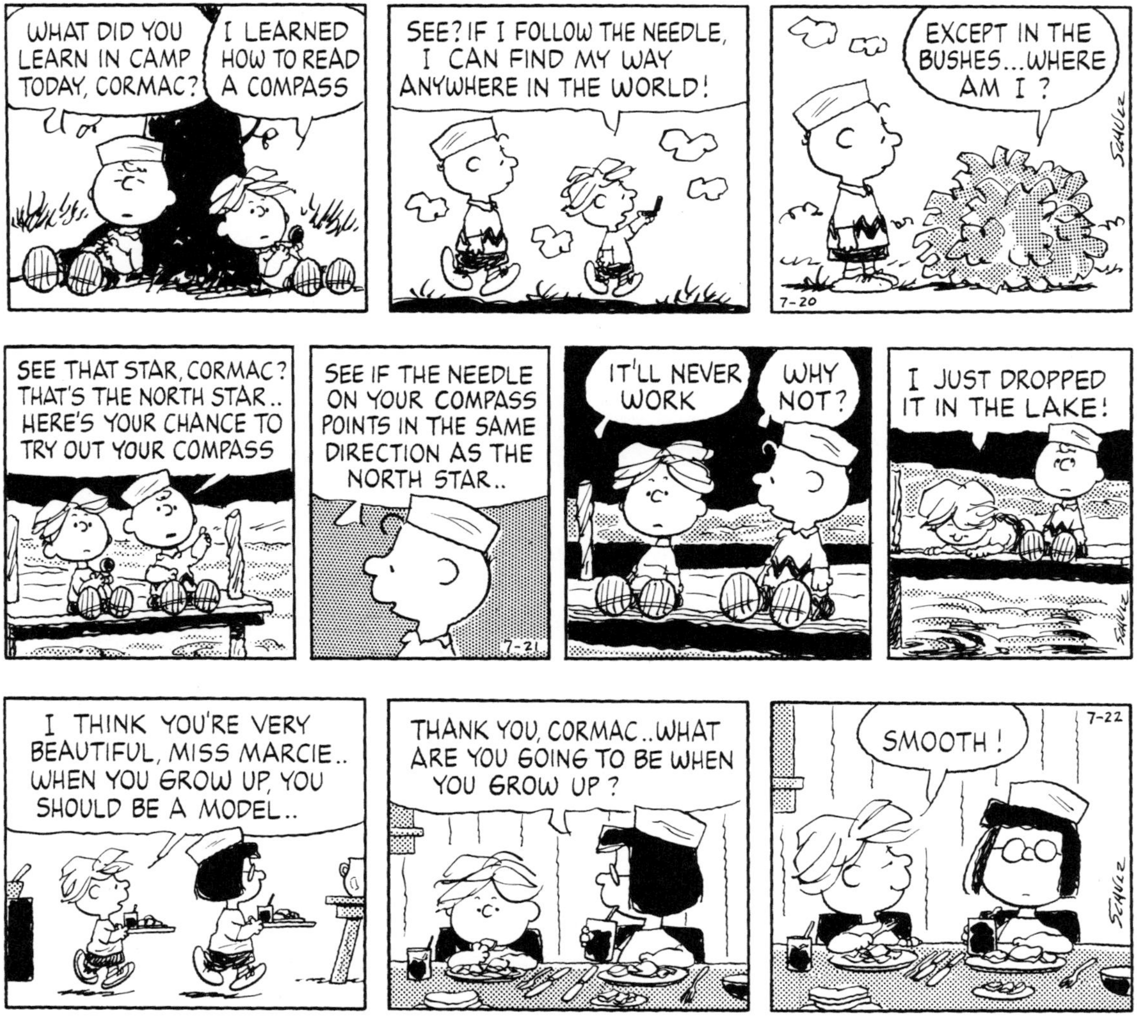
WHAT DID YOU LEARN IN CAMP TODAY, CORMAC?
I LEARNED HOW TO READ A COMPASS
SEE? IF I FOLLOW THE NEEDLE, I CAN FIND MY WAY ANYWHERE IN THE WORLD!
EXCEPT IN THE BUSHES...WHERE AM I?
SCHULZ
7-20
SEE THAT STAR, CORMAC? THAT'S THE NORTH STAR.. HERE'S YOUR CHANCE TO TRY OUT YOUR COMPASS
SEE IF THE NEEDLE ON YOUR COMPASS POINTS IN THE SAME DIRECTION AS THE NORTH STAR..
7-21
IT'LL NEVER WORK
WHY NOT?
I JUST DROPPED IT IN THE LAKE!
SCHULZ
I THINK YOU'RE VERY BEAUTIFUL, MISS MARCIE.. WHEN YOU GROW UP, YOU SHOULD BE A MODEL..
THANK YOU, CORMAC..WHAT ARE YOU GOING TO BE WHEN YOU GROW UP?
7-22
SMOOTH!
SCHULZ

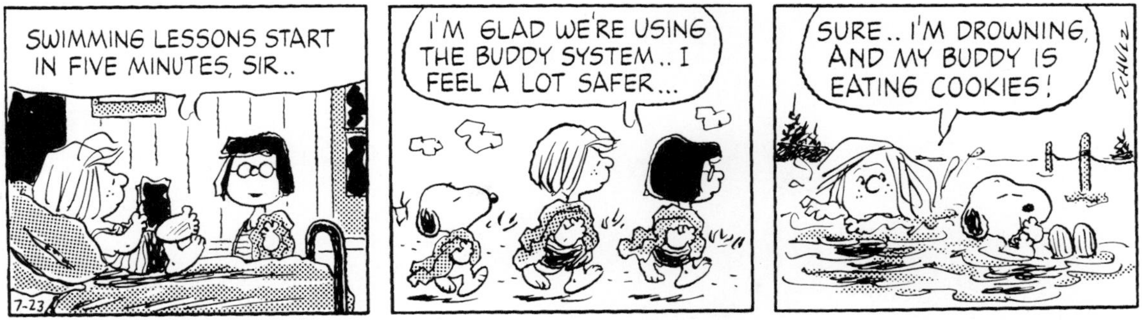
SWIMMING LESSONS START IN FIVE MINUTES, SIR..
I'M GLAD WE'RE USING THE BUDDY SYSTEM.. I FEEL A LOT SAFER...
SURE.. I'M DROWNING, AND MY BUDDY IS EATING COOKIES!

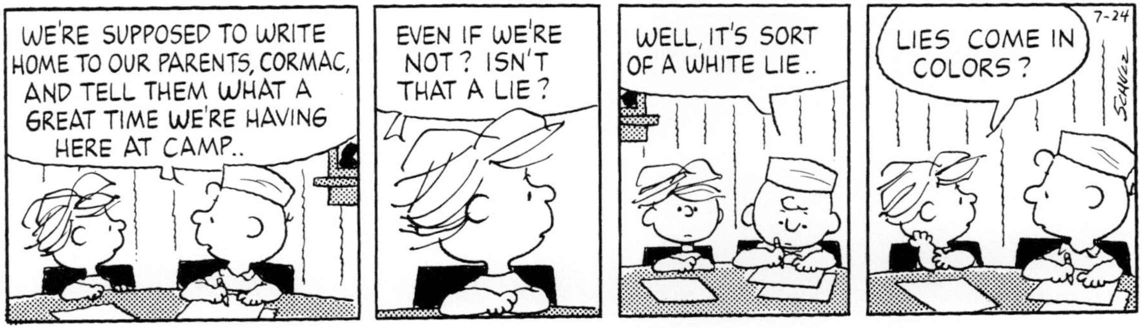
WE'RE SUPPOSED TO WRITE HOME TO OUR PARENTS, CORMAC, AND TELL THEM WHAT A GREAT TIME WE'RE HAVING HERE AT CAMP..
EVEN IF WE'RE NOT? ISN'T THAT A LIE?
WELL, IT'S SORT OF A WHITE LIE..
LIES COME IN COLORS?

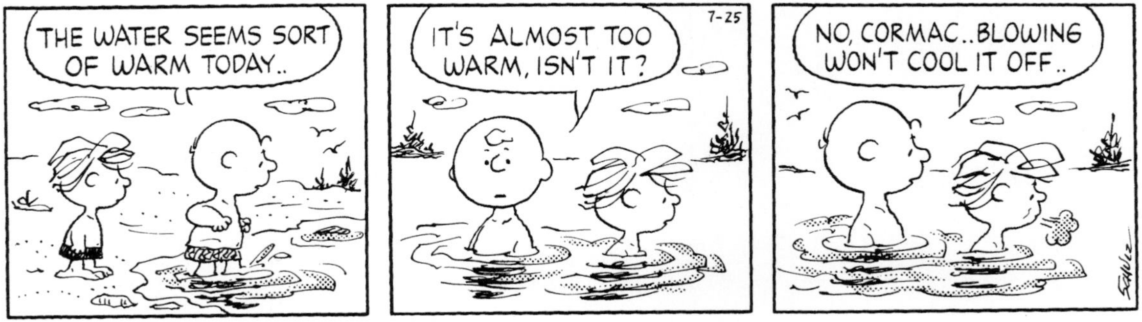
THE WATER SEEMS SORT OF WARM TODAY..
IT'S ALMOST TOO WARM, ISN'T IT?
NO, CORMAC.. BLOWING WON'T COOL IT OFF..

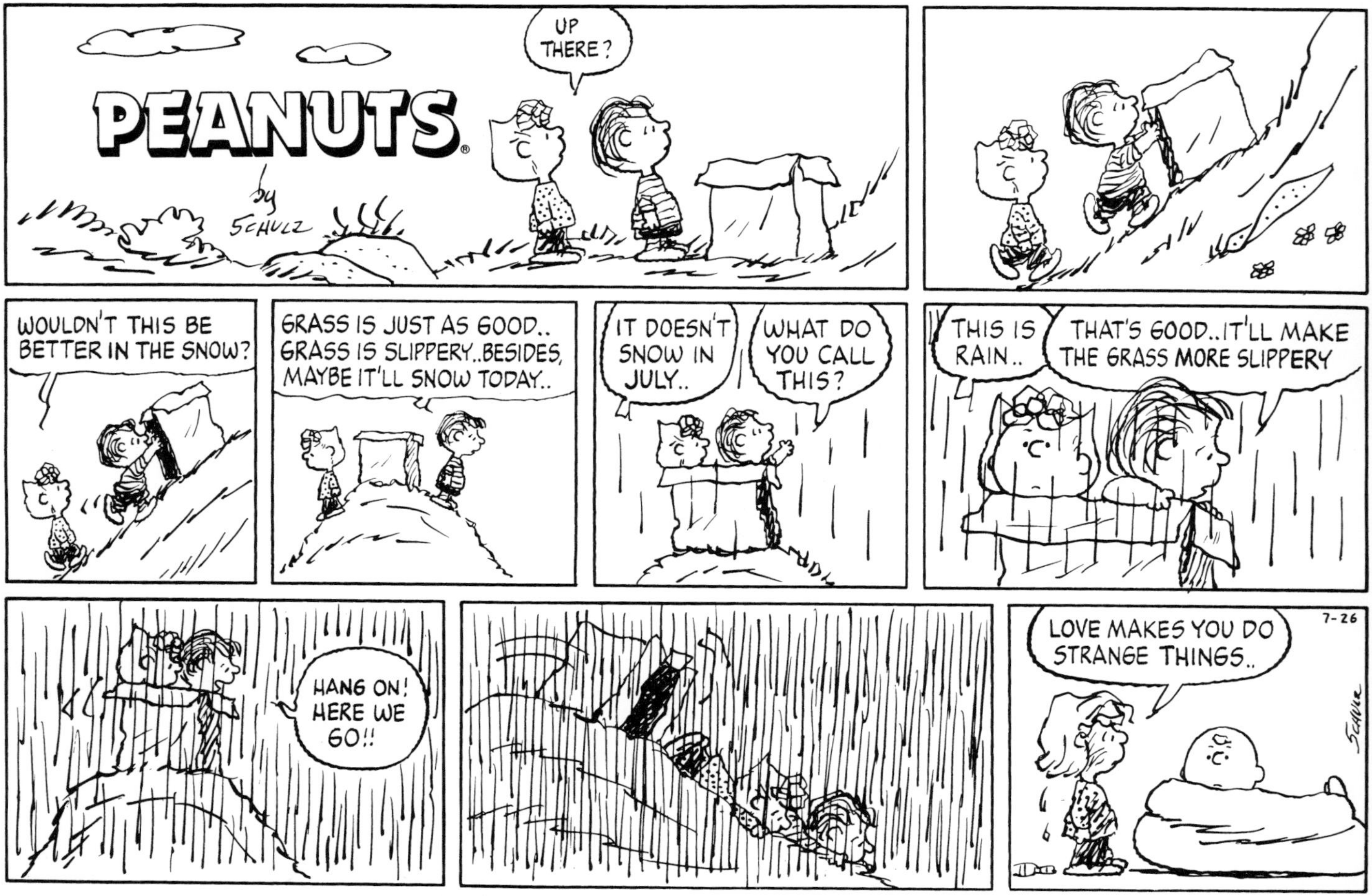
PEANUTS
by SCHULZ
UP THERE?
WOULDN'T THIS BE BETTER IN THE SNOW?
GRASS IS JUST AS GOOD.. GRASS IS SLIPPERY..BESIDES, MAYBE IT'LL SNOW TODAY..
IT DOESN'T SNOW IN JULY..
WHAT DO YOU CALL THIS?
THIS IS RAIN..
THAT'S GOOD..IT'LL MAKE THE GRASS MORE SLIPPERY
HANG ON! HERE WE GO!!
7-26
LOVE MAKES YOU DO STRANGE THINGS..
SCHULZ

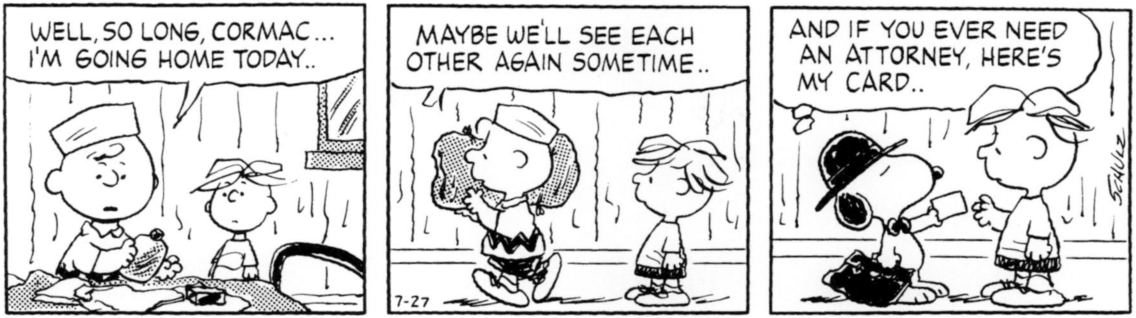
WELL, SO LONG, CORMAC... I'M GOING HOME TODAY..
MAYBE WE'LL SEE EACH OTHER AGAIN SOMETIME..
AND IF YOU EVER NEED AN ATTORNEY, HERE'S MY CARD..

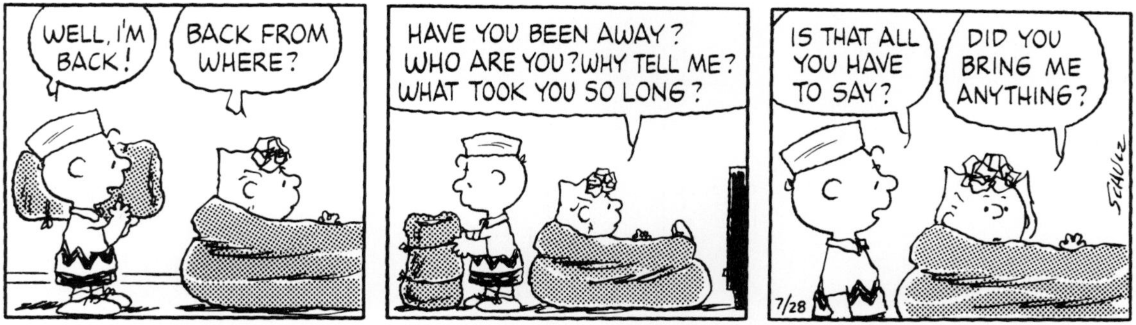
WELL, I'M BACK!
BACK FROM WHERE?
HAVE YOU BEEN AWAY? WHO ARE YOU? WHY TELL ME? WHAT TOOK YOU SO LONG?
IS THAT ALL YOU HAVE TO SAY?
DID YOU BRING ME ANYTHING?

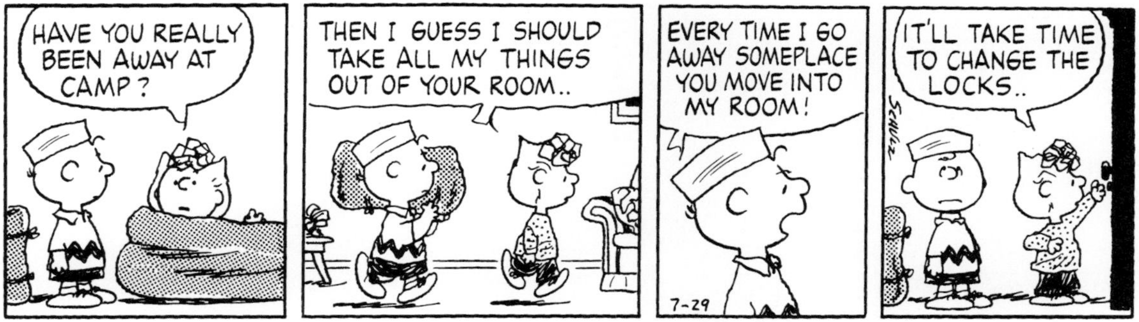
HAVE YOU REALLY BEEN AWAY AT CAMP?
THEN I GUESS I SHOULD TAKE ALL MY THINGS OUT OF YOUR ROOM..
EVERY TIME I GO AWAY SOMEPLACE YOU MOVE INTO MY ROOM!
IT'LL TAKE TIME TO CHANGE THE LOCKS..

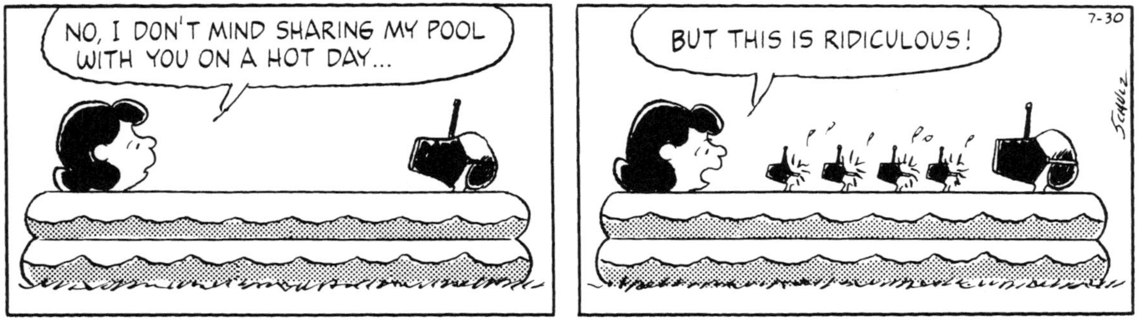
NO, I DON'T MIND SHARING MY POOL WITH YOU ON A HOT DAY...
7-30
BUT THIS IS RIDICULOUS!

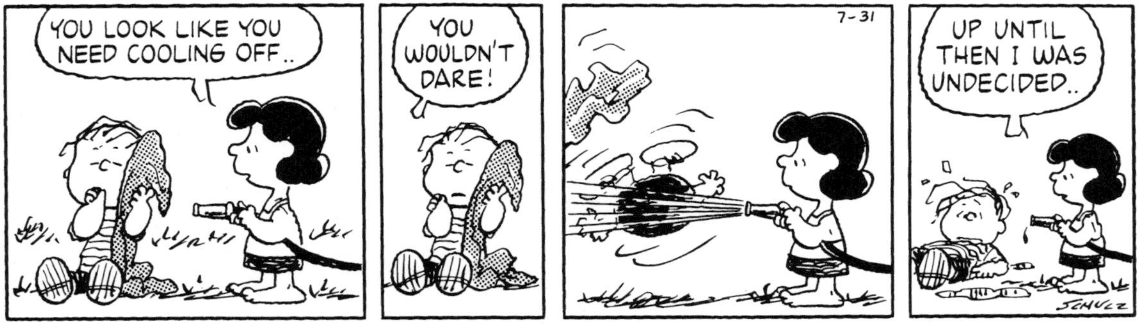
YOU LOOK LIKE YOU NEED COOLING OFF..
YOU WOULDN'T DARE!
7-31
UP UNTIL THEN I WAS UNDECIDED..

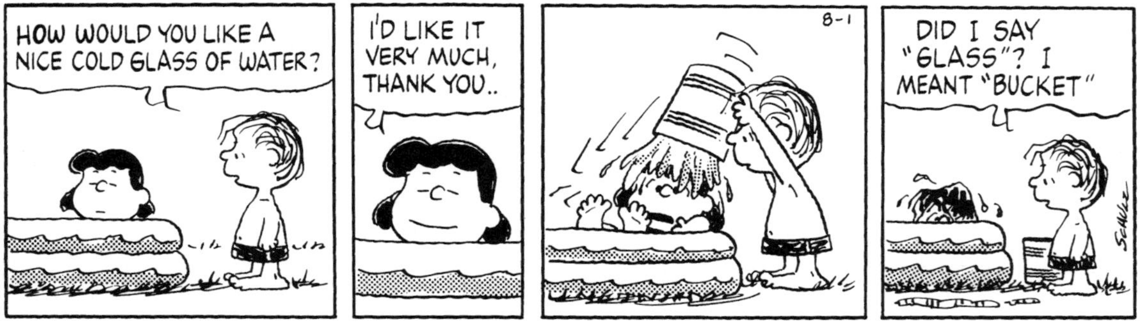
HOW WOULD YOU LIKE A NICE COLD GLASS OF WATER?
I'D LIKE IT VERY MUCH, THANK YOU..
8-1
DID I SAY "GLASS"? I MEANT "BUCKET"

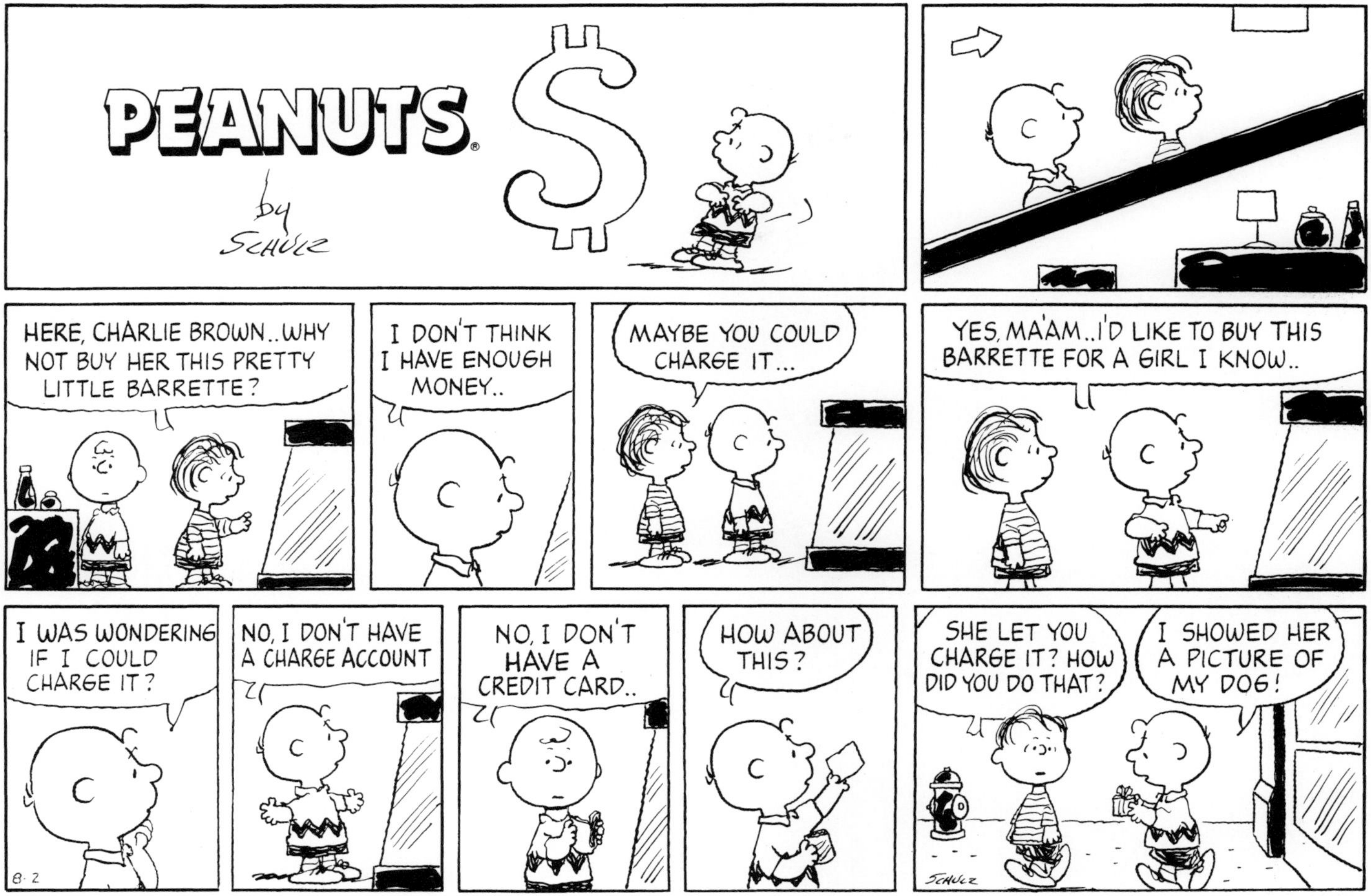
PEANUTS
by SCHULZ
HERE, CHARLIE BROWN..WHY NOT BUY HER THIS PRETTY LITTLE BARRETTE?
I DON'T THINK I HAVE ENOUGH MONEY..
MAYBE YOU COULD CHARGE IT...
YES, MA'AM..I'D LIKE TO BUY THIS BARRETTE FOR A GIRL I KNOW..
I WAS WONDERING IF I COULD CHARGE IT?
NO, I DON'T HAVE A CHARGE ACCOUNT
NO, I DON'T HAVE A CREDIT CARD..
HOW ABOUT THIS?
SHE LET YOU CHARGE IT? HOW DID YOU DO THAT?
I SHOWED HER A PICTURE OF MY DOG!
8-2
SCHULZ

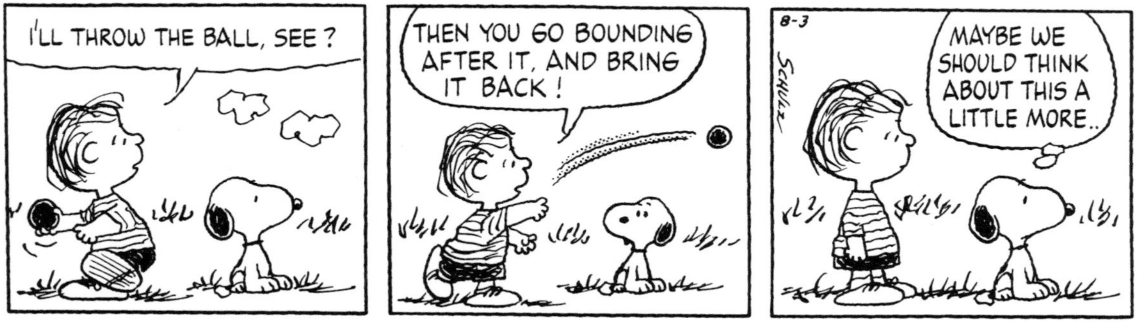
I'LL THROW THE BALL, SEE?
THEN YOU GO BOUNDING AFTER IT, AND BRING IT BACK!
8-3
SCHULZ
MAYBE WE SHOULD THINK ABOUT THIS A LITTLE MORE..

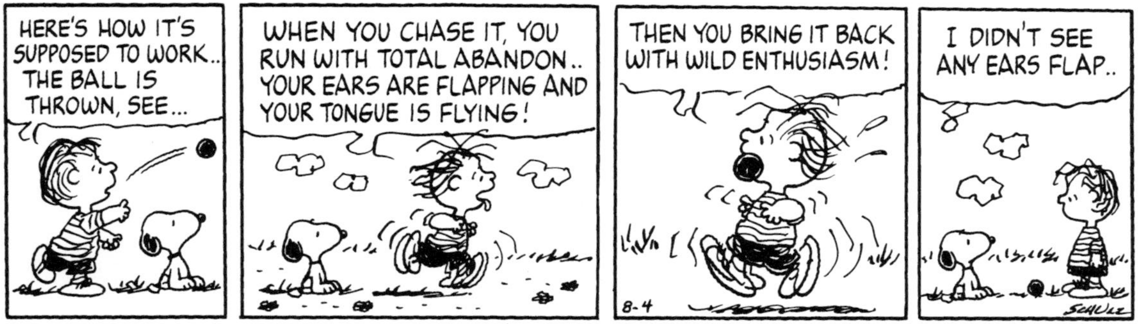
HERE'S HOW IT'S SUPPOSED TO WORK.. THE BALL IS THROWN, SEE...
WHEN YOU CHASE IT, YOU RUN WITH TOTAL ABANDON.. YOUR EARS ARE FLAPPING AND YOUR TONGUE IS FLYING!
THEN YOU BRING IT BACK WITH WILD ENTHUSIASM!
8-4
I DIDN'T SEE ANY EARS FLAP..
SCHULZ

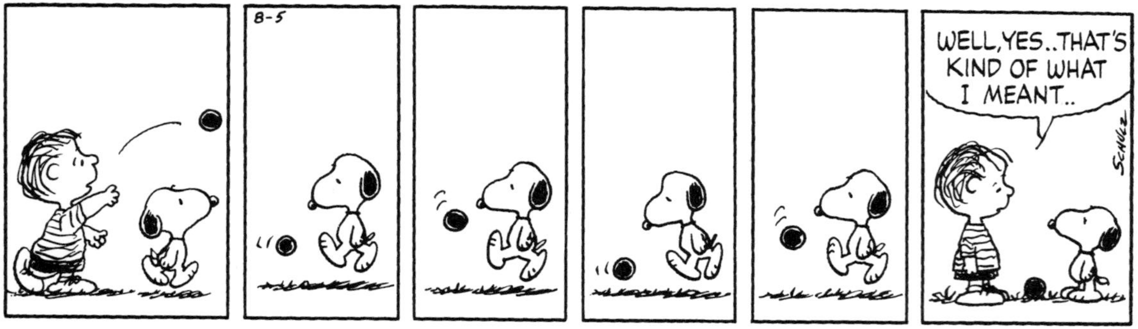
8-5
WELL, YES..THAT'S KIND OF WHAT I MEANT..
SCHULZ

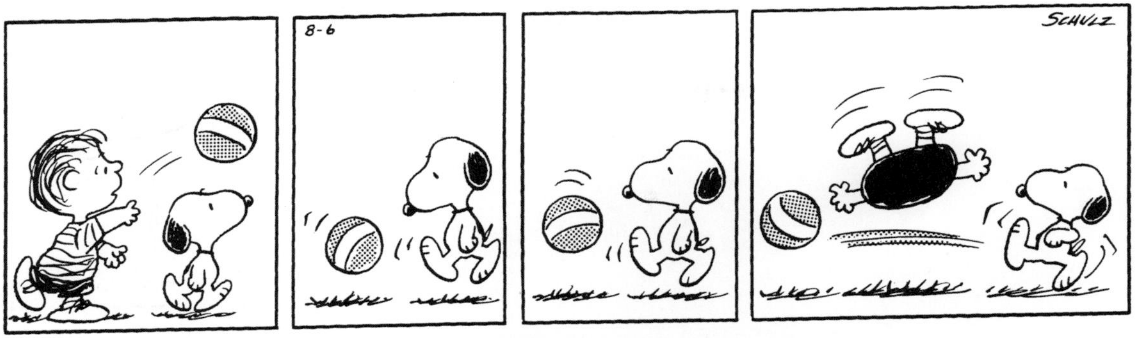
8-6
SCHULZ

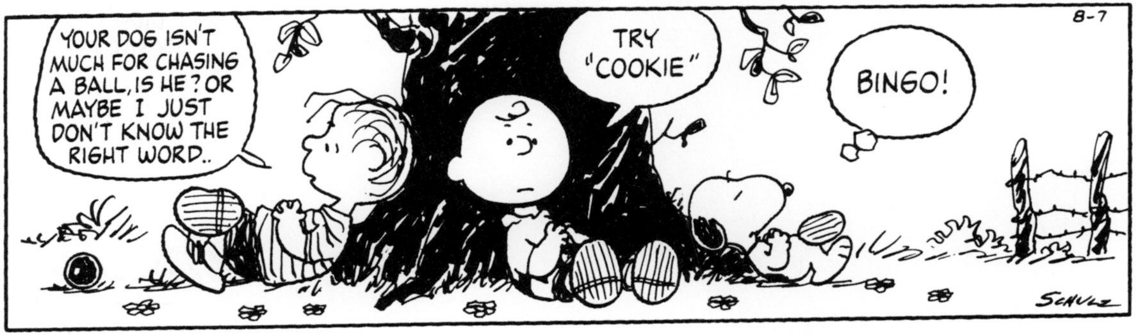
8-7
YOUR DOG ISN'T MUCH FOR CHASING A BALL, IS HE? OR MAYBE I JUST DON'T KNOW THE RIGHT WORD..
TRY "COOKIE"
BINGO!
SCHULZ

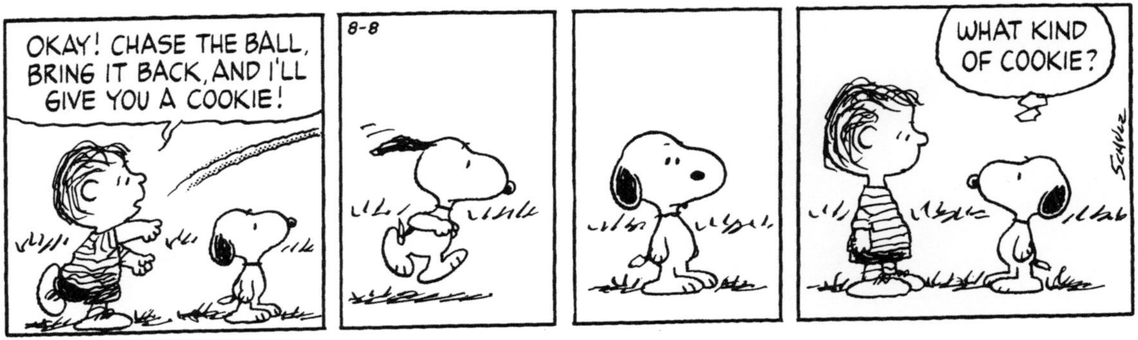
OKAY! CHASE THE BALL, BRING IT BACK, AND I'LL GIVE YOU A COOKIE!
8-8
WHAT KIND OF COOKIE?
SCHULZ

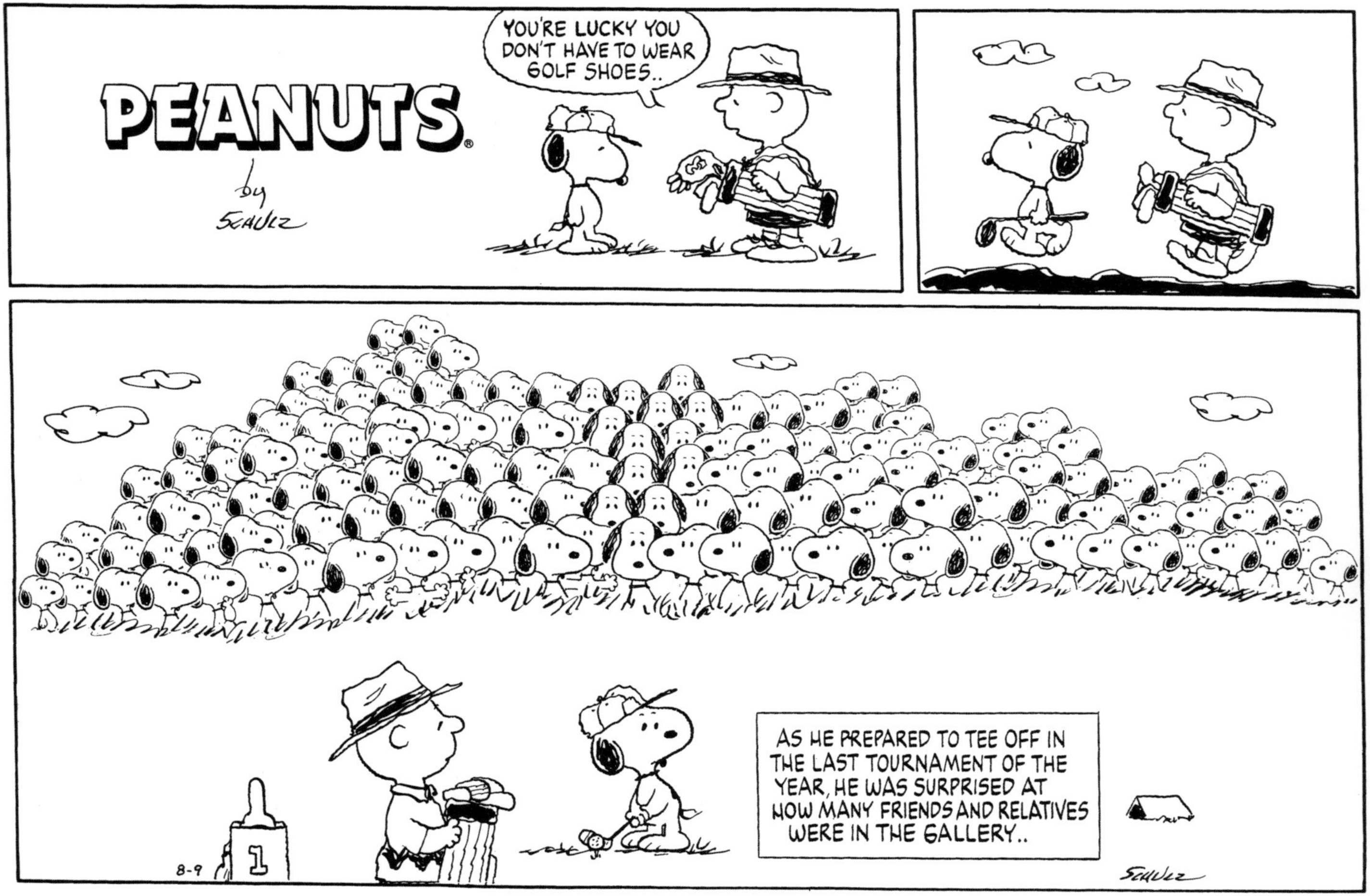
PEANUTS®
by SCHULZ
YOU'RE LUCKY YOU DON'T HAVE TO WEAR GOLF SHOES..
1
8-9
AS HE PREPARED TO TEE OFF IN THE LAST TOURNAMENT OF THE YEAR, HE WAS SURPRISED AT HOW MANY FRIENDS AND RELATIVES WERE IN THE GALLERY..
SCHULZ

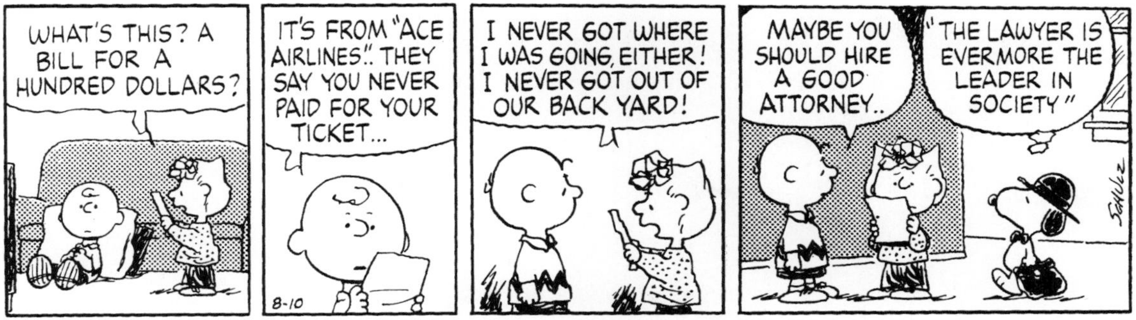
WHAT'S THIS? A BILL FOR A HUNDRED DOLLARS?
IT'S FROM "ACE AIRLINES". THEY SAY YOU NEVER PAID FOR YOUR TICKET...
8-10
I NEVER GOT WHERE I WAS GOING, EITHER! I NEVER GOT OUT OF OUR BACK YARD!
MAYBE YOU SHOULD HIRE A GOOD ATTORNEY..
"THE LAWYER IS EVERMORE THE LEADER IN SOCIETY"
SCHULZ

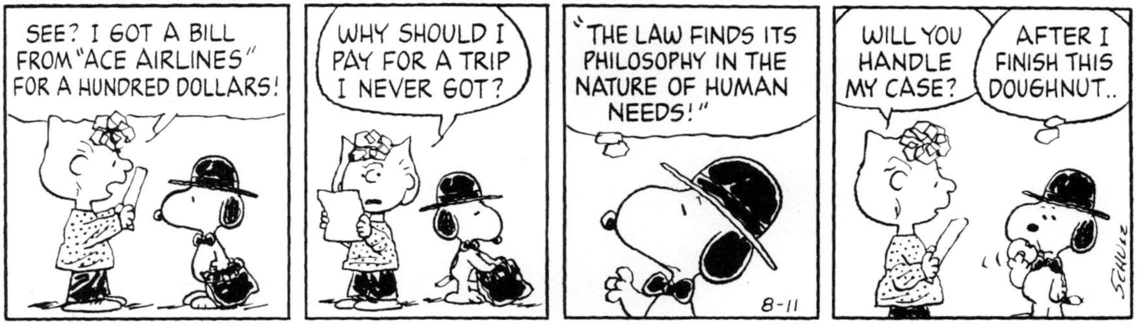
SEE? I GOT A BILL FROM "ACE AIRLINES" FOR A HUNDRED DOLLARS!
WHY SHOULD I PAY FOR A TRIP I NEVER GOT?
"THE LAW FINDS ITS PHILOSOPHY IN THE NATURE OF HUMAN NEEDS!"
8-11
WILL YOU HANDLE MY CASE?
AFTER I FINISH THIS DOUGHNUT..
SCHULZ

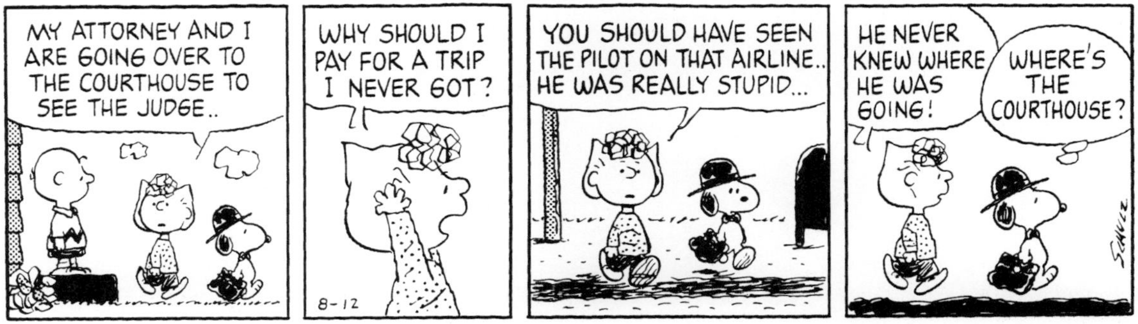
MY ATTORNEY AND I ARE GOING OVER TO THE COURTHOUSE TO SEE THE JUDGE..
WHY SHOULD I PAY FOR A TRIP I NEVER GOT?
8-12
YOU SHOULD HAVE SEEN THE PILOT ON THAT AIRLINE.. HE WAS REALLY STUPID...
HE NEVER KNEW WHERE HE WAS GOING!
WHERE'S THE COURTHOUSE?
SCHULZ

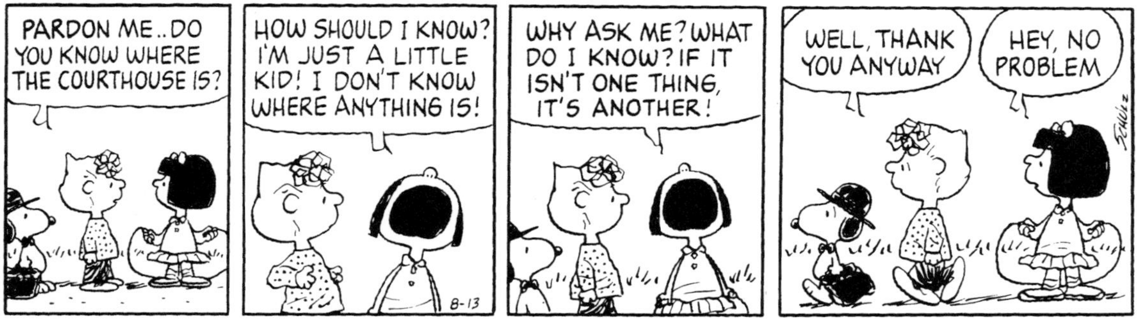
PARDON ME..DO YOU KNOW WHERE THE COURTHOUSE IS?
HOW SHOULD I KNOW? I'M JUST A LITTLE KID! I DON'T KNOW WHERE ANYTHING IS!
8-13
WHY ASK ME? WHAT DO I KNOW? IF IT ISN'T ONE THING, IT'S ANOTHER!
WELL, THANK YOU ANYWAY
HEY, NO PROBLEM
SCHULZ

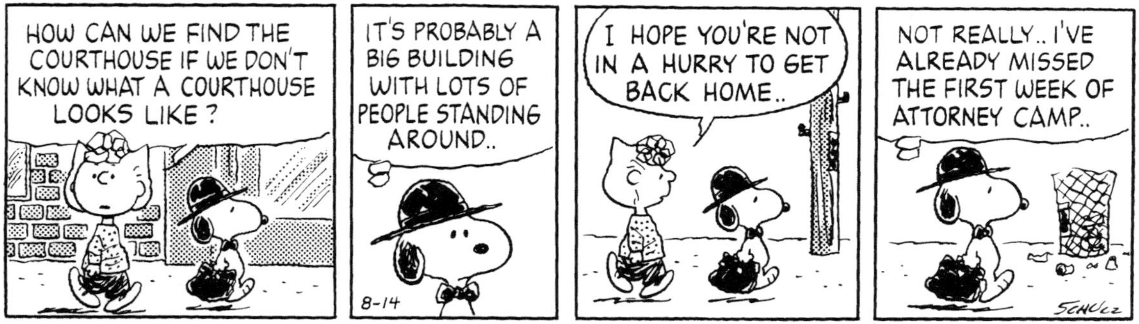
HOW CAN WE FIND THE COURTHOUSE IF WE DON'T KNOW WHAT A COURTHOUSE LOOKS LIKE?
IT'S PROBABLY A BIG BUILDING WITH LOTS OF PEOPLE STANDING AROUND..
8-14
I HOPE YOU'RE NOT IN A HURRY TO GET BACK HOME..
NOT REALLY.. I'VE ALREADY MISSED THE FIRST WEEK OF ATTORNEY CAMP..
SCHULZ

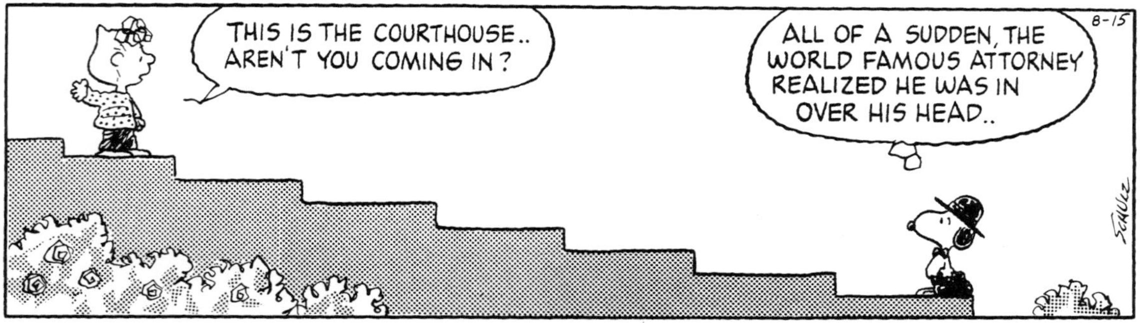
THIS IS THE COURTHOUSE.. AREN'T YOU COMING IN?
8-15
ALL OF A SUDDEN, THE WORLD FAMOUS ATTORNEY REALIZED HE WAS IN OVER HIS HEAD..
SCHULZ

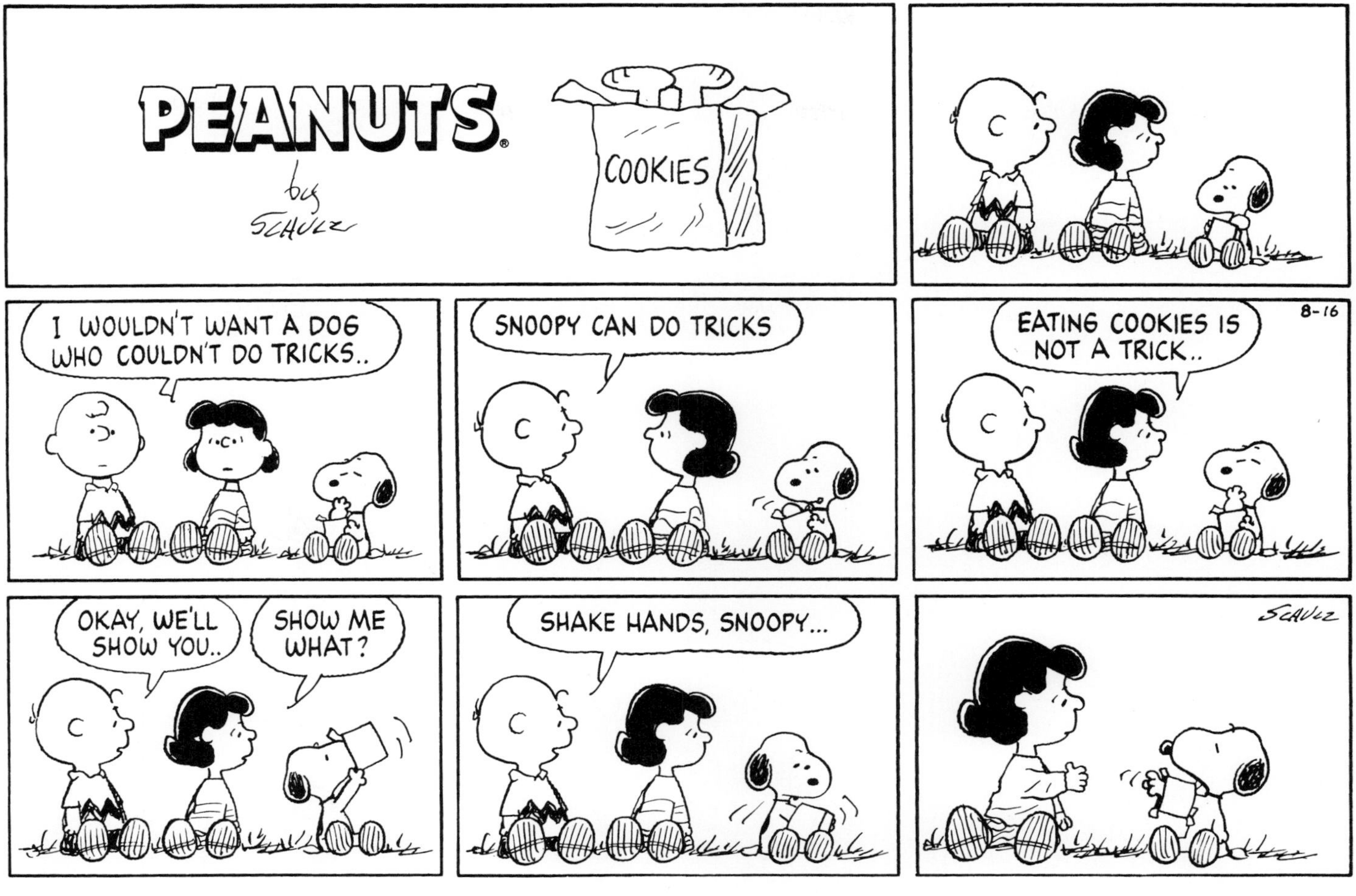
PEANUTS
by SCHULZ
COOKIES
I WOULDN'T WANT A DOG WHO COULDN'T DO TRICKS..
SNOOPY CAN DO TRICKS
EATING COOKIES IS NOT A TRICK..
8-16
OKAY, WE'LL SHOW YOU..
SHOW ME WHAT?
SHAKE HANDS, SNOOPY...
SCHULZ

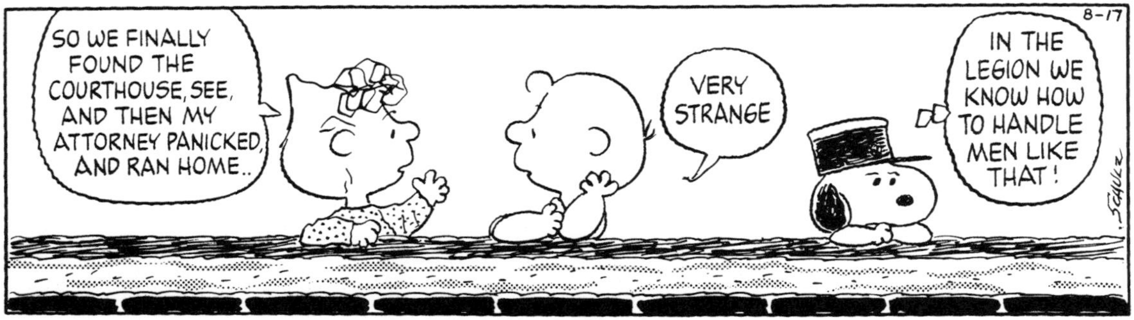
SO WE FINALLY FOUND THE COURTHOUSE, SEE, AND THEN MY ATTORNEY PANICKED, AND RAN HOME..
VERY STRANGE
IN THE LEGION WE KNOW HOW TO HANDLE MEN LIKE THAT!
8-17
SCHULZ

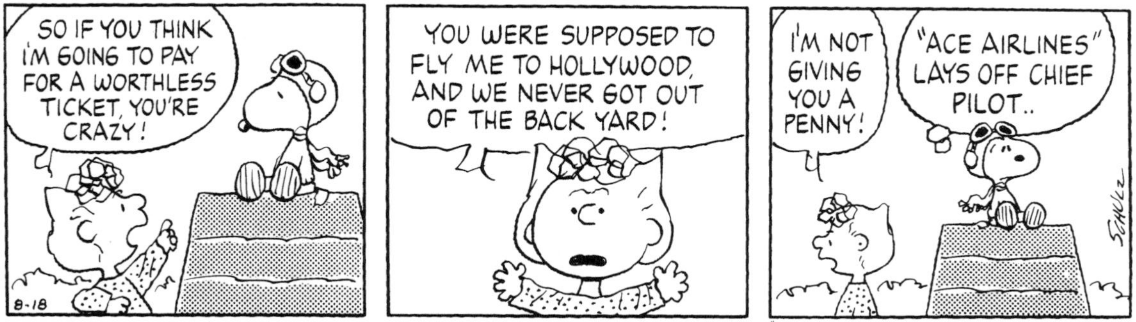
SO IF YOU THINK I'M GOING TO PAY FOR A WORTHLESS TICKET, YOU'RE CRAZY!
8-18
YOU WERE SUPPOSED TO FLY ME TO HOLLYWOOD, AND WE NEVER GOT OUT OF THE BACK YARD!
I'M NOT GIVING YOU A PENNY!
"ACE AIRLINES" LAYS OFF CHIEF PILOT..
SCHULZ

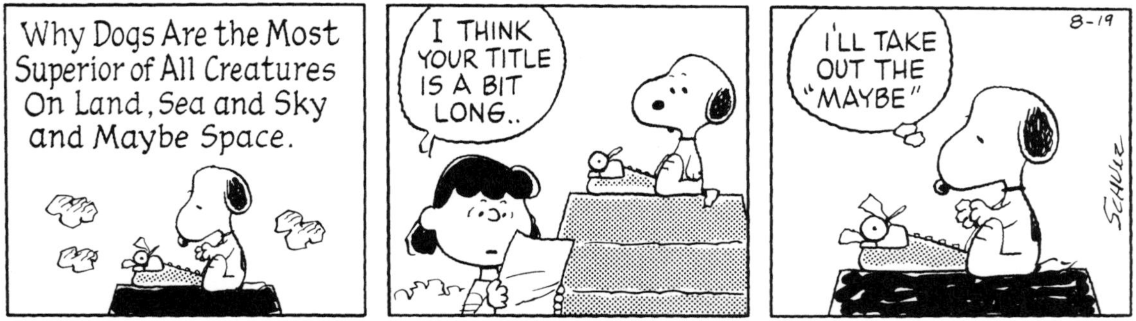
Why Dogs Are the Most Superior of All Creatures On Land, Sea and Sky and Maybe Space.
I THINK YOUR TITLE IS A BIT LONG..
I'LL TAKE OUT THE "MAYBE"
8-19
SCHULZ

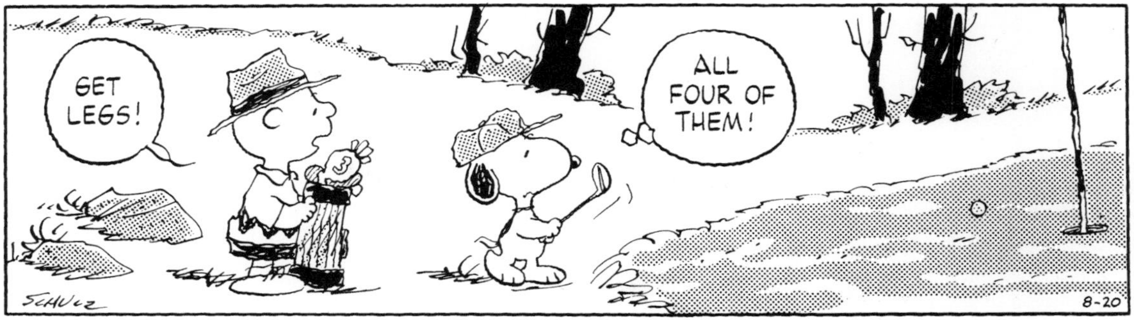
GET LEGS!
ALL FOUR OF THEM!
SCHULZ
8-20

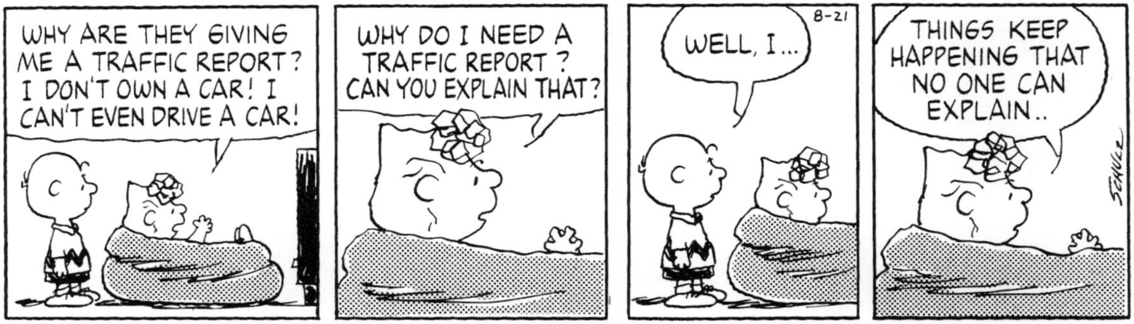
WHY ARE THEY GIVING ME A TRAFFIC REPORT? I DON'T OWN A CAR! I CAN'T EVEN DRIVE A CAR!
WHY DO I NEED A TRAFFIC REPORT? CAN YOU EXPLAIN THAT?
8-21
WELL, I...
THINGS KEEP HAPPENING THAT NO ONE CAN EXPLAIN..
SCHULZ

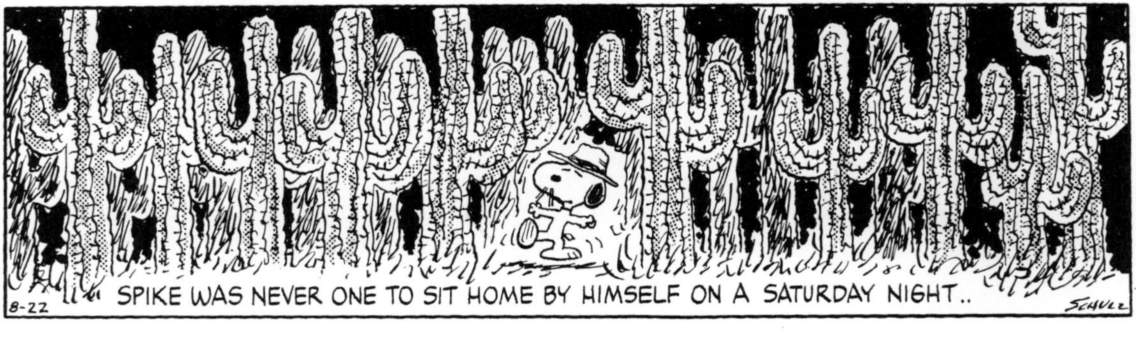
8-22
SPIKE WAS NEVER ONE TO SIT HOME BY HIMSELF ON A SATURDAY NIGHT..
SCHULZ

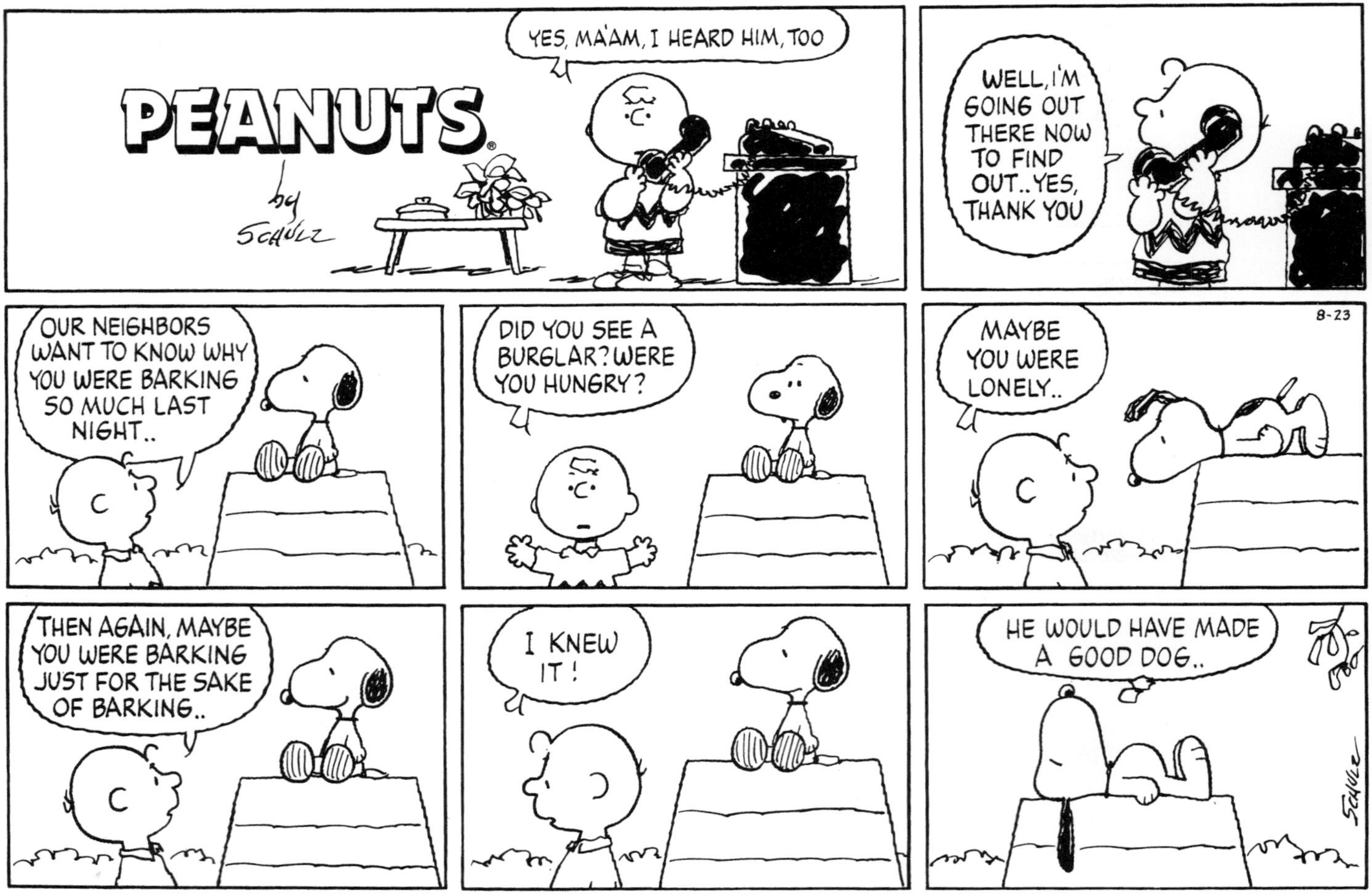
PEANUTS
by SCHULZ
YES, MA'AM, I HEARD HIM, TOO
WELL, I'M GOING OUT THERE NOW TO FIND OUT.. YES, THANK YOU
OUR NEIGHBORS WANT TO KNOW WHY YOU WERE BARKING SO MUCH LAST NIGHT..
DID YOU SEE A BURGLAR? WERE YOU HUNGRY?
8-23
MAYBE YOU WERE LONELY..
THEN AGAIN, MAYBE YOU WERE BARKING JUST FOR THE SAKE OF BARKING..
I KNEW IT!
HE WOULD HAVE MADE A GOOD DOG..
SCHULZ

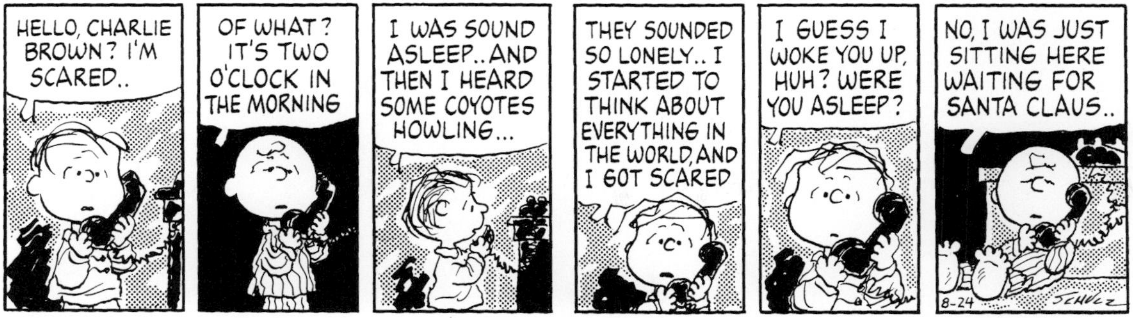
HELLO, CHARLIE BROWN? I'M SCARED..
OF WHAT? IT'S TWO O'CLOCK IN THE MORNING
I WAS SOUND ASLEEP..AND THEN I HEARD SOME COYOTES HOWLING...
THEY SOUNDED SO LONELY.. I STARTED TO THINK ABOUT EVERYTHING IN THE WORLD, AND I GOT SCARED
I GUESS I WOKE YOU UP, HUH? WERE YOU ASLEEP?
NO, I WAS JUST SITTING HERE WAITING FOR SANTA CLAUS..
8-24
SCHULZ

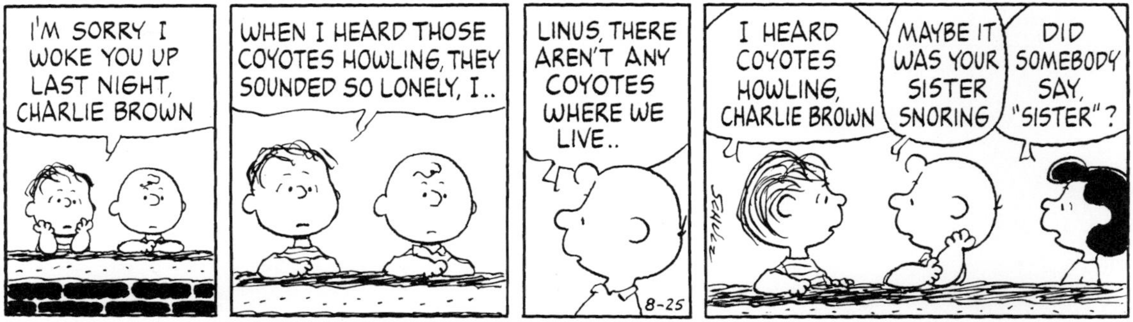
I'M SORRY I WOKE YOU UP LAST NIGHT, CHARLIE BROWN
WHEN I HEARD THOSE COYOTES HOWLING, THEY SOUNDED SO LONELY, I..
LINUS, THERE AREN'T ANY COYOTES WHERE WE LIVE..
8-25
SCHULZ
I HEARD COYOTES HOWLING, CHARLIE BROWN
MAYBE IT WAS YOUR SISTER SNORING
DID SOMEBODY SAY, "SISTER"?

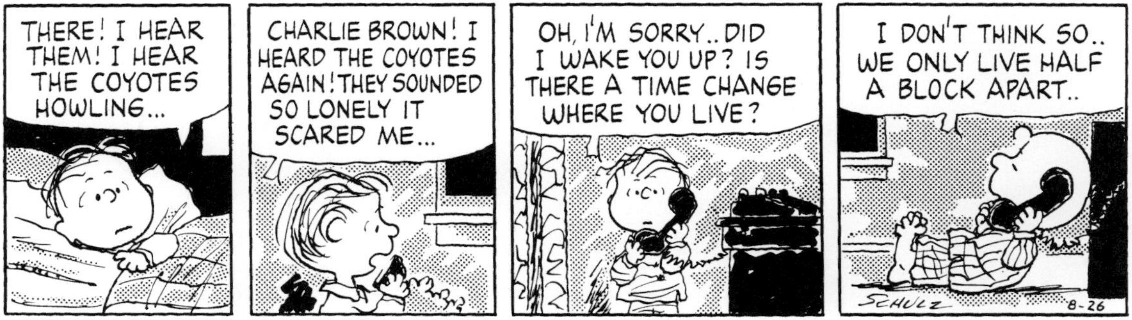
THERE! I HEAR THEM! I HEAR THE COYOTES HOWLING...
CHARLIE BROWN! I HEARD THE COYOTES AGAIN! THEY SOUNDED SO LONELY IT SCARED ME...
OH, I'M SORRY..DID I WAKE YOU UP? IS THERE A TIME CHANGE WHERE YOU LIVE?
I DON'T THINK SO.. WE ONLY LIVE HALF A BLOCK APART..
SCHULZ
8-26

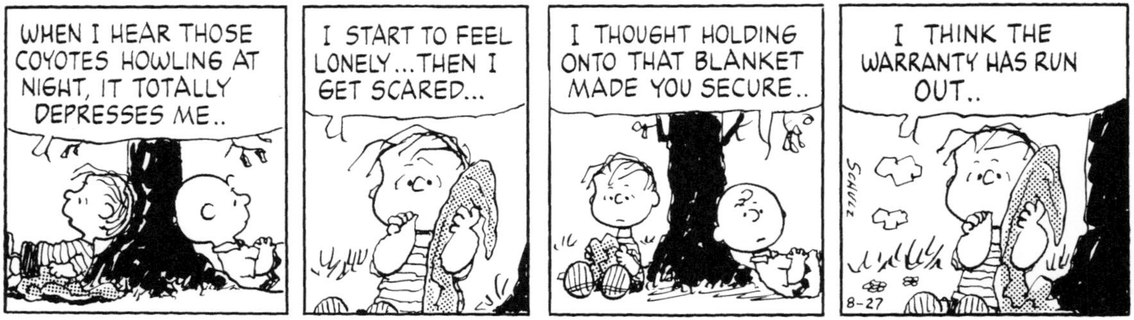
WHEN I HEAR THOSE COYOTES HOWLING AT NIGHT, IT TOTALLY DEPRESSES ME..
I START TO FEEL LONELY...THEN I GET SCARED...
I THOUGHT HOLDING ONTO THAT BLANKET MADE YOU SECURE..
I THINK THE WARRANTY HAS RUN OUT..
SCHULZ
8-27

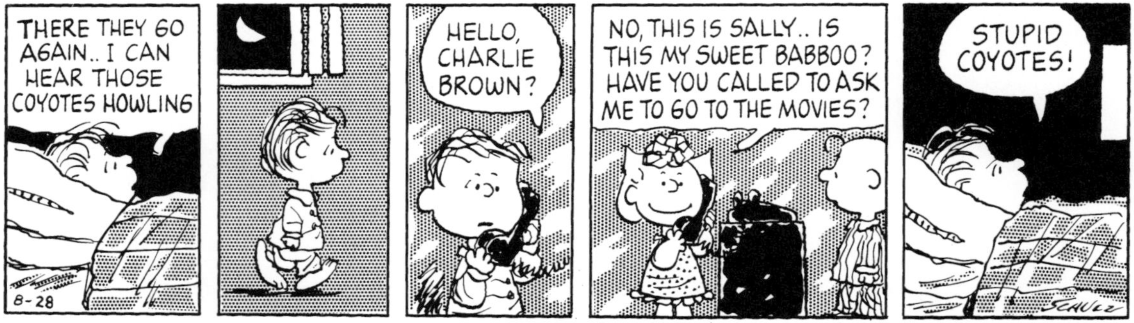
THERE THEY GO AGAIN.. I CAN HEAR THOSE COYOTES HOWLING
8-28
HELLO, CHARLIE BROWN?
NO, THIS IS SALLY.. IS THIS MY SWEET BABBOO? HAVE YOU CALLED TO ASK ME TO GO TO THE MOVIES?
STUPID COYOTES!
SCHULZ

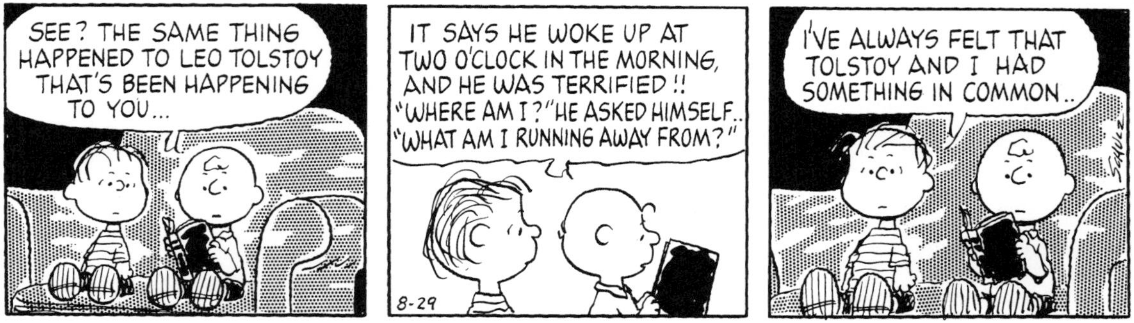
SEE? THE SAME THING HAPPENED TO LEO TOLSTOY THAT'S BEEN HAPPENING TO YOU...
IT SAYS HE WOKE UP AT TWO O'CLOCK IN THE MORNING, AND HE WAS TERRIFIED!! "WHERE AM I?" HE ASKED HIMSELF.. "WHAT AM I RUNNING AWAY FROM?"
8-29
I'VE ALWAYS FELT THAT TOLSTOY AND I HAD SOMETHING IN COMMON..
SCHULZ

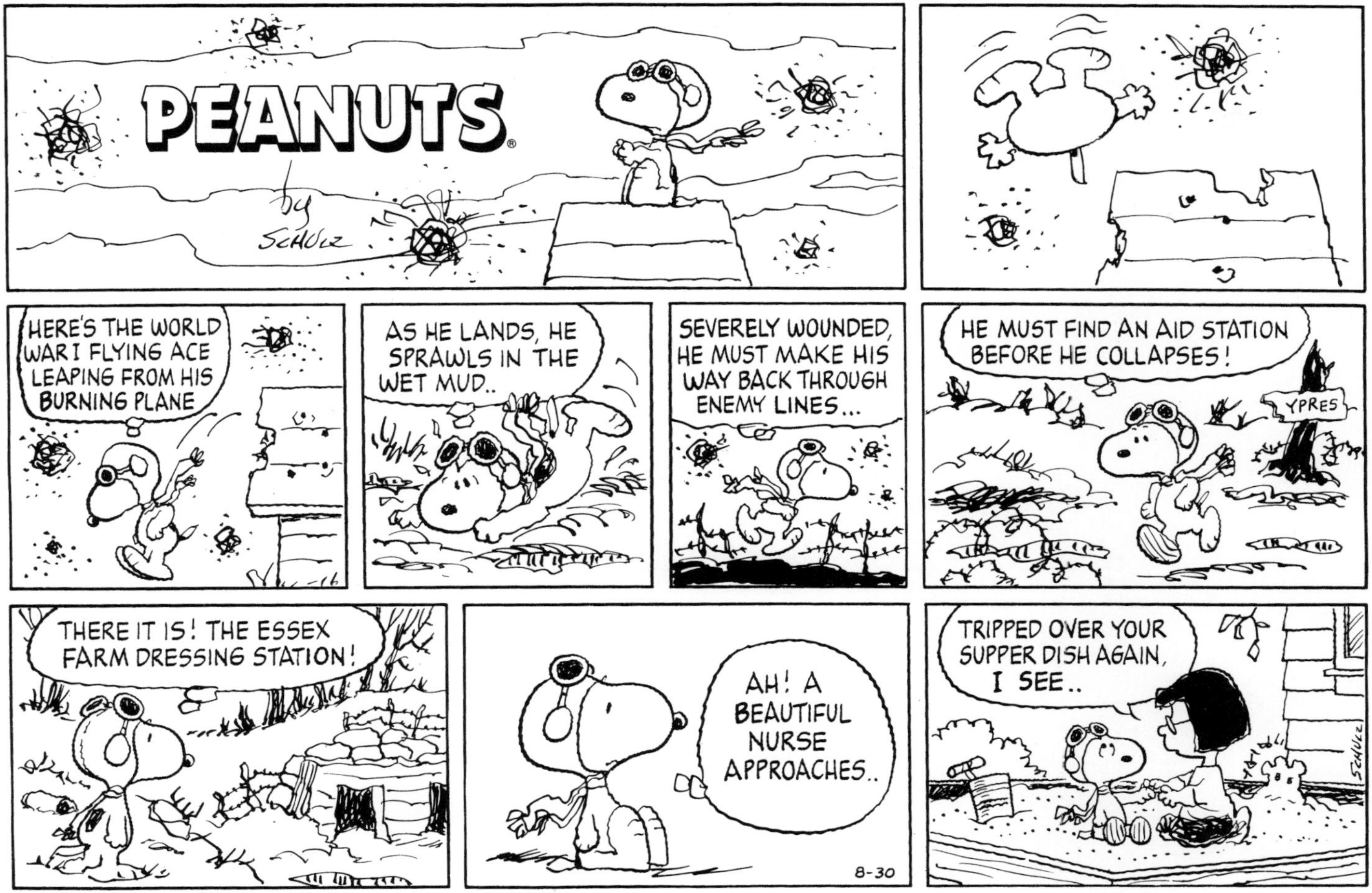
PEANUTS
by SCHULZ
HERE'S THE WORLD WAR I FLYING ACE LEAPING FROM HIS BURNING PLANE
AS HE LANDS, HE SPRAWLS IN THE WET MUD..
SEVERELY WOUNDED, HE MUST MAKE HIS WAY BACK THROUGH ENEMY LINES...
HE MUST FIND AN AID STATION BEFORE HE COLLAPSES!
YPRES
THERE IT IS! THE ESSEX FARM DRESSING STATION!
AH! A BEAUTIFUL NURSE APPROACHES..
8-30
TRIPPED OVER YOUR SUPPER DISH AGAIN, I SEE..
SCHULZ

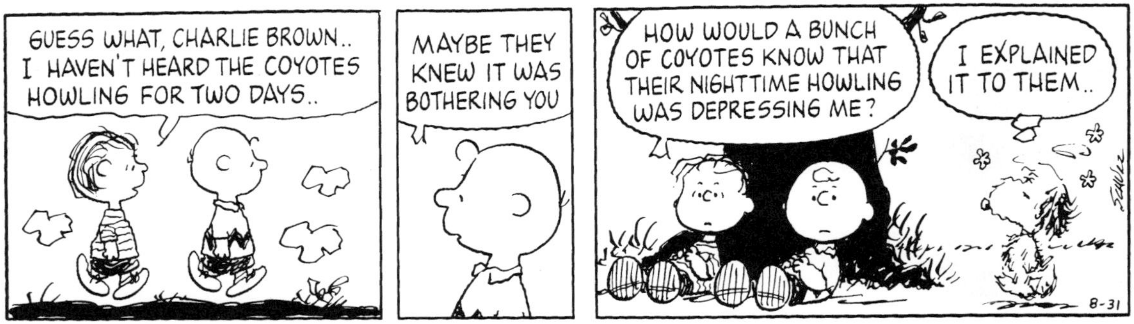
GUESS WHAT, CHARLIE BROWN.. I HAVEN'T HEARD THE COYOTES HOWLING FOR TWO DAYS..
MAYBE THEY KNEW IT WAS BOTHERING YOU
HOW WOULD A BUNCH OF COYOTES KNOW THAT THEIR NIGHTTIME HOWLING WAS DEPRESSING ME?
I EXPLAINED IT TO THEM..
SCHULZ
8-31

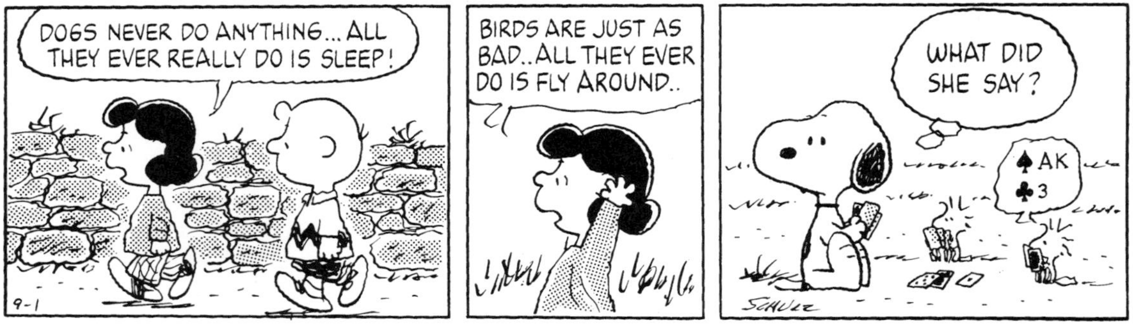
DOGS NEVER DO ANYTHING... ALL THEY EVER REALLY DO IS SLEEP!
9-1
BIRDS ARE JUST AS BAD.. ALL THEY EVER DO IS FLY AROUND..
WHAT DID SHE SAY?
♠AK
♣3
SCHULZ

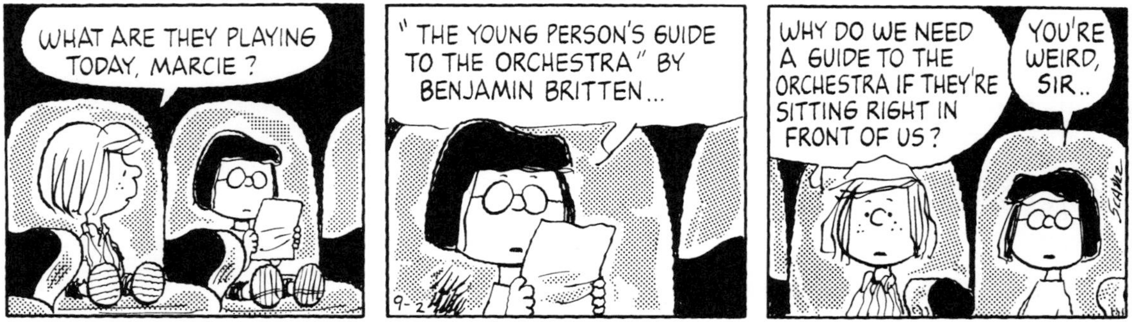
WHAT ARE THEY PLAYING TODAY, MARCIE?
"THE YOUNG PERSON'S GUIDE TO THE ORCHESTRA" BY BENJAMIN BRITTEN...
9-2
WHY DO WE NEED A GUIDE TO THE ORCHESTRA IF THEY'RE SITTING RIGHT IN FRONT OF US?
YOU'RE WEIRD, SIR..
SCHULZ

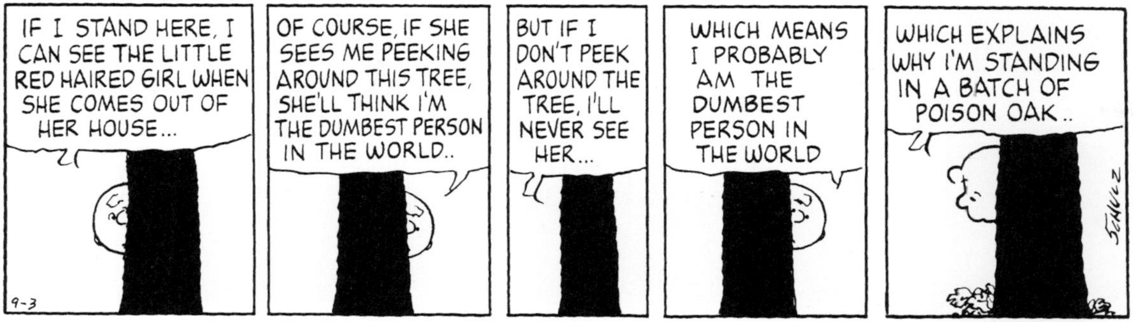
IF I STAND HERE, I CAN SEE THE LITTLE RED HAIRED GIRL WHEN SHE COMES OUT OF HER HOUSE...
OF COURSE, IF SHE SEES ME PEEKING AROUND THIS TREE, SHE'LL THINK I'M THE DUMBEST PERSON IN THE WORLD..
BUT IF I DON'T PEEK AROUND THE TREE, I'LL NEVER SEE HER...
WHICH MEANS I PROBABLY AM THE DUMBEST PERSON IN THE WORLD
WHICH EXPLAINS WHY I'M STANDING IN A BATCH OF POISON OAK..
9-3
SCHULZ

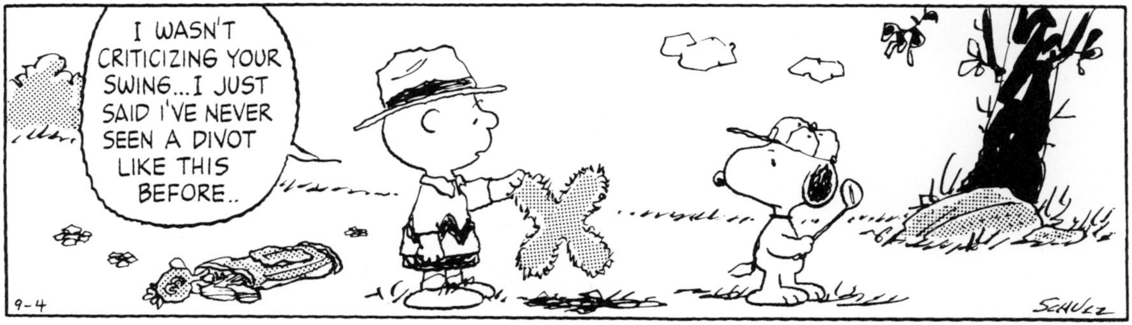
I WASN'T CRITICIZING YOUR SWING...I JUST SAID I'VE NEVER SEEN A DIVOT LIKE THIS BEFORE..
9-4
SCHULZ

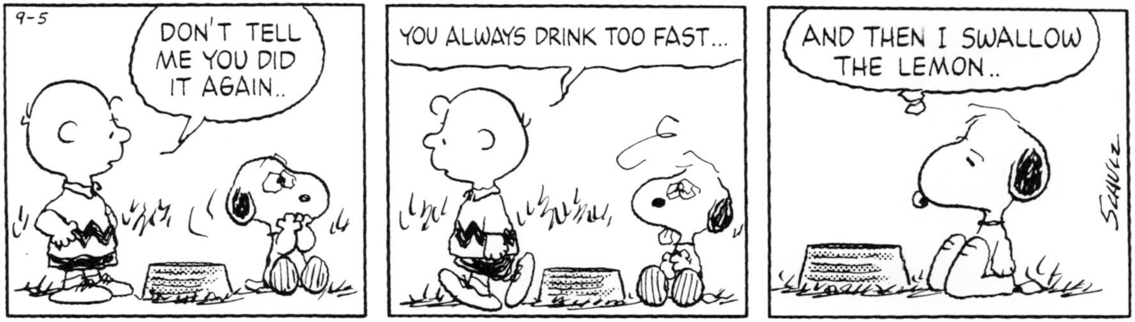
9-5
DON'T TELL ME YOU DID IT AGAIN..
YOU ALWAYS DRINK TOO FAST...
AND THEN I SWALLOW THE LEMON..
SCHULZ

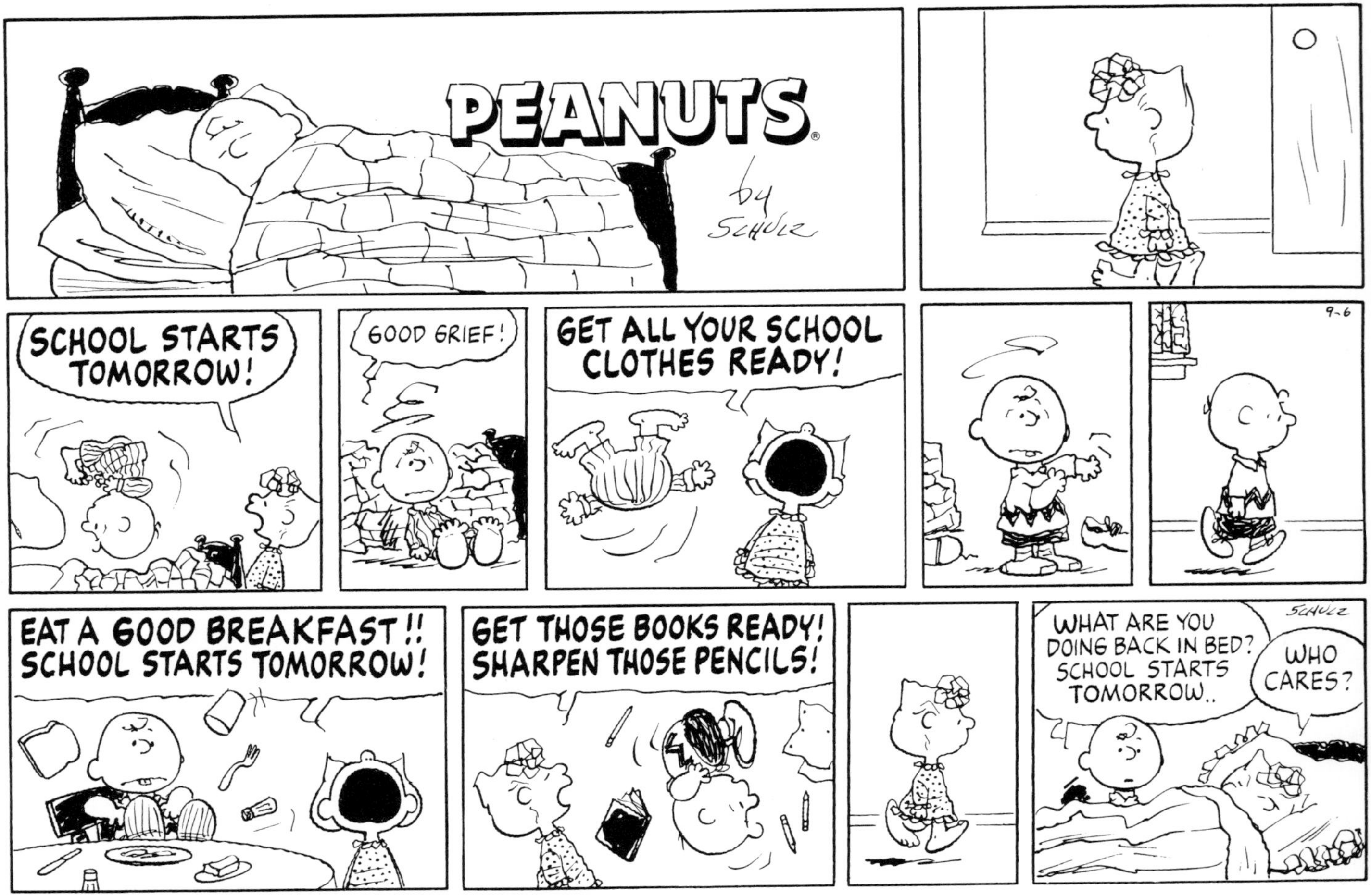
PEANUTS
by SCHULZ
SCHOOL STARTS TOMORROW!
GOOD GRIEF!
GET ALL YOUR SCHOOL CLOTHES READY!
9-6
EAT A GOOD BREAKFAST!! SCHOOL STARTS TOMORROW!
GET THOSE BOOKS READY! SHARPEN THOSE PENCILS!
SCHULZ
WHAT ARE YOU DOING BACK IN BED? SCHOOL STARTS TOMORROW..
WHO CARES?

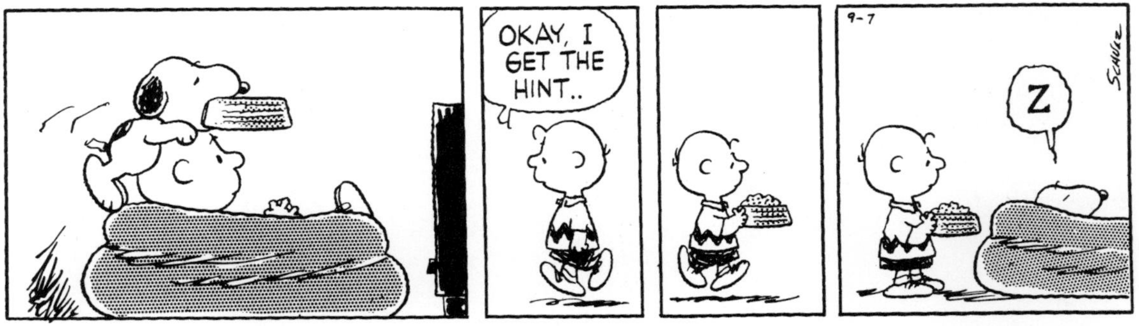
OKAY, I GET THE HINT..
9-7
SCHULZ
Z

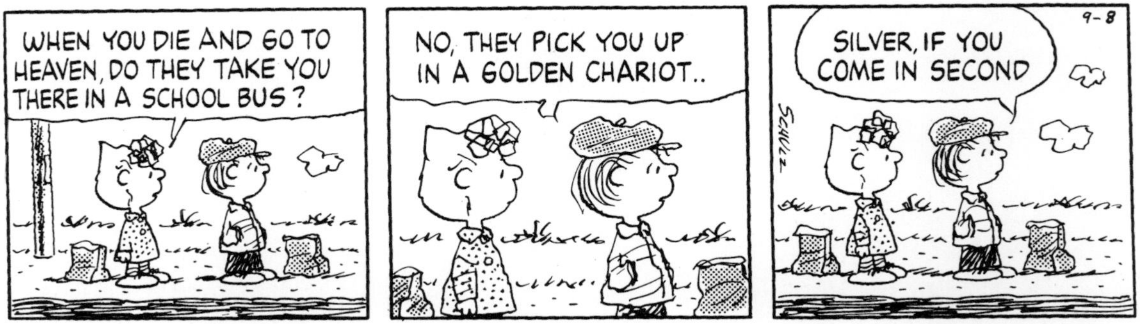
WHEN YOU DIE AND GO TO HEAVEN, DO THEY TAKE YOU THERE IN A SCHOOL BUS?
NO, THEY PICK YOU UP IN A GOLDEN CHARIOT..
9-8
SCHULZ
SILVER, IF YOU COME IN SECOND

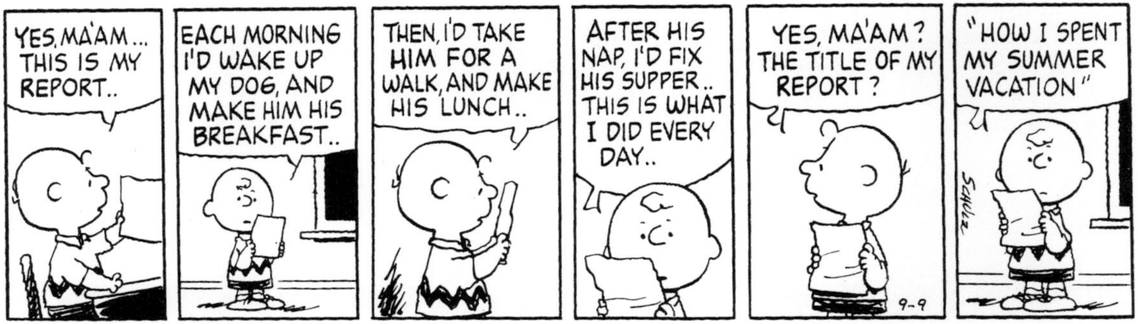
YES, MA'AM... THIS IS MY REPORT..
EACH MORNING I'D WAKE UP MY DOG, AND MAKE HIM HIS BREAKFAST..
THEN, I'D TAKE HIM FOR A WALK, AND MAKE HIS LUNCH..
AFTER HIS NAP, I'D FIX HIS SUPPER.. THIS IS WHAT I DID EVERY DAY..
YES, MA'AM? THE TITLE OF MY REPORT?
9-9
"HOW I SPENT MY SUMMER VACATION"
SCHULZ

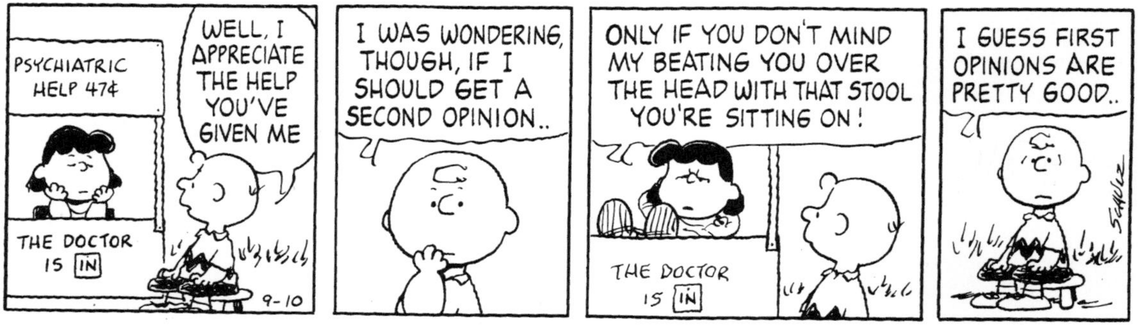
PSYCHIATRIC HELP 47¢
THE DOCTOR IS IN
WELL, I APPRECIATE THE HELP YOU'VE GIVEN ME
I WAS WONDERING, THOUGH, IF I SHOULD GET A SECOND OPINION..
ONLY IF YOU DON'T MIND MY BEATING YOU OVER THE HEAD WITH THAT STOOL YOU'RE SITTING ON!
THE DOCTOR IS IN
I GUESS FIRST OPINIONS ARE PRETTY GOOD..
9-10
SCHULZ

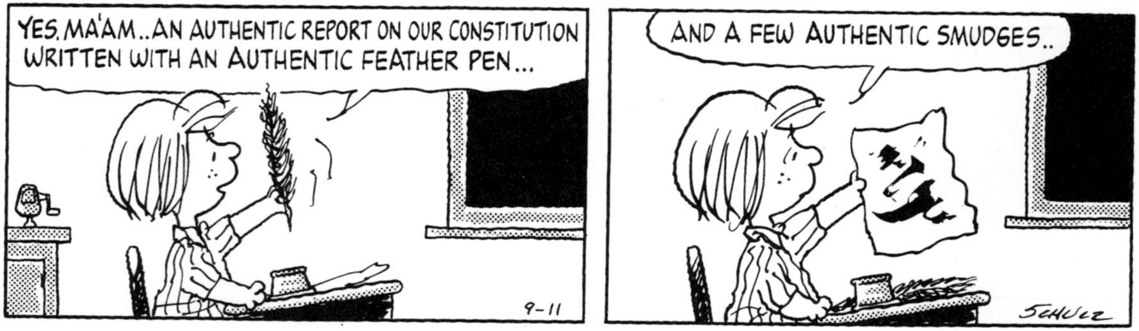
YES, MA'AM..AN AUTHENTIC REPORT ON OUR CONSTITUTION WRITTEN WITH AN AUTHENTIC FEATHER PEN...
9-11
AND A FEW AUTHENTIC SMUDGES..
SCHULZ

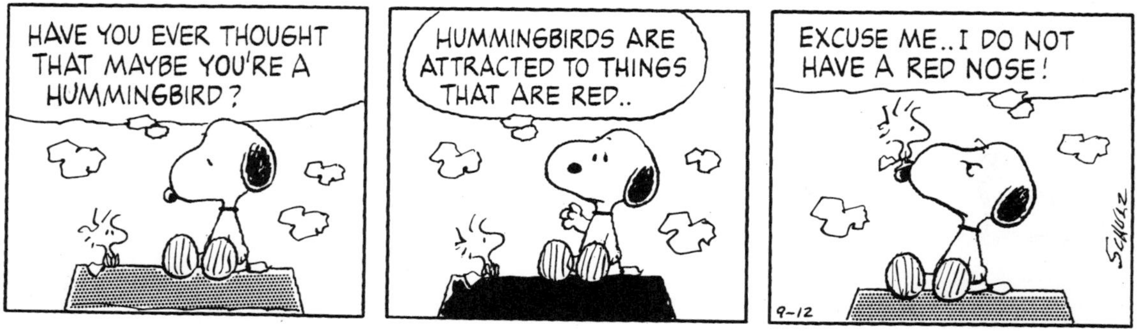
HAVE YOU EVER THOUGHT THAT MAYBE YOU'RE A HUMMINGBIRD?
HUMMINGBIRDS ARE ATTRACTED TO THINGS THAT ARE RED..
EXCUSE ME..I DO NOT HAVE A RED NOSE!
9-12
SCHULZ

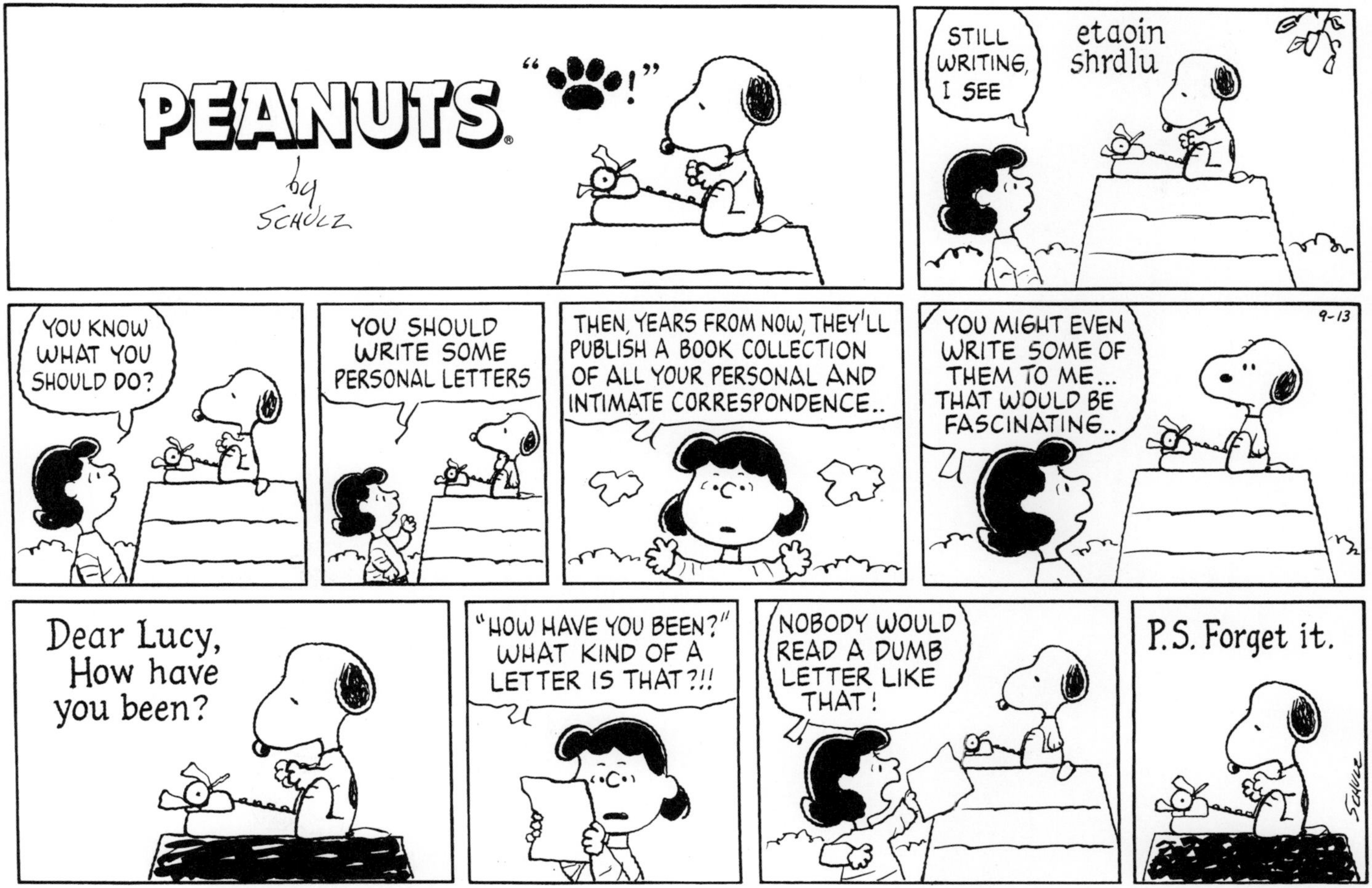
PEANUTS
by SCHULZ
"🐾!"
STILL WRITING, I SEE
etaoin shrdlu
YOU KNOW WHAT YOU SHOULD DO?
YOU SHOULD WRITE SOME PERSONAL LETTERS
THEN, YEARS FROM NOW, THEY'LL PUBLISH A BOOK COLLECTION OF ALL YOUR PERSONAL AND INTIMATE CORRESPONDENCE..
9-13
YOU MIGHT EVEN WRITE SOME OF THEM TO ME... THAT WOULD BE FASCINATING..
Dear Lucy, How have you been?
"HOW HAVE YOU BEEN?" WHAT KIND OF A LETTER IS THAT?!!
NOBODY WOULD READ A DUMB LETTER LIKE THAT!
SCHULZ
P.S. Forget it.

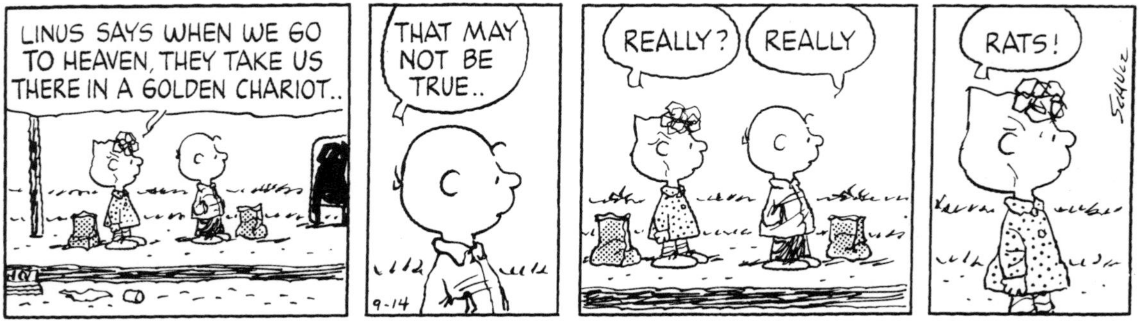
LINUS SAYS WHEN WE GO TO HEAVEN, THEY TAKE US THERE IN A GOLDEN CHARIOT..
THAT MAY NOT BE TRUE..
9-14
REALLY?
REALLY
RATS!
SCHULZ

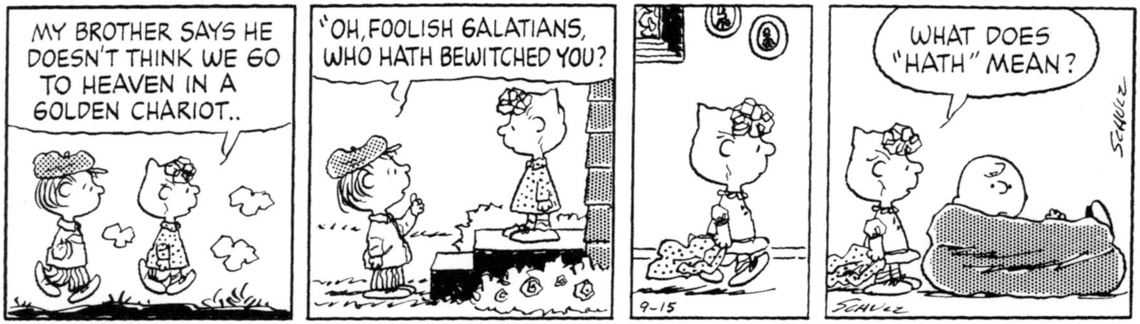
MY BROTHER SAYS HE DOESN'T THINK WE GO TO HEAVEN IN A GOLDEN CHARIOT..
"OH, FOOLISH GALATIANS, WHO HATH BEWITCHED YOU?
9-15
WHAT DOES "HATH" MEAN?
SCHULZ
SCHULZ

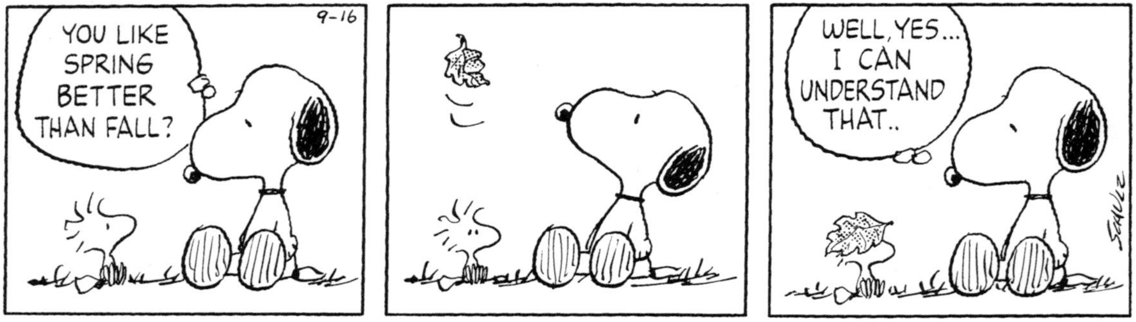
9-16
YOU LIKE SPRING BETTER THAN FALL?
WELL, YES... I CAN UNDERSTAND THAT..
SCHULZ

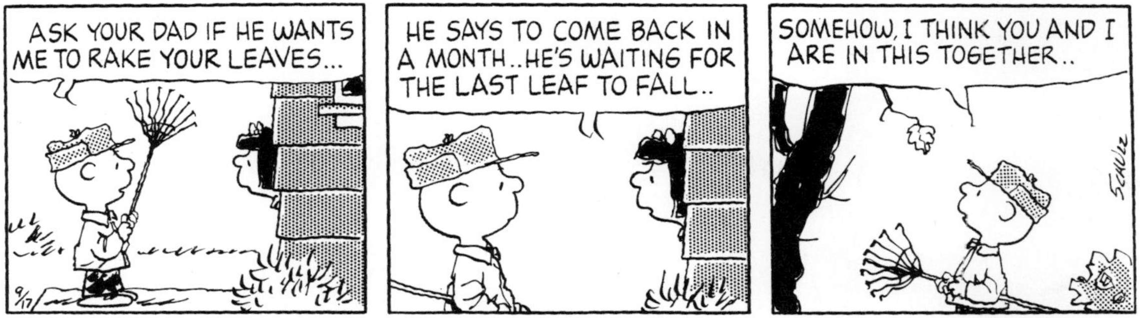
ASK YOUR DAD IF HE WANTS ME TO RAKE YOUR LEAVES...
HE SAYS TO COME BACK IN A MONTH..HE'S WAITING FOR THE LAST LEAF TO FALL..
SOMEHOW, I THINK YOU AND I ARE IN THIS TOGETHER..

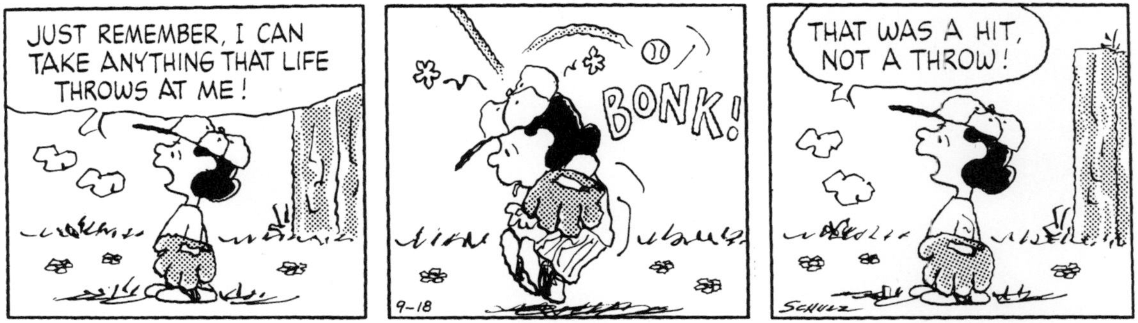
JUST REMEMBER, I CAN TAKE ANYTHING THAT LIFE THROWS AT ME!
BONK!
THAT WAS A HIT, NOT A THROW!

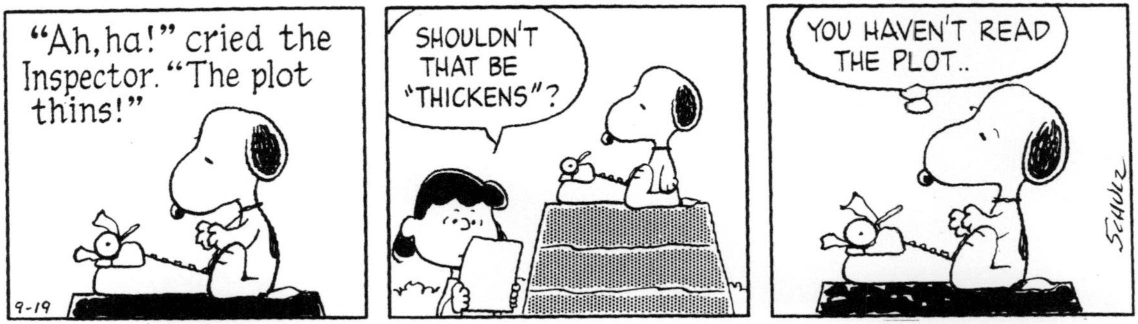
"Ah, ha!" cried the Inspector. "The plot thins!"
SHOULDN'T THAT BE "THICKENS"?
YOU HAVEN'T READ THE PLOT..

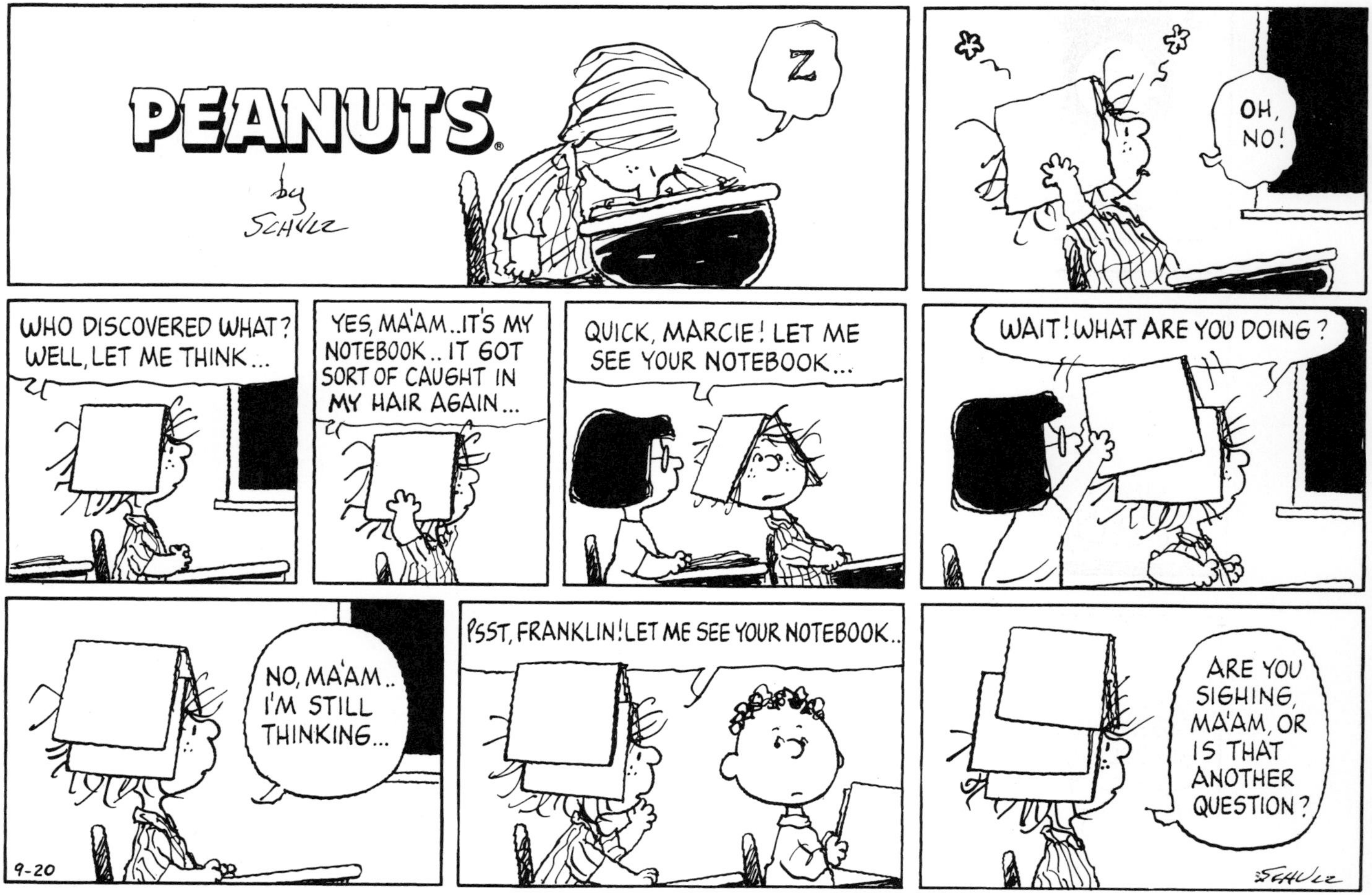
PEANUTS
by SCHULZ
Z
OH, NO!
WHO DISCOVERED WHAT? WELL, LET ME THINK...
YES, MA'AM..IT'S MY NOTEBOOK.. IT GOT SORT OF CAUGHT IN MY HAIR AGAIN...
QUICK, MARCIE! LET ME SEE YOUR NOTEBOOK...
WAIT! WHAT ARE YOU DOING?
NO, MA'AM.. I'M STILL THINKING...
9-20
PSST, FRANKLIN! LET ME SEE YOUR NOTEBOOK..
ARE YOU SIGHING, MA'AM, OR IS THAT ANOTHER QUESTION?
SCHULZ

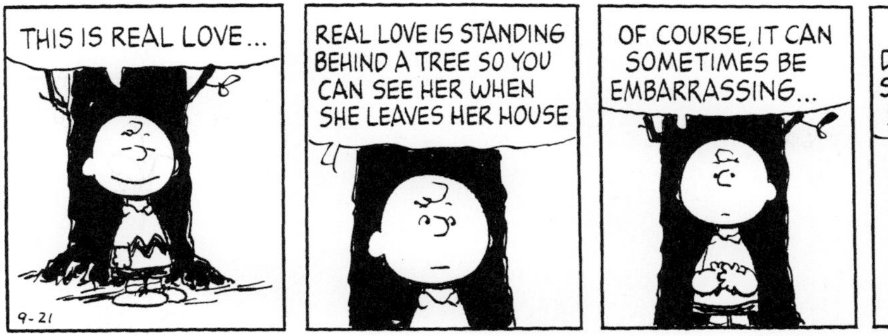
THIS IS REAL LOVE...
REAL LOVE IS STANDING BEHIND A TREE SO YOU CAN SEE HER WHEN SHE LEAVES HER HOUSE
OF COURSE, IT CAN SOMETIMES BE EMBARRASSING...
LIKE WHEN YOU DISCOVER YOU'VE BEEN STANDING ON THE WRONG SIDE OF THE TREE..
9-21

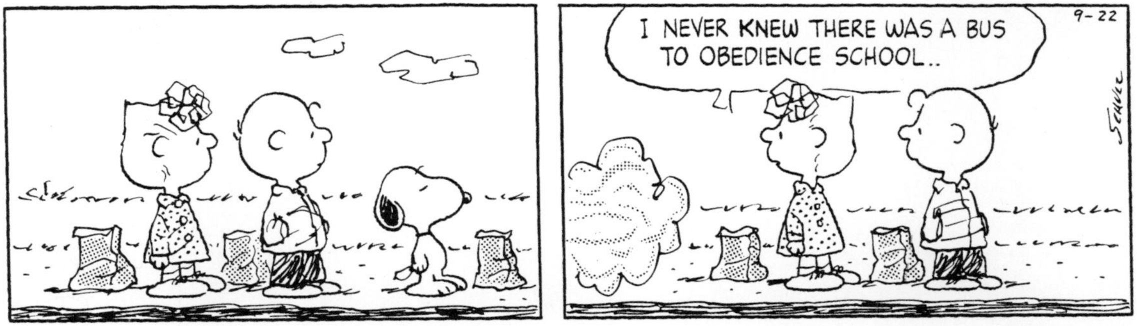
I NEVER **KNEW** THERE WAS A BUS TO OBEDIENCE SCHOOL..
9-22

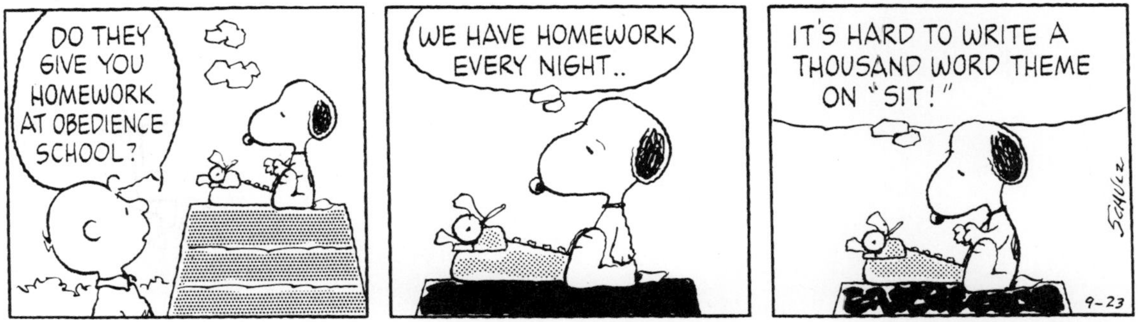
DO THEY GIVE YOU HOMEWORK AT OBEDIENCE SCHOOL?
WE HAVE HOMEWORK EVERY NIGHT..
IT'S HARD TO WRITE A THOUSAND WORD THEME ON "SIT!"
9-23

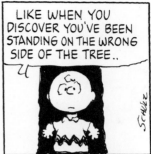

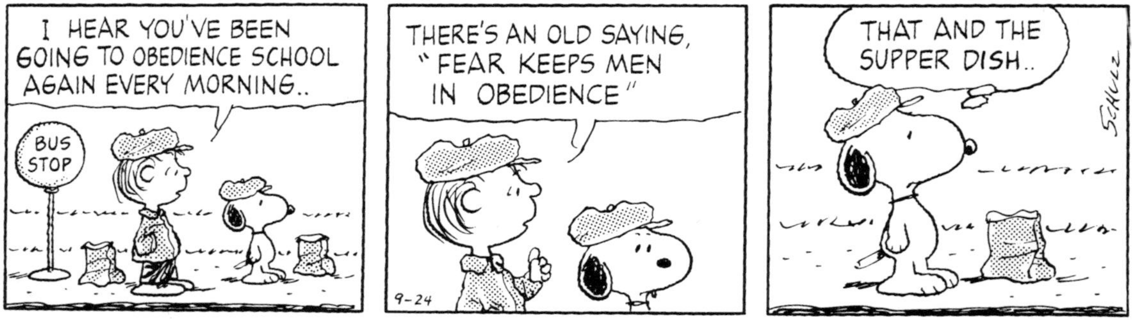
I HEAR YOU'VE BEEN GOING TO OBEDIENCE SCHOOL AGAIN EVERY MORNING..
BUS STOP
THERE'S AN OLD SAYING, "FEAR KEEPS MEN IN OBEDIENCE"
9-24
THAT AND THE SUPPER DISH..
SCHULZ

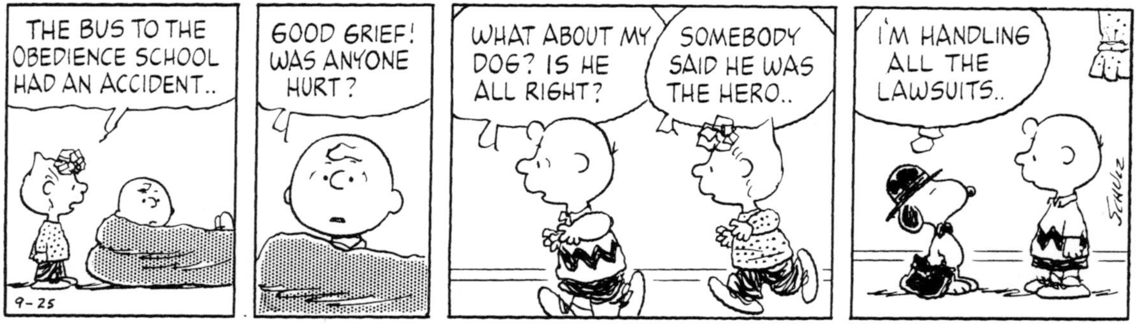
THE BUS TO THE OBEDIENCE SCHOOL HAD AN ACCIDENT..
9-25
GOOD GRIEF! WAS ANYONE HURT?
WHAT ABOUT MY DOG? IS HE ALL RIGHT?
SOMEBODY SAID HE WAS THE HERO..
I'M HANDLING ALL THE LAWSUITS..
SCHULZ

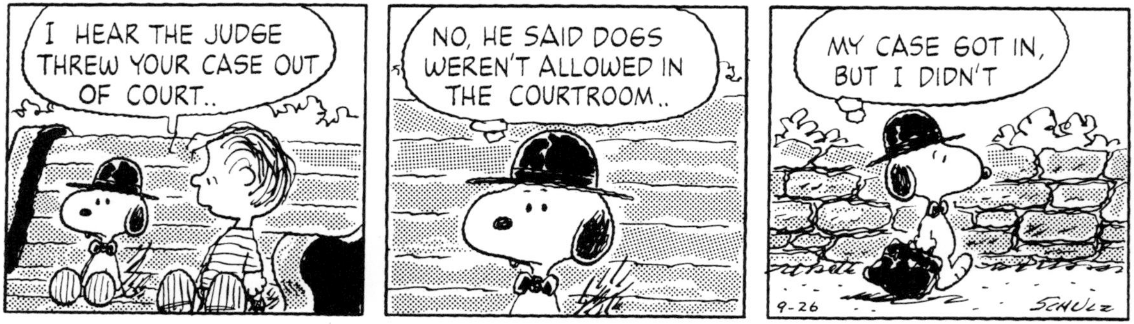
I HEAR THE JUDGE THREW YOUR CASE OUT OF COURT..
NO, HE SAID DOGS WEREN'T ALLOWED IN THE COURTROOM..
MY CASE GOT IN, BUT I DIDN'T
9-26
SCHULZ

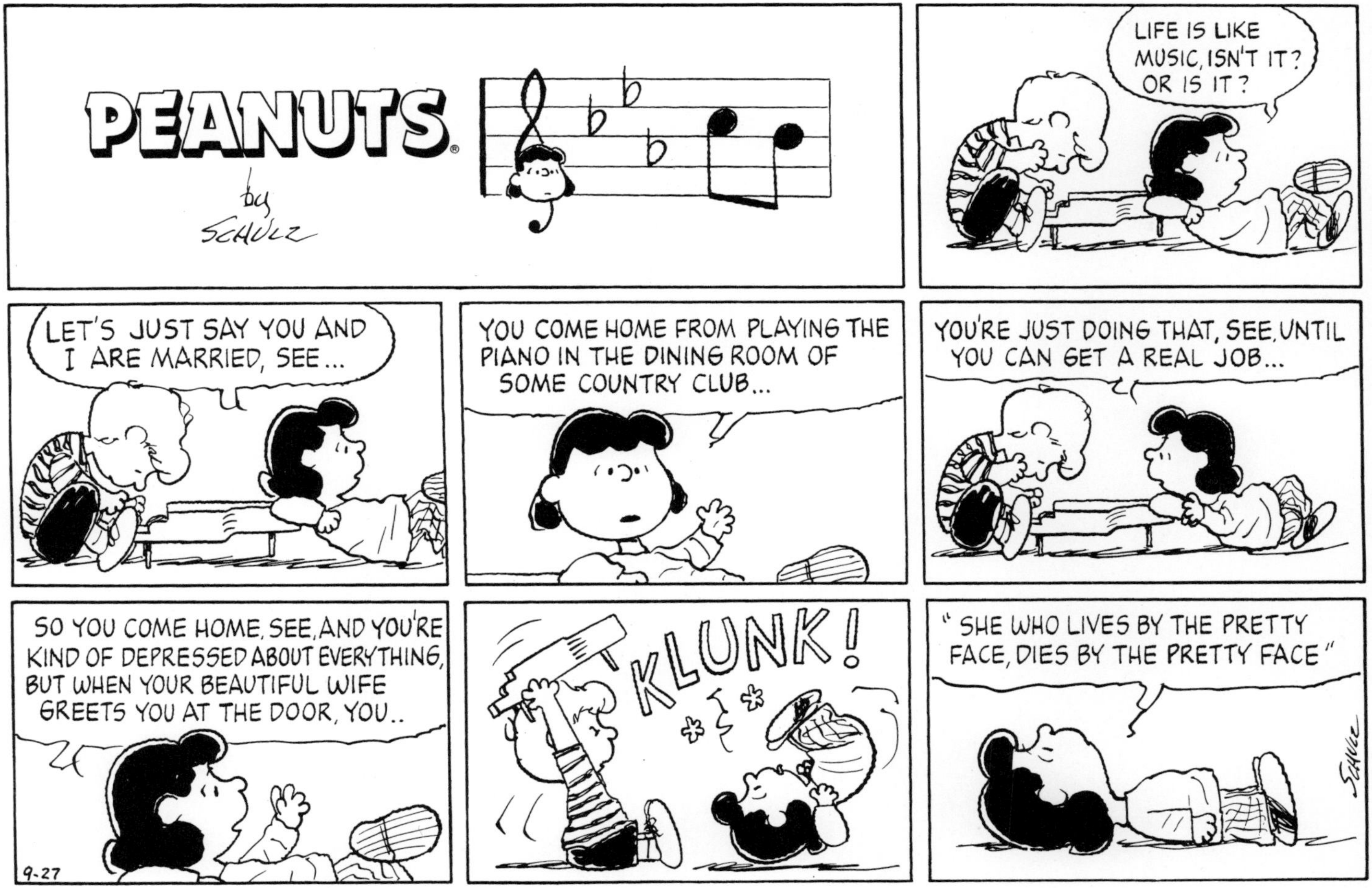
PEANUTS
by SCHULZ
LIFE IS LIKE MUSIC, ISN'T IT? OR IS IT?
LET'S JUST SAY YOU AND I ARE MARRIED, SEE...
YOU COME HOME FROM PLAYING THE PIANO IN THE DINING ROOM OF SOME COUNTRY CLUB...
YOU'RE JUST DOING THAT, SEE, UNTIL YOU CAN GET A REAL JOB...
SO YOU COME HOME, SEE, AND YOU'RE KIND OF DEPRESSED ABOUT EVERYTHING, BUT WHEN YOUR BEAUTIFUL WIFE GREETS YOU AT THE DOOR, YOU..
9-27
KLUNK!
"SHE WHO LIVES BY THE PRETTY FACE, DIES BY THE PRETTY FACE"
SCHULZ

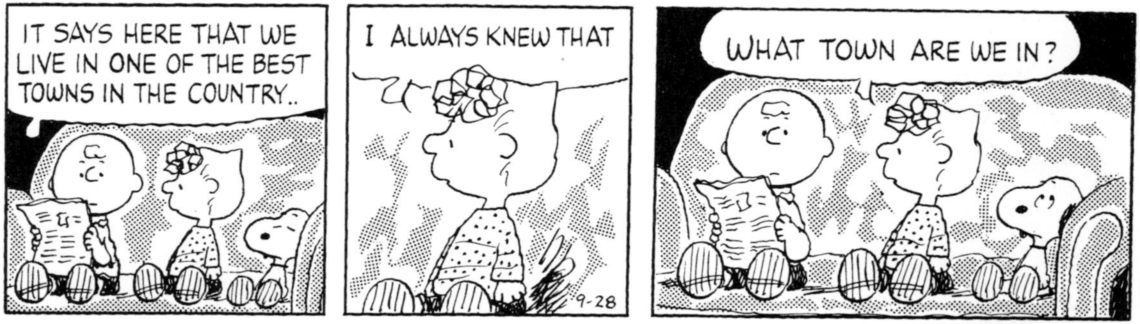
IT SAYS HERE THAT WE LIVE IN ONE OF THE BEST TOWNS IN THE COUNTRY..
I ALWAYS KNEW THAT
WHAT TOWN ARE WE IN?
9-28

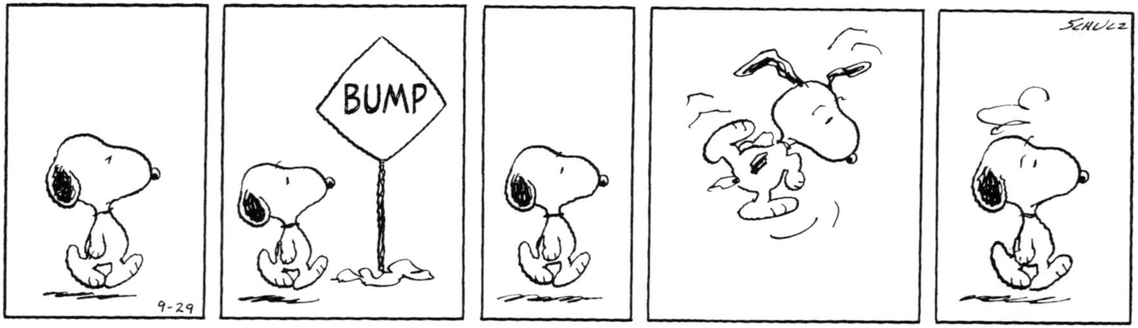
9-29
BUMP
SCHULZ

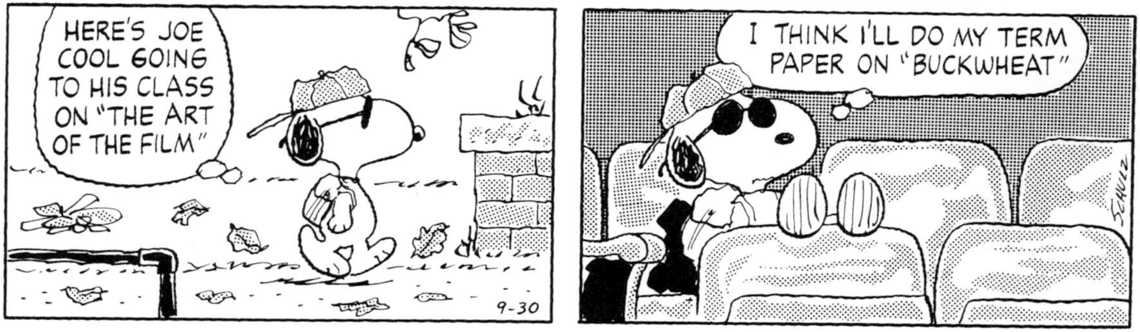
HERE'S JOE COOL GOING TO HIS CLASS ON "THE ART OF THE FILM"
9-30
I THINK I'LL DO MY TERM PAPER ON "BUCKWHEAT"
SCHULZ

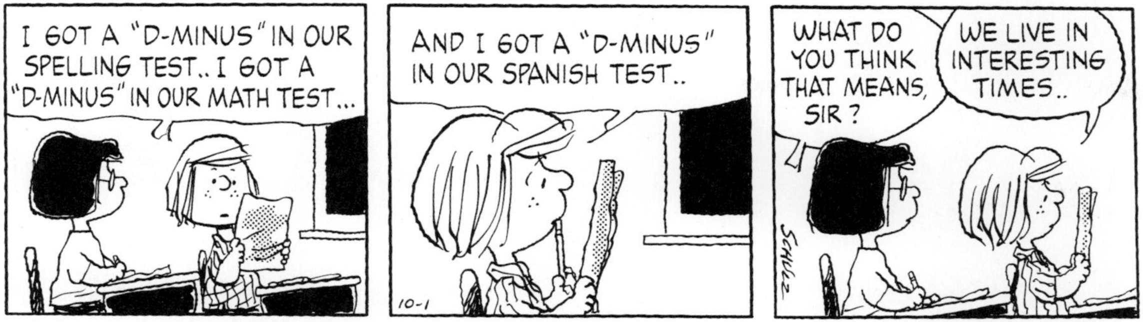
I GOT A "D-MINUS" IN OUR SPELLING TEST.. I GOT A "D-MINUS" IN OUR MATH TEST...
AND I GOT A "D-MINUS" IN OUR SPANISH TEST..
WHAT DO YOU THINK THAT MEANS, SIR ?
WE LIVE IN INTERESTING TIMES..
10-1
SCHULZ

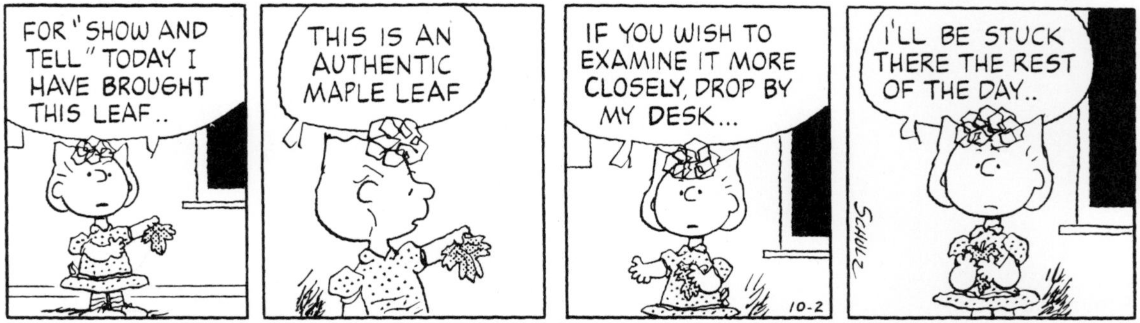
FOR "SHOW AND TELL" TODAY I HAVE BROUGHT THIS LEAF..
THIS IS AN AUTHENTIC MAPLE LEAF
IF YOU WISH TO EXAMINE IT MORE CLOSELY, DROP BY MY DESK...
I'LL BE STUCK THERE THE REST OF THE DAY..
10-2
SCHULZ

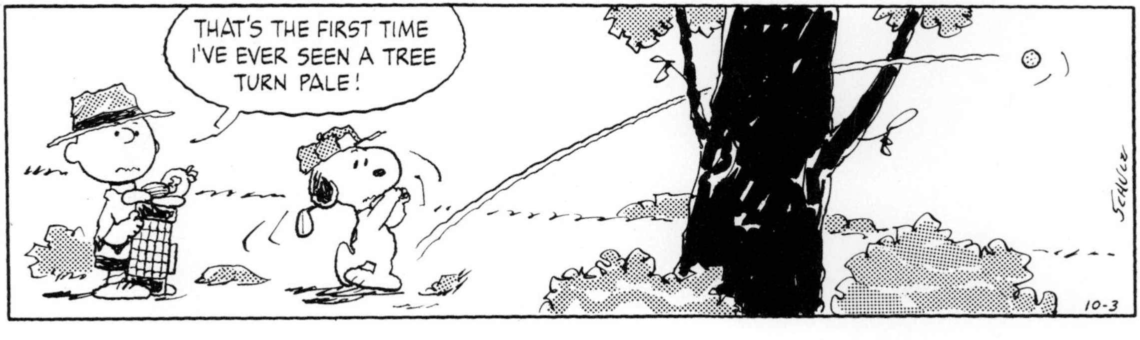
THAT'S THE FIRST TIME I'VE EVER SEEN A TREE TURN PALE!
SCHULZ
10-3

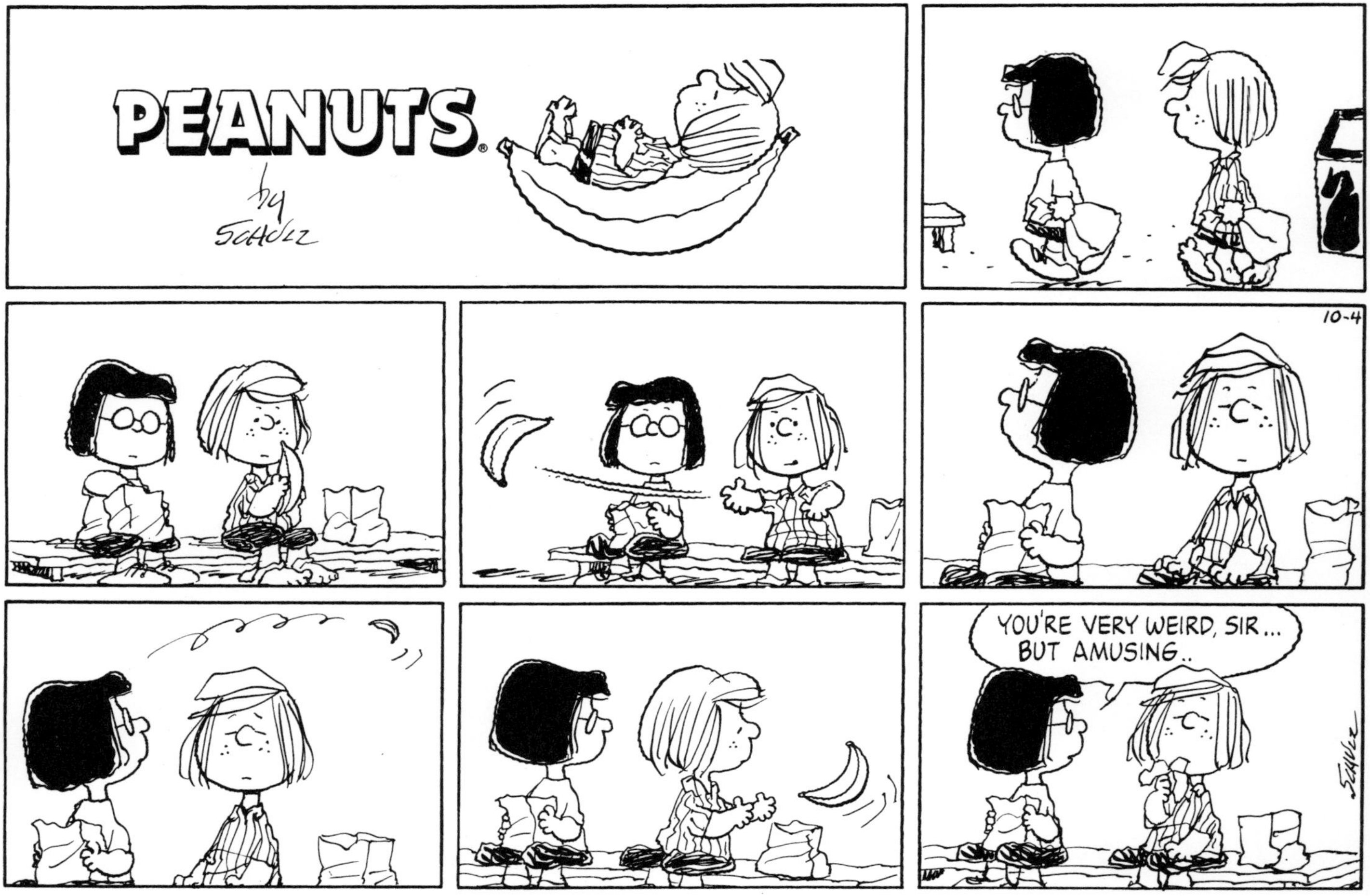
PEANUTS
by SCHULZ
10-4
YOU'RE VERY WEIRD, SIR...
BUT AMUSING..
SCHULZ

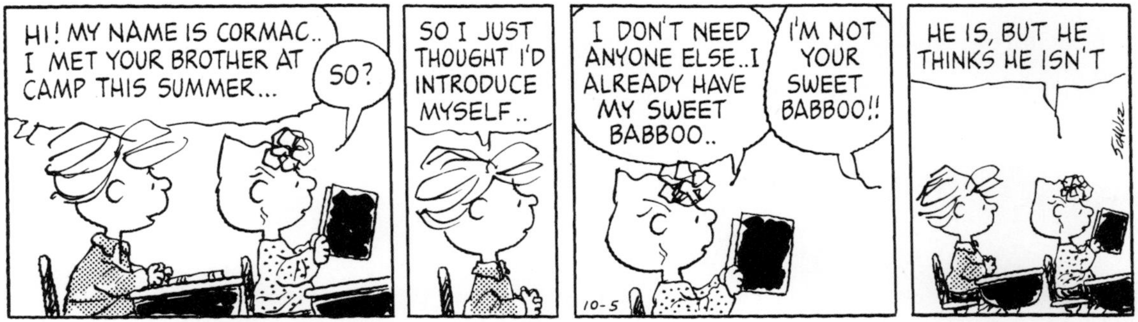
HI! MY NAME IS CORMAC.. I MET YOUR BROTHER AT CAMP THIS SUMMER...
SO?
SO I JUST THOUGHT I'D INTRODUCE MYSELF..
I DON'T NEED ANYONE ELSE..I ALREADY HAVE MY SWEET BABBOO..
I'M NOT YOUR SWEET BABBOO!!
10-5
HE IS, BUT HE THINKS HE ISN'T
SCHULZ

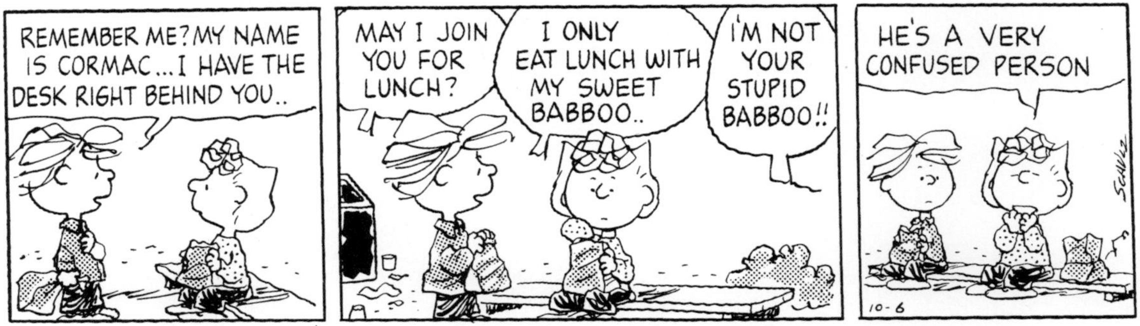
REMEMBER ME? MY NAME IS CORMAC...I HAVE THE DESK RIGHT BEHIND YOU..
MAY I JOIN YOU FOR LUNCH?
I ONLY EAT LUNCH WITH MY SWEET BABBOO..
I'M NOT YOUR STUPID BABBOO!!
HE'S A VERY CONFUSED PERSON
SCHULZ
10-6

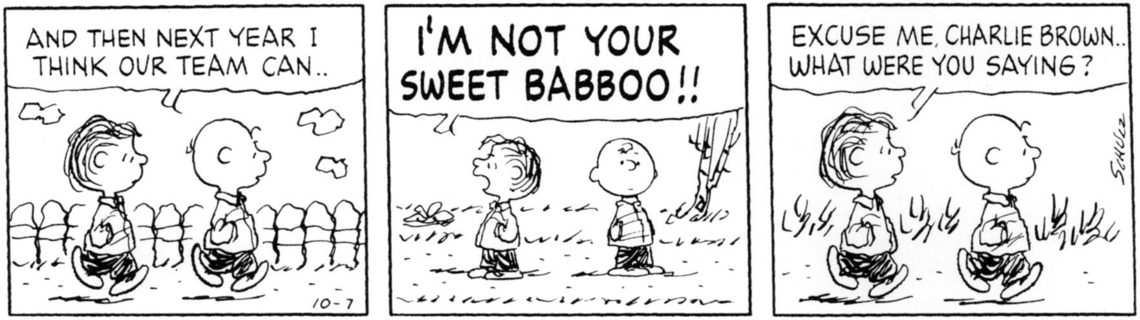
AND THEN NEXT YEAR I THINK OUR TEAM CAN..
10-7
I'M NOT YOUR SWEET BABBOO!!
EXCUSE ME, CHARLIE BROWN.. WHAT WERE YOU SAYING?
SCHULZ

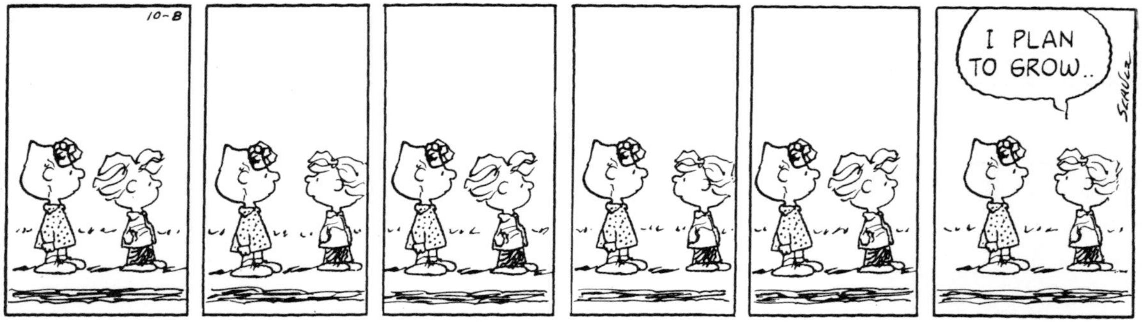
I PLAN TO GROW..

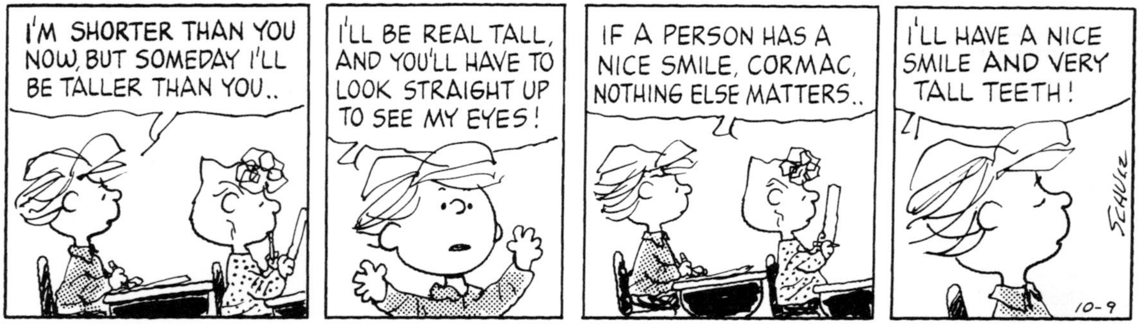
I'M SHORTER THAN YOU NOW, BUT SOMEDAY I'LL BE TALLER THAN YOU..
I'LL BE REAL TALL, AND YOU'LL HAVE TO LOOK STRAIGHT UP TO SEE MY EYES!
IF A PERSON HAS A NICE SMILE, CORMAC, NOTHING ELSE MATTERS..
I'LL HAVE A NICE SMILE AND VERY TALL TEETH!

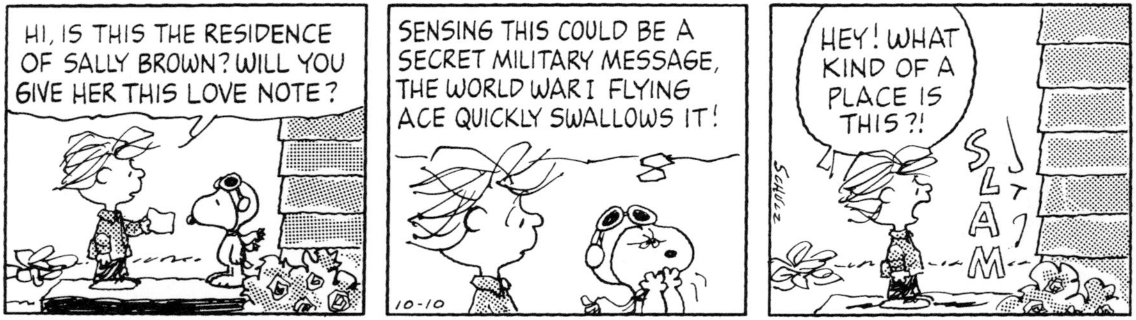
HI, IS THIS THE RESIDENCE OF SALLY BROWN? WILL YOU GIVE HER THIS LOVE NOTE?
SENSING THIS COULD BE A SECRET MILITARY MESSAGE, THE WORLD WAR I FLYING ACE QUICKLY SWALLOWS IT!
HEY! WHAT KIND OF A PLACE IS THIS?!
SLAM

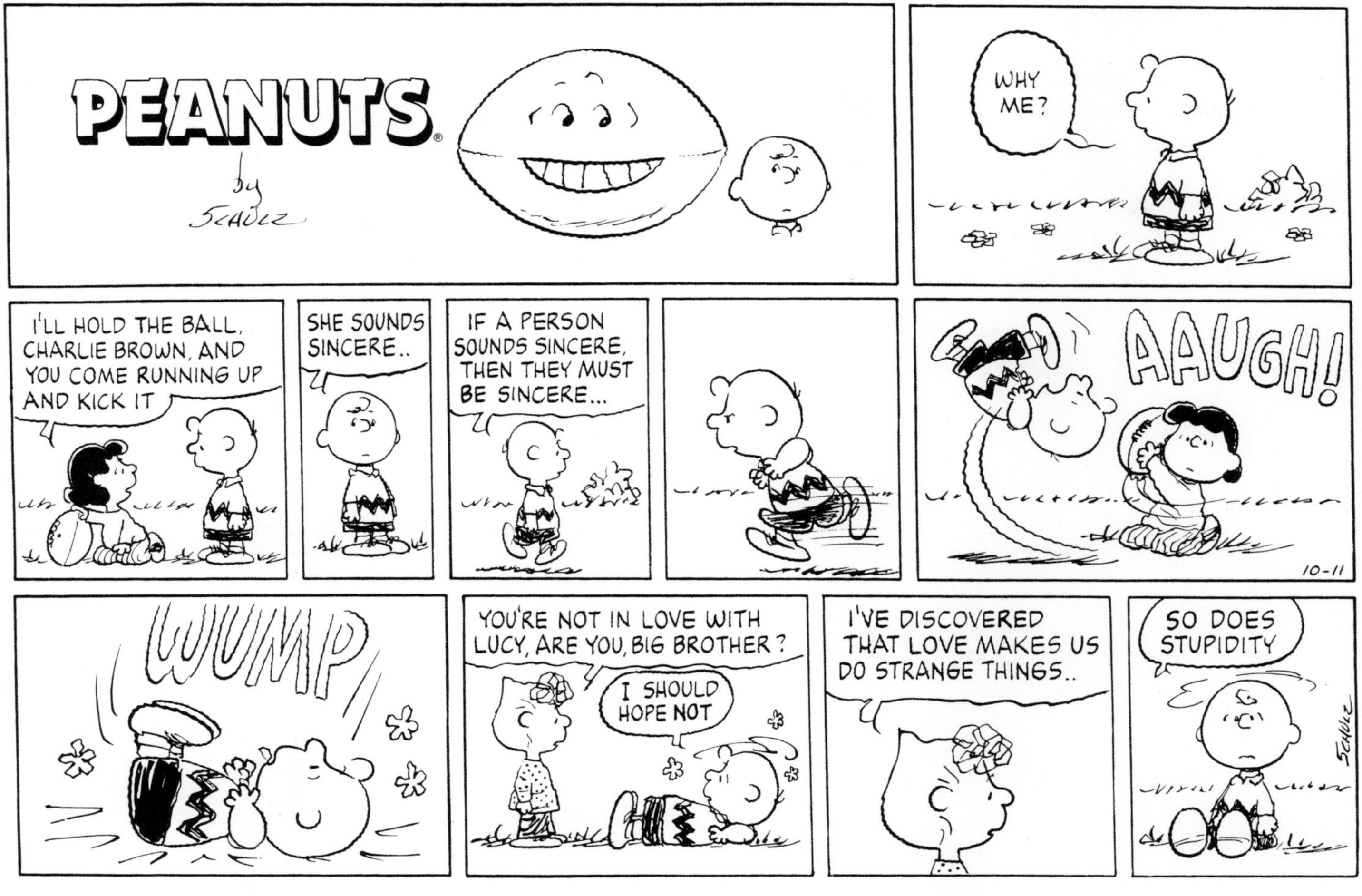
PEANUTS
by SCHULZ
WHY ME?
I'LL HOLD THE BALL, CHARLIE BROWN, AND YOU COME RUNNING UP AND KICK IT
SHE SOUNDS SINCERE..
IF A PERSON SOUNDS SINCERE, THEN THEY MUST BE SINCERE...
AAUGH!
10-11
WUMP
YOU'RE NOT IN LOVE WITH LUCY, ARE YOU, BIG BROTHER?
I SHOULD HOPE NOT
I'VE DISCOVERED THAT LOVE MAKES US DO STRANGE THINGS..
SO DOES STUPIDITY
SCHULZ

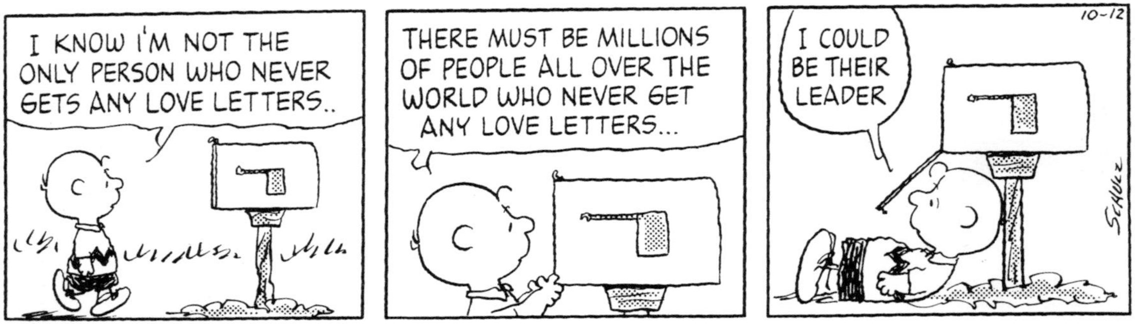
I KNOW I'M NOT THE ONLY PERSON WHO NEVER GETS ANY LOVE LETTERS..
THERE MUST BE MILLIONS OF PEOPLE ALL OVER THE WORLD WHO NEVER GET ANY LOVE LETTERS...
10-12
I COULD BE THEIR LEADER
SCHULZ

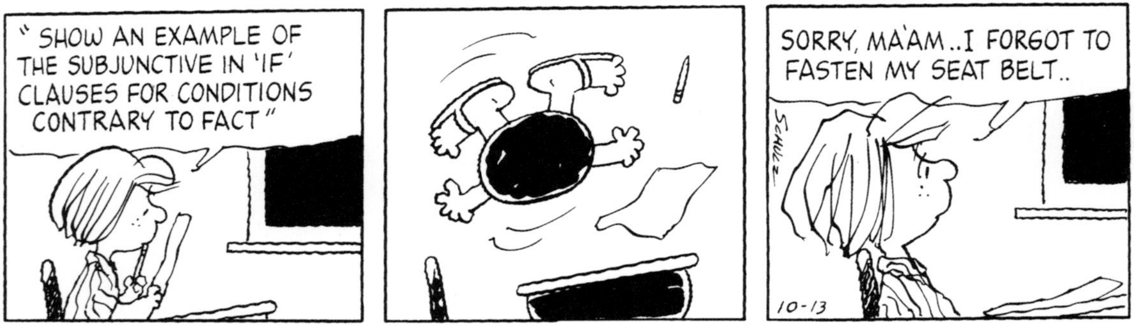
" SHOW AN EXAMPLE OF THE SUBJUNCTIVE IN 'IF' CLAUSES FOR CONDITIONS CONTRARY TO FACT "
SORRY, MA'AM..I FORGOT TO FASTEN MY SEAT BELT..
SCHULZ
10-13

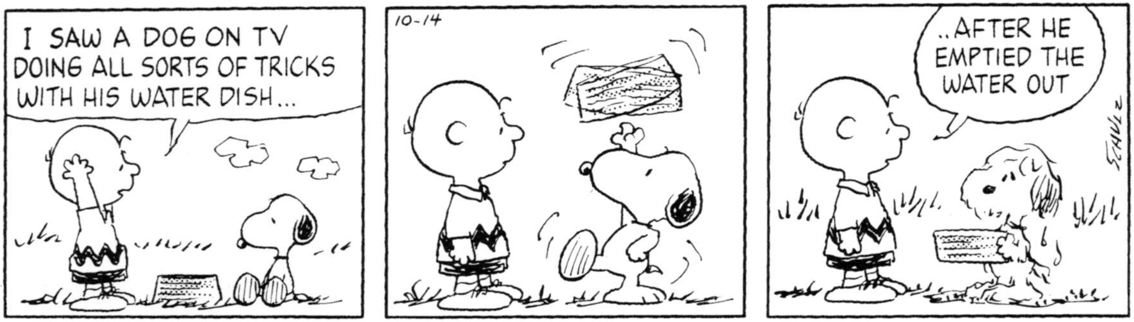
I SAW A DOG ON TV DOING ALL SORTS OF TRICKS WITH HIS WATER DISH...
10-14
..AFTER HE EMPTIED THE WATER OUT
SCHULZ

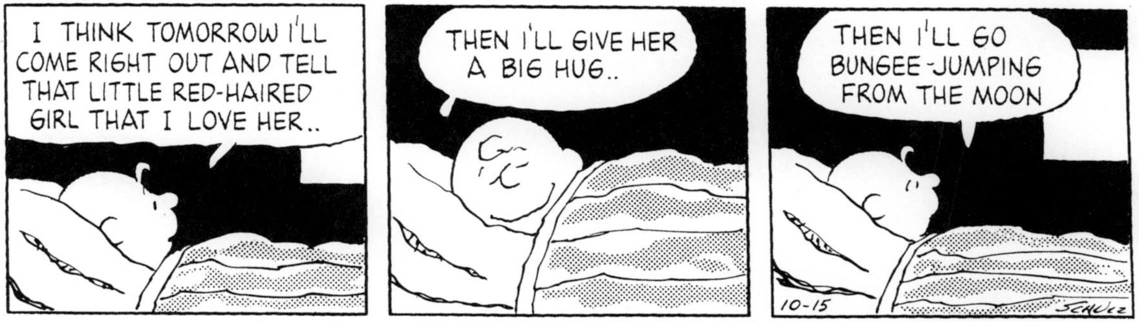
I THINK TOMORROW I'LL COME RIGHT OUT AND TELL THAT LITTLE RED-HAIRED GIRL THAT I LOVE HER..
THEN I'LL GIVE HER A BIG HUG..
THEN I'LL GO BUNGEE-JUMPING FROM THE MOON
10-15
SCHULZ

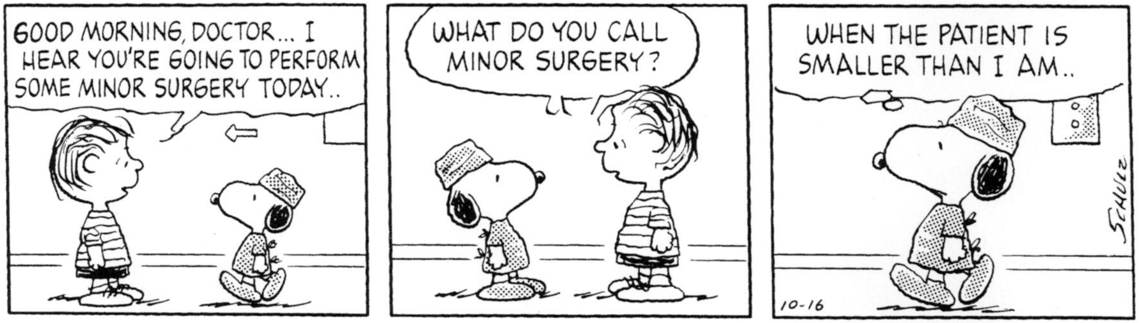
GOOD MORNING, DOCTOR... I HEAR YOU'RE GOING TO PERFORM SOME MINOR SURGERY TODAY..
WHAT DO YOU CALL MINOR SURGERY?
WHEN THE PATIENT IS SMALLER THAN I AM..
SCHULZ
10-16

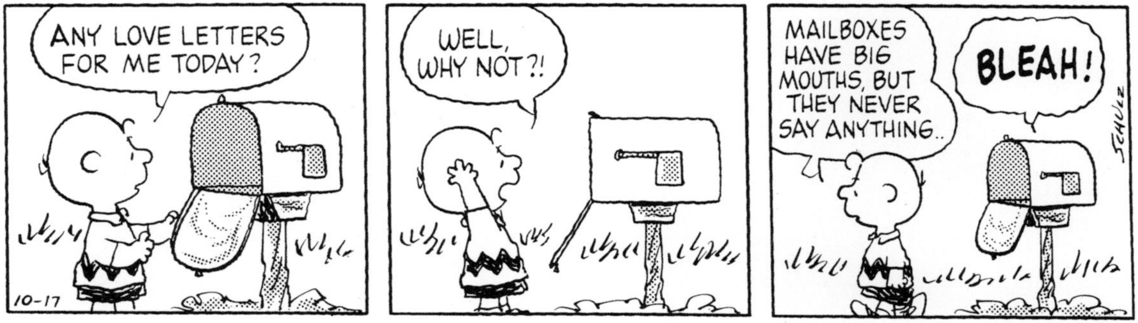
ANY LOVE LETTERS FOR ME TODAY?
10-17
WELL, WHY NOT?!
MAILBOXES HAVE BIG MOUTHS, BUT THEY NEVER SAY ANYTHING..
BLEAH!
SCHULZ

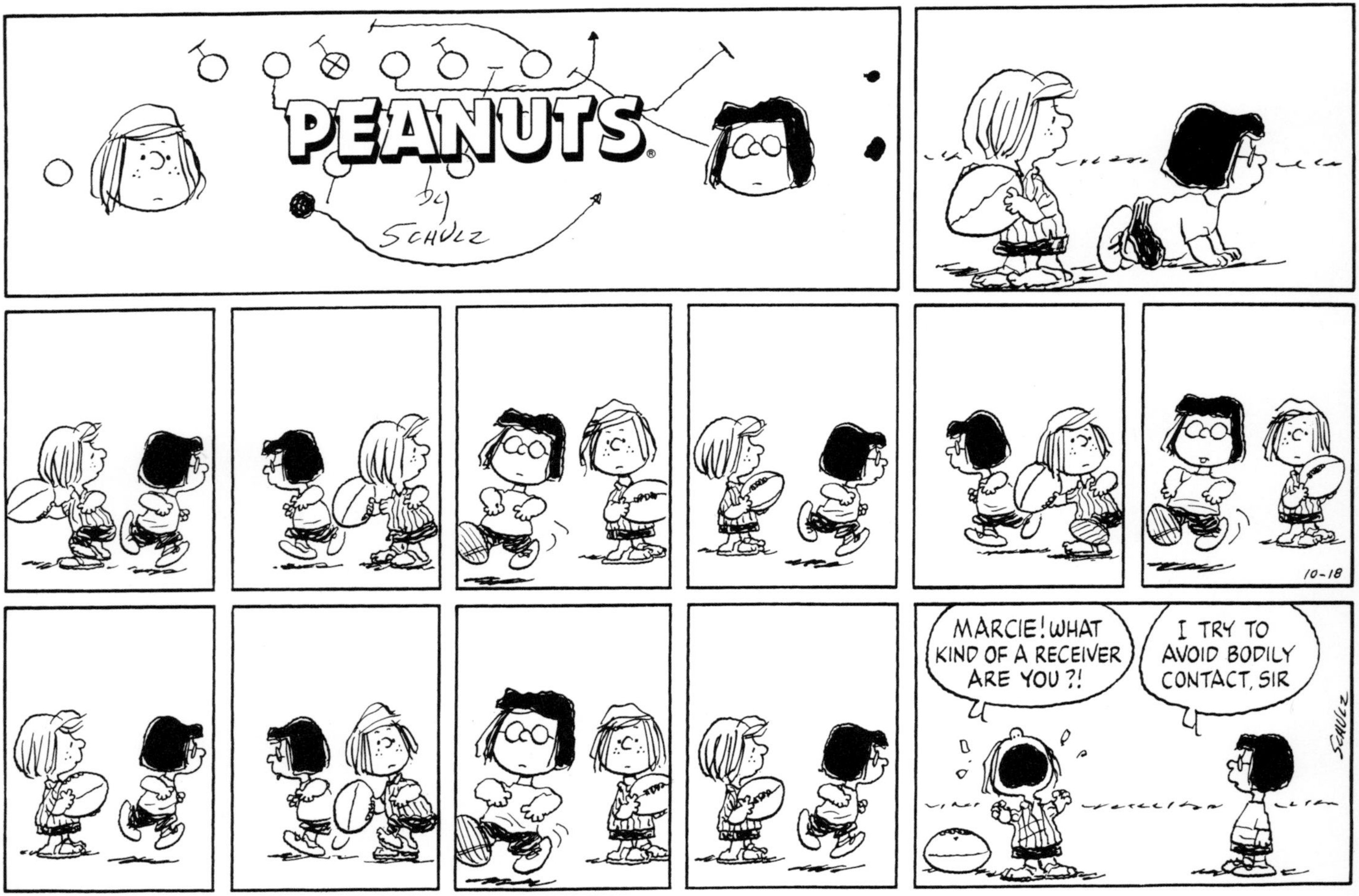
PEANUTS®
by
SCHULZ
10-18
MARCIE! WHAT KIND OF A RECEIVER ARE YOU ?!
I TRY TO AVOID BODILY CONTACT, SIR
SCHULZ

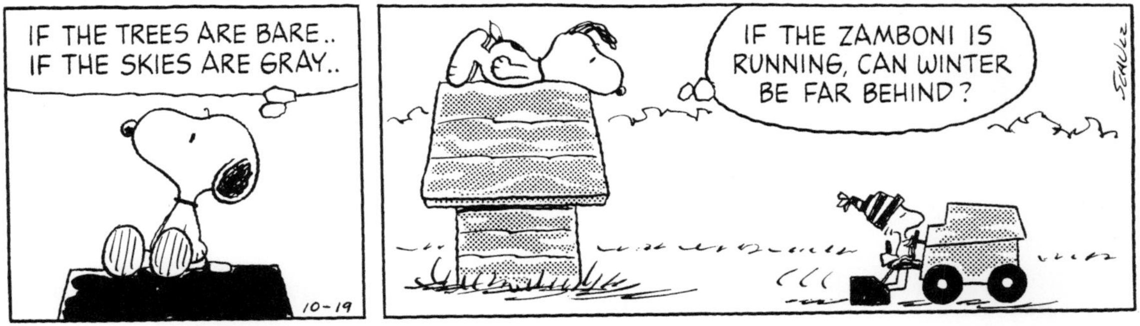
IF THE TREES ARE BARE..
IF THE SKIES ARE GRAY..
10-19
IF THE ZAMBONI IS RUNNING, CAN WINTER BE FAR BEHIND?
SCHULZ

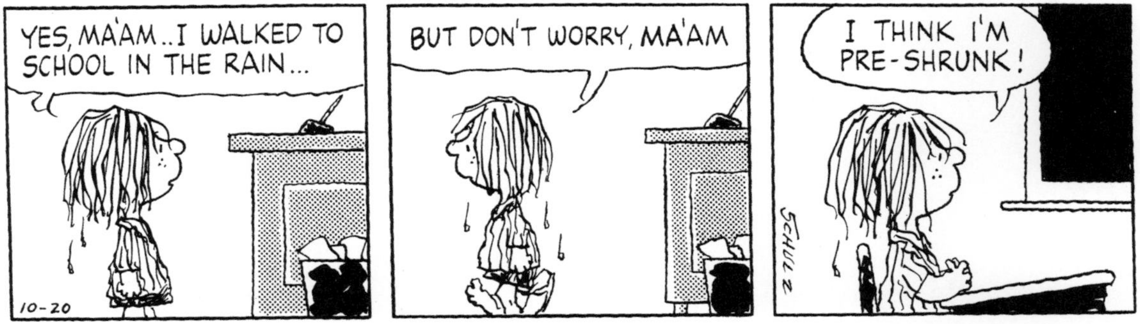
YES, MA'AM..I WALKED TO SCHOOL IN THE RAIN...
10-20
BUT DON'T WORRY, MA'AM
I THINK I'M PRE-SHRUNK!
SCHULZ

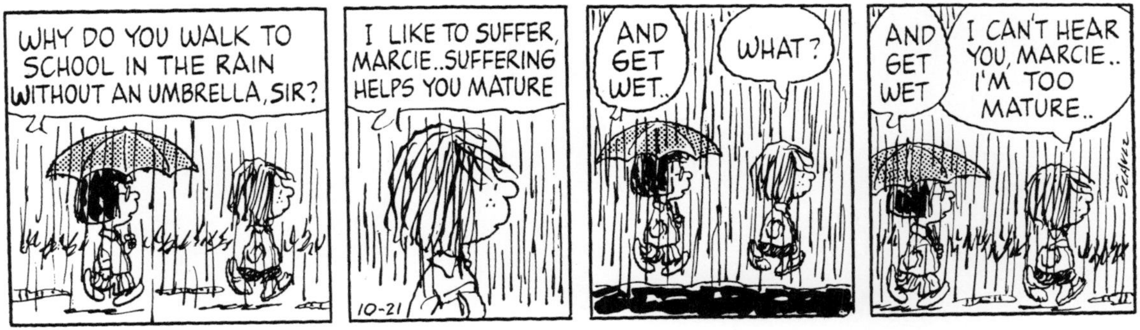
WHY DO YOU WALK TO SCHOOL IN THE RAIN WITHOUT AN UMBRELLA, SIR?
I LIKE TO SUFFER, MARCIE..SUFFERING HELPS YOU MATURE
10-21
AND GET WET..
WHAT?
AND GET WET
I CAN'T HEAR YOU, MARCIE.. I'M TOO MATURE..
SCHULZ

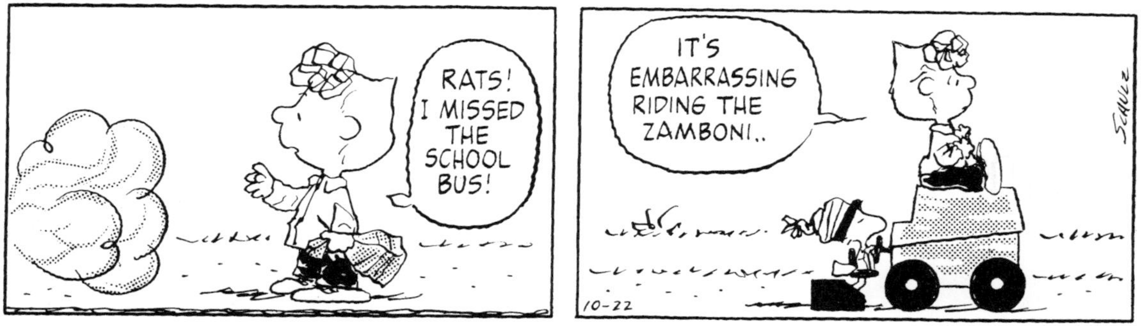
RATS! I MISSED THE SCHOOL BUS!
IT'S EMBARRASSING RIDING THE ZAMBONI..
10-22
SCHULZ

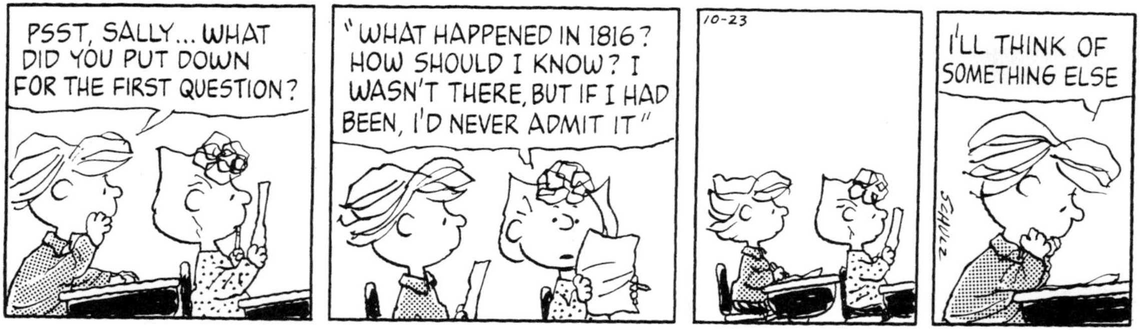
PSST, SALLY... WHAT DID YOU PUT DOWN FOR THE FIRST QUESTION?
"WHAT HAPPENED IN 1816? HOW SHOULD I KNOW? I WASN'T THERE, BUT IF I HAD BEEN, I'D NEVER ADMIT IT"
10-23
SCHULZ
I'LL THINK OF SOMETHING ELSE

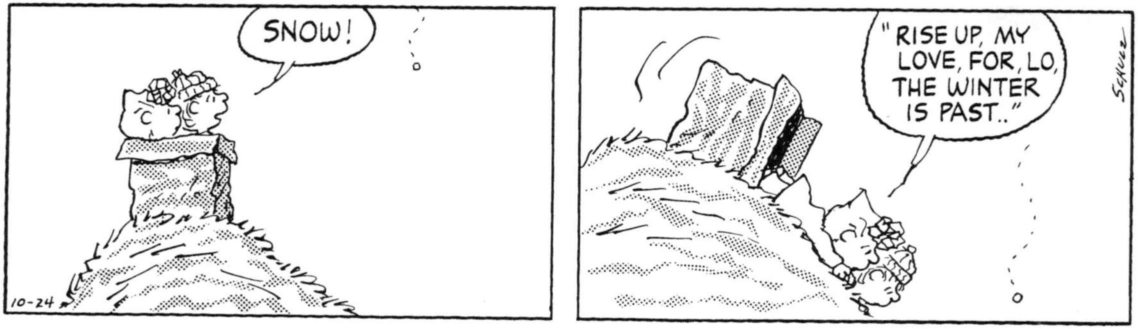
SNOW!
10-24
"RISE UP, MY LOVE, FOR, LO, THE WINTER IS PAST.."
SCHULZ

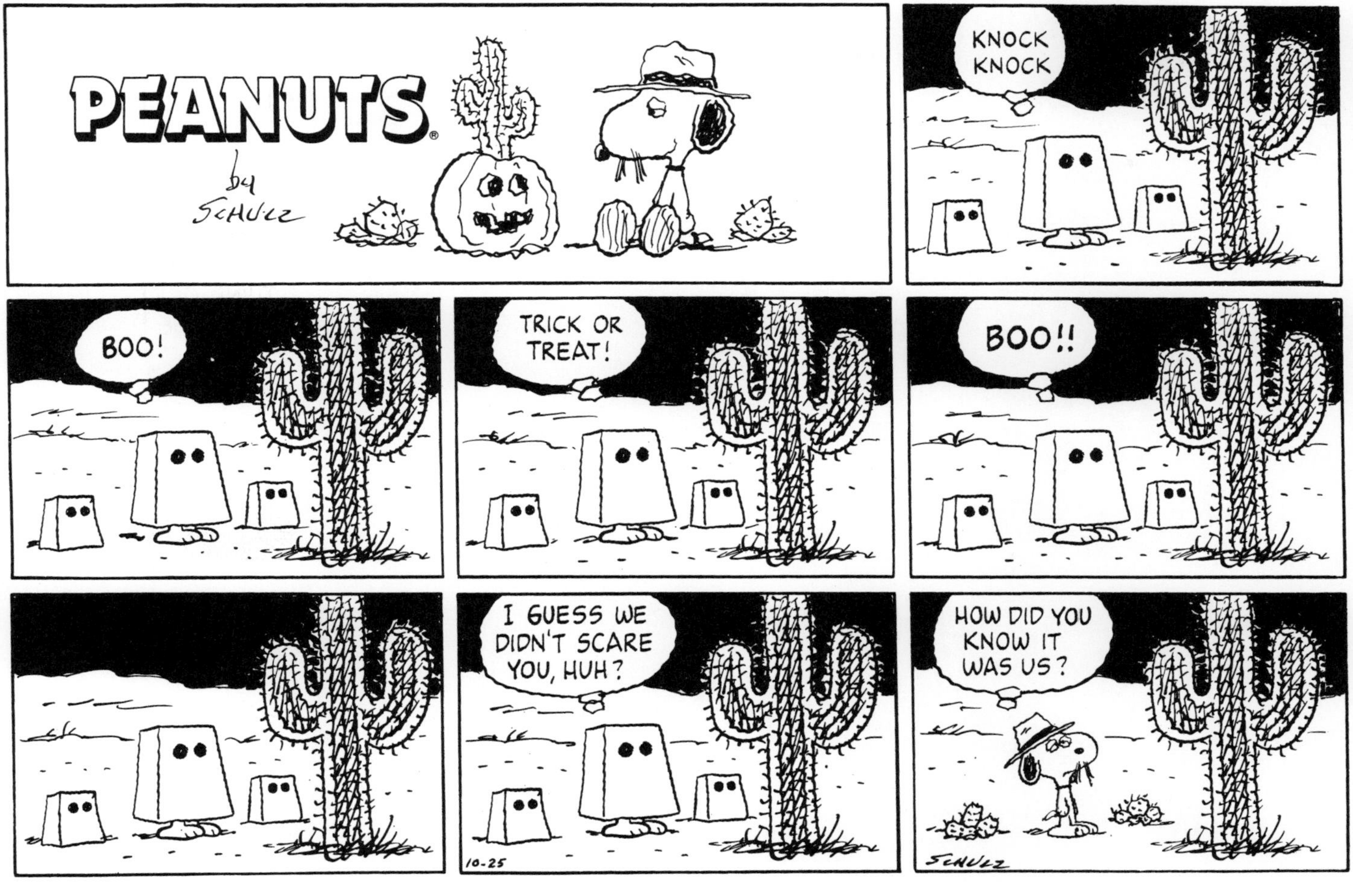
PEANUTS®
by SCHULZ
KNOCK KNOCK
BOO!
TRICK OR TREAT!
BOO!!
I GUESS WE DIDN'T SCARE YOU, HUH?
10-25
HOW DID YOU KNOW IT WAS US?
SCHULZ

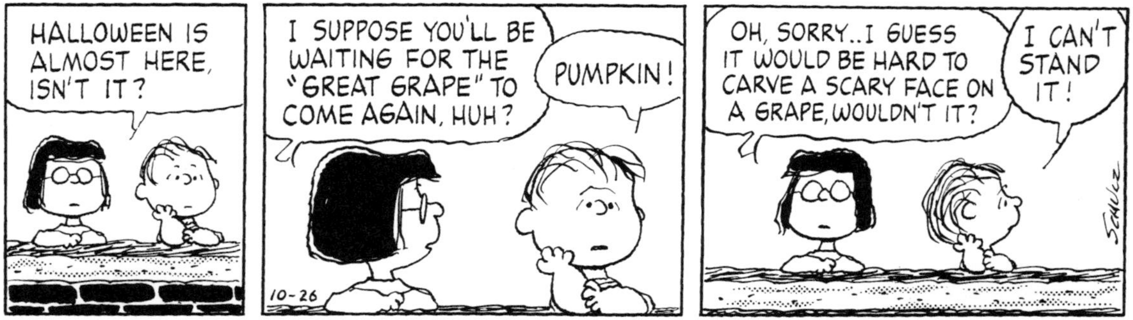
HALLOWEEN IS ALMOST HERE, ISN'T IT?
I SUPPOSE YOU'LL BE WAITING FOR THE "GREAT GRAPE" TO COME AGAIN, HUH?
PUMPKIN!
10-26
OH, SORRY..I GUESS IT WOULD BE HARD TO CARVE A SCARY FACE ON A GRAPE, WOULDN'T IT?
I CAN'T STAND IT!
SCHULZ

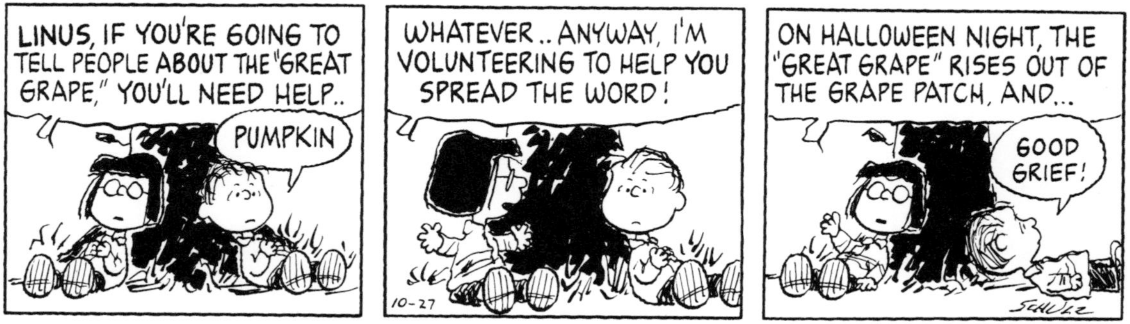
LINUS, IF YOU'RE GOING TO TELL PEOPLE ABOUT THE "GREAT GRAPE," YOU'LL NEED HELP..
PUMPKIN
WHATEVER.. ANYWAY, I'M VOLUNTEERING TO HELP YOU SPREAD THE WORD!
10-27
ON HALLOWEEN NIGHT, THE "GREAT GRAPE" RISES OUT OF THE GRAPE PATCH, AND...
GOOD GRIEF!
SCHULZ

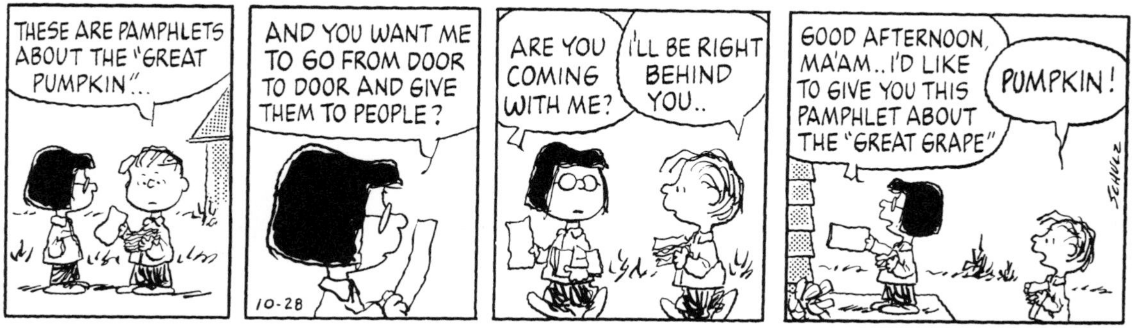
THESE ARE PAMPHLETS ABOUT THE "GREAT PUMPKIN"..
AND YOU WANT ME TO GO FROM DOOR TO DOOR AND GIVE THEM TO PEOPLE?
10-28
ARE YOU COMING WITH ME?
I'LL BE RIGHT BEHIND YOU..
GOOD AFTERNOON, MA'AM.. I'D LIKE TO GIVE YOU THIS PAMPHLET ABOUT THE "GREAT GRAPE"
PUMPKIN!
SCHULZ

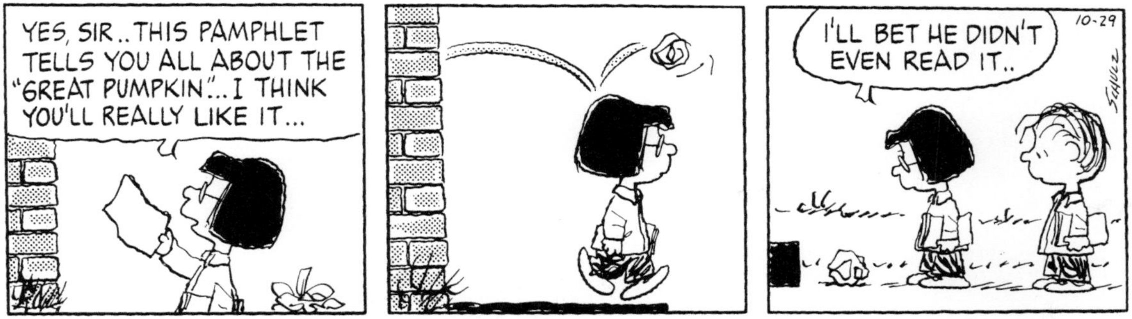
YES, SIR.. THIS PAMPHLET TELLS YOU ALL ABOUT THE "GREAT PUMPKIN"... I THINK YOU'LL REALLY LIKE IT...
I'LL BET HE DIDN'T EVEN READ IT..

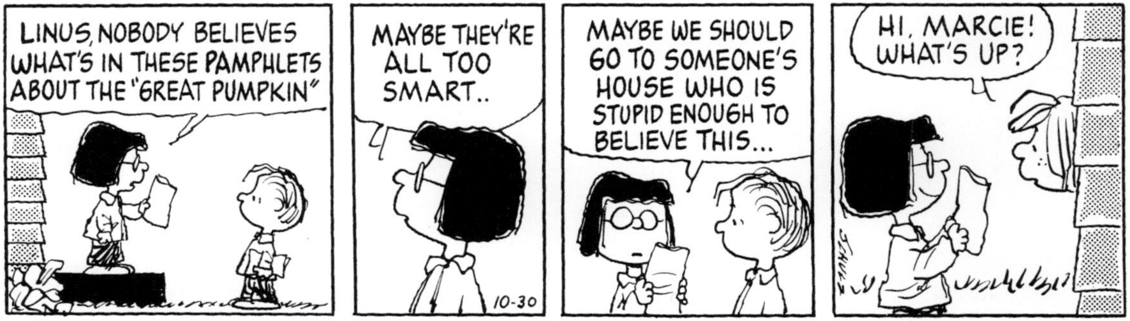
LINUS, NOBODY BELIEVES WHAT'S IN THESE PAMPHLETS ABOUT THE "GREAT PUMPKIN"
MAYBE THEY'RE ALL TOO SMART..
MAYBE WE SHOULD GO TO SOMEONE'S HOUSE WHO IS STUPID ENOUGH TO BELIEVE THIS...
HI, MARCIE! WHAT'S UP?

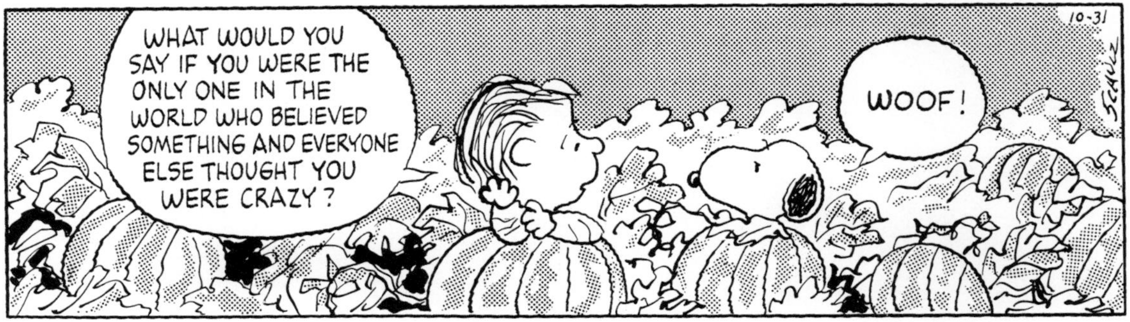
WHAT WOULD YOU SAY IF YOU WERE THE ONLY ONE IN THE WORLD WHO BELIEVED SOMETHING AND EVERYONE ELSE THOUGHT YOU WERE CRAZY?
WOOF!

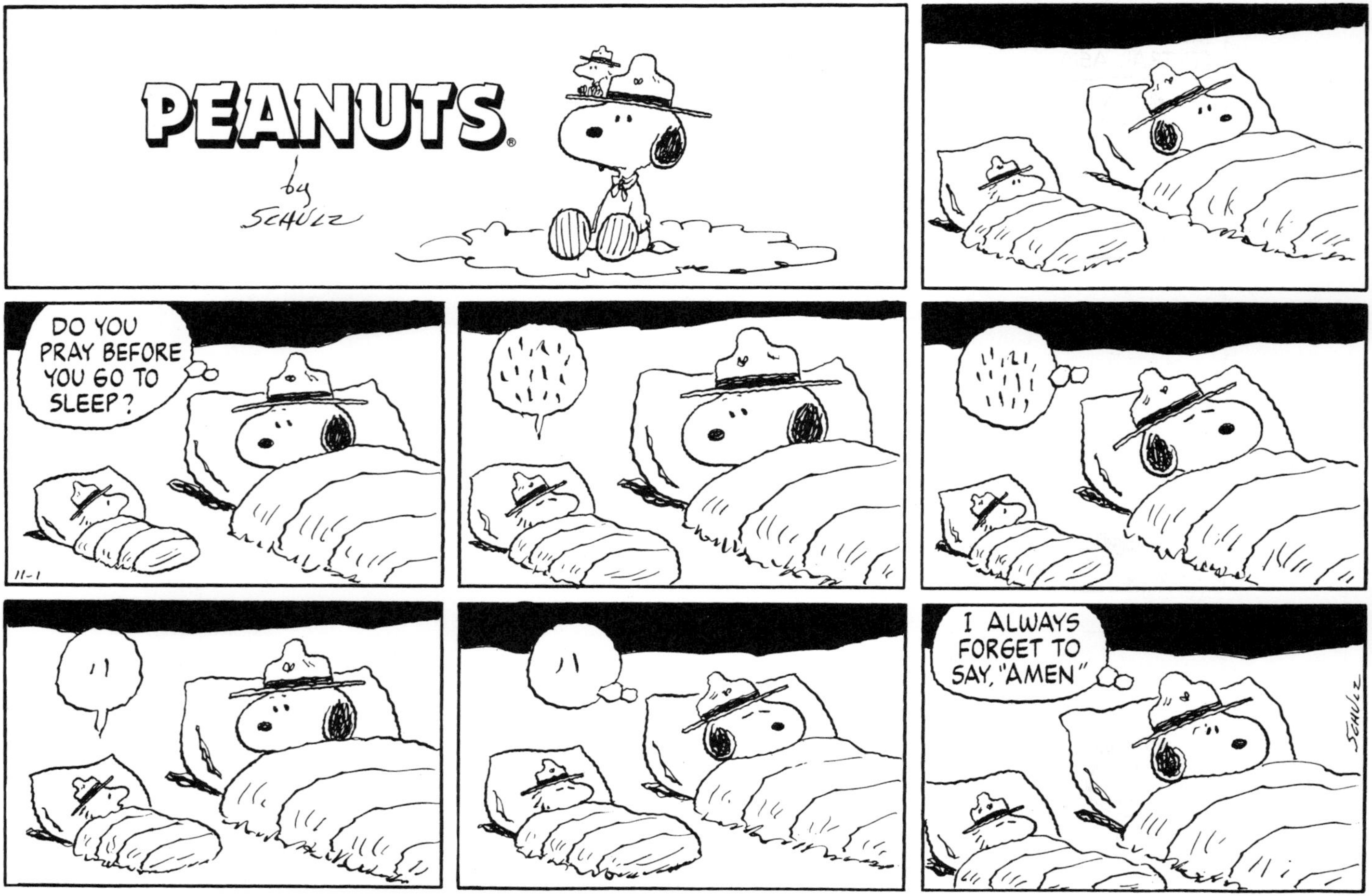
PEANUTS
by SCHULZ
DO YOU PRAY BEFORE YOU GO TO SLEEP?
11-1
I ALWAYS FORGET TO SAY, "AMEN"
SCHULZ

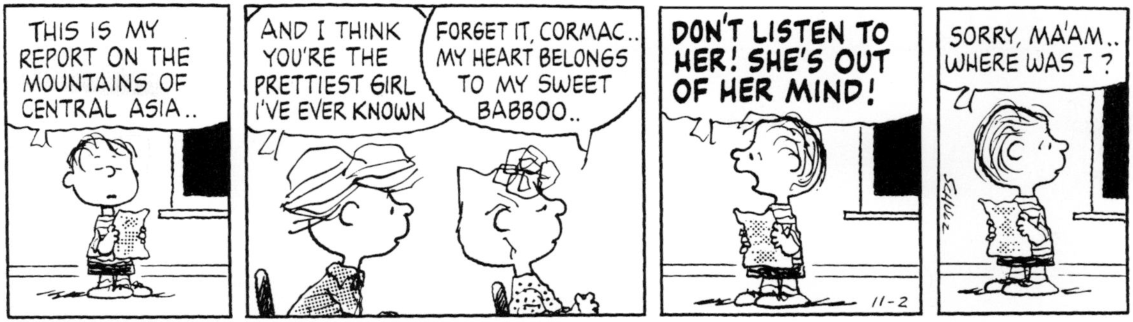
THIS IS MY REPORT ON THE MOUNTAINS OF CENTRAL ASIA..
AND I THINK YOU'RE THE PRETTIEST GIRL I'VE EVER KNOWN
FORGET IT, CORMAC.. MY HEART BELONGS TO MY SWEET BABBOO..
DON'T LISTEN TO HER! SHE'S OUT OF HER MIND!
11-2
SORRY, MA'AM.. WHERE WAS I?

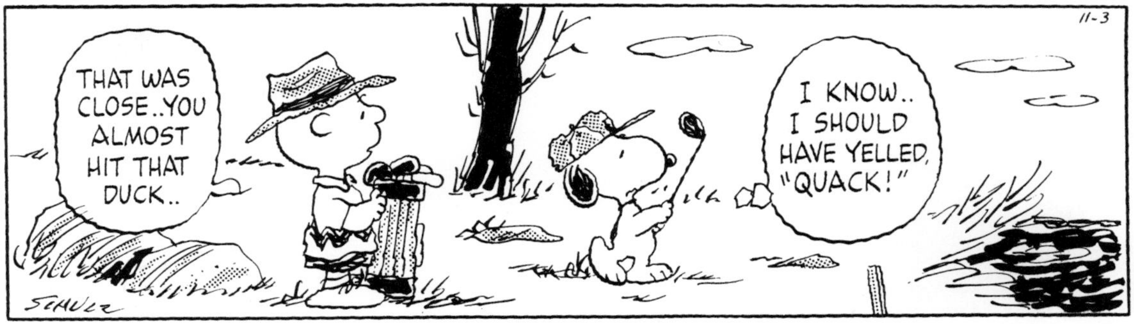
11-3
THAT WAS CLOSE..YOU ALMOST HIT THAT DUCK..
I KNOW.. I SHOULD HAVE YELLED, "QUACK!"

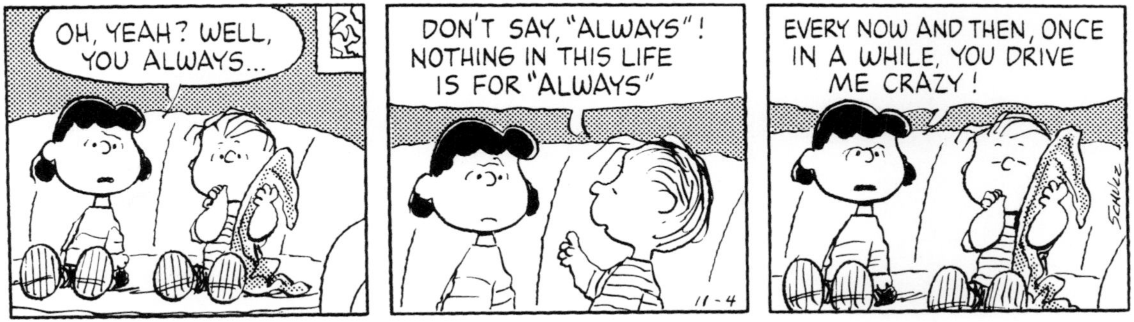
OH, YEAH? WELL, YOU ALWAYS...
DON'T SAY, "ALWAYS"! NOTHING IN THIS LIFE IS FOR "ALWAYS"
11-4
EVERY NOW AND THEN, ONCE IN A WHILE, YOU DRIVE ME CRAZY!

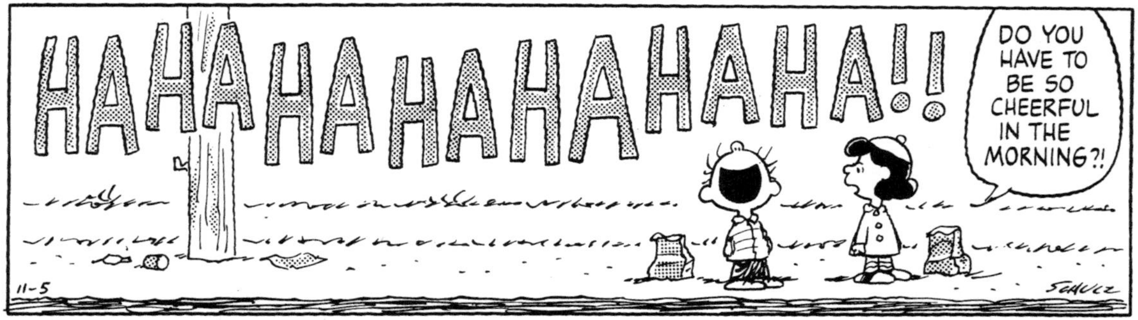
HAHAHAHAHAHAHAHAHA!!
DO YOU HAVE TO BE SO CHEERFUL IN THE MORNING?!
11-5
SCHULZ

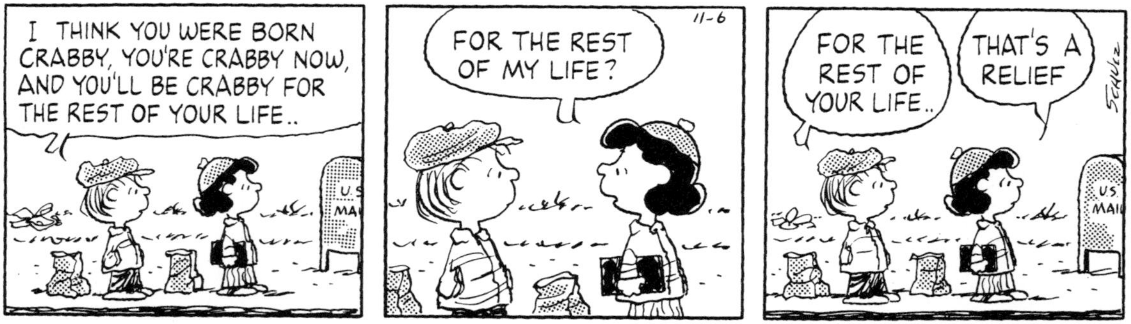
I THINK YOU WERE BORN CRABBY, YOU'RE CRABBY NOW, AND YOU'LL BE CRABBY FOR THE REST OF YOUR LIFE..
11-6
FOR THE REST OF MY LIFE?
FOR THE REST OF YOUR LIFE..
THAT'S A RELIEF
SCHULZ

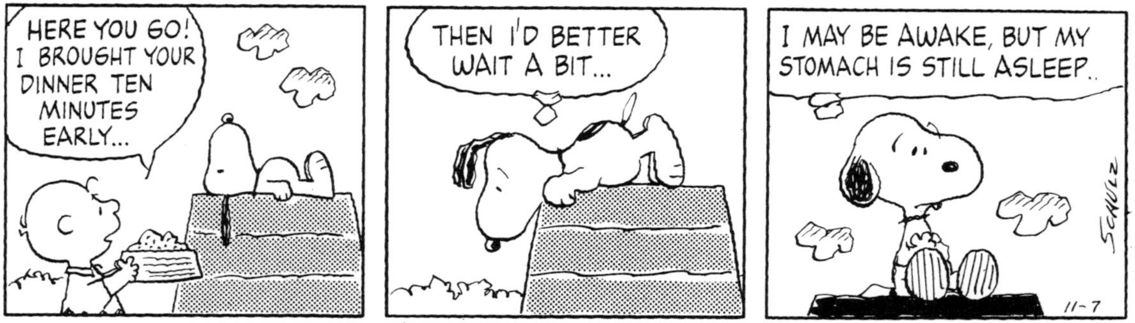
HERE YOU GO! I BROUGHT YOUR DINNER TEN MINUTES EARLY...
THEN I'D BETTER WAIT A BIT...
I MAY BE AWAKE, BUT MY STOMACH IS STILL ASLEEP..
SCHULZ
11-7

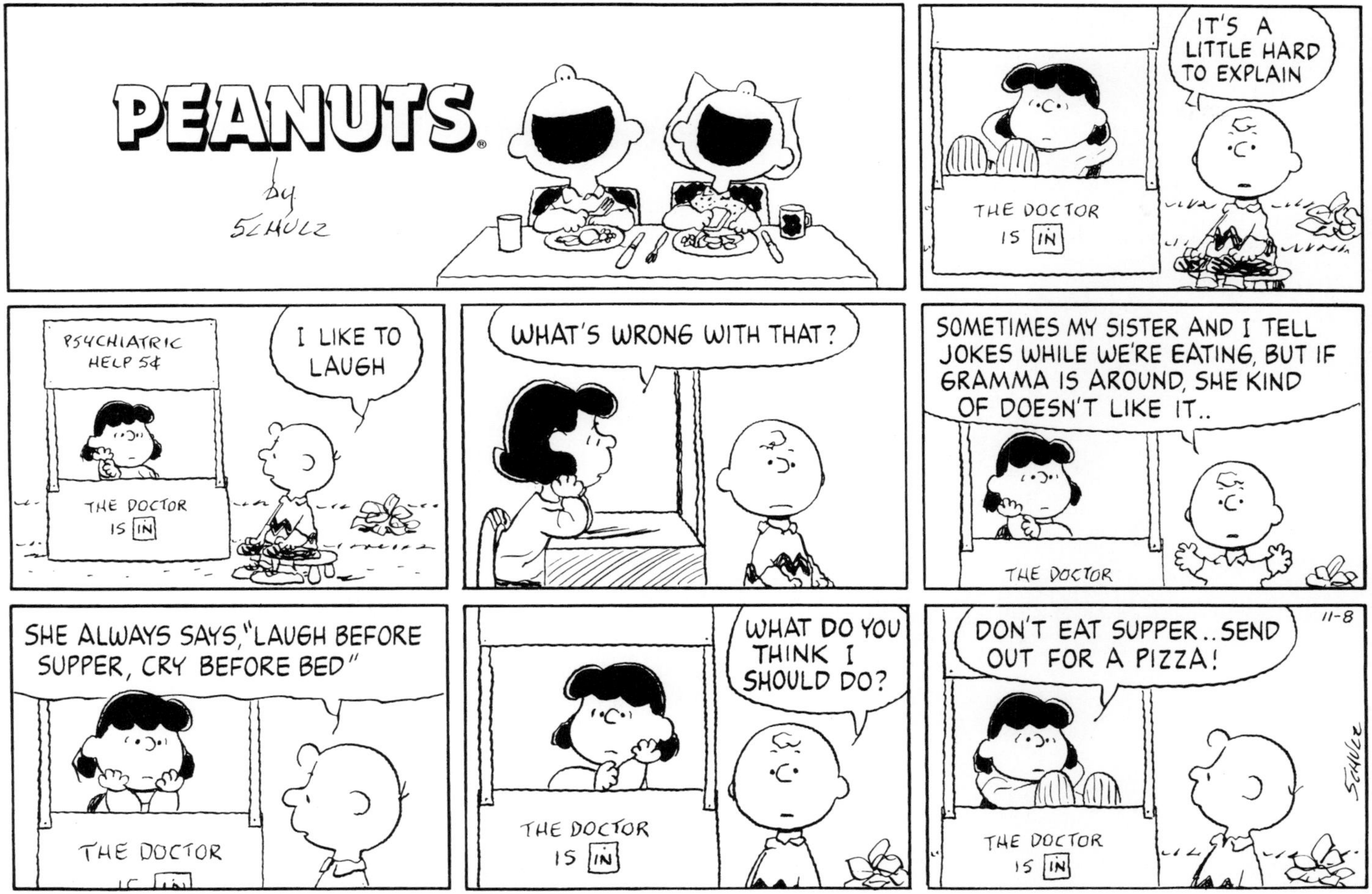
PEANUTS
by SCHULZ
IT'S A LITTLE HARD TO EXPLAIN
THE DOCTOR IS IN
PSYCHIATRIC HELP 5¢
I LIKE TO LAUGH
THE DOCTOR IS IN
WHAT'S WRONG WITH THAT?
SOMETIMES MY SISTER AND I TELL JOKES WHILE WE'RE EATING, BUT IF GRAMMA IS AROUND, SHE KIND OF DOESN'T LIKE IT..
THE DOCTOR
SHE ALWAYS SAYS, "LAUGH BEFORE SUPPER, CRY BEFORE BED"
THE DOCTOR
WHAT DO YOU THINK I SHOULD DO?
THE DOCTOR IS IN
11-8
DON'T EAT SUPPER.. SEND OUT FOR A PIZZA!
THE DOCTOR IS IN
SCHULZ

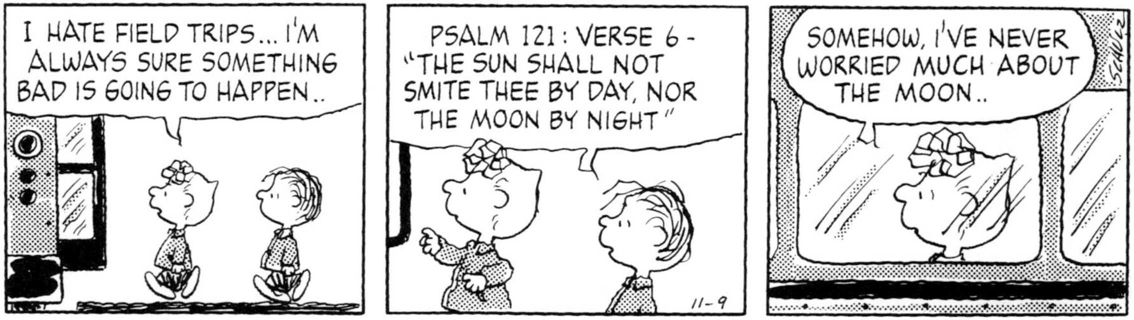
I HATE FIELD TRIPS... I'M ALWAYS SURE SOMETHING BAD IS GOING TO HAPPEN..
PSALM 121 : VERSE 6 - "THE SUN SHALL NOT SMITE THEE BY DAY, NOR THE MOON BY NIGHT"
11-9
SCHULZ
SOMEHOW, I'VE NEVER WORRIED MUCH ABOUT THE MOON..

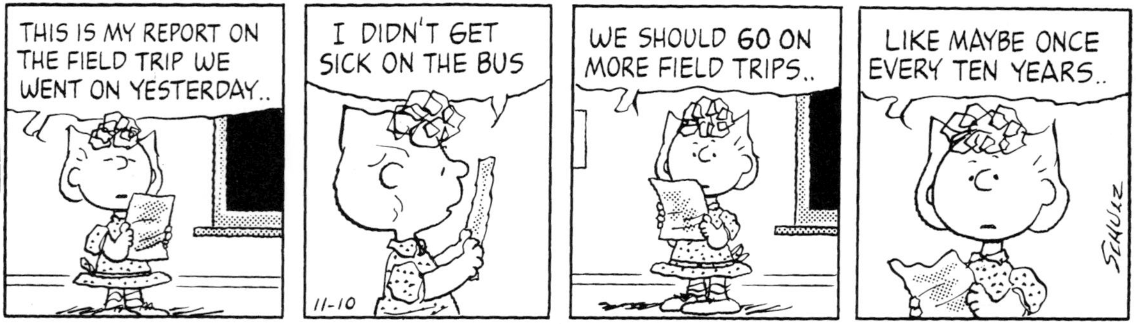
THIS IS MY REPORT ON THE FIELD TRIP WE WENT ON YESTERDAY..
I DIDN'T GET SICK ON THE BUS
11-10
WE SHOULD GO ON MORE FIELD TRIPS..
LIKE MAYBE ONCE EVERY TEN YEARS..
SCHULZ

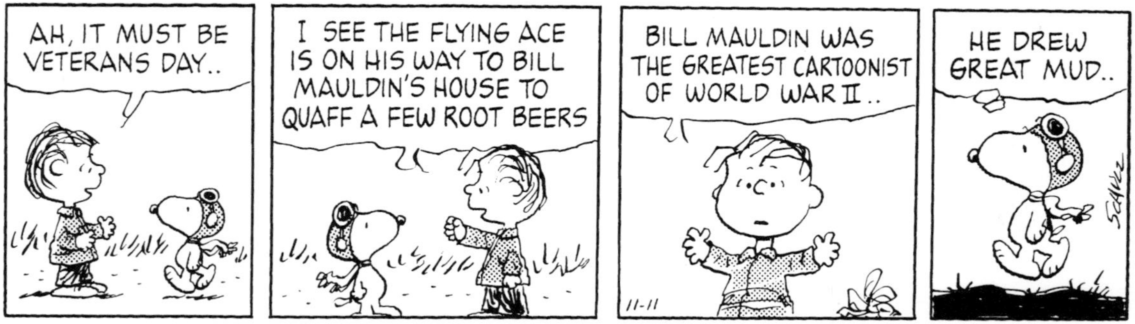
AH, IT MUST BE VETERANS DAY..
I SEE THE FLYING ACE IS ON HIS WAY TO BILL MAULDIN'S HOUSE TO QUAFF A FEW ROOT BEERS
BILL MAULDIN WAS THE GREATEST CARTOONIST OF WORLD WAR II ..
11-11
HE DREW GREAT MUD..
SCHULZ

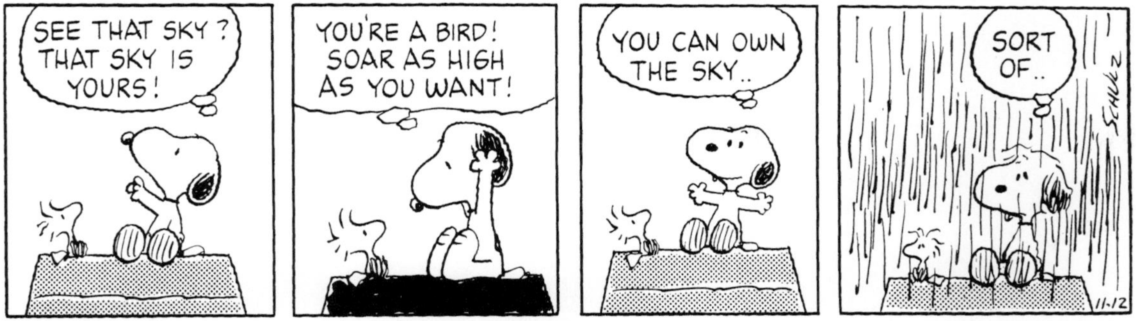
SEE THAT SKY ? THAT SKY IS YOURS !
YOU'RE A BIRD! SOAR AS HIGH AS YOU WANT!
YOU CAN OWN THE SKY..
SORT OF..
SCHULZ
11-12

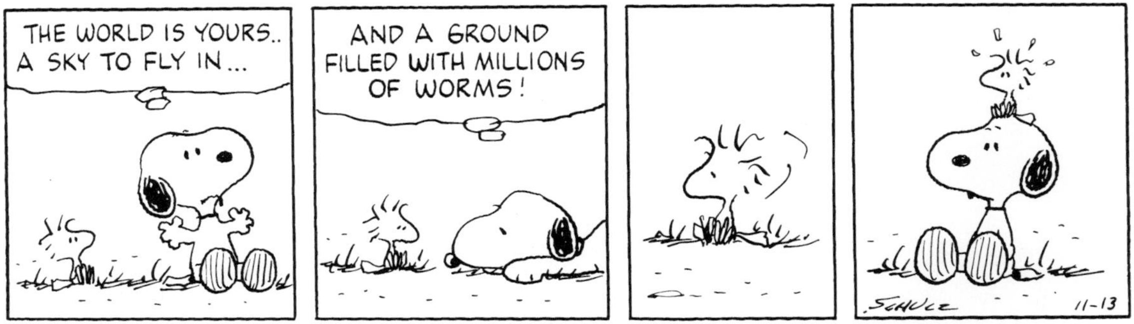
THE WORLD IS YOURS.. A SKY TO FLY IN...
AND A GROUND FILLED WITH MILLIONS OF WORMS!
SCHULZ
11-13

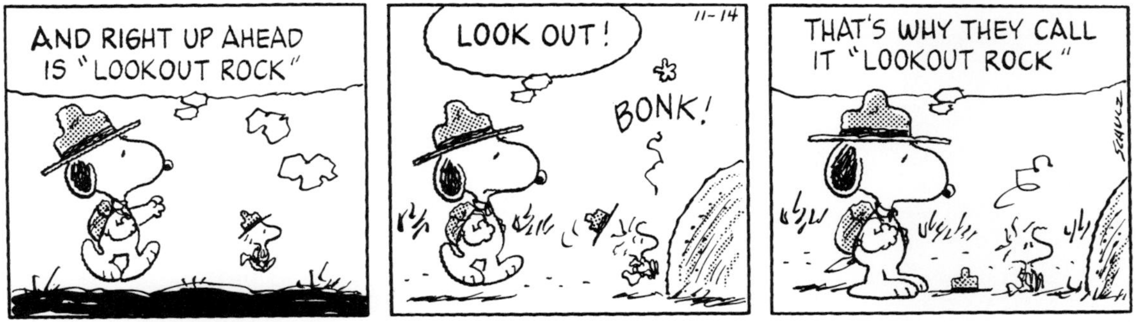
AND RIGHT UP AHEAD IS "LOOKOUT ROCK"
11-14
LOOK OUT!
BONK!
THAT'S WHY THEY CALL IT "LOOKOUT ROCK"
SCHULZ

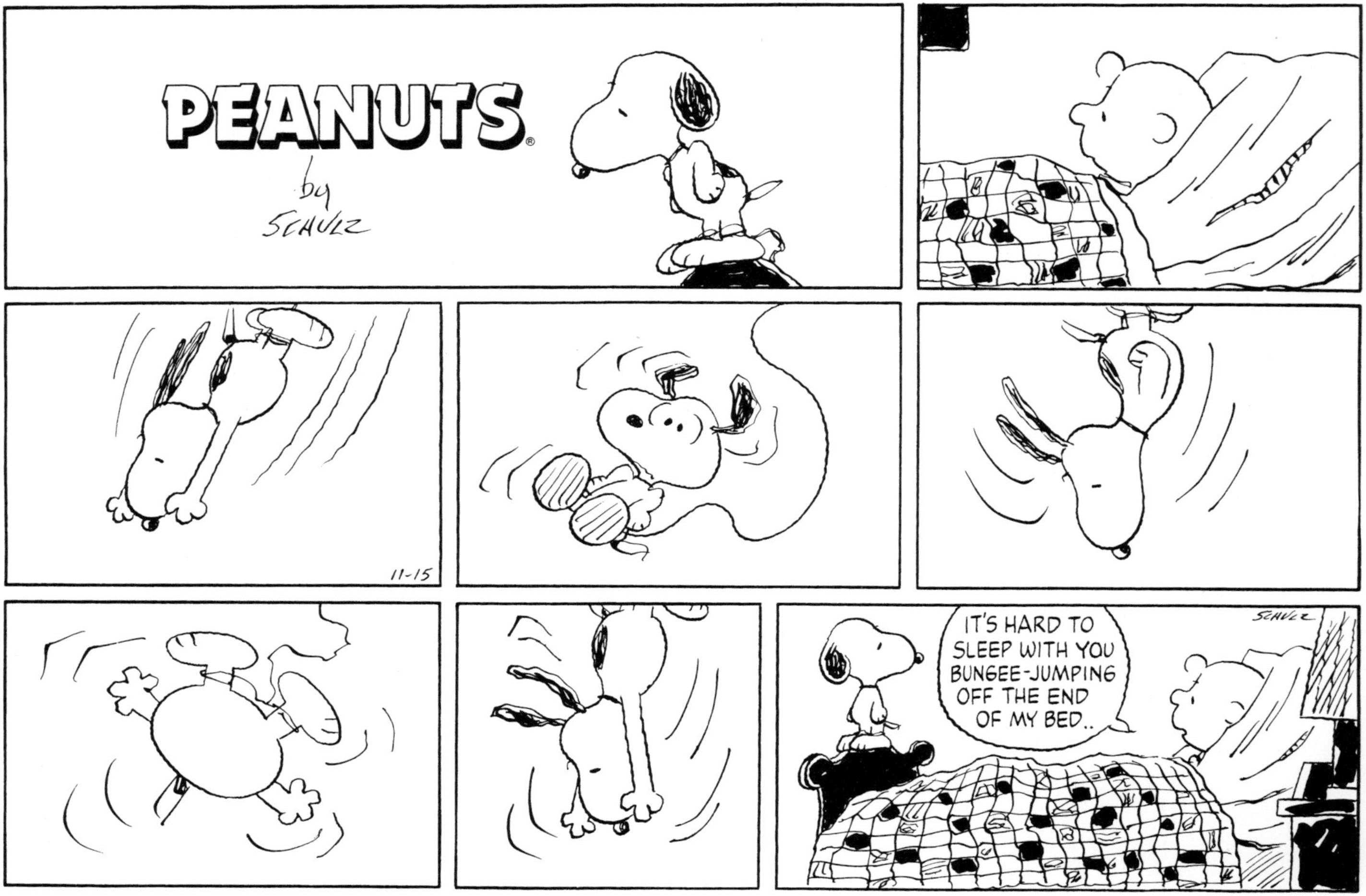
PEANUTS®
by SCHULZ
11-15
SCHULZ
IT'S HARD TO SLEEP WITH YOU BUNGEE-JUMPING OFF THE END OF MY BED..

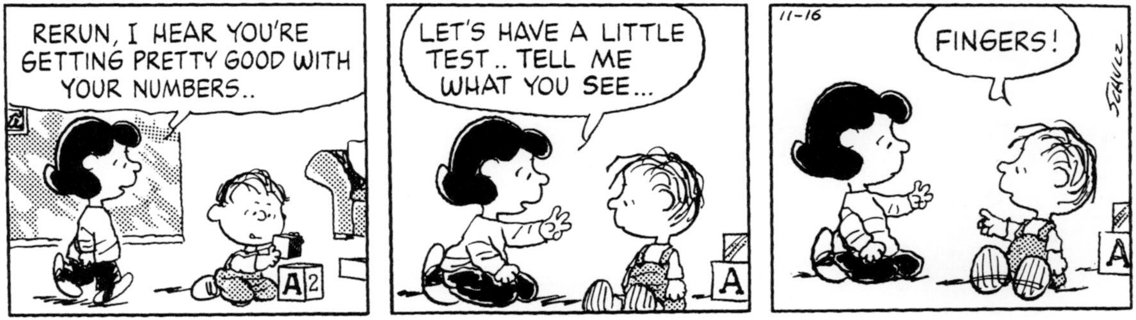
RERUN, I HEAR YOU'RE GETTING PRETTY GOOD WITH YOUR NUMBERS..
LET'S HAVE A LITTLE TEST.. TELL ME WHAT YOU SEE...
11-16
FINGERS!

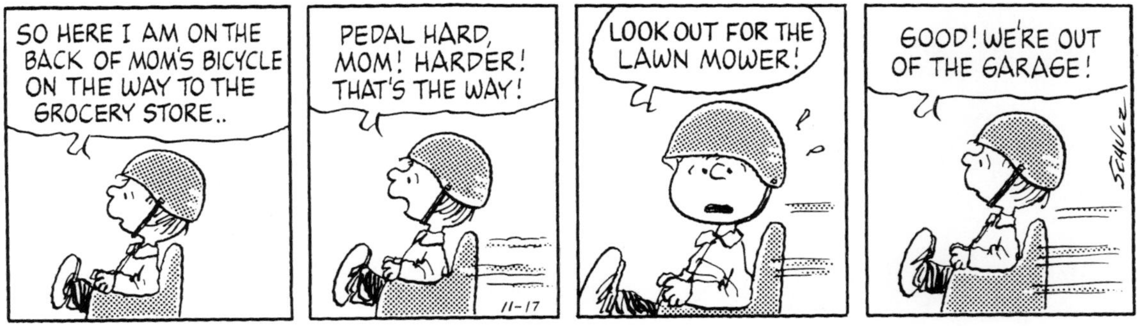
SO HERE I AM ON THE BACK OF MOM'S BICYCLE ON THE WAY TO THE GROCERY STORE..
PEDAL HARD, MOM! HARDER! THAT'S THE WAY!
11-17
LOOK OUT FOR THE LAWN MOWER!
GOOD! WE'RE OUT OF THE GARAGE!

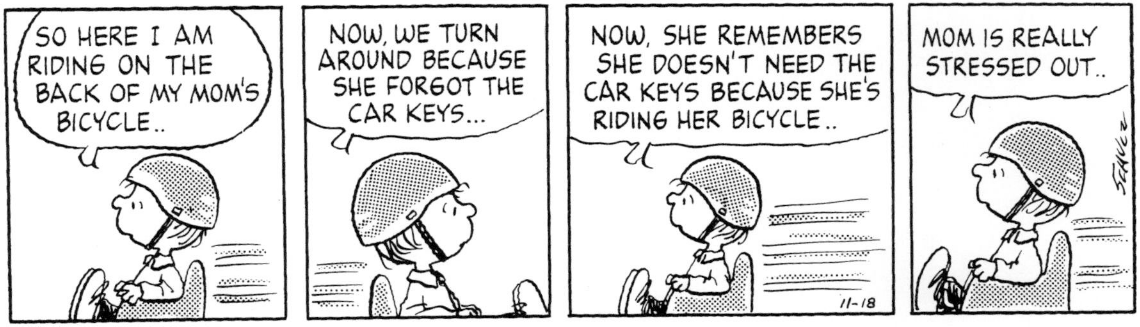
SO HERE I AM RIDING ON THE BACK OF MY MOM'S BICYCLE..
NOW, WE TURN AROUND BECAUSE SHE FORGOT THE CAR KEYS...
NOW, SHE REMEMBERS SHE DOESN'T NEED THE CAR KEYS BECAUSE SHE'S RIDING HER BICYCLE..
11-18
MOM IS REALLY STRESSED OUT..

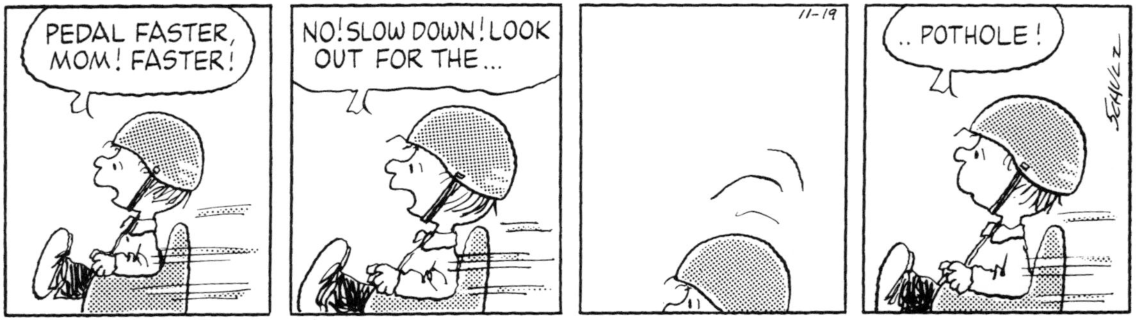
PEDAL FASTER, MOM! FASTER!
NO! SLOW DOWN! LOOK OUT FOR THE...
11-19
.. POTHOLE!
SCHULZ

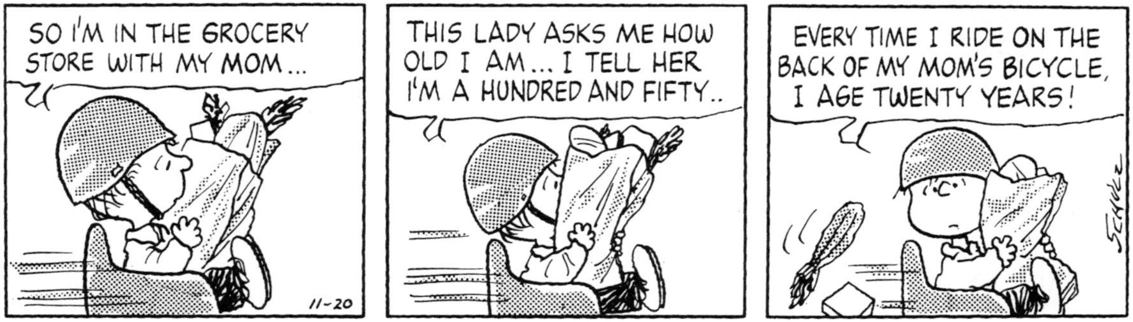
SO I'M IN THE GROCERY STORE WITH MY MOM...
11-20
THIS LADY ASKS ME HOW OLD I AM... I TELL HER I'M A HUNDRED AND FIFTY..
EVERY TIME I RIDE ON THE BACK OF MY MOM'S BICYCLE, I AGE TWENTY YEARS!
SCHULZ

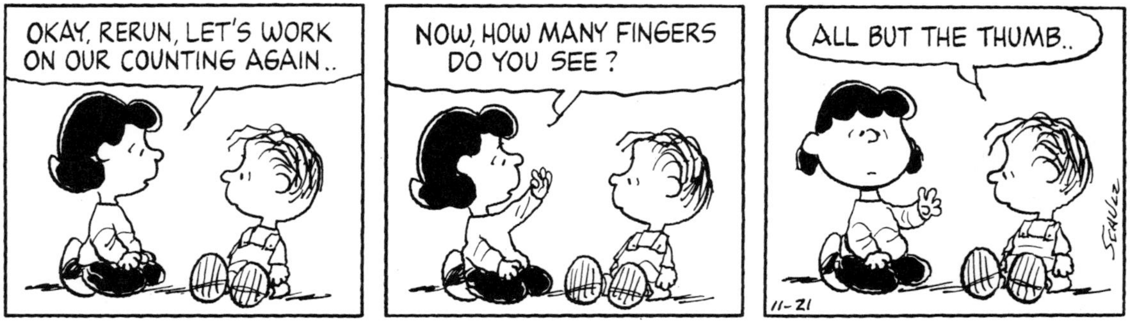
OKAY, RERUN, LET'S WORK ON OUR COUNTING AGAIN..
NOW, HOW MANY FINGERS DO YOU SEE?
ALL BUT THE THUMB..
SCHULZ
11-21

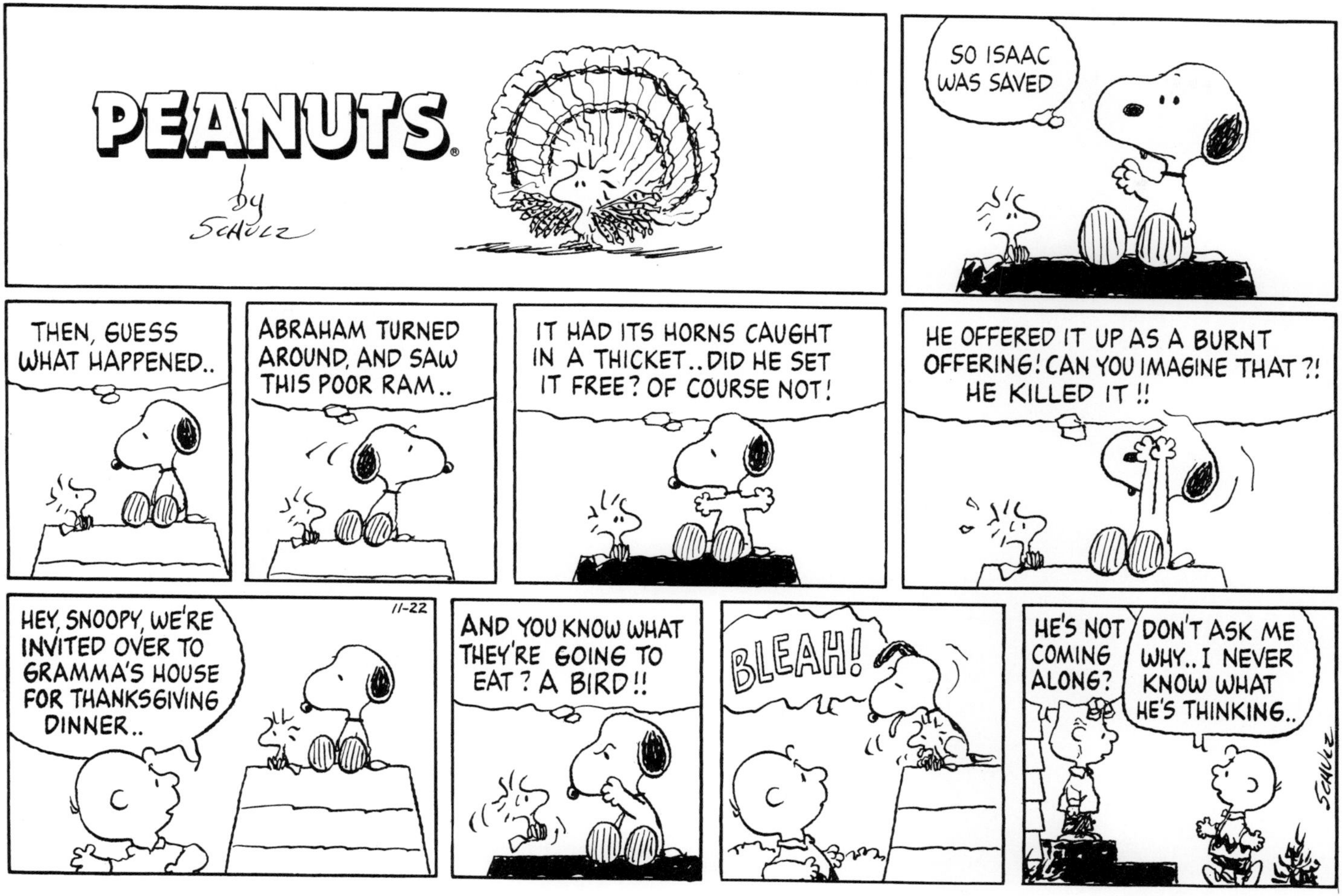
PEANUTS
by SCHULZ
SO ISAAC WAS SAVED
THEN, GUESS WHAT HAPPENED..
ABRAHAM TURNED AROUND, AND SAW THIS POOR RAM..
IT HAD ITS HORNS CAUGHT IN A THICKET..DID HE SET IT FREE? OF COURSE NOT!
HE OFFERED IT UP AS A BURNT OFFERING! CAN YOU IMAGINE THAT?! HE KILLED IT!!
11-22
HEY, SNOOPY, WE'RE INVITED OVER TO GRAMMA'S HOUSE FOR THANKSGIVING DINNER..
AND YOU KNOW WHAT THEY'RE GOING TO EAT? A BIRD!!
BLEAH!
HE'S NOT COMING ALONG?
DON'T ASK ME WHY..I NEVER KNOW WHAT HE'S THINKING..
SCHULZ

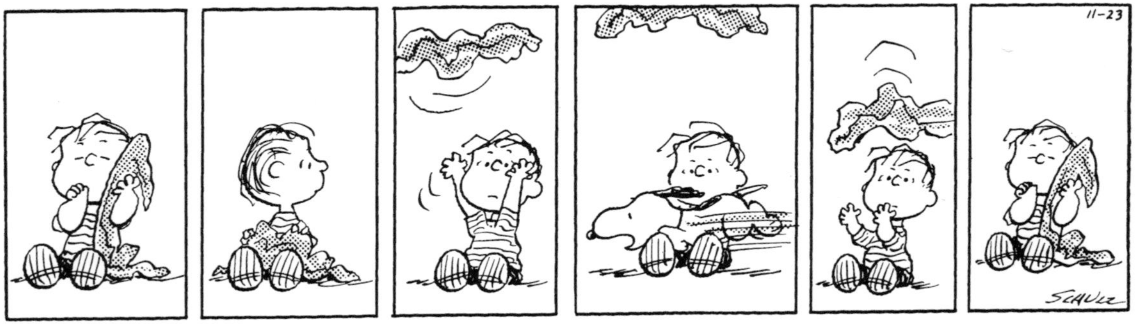
11-23
SCHULZ

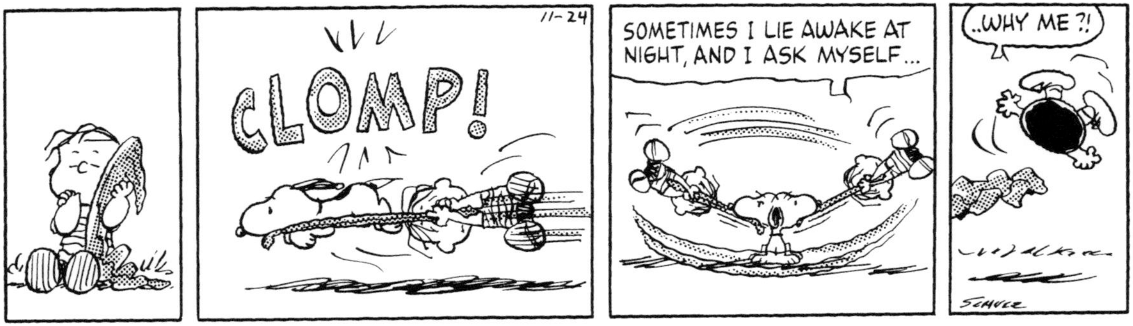
11-24
CLOMP!
SOMETIMES I LIE AWAKE AT NIGHT, AND I ASK MYSELF...
..WHY ME ?!
SCHULZ

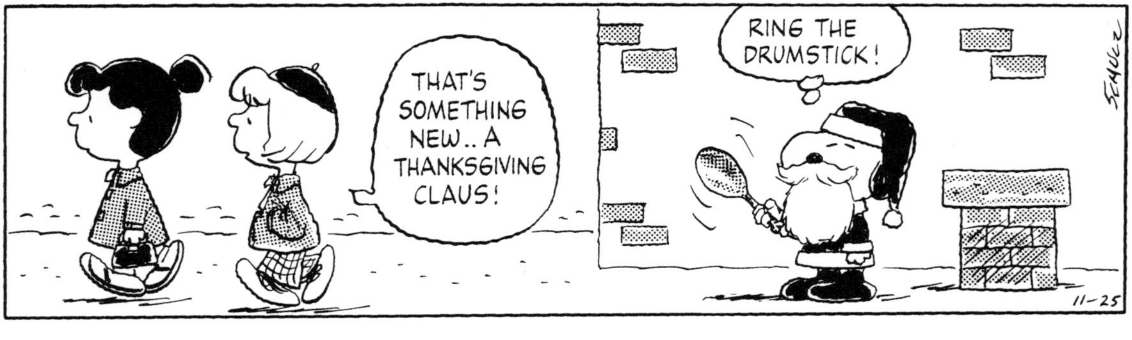
THAT'S SOMETHING NEW.. A THANKSGIVING CLAUS!
RING THE DRUMSTICK!
SCHULZ
11-25

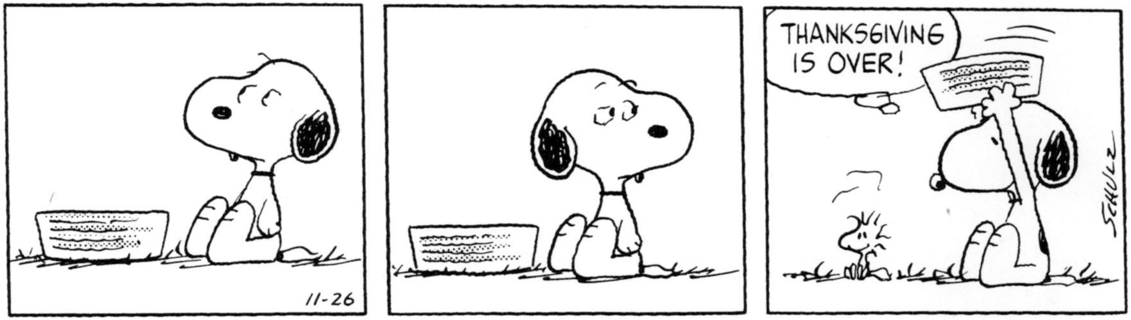
11-26
THANKSGIVING IS OVER!
SCHULZ

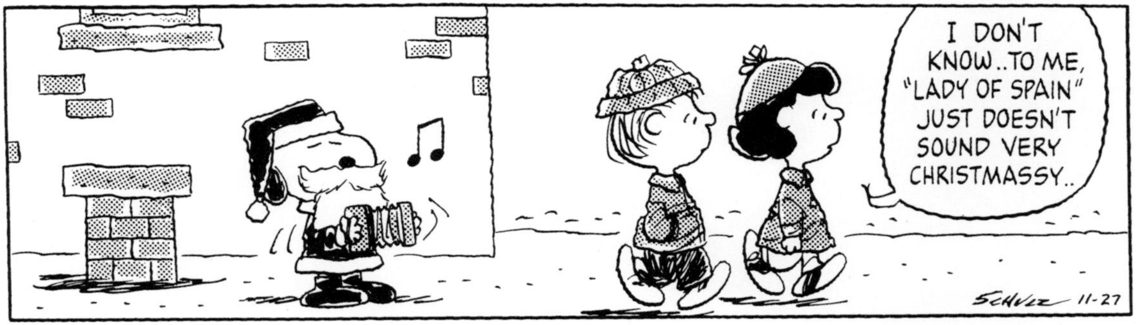
I DON'T KNOW..TO ME, "LADY OF SPAIN" JUST DOESN'T SOUND VERY CHRISTMASSY..
SCHULZ 11-27

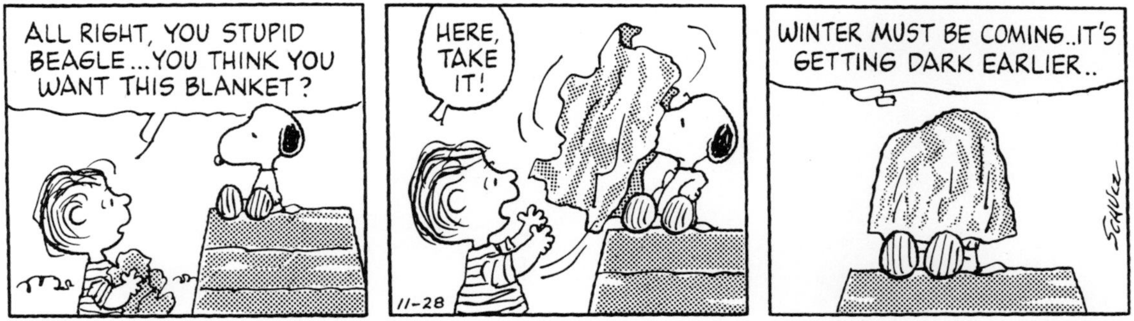
ALL RIGHT, YOU STUPID BEAGLE...YOU THINK YOU WANT THIS BLANKET?
HERE, TAKE IT!
11-28
WINTER MUST BE COMING..IT'S GETTING DARK EARLIER..
SCHULZ

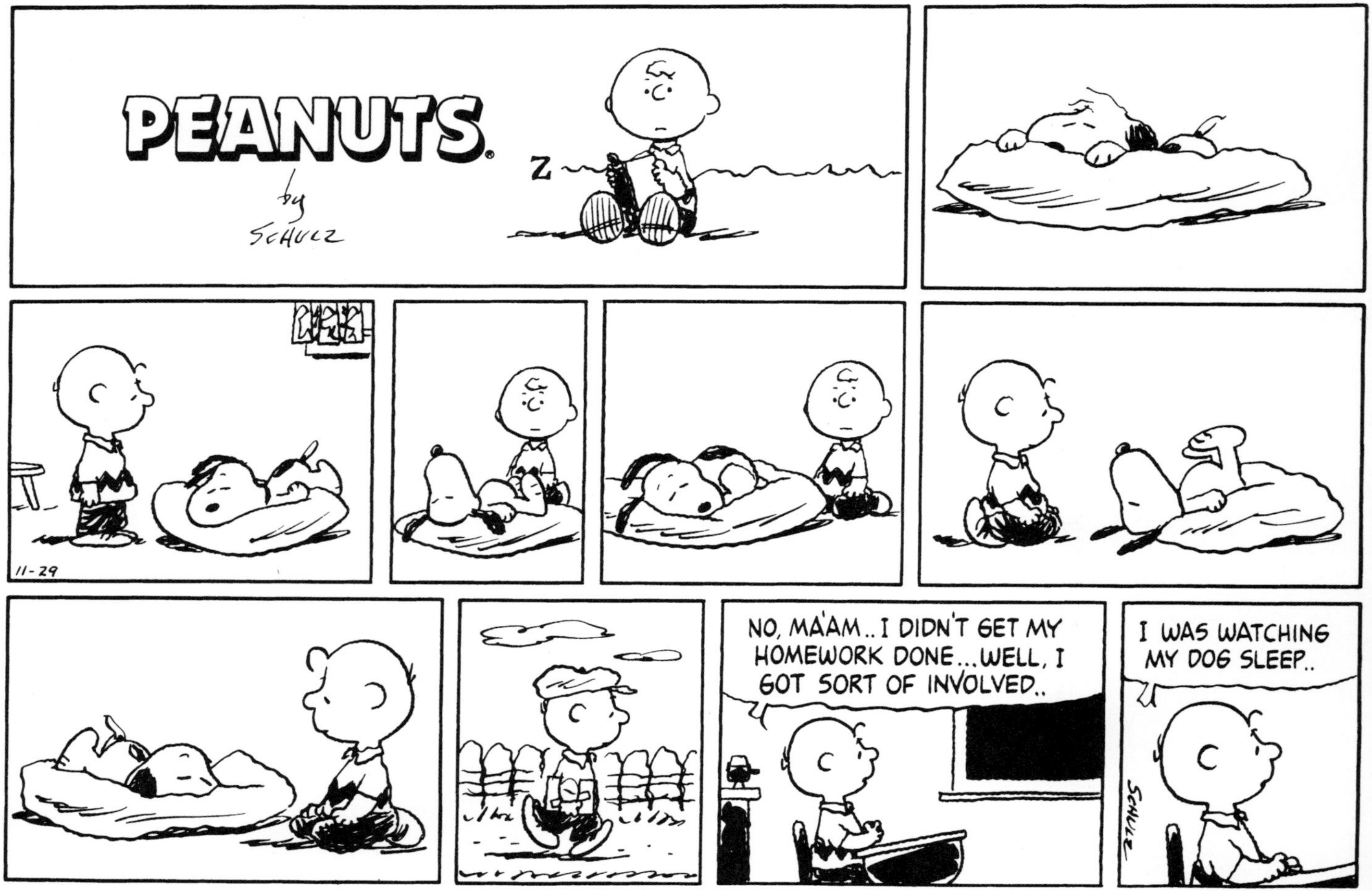
PEANUTS
by SCHULZ
Z
11-29
NO, MA'AM..I DIDN'T GET MY HOMEWORK DONE...WELL, I GOT SORT OF INVOLVED..
I WAS WATCHING MY DOG SLEEP..
SCHULZ

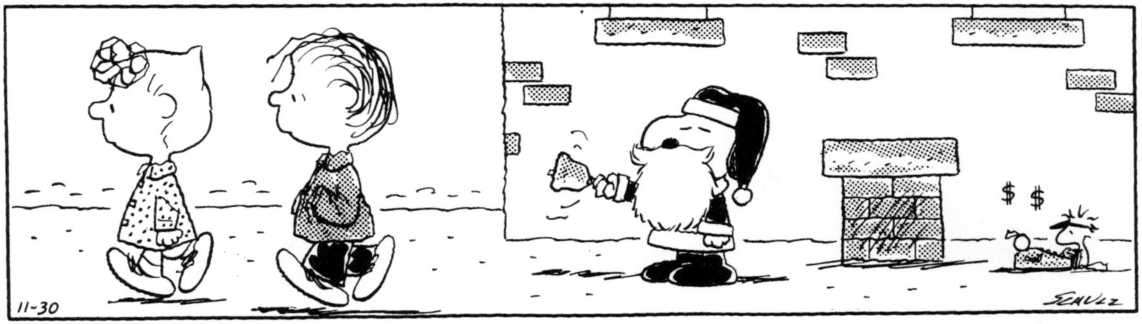
11-30

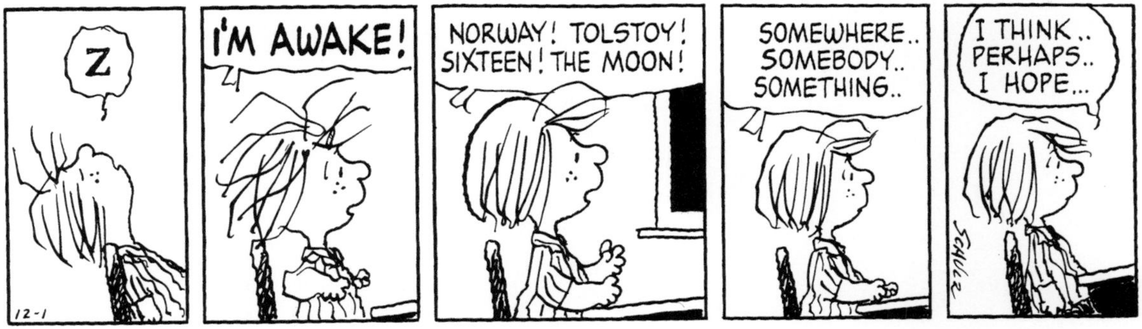
Z
I'M AWAKE!
NORWAY! TOLSTOY! SIXTEEN! THE MOON!
SOMEWHERE.. SOMEBODY.. SOMETHING..
I THINK.. PERHAPS.. I HOPE...
12-1

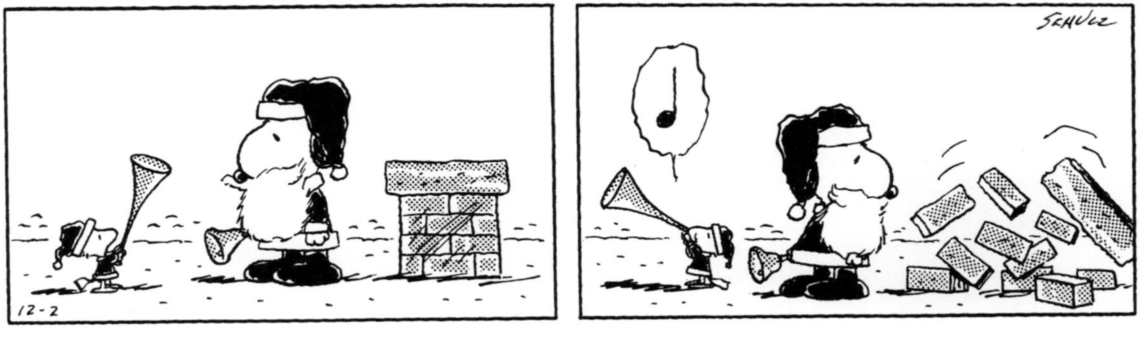
12-2

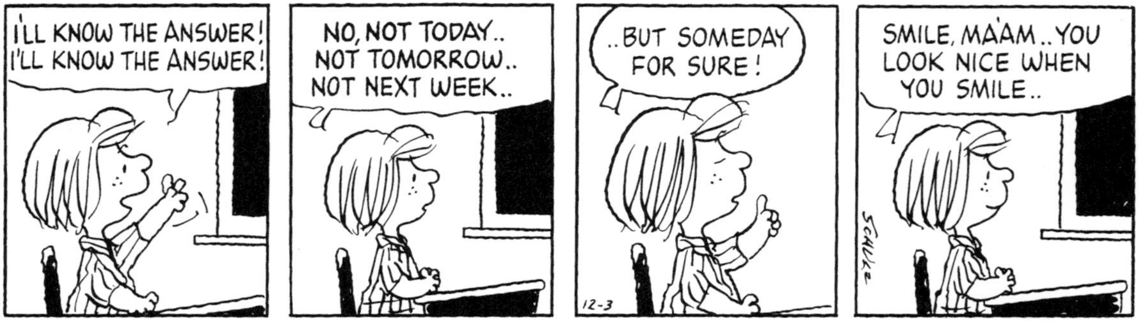
I'LL KNOW THE ANSWER! I'LL KNOW THE ANSWER!
NO, NOT TODAY.. NOT TOMORROW.. NOT NEXT WEEK..
..BUT SOMEDAY FOR SURE!
12-3
SMILE, MA'AM..YOU LOOK NICE WHEN YOU SMILE..
SCHULZ

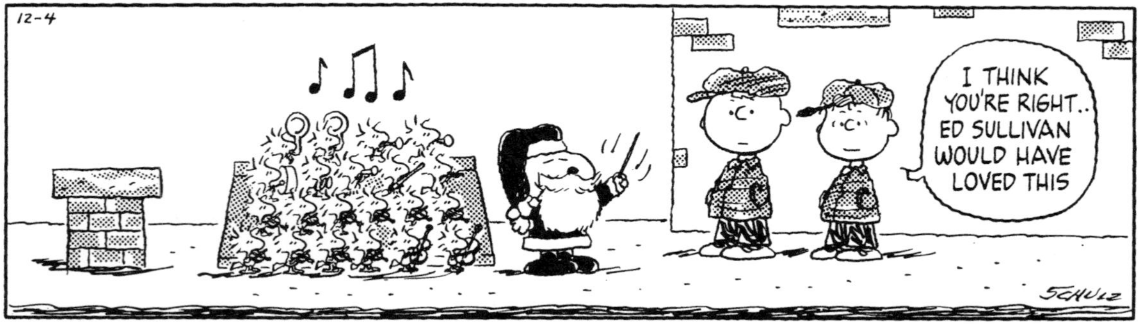
12-4
I THINK YOU'RE RIGHT.. ED SULLIVAN WOULD HAVE LOVED THIS
SCHULZ

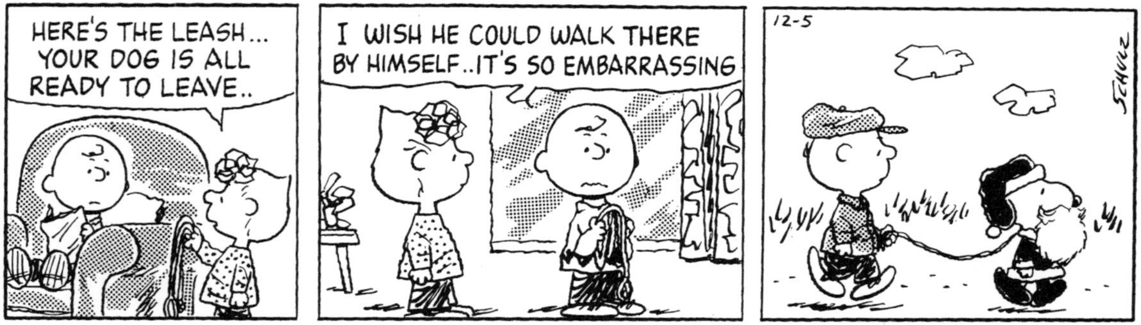
HERE'S THE LEASH... YOUR DOG IS ALL READY TO LEAVE..
I WISH HE COULD WALK THERE BY HIMSELF..IT'S SO EMBARRASSING
12-5
SCHULZ

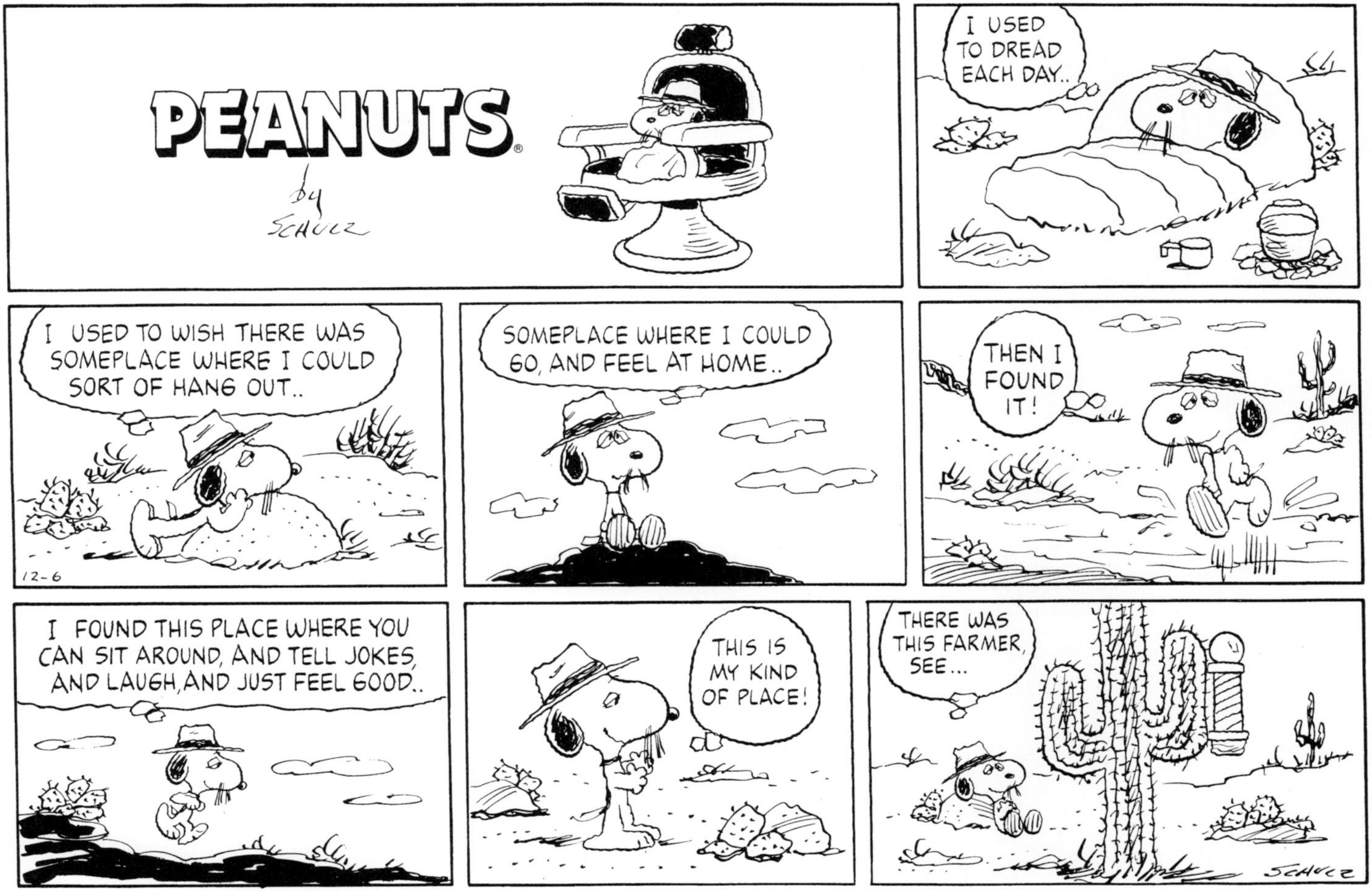
PEANUTS
by SCHULZ
I USED TO DREAD EACH DAY..
I USED TO WISH THERE WAS SOMEPLACE WHERE I COULD SORT OF HANG OUT..
12-6
SOMEPLACE WHERE I COULD GO, AND FEEL AT HOME..
THEN I FOUND IT!
I FOUND THIS PLACE WHERE YOU CAN SIT AROUND, AND TELL JOKES, AND LAUGH, AND JUST FEEL GOOD..
THIS IS MY KIND OF PLACE!
THERE WAS THIS FARMER, SEE...
SCHULZ

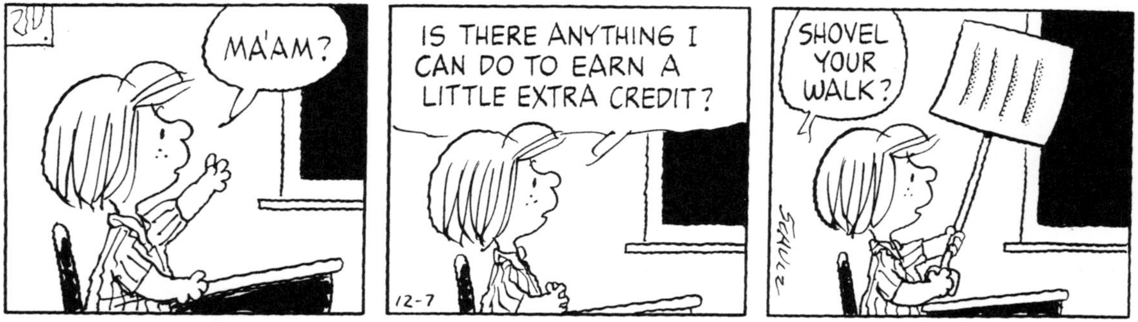
MA'AM?
IS THERE ANYTHING I CAN DO TO EARN A LITTLE EXTRA CREDIT?
SHOVEL YOUR WALK?
SCHULZ
12-7

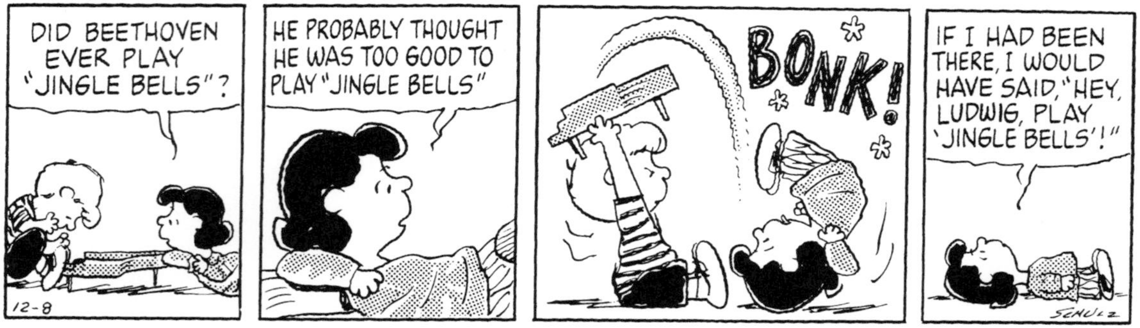
DID BEETHOVEN EVER PLAY "JINGLE BELLS"?
12-8
HE PROBABLY THOUGHT HE WAS TOO GOOD TO PLAY "JINGLE BELLS"
BONK!
IF I HAD BEEN THERE, I WOULD HAVE SAID, "HEY, LUDWIG, PLAY 'JINGLE BELLS'!"
SCHULZ

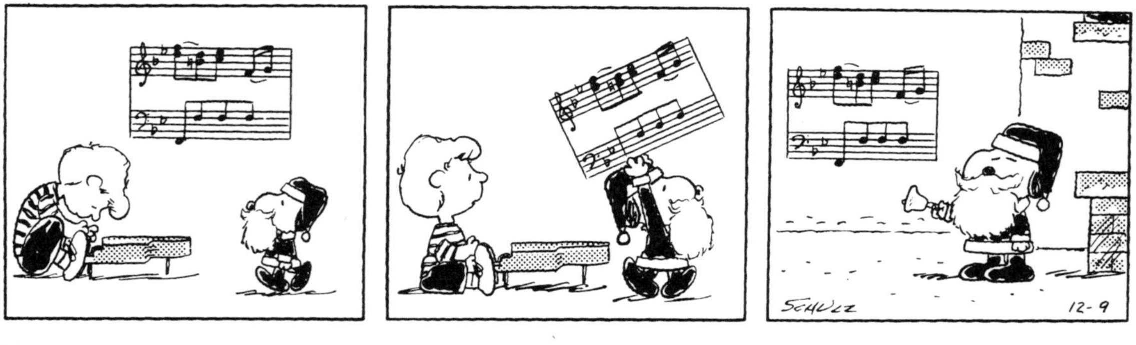
SCHULZ
12-9

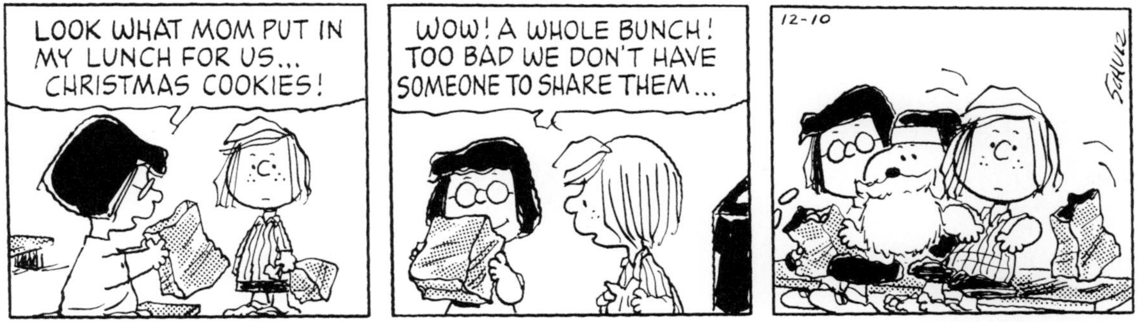
LOOK WHAT MOM PUT IN MY LUNCH FOR US... CHRISTMAS COOKIES!
WOW! A WHOLE BUNCH! TOO BAD WE DON'T HAVE SOMEONE TO SHARE THEM...
12-10
SCHULZ

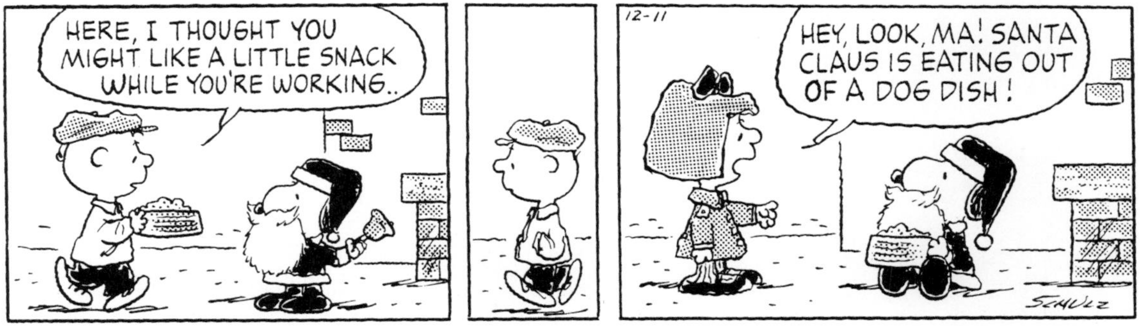
HERE, I THOUGHT YOU MIGHT LIKE A LITTLE SNACK WHILE YOU'RE WORKING..
12-11
HEY, LOOK, MA! SANTA CLAUS IS EATING OUT OF A DOG DISH!
SCHULZ

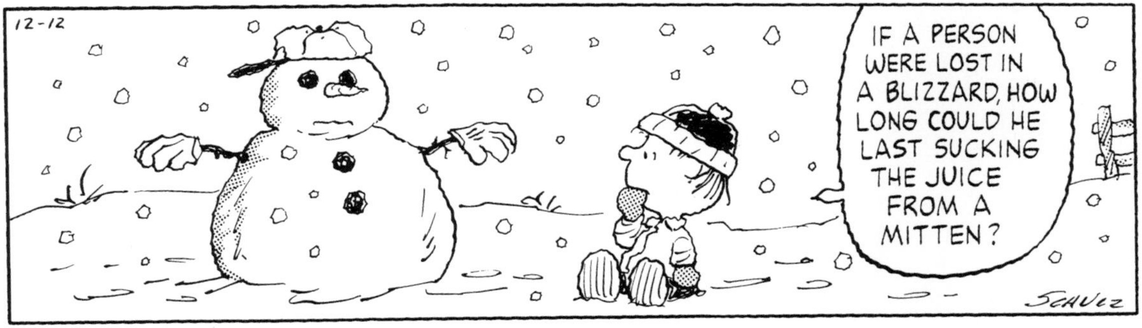
12-12
IF A PERSON WERE LOST IN A BLIZZARD, HOW LONG COULD HE LAST SUCKING THE JUICE FROM A MITTEN?
SCHULZ

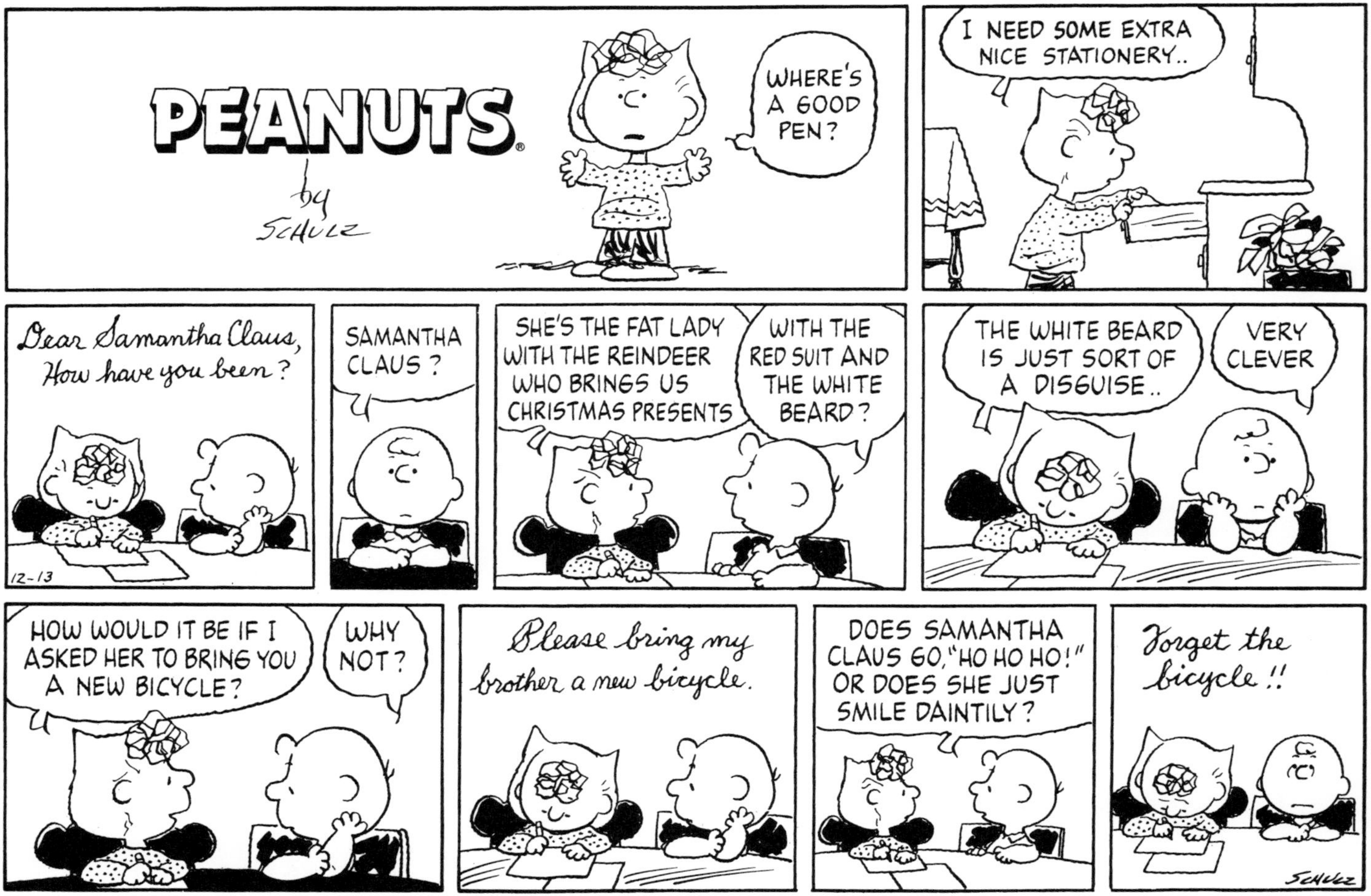
PEANUTS
by SCHULZ
WHERE'S A GOOD PEN?
I NEED SOME EXTRA NICE STATIONERY..
Dear Samantha Claus, How have you been?
12-13
SAMANTHA CLAUS?
SHE'S THE FAT LADY WITH THE REINDEER WHO BRINGS US CHRISTMAS PRESENTS
WITH THE RED SUIT AND THE WHITE BEARD?
THE WHITE BEARD IS JUST SORT OF A DISGUISE..
VERY CLEVER
HOW WOULD IT BE IF I ASKED HER TO BRING YOU A NEW BICYCLE?
WHY NOT?
Please bring my brother a new bicycle.
DOES SAMANTHA CLAUS GO, "HO HO HO!" OR DOES SHE JUST SMILE DAINTILY?
Forget the bicycle!!
SCHULZ

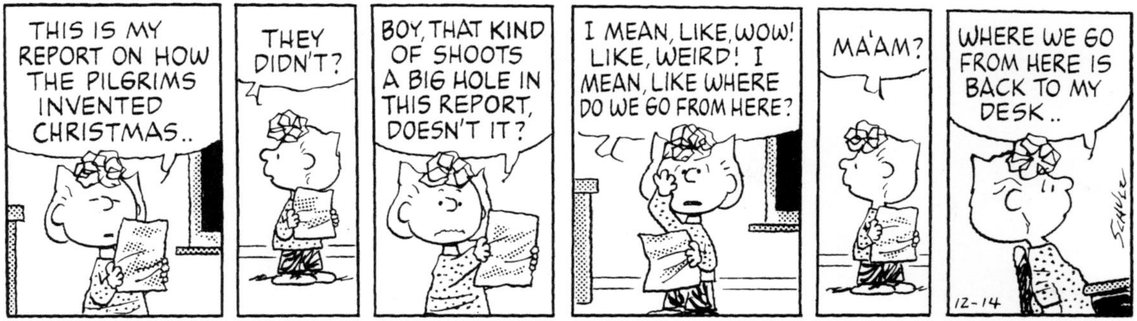
THIS IS MY REPORT ON HOW THE PILGRIMS INVENTED CHRISTMAS..
THEY DIDN'T?
BOY, THAT KIND OF SHOOTS A BIG HOLE IN THIS REPORT, DOESN'T IT?
I MEAN, LIKE, WOW! LIKE, WEIRD! I MEAN, LIKE WHERE DO WE GO FROM HERE?
MA'AM?
WHERE WE GO FROM HERE IS BACK TO MY DESK..
SCHULZ
12-14

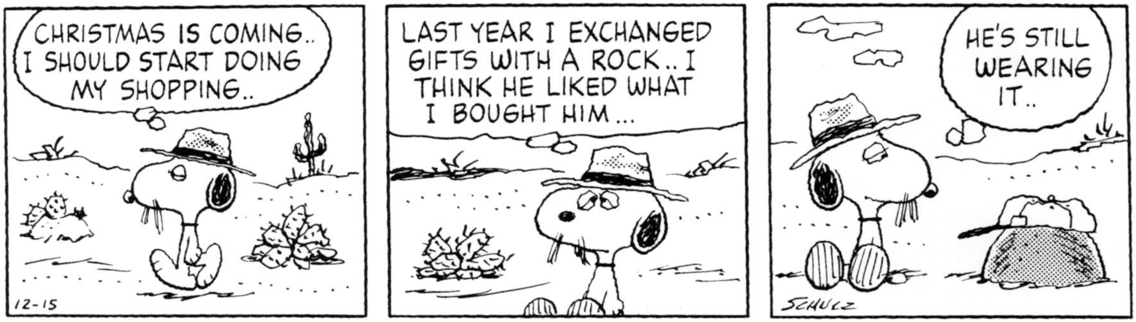
CHRISTMAS IS COMING.. I SHOULD START DOING MY SHOPPING..
12-15
LAST YEAR I EXCHANGED GIFTS WITH A ROCK.. I THINK HE LIKED WHAT I BOUGHT HIM...
HE'S STILL WEARING IT..
SCHULZ

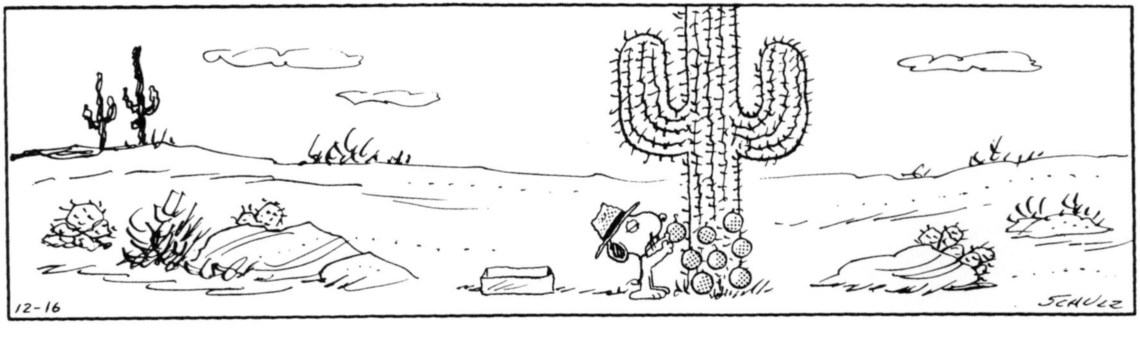
12-16
SCHULZ

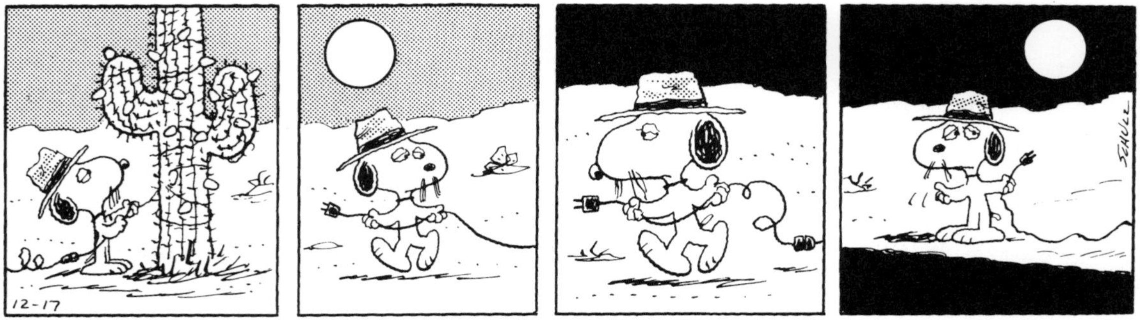
12-17
SCHULZ

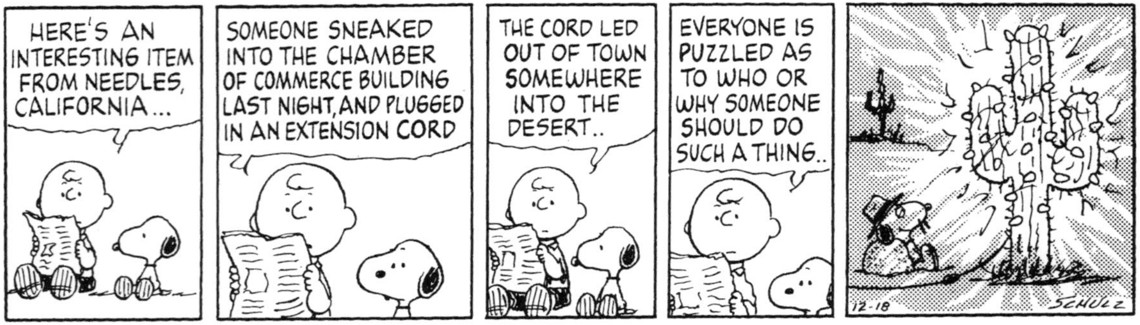
HERE'S AN INTERESTING ITEM FROM NEEDLES, CALIFORNIA...
SOMEONE SNEAKED INTO THE CHAMBER OF COMMERCE BUILDING LAST NIGHT, AND PLUGGED IN AN EXTENSION CORD
THE CORD LED OUT OF TOWN SOMEWHERE INTO THE DESERT..
EVERYONE IS PUZZLED AS TO WHO OR WHY SOMEONE SHOULD DO SUCH A THING..
12-18
SCHULZ

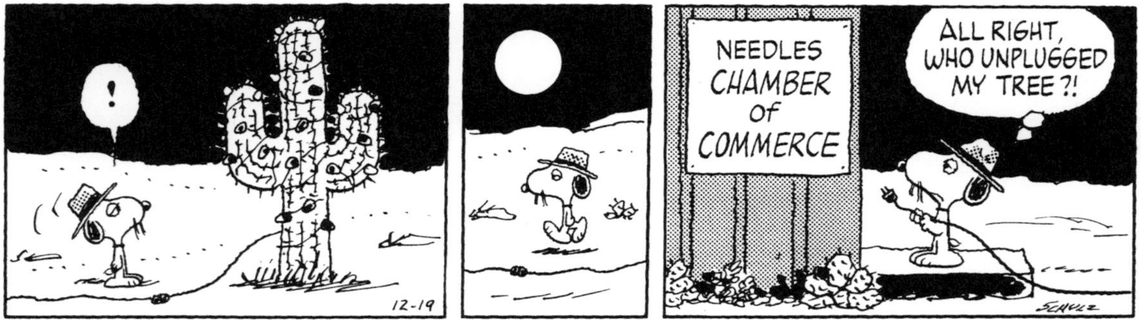
!
12-19
NEEDLES CHAMBER OF COMMERCE
ALL RIGHT, WHO UNPLUGGED MY TREE ?!
SCHULZ

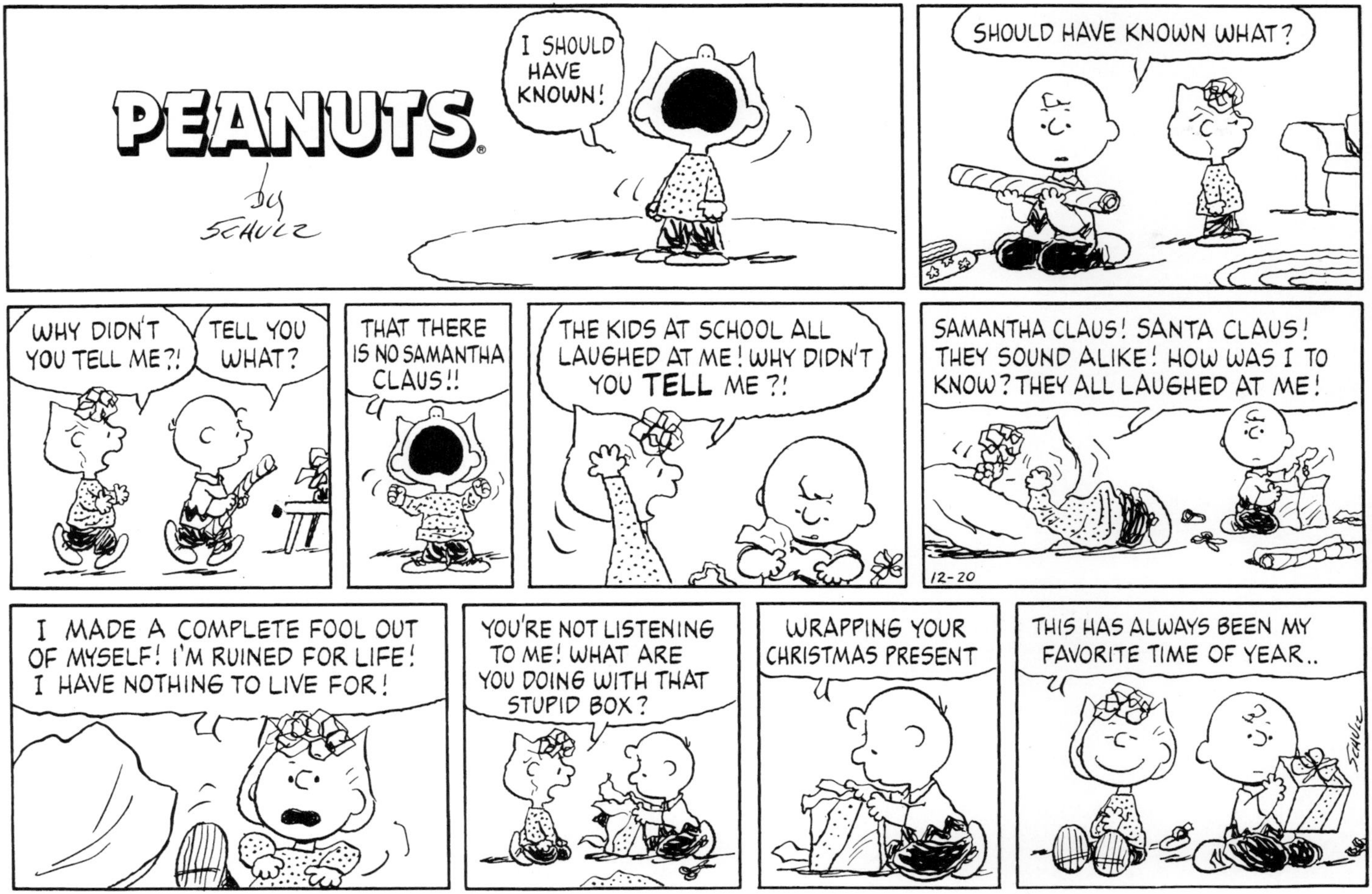
PEANUTS
by SCHULZ
I SHOULD HAVE KNOWN!
SHOULD HAVE KNOWN WHAT?
WHY DIDN'T YOU TELL ME?!
TELL YOU WHAT?
THAT THERE IS NO SAMANTHA CLAUS!!
THE KIDS AT SCHOOL ALL LAUGHED AT ME! WHY DIDN'T YOU TELL ME?!
SAMANTHA CLAUS! SANTA CLAUS! THEY SOUND ALIKE! HOW WAS I TO KNOW? THEY ALL LAUGHED AT ME!
12-20
I MADE A COMPLETE FOOL OUT OF MYSELF! I'M RUINED FOR LIFE! I HAVE NOTHING TO LIVE FOR!
YOU'RE NOT LISTENING TO ME! WHAT ARE YOU DOING WITH THAT STUPID BOX?
WRAPPING YOUR CHRISTMAS PRESENT
THIS HAS ALWAYS BEEN MY FAVORITE TIME OF YEAR..
SCHULZ

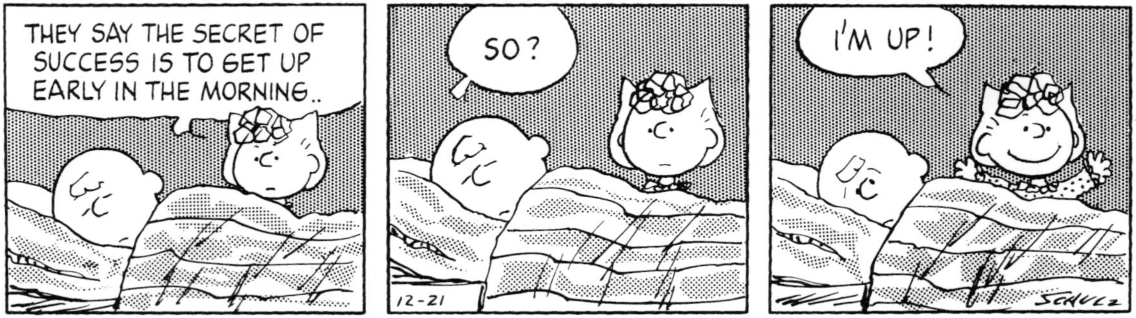
THEY SAY THE SECRET OF SUCCESS IS TO GET UP EARLY IN THE MORNING..
SO?
12-21
I'M UP!
SCHULZ

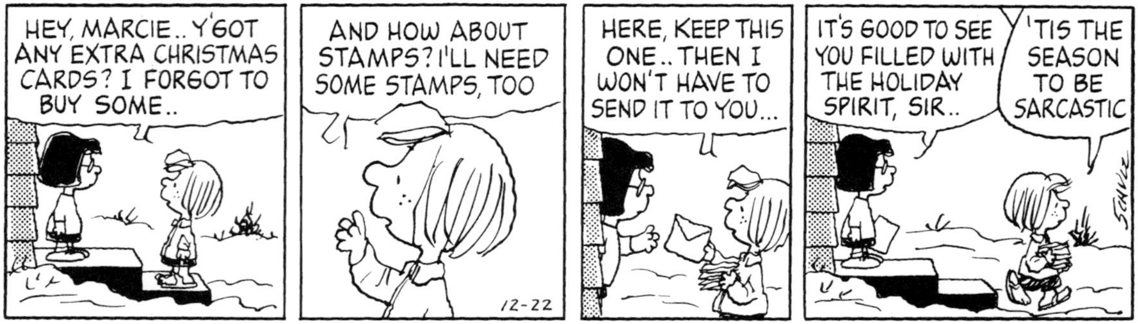
HEY, MARCIE.. Y'GOT ANY EXTRA CHRISTMAS CARDS? I FORGOT TO BUY SOME..
AND HOW ABOUT STAMPS? I'LL NEED SOME STAMPS, TOO
12-22
HERE, KEEP THIS ONE.. THEN I WON'T HAVE TO SEND IT TO YOU...
IT'S GOOD TO SEE YOU FILLED WITH THE HOLIDAY SPIRIT, SIR..
'TIS THE SEASON TO BE SARCASTIC
SCHULZ

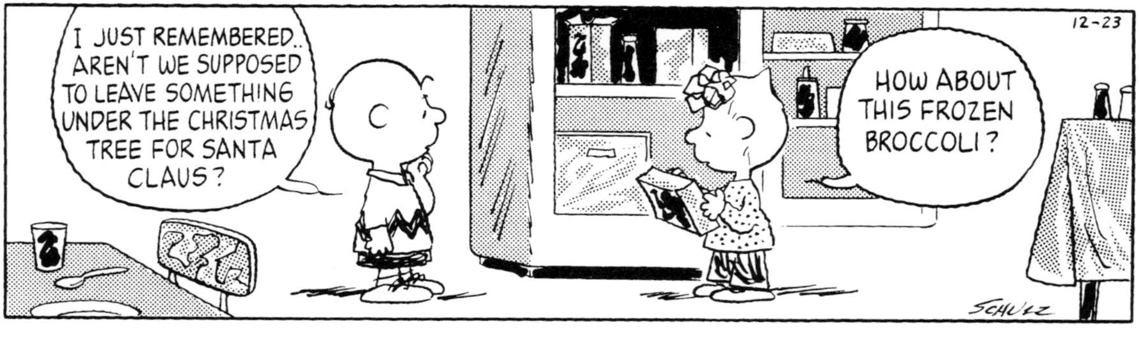
12-23
I JUST REMEMBERED.. AREN'T WE SUPPOSED TO LEAVE SOMETHING UNDER THE CHRISTMAS TREE FOR SANTA CLAUS?
HOW ABOUT THIS FROZEN BROCCOLI?
SCHULZ

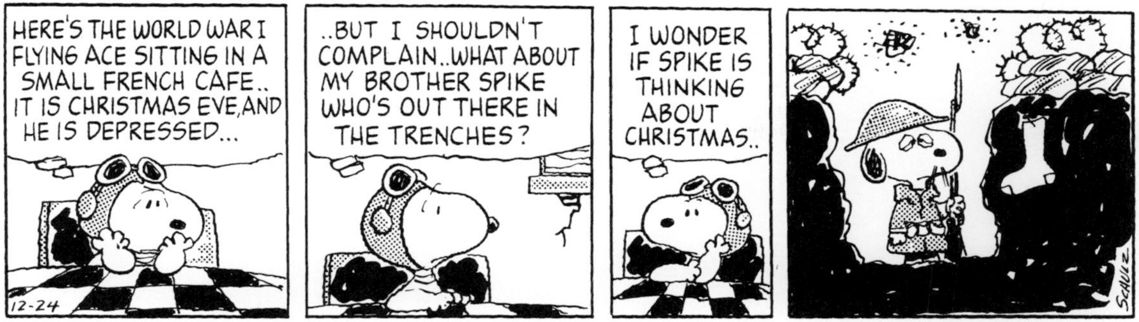
HERE'S THE WORLD WAR I FLYING ACE SITTING IN A SMALL FRENCH CAFE.. IT IS CHRISTMAS EVE, AND HE IS DEPRESSED...
..BUT I SHOULDN'T COMPLAIN..WHAT ABOUT MY BROTHER SPIKE WHO'S OUT THERE IN THE TRENCHES?
I WONDER IF SPIKE IS THINKING ABOUT CHRISTMAS..
12-24
SCHULZ

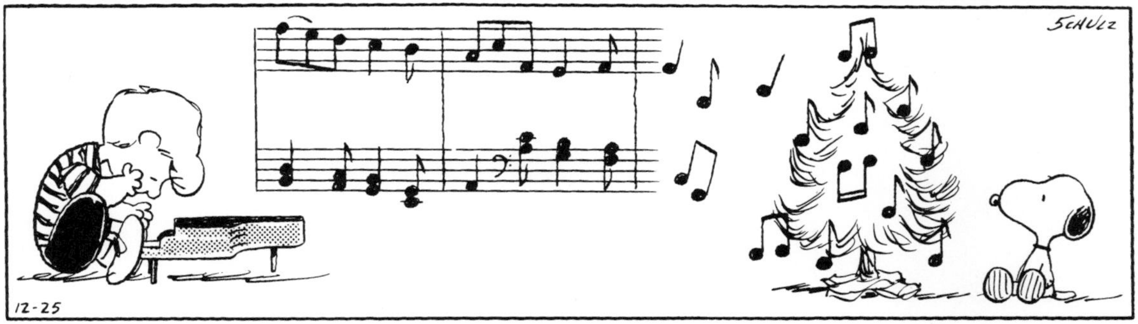
SCHULZ
12-25

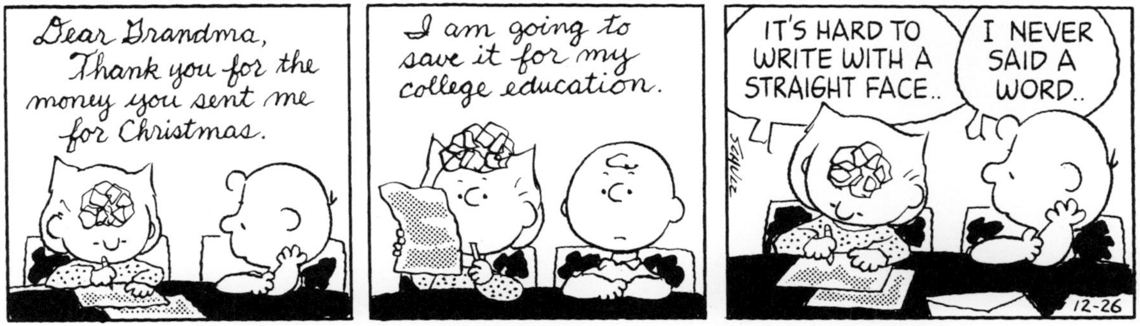
Dear Grandma,
Thank you for the money you sent me for Christmas.
I am going to save it for my college education.
IT'S HARD TO WRITE WITH A STRAIGHT FACE..
I NEVER SAID A WORD..
SCHULZ
12-26

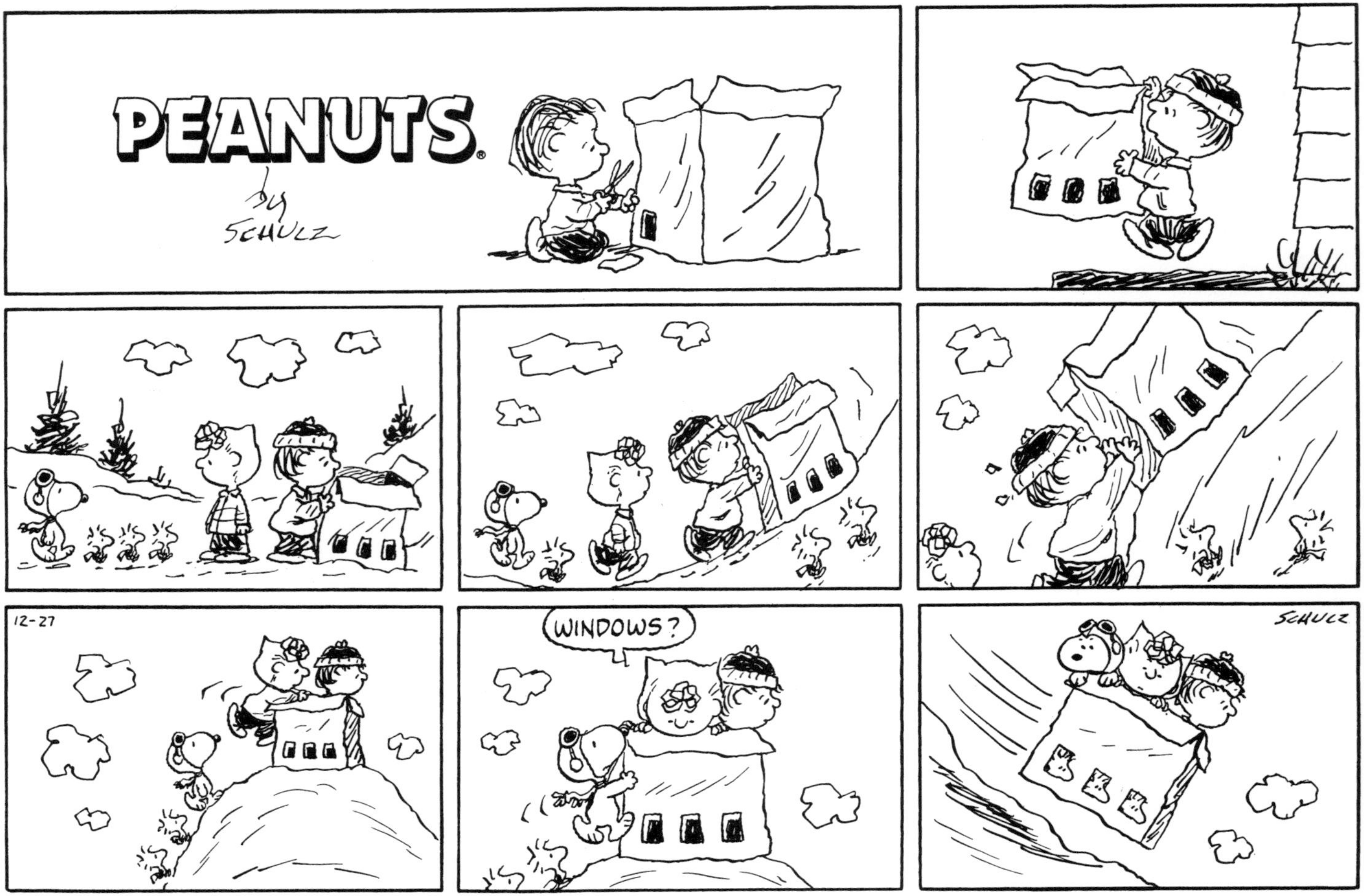
PEANUTS
by
SCHULZ
12-27
WINDOWS?
SCHULZ

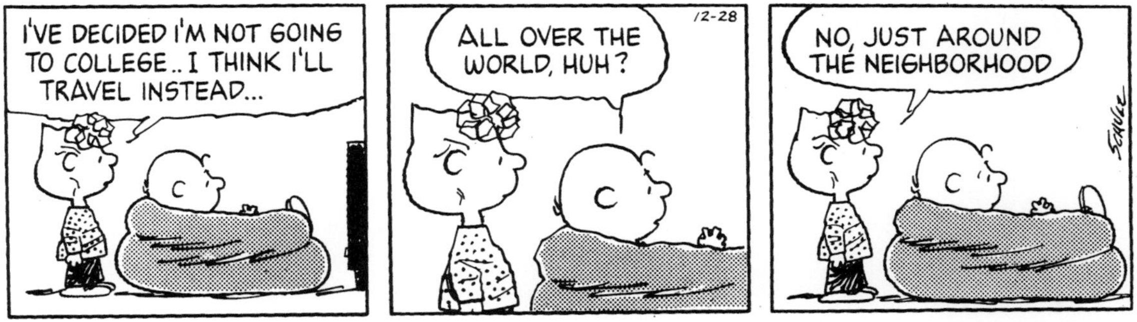
I'VE DECIDED I'M NOT GOING TO COLLEGE.. I THINK I'LL TRAVEL INSTEAD...
ALL OVER THE WORLD, HUH ?
12-28
NO, JUST AROUND THE NEIGHBORHOOD

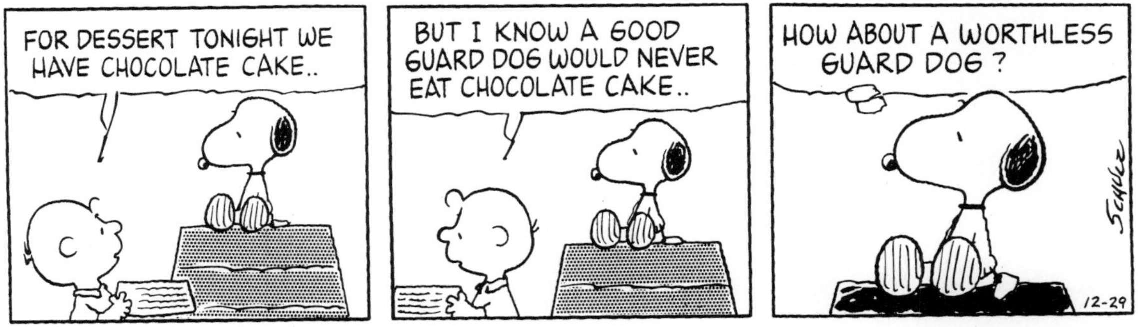
FOR DESSERT TONIGHT WE HAVE CHOCOLATE CAKE..
BUT I KNOW A GOOD GUARD DOG WOULD NEVER EAT CHOCOLATE CAKE..
HOW ABOUT A WORTHLESS GUARD DOG ?
12-29

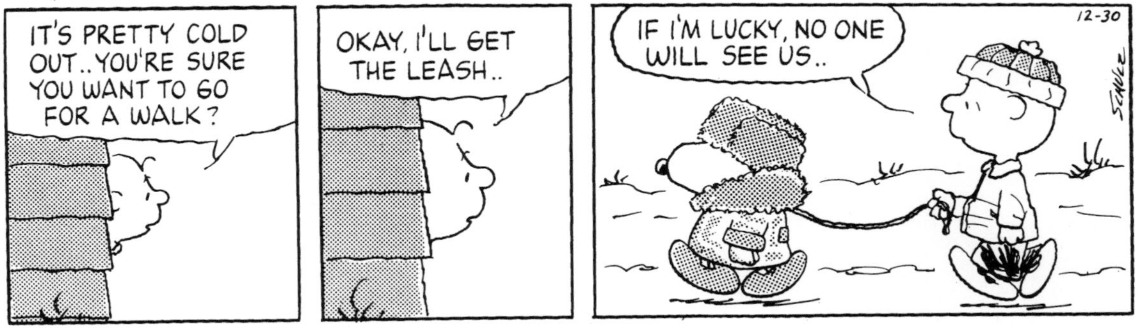
IT'S PRETTY COLD OUT.. YOU'RE SURE YOU WANT TO GO FOR A WALK ?
OKAY, I'LL GET THE LEASH..
12-30
IF I'M LUCKY, NO ONE WILL SEE US..

1922 CHARLES M. SCHULZ 2000

CHARLES M. SCHULZ WAS BORN NOVEMBER 26, 1922, in Minneapolis. His destiny was foreshadowed when an uncle gave him, at the age of two days, the nickname "Sparky" (after the racehorse Spark Plug in the newspaper strip *Barney Google*).

Schulz grew up in St. Paul. By all accounts, he led an unremarkable, albeit sheltered, childhood. He was an only child, close to both parents, his eventual career path nurtured by his father, who bought four Sunday papers every week — just for the comics.

An outstanding student, he skipped two grades early on, but began to flounder in high school — perhaps not so coincidentally at the same time kids are going through their cruelest, most status-conscious period of socialization. The pain, bitterness, insecurity, and failures chronicled in *Peanuts* appear to have originated from this period of Schulz's life.

Although Schulz enjoyed sports, he also found refuge in solitary activities: reading, drawing, and watching movies. He bought comic books and Big Little Books, pored over the newspaper strips, and copied his favorites — *Buck Rogers*, the Walt Disney characters, *Popeye*, *Tim Tyler's Luck*. He quickly became a connoisseur; his heroes were Milton Caniff, Roy Crane, Hal Foster, and Alex Raymond.

In his senior year in high school, his mother noticed an ad in a local newspaper for a correspondence school, Federal Schools (later called Art Instruction Schools). Schulz passed the talent test, completed the course, and began trying, unsuccessfully, to sell gag cartoons to magazines. (His first published drawing was of his dog, Spike, and appeared in a 1937 *Ripley's Believe It or Not!* installment.)

After World War II had ended and Schulz was discharged from the army, he started submitting gag cartoons to the various magazines of the time; his first breakthrough, however, came when an editor at *Timeless Topix* hired him to letter adventure comics. Soon after that, he was hired by his alma mater, Art Instruction, to correct student lessons returned by mail.

Between 1948 and 1950, he succeeded in selling seventeen cartoons to the *Saturday Evening Post* — as well as, to the local *St. Paul Pioneer Press*, a weekly comic feature called *Li'l Folks*. It was run in the women's section and paid ten dollars a week. After writing and drawing the feature for two years, Schulz asked for a better location in the paper or for daily exposure, as well as a raise. When he was turned down on all three counts, he quit.

He started submitting strips to the newspaper syndicates. In the spring of 1950, he received a letter from the United Feature Syndicate, announcing its interest in his submission, *Li'l Folks*. Schulz boarded a train in June for New York City; more interested in doing a strip than a panel, he also brought along the first installments of what would become *Peanuts* — and that was what sold. (The title, which Schulz loathed to his dying day, was imposed by the syndicate.) The first *Peanuts* daily appeared October 2, 1950; the first Sunday, January 6, 1952.

Prior to *Peanuts*, the province of the comics page had been that of gags, social and political observation, domestic comedy, soap opera, and various adventure genres. Although *Peanuts* changed, or evolved, during the fifty years Schulz wrote and drew it, it remained, as it began, an anomaly on the comics page — a comic strip about the interior crises of the cartoonist himself. After a painful divorce in 1973 from which he had not yet recovered, Schulz told a reporter, "Strangely, I've drawn better cartoons in the last six months

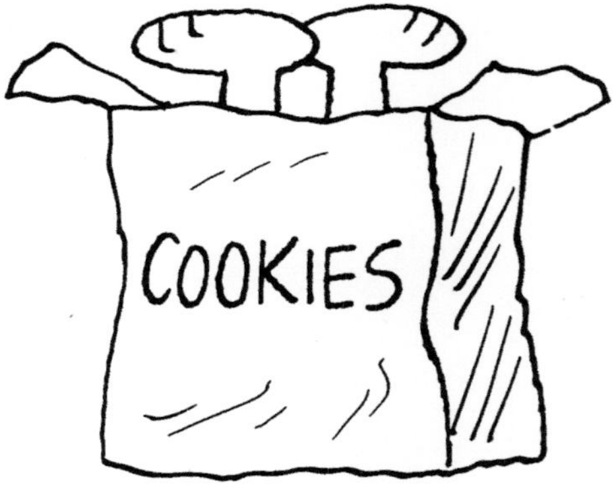
COOKIES

— or as good as I've ever drawn. I don't know how the human mind works." Surely, it was this kind of humility in the face of profoundly irreducible human question that makes *Peanuts* as universally moving as it is.

Diagnosed with cancer, Schulz retired from *Peanuts* at the end of 1999. He died on February 12, 2000, the day before his last strip was published (and two days before Valentine's Day) — having completed 17,897 daily and Sunday strips, each and every one fully written, drawn, and lettered entirely by his own hand — an unmatched achievement in comics.

— GARY GROTH

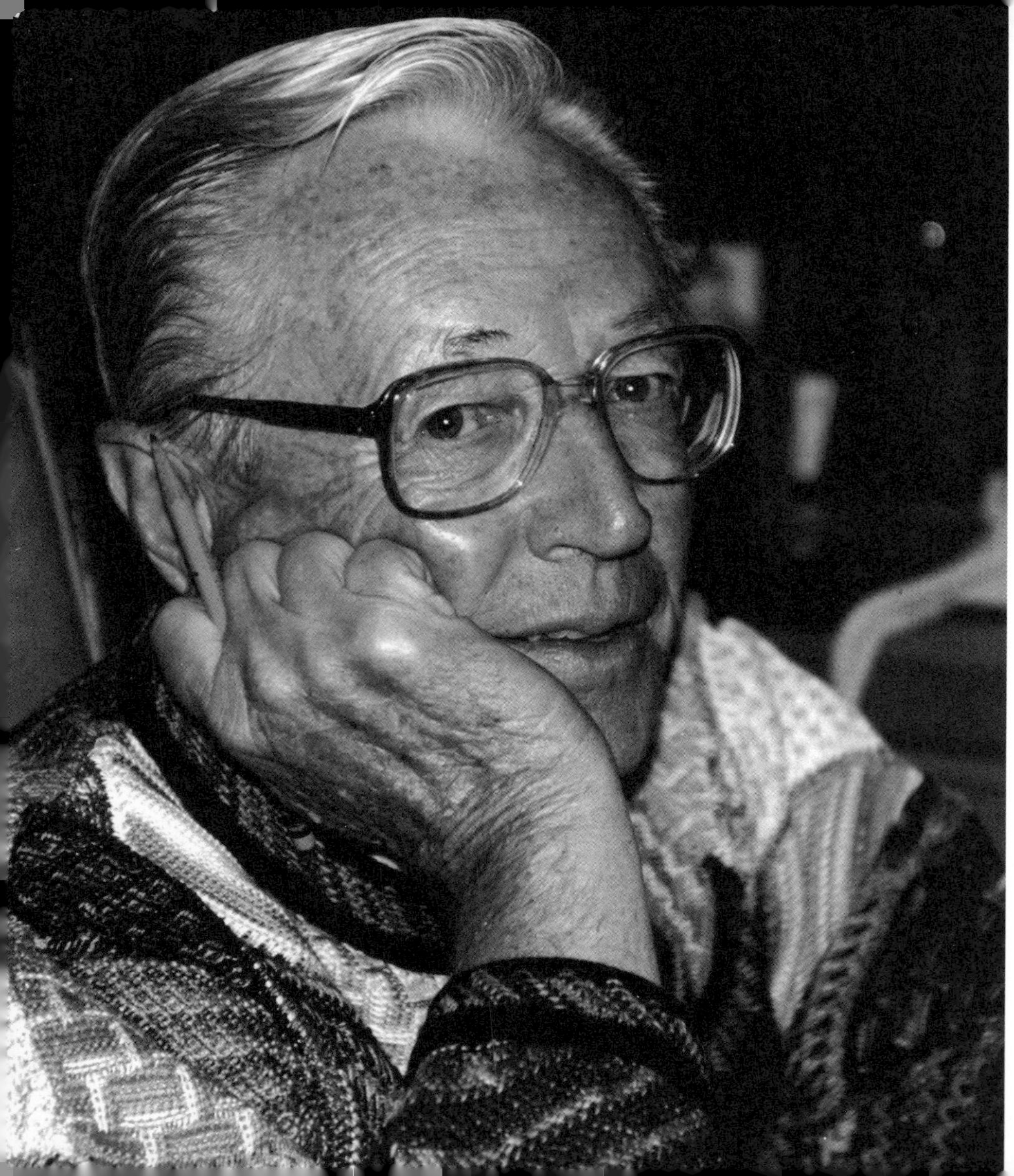

Charles M. Schulz in his home studio at the drawing board, Santa Rosa, California, mid-1990s: courtesy of the Charles M. Schulz Museum.